Genetics and the Law

National Symposium on Genetics and the Law
II

Genetics and the Law

Edited by

AUBREY MILUNSKY, MB. B. Ch., M. R. C. P., D. C. H.

Assistant Professor of Pediatrics, Harvard Medical School;
Director, Genetics Laboratory, Eunice Kennedy Shriver Center
at the Walter E. Fernald State School;
Medical Geneticist, Massachusetts General Hospital and the
Center for Human Genetics, Harvard Medical School,
Boston, Massachusetts

and

GEORGE J. ANNAS, J. D., M. P. H.

Director, Center for Law and Health Sciences, Boston University School of Law;
Assistant Professor, Department of Socio-Medical Sciences and Community Medicine
(Law and Medicine), Boston University School of Medicine, Boston, Massachusetts;
Lecturer in Legal Medicine, Boston College Law School,
Newton, Massachusetts

PLENUM PRESS · NEW YORK AND LONDON

4417577

Library of Congress Cataloging in Publication Data

National Symposium on Genetics and the Law, Boston, 1975.
Genetics and the law.

"Proceedings of a National Symposium on Genetics and the Law held in Boston,
Mass., May 18-20, 1975, and co-sponsored by the Boston Chapter of the National
Genetics Foundation and the American Society of Law and Medicine."
Bibliography: p.
Includes index.
1. Medical genetics—Law and legislation—United States—Congresses. 2. Medicine,
Experimental—Law and legislation—United States. I. Milunsky, Aubrey. II. Annas,
George J. III. National Genetics Foundation. Boston Chapter. IV. American Society
of Law and Medicine. V. Title. [DNLM: 1. Genetic counseling—Congresses. 2. Ethics,
Medical—Congresses. 3. Hereditary diseases—Prevention and control—United States—
Legislation—Congresses. 5. Human experimentation—United States—Legislation—
Congresses. 6. Eugenics—United States—Legislation—Congresses. QZ50 N28g 1975]
KF3827.G4N38   1975   344'.73'041   75-38569
ISBN 0-306-30906-8

First Printing — January 1976
Second Printing — December 1976

Proceedings of a National Symposium on Genetics and the Law
held in Boston, Mass., May 18-20, 1975, and cosponsored by the
Boston Chapter of the National Genetics Foundation and the
American Society of Law and Medicine, Inc.

©1976 Plenum Press, New York
A Division of Plenum Publishing Corporation
227 West 17th Street, New York, N.Y. 10011

United Kingdom edition published by Plenum Press, London
A Division of Plenum Publishing Company, Ltd.
Davis House (4th Floor), 8 Scrubs Lane, Harlesden, London, NW10 6SE, England

Printed in the United States of America

Preface

Society has historically not taken a benign view of genetic disease. The laws permitting sterilization of the mentally retarded, and those proscribing consanguineous marriages are but two examples. Indeed as far back as the 5th-10th centuries, B.C.E., consanguineous unions were outlawed (Leviticus XVIII, 6).

Case law has traditionally tended toward the conservative. It is reactive rather than directive, exerting its influence only after an individual or group has sustained injury and brought suit. In contrast, state legislatures have not been inhibited in enacting statutes. Many of their products can be characterized as hasty, unnecessary, ill-conceived, and based on the heart rather than the head. Moreover the lack of expert consultation sought has also been remarkable. One state legislature, for example, has advocated immunization for sickle cell anemia! Many others have enacted laws for the screening of inborn errors of metabolism, e.g., phenylketonuria, but have poorly defined the lines of responsibility to secure compliance.

A spate of specific disease-related bills has emerged in the U.S. Congress, each seeking recognition and appropriations. Sickle cell anemia, hemophilia, Cooley's anemia and Tay-Sachs disease have been among the front-runners for support. Finally, in 1975, Congress has begun to examine an omnibus bill concerning all forms of genetic disease. The bill, termed the National Genetic Diseases Act is, however, still far from being enacted.

The striking recent advances in medical technology have brought the basic confrontations between Genetics and the Law into sharp relief. Informed consent and confidentiality are terms that have had to be added to the lexicon of genetic counselors. In the research area, a rash of state statutes appeared in 1973-1974 aimed at prohibiting fetal experimentation. Since physicians, lawyers, philosophers and theologians have not been able to settle the question of when life begins, these laws have served mainly to mirror, and on occasion compound, the problem. The legal literature is replete with differences of opinion concerning court de-

cisions on fetal viability, legal personality and personhood. The
recent Boston trial of Dr. Kenneth Edelin simply focused attention
on these now glaring medicolegal problems.

   Society has manifested increasing concern about experiments
involving gene manipulation, cloning and in vitro fertilization.
Calls have been made to interdict further study into gene manipulation. Should legislation be enacted to restrict certain types
of research it may prove harmful to science and society in the
long run. A balance between the apparent dangers of uncontrolled
scientific initiatives and restricted research must be sought.
Intrusion by government into what may or may not be researched by
individual scientists does, however, raise very serious societal
issues.

   Heated professional and public controversy has enveloped a
large newborn chromosomal screening program in Boston. Problems
arose concerning informed consent, self-fulfilling prophecy, psy-
chologic risks, and especially the relevance of an XYY karyotype
to deviant behavior. These and other aspects of the XYY controversy are discussed in detail in these Proceedings.

   Because of serious concerns about fetal and human rights, a
moratorium on fetal research was imposed by the U.S. Congress in
1974 while a specially created commission studied and reported on
the issues. The commission recently recommended that such research
resume under strict review procedures. Meanwhile, a number of
Boston medical researchers are about to be tried for grave-robbing
- a charge arising out of their experiments on the effects of anti-
biotic transfer from mother to fetus. Their protocols had passed
through the then-required research review committees. The trial
will necessarily raise issues concerning both the adequacy of the
review procedure and the relevance of a 19th century criminal
statute to 20th century medical experimentation.

   Advances in the medical care of sick and malformed newborns
now enables many genetically defective infants to survive. Decisions by parents, physicians, or both, to allow such infants to die
may be homicide if treatment could permit their survival. In this
volume are eloquent arguments that the admittedly harsh and unen-
forced state of the law should nevertheless not be changed. Such
advocacy may appear untenable, but there are few unequivocal answers to this or the other dilemmas in genetics which now confront
the law.

Against this background of legislative and judicial activity we decided to examine the issues and to present as best an overall perspective as was possible. To this end a distinguished faculty of scientists, physicians and lawyers was assembled. It is our hope that their deliberations in these Proceedings and the appended selected bibliography will help provide a basis upon which a balanced informed public policy can be formulated. There is nothing inherent preventing the law from responding in a productive and humane manner to genetic advances.

Boston   Aubrey Milunsky

September, 1975   George J. Annas

Acknowledgments

We acknowledge with appreciation the support and sponsorship of the Boston Chapter of the National Genetics Foundation and the American Society of Law and Medicine. The guidance and help of Dr. Elliot L. Sagall, President of the American Society of Law and Medicine, in the organization of this meeting was very much appreciated. Special thanks are due to Debbie Sack, Karen Brockman, and Myra Fraidin for their help in organizing the Symposium. We are indebted to Babette Milunsky for her major efforts, eye for detail and wise counsel in organizing this meeting. The manuscript was typed by Carmela M. Ryan, whose expertise, patience and charm is again gratefully acknowledged. The manuscript was prepared through the combined efforts of Elizabeth Keel, Patricia Callahan, Judy Heck and Babette Milunsky.

Contents

THE FETUS AND THE NEWBORN

EUGENICS, ETHICS, LAW AND SOCIETY

The Fetus and the Newborn

LEGAL STATUS OF THE FETUS

Margery W. Shaw and Catherine Damme

Medical Genetics Center, The University of Texas Health

Science Center at Houston

INTRODUCTION

When does life begin? There are two moments in time - the moment of conception and the moment of birth - which have most often been used to mark the existence of a new human being. The moment of birth is easily ascertainable and has often been cited by the courts to define the entry into human society of a "person" within the meaning of the Fourteenth Amendment. It is a convenient landmark, but it is not universally accepted in the social or legal sense.

Biologically, the moment of conception is a more accurate definition of the beginning of a new life, but this moment can never be precisely determined except when fertilization occurs outside the body and under microscopic observation. Some biologists have argued that the beginning of life is a cosmic concept since all life is cyclic. It is important to remember that all new life comes from pre-existing life in a never-ending continuum.

Philosophers, ethicists and others have grappled with the concepts of the meaning of personhood, the sanctity of human life and the moral dilemmas posed by the explosion of scientific knowledge. The new technologies have raised issues which demand that ethical decisions be made, not in the future, but today. This paper will not deal with these knotty problems. Instead we will examine the historical framework of legal questions involving the rights and interests of the fetus.

PROPERTY RIGHTS

Within the Anglo-American common law tradition the earliest enunciation of the rights of the unborn child are found in property law. This was the beginning of an unbroken line of cases establishing the unborn child's ability to inherit for his benefit. In 1762 Blackstone wrote "An infant...in the mother's womb is supposed in law to be born for many purposes. It is capable of having a legacy...made to it. It may have a guardian assigned to it; and it is enabled to have an estate...as if it were actually born" (1). Thus, a fetus in utero is considered to be a person in being for the purposes of inheritance.

We will cite several seventeenth century cases which uphold this legal dictum. It is important to note that the testator's intent was the primary concern of the courts, not the personhood of the fetus. To deny the fetus property rights would frustrate that intent. In Burdett v. Hopegood, a posthumous child (born after the death of the testator) was allowed to take under his father's will (2). In Hale v. Hale the court ruled that a trust must be construed to allow a posthumous child to be "living" and permitted to take under the trust (3). In Marsh v. Kirby a testator devised by will a life estate to his wife with remainder to children. At the time of death his wife was pregnant. The child later inherited the estate in preference to collateral relatives (4).

Hundreds of modern cases which descended from these precedents could be cited. In fact, this principle - the right of the fetus to inherit - has often been used as a rationale for allowing recovery for prenatal torts.

WRONGFUL DEATH DUE TO PRENATAL INJURIES

This brings us to another area of law which has considered the rights of the fetus: the law of torts. A tort is a wrong done to one individual by another.

Injury to the fetus may have three different outcomes: 1) miscarriage or stillbirth caused by the injury; 2) livebirth followed by death; and 3) livebirth with injuries not resulting in death. The first two will be considered here while the third is considered in the next section.

A cause of action for wrongful death is purely statutory. It is not based on common law, which is the case for prenatal injury (5).

In 1884, Justice Holmes wrote the opinion in a landmark
case involving prenatal injury resulting in death (6). A woman
who was in the second trimester of pregnancy miscarried as a
result of a fall on a defective highway. The abortus soon ex-
pired but did move its limbs for several minutes before death.
Holmes stated that a cause of action did not lie because the
unborn child was a part of the mother at the time of the injury.
He went on to note that the decision to deny recovery was not
based on the degree of maturity of the fetus. This precedent
survived until 1946.

American courts have been inconsistent in allowing recovery
for stillbirths and viable fetuses born alive but later dying of
injuries received in utero. Part of the inconsistency may be
traced to variation in wording in the wrongful death statutes
of the different states, i.e., as to whether the legislature intended the word "person" to include fetuses. Also, courts differ
in the emphasis placed on viability or maturity of the fetus at the
time of injury. Many of them require viability, some require
quickening, and some have allowed recovery even though the injury
occurred during the early weeks of pregnancy (7). Some examples
of different outcomes of recent cases on wrongful death actions
are given in the footnotes (8-12).

PRENATAL INJURIES NOT RESULTING IN DEATH

As we have seen, recovery for prenatal injuries, including
wrongful death, was denied following the precedent established
by Justice Holmes in 1884. But as early as 1900 this doctrine
was questioned in a dissenting opinion by Justice Boggs in
Allaire v. St. Luke's Hospital (13). He stated that once a fetus
became viable, it must be considered to constitute life separate
and apart from its mother. This dissent formed the basis for the
later trend to allow recovery.

In 1946, in Bonbrest v. Kotz (14) a federal district court
held the physician liable for injuries to the fetus when it was
being removed from the womb. To allow recovery, the court looked
to fetal viability and references to property law. The court said
that if the child was viable and born alive, then it is "but
natural justice" to allow it to maintain a cause of action. Although Bonbrest restored "natural justice" to prenatal injuries,
it established the issue of viability as the crucial determinant
in allowing recovery. However, in a 1956 case, viability at the
time of injury was not the deciding issue. A child was born with
deformities of one leg, ankle and foot allegedly due to tortious
conduct during the sixth week of pregnancy. Recovery was allowed
based on the reasoning that any injury sustained after the time of
conception should be recognized as a cause of action (15). A

concurring opinion disagreed with the majority in calling a "cell"
a person: "Whether a cell becomes a person is dependent on the
processes of nature..." A dissenting justice argued that the
time of conception cannot be ascertained but the time of quickening can be determined.

The case of Bennet v. Hymers underscores the irrelevance of
viability to recovery. The court stated "We adopt the opinion
that the fetus from the time of conception becomes a separate
organism and remains so..." (16).

The opinion in Smith v. Brennan went even further (17). In
allowing recovery for prenatal injuries followed by livebirth,
the court held that "the child has a legal right to begin life
with a sound mind and body..." If this reasoning ever becomes
widely recognized, or if it is raised to a constitutional right
then there would be far-reaching consequences in cases of genetic
defects.

Courts do not always rely on scientific facts. A mother was
injured during the first month of pregnancy and later a mongoloid
child was born. Recovery was allowed for prenatal injury, even
though the extra chromosome in Down's syndrome had been discovered
a year earlier (18).

In two other cases, mental retardation allegedly resulted
from injuries early in pregnancy. Although this would be difficult
to prove, the courts allowed recovery (19).

We have reviewed a spectrum of cases on prenatal torts;
many other cases could be cited. The reader is referred to an
excellent annotation by Chase (20) on liability for prenatal injuries.

Finally, a very interesting fact situation arose in connection
with a tort action for preconception injury rather than prenatal
injury. In Jorgensen v. Meade-Johnson Laboratories (21), the
mother took contraceptive pills prior to the conception of mongoloid twins, one of whom died after birth. The plaintiff father
sought recovery, alleging a breach of express and implied warran-
ties of the pills which allegedly caused chromosome abnormalities
in the mother's ovum before conception. The lower court dismissed
the case, finding no precedent for recovery due to injury to a
sperm or ovum. The court relied on Morgan v. U.S. (22) which dismissed the complaint of an infant's injuries allegedly caused by a
blood transfusion to the mother prior to conception. According to
the Jorgensen court, a cause of action arising from maternal chromosome damage by oral contraceptives must be created by the legislature, not by judicial decision. The appellate court, however,
vacated the lower court's holding and remanded the case for trial,

stating that an injury before conception is actionable when the
injured party, the infant, is born alive. Since tort law for
prenatal injuries has evolved from court decisions, no legislative
action is necessary (23).

WRONGFUL DEATH OF A PARENT

In two cases of wrongful death of a father when the fetus was
in utero, a cause of action ripened at birth, allowing the posthumous child to recover (24). Both courts held that a fetus is
in esse even though it is not yet viable at the time of death
of the father.

WRONGFUL LIFE

The tort of wrongful life has a colorful history and is
reviewed in a recent annotation (25). The cases discussed here
concern liability of one person for wrongfully causing the birth
of another. The issue is not between being born with health or
without it, but rather the choice between a worldly existence and
no life at all. If the cause of action of "wrongful life" can
be sustained, then this tort could touch upon situations where a
genetically defective child is negligently conceived or knowingly
carried to term after a prenatal diagnosis has been made. The
defective infant could theoretically bring suit against the physician or against its parents.

In a 1963 Illinois case, a bastard sued his father for damages, alleging that a tort had been committed at the moment of
conception. He claimed stigmatization because of his illegitimate
status. The court not only allowed the action but they agreed
that injury had occurred. However, they refused to award damages,
arguing that this was the province of the legislature after a
"thorough study of all of the consequences" (26).

Several courts have reached the question of "wrongful life"
when a child was born after the mother was purportedly sterilized.
In Jackson v. Anderson (27) the court held that a cause of action
could be maintained and damages assessed for the expenses of
rearing an unplanned child. Another court, however, has denied
recovery, reasoning that any child is a joy and benefit, even
though unplanned (28). In another case the court distinguished
between "wrongful pregnancy" and "wrongful life", allowing recovery to the parents for the ineffective salpingectomy but dis-
allowing the expenses of rearing the child (29).

Three cases of rubella during early pregnancy resulting in
fetal deformities have also been decided. The outcomes of the

three cases were quite different although the fact situations
were similar. In each case the pregnancy and birth occurred at a
time when abortions for grave risks to the fetus were illegal
in those states. In two cases the physician or hospital had failed
to warn the mother of the risks to the child and in one the diagnosis of rubella was not made prenatally.

        In <u>Gleitman v. Cosgrove</u> (30), the New Jersey court disallowed
the cause of action because the law did not recognize damages for
allowing the birth of a child, even with defects. Also, the parents had sought recovery for emotional pain and suffering and expenses for caring for the defective child. This was denied because of the impossibility of measuring damages and because of
substantial policy reasons in support of the preciousness of human
life.

        In contrast, a New York court, in <u>Stewart v. Long Island
Hospital</u> (31), held that the jury was justified in finding that the
hospital breached duties it owed the mother to make a "reasonable
disclosure" to her, thus giving her the false assurance that an
abortion was not indicated for rubella. However, the court said
no remedy exists for having been born with a handicap when the
alternative is not to have been born at all. Thus, the hospital
was not liable for damages to the infant. The parents, but not
the child, were awarded money damages.

        Recently, the Texas Supreme Court ruled, in <u>Jacobs v.Theimer</u>
(32), that a cause of action exists against a doctor who negligently failed to diagnose rubella and to advise the mother of the
attendant risks. They held that recovery could be had for all
past and future medical expenses.

ABORTION LEGISLATION AND JUDICIAL DECISIONS BEFORE 1973

        The legal prohibitions against abortions have a relatively
recent history. Abortion before quickening was not proscribed by
religion or law until the 19th century in the Western world. The
first U.S. anti-abortion law was passed in 1835 in Missouri. In
1861 early abortion was forbidden in England as an offense against
the person. Not until 1869 was early abortion equated with murder
by the Roman Catholic Church (33).

        All of the state statutes passed during the past century
have recognized the legal right of abortion to save the life of
the mother. Many states have also permitted abortion to save the
life and health of the mother (sometimes including mental health),
if there is a substantial risk to the fetus of grave physical or
mental defects, or if the pregnancy resulted from rape or incest.

Many of the court decisions pertaining to illegal abortions were inconsistent and reflected either statutory differences or variations in court interpretations of legislative intent. In general, the woman is considered to be the victim of the abortionist and not the perpetrator of the crime (34). Women were seldom prosecuted for seeking and obtaining an illegal abortion. Usually the pregnant woman was held not to be an accomplice (35) even though she willingly submitted to an abortion (36). A few courts have held that the mother is a participant and legally responsible for her act of submission (37). On rare occasions she was prosecuted as a principal in the crime (38), or for self-induced abortion. In certain states there was statutory punishment for the woman who caused a self-abortion or who submitted her body for one (39).

During the early 1970s several abortion decisions addressed the question of the status of the fetus and weighed the relative rights of the mother and the fetus. However, the issue of maternal versus fetal rights arose years earlier in another setting. In Raleigh-Fitkin Hospital v. Anderson (40) the hospital sought authority to give a blood transfusion to a woman who was in the seventh month of pregnancy. She objected on religious grounds. The court required her to submit to the transfusion because "the unborn child is entitled to the law's protection." The judge said it was unnecessary to decide the question of whether the transfusion is ordered to save the mother's life or the child's life because "the welfare of the child and mother are so intertwined and inseparable that it would be impracticable to attempt to distinguish between them..."

This raises the possibility that the courts, at some time in the future, may find a rationale to require a pregnant woman with phenylketonuria to adhere to a special low-phenylalanine diet in order to protect the fetus from brain damage. In both transfusions and diets, the mother's treatment would benefit the child.

Returning to abortion, we will examine four cases which may be considered a prelude to the United States Supreme Court decision of 1973. In Babbitz v. McCann (41), the court stated that the state's interest in the fetus was not compelling enough to invade the right of privacy of the mother even though the fetus was four months in utero. The question of personhood was not addressed; only the superior interest of the mother vis-a-vis the fetus was recognized.

In Abele v. Markle (42), the court invalidated a statute protecting human life from the moment of conception by failing to find a compelling state interest in the fetus, reasoning on the basis of the mother's right to privacy. In the opinion it was

pointed out that the U.S. census did not enumerate fetuses, imply-
ing that a fetus is not a person under the Constitution.

An Indiana court, on the other hand, upheld the state's
abortion statute which forbade abortion except to save the life of
the mother (43). It reached the question of privacy but distinguished its holding from Griswold v. Connecticut (44) which
legalized the right to use contraceptives by arguing that prevention of life is not the same as destruction of life after
conception.

In Pennsylvania, a doctor sued as guardian ad litem for a
class of unborn children, who, as alleged citizens, had their lives
terminated before birth (45). The court could find nothing in the
Constitution which indicated that the Fourteenth Amendment right
of due process could be applied to the fetus.

THE ROE v. WADE DECISION AND ITS AFTERMATH   .

On January 22, 1973 the United States Supreme Court handed
down a landmark decision, entitled Roe v. Wade (46), and a companion case, Doe v. Bolton (47). It is not the purpose of this
paper to review the numerous publications (48) which have emanated
from this far-reaching decision. It may be summarized by quoting
a footnote from Fletcher (49): "This decision knocked down restrictive abortion statutes in forty-six of the fifty states of the
Union. It means that freedom of abortion may not be regulated in
the first six or seven months - and even then, after the first
six months, it would only be allowed to the states, not required.
The Court rejected any assignment of personal status to the fetus
at any stage, and allowed only that a government might find a
public interest in potential human life, and even then not until
the fetus has become capable of survival independently of the
maternal body".

Following the Roe pronouncement a number of courts and
legislatures have attempted to undermine the right of the mother
to abortion on demand.

The state of Rhode Island, by legislative fiat, declared that
human life begins at the moment of conception and that such life
is a person under the Fourteenth Amendment. This statute was
challenged in Doe v. Israel (50) by an action brought for declara-
tory judgement on the constitutionality of this law. It was held
that the Rhode Island legislature cannot establish a law contrary
to the Roe v. Wade decision. The Supreme Court has the ultimate
authority to interpret the meaning of the Fourteenth Amendment and
no state may pass a law which, by declarations or presumptions, is

contrary to the Supreme Court's holding. Later, the Supreme
Court declined to hear the appeal (51).

In another case (52), three doctors brought suit for a de-
claratory ruling and injunctive relief of Florida's post-Roe
abortion statute which required consent of the husband of a pregnant woman or consent of the parents of a minor in order to perform a legal abortion. In relying on Roe, the court held that
the state cannot interfere on behalf of husbands or parents until
the third trimester. The state cannot delegate by statute an
authority it does not possess and which, in fact, has been proscribed by the Supreme Court in Roe. Therefore, that clause of
the statute pertaining to third party consent is held to be unconstitutional, infringing upon the paramount right of privacy of the
mother.

In spite of the Florida holding, the issue of consent is
still alive in other jurisdictions. The Pennsylvania legislature
has enacted an abortion statute (over the governor's veto) requiring that married women obtain consent of their husbands prior
to obtaining an abortion and both Ohio and Pennsylvania now require
third party consent for abortions on unmarried minors (53). Both
of these statutes will undoubtedly be challenged as unconstitutional.

There have been other attempts to provide protection for the
fetus under law. A lower court in California has granted extra
food stamps to a pregnant woman (54). The Supreme Court has
addressed a similar issue involving increased welfare payments to
expectant mothers under the Social Security Act. In a 7-1 decision the majority held that federally funded benefits for needy
children (under the Aid to Families with Dependent Children assistance program) were intended for "children already born, with an
existence separate and apart from its mother" (55). Prior to
this ruling most lower courts had interpreted the Social Security
Act broadly to include the unborn within the definition of a
"dependent child" (56). Now, the states are given the option of
including extra benefits to pregnant women but are not required to
do so.

We cannot gauge what impact this decision will have on other
issues now wending their way toward the Supreme Court, such as the
food stamps case, and it would be foolhardy to attempt to do so.
We can be sure that continued challenges to Roe will arise in the
months ahead as the legislatures and courts wrestle with other
questions related to pregnancy and abortion.

CONCLUSION

The final chapter on the legal status of the fetus has not

yet been written. The law evolves as social customs, moral codes, and ethical issues change. Much of the momentum for legal innovation derives from scientific advancements which pose new questions for judicial decisions. As this brief review has demonstrated, many questions are left unanswered. Other presentations and discussions at this symposium may provide us with guidelines in searching for solutions.

ACKNOWLEDGEMENTS

Supported in part by U.S. P.H.S. Grant GM 19513.

REFERENCES

1. W. Blackstone, Commentaries 130 (1762).

2. Burdett v. Hopegood, 24 Eng. Rep. 485 (1718).

3. Hale v. Hale, 24 Eng. Rep. 25 (1692).

4. Marsh v. Kirby, 21 Eng. Rep. 512 (1634). Wallis v. Hodson,
    26 Eng. Rep. 472 (1740) is in accord with the Marsh holding
    more than a century later.

5. Stephen E. Segal, Wrongful Death and the Stillborn Fetus - A
    Current Analysis, 7 Houston L. Rev. 449 (1970).

6. Dietrich v. Inhabitants of Northampton, 138 Mass. 14, 52 Am.
    Rep. 242 (Sup. Jud. Ct. 1884).

7. William L. Prosser, Law of Torts 356 (3d ed. 1964).

8. Polquin v. Macdonald, 135 A. 2d 249 (N.H., 1957). The
    Supreme Court of New Hampshire stated that if the fetus was
    viable at the time of injury and could have lived apart from
    its mother if the mother died, then recovery may be allowed,
    even if such a "child" dies in the womb.

9. Carroll v. Skiff, 202 A. 2d 9 (Pa., 1960). Plaintiff-father
    sued physician for negligently destroying an allegedly
    "viable fetus" in utero at ten weeks. The Supreme Court of
    Pennsylvania stated it was not the legislature's intent to
    provide relief to estates of unborn children. Since the
    estate of the unborn fetus is nothing, it cannot take property
    by descent or devise unless it is born alive.

10. Keys v. Construction Service, Inc., et al, 165 N.E. 2d 912
    (Mass., 1960). The court held that if the fetus is so well
    developed in its mother's womb that it is capable of sustaining
    life if parturition occurs and if the child is born alive and
    then dies, a cause of action exists.

11. Panagopoulos v. Martin, 295 F. Supp. 220 (S.D.W.V. 1969). A
    stillbirth resulted from mother's injury during the eighth
    month of pregnancy. The court held that if death occurs in
    utero, a viable fetus should be considered a person, for
    biologically speaking, it is. Damages were awarded solely for
    sorrow, mental anguish and bereavement, since pecuniary loss
    is purely speculative.

12. State v. Dickenson, 275 N.E. 2d 599 (Ohio, 1971). A viable

fetus died <u>in utero</u> from placental hemorrhage incurred in an automobile accident caused by a drunken driver. The court found that the child must be born alive to be a person within the meaning of the vehicular homocide statute. The <u>Dickenson</u> case here construes the Ohio <u>vehicular</u> homicide statute; generally the courts have held that the killing of an unborn child is not a homicide under other statutes, a notion rooted in common law principle that the fetus must be born alive, independent of its mother, before it could be subject of a homicide. Leading cases which uphold this view are <u>Clark v. State</u>, 117 Ala. 1, 23 So. 671 (Ala., 1878); <u>Keeler v. Superior Court of Amador County</u>, 2 Cal. 3d 619, 817 Cal. Rptr. 481, 470 P. 2d 617, 40 A.L.R. 3d 420 (Cal. 1970); <u>Passley v. State</u> 194 Ga. 327, 21 S.E. 2d (Ga., 1942); <u>Abrams v. Foshee</u>, 3 Iowa 274 (1856); <u>Morgan v. State</u>, 148 Tenn. 417, 256 S.W. 433 (Tenn., 1923). An excellent annotation on this subject can be found in 40 A.L.R. 3d 444 (1971).

13. <u>Allaire v. St. Luke's Hospital</u>, 56 N.E. 638 (Ill., 1900). Recovery denied for prenatal injuries resulting in limb deformities. The court reasoned that the child is part of the mother during pregnancy and only severed at birth. A long line of cases followed the <u>Dietrich</u> and <u>Allaire</u> rationale, e.g. <u>Gorman v. Budlong</u>, 49 A. 704 (R.I., 1901); <u>Nugent v. Brooklyn Hts. Ry. Co.</u>, 139 N.T.S. 367 (N.Y. App. 1913), <u>appeal dismissed</u>, 102 N.E. 1107 (1913); <u>Buel v. United Rys. Co. of St. Louis</u>, 154 S.W. 71 (Mo., 1913); <u>Lipps v. Milwaukee Electric Ry. & Light Co.</u>, 199 N.W. 916 (Wis., 1916); <u>Drobner v. Peters</u>, 133 N.E. 567 (N.Y. 1921); <u>Stanford v. St. Louis-SF Ry. Co.</u>, 108 So. 566 (Ala. 1926); <u>Magnolia Coca-Cola Bottling Co. v. Jordan</u>, 78 S.W. 2d 944 (Tex. 1935); <u>Newman v. City of Detroit</u>, 274 N.W. 710 (Mich., 1937); <u>Berlin v. J.C. Penney Co.</u>, 16 A. 2d 28 (Pa., 1940).

14. <u>Bonbrest v. Kotz</u>, 65 F. Supp. 138 (D.C.D.C. 1946). This was the first case allowing for recovery for prenatal injuries not resulting in death. Cases which followed the <u>Bonbrest</u> precedent include <u>Amman v. Faidy</u>, 114 N.E. 2d 412 (Ill., 1953); <u>Woods v. Lancet</u>, 102 N.E. 2d 691 (N.Y., 1951); <u>Stegall v. Morris</u>, 258 S.W. 2d 577 (Mo., 1953); <u>Tursi v. N.E. Windsor Co.</u>, 111 A. 2d 14 (Ct., 1955); <u>Von Elbe v. Studebaker Packard Corp.</u>, 15 Pa. D. & C. 2d 635 (1958); <u>Rainey v. Horn</u>, 72 So. 2d 434 (Miss., 1950); <u>Tucker v. Carmichael & Sons. Inc.</u>, 65 S.E. 2d 909 (Ga. 1951); <u>Damasiewicz v. Gorush</u>, 79 A. 2d 550 (Md., 1951); <u>Mitchell v. Couch</u>, 258 S.W. 2d 901 (Ky., 1955); <u>Mallison v. Pomeroy</u>, 291 P. 2d 225 (Ore., 1955); <u>Worgen v. Greggo & Ferrara</u>, 128 A. 2d 557 (Del., 1956); <u>Polquin v. Macdonald</u>, 135 A. 2d 249 (N.H., 1957).

15. <u>Hornbuckle v. Plantation Pipe Line</u>, 93 S.E. 2d 727 (Ga., 1956).

16. Bennet v. Hymers, 147 A. 2d 108 (N.H., 1958).

17. Smith v. Brennan, 157 A. 2d 497 (N.J., 1960).

18. Sinkler v. Kneale, 164 A. 2d 93 (Pa., 1960).

19. Daley v. Meier, 178 N.E. 2d 691 (Ill., 1961) and Sana v. Brown, 183 N.E. 2d 187 (Ill., 1962).

20. Annot., 40 A.L.R. 3d 1222 (1971).

21. Jorgensen v. Meade-Johnson Lab. Inc., 336 F. Supp. 961 (W.D. Okla. 1972).

22. Morgan v. U.S., 143 F. Supp. 580 (D.C.N.J. 1956).

23. Jorgensen v. Meade-Johnson Lab. Inc., 483 F. 2d 237 (10th Cir. 1973). This holding, which recognizes a cause of action for damage to the sperm or egg resulting in an injury to the infant could have far-reaching consequences. A library search for a case of radiation to the gonads prior to conception, resulting in a genetically-defective baby, was unproductive. But as physical and chemical mutagens in the environment increase (e.g., industrial hazards, drugs, food additives, and air pollutants) the possibility of suits for preconception injury becomes more likely.

24. La Blue v. Specker, 100 N.W. 2d 445 (Mich., 1960). In a similar case, Weaks v. Mounter, 493 P. 2d 1307 (Nev., 1972). the court relied on the La Blue reasoning.

25. Annot., 22 A.L.R. 3d 1441 (1968).

26. Zepeda v. Zepeda, 41 Ill. App. 2d 240 (1963). In another case involving wrongful life by reason of illegitimacy, an infant was conceived when her mother, a mental retardate, was raped by another patient in the state hospital. The child claimed the state was negligent in allowing her conception. But the court concluded that there are strong policy and social reasons against providing such compensation. Williams v. New York, 223 N.E. 2d 849 (App. Ct. 1963); cert. denied, 379 U.S. 945 (1964). In Pinkney v. Pinkney, 198 So. 2d 52 (Fla., 1967), the court similarly denied a cause of action for wrongful life brought by a bastard on the grounds that such a tort could only be created by statute.

27. Jackson v. Anderson, 230 So. 2d 503 (Fla., 1970).

28. Terrey v. Garcia, 496 S.W. 2d 124 (Tex., 1973).

29. Coleman v. Garrison, 1 Fam. L. Rep. 2013 (1974). In accord
     with Coleman is Aronoff v. Snider, 292 So. 2d 418 (Del., 1974).

30. Gleitman v. Cosgrove, 227 A 2d 689 (N.J., 1967).

31. Stewart v. Long Island College Hospital, 296 N.Y.S. 2d
     41 (1968).

32. Jacobs v. Theimer, 18 Tex. Sup. Ct. J. 222 (1975).

33. Blair L. Sadler, The Law and the Unborn Child: A Brief Review
     of Emerging Problems, in Early Diagnosis of Human Genetic
     Defects - Scientific and Ethical Considerations. Fogarty
     International Center Proc. No. 6, a symposium sponsored by
     the John F. Fogarty International Center for Advanced Study
     in Health Sciences, National Institutes of Health, Bethesda,
     Maryland, May 18-19, 1970, pp. 211-218, U.S. Government
     Printing Office.

34. 1 C.J.S. Abortion § 14 (1936) note 48.

35. Id., note 49.

36. Id., note 50.

37. Id., note 51.

38. Id., note 52, note 52.5

39. Id., note 47.

40. Raleigh-Fitkin Hospital v. Anderson, 201 A 2d 537 (N.J., 1964).
     A strong precedent had been established in Jehovah's
     Witnesses cases where a court exercises its powers of parens
     patriae by ordering transfusions to children when the parents
     refuse. See, for example, State v. Perricone, 181 A 2d
     751 (1962).

41. Babbitz v. McCann, 310 F. Supp. 293 (E.D. Wis., 1970). In
     Rosen v. La. State Board of Med. Examiners, 380 F. Supp.
     1217 (E.D. La. 1970). The court came to the opposite conclu-
     sion, announcing that embryonic and fetal life may be protected
     by the state from destruction by another. In protecting
     the right of the fetus to survive, on the basis of equality
     with human beings generally, the state is not violating the
     Fourteenth Amendment rights of the mother.

42. Abele v. Markle, 351 F. Supp. 224 (D.C.Ct., 1972), judgment
     vacated, 41 U.S.L. Week 3462 (U.S.   ) rehearing den-
     ied, 41 U.S.L. Week 355 (U.S. April 17, 1975).

43. Cheaney v. State of Indiana, 285 N.E. 2d 265 (Ill., 1972).

44. Griswold v. Connecticut, 381 U.S. 479 (1965).

45. McGarvey v. McGee-Womens Hospital, 340 F. Supp. 751 (W.D.
     Pa. 1972).

46. Roe v. Wade, 410 U.S. 113 (1973). Footnote 54, at page 157
     sets forth the difficulty of applying Fourteenth Amendment
     rights to the non-viable fetus:
     "When Texas argues that a fetus is entitled to Fourteenth
     Amendment protection as a person, it faces a dilemma.
     Neither in Texas nor in any other State are all abortions
     prohibited. Despite broad proscription, an exception always
     exists. (Saving the mother's life is a typical exception).
     But if a fetus is a person who is not to be deprived of life
     without due process of law, and if the mother's condition is
     the sole determinant, does not the Texas exception appear to
     be out of line with the Amendment's command?

     "There are other inconsistencies between Fourteenth Amendment
     status and the typical abortion statute. It has already
     been pointed out, in 49 supra that in Texas the woman is not
     a principal or an accomplice with respect to an abortion upon
     her. If a fetus is a person, why is the woman not a principal
     or accomplice? Further, the penalty for criminal abortion
     (in Texas and in most states) is significantly less than
     the maximum penalty for murder...If the fetus is a person,
     may the penalties be different?"

47. Doe v. Bolton, 410 U.S. 179 (1973).

48. See especially Tribe, Laurence H., Toward a Model of Roles
     in the Due Process of Life and Law, 87 Harv. L. Rev.(1973),
     and State Restrictions on Abortion as Violation of Due Process
     Right of Privacy, Harv. L. Rev. 75 (1973).

49. Joseph Fletcher, Humanness and Abortion, in The Ethics of
     Genetic Control: Ending Reproductive Roulette, New York:
     Doubleday & Co., Inc. (1974).

50. Doe v. Israel, 358 F. Supp. 1193 (D.C.R.I. 1973).

51. Amer. Med. Assn. News, June, 1974.

52. Coe v. Gerstein, 376 F. Supp. 695 (S.D. Fla. 1973). In a
     similar case a husband brought an action to enjoin his wife
     from having a voluntary abortion. The Massachusetts Supreme
     Court said "No", reasoning"... the state cannot interfere
     with the woman's abortion decision before the fetus is

viable..." Doe v. Doe, 1 Fam. L. Rep. 2019 (Nov. 12, 1974);
see also Washington v. Koome, 43 U.S.L. Week (U.S. Feb. 2,
1975).

53. Legislative Briefs, 1 Fam. L. Rep. 2067 (Nov. 26, 1974).

54. Houston Post, § A, p. 12, Col. 2 (Feb. 1, 1975). A U.S.
     District Court judge in California ordered the Department
     of Agriculture to give a pregnant woman extra food stamps to
     feed her unborn child after her attorneys argued she needed
     better nutrition.

55. Burns v. Alcala, 43 U.S.L. Week 4374 (U.S. Mar. 18, 1975).

56. In the last two years six federal courts of appeals and 18
     federal district courts have considered the question of
     whether the fetus is a "dependent child" under 42 U.S.C.
     606(a), thus entitling the pregnant woman to AFDC benefits.
     Most of the lower court decisions have leaned heavily in
     favor of eligibility. See Keller v. Mixon, 372 F. Supp.
     51, 371 F. Supp. 1379, 42 U.S.L. Week 2492 (U.S. Mar. 26,
     1974); 1 Fam. L. Rep. 2034 (Nov. 12, 1974); Lukhard v. Doe,
     493 F. 2d 54, 1 Fam. L. Rep. 2035 (Nov. 12, 1974); Hooker v.
     Carver, 43 U.S.L. Week 2057 (U.S. Aug. 13, 1974); 1 Fam. L.
     Rep. 2036 (Nov. 12, 1974); Brian v. California Welfare Rights
     Organization, 11 Cal. 3d 237, 520 P. 2d 970, 1 Fam. L. Rep.
     2036 (Nov. 12, 1974), 1 Fam. L. Rep. 2053 (Nov. 19, 1974);
     Parks v. Harden, 1 Fam. L. Rep. 2116 (Dec. 17, 1974.

THE FETUS AND THE LAW

Harold P. Green

The George Washington University National Law

Center, Washington, D.C.

The present state of the law with respect to the fetus can best be characterized as amorphous. Legal principles relating to the fetus are for the most part fragmentary and are much more suggestive than definitive from the standpoint of the kinds of issues that are likely to arise in the context of human use of the genetic techniques that are the subject of this Symposium.

The common law has recognized that the fetus has a legal personality for certain purposes. The legal principles applicable to the unborn child have been fully discussed elsewhere (1), and I shall merely summarize them in capsule form. In various areas of the common law, a fetus has been held to be capable of possessing legal rights. In most cases, however, these legal rights are contingent upon live birth of the fetus. For example, where a man's will devises property to his children, a child unborn at the time of the man's death is entitled, if the child is ultimately born alive, to share in the father's estate to the same extent as if he were living when the father died. Similarly, most states now recognize the right of a child, after live birth, to sue for damages on account of prenatal injuries (2). Although the law in many states permits the child to recover damages only if the injuries were inflicted after the fetus is viable, the general trend of the law seems to be in the direction of ignoring the distinction between viability and pre-viability (3). There are also a few cases in which it has been held that certain legal rights of the fetus are not contingent on live birth. It has been stated, for example, that an unborn child may bring a legal action to enjoin the waste of an estate in which it has an interest contingent on live birth (4); and in at least one case it has been held that an unborn child may sue its father for support (5). In addition, it has been held that

an unborn child is entitled to the law's protection so as to require a pregnant woman, notwithstanding religious objections, to
submit to blood transfusions necessary to preserve her own life
and the life of the fetus (6).

Whatever may be the common law rights of the fetus, it is
clear that they may be extinguished to the extent that the woman
carrying the fetus has a right to abortion. The 1973 decision by
the Supreme Court in Roe v. Wade (7) is, of course, relevant in
this connection, but it is important to understand that this
decision says very little about the legal status and rights of the
fetus. The issue in Roe v. Wade was whether a state has the constitutional power to interfere with the decision of a woman, in
consultation with her physician, to have an abortion performed.
The Supreme Court's decision was, therefore, solely in the context
of the clash of interests between the power of the state to prohibit
abortion and the right of a woman to have an abortion. The interests and rights of the fetus were not directly in issue.

The Supreme Court held in Roe v. Wade that a woman's decision,
in consultation with her physician, to have an abortion was encompassed within the previously recognized fundamental right of
privacy which could be infringed upon by a state only upon a showing of a compelling state interest. Avoiding precise definition
of the time at which these state interests attach, the court concluded that the state has an important and legitimate interest in
preserving and protecting the health of the pregnant woman and in
protecting the potentiality of human life, that these interests are
separate and distinct, that "each grows in substantiality as the
woman approaches term," and that each "becomes compelling" at some
point during pregnancy. Translating these conclusions into operative
rules, the court held that a state may not interfere with or regulate the medical judgment of the attending physician, in consultation with the pregnant woman, until "approximately the end of the
first trimester" of pregnancy. Thereafter, the state may regulate
abortion procedures to an extent reasonably related to the preservation and protection of the mother's health. Once, however, the
fetus is viable, i.e., "has the capability of meaningful life
outside the mother's womb," abortion may be prohibited, except where
necessary, as a matter of medical judgment, to preserve the life or
health of the mother. This exception means, as a matter of constitutional interpretation, that the interest of the mother in her
life and health, where her physician finds abortion necessary in
such interest, outweighs the state interest in the life of the fetus.

The Supreme Court did, however, consider the legal rights of
the fetus in one respect and held unequivocally that the fetus is
not a "person" within the meaning of the Fourteenth Amendment.
Thus, destruction of the fetus is not the taking of a person's
life prohibited by the Fourteenth Amendment.

The focus of this Symposium, to the extent that the interests of the fetus are relevant, is on deliberate reproductive interventions of two general types. The first type, which can be characterized as experimental, will occur primarily in the cases of fetuses destined for abortion, and is intended to develop scientific knowledge that will enable biomedical science to deal more effectively with future reproductions. The second type of intervention may be characterized, although somewhat loosely, as therapeutic, and involves procedures looking towards the birth of a live human being. The intention in this latter type of intervention is to produce a healthier or a better child, or at least one that the parents and/or the biomedical practitioners will regard as healthier, better, or more desirable. The line between experimental and therapeutic interventions, as I use these terms, is not always entirely clear, since the initial use of these procedures in human beings for therapeutic purposes will always involve some element of experimentation.

The existing body of law relating to the fetus has evolved in what can be termed a largely pre-technological context. The legal system has to date taken little if any cognizance of the various possibilities inherent in the application of genetic technologies to human beings. It is not difficult to visualize the kinds of novel legal issues that may arise in varied factual contexts in the years ahead as these technologies come into use for human purposes. Although the full range of these issues is beyond present comprehension, it would be useful to list and briefly describe a few of the more obvious ones.

1. There are some unresolved questions about abortion.

First, bearing in mind that the Supreme Court's decision in Roe v. Wade dealt only with the right of a state to prohibit abortion, there remains a question whether the fetus itself has a legal right not to be the victim of abortion. This question might arise where the father who objects to abortion, or where another party with an interest in the birth of the child, brings an action on behalf of the fetus to enjoin a contemplated abortion. Having raised this as an unanswered question, I should add that I have little doubt that, should such a question arise, the courts will extend Roe v. Wade so as to reject any such interest on the part of the fetus.

Second, although the Supreme Court held that a state has no adequate interest in prohibiting pre-viability abortion, it is possible that, with changing circumstances and advancing technology, a state could show such an interest in some cases. For example, if abortion were widely used for purposes of choosing the sex of children with a resultant imbalance in the male-female ratio, it is possible that a state might be able to show an adequate interest in prohibiting abortion for such a purpose.

Third, there remains a question as to the legal status of
abortion if, as can be expected, biomedical technology pushes
back the point in time at which a fetus is capable of meaningful
life outside the mother's womb. For example, would a state be
justified in prohibiting abortion if biomedical science should
make it possible to sustain the life of a first or second trimester
abortus?

2. A second group of questions centers upon the fate of the
abortus. Some state laws require that abortions performed during
the period of viability be performed through procedures that will
preserve the life of the fetus. Since Roe v. Wade recognizes
that a state may regulate abortion during the period of viability
to promote its interest in the potentiality of human life, such
statutes are probably constitutional. This invites the questions
whether, apart from such a statute, a viable fetus has a legal
right to have an abortion performed in a manner that will preserve
its life and whether a woman has a legal right to have an abortion
that will result in a dead abortus.

Another question relates to the physician's duties with
respect to a live abortus that is either seemingly non-viable or of
borderline viability. As suggested by recent events in this
Commonwealth, conservatism may require a physician to attempt
heroic measures to sustain the life of such an abortus. But since
such measures, if successful, could result in a disadvantaged
child, does a fetus which is to be aborted have a legal right not
to be kept alive?

3. A third group of questions involves experimentations on
the fetus, with the consent of the parents,* in anticipation of
abortion. If an abortion resulting in destruction of the fetus is
in fact performed, the fetus will not be injured by the experiment.
On the other hand, it cannot be certain at the time the experiment
is performed that an abortion will be performed - since the mother
may change her mind - or that a live abortus will not result under
circumstances requiring an effort to sustain its life. Moreover,
the mother's consent to the experiment may operate as a deterrent
to change of mind about the abortion decision and thereby prejudice

---

*For purposes of simplicity, I refer in this paper to consent by
 the "parents" even though, as a matter of law, the consent of
 only one parent - the one on whom the procedure is performed -
 may be required. In Roe v. Wade, the Supreme Court explicitly
 left unanswered the question of the father's rights with respect
 to abortion decisions.

the interests of the fetus. The fetus is, therefore, at risk,
theoretically at least, and there is the question whether such
experiments should be performed with the consent only of the
mother (or mother and father), since her interests at the time
of consent are in conflict with the interests of the potential
child. The Department of Health, Education and Welfare's proposed
regulations on fetal experimentation (8) attempt to deal with
this problem by excluding those conducting the experiment from
any role in determining when and how the abortion will be performed
and whether or not the fetus is viable. It is questionable
whether these procedures provide adequate protection against the
possibility that a live child will result.

    4. Another group of problems relates to interventions that
may occur in connection with conception, i.e., _in vitro_ fertilization and cloning. The first and early children born as a
consequence of these techniques, especially the latter, will be
"different." Each will enter life as a unique kind of human being.
One cannot predict whether they will be, or will come to regard
themselves as, advantaged or disadvantaged by the circumstances of
their conception. There are obvious ethical questions concerning
the propriety of deliberate technological interventions looking
towards the birth of a child that may, as a consequence of the
intervention, be born in a disadvantaged condition. There may
also be substantial legal questions. Does a potential child have
a legal right to be born with such biological advantages and disadvantages as are bestowed by nature's own lottery rather than to
be subject to the risk of disadvantages resulting from deliberate
technological interventions of this kind?

    Such questions are easy to raise but difficult to answer at
this time. Any attempt to predict how the law will respond to
these questions would be sheer and unproductive speculation.
Accordingly, instead of trying to predict the course of the law's
response, I would like to discuss the general framework within
which these questions will ultimately be resolved by the law.

    The genetic technologies relevant to this Symposium exist and
will exist primarily as a result of direct or indirect public
funding of scientific research. The fact that public funds are
made available for this purpose connotes a public policy decision
reflected in appropriations legislation - a form of law - that this
research is beneficial in itself and may lead to beneficial
applications. As this research opens doors to the previously unknown and is applied in animal experimentation, the possibilities
for beneficial human application become apparent. Initial human
application is on an experimental basis, and as this human experimentation demonstrates the feasibility of beneficial application
in human beings, the techniques are introduced on a clinical basis.

Human application, whether experimental or clinical, requires
the consent of the parents whose child will ultimately be born.
It is clear that the initial experiments on human beings involve
risk to the potential child. Parents who consent to an experiment
involving the fetus will probably do so on the basis of a
calculation that the potential benefits outweigh the risks. The
parents make this decision not only for themselves, but also for
the potential child. Later, when the technology is used on a
clinical basis, consent is based on the same kind of calculation
except that the parents can presumably have a higher degree of
confidence that the prospective benefits are real and that the
risks, if any, are small, or at least more clearly known.

It should be observed that the parents' consent to the use
of these techniques is based on their own interests, needs, and
desires. In most situations, there may well be an identity of
interest between the parents and their potential child. This is
not, however, necessarily the case. An attribute which the parents
seek for their child through use of these techniques may turn out
not to be advantageous from the child's standpoint in itself or in
relation to the risks to which the unborn child is exposed. While
it may be true that no one is better able to determine what is
in the unborn child's best interests than the parents, there is an
unsettling conflict of interest, exacerbated by the ambiguity of
the physician's legal duty to the unborn child, that would seem to
invite a legal response in the direction of enhancing the legal
protection afforded the unborn child.

Over and above the questions raised about the impact of genetic
technology on the interests of unborn children, there are also
questions that arise because of the potentially substantial impact
on society. The most dramatic potential societal impacts are those
relating to cloning and various scenarios for in vitro fertilization.
These potential impacts may also invite a legal response, particularly by the legislatures, based more on concern for broad social
values than on concern for the interests of unborn children.

To the extent that legal issues involving human application
of these technologies are considered by the courts, the decisions
in individual cases will generally involve the determination of
legal rights and interests in the context of factual situations
that arose in the past. The judicial system is essentially back-
wards-looking. It cannot operate to prevent the occurrence of
abuse but only to vindicate the rights of plaintiffs who have
suffered abuse. Of course, once a rule of law has emerged in a
judicial decision holding a defendant liable, this rule will
operate prospectively as precedent and should discourage, but
cannot prevent, similar abuse in the future. An exception to this
is in the case of judicial proceedings to enjoin use of the technology in a specific case, but it is unlikely that a court would

in fact issue an injunction in the absence of some experience
showing the probability of abuse. If, therefore, the use of these
technologies involves the potentiality for abuse, the most effective preventative would be legislation regulating or prohibiting
the technology. It is unlikely, however, that legislatures would
enact regulatory or prohibitory measures in the absence of demonstrable abuse since legislatures are generally too busy to devote
their attention to hypothetical problems, particularly where the
benefits are obvious and the possibility of abuse is merely speculative. It should be noted, moreover, that legislation that
anticipates abuse is generally undesirable in that it would operate
to forestall beneficial developments.

These difficulties are compounded by the problem of incrementalism. Initial human use of a genetic technology will probably
be in a context in which the use, viewed objectively, is clearly
beneficial and desirable. Subsequent uses will probably be in
successively more questionable contexts. Each successive step
will, however, operate as a precedent justifying subsequent
incremental steps. To the extent that there is a legal response
to the earlier steps, the response, if affirmative from the
standpoint of use of the technology, will operate as a legal precedent clearing the way for future steps, even though the future
steps may involve the potential for substantially greater abuse.
For example, the technology of artificial insemination and the
judicial decisions dealing with this technology would appear to
invite the taking of a next step, in vitro fertilization. It is
obvious, however, that in vitro fertilization involves issues of a
substantially different dimension and that the courts that have
considered artificial insemination questions did not consider, and
could not have considered, the implications of their decisions
with respect to in vitro fertilization. It should be observed,
moreover, that even though use of genetic technology will be on an
incremental basis, human application is likely to proceed through
various incremental steps at a very rapid rate so that subsequent
steps are likely to be taken before there is full information about
the human and legal consequences of earlier steps.

If, therefore, one is concerned about the potential adverse
consequences of the genetic technologies, it should be recognized
that remedial laws will probably be formulated only after adverse
consequences are clearly demonstrable. Even then, moreover, the
law-makers will be faced with the difficult task of balancing the
obvious benefits against the adverse consequences, and the outcome
of such balancing is problematical.

Genetic technology, like most technologies, has an inherent
momentum of its own fueled by the ambitions of its proponents
and their desire to bring the benefits of the technology to
mankind. There appears to be an inexorable linkage between

scientific research that points the way towards beneficial human
applications and the actual use of the fruits of the research for
human purposes. What man can do for his benefit, he will do.
Potential adverse consequences are, of course, considered concomitantly with prospective benefits by the biomedical community
when a new technology is available for human use, as well as by
courts and legislatures confronted with the necessity of deciding
questions involving the use of the technology. The fact of the
matter is, however, that at that stage benefits, which are usually
obvious and relatively immediate, almost always outweigh the risks
of adverse consequences, which are usually speculative and relatively remote.

      One cannot, therefore, offer comfort to those who look to the
law to slow the march, or to bar the doors, to the brave new
world. It seems inevitable that biomedical science will develop
new genetic technologies that offer substantial benefits, and that
our institutions of government will not interfere with the use of
these technologies where individuals desire their benefits and
the practitioners of the technology are willing to employ them.
Indeed, it seems today to be a cardinal principle of public policy
that beneficial biomedical technology, like beneficial technologies
generally, should be vigorously developed and reduced to practice,
and that purely hypothetical adverse consequences should not stand
in the way. It is implicit in the view that it is time enough to
worry about adverse consequences when they are shown to be real,
that adverse consequences are acceptable, at least for a time. It
may, however, be a difficult or impossible political and legal
exercise to reverse the thrust of a technology after people come
to enjoy and expect its benefits. If, therefore, the march to the
brave new world is to be slowed, this will probably come about only
through the self-restraint of the biomedical community. Such self-
restraint would reflect a greater propensity to give weight to
potential, albeit still hypothetical, risks including those risks
that may transcend the biological well-being of those directly
involved in the use of the technology and impinge upon the values
of the community as a whole. Self-restraint of this kind may
indeed be necessary if the biomedical community is to be permitted
the degree of independence and self-regulation that it presently
enjoys.

      In conclusion, I would note that the issues raised by genetic
technology involve a complex amalgam of diverse and potentially
conflicting interests: the interests of the fetus, the potential
child, the mother, the father, the family unit, the physician,
biomedical science, and society as a whole. In the present state
of the law, there has been only a meager beginning of the process
of sorting out and attempting to reconcile these interests. My
speculations in this paper are necessarily fragmentary and far less
than exhaustive. It can, however, be regarded as a certainty that

the kinds of questions I have discussed will ultimately have to
be resolved by our courts and legislatures. The exciting prospects
for biomedical advance in the areas discussed in this Symposium
will inevitably be matched by exciting legal developments as the
law responds to the challenges posed by technology. We can all -
scientists, physicians, and lawyers - look forward to an interesting and challenging future.

REFERENCES

1. The Law and The Unborn Child: The Legal and Logical Inconsis-
    tencies, 46 Notre Dame Law. 349 (1971); The Unborn Child and the
    Constitutional Conception of Life, 56 Iowa L. Rev. 994 (1971);
    Louisell, The Practice of Medicine and Due Process of Law,
    16 UCLA L. Rev. 233 (1969); Kindregan, Abortion, The Law and
    Defective Children: A Legal-Medical Study, 3 Suff. U.L. Rev.
    226, 258-271 (1969).

2. Anno. 40 ALR 3rd 1222.

3. Ibid.

4. Waters v. Duvall, 1 Bland Ch. (Md.) 569 (1827).

5. Kyne v. Kyne, 38 Cal. App. 2d 122, 100 P.2d 806 (1940).

6. Raleigh Fitkin-Paul Morgan Memorial Hospital v. Anderson,
    42 N.J. 421, 201 A 2d 537, cert. den. 377 U.S. 985 (1964).

7. 410 U.S. 113 (1973).

8. 39 Fed. Reg. 30648, et seq. (Aug. 23, 1974).

THE LEGAL ASPECTS OF FETAL VIABILITY

Leonard H. Glantz

Center for Law and Health Sciences

Boston University School of Law, Boston

THE CRIMINAL LAW

The issue of the legal aspects of fetal viability is an important one for those involved in the practice of genetic counseling. Amniocentesis is usually performed after the 14th week of pregnancy. Although chromosomal karyotyping can be performed within fourteen days, biochemical analysis usually takes between 21-40 days (1). As a result of this, a woman will be in her 20th or 21st week of pregnancy before she would be able to make an informed decision as to the termination or continuation of her pregnancy based on the results of these diagnostic tests. At this stage in fetal development there is the problem that the fetus is approaching "viability" and the state may then outlaw non-therapeutic abortions (2). Even assuming the state has not outlawed such procedures, the physician who performs the abortion procedure at this stage may be subject to criminal liability if the fetus does not survive. Such was the case of Dr. Kenneth Edelin who, after a trial in Boston, was found guilty of manslaughter for the death of a "baby boy" who died following a hysterotomy.

The prosecution in this case alleged that the "baby" was viable, was "born alive", and therefore Dr. Edelin had a duty to try to preserve its life. In attempting to try to prove viability the prosecution stressed the gestational age of the fetus. It made every attempt to show that the fetus was "killed" between the 24th and 28th weeks of pregnancy. Apparently, the prosecution believed that the Supreme Court in Roe v. Wade (3) had determined, as a matter of law, that viability occurs at the 24th week. Whether or not this is in fact the case, the prosecution claimed that a duty to try to save the life of such a fetus arose after viability. Implied in this argument is the allegation that abortion is not necessarily the termination of fetal life, but only the termination of a woman's pregnancy. If this interpretation of the meaning of abortion is correct, it could have serious consequences on genetic counseling. When a woman decides to abort her pregnancy as a result of discovering that the fetus is abnormal, it is most likely that she intends to destroy the fetus. If she wanted the fetus to be born alive, she would not undergo the abortion procedure. If the Edelin decision is allowed to stand, doctors would be forced to try to save the lives of fetuses which are aborted late in the pregnancy, and women who undergo abortions after amniocentesis may be presented with the defective child they wished to avoid.

The culprit of the case is the concept of viability, meaning the ability of the fetus to live separate and apart from the mother. In the Edelin case, the prosecution sought to prove, in addition to viability, that the fetus was born alive. This concept of live birth is integrally tied to the concept of viability, because proof of live birth following an abortion is proof of viability, and proof of viability may be a strong indicator of live birth. To prove live birth, the prosecution presented evidence that the fetus breathed after the placenta was separated from the uterine wall. Under the common law of homicide, these elements are necessary to prove the murder of a "newborn."

One of the problems the prosecution had to face was that the murder of a viable fetus, not born alive, was impossible. Homicide requires the taking of a "person's" life, and for purposes of the criminal law, no person existed until birth. Generally, birth required complete expulsion from the mother, breathing and an independent circulation (4). These three requirements have caused some relatively bizarre results. For example, in one case a woman was tried for murder for cutting off the head of her child during delivery. An examination of the lungs showed that the infant breathed, but the court stated that since the infant could have breathed prior to complete expulsion, there was insufficient evidence to convict the woman (5). Fetal viability was never mentioned. At common law there was some split as to whether or not a child was a "person" for purposes of homicide if it was expelled but the umbilical cord was not cut (6). An examination of one of these cases shows how a court used medical evidence to arrive at its decision a century ago.

In State v. Winthrop (7) a doctor was accused of the murder of a child while attending a woman at birth. The state claimed that the child respired and had independent circulation. The trial court instructed the jury that the child could have independent

existence even when attached to the mother by the umbilical
cord, whether or not it breathed or had independent circulation.
This instruction comes very close to stating that viability of the
child (i.e., the potential for independent life) is enough. The
Supreme Court of Iowa, in reversing, pointed out that the evidence
demonstrated that the fetus' ductus arteriosus was not closed
and that this indicated lack of independent circulation. This
means that the child had a potential for independence (viability?)
but not actual independence. The court, in continuing its scientific analysis went on to say that:

> While the blood of this child circulates through the
> placenta, it is renovated through the lungs of the
> mother. In such a sense it breathes through the
> lungs of the mother (8).

It went on to cite Beck, Medical Jurisprudence, vol. 1, page 498,
in which it is stated:

> It must be evident that when a child is born alive,
> but has not yet respired, its condition is precisely
> like that of the fetus in utero. It lives merely
> because the fetal circulation is still going on.
> In this case none of the organs undergo any change (9).

The court goes on to state that if a child is not independent,
the possibility of independence is merely conjecture and not
enough to convict a person of murder. The comment has been made
that due to the state of medicine at the time the common law was
developing there was probably a presumption that a child would not
be born alive and therefore the requirement of live birth made some
sense (10). Another commentator has pointed out that the use of
the live birth tests could (and have) lead to some strange results.
In an admittedly absurd example he states that if a woman wants to
kill her child at birth and not worry about criminal prosecution
she should give birth in a bath full of water. This way the baby
could never breathe and would not have an independent circulation,
since it would be dead prior to the severance of the umbilical
cord (11).

The California court took a step in amending this situation in
the case of People v. Chavez (12). In this case a woman was
accused of killing her newborn child, and there was evidence of
breathing and independent heart action. The defense established
that both of these functions could have occurred prior to complete
expulsion from the mother. The court stated that there is not
much difference between a child the moment before birth and the
moment after birth. It went on to say:

(A)viable child in the process of being born is a

human being within the meaning of the homicide statute,
whether or not the process has been fully completed.
It should at least be considered a human being where
it is a living baby and where in the natural course
of events a birth which is already started would
naturally be successfully completed (13).(emphasis added)

Under a ruling such as this, if an abortion can be perceived as a
birth process, and if the fetus is "viable" it is possible that
one could be guilty of infanticide if one does not try to save the
fetus.

The impact of this decision has been somewhat narrowed in
the later case of Keeler v. Superior Court (14). In this case
Mrs. Keeler had received an interlocutory decree of divorce from
her husband and was living with another man. She became pregnant
and Mr. Keeler discovered this fact. He sought out Mrs. Keeler
and said to her,"I'm going to stomp it out of you." He then proceeded to kick her in the abdomen several times. Mrs. Keeler was
thirty-one to thirty-six weeks pregnant at the time of this incident. She went to the hospital where a caesarian section was
performed. The fetus which weighed five pounds and was 18 inches
long was stillborn, the result of a fractured skull. Mr. Keeler
was indicted for murder of the child. The lower court found that
the fetus was viable and that it became a "person" at the time of
viability for purposes of the homicide statute (15). The Supreme
Court reversed, relying on the common-law rules of homicide discussed above. The court distinguished this case from Chavez
stating that Chavez was dealing with a viable child in the process
of being born (16). In Keeler this process had not yet begun.
Thus, for the purposes of the homicide statute a viable fetus in
utero is not a person and therefore one who kills such a fetus
is not guilty of homicide.

The strong dissent in Keeler argues that advances in medicine
must be followed by advances in the law. It states that all would
agree that shooting a corpse is not murder because a corpse is not
a human being. However our concept of what constitutes a corpse
is continually being modified by advances in the field of medicine.
It then goes on to ask:

Would this court ignore the developments and ex-
onerate the killer of an apparently "drowned"
child merely because their child would have been
pronounced dead in 1648 or 1850? Obviously not.
Whether a homicide occurred in that case would be
determined by medical testimony regarding the capability of the child to have survived prior to the
defendant's acts. And that is precisely the test
which this court should adopt in the instant case (17).

In discussing the policy issues involved, a relatively rare occurrence in this line of cases, the dissent asks, "what justice will be promoted, what objects effectuated" by not considering this child a human being for the purposes of the homicide statute? It asks if the defendant's violent act of stomping this child to death is any different than killing a newborn. It states that this fetus with "its unbounded potential for life" must be protected (18).

Following the Keeler case, the California state legislature passed a feticide statute (19) which states that it is unlawful to kill a human being or fetus regardless of age. This however makes it very different from most of the feticide statutes in this country which make it a crime to kill a "quick" fetus, not a viable fetus.

Thus, it appears that the concept of viability is really unheard of in the criminal law. However, the courts' unwillingness to confront this issue and to rely on law centuries old for their answers raises questions as to the responsiveness of the courts to medical advances, and points to their propensity for using old law to confront new problems.

THE CIVIL LAW

During the past thirty years the courts have been more willing to examine the policy issues surrounding compensation of fetuses for harm caused to them while in utero.

The first case dealing with the issue of compensating a fetus for harm done to it in utero arose, interestingly enough, in Massachusetts. In Dietrich v. Inhabitants of Northampton (20), a woman slipped on a highway due to a defect in the road. She was four to five months pregnant at the time and prematurely gave birth. Justice Holmes in his opinion pointed out that the fetus was too little advanced to survive although there was testimony that the fetus lived for 10-15 minutes. He said that the fetus is not a person in being and thus no one could owe a duty to it. In addition, he held that this rule would not be affected by the "degree of maturity reached by the embryo at the moment of the organic lesion or act."

Thus, neither quickening nor viability entered the picture at this stage. This rule was followed by virtually all courts until 1946, although as early as 1900 Judge Boggs in a dissent in Allaire v. St. Luke's Hospital (21), strenuously argued that viable fetuses born alive should be compensated for harm caused them while in utero.

In 1946 the case of Bonbrest v. Kotz (22) arose. A child was

injured by a physician during delivery and sued the doctor for
malpractice. The court readily conceded that at common law a child
en ventre sa mere has no judicial existence and could not successfully bring suit. The court refers to the Dietrich case but dis-
tinguishes it by pointing out that in the present case the court
is dealing with a direct injury to a viable child. The court
claimed that the child's viability was proved by its existence at
the time of the suit. It then flatly states that a viable fetus
is not part of the mother, as the mother could die but the fetus
could continue to live. The court attempts to outline the significance of viability - the viable fetus has its own bodily form
and members, manifests all of the anatomical characteristics of
individuality, possesses its own circulatory, vascular and excre-
tory systems, and is now capable of living (23).

The court argues that as a matter of policy the fetus must be
allowed to recover for damage which it will suffer for the rest
of its life. If the child is not allowed to recover then a wrong
will have been inflicted for which there is no remedy. Quoting a
Canadian decision the court finds:

> If a right of action be denied to the child it will
> be compelled without any fault on its part, to go
> through life carrying the seal of another's fault
> and bearing a very heavy burden of infirmity and
> inconvenience without any compensation therefor.
> To my mind it is but natural justice that a child,
> if born alive and viable should be allowed to maintain
> an action in the courts for injuries wrongfully com-
> mitted upon its person while in the womb of its
> mother (24).

Thus we have a court trying to utilize scientific facts to show
the separate nature of the fetus from the mother, and struggling
with notions of natural justice.

Since 1946 a number of courts have decided that for a fetus to
recover for prenatal injuries after it is born alive, the injury
had to occur while it was viable (25). This is because the courts
state that the injury must be done to a "person," and prior to
viability there is no person in existence. A number of courts have
decided that the viability of the infant at the time of the injury
is an irrelevant factor as long as the fetus is born alive. In
Hornbuckle v. Plantation Pipe Line (26), it was decided that if a
child born after an injury sustained at any period of its prenatal
life can prove the ill effect, it would have the right to recover.
One justice of the court concurring specially stated that he
believed the fetus had to be quick at the time of the injury to
recover. The law requires injury to be done to a person and no
such person exists prior to quickening (27).

In 1960 the New Jersey Court also decided that the child could recover for injuries occurring at any time after conception (28). In this case the court recognized that recovery for such injuries was generally not allowed because the child was a part of the mother and not an independent person to whom a duty could be owed. It then discusses the scientific basis for disputing this proposition. The court states that medical authorities have recognized that a child "is in existence" at the moment of conception and not merely a part of its mother's body. The unborn child has its own system of circulation, a heart beat not in tune with the mother's but which is more rapid and with no dependence on the mother except for sustenance, which is also true after birth. It scorns the "semantic argument" whether or not an unborn child is a person. The court found that from the moment of conception a process is placed in motion that will produce a person if left undisturbed, and that "a child has a legal right to begin life with a sound mind or body " (29). While the court admits that most courts require viability at the time of injury as a precondition to recovery, it states that the "viability rule is impossible of practical application" since viability is so difficult to ascertain (30).

An interesting case in regard to the viability issue is Torigan v. Watertown News Co. (31). A woman who was three and one-half months pregnant was injured in a motor vehicle accident. The child was born two and one-half months later and lived for two and one-half hours. The court held that non-viability of the fetus at the time of the injury was not a bar to recovery. However, the court did not discuss the fact that the child may not have been viable at the time of birth. The fact that it "lived" for two and one-half hours was enough to permit recovery. It should be remembered that in 1884, the child in the Dietrich case decided in the same jurisdiction, also "lived" after birth for 15 minutes, but recovery was denied.

In a case a few years after Torigan the Massachusetts court had to decide if a fetus which is born dead could recover for prenatal injuries. The court said that if a fetus is born alive it becomes a "person" within the meaning of the wrongful death statute as it has "the theoretical possibility of survival and of enduring the consequences of prenatal injury throughout life" (32).

If it is not born alive it is not such a person and will not suffer continuing injury. The court is really setting forth a compensation concept by stating that recovery should only be for those who will suffer in the future, and that funds should be made available for treatment. This, of course, is not necessary when the child dies (33). There might appear to be an injustice in the outcome as one who injures a fetus only enough to cause damages must pay for his actions, while one who injures the fetus severely enough to kill it does not.

Some courts do allow recovery for wrongful death even when
the fetus is not born alive. In Chrisafogeorgis v. Brandenburg (34)
a woman in her 36th week of pregnancy was struck by a car which
caused the death of the fetus. The court, now arguing logic, not
medicine or law, states that it is indefensible not to allow recovery in this case. For the purpose of wrongful death actions the
fetus is a person at the time of viability as it was alive, and
would have stayed alive but for the actions of the tortfeasor.
The difference between death in utero or ex utero, states the
court, is the time of death, not the cause of death or the character
of injury (35). The dissenting opinion argues that the Supreme
Court's abortion decision held that a fetus is not a person. It
also argued that viability was an unusable standard as it was
difficult to ascertain, indefinite and depends on several factors
other than length of pregnancy (36).

WHAT INTERESTS ARE WE PROTECTING?

The law concerning civil suits has tried to progress through
the years, relying on medical evidence, logic and social policies
to compensate individuals to whom harm has been done. Although it
may sound logically indefensible to state that recovery can be had
for injury to a fetus but not for its death, the courts that decide
cases in this way are trying to help the living, and are not
concerned with punishing the wrongdoer. It is for this reason that
the courts have disregarded the concept that the injury must occur
during viability. In compensating those infants who have been
harmed as the result of prenatal injuries and were born alive, the
courts have implicitly found that the true damage is suffered after
birth, i.e., having to go through life with some defect or deformity.
Thus, the damage has not actually been suffered by the viable or
non-viable fetus, but by the human being who must now live with
the handicap caused by the tortfeasor. This is one interest the
court is protecting.

With fetuses that are born dead, recovery is denied because
no protectable interest seems to have been harmed. No one has been
deprived of "life," because no life has truly existed. In addition,
no future medical or custodial care is required and no future
suffering will occur (37). One might argue that recovery should be
allowed so that the potential wrongdoers will be deterred from
harming fetuses. However, in injuring the fetus so severely that
it will be stillborn, the wrongdoer will probably have to also
injure the mother, and her possibilities for recovery should discourage harm to her and her fetus.

The courts' reluctance to expand the area of the criminal law
in cases such as Keeler (38) does not display a callousness on
the part of the court, but instead indicates the courts' desire to

protect a countervailing interest - the right of the defendant.
The Keeler court's reversal of the lower court's decision that the
killing of a viable fetus in utero is murder was based on constitutional law. Basically, the California court stated that no such
crime existed in common law, that the California statutes do not
include a feticide law, and therefore the defendant could not have
known that he was breaking a law at the time of his actions. To
convict him in this situation would be a denial of due process
(39). The court then passed the burden of righting this perceived
wrong onto the legislature which it felt was the proper decision-
maker.

The common law, then, had three reference points in pre
existence that it found meaningful - conception, quickening and live
birth (40). Each had something to offer and was based on some
kind of logic. For example, after conception if the child's father
died, the unborn child can inherit from his father upon being born
alive (41). The common law had a strong bias for insuring that
property would go from the father to the son so as to keep the
property within blood lines. The law, to accomplish this purpose,
was willing to ignore the fact that there was "no person in being"
at the time of the father's death. If a child were born within
forty weeks of the father's death, that child would inherit the
father's property (42). The forty week limitation added some
definiteness to the scheme as the exact time of conception would
have been impossible to ascertain centuries ago.

The concept of quickening at common law could have served two
purposes. One was religious, i.e. at the moment of quickening the
fetus became infused with a soul and therefore a "person" came
into being (43). From a more scientific basis, however, quickening was really the first concrete indication that there was a live
fetus within the mother. Although quickening usually refers to
the first recognizable movement of the fetus, usually from the
16th to the 18th week (44), theologians and cannon lawyers fixed
this point at forty days for males and eighty days for females
(45). One American court set the date of quickening at four months
after conception (46). Interestingly, the draftsmen of the 1965
New York abortion law (47) used the 24th week as the point which
separates the degree of the crime. The draftsmen referred to the
24th week as the point of quickening. As only the mother could
truly testify as to the quickening it was felt that a fixed period
would make proof of the crime easier (48).

Live birth, of course, was the moment when the fetus became
a person in the eyes of the law.

Assuming that these common-law concepts have some basis in
logic, we must ask, can we say the same about the concept of
viability? On the most basic level, what does the term mean?

Dorland's Medical Dictionary tells us it is the "ability to live
after birth" (49). In 1965 the American College of Obstetrics and
Gynecology defined "live born infant" as "one that weighs 500 grams
or more and shows any sign of life, such as heart beat, voluntary
muscular activity or respiration" (50). A fetus that could meet
these criteria would be viable. Williams' Obstetrics in 1971
stated that although there is a report of 397 gram fetus surviving,
and the authors personally cared for a 540 gram fetus that survived,
survival is rare before a weight of 700-800 gram fetus surviving,
The authors recommend that at 1,000 grams the fetus has a substantial chance of survival and that therefore this could be considered
the point of viability. Williams' defines the word viability in
terms of survival while Dorland defines viability in terms of the
ability to live. This is an important distinction. The prosecution
in the Edelin case alleged that if the fetus was separated from
its mother and took one breath, it "lived." The common law is in
agreement. But what interests do we further by defining viability
as the ability to take one breath? I suggest that as important as
viability may be in making determinations of fetal rights we
must look to the interests we seek to protect and get away from
setting arbitrary points in the prenatal period as a means of
guiding our action. This is a more difficult task, but it would
also be a more rewarding one.

We can look at a couple of examples in which an interest
analysis could be performed that might change the results in a
specific case. Means,in his article (51),discusses a case (52)
in which a woman created a trust which she later decided to revoke.
Prior to the revocation she had to obtain the consent of every
"person beneficially interested" in the trust. At this time she
was eight months pregnant and after the birth of the child it would
have been a beneficially interested person under the terms of the
trust. The trustee bank went to court to determine if the consent
of the fetus (or someone acting in its behalf) was required. The
court said that the fetus was not a person until it "sees the light
of day," and therefore no consent was required. Since the fetus
was almost certain to be born, one wonders whether or not the court
should have treated it as a child who might be deprived of a benefit
by the mother's action. The court rejected this type of analysis
and instead relied upon old common-law rules.

Or we can look at the case set forth at the beginning of the
paper, dealing with amniocentesis. Suppose a woman undergoes this
procedure and discovers that the child will be born with a serious
defect. She decides to terminate the pregnancy which is now in
the 20th or 21st week. Let us further suppose that she resides in
a state where the legislature has decided that viability occurs
at the 20th week and proscribes all abortions not done to preserve
the woman's life or health. By allowing this situation to arise
the legislature may have protected fetal life, but it has deprived

the woman of making her decision to terminate pregnancy on the
basis of full information. Thus, the hypothetical state has decided that a woman can have an abortion on the basis of no information but if she undergoes a test which would enable her to make
her decision based on full information, she will not be able to
terminate her pregnancy.

As another example one can examine the regulations pertaining to experimentation with fetuses proposed by the Department
of Health, Education and Welfare (53). These regulations would
prevent experimentation which is of no benefit to that particular
fetus, but would allow certain types of experimentation "as part
of (but not prior to the commencement of) a procedure to
terminate the pregnancy." Thus the fetus loses certain rights
when the procedure begins. If we look back to the Chavez case
(54), we see the court gave the fetus greater rights after the
birth process began than prior to the beginning of the process.
The regulation in question is only indirectly concerned with
the rights of the fetus. If experimentation were permitted
prior to the abortion procedure but in contemplation of such procedure, and there was a chance that the fetus would be damaged by
the experiment, then the woman would not be able to change her
mind after the experimental procedure and undergo the abortion.
In effect, this regulation protects the mother's right to change
her mind, and in this way indirectly may protect the fetus. After
the abortion procedure has commenced, the mother has given up her
right to change her mind. The interests to be furthered by the
criminal law and the interests to be furthered by the regulation
of experimentation are different, and thus fetal rights are
defined in a different manner.

Let us assume that a court requires a fetus to be viable at
the time an injury occurs as a precondition to its recovering damages after it is born. As noted above, this is not a completely
hypothetical situation. By adhering to such a rule the court would
satisfy the purely legal requirement that a "person" must be injured
prior to recovery. But it would be ignoring the fact that the
fetus would be deprived of protection throughout the first three
months of gestation, during which time the fetus is very susceptible
to prenatal injuries (55).

The point to be made is that in defining the rights of fetuses,
it is not enough to determine viability or quickening, or conception,
without an examination of the interests we seek to protect.
Purpura has reported that "brain life" in humans begins between
the 28th and 32nd weeks of pregnancy (56). Brain life according
to Purpura means the capacity of the cerebral cortex to begin to
develop consciousness, self-awareness and other generally recognized cerebral functions. Therefore Purpura suggests that
viability should be deemed to begin at this stage and not at 24

weeks. The concept is very appealing because if death occurs when
the brain stops functioning (57), then should "life" begin prior
to its functioning? The concept of "brain life" may be relevant
in the future interpretation of the viability requirement in Roe
v. Wade, but should it determine property rights of fetuses
in utero?

What is needed is a committee similar to the Ad Hoc Committee
of the Harvard Medical School to Examine the Definition of Brain
Death. The purpose of the committee would be to determine the
possible interests that a fetus might have at various stages in
development, a scientific analysis of the developmental stages of
the fetus (when does brain life, ability to survive, ability to
live for a short period of time, ability to feel pain, occur,
for example) and the interaction between the policy considerations
and the scientific knowledge we possess. Only through the detailed
analysis of these policy and legal considerations in the light of
recent scientific and medical advances can we rationally and fairly
protect the rights of the fetus, and the rights of those who make
decisions concerning the fetus.

REFERENCES

1. Friedman, Legal implications of amniocentesis, <u>Univ. of Pa.
    L. Rev.</u> 123:92 at 97-98.

2. Roe v. Wade, 410 U.S. 113 at 165 (1973).

3. <u>Id.</u>, at 112.

4. American Law Report Annotation, 159:525 (1945).

5. <u>Id.</u>, at 525.

6. <u>Id.</u>, at 528.

7. 43 Iowa 519 (1876).

8. <u>Id.</u>, at 521.

9. <u>Id.</u>, at 522.

10. Comment, The non-consensual killing of an unborn infant: a
    criminal act, <u>Buffalo Law Rev.</u> 20:563 (1970-71).

11. Note, The killing of a viable fetus is murder, <u>Maryland Law
    Rev.</u> 30:140 (1970).

12. 176 P.2d 92 (Cal. App. 1947).

13. <u>Id.</u>, at 94.

14. 87 Cal. Reporter 481, 470 P.2d 617 (1970).

15. Keeler v. Superior Court, 80 Cal. Rptr. 865, at 868 (1969).

16. 470 P.2d, at 629.

17. 470 P.2d, at 632.

18. 470 P.2d, at 633.

19. California Penal Code §187.

20. 138 Mass. 14(1884).

21. 184 Ill. 359, 56 N.E. 638 (1900).

22. 65 F. Supp. 138 (1946).

23. <u>Id.</u>, at 141.

24. Id., at 141-2, quoting from Montreal Tramways v. Leveille, 4 Dom. L.R. 337 (1933).

25. Prosser, "Law of Torts" section 55 (4th ed. 1971).

26. 212 Ga. 504, 93 S.E.2d 727 (1956).

27. Id., at 729.

28. Smith v. Brennan, 31 N.J. 353, 157 A.2d 497 (1960).

29. Id., at 503.

30. Id., at 504.

31. 352 Mass. 446, 225 N.E.2d 926 (1967).

32. Lecesse v. McDonough, 279 N.E.2d 339 (1972).

33. Gordon, The unborn plaintiff, Michigan Law Rev. 63:594-5, (1965).

34. 55 Ill. 2d 368, 304 N.E.2d 88 (1973).

35. Id., at 91.

36. Id., at 92.

37. Gordon, supra note 33.

38. See, footnote 13 and accompanying text.

39. 407 P.2d, at 626.

40. Means, The law of New York concerning abortion and the status of the fetus, 1664-1968: a case of cessation of constitutionality, New York Law Forum 14:411 at page 424.

41. Id., at 421.

42. Id., at 421.

43. Id., at 412.

44. 410 U.S., at 132.

45. Supra note 40 at 412.

46. Segur v. State, 206 Ga. 618, 58 S.E.2d 149, cited in Hornbuckle, supra note 26 at 729.

47. N.Y. Penal Code, 1965 section 125.00.

48. Means, supra note 40 at pages 498 and 502.

49. Dorland's Medical Dictionary, 25th ed. (1974).

50. Terminology Bulletin #1, Sept. 1965.

51. Supra note 40.

52. Matter of Peabody, 5 N.Y.2d 541, 158 N.E.2d 841 (1959).

53. Federal Register 39:30654 section 43.306 (August 23, 1974).

54. See, footnote 11 and accompanying text.

55. Gordon, supra note 33 at 589.

56. New York Times, page 30 (May 9, 1975).

57. See, A definition of irreversible coma, J.A.M.A. 205:
    337 (1968).

DISCUSSION

Papers of Prof. M.W. Shaw, Prof. H.P. Green and Mr. L.H. Glantz.
<u>Principal Discussants</u>: Prof. F.D. Frigoletto, Mr. N.L. Chayet,
Dr. S. Bok and Prof. A.J. Dyck.
<u>Moderator</u>: Prof. A.M. Capron.

CAPRON: We talk about legal rules, but do so in a context
in which there is rapid change. In the 19th century, before
there was what is called a wrongful death statute (which applies
to the fetus as well as to adults) it was sometimes said that
railroad conductors were instructed that if a passenger was
badly injured, they should make sure that he was dead, because a
dead person lost the right to suit. It died with him, and it was
better that he arrive in the station dead and there be no right of
action, than he arrive live and severely injured with a cause of
action against the railroad. All that was changed by statute.

FRIGOLETTO: It certainly would be presumptuous of me to
comment in a legalistic way on these interesting papers that have
been presented to us this morning. I don't have the capacity to
respond to a law or a body of law that on the one hand awards for
damages, so-called damages, of mongolism following some kind of an
accident and a law, on the other hand, that can respond in one
state to damages for rubella and damages for a lack of action with
respect to rubella.

The law, again, has not been consistent, and I perhaps recognize that another discipline in addition to my own, namely medicine,
is as inconsistent and has contributed to some of the problems
that we have been trying to identify here this morning. The questions have been asked. They haven't been answered. I don't have
the answers. I appreciate through each of the comments that all of
these questions cannot be lumped together, but that each will have
to be individualized. Moreover, we will not be able to fall back
necessarily on precedents that have been set which do not apply to
things that are presently of concern, but which will become a
concern in the future.

CHAYET: A few months ago I received a notification from the
clerk of our Supreme Court here in Massachusetts that I had just
been appointed <u>guardian ad litem</u> for an unborn fetus. I asked for
a repeat of that, since I didn't think that was possible. I was
told that a case had arisen where a woman had become pregnant,
wanted to abort the child, and her estranged husband had just secured a restraining order against the hospital, preventing the
abortion.

I still haven't really gotten over the impact of that case
because for the first time one was not asked to give a speech about

abortion or argue a case for a client in the usual sense, but
rather one was given the legal guardianship of an unborn fetus.
After three sleepless nights and some research, I reported to the
court in a rather lengthy brief that I simply did not have a
client and that under the Roe v. Wade case there was no person
for whom a guardian ad litem could be appointed. I felt so badly
about that situation because whatever it was, if I wasn't going to
speak for it, who was? I called Prof. Kindregan and he thought
that the law was wrong in this area. He argued very well that
life begins at conception and the person does have personhood from
that time and also he filed a brief and we argued together before
the Supreme Court. The court did accept the non-person implications of the Roe v. Wade case and did allow the abortion.

The second situation that I'd just like to put before you was
a call that I received asking if I would defend for grave-robbing
a physician who had tried to find the best medication to treat
congenital syphilis. The statute reads, "Whoever conveys away
without being lawfully authorized the remains of a human body may
be sentenced to a term of years in the state prison and fined."

The argument goes that when the abortion occurred and the
abortus was taken from the delivery room to the pathology laboratory
for assay of the tissue, that this was a conveyance of the remains
of the human body. And since there were no burial permits that
the physicians had as an undertaker would have, they, therefore,
were properly indicted. This case will be coming up with motions
for discovery heard on May 27th and motions to dismiss heard on
June 24th, in just a few weeks. I still have great difficulty
forgetting the sight of these physicians placed in the back of a
police cruiser to be taken to headquarters for fingerprinting and
booking because they were trying to do some of the work that many
of you are interested in, which is to find out how to prevent certain types of congenital and other diseases.

Lastly - and this has been quite a year - becoming involved
with the physicians and the legislature in trying to develop some
kind of reasonable case to present to the legislature, as to why
we should not have such restrictive fetal experimentation legislation. How it finally came out is still difficult to accept. This
law allows experimentation only on fetuses which are going to go
full term and does not permit experimentation on fetuses which are
to be aborted. Now this does not refer to amniocentesis or work
particularly aimed at that particular fetus, but for any broad
experimentation or research. Only those fetuses which are scheduled
to go full term can be so worked with.

What are your conclusions at the end of all this? The ultimate
question is if viability is moved backwards, will abortion of
fetuses that could be kept alive be allowed? That becomes a

population control question, and a moral and ethical question.
Parties involved are very vocal, well financed, and very difficult
to deal with. Now, what advice can I give you? You have heard
two pieces of advice, don't be negligent, and scrupulously conform
to informed consent. Well, my opinion is that both of those
suggestions are virtually impossible for you to accept at the
present time.

First of all, informed consent is not only difficult when you
are dealing with a patient who can understand and listen to you.
What you have to tell that patient is so far from being known at
the present time that it's ridiculous. For us lawyers to impose
upon you the legal restraints of informed consent which is so
medically and scientifically unrealistic at this time is really an
impossibility. Yet we are doing it left and right in the courts.
What you have to do gets really to the thrust of my remarks. If
you don't start building your case for what you are doing in an
effective way, then you are in fact going to lose the battle,
because those who are arguing against research, against scientific
progress, against genetic technology and engineering, are very
vocal and being heard regularly. You can talk about what the
courts are doing, but remember, the legislatures every week are
passing laws contrary to the Supreme Court's opinion. It is true
when they get to federal court very often they are thrown out.
But how long can the courts keep the will of the people, and I use
the term "people" rather narrowly, as it is being expressed?
In my opinion, not indefinitely.

BOK: The various speakers have described the present status
of the fetus and the law and have raised a number of questions for
policy making and legislation. I would like to use the present
debate about fetal research as an example in commenting on Prof.
Green's conclusion regarding attitudes to dangers and abuses which
might flow from progress in genetics and the nature of the
restraints that we may need.

Prof. Green sees little hope that the law will respond to any
dangerous developments before they take place. Firstly, because
of an unwillingness to pronounce about hypothetical abuses and
risks, and secondly, because of difficulties in legislation even
after abuses and risks have arisen, in view of a resistance to
removing techniques which do seem to benefit some people, and which
are currently in use, and where the momentum is as strong as he
has indicated. Prof. Green suggests instead that there should be
self-restraint on the part of the biomedical community. Another
speaker has just mentioned there should be a sense of battle on
the part of this community as well, in order to replace the res-
straints that the law fails to impose and in order to see that some
research will continue and to avoid outside regulation which might,
in spite of all, come about if there are excesses or abuses.

My view is a very strong one. I think that the regular
professional self-restraint and self-regulation is not a very
impressive one. It would be admirable in the best of all worlds
if professions regulated themselves entirely. But we as a society
cannot count on this and on the result. I speak here not as a
lawyer or as a physician, but rather perhaps as a representative
of those human beings who in the long run will bear the burdens
and receive the benefits of all the research that will take place.
I think that professional self-restraint is insufficient because
in the first place all that is needed is a few who could refuse to
comply for some of the dangers to arise. I think people are justly
worried about that possibility. Secondly, the past record of
professional self-restraint has not been overwhelming.

The incentives not to comply are powerful and also in order
to exercise restraint, it would be necessary to know exactly
what kinds of procedures should not be undertaken and why. This
usually requires a debate and a profound analysis, yet frequently
there is no such debate before the abuses do take place. I will
give psychosurgery as an example. While it was being performed
most often, the self-restraint on the part of all those participating, even though a great many may have been very well meaning, was
so poor that we still have no data as to what was done, how often
it was done, or what the results were - good or bad. There has
been very little follow-up in the field of psychosurgery.

I think it is important to keep in mind, therefore, that the
self-restraints are not sufficient. If we shared Prof. Green's
concerns that legislation may not do the job, and Mr. Chayet's
concern that perhaps legislation may do the wrong job - and I agree
with him about that - and if we add my fears that professional
self-restraint will not suffice, we need to turn to a third alternative which could, as it were, stimulate both the legislation and
the self-restraint to going in the right directions. This alternative for which this conference is ideally suited is to begin a
thorough public debate about what we hope for and what we fear from
progress in genetics, in vitro fertilization, cloning, and fetal
research. There are a number of very important things that we
have to keep on doing. There are a number of things not so important that perhaps it would be dangerous to keep on doing. Most
importantly, we have to ask ourselves who should be making choices
about this kind of research.

Some may point a warning finger to the present debate about
fetal research where there has been great emotion and excessive
charges, while some important research is presently at a standstill.
But I do want to suggest that when the process is over, much will
have been gained and has already been gained.

I think it would be wrong to take the present Massachusetts

situation as being permanent. I think it will be bypassed very shortly. But we will have then restraints which do matter, and we will know what kind of research is important enough, what risks we want to take and what risks we don't want to take.

DYCK: I would like to make only two points. One is a minor factual point and the other, I trust, is a major moral issue. The first point stems from something that was said in Dr. Shaw's paper that religion did not consider abortion before quickening as homicide until 1869. It was then, she said, the Roman Catholics equated early abortion with murder. I believe that anyone who is acquainted with the early writings and early behavior of Christians as they entered the Greco-Roman world where abortion and infanticide were both very prevalent would note that abortion was considered akin to homicide in most of these writings. It was only later in Augustine and in Aquinas that we had some distinctions made between quickening as the critical period for deciding when an act of abortion was homicide.

The second point that I want to make is one that is raised somewhat in passing by these papers. Dr. Shaw says the law changes as ethics change. Dr. Green says that the courts are backward-looking, that the scientists will have to exercise constraint, and he talks about the benefits in medicine, weighing the benefits against the cost or the risks. I have no question in my mind that we have all benefitted greatly from medicine and research. So any of the remarks that I now make have nothing to do with the vendetta against research or against the benefits of medicine. It has to do with how we understand them.

As I understand some of the simplest benefits of medicine, because after all, I am mainly a consumer (although I try not to be), those benefits have to do with the treatment and/or the care of persons who have diseases or handicaps or whatever that medical intervention can do something about. Or in the case of care, it can bring comfort and health and alleviation of suffering. We have controlled or virtually eliminated certain diseases, such as smallpox or polio, through the use of vaccinations. Presumably these benefits are very clear. These benefits save lives and they enhance the health of persons and individuals.

But when we come to the area of genetics, the situation becomes much less clear. When we diagnose someone or some individual or some organism as having Down's syndrome, and when we diagnose Down's syndrome in a fetus or in a newly born, it is not clear that that fetus or that newly born benefits in any way, certainly not in any life-saving way. And when we apply diagnoses like XYY, it is not clear to me what is going to happen to some of the people who have these labels, these diagnoses, affixed to them.

There are great difficulties raised by genetic diagnoses. So we are not clear that we will benefit or that certain individuals will benefit when they receive certain genetic diagnoses. Vaccinations, appendectomies, polio shots do not create second-class citizens. Genetic diagnoses sometimes do create second-class citizens.

I would think that one of the greatest benefits that all of us have received and which goes far beyond medicine, is a presumption of equal rights. Equal right to life and equal right to liberty. What we have to look out for in the area of genetics is that genetic diagnoses and genetic labels are not used to deny these rights to life and to liberty.

Let me refer briefly here about the mention of incrementalism, or edge and wedge. The interesting thing about edge of the wedge is not that certain actions may lead to other actions, but that certain categories may logically apply much more widely than we had hoped they would apply. In fact, some of the genetic categories do not stop with live births and do not stop with the fetus. If we think it is of benefit to someone to die rather than to live with mongolism, something that I cannot understand is why to die should be a benefit. If persons with mongolism should benefit from death, then this thinking will extend and does extend beyond the fetus, because it is the mongolism that is a bad thing. We do have cases where infants with mongolism are simply not treated with life-saving intervention and they are by any of these slippery categories, viable, living, or whatever. I therefore feel that we need to think very seriously about using categories and to consider whether what we are actually doing will benefit the individuals to whom these categories and labels apply.

S.F. SPICKER: (The University of Connecticut School of Medicine) I also bring good and bad news: Philosophers (especially when teaching undergraduates) have prided themselves in remarking that they raise many questions, but should not be expected to provide any answers. That is the bad news. The good news is that we all now know that the law makes precisely the same claim.

I step up here because every such meeting should have its Jeremiah who, in this case, should caution on the use of the so-called ontological distinction that is introduced to distinguish being human from being a person. I have heard this distinction mentioned in the previous remarks of a few speakers and though they may not specifically intend to employ this ontological distinction, it does sound as if that is the case. The distinction has been employed to serve as a wedge within legal, philosophical, and biomedical debates on such issues as abortion and euthanasia. In the role of Jeremiah, I must say that I believe the distinction is overworked and cannot possibly serve as an adequate conceptual

distinction to do the job that some philosophers and others think
it can. This is revealed in discussions that attempt to define
the existential status of the fetus. Some suggest that whether
the fetus is <u>human</u> or a <u>person</u> primarily determines the way to
the correct moral point of view on abortions and experiments on
fetuses. The same distinction is often employed to enable us
to determine the moral justification of acts of euthanasia. Consider recent suggestions to redefine death, which permit us to
declare that X is no longer a person when deeply comatose, thereby
enabling the removal of organs from X without having to face any
legal accusations which hinge on ending the life of a person.

Thus I do not believe that the notion of 'person' can do the
conceptual work and carry the moral burden, as it were, that some
philosophers and theologians believe it can. Would that it could!
How easy certain practical decisions would become.

I think we also have to look more deeply into the complex
notion of rights, as well as of duties. Having read George
Annas' book, I know that he has reflected a good deal on rights.
But I am more concerned with the kind of 'things' rights are.
Dr. Green made a most important comment when he said that rights
may be <u>extinguished</u>. They seem, too, to be transferrable, for-
feitable, waivable, acquirable, and even made available. Rights
are peculiar kinds of things; we would do well to probe further
into their nature. Dr. Green's comment that rights are extinguishable brings to mind the prisoner who clearly relinquishes certain
rights <u>qua</u> prisoner. But I do not believe prisoners relinquish all
rights. Dr. Annas seems to argue that patients never give up
any rights when they enter the hospital. Although I have not
thought through counterexamples to show that patients do give up
certain rights, it is surely the case that they relinquish certain
rights to privacy in the hospital which they otherwise retain while
at home.

My question to Dr. Green, then, is whether he agrees that this
line of approach is worth pursuing. Perhaps we could then begin
to resolve the question as to when and in what cases the fetus has
rights <u>qua</u> fetus and not <u>qua</u> person, for the former already has
rights to inheritance and property. That is, when are rights
appropriately extinguished and when are they inappropriately
extinguished? If the rights of a fetus are extinguishable, that
is one view; if attorneys, philosophers, and the general public
do not accept this view, will it be because such a claim assumes
that the taking of the life of a particular fetus is immoral or will
a preconceived view or morality color our view of the rights of
the fetus?

GREEN: Unfortunately, it is necessary to think to some extent

in compartments. Whatever my views may be on the subject of
extinction of rights philosophically, ethically, morally or
theologically, the fact of the matter is that in that compartment
that is known as the law, rights are subject to extinction.
The Supreme Court in Roe v. Wade certainly very clearly indicated
that there are circumstances under which whatever rights the fetus
may have may be extinguished by the decision of the mother to kill
the fetus.

MEDICO-LEGAL ISSUES IN PRENATAL GENETIC DIAGNOSIS

Aubrey Milunsky

Harvard Medical School, The Eunice Kennedy Shriver

Center and the Massachusetts General Hospital

The essential thrust and philosophy of prenatal genetic diagnosis is to provide the opportunity to parents at risk to selectively have unaffected offspring. Utilizing current indications for amniocentesis approximately 95% of all studies reveal an unaffected fetus (1, 2). The need to consider therapeutic abortion only arises in about 5% of cases. This emphasis focuses on the point that these studies secure the birth of children that would ordinarily not even have been born, in contrast to the probably smaller number in which abortion would be a considered option. The aim of prenatal studies is to detect serious or fatal genetic defect in the fetus, and not to determine carrier status. Indeed all of us are carriers of 4-8 deleterious genes, and any such goal would therefore be regarded as simply absurd.

New technological developments have lead to striking advances in prenatal genetic diagnosis in which significant issues now confront the law (3). The aim of this presentation is to recognize these issues and to initiate a meaningful and constructive discourse that could form the basis for innovative and informed planning. Few undisputed answers exist and those that do stem directly from legal precedent concerned with issues other than prenatal diagnosis - a procedure which has become generally available only in these past five years. What legal precedents do exist are based mainly on extrapolations from confrontations arising over matters unrelated to prenatal genetic diagnosis.

ISSUES PRIOR TO AMNIOCENTESIS

Prenatal genetic study is undertaken to answer a sharply defined

question. Presently its main purpose is as a diagnostic and not
as a screening tool. Hence, if there has been a previously
affected child the exact diagnosis must be known before efforts
are undertaken to determine the fetal status for that genetic disorder. It is unacceptable for example, to seek for a mucopoly-
saccharide disorder in a fetus when a specific diagnosis has not
yet been attempted on a living affected child where the enzyme
defect could accurately be determined. Problems could therefore
arise at the initiation of the prenatal diagnostic process when
the wrong question is asked and the mother duly delivers an
affected infant that could have been prenatally diagnosed if due
care had been exercised prior to study.

The commonest reason by far for prenatal genetic studies is
advanced maternal age. Failure by the obstetrician or medical
practitioner to apprise a woman over 35 years of age about her risk
of having a child with a chromosomal abnormality may initiate
litigation. Recently one court has ruled that in at least 1971
this was not common practice (4). Plaintiffs may be more fortunate
today. It is also conceivable that an obstetrician may fail to
take action following the prenatal diagnosis of a genetic defect.
Indeed we have had one experience where the obstetrician communi-
cated "normal results" to the patient when indeed cell growth had
failed completely and no answer in fact existed!

Such an eventuality may also occur if the obstetrician argued
that the fetal defect diagnosed was not sufficiently serious as to
warrant termination of pregnancy, and refused to take action simply
in the light of his best judgement. While the woman has constitutional rights to control her own body in this instance, the physician too has the freedom through his best medical judgement to
determine the need for pregnancy termination (5). As Friedman
has argued (6), this problem cannot be circumvented by this woman
seeking a second physician, because the passage of time may be
sufficiently crucial as to have the pregnancy progress from the
second to third trimester of pregnancy. She might then find herself
in a situation where the state would prohibit her from terminating
such a pregnancy, unless in the light of the Roe v. Wade decision,
even abortion is then considered necessary for the preservation of
her life or health.

There are at least 66 different biochemical disorders of metabolism which are presently diagnosable in utero (1, 2). For an
increasing number of these disorders, determination of heterozygosity
is possible. Careful elucidation of the family history will alert
the physician to such possibilities and will hopefully initiate
a search for the particular carrier state. Such efforts are best
made prior to pregnancy, since misleading or spurious answers
may be obtained from serum studies during pregnancies (e.g. hexo-
saminidase assays for Tay-Sachs disease carriers). Indeed a failure

by the physician (especially having been primed by the family history) to determine the carrier status of both parents has already
formed the basis for legal action, where the offspring was born
with a preventable genetic defect.

Given the rarity of genetic disorders, obstetricians in particular will often be faced with questions concerning carrier detection, modes of inheritance, etc., that they will be unable to answer. Little emphasis is needed here to remind such practitioners
that their legal responsibilities are to seek or advise consultation
for their patients. Ignoring this duty to consult opens the
practitioner to malpractice actions.

Not infrequently a physician is faced with questions concerning
prenatal diagnosis when the options of abortion run contrary to
his own religious or other dictates. It would seem obvious that due
responsibility would be to refer such patients to another physician.
However, I am familiar with a number of cases where the obstetrician
has simply not offered prenatal studies nor referred the patient
elsewhere because of his own religious beliefs. Every physician
has the constitutional right to pursue his own religious beliefs,
but these should be exercised in a way as not to interfere with
the rights of his patients. On occasion both obstetricians and
geneticists will withhold prenatal studies unless a prior commitment to abortion is given by the parents if fetal defect is found.
I have espoused the view that this is untenable since I believe all
parents have a right to know as much as is possible about their
fetus. This right should extend all the way along the line up
to the point of pregnancy termination. Indeed those parents ambivalent about abortion in general may never have to address that
specific question and will receive the reassurance so frequently
provided by prenatal genetic studies. Withholding such diagnostic
studies from these parents may be ruled as an infringement of their
basic rights.

Introduction of a needle into the uterus carries with it a
risk to both mother and fetus (1, 2). Hemorrhage and infection in
the mother are real but rare sequelae. The amniocentesis needle
may disrupt the pregnancy (e.g. retroplacental bleeding), damage
the fetus (e.g. pierce the eye), or cause early fetal death or
conceivably even stillbirth. The amniotic fluid sample obtained
may become contaminated in culture, the cells may fail to grow,
no answer may be obtained and finally certain errors may be made.
The fetal sex could be incorrectly diagnosed, the karyotype may
be misinterpreted or maternal rather than fetal cells may have
been studied, or an error in biochemical assay may occur yielding
an incorrect diagnosis. All of these errors have already been
reported and suit has been entered in at least one case. An error
rate of between 6-7 per 1,000 cases studied is the general experience these past 8 years (7). All of the above issues require the

most careful delineation to parents prior to amniocentesis, with
careful verbal disclosure tailored to the comprehension of the
particular patients involved and including their written consent.

ISSUES ARISING FROM AMNIOCENTESIS AND PRENATAL STUDIES

Results provided from amniocentesis pertain to only one
fetus. Hence in the case of undiagnosed twins, no answer may be
available on the other twin who may be delivered with a genetic
defect. Prior ultrasound studies are available to mitigate this
disaster by at least being able to offer therapeutic abortion if
it has not been technologically possible to aspirate amniotic
fluid from the other twin sac.

Dilemmas rarely arise in situations where well described
genetic abnormalities are found in the fetus. On occasion however,
unexpected observations are made and may for example include a
fetus with an XYY karyotype or an unusual or undescribed chromosome
abnormality whose significance is unknown. In either event the
parents have the right to know all the information available,
and for the XYY fetus, this would mean an admission by the physician
that it is not yet possible to prognosticate with any certainty
about the ultimate development - normal, criminal or otherwise of
such offspring. No reassurance could or should be offered to
parents involved in the second situation of karyotypes of unknown
significance lest they be misled that some data base exists.

The prenatal diagnosis of a "treatable disorder" may be made
(e.g. galactosemia). Again the most careful and sophisticated
counseling is necessary in these situations lest the parents believe
that not only is treatment available but that it is invariably
successful. While there is only one genetic disorder (methylmalonic
aciduria) in which treatment of the fetus is available in utero via
the mother (8), other such disorders are likely to develop. Great
caution need be exercised in communicating any prognostication
on the developmental outcome of any such offspring.

Notwithstanding the problems of morality and ethics concerning
the fetus, some difficult legal questions remain that pertain to
fetal rights. The U.S. Supreme Court has acknowledged that the
state has an important interest in protecting potential life, and
that this interest may become compelling when the fetus has achieved
the capability of extra-uterine existence (9). Considered in
parallel is the view that a woman's right to privacy encompasses
the decision whether or not to terminate her pregnancy. Hence,
this qualified right to abort a fetus remains in sharp contradis-
tinction to the already established evidence from common law in
which the fetus has been seen to have legal rights. Some jurisdictions for example, have acknowledged the existence of estate

rights and property rights by the fetus as referred to by Prof.
Shaw today.

Problems may on occasion develop when a false positive test
leads to the termination of pregnancy with a healthy fetus. For
example the false elevation of alpha-fetoprotein concentration in
the amniotic fluid in one case resulted in the abortion of an
unaffected fetus. It is conceivable that a cause for action for
wrongful death might lie following the misdiagnosis resulting in
the abortion of a "healthy fetus." Many jurisdictions have already
recognized the right of prospective parents to bring such suits
in cases of fetal death caused by negligence (in such cases referring to the operation of motor vehicles).

Certain unanswered questions remain about the rights of a
fetus viewed from the standpoint of genetic defect. The courts
have examined actions where a defective child (affected in utero)
has entered suit because of the preventable nature of the defect.
The tort of wrongful life concerns the liability of one individual
for wrongfully causing the birth of another. The issue then is
between the difference of nonexistence and existence with defective
life.

The argument could be pursued that those who advocate legal
rights and personality as well as humanhood to the fetus could be
asked to acquiesce that such a fetus may indeed exercise the right
to be born unaffected rather than be born at all. Indeed the
Supreme Court of Rhode Island held that "justice requires that the
principle be recognized that a child has a legal right to begin
life with a sound mind and body" (6).

GENERAL ISSUES

Cost-benefit analyses for prenatal genetic diagnosis (2) have
demonstrated the major economic benefits of genetic disease prevention. Society, assailed by spiraling costs of health care, is not
likely to sit idly by in the face of such evidence. Indeed historically, the ability to test for homozygotes or screen for heterozygotes has rapidly been followed by hurried, poorly considered and
often inappropriate legislation. It can therefore safely be
anticipated that government will ultimately concern itself directly
with or even regulate prenatal genetic studies.

The prevention of genetic disease through prenatal genetic
diagnosis exists at present as a voluntary program. However even
in states such as Massachusetts where the public has been well
exposed to the availability of such studies, only a small percentage
of women at risk because of their age elect to have an amniocentesis.
While these figures are continually rising, it is obvious that an

effective program will need legislative support. The problem
then would be to distinguish between voluntary and mandatory
amniocentesis, and voluntary and mandatory selective abortion of
defective progeny.

A voluntary program of amniocentesis followed by voluntary
abortion of genetically defective fetuses would appear to be the
most equitable and to least assail the religious and other beliefs
of society. Because current evidence clearly indicates the in-
effectiveness of such a program, government will inevitably
assess the merits of continuation.

A mandatory program of amniocentesis followed by voluntary
selective abortion of defective fetuses increases the likelihood
of a more effective program of prevention. The indications for
amniocentesis in such cases would be for known carriers of genetic
disease or for those mothers who are over 35 years of age. Decisions to terminate such pregnancies would still remain in the
province of the parents. Conflict could arise if prenatal studies
are initiated later in pregnancy than when routinely recommended
(14-16 weeks). Such inadvertent activity may result in answers of
fetal abnormality becoming available at the beginning of the
third trimester of pregnancy. The state, acting in accordance with
the Roe v. Wade decision may proscribe postviability abortion at
that stage of pregnancy. Further, serious objections may arise
concerning the ethics of a program compelling amniocentesis even
for a patient who has indicated her intent not to have an abortion
regardless of the prenatal genetic study results. Additional
considerations arise in regard to the risks of injury and the invasion of privacy, not to mention the real questions of constitutionality. It should be noted however that many courts have upheld
the validity of statutes mandating specific treatment and care of
children, including considerations of vaccination, blood transfusions
and operations, despite parental objections on the grounds of
religion. Friedman has pointed out (6) that any statutory scheme
mandating amniocentesis for those at risk would likely be challenged
on the grounds of violating the Fourth Amendment's proscription of
"unreasonable searches and seizures." To be ultimately effective,
statutory amniocentesis would have to include a penalty for non-
compliance.

Friedman has considered at length the questions of mandatory
amniocentesis followed by compulsory abortion (6). Since compulsory
sterilization statutes exist in at least 21 states, society has
clearly established the power to prevent the conception of potentially defective offspring. Legislation therefore mandating abortion
of genetically defective fetuses can be considered under the
same rubric, more especially since after Roe v. Wade held that a
fetus prior to viability is not a person within the meaning of the
Fourteenth Amendment.

Major objections arise against the introduction of mandatory abortion for genetic defect. For example the problem of arbitrariness in determining which genetic disorder was sufficiently serious to merit mandatory action. Which of the disorders presently treatable but not curable would be included? On what basis? On whose 'discretion'?

Much argument has centered on the question whether the state has a compelling interest in preventing the birth of genetically defective offspring. Justifications that could be advanced include consideration of the "health of society" (eugenics), the suffering of the defective child when born (euthanasia), and the more banal consideration of economics. Any statute aiming at mandatory amniocentesis and compulsory abortion is likely to fail in view of its assault on the rights to procreational privacy and those rights prohibiting unreasonable searches and seizures (6).

Insurance carriers are likely to move with even greater dispatch than government, and develop specific "conditions of coverage." Hence demands could be made for carrier detection tests (after reliability has been proved) for an increasing number of genetic disorders. Pregnancies at risk following demonstrated carrier states for autosomal recessive and sex-linked disorders may require mandatory study for inclusion in that insurance program. Included in such imperatives could be women over 35 years of age. It need only be recalled that until recently over 50% of all offspring with Down's syndrome were born to mothers aged 35 and over - who constitute only about 10% of the childbearing population! (1). One corollary of the insurance carrier is likely to declare that while amniocentesis and prenatal genetic studies will be covered as will the abortion of an affected fetus, failure to terminate such a pregnancy will result in a lack of insurance coverage after birth. The morality, ethics and constitutionality of such actions remain in question.

ACKNOWLEDGMENTS

Supported in part by US PHS Grants 1-P01-HD-05515, 1-R01-HD09281-01 and 1-T32-GM0701501

REFERENCES

1. Milunsky, A., "The Prenatal Diagnosis of Hereditary Disorders", Charles C. Thomas, Springfield (1973).

2. Milunsky, A., "The Prevention of Mental Retardation and Genetic Disease", W.B. Saunders Company, Philadelphia (1975).

3. Milunsky, A. and Reilly, P., Medico-legal issues in the prenatal diagnosis of hereditary disorders, Amer. J. Law Med. 1:71 (1975).

4. Park v. Nissen, Cal. Super. Ct., Orange Co., Docket No. 190033, Dec. 13, 1974.

5. Doe v. Bolton, 410 U.S. 179, 192 (1973).

6. Friedman, J.M., Legal implications of amniocentesis, Univ. Penn. Law Rev. 123:92 (1974).

7. Milunsky, A., Prenatal genetic diagnosis: risks and needs, in "Genetic Counseling", H. Lubs and F. DeLa Cruz (eds.). Proceedings of a NIH Workshop, Denver, February 1975 (in press).

8. Ampola, M.G., Mahoney, M.J., Nakamura, E., et al, In utero treatment of methylmalonic acidemia (MMA-EMIA) with vitamin B_{12}, Pediat. Res. 8:113 (1974).

9. Roe v. Wade, 410 U.S. 113, (1973).

DISCUSSION

Paper of Prof. A. Milunsky
<u>Moderator</u>: Prof. A.M. Capron

J. HAMERTON: University of Manitoba, Winnipeg: Dr. Milunsky raised the point about not doing amniocentesis unless there is a prior commitment to a therapeutic abortion if the test shows the prognosis for the fetus to be bad. He then raised what I thought was a principle - the right of parents to knowledge. If this was established, it seems to raise a number of dangerous precedents. First of all, the test does carry, I think we'd all accept, some definable risk. I wonder, therefore, whether it should be done without some prior commitment to undergo treatment, which in this case is, in most cases, therapeutic abortion.

Secondly, if the principle is fully established, it would seem to me that any mother, whatever her age, whatever the indications, would then have the right to demand an amniocentesis. She may want to know the sex of the infant. Should amniocentesis be done simply for the determination of sex. Finally, in the situation of limited health resources that we have at the moment, should such a principle, as established by Dr. Milunsky, stand?

MILUNSKY: There is a clear need for parents to understand the risks prior to amniocentesis. There is little point in my view, for somebody to undergo an amniocentesis if they have no plan to terminate the pregnancy. There may be little point in your mind and my mind. However, they certainly have the right to undertake a risk which they perceive and which they understand. So my feeling is since they have the right to know, they don't need to make a commitment to abortion.

So as long as they understand that the sequence of events involves additional risk, we can give them a fairly sharp idea of the risks. I can share with you the fact that the Collaborative Amniocentesis Registry Project will shortly be making their data public. I would guess that the Registry will simply echo the experience in our laboratory that the risk is extremely small. The answer to the question "should everybody be able to demand an amniocentesis," is undoubtedly yes. All parents should have the opportunity of knowing about their fetus.

But, of course, it is totally impossible technologically to provide that kind of service at this time. Parents also have a right to know the fetal sex for family planning or other reasons. However, this is a most inappropriate use of a very scarce and expensive technology at this time and, therefore, it is something which we cannot even begin to offer for another five to ten years.

STEINBERG: The point that Dr. Milunsky raised leads to another one.   The cost of prenatal genetic studies is not trivial. There is a problem of who will fund these studies?   I think the question that came from Dr. Hamerton was raised because he comes from a country (Canada) in which the government pays for amnio-centesis.   In this country, some will be paid by the government, but others will be paid by third party insurance.

Who is entitled to amniocentesis?   Will the insurance pay for it?   Will the government pay for it?   Will some other third party pay for it?   Or will only those who can afford it pay for it?   Then we raise the question concerning an equitable distribution of the right to knowledge.   I am not sure that the right to know-ledge should extend to all questions at issue, particularly a question of simple curiosity that will resolve itself in the near future - the sex of the child usually is determinable within a period of nine months!

KARYOTYPE, PREDICTABILITY AND CULPABILITY

Alan M. Dershowitz

Harvard Law School

From the beginning of recorded history, prophets have attempted to foresee harmful occurrences, such as flood, famine, pestilence, earthquake and volcanic eruption. Attempting to predict crime - - to determine who is likely to become a criminal - - has also captured the imagination of mankind for centuries. From the Bible's "stubborn and rebellious son," identifiable by his gluttony and drunkenness; to Lombroso's "born criminal and criminaloid," identifiable by the shape of his cranium; to Sheldon and Eleanor Glueck's 3 year-old delinquent, identifiable by a composite score derived from familial relationships - - "experts" have claimed the ability to spot the mark of the potential criminal before he or she has committed serious crimes. Though the results have not generally met with scientific approval, it is still widely believed - - by many policemen, judges, psychiatrists, lawyers and members of the general public - - that there are ways of distinguishing real criminals from the rest of us. Most recently, it has been suggested that the presence of the XYY karyotype in a man may be associated with - - and consequently predictive of - - certain kinds of violent crime.

One can sympathize with efforts to predict and prevent crimes before they occur, rather than to wait until the victim lies dead. Indeed, Lewis Carroll put in the Queen's mouth an argument for preventive confinement of predicted criminals that Alice found difficult to refute. The Queen says:

> "There's the King's Messenger. He's in prison now, being punished; and the trial doesn't even begin till next Wednesday; and of course the crime comes last of all."

"Suppose he never commits the crime?" asked Alice.

"That would be all the better, wouldn't it?" the
Queen responded ...

Alice felt there was no denying that. "Of course
that would be all the better," she said: "But it wouldn't
be all the better his being punished."

"You're wrong..." said the Queen. "Were you ever
punished?"

"Only for faults," said Alice.

"And you were all the better for it, I know!" the
Queen said triumphantly.

"Yes, but then I had done the things I was punished
for," said Alice. "That makes all the difference."

"But if you hadn't done them," the Queen said, "that
would have been even better still; better, and better, and
better!" Her voice went higher with each "better,"
till it got quite to a squeak...

Alice thought, "There's a mistake here somewhere--"

There are at least two mistakes prevalent in current discussions of the XYY karyotype that this essay will focus on: The
first concerns whether the presence of such karyotype, alone or in
combination with other factors, should be deemed predictive of
violent crime; the second concerns whether the presence of such
karyotype, alone or in combination with other factors, should be
deemed an excusing or mitigating condition in assessing criminal
responsibility.

First a few words of introduction: In 1961, the first report
of a 47, XYY human appeared in a letter by Sandberg et al (1). The
XYY characteristic or karyotype is a chromosome abnormality in which
a man has 47 as compared to the normal 46 chromosomes. It is the
result of non-disjunction, or the failure of the chromosomes to
properly separate during the meiotic division which gives rise to
the sperm. This phenomenon remained but a biological curiosity until
the paper in Nature in 1965 by Jacobs et al (2) which associated
this extra Y chromosome with tall stature, mental retardation, and
aggressive behavior. Thus began a long series of studies attempting
to substantiate or disprove this claim which, if true, would have
the most profound consequences for society.

The original Jacobs study in England justifiably caused much commotion, as it found 7 XYY males in a mental hospital of 197 patients when previously only 11 XYY males had been identified throughout the world. A number of retrospective validation studies confirmed the higher incidence, but nowhere near the 7 out of 197 of the Jacobs study. Aggregating 12 studies (3) of mental sub-normals and mental hospital patients, yields a rate of approximately 10 XYY males out of 8,500 or 0.12% of the subnormal population. The alleged association of XYY and violence naturally led investi-gators to criminal populations in prisons. Putting together the data from 16 separate studies, there is an incidence of approxi-mately 55 out of 17,500 or 0.32% of inmates who are XYY. More information is necessary, however, before it is possible to judge the significance of this data. The incidence rates are worthless until we know the natural incidence of XYY in the total male popu-lation. Three studies of consecutively born males have found a population rate of 12 out of 6,746 or 0.18%, somewhat higher than the incidence in mental hospitals and somewhat more than one-half the incidence in prison.

Since the validation studies have all been retrospective, they tell us very little about the percentage of XYY individuals in the total population that becomes aggressive, much less become pri-son inmates. This latter figure is crucial to establishing any sort of reliable predictive criteria. At present there is no published data on a prospective study of XYY individuals, although such studies are in progress. Walzer, for example, has been examining every newborn male at a hospital in Boston for several years and is keeping track of all the XYY children. If the study is permitted to continue, these subjects will be followed into maturity so as to get as complete a report as possible. For ethi-cal reasons, Walzer is informing the families about the nature of what they are studying in the children. From a purely experimental point of view this threatens to contaminate the results, but is necessary for the reason that parents have a right to know what is being measured in their children.

Methodological problems aside, there would still be great problems in the application of the data to a group of XYY males for predictive purposes. Using the data above, if the United States has a population of 110,000,000 males, it will have approximately 200,000 males with the XYY karyotype. If there are 1,000,000 American males who have at one time commited a seriously violent crime, then by these incidence rates 3,200 of them have the XYY karyotype. Thus, to line up all XYY males and try to predict which of them will be criminally violent without any other information, one would have to select 3,200 out of 200,000 or a mere 1.5%. To predict that all the XYY persons will be violent would result in a false positive rate of 98.4%.

This data may very well later be proved inaccurate. If the

incidence of the XYY individual is either greater in prison
populations or lower in the total population than presently believed, the predictability of violence or criminality in XYY
individuals would increase proportionately. Thus, if the total
population incidence were actually half of the estimate in use
here there would only be 100,000 males in the United States
with the XYY karyotype. For a target population of 1,000,000
criminals this would increase the prediction accuracy to 3,2%;
that would still result in an unacceptably high false positive rate
for virtually any program of incarceration or serious constraint
on liberty.

To show how far from the mark we currently are, hypothesize
the following situation:

Assume that 1 out of 200 in prison has an XYY karyotype.

Assume that 1 out of 10,000 in normal population has such a
karyotype. Under this hypothetical situation - - which exaggerates
any likely predictive strength of the XYY karyotype - - the incidence of the alleged predictor would be 50 times greater in the
prison than in the normal population. The total population of normal males (110,000,000) would include only 11,000 XYY males; the
hypothetical prison population (1,000,000) would include 5,000
XYY males. If all the XYY individuals were to be confined, there
would still be more than twice as many false positives as true
positives (16,000 confined of which 11,000 were false positives
and 5,000 true positives). Moreover, only a small amount of the
potential target population (less than one-half of 1%) would have
been correctly identified. Even if one were to expand the target
population 10-fold to include all persons who will ever engage in
any serious violence, the predictive utility of the XYY karyotype
would prove unsatisfactory. Assume that 10,000,000 American males
would fit into this expanded category. Assume - - an even more
unlikely situation - - that the ratio of XYY males in this expanded target group remained the same as in the original target
group (1 out of 200). Now the number of XYY males in the target
group would increase to 10,000 (1/200 x 10,000,000) and the number
of XYY's in the normal population would decrease slightly to
10,100 (1/10,000 x 101,000,000). Thus, the total number of persons
confined uner an XYY preventive confinement program would come to
20,100, of whom 10,000 would be true positives and 10,100 would be
false positives. Even under this absolutely unreachable plateau,
the number of false positives would slightly exceed the number of
true positives.

There is simply no way to reduce the number or percentage of
false positives to manageable figures, while still spotting any
significant number or percentage of true positives. The reason for
this inheres in the mathematics of the situation: whenever the base

rate expectancy for a predicted human act is low, it becomes extremely difficult to spot those who would commit the act without also including a large number of false positives -- unless, of course, the predictor being employed is far more discriminating than the XYY karyotype is ever likely to be. And since the percentage of American males who will engage in seriously violent conduct is relatively low, it is not feasible to use the XYY karyotype as a predictive criterion capable of sorting out the future offenders from the future non-offenders. Nor is it likely that the XYY karyotype, even in combination with other factors, could be used to predict violence. Current efforts at violence prediction -- employing sophisticated and multifaceted approaches -- have also produced extraordinarily large numbers and percentages of false positives. There is simply no hard evidence establishing that any combination of factors can accurately spot a large percentage of future violent criminals without also including an unsatisfactorily large number and percentage of false positives (4).

On the opposite side of the coin from the prediction problem is the question what to do with the defendant who has committed a serious violent crime and who claims -- in defense or in mitigation -- that he is affected with an XYY karyotype. Even if such a karyotype does not have predictive significance, it can be argued, that does not mean it should not be deemed an excusing or mitigating condition. After all, such a condition would help the bearer of the XYY karyotype, would it not? The answer to that question is complex, both as it relates to the particular criminal defendant raising the XYY karyotype as a defense, and as it relates to the particular criminal defendant raising the XYY karyotype as a defense, and as it relates to the general class of persons afflicted with that abnormality. As to the particular individual: since there is no known cure for this type of chromosomal abnormality, the likely result of a successful "chromosomal defense" would be long term -- perhaps lifetime -- confinement.*

As to the general class of XYY males, there has always been a direct relationship between a class's lack of criminal accountability and the power of the state to confine that class preventively. The relationship is a natural one: most people believe, and probably always have, that someone who has committed a serious crime and who continues to be dangerous should be incapacitated in some manner. Accordingly, if the formal criminal process is incapable of dealing with him effectively, then he must be dealt with by some other, perhaps less formal but equally effective, mechanism of control.

---

*Editor's note
    The XYY karyotype has been raised in a number of criminal trials around the world as a defense. In general, however, it can

Even if a dangerous "madman" has not "yet" committed a serious crime, the fact that he could not be held answerable for any future criminality would suggest the need for preventive intervention.

---

be said that its use has been infrequent and unsuccessful. It was first raised in April, 1968 in France in a murder trial. Defendant Daniel Hugon was accused of murdering a 65 year-old prostitute in a Paris hotel. A chromosome analysis taken after he attempted suicide indicated that Hugon had an XYY karyotype. He was, nonetheless, found legally sane and convicted of murder. The prosecution asked for a 5-10 year sentence rather than the normal 15 years for similar crimes. The jury considered chromosome aberration during sentencing and Hugon received a seven year sentence. In the same year 21 year-old Lawrence Hannel came to trial charged with the stabbing death of his 77 year-old landlady in Australia. He urged the court to accept an insanity defense based upon the allegation that his behavior was adversely affected by his XYY genotype. The only witness who appeared for the defense was a psychiatrist who testified both to defendant's karyotype and to abnormal EEG readings indicating right temporal lobe epilepsy. While his competency to stand trial was questioned during the trial, the judge let the case go to the jury. After only eleven minutes of deliberation the jury delivered a not guilty by reason of insanity verdict and Hannel was committed to a maximum security hospital until cured. In another case, Ernest D. Beck, a 20 year-old farm worker, was tried in Bielefeld, West Germany, in November, 1968, and sentenced to life imprisonment for the murder of three women. Scientists informed the court that Beck had an extra Y chromosome and that this made him unable to control his impulses to commit crimes from house breaking to murder. The court, however, accepted the prosecution's argument that Beck was fully aware that he was committing murders even though he might not be able to control his impulse to kill, and Beck received the maximum sentence.

As little success as the XYY defense has achieved abroad, in the United States its effect in criminal proceedings has been even more limited. In April, 1969, Sean Farley of New York, a 6'8" 26 year-old male pleaded not guilty on the ground of insanity to the alleged brutal murder and rape of a 40 year-old woman in an alley near her home (People v. Farley, No. 1827 (Sup. Ct., Queens County, April 30, 1969). No attempt was made to deny the act, the defense being based upon Farley's XYY karyotype. Dr. E. Schutta, called as an expert witness in the field of genetics, described the physical and behavioral characteristics of XYY males, emphasizing their frequently aggressive behavioral characteristics, and the belief that the XYY abnormality could have a causative effect on Farley's behavior pattern. On cross examination the prosecutor elicited the admission that it is possible to live a normal life although possessing the XYY karyotype. The prosecution also

After all, an important assumption underlying most criminal punishment is that the threat of its imposition will, in most cases,
deter potential criminals. When that assumption is negated -- when

---

argued that Farley was sane under New York's version of the
M'Naughten Rule, and that he murdered the victim in a drunken rage.
The jury found him guilty of murder in the first degree.

   In People v. Tanner, 13 Cal. App. 3d 596, 91 Cal. Rpt. 656
(1970), the XYY defense was held to be insufficient to prove legal
insanity under the California version of the M'Naughten Rule.
The defendant, Raymond Tanner, had originally pleaded guilty to a
charge of assault with intent to commit murder, stemming from a
brutal rape. While confined at Atascadero State Hospital for
study, he was discovered to possess the XYY karyotype.   Thereafter
he attempted to change his guilty plea to not guilty by reason of
insanity. At a hearing held on this motion, the defense introduced expert testimony and studies attempting to prove to the court
that XYY individuals are likely to exhibit certain aggressive behavioral traits. Despite the presentation of considerable expert
testimony, supporting evidence, and recent work done at the Atascadero State Hospital in California, the court denied the motion.
Examining the data, the court observed that present studies based
upon populations of institutionalized mental defectives and criminals, are prejudiced since they are a biased sample population.
Further, the court found weakness in the experts' inability to
determine whether the appellant's aggressive behavior, namely the
commission of an assault, resulted from the XYY chromosomal abnormality. The court concluded that, at this time, there is not
sufficient information or knowledge of any relationship between
behavior and the XYY karyotype. Also in 1970, in the Maryland case
of Millard v. State, 8 Md. App. 419, 261 A. 2d 227 (1970), the
XYY defense was adjudged insufficient to bring the question of
insanity before a jury. In that case the defendant was charged
with robbery with a deadly weapon. Using the testimony of a geneticist and the introduction of 40 XYY research papers, an attempt
was made to have him declared not guilty by reason of insanity in
accordance with Maryland's version of the M'Naughten Rule. The
judge ruled as a matter of law that the XYY anomaly as a "mental
defect" was not of itself sufficient to show the defendant lacked
substantial capacity to appreciate the criminality of his conduct.
An additional handicap to the defense was that counsel called only
one expert witness, the geneticist, who admitted having no psychiatric training, and to being unfamiliar with the legal standards for
sanity in general and the Maryland test in particular. The jury
found the defendant guilty as charged.

   While there have thus been very few cases involving XYY as a
defense to a criminal charge, those in which it has been used indic-

there is no threat of criminal punishment or when the potential
crime-doer is seen as incapable of exercising choice in a rational
manner -- then a need is perceived for some other mechanism of
social control. Thus, there has always been a direct relationship
between the size and nature of the category of persons deemed
ciminally nonresponsible and the size and nature of the category
of persons regarded as preventively confinable. This relationship
has been most direct, and most easily observable, in the context
of madmen who have committed criminal acts and been acquitted by
reason of insanity, or found incompetent to stand trial. But
there has also been a significant relationship in the context of
what has come to be called "civil commitment," i.e., the confinement
of insane persons who have not "yet" engaged in criminal behavior,
but who are thought "likely" to do so in the future.

Blackstone tied the power to confine the mentally ill directly
to the lack of answerability and responsibility in the formal
criminal process:

> "(I)n the case of absolute madmen, as they are not
> answerable for their actions, they should not be
> permitted the liberty of acting, unless under proper
> control; and, in particular, they ought not be suffered
> to go loose, to the terror of the king's subjects.
> It was the doctrine of our ancient law, that persons
> deprived of their reason might be confined till they
> recovered their senses, without waiting for the forms
> of a commission or other special authority from the
> crown...(5).

My fear is that if the XYY karyotype came to be recognized as an
excusing or mitigating condition, this would create increasing
pressure to preventively confine persons with such karyotypes.

CONCLUSION

The XYY karyotype is an intriguing phenomenon in search of
employment. It is the thesis of this essay that the time is not
ripe for it to find any employment in the service of crime prevention or criminal responsibility. Nor is there any basis for ex-
pecting that such a time is close at hand. Further research should
not, however, be throttled in the name of misguided certainty that
chromosomal abnormality is a blind alley, or misguided fear of the
consequences of a finding that there is a relationship between such
abnormality and violence. We should be vigilant to control the

---

ate that courts will not excuse criminal behavior on the basis of
XYY, but may sometimes take it into account in determining sentence.

uses to which scientific research may be put, while at the same time remaining vigilant to the dangers of scientific censorship.

REFERENCES

1. Sandberg, A., Koepf, G.F., Ishihara, T., et al, XYY human male, Lancet 2:488 (1961).

2. Jacobs, P.A., Brunton, M., Melville, M.M., et al, Aggressive behavior, mental subnormality and the XYY male, Nature 208:1351 (1965).

3. Owen, D.R., The 47 XYY male: A review, Psychol. Bull. 78: 209 (1972).

4. Dershowitz, A.M., Preventive disbarment, The numbers are against it, 58 A.B.A.U. 815 (1972).

5. Blackstone, W., "Blackstone commentaries on the Laws of England," Vol. 4, J. Murray, London, 1857, p. 25.

GENETICOPHOBIA AND THE IMPLICATIONS OF SCREENING FOR THE XYY GENOTYPE IN NEWBORN INFANTS

Ernest B. Hook

Birth Defects Institute, New York State Department of

Health, and Albany Medical College

The programs involving screening of newborn populations for abnormal chromosome genotype, in particular the study at the Boston Hospital for Women, have been subject to well publicized criticism because of the alleged consequences for infants (and their families) with XYY genotype detected in such studies (1-5). These criticisms have focused on some specific aspects of the Boston study, but they have much broader significance. Among other issues, they directly raise the question of the relationship of the XYY geno-type to behavior and the broader social implications of such a purported relationship.

The main criticisms (1, 2, 4) of the newborn studies have been:
1). The sole purpose of these studies is to determine the nature and extent of the alleged excess psychopathology associated with an extra Y chromosome.
2). This alleged excess psychopathology however, is a myth based primarily on methodologically flawed studies (or if it exists involves only a trivial fraction of XYY indiv-iduals). The alleged excess moreover, may simply result from the possibility that the XYY genotype is a marker of adverse social factors in the parents' background, that have resulted for some reason in this chromosomal disorder.
3). If parents are told that their infant has a chromosome abnormality as they are in the Boston study - or speci-fically of the presence of the XYY genotype - and are familiar with or learn of the allegedly specious evidence linking the genotype with possible behavioral consequences, their handling of the child may result in the very behavior feared.

73

4). There is no behavioral therapy or intervention that can be provided those with chromosome abnormalities (or specifically the XYY genotype) detected in the study that could benefit the child, certainly none that could outweigh the behavioral consequences of telling the parent of the diagnosis.

5). These studies are ideologically influenced and undermine programs which attempt to eliminate environmental inequality and improve social conditions of those who are deprived.

6). "Informed consent"is mandated at the Boston institution but is, essentially, impossible to obtain for the study.

Before considering these claims in detail, consideration of some background material is necessary. For the purposes of the discussions below some conventions will be used. The terms "penal", and "mental-penal" setting are as defined elsewhere (6) and "security setting" refers to a "penal" or "mental-penal" setting. "Deviance" denotes behavior which leads to placement in security settings in a particular jurisdiction, which is to give the term an operational definition depending upon social context. This is not to imply that anyone in such a setting is there appropriately, or conversely. By "abnormal behavior" or "behavioral problems" or "difficulties" I mean a significant negative deviation from a generally agreed upon mean in speech, reading, learning, overall "intelligence", social development, adjustment, or related areas. This is much harder to define in an operational sense. I can be no more specific than to say that they are such deviations of behavioral patterns which, if exhibited by a child, I would hope parents would be concerned about and seek help for.

Of course environmental deprivation or other psychosocial factors may well result in behavioral difficulties in children, but there is no question that for some specific "problems", e.g. mental retardation, genetic factors may contribute strongly in some children e.g. those with trisomy 21, phenylketonuria, etc. Investigation of a genetic contribution to deviance is more difficult however, not only because of the many probable additional confounding environmental factors, but because of the relatively late manifestation of the "phenotype". Concerning extra Y chromosomes, the evidence suggests a 20-fold greater rate of XYY individuals in mental-penal settings (6) and perhaps a 4-fold greater rate in exclusively penal settings (7) over the newborn rate, in those studied to date, but the reasons for this difference are still not known. Three types of hypotheses may be considered (6): associative (the XYY genotype occurs in infants in which for independent reasons e.g. socioeconomic deprivation, deviant behavior is more frequent); social (some external correlate of the genotype e.g. tall stature, makes eventual deviance more likely); or neural: some aspect of central servous system function, (either direct, through neural organization or indirect, e.g. through hormonal effect) makes deviance more likely. (See (6) for elaboration.) These hypotheses are not mutually exclusive. The tenor of many discussions and critiques has been that a "neural" etiology must have fatalistic and "demonistic" implications for those with an extra Y chromosome. This is not necessarily the case, and a neural model which is neither fatalistic nor "demonistic" can readily be postulated. (See appendix).

That such a model can be postulated does not mean it is correct, of course, but it has heuristic value for the purpose of the discussion below. (It also appears to me to be the most plausible explanation of the observed association of the XYY genotype with deviance, on the basis of evidence available to date.)

With regard to the published criticisms (1, 2) of the studies of abnormal karyotypes in infants:

1.   These are written as if there are no other possible benefits of such studies for the individuals involved or society. But determinations of newborn chromosomal genotype in fact:

   a.   Provide estimates of the incidence rate of all chromosomal disorders, and ultimately allow study of possible environmental factors that may contribute causally to these conditions. Knowledge derived from such studies may help to clarify or negate claims of chromosomal "mutations" of number or structure.
   b.   Identify ostensibly normal individuals (infants, and ultimately parents and siblings) at particular risk for having offspring with adverse chromosomal constitution, e.g. mosaics, or carriers of balanced translocations, who may find this information of great pertinence to their subsequent personal decisions concerning child bearing.
   c.   Identify individuals other than with the XYY genotype who may benefit from particular therapeutic support and intervention who would not otherwise be identified (see below).
   d.   Contribute further to knowledge of phenotypic-genotypic correlation concerning karyotypes where questions now exist, quite separate from the XYY genotype, for example the suggested association of sporadic (but not familial) balanced Robertsonian translocations with mental retardation.
   e.   Identify which children do not have a detectable chromosome abnormality, providing such reassurance, for what it is worth, to their families.

Each of these goals, of course, raises certain methodological, not to mention ethical questions of its own, but they illustrate that despite the implicit claims of the critics, studies of newborn chromosomal genotype are more than simple attempts to incriminate the XYY genotype.

     2. An increase in probability of deviance of the XYY is not a "myth."* Moreover, there is not and never has been any direct evidence for the associative hypothesis. The history of this suggestion, however, is worth examining in detail. In 1966 Robinson and Puck (8) noted a suggestive increase of abnormal geno-types associated with X chromosome abnormalities (XXY, XXX, XO) in newborns of parents with lower socioeconomic status. Kessler and Moss (9) then suggested that perhaps an extra Y chromosome had the same association, arguing only by analogy, without benefit of any data concerning the XYY genotype. Subsequently, Baker et al (10) and Casey et al (11) among others noted that many XYY's in security settings had come from adverse backgrounds and difficult circumstances suggesting that adverse environmental factors may have contributed to their presence in these settings. (This was contrary to the impression left by an earlier study by Price and Whatmore (12, 13) in which there was very little to suggest that adverse circumstances had contributed to institutionalization in mental-penal settings.) These reports for some reason, lent weight to the view that adverse circumstances were exclusively responsible for the increased frequency of XYY individuals in custody, as if the risks of deviance for those with the XYY geno-type must be entirely environmental or entirely genetic, with no middle ground. The claim is: showing that risk is not just genetic proves it is not genetic at all. The most recent apparent expres-sion of such views comes from Borgaonkar and Shah (14) cited appro-vingly by Beckwith et al (1) in a recent exposition of their criti-cisms of the newborn studies: "...the frequency of antisocial behavior of the XYY male is probably not very different from non-XYY persons of similar background and social class." (This can be readily shown to be false, incidentally, since the term "persons" denotes both males and females of course, and the frequency of "deviance" in females is at least one order of magnitude less than that in males. Thus the mean rate for deviance in all non-XYY persons, which includes females and males, is considerably lower than that of XYY males.) For the statement to have relevance in the context of the quotation, I presume "non-XYY males," particu-larly "XY males", was intended by the phrase "non-XYY persons."

---

* Much criticism has been directed at those suggesting an XYY syndrome, and some of the disagreement may derive from differences in understanding of the term "syndrome". One interpretation views this as denoting an almost inevitable association of two or more descriptive aspects of an individual. Clinical usage of the term "syndrome" however is variable, and often denotes, in a less res-trictive sense, a spectrum of signs and symptoms which occur in some individuals more often than would be expected by chance.

Borgaonkar and Shah probably meant by this statement the canonical interpretation I gave it at first reading: no risk for the XYY after correction for social factors (and of course, sex of the subject). After reflection, I realized their statement is really a pseudo-conclusion whose meaning varies widely with the interpretation of the terms "probably" and "not very different." (For example, a 4-fold difference e.g. between 0.3% and 1.3% or 1% and 4% might appear "not very different" to them but considerably different to others.) Borgaonkar and Shah cite, incidentally, no evidence to support their view except that similar to evidence already discussed concerning adverse circumstances in the background of many incarcerated XYY persons, evidence irrelevant to the existence of other contributing factors associated with the XYY genotype.

But the most extreme form of the associative hypothesis in fact has come from Beckwith and King: "...it has been pointed out there are data suggesting that the rate of chromosomal non-disjunction, leading to the XYY karyotype is increased among lower socio-economic groups. This may be due to nutritional deprivation" (2). There is no reference to such data, in fact none exists. The pertinent observations concern X chromosome abnormalities (e.g. XXY) of the type already discussed above (8). I suspect this represents a (probably subconscious) mutation of the literature, resulting either from an insertion, or at least a transition (XXY to XYY) in accord with the argument and ideologies of the 'mutagenic agents' here.

There are several facts which were available to these authors, however, which should have been considered when they postulated the malnutrition hypothesis. These are: a) fragmentary data available in 1972 from newborn studies and published in 1973 did not reveal any evidence for a marked association of the XYY genotype with the lowest parental social class in which malnutrition, if it existed, should be concentrated - certainly none suggestive of the 20-fold increase in magnitude noted for the presence of XYY males in mental-penal settings (6); b) perhaps more significantly, the newborn rate of the XYY genotype in blacks in the U.S.A. was reported as not increased compared to the rate in whites in studies to date, and if anything, in fact the rate of the XYY genotype is lower in black newborns studied to date (15). Yet adverse social circumstances and malnutrition are notoriously greater in blacks in the U.S.A. Without some additional ad hoc hypothesis on a racial difference in rates, these data suggest that adverse circumstances do not increase the rate of the XYY genotype in newborns. (If anything the data are consistent with a trend in the other direction.) The additional direct data now accumulating from newborn studies further support this view. In the largest newborn study to date in Europe, of 14 XYY males detected, 8 were born to parents in social classes I and II, the highest, 6 to those in class III, and none to those in the lowest social classes IV and V. The expected frequencies were 2.6%, 7.4%, and 4.0% respectively.

This does not prove incidentally that there are not some adverse environmental circumstances, e.g. heavy irradiation, which could result in a higher rate of XYY offspring by inducing paternal secondary nondisjunction, or preferential fertilization by YY sperm, or maternal retention of an XYY zygote. But if there are, there is no reason to believe such environmental factors are responsible for the observed association to date of the XYY genotype with deviance.

It is likely that only a small fraction of XYY individuals ultimately become deviant as defined here, but it does not follow that it is only these deviant XYY males in which there is an increase in behavioral problems. Cross-sectional studies of "normal" populations will provide the answers here. (See also 17 and 7, a rejoinder, for discussion of related issues.)

Results of several studies of XYY persons detected in investigation of normal populations compared with background or control group are now becoming available. Three XYY infant males (whose parents did not know of the genotype) evaluated at age 2½ years had lower developmental quotients and language quotients than XY males, with more apparent difficulty in language than in development (18). (The controls were matched by sex, race, length of gestation and as closely as possible by age but further details are not given. The XYY infants in this population were on the average, born to a higher socioeconomic background than those in the total newborn population screened and examined (19)). Five adult XYY males found in a general population study in Denmark (20) (military service examinees) were said to be, compared to their siblings, more immature, more impulsive, and to have had greater "contact" difficulties. Two of the five had criminal records, compared to 50 of 1,010 XY males in the population sampled (p $<$ .05) but no comparison with siblings is provided concerning criminality. Seven adult XYY males detected in a general population study in France (21) were compared to a control group matched for age, social class, and level of education. These XYY males showed less tolerance concerning fits of temper, compulsive behavior, and aggression. The most significant impression of these seven as well as seven others detected in other screening of normal adult male population was said to be their inability to integrate aggression normally. (Yet only 1 of 14 after "check on police files" was found to have had a conviction. Data concerning convictions in controls are not provided.)

The data are fragmentary and a great deal more description of the methods and results would be useful. But in sum these data suggest (but do not prove) it is not just those few XYY's in security settings who have an increased frequency in behavioral problems.

    3. The criticism concerning the "self-fulfilling prophecy" assumes parents are told of the diagnosis, and something of its prognosis and consequent uncertainties. Counseling in the face of uncertain expectation is always difficult and a great deal depends on precisely what parents are told after being informed of a chromosome abnormality. Knowledge of the possibility of future difficulties in an ostensibly normal infant may well induce parental anxieties (22), but what reason is there to think that such anxieties will induce social problems? Beckwith and King cite (2) in sole support of this claim an article (in the lay journal Psychology Today) by Rosenthal (23) on the "Pygmalion effect". Aside from the fact that 1) the work itself has been challenged by many investigators, and 2) there is a logical question as to how one could prove that evidence for the "Pygmalion effect" is not just a "Pygmalion effect" itself -- a problem as old as the ancient paradox of Epimenides of Crete who declared "all Cretans are liars" -- the nature of the effect Rosenthal discusses is quite different from that postulated by Beckwith et al. Those in a position to influence the outcome in Rosenthal's experiments, (i.e. experimenters or teachers) were in some way "manipulating" their subjects or students unconsciously so that the ultimate data agreed with a hypothesis in which they had full trust and confidence or in which they had a personal stake - the validity of psychological tests as a predictor of student performance, or some personal scientific hypothesis.

    Of course under some circumstances these or similar effects might appear plausible. But the situation we are discussing in newborn studies is quite different. Parents have a vested interest in avoiding difficulties, not in producing them. If support such as psychiatric intervention, counseling, speech therapy, special education, etc. are provided should any difficulties arise, (as they are in the Boston study), then subsequent social problems would be expected to diminish. Knowing of risks, parents would if anything be more likely to avail themselves of strategies which would avoid difficulties, not induce them. Beckwith et al might argue that, plausible as such effects might be, we don't have proof that the change would be in the direction expected. But certainly no more proof than that any environmental help will avoid subsequent problems in any child, if we believe in the significance of environmental help at all.

    Counseling as to risk does raise questions as to the possible conclusions that could stem from the observations in these studies. But if anything, studies associated with intervention would be expected to diminish the estimate of associated risks, if they find any at all. At least they will provide estimates of "risk" associ-

ated with some intervention strategies designed to diminish that
risk. Such studies as described here will, then, not provide an
answer as to the "natural" history of the XYY genotype (i.e.
without intervention), but that does not diminish their importance
or their likely value to those enrolled.

4. Regarding "specific" therapy, none is likely to be available until we better understand the precise nature of the association of the XYY genotype with behavioral abnormalities but that
does not negate the value of "non-specific" intervention for behavioral problems that may emerge, as discussed above. With regard
to the XXY karyotype incidentally, there are already suggestions that
testosterone administration in childhood may diminish the likelihood
of behavioral problems (24-26), but this is not exactly analagous,
as the hormones would also affect the structural aspects of the
phenotype, e.g. diminished secondary sex characteristics, which
could contribute to difficulties for social reasons as well.

5. The underlying motivation for the criticisms of studies
of the XYY genotype that have been raised are best illustrated by
the following quotation from Beckwith and King:

> "...the pursuit of such studies on the XYY genotype and the
> publicity they receive, help to reinforce a growing
> tendency to explain away the problems of society in terms
> of the genes or biology of individuals. These arguments
> support the concept that it is not deprived social con-
> ditions that generate social unrest and antisocial
> behavior. Thus, according to this position social pro-
> grammes designed to eliminate inequality will not solve
> the problem. The implication is that only programmes
> aimed at controlling the "deviant" individuals will work."
> (2) (Emphasis added)

There is a very tenuous thread in this passage which links
those doing XYY studies at the beginning with the police state
mentality described at the end. But tenuous as it may be, it is
not intended as an innocent connection, for elsewhere in the same
article these studies are said to be "ideologically influenced" as
if those engaged in them at least unconsciously are supporting the
alleged social effects described. (The possibility that individuals
doing those studies might themselves oppose the use of studies to
justify such predicted consequences is not considered.)

But in any event, how plausible are these alleged consequences?
Is the generally accepted belief in environmental influence upon
social unrest so fragile? Does discussion of a contribution of an
extra Y chromosome to deviance of XYY individuals ultimately argue
against the significance of any environmental contribution to the
deviance of men with normal (XY) genotype? There are deep seated

fears that appear to have led Beckwith et al to attempts to polarize the issues. I believe such fears result from what I will define as "geneticophobia": The fear that the search for evidence of a genetic contribution to the observed variation in human behavior must undermine the necessity for attention to the complexity of the human environment. I regard it as an irrational fear (hence "phobia") but it afflicts many individuals and sometimes has unexpected consequences. I have observed for instance what appeared to be an acute anxiety reaction in one student of the behavioral sciences prompted by a seminar on the XYY genotype.

Geneticophobes find the issue of the XYY genotype a personal and social threat. They are unaware of a rich and full tradition in the history of human genetics, which recognizes the importance of characterizing the genetic basis of human diversity so that environmental help may be made as specific as possible to human needs. The geneticophobes however, are only aware of abuses of human genetics, so for them the issues are already decided. Such discussion of human genetic diversity, particularly as it touches on behavior, undermines the ideological necessity to direct all resources to those already identified areas of human social needs. Each cent spent on genetics, is one less spent on environment! And why investigate (or even discuss) genetics when we already know the answers to what causes human problems and what their ultimate solutions are? They argue with the same intransigence with which other social movements have argued their final solutions to various social problems.

The answers are quite simple. The genetic studies I have discussed may reveal, among other things, who is in particular need of what environmental help. Their aim is not to deny the contribution of environment but to help optimize its effects. Evidence for genetic influence is not evidence for genetic fatalism. Of course there have been and still are those who would abuse knowledge of human genetics or any other scientific knowledge, for unhumanitarian ends. But the answer is not to stop studies in human genetics or to launder them until they meet some prescribed test for ideological "purity", but rather to examine, case by case, the precise implications for individuals involved. And here doctrinaire ideology has no place.

6. True "informed consent" (as understood by the lay individual) is probably literally impossible to obtain for any therapeutic or investigative procedure for which it is requested, even for intelligent adults, in that all possible consequences can never be spelled out.* Thus we must recognize that if there is intense

---

* While "informed consent" has a specific legal meaning as stated by Mr. Annas (p.104) which is achievable in a legal sense (at least what the courts hold it to be) it is not congruent to what the term denotes to many non-legal commentators who in essence give it a

ideological objection to the implications of any therapy or research, intense efforts are likely to be made to demonstrate in
that particular instance why "informed consent" appears impossible.
After reviewing the data available to me on the controversy in
Boston (2-5, 14) I believe that the charges that "informed consent"
obtained was unsatisfactory was not the real motive for objection
to the study, but essentially a tactic to stop work whose implications were found objectionable on other grounds. The focus of
the controversy of the consent procedures was to insist at each
step that the "true" consequences were not spelled out in sufficient detail in accord with the ideology of those objecting. Successive modifications were introduced into the "consent" procedure
used in the Boston study but these were. of course, never sufficient
to please the vocal critics, and indeed, the argument was that they
never could be sufficient. How could they ever to be anyone who
saw in such studies the roots of social disaster?

Further Questions

     In some jurisdictions in Europe a systematic search for ab-
normal karyotypes in newborns is done without informing parents
specifically of the test (27). In such social milieux the populations at large appear less concerned about the issues involved in
human "research", and are less troubled about issues of this type,
perhaps because they have greater faith than Americans in the
ultimate good will of their own institutions.

     Under such circumstances, where this approach is culturally
acceptable, (and children are still followed and derive the benefits
of therapeutic intervention where necessary), the affected individuals may do just as well in such a study, but matters may be much
more tranquil for the uninformed parents. There are a great many
complications latent in this approach however, since questions arise
as to whether and when the parents or the individual himself would
be told of the finding and what explanations they receive before
this. (See 6, 27, 28 for further discussion of some of these issues).
Indeed these and similar questions arise concerning any XYY individual detected postnatally.

     When further data are accumulated concerning the frequency of
behavioral difficulties in young children with XYY (and XXY) genotypes, we will be in a better position to answer these questions.
If only a very small fraction of XYY persons have such problems in
early childhood, one could argue that there is a stronger rationale
for not worrying parents about very unlikely outcomes. But if, as
seems increasingly likely, there is a significant increase in some

---

meaning which makes it impossible to attain, in the sense discussed
here.

types of behavioral difficulties in these individuals in early childhood (only a small fraction of whom go on to become "deviant"), there is a much greater rationale for discussing the diagnoses openly with parents, so they might be more likely to avail themselves of such intervention as may be appropriate.

In the U.S.A. however, such discussions appear to become increasingly "academic" since legal commentators are insisting to an ever greater extent upon complete disclosure of all diagnostic information. (See 29 for discussion of related issues.)

Lastly, a recurrent theme throughout the entire XYY "controversy" has been the assumption concerning "stigmatization" in the public mind about the XYY genotype. In an attempt to determine the order of magnitude of such an effect, I had a street corner poll taken in Albany, New York on May 15th and 16th, 1975 of women of childbearing age. Of 31 interviewed, only six had heard of the XYY genotype (or of a "criminal chromosome"), none of whom thought the association with criminality was inevitable. Indeed, several expressed doubts that the association was a real one. All six stated that if they had an affected child they would want to be informed. Obviously, this is only a fragmentary result in one community, but it suggests that the views of the "public" have not been irremediably shaped by the unfortunate publicity on the XYY genotype in 1968 and 1969.

APPENDIX

The neural model mentioned in the text posits:

1) The XYY genotype (and probably the XXY genotype) is more likely than the XY genotype (in individuals born to the same social circumstances) to result in a neural organization which produces (after interaction with the child's microenvironment) some "behavioral difficulties" in the infant and child. These "behavioral difficulties" need not be global, but may be specific, e.g. in speech, language, or other areas. (It is emphasized that such a model makes no assumption about the magnitude, specificity or possible amelioration of such difficulties. Such patterns of neural organization that may be produced by the extra Y chromosome presumably could be modified by other as yet unknown genetic, intrauterine, and postnatal environmental factors, as well as by internal-physiologic factors, e.g. variation in quantity, quality or sensitivity to sex hormones in the XYY. The resultant "behavioral difficulties" postulated need not be (necessarily) specific to males with extra Y (or X) chromosomes (or even males), but presumably could be produced by other genetic as well as preventable environmental factors. These "behavioral difficulties" particularly in the area of speech, reading, learning, and social adaptation could be at least partially amenable).

2) A child with such "behavioral difficulties", particularly one also encountering unfortunate environmental circumstances, will be more likely eventually to come into conflict with the law and wind up at sometime in his (or her) life in a security setting of some type.

This model makes no estimate for the increase of "behavioral difficulties" postulated in XYY children or infants, or of which specific "difficulties" may be relevant (after adjustment for appropriate environmental effects) to ultimate "deviance". (Under the "continuum" sub-hypothesis discussed elsewhere (6), the 20-fold greater rate of XYY males in mental-penal settings than in newborns would be accompanied by a marked increase in at least some "behavioral difficulties" in non-deviant XYY males (compared to XY males born to similar circumstances) but on the "threshold sub-hypothesis (6) the postulated increase in "behavioral difficult-ies" (adjusted for environmental background) would be concentrated only in the relatively few XYY individuals exhibiting "deviant" behavior.)

ACKNOWLEDGMENTS

The interviews for the poll described were conducted by Margaret A. Aldrich. I thank Norma H. Hatcher and Geraldine Chambers for suggestions concerning the manuscript.

REFERENCES

1. Beckwith, J., Elseviers, D., Gorini, L. et al, Harvard XYY study, Science 187:298 (1975).

2. Beckwith, J. and King, J., The XYY syndrome: a dangerous myth, New Scientist, 64:474 (1974).

3. Brody, J.E., Scientists group terms Boston study of children with extra sex chromosome unethical and harmful, The New York Times, Friday, Nov. 15, 1974, p. 16.

4. Culliton, B.J., 'Patients' rights: Harvard is site of battle over X & Y chromosomes, Science 186:715 (1974).

5. Culliton, B.J., Harvard faculty says XYY study should continue, Science 186:1189 (1974).

6. Hook, E.B., Behavioral implications of the human XYY genotype, Science 179:139 (1973).

7. Hook, E.B., Rates of XYY genotype in penal and mental settings,

Lancet 1:98 (1975).

8. Robinson, A. and Puck, T.T., Studies in chromosomal non-disjunction in man. II, Amer. J. Hum. Genet. 10:112 (1967).

9. Kessler, S. and Moos, R.H., The XYY karyotype and criminality: A review, J. Psychiat. Res. 7:153 (1970).

10. Baker, D., Telfer, M.A., Richardson, C.E. et al, Chromosome errors in man with anti-social behavior, J.A.M.A. 214:869 (1970).

11. Casey, M.D., Blank, C.E., Mobley, T. et al, Special hospital research report number 2 (Broadmoor Hospital, Berks, U.K.) p. 1 (1971).

12. Price, W.H. and Whatmore, P.B., Criminal behaviour and the XYY males, Nature 213:815 (1967).

13. Price, W.H. and Whatmore, P.B., Behaviour disorders and pattern of crime among XYY males identified at a maximum security hospital, Brit. Med. J. 1:533 (1967).

14. Bordaonkar, D.S. and Shah, S.A., The XYY chromosome male -- or syndrome?, Prog. Med. Genet. 10:135 (1974).

15. Hook, E.B.: Racial differentials in the prevalence rates of males with sex chromosome abnormalities (XXY, XYY) in security settings in the U.S.A., Amer. J. Hum. Genet. 26:504 (1974).

16. Ratcliffe, S.G. and Evans, H.J., Sex chromosome abnormalities and social class, Lancet 1:1144 (1975).

17. Anonymous, What becomes of the XYY male? Lancet 2:1297 (1974).

18. Leonard, M.F., Landy, G., Ruddle, F.H. et al, Early development of children with abnormalities of the sex chromosomes: A prospective study, Pediatrics 54:208 (1974) and Leonard, M.F., Personal communication (1974). The paper cited pools all data on those with sex chromosome abnormalities; data on the specific genotypes were provided by the senior author.

19. Lubs, H.A., Personal communication.

20. Zeuthen, E., Hanse, M., Christensen, A.L. et al, A psychiatric-psychological study of XYY males found in a general male population, Acta Psychiat. Scand. 51:3 (1975).

21. Noel, B., Duport, J.P., Revil, D., et al, The XYY syndrome: Reality or myth? Clin. Genet. 5:387 (1974).

22. Valentine, G.H., McClelland, M.A. and Sergovich, F.R., The
     growth and development of four XYY infants, Pediatrics 48:
     583 (1971). This paper is cited by Beckwith et al (Science
     187:298 (1975))concerning anxieties induced by parents learning
     of the XYY genotype. Ironically, the child of the parents
     who did learn of the diagnosis had a better outcome than
     those of parents who were not informed but of course other
     factors probably contributed to the difference in outcome.
     The paper describes a parental reaction in the early part of
     1968 incidentally when the publicity, a good deal of it false,
     was at its peak on this issue.

23. Rosenthal, R., The Pygmalion effect lives, Psychology Today
     7:56 (1973).

24. Caldwell, P.D. and Smith, D.W., The XXY (Klinefelter's)
     syndrome in childhood: Detection and treatment, J. Pediat.
     80:250 (1972).

25. Mellman, W.J., Chromosomal screening of human populations,
     in "Ethical, Social, and Legal Dimensions of Screening for
     Human Genetic Disease, Bergsma, D. (ed.), Birth Defects
     Original Article Series, X:123 (1974), Symposia Specialists,
     Miami.

26. Myhre, S.A., Ruvalcaba, R.H.A., Johnson, H.R., The effects of
     testosterone treatment in Klinefelter's syndrome. J. Pediat.
     76:267 (1970).

27. Nielsen, J., Chromosome examination of newborn children,
     Humangenetik 26:215 (1975).

28. Eller, E., Frankenburg, W., Puck, M. et al, Prognosis in
     newborn infants with X-chromosomal abnormalities, Pediatrics
     47:681 (1971).

29. Hilton, B., Callahan, D., Harris, M. et al, (eds.) "Ethical
     Issues in Human Genetics. Plenum Press, New York, pp.275-
     281 (1973).

DISCUSSION

Papers of Profs. A.M. Dershowitz and E.B. Hook
Principal Discussant: Prof. J.R. Beckwith
Moderator: Prof. A.M. Capron

BECKWITH: Well, it is clearly going to be impossible to respond
to the great number of points made in the papers of Prof. Dershowitz
and Prof. Hook. I'd like to make a few specific and some more
general points. Prof. Capron just referred to discussion of dangers in advances in science and their uses, and I would emphasize
my belief that it is not just the matter of the danger in advances.
It is a question of which advances are made, which directions are
taken. And I think these are not neutral.

What kind of research is done in a particular society is very
much influenced by a large number of factors. One portion of that
is the scientific and medical community. But also ideological
inferences, the influences of funding by government, may play a
very important role.

Now, as far as the XYY story goes, I feel this has played a
very important role in the development of that particular field.
First of all, I'd like to raise the general question as to whether
studies on such complex behavioral traits as intelligence and criminality can in fact lead to any meaningful and useful results,
when the very complex interaction between environment and genetics
in these particular cases make it so difficult. This point has
been made by a number of critics of this particular field of research.
Prof. Dershowitz commented on XYY and violence, although he did not
make any particular statement about it. One thing that's been pointed out in most of the reviews that I am aware of is that in fact most
XYY individuals have not tended to commit crimes of violence. In
fact, at least Borgaonkar and Shah reviewed their claims
that they tend to be less violent than other individuals in prisons.
I still feel very strongly, together with the group with whom I work,
that the whole XYY story is a myth, and that part of the reason
this myth has grown and been generated does in fact have to do with
the perspective of at least some of the people doing the research.

This comes again - and it is obviously a subjective opinion -
from an analysis of the literature, reading introductions to papers,
public statements by those involved in the field and conclusions of
papers which often suggest social programs as a result of this
research. In addition, I should point out that in the United States
not an insignificant amount of the funding for this research has
come from such institutions as the Law Enforcement Assistance
Administration and the Center for the Study of Crime and Delinquency.
So here again we see instances where at least from our perspective,
ideology and the funding interests of the government itself determine

the directions that a particular field of research will take.

I have been somewhat disturbed at some of the comments earlier in the morning and I would like to emphasize or expand on some of the things that Dr. Bok said. At least from some of the earlier presentations and the reaction of the audience, I had a feeling of an attitude of rejection of society's rights for the control over what directions science and what application science and medicine will have. In fact, there is some sense of self-protection that is going on here.

I realize that there are many problems in involving the public in determining what is done with the areas of research and how those areas are applied. But I think we have to realize that directions are already given in many ways by the society we live in. I have already tried to point out in the example of the XYY case the ways in which funding, the ways in which particular ideological perspectives have affected a particular area of research. I certainly don't see why the ethics and ideology of the medical community in particular should be the dominant factor in determining how screening programs, etc., are used. So I do feel that in as many ways as possible, we have to begin to communicate with the public, scientists, doctors, etc., to bring them into the discussion of these problems. I recognize the argument will be made that when attempts have been made, the lay public is so poorly informed on these issues that there is no way to really involve them in a meaningful way.

Well, I'm afraid that is a price that we are going to have to pay for our failure for many, many years in fact to communicate what is happening and what the implications of research in science and medicine are. I think we should be making an effort now, and I essentially reinforce what Dr. Bok said, to communicate in much better ways with the public and to point out how research in science and medicine are applied through political decisions which are not particular decisions that the scientific and medical community should be able to make.

LAPPE: Let me emphasize that these comments were sparked by the debate which we have just seen and have not been prepared in advance. The key issue, which perhaps we have overlooked in the discussion of screening for cytogenetic or biochemical defects so far, is the question of morality or ethics raised by screening for potential defects where we have not anticipated the therapeutic options which we would provide once we have found them. We have discussed screening for an XYY karyotype and have not anticipated the kinds of structures which a free society must deal with once a presumptive defect is found. This, it seems to me, does leave open a serious possibility of misuse. Rather than a geneticophobia, as Dr. Hook has encountered it, it is

possible that in society's view the glaring publicity given to
occasional cases (and sometimes mistakenly identified cases of
individuals with purported chromosome aneuploidies), can lead to
anticipation and labeling that in psychiatric circles is considered
a highly contagious and potentially dangerous means of structuring
a society. I am speaking about a labeling theory that has been
developed for explaining some kinds of schizophrenia. But like this
labeling theory, the notion that an XYY genotype or any other condition is causally linked with deviant behavior or that specific
environments are causally linked with deviant behavior have not
been adequately studied at all.

Ultimately, then, what we are talking about is the kind of
response which society is prepared to give to individuals who by
virtue of particular genetic susceptibility or environmental
deprivation may be prone to behaviors or inabilities towards which
we would like to offer remedial help. It would seem to me that
we could spend an equal portion of time designing programs like
we have begun to do for individuals with the XXY genotype, which
would begin to organize therapies which may help these individuals
lead a more normal and productive life.

DAVIS: The term "geneticophobe" is a new and interesting one.
I have used the term "social determinist" to describe the attitude
that Dr. Hook has just referred to. People who fall into this
category seem to make the curious assumption that anybody who
talks about any genetic contribution to human behavior is trying to
ascribe all differences to genetic causes. But I don't know any
such 100 percent hereditarians. They existed in the 19th century,
but this is an ancient and now thoroughly dead horse that is being
flogged. On the other hand, there still seem to be a lot of 100
percent environmentalists, for political purposes, even though
those who know anything about genetics understand that genes determine potentials, and the environment conditions behavior within an
individual's range of potentials.

The problem of XYY, unfortunately, has reached the public in an
over-simplified and confusing way. It has been discussed as though
it involved a Mendelian kind of inheritance, in which a genetic abnormality, such as a pair of genes for phenylketonuria or the extra
chromosome 21 of Down's syndrome, produces a definite, predictable
phenotypic effect in every subject. In fact, the limited data
available suggest that with XYY we are dealing with an example of
a more complex genetic mechanism (limited penetrance), in which the
genotypic abnormality only increases the probability of, rather
than determines, a phenotypic abnormality.

The problem seems to resemble that of schizophrenia, where the
presence of a large genetic factor is shown by the fact that the
identical twin of a schizophrenic has a 50% chance of being schizo-

phrenic, while the incidence in the population is only 1%. Moreover, in Kety's large, definitive study of adopted children in
Denmark who became schizophrenic, their biological relatives showed
a several-fold increase in the incidence of schizophrenia, while
the biologically unrelated adoptive relatives showed only the
background incidence. Since the role of genetic factors is thus
so prominent, while that of the environment could not be demonstrated, the mystery is why 50% of the identical twins of schizo-
phrenics do not develop the disease.

XYY seems to involve a similar mystery in developmental genetics. In addition, it is theoretically possible that some Y chromosomes have, and others lack, genes whose duplication would predis-
pose to behavioral difficulties. Hence there is little sense in
newspaper articles that identify XYY with predestined criminality,
and it is premature for lawyers to be writing articles based on
this deterministic concept. But it is equally false to conclude,
from the absence of a defined and deterministic syndrome, that XYY
has no relation to deviant behavior. The "XYY syndrome" is a myth,
but the XYY problem is not, for the 20-fold increased incidence in
mental penal institutions is a reality. And since karyotyping is
here to stay we are going to continue to encounter XYY individuals,
in fetuses and newborns as well as adults. We had better learn
what it means - whether one in two or one in fifty is likely to
have serious behavioral problems, and whether the others have less
serious but significant problems, or whether they fall in the
normal range.

It is true that the sensational publicity aroused by the early
observations now unfortunately complicates any long-term longi-
tudinal study. However, since such a study, like most clinical
research, inevitably combines fact-finding with therapy where indicated, I am not convinced by the argument that the subject families
are being harmed. Neither am I convinced by the argument that the
studies are valueless because they lack the ideal controls, i.e.,
normal children falsely labeled as XYY. For when the scientific method is applied to epidemiological studies in man it often has to
settle for less than ideal controls. Both these objections are
based on the alleged danger of self-fulfilling prophecy -- an
effect that is real in some circumstances, but is not generalizable
or predictable in its magnitude. In fact, in the present study of
Dr. Walzer at Harvard this effect seems to be negligible, in the
light of preliminary results: the XYY subjects have so far failed
to exhibit behavioral problems. It thus seems likely that the
popular impression of the dangerous consequences of an extra Y
chromosome are grossly exaggerated, and it is ironical that the
critics, who properly decry this unwarranted genetic determinism,
are attacking the kind of study that seems to offer the best hope
of refuting it.

The basis of geneticophobia, of course, is the fear that any attention to genetic factors in behavior will divert energy from the effort to eliminate the environmental inequalities, particularly in educational and economic opportunity, that have been the cause of enormous injustice and waste of talent. But while we are breaking down these barriers we will attain the goal of greater social equality in a more realistic way if we define it in terms that recognize our genetic diversity. People differ widely in their intellectual potentials, artistic talents, motor skills, temperaments, and drives, and we know that different environments have different effects on different genotypes. Denial of this principle will lead to a shallow and self-defeating extreme egalitarianism. On the other hand, advances in the young (and threatened) field of behavioral genetics should help us to individualize our manipulations of the environment in ways that will increase the opportunity for self-fulfillment.

CAPRON: We may wish in this discussion to focus in on some of the particular human experimentation problems that are raised by the kinds of screening tests that Prof. Hook was talking about and that have been addressed by the last three speakers. Specifically one of the difficulties that was faced in the design of these experiments is this question of a self-fulfilling prophecy. One way of testing that is to have included in the group of children who will be studied and followed, is a group who are not XYY, but who are XY. The question then arises, which some of you may wish to comment on, should the parents of those children be told that their child is XYY for the period of the study to see if the problems are caused by the environment. Is this an unethical type of experimentation?

Indeed the question arises about what should the parents themselves be told of the children who are XYY. There have been variations in the design of these studies. A number of studies have been conducted and they have changed their pattern. One thought which some of the physicians had at first was they would not reveal the diagnoses at all initially so as to avoid the self-fulfilling prophecy. Would any of the speakers care to comment on this?

CHOROVER: I'd like to comment on Prof. Capron's suggestion. What he has done is to point out what the necessary control group would be for the study. Lest the point be missed, let me restate it. What would be required in order to turn the study into an experiment, would be to have a control group of perfectly normal children, whose parents are told for the purposes of the study that they are genetically abnormal. That is required in order to control for the effects of the information that is given to the parents in the present study. I trust that everyone can recognize an atrocity when they see one. Would anyone here be interested in being participants in such a study with their normal children?

But there is another point at issue here also. It is the fact of enrichment that Prof. Davis mentioned. I think the introduction of the term "geneticophobia" is unfortunate. It only serves to obscure a more fundamental defect in the way in which we tend to think about social problems. The defect is not unique to the genetic approach. Let us assume that it is a fact that there is enrichment for the XYY karyotype among incarcerated populations. What are we to make of that fact? Let me point out to you that if you take the posture of an investigator from Mars coming down to look at the prisons in the United States today, you would very quickly make a discovery of two factors, both of them genetically-determined for which there is extensive enrichment in these institutions. One of these is the character of maleness and the other is the character of non-white skin. Both show enrichment within such institutions and both are genetically determined. What is one going to make of these facts? Would it be 'scientific' to propose a study that would focus upon the biology of non-white males as a means of 'explaining' the enrichment. Or might it be more reasonable to study the social system of which they are a part? It is not merely a matter of 'science' when someone proposes studies on incarcerated individuals or people of the class that they represent.

I suggest that it is perfectly possible to examine the process whereby individuals who are different from what is seen as the standard of perfection or adequacy in the society end up in such institutions. The fundamental error, it seems to me, is in the assumption which Prof. Hook made at the outset of his talk that there is a meaningful correlation in a scientific sense between the fact of incarceration and the concept of deviance or abnormal behavior. Let me suggest further, that a large number of individuals who engage in antisocial, deviant, and socially disruptive behavior are not identified as deviant and do not end up incarcerated in such institutions. The people who do commit acts which end them in such institutions tend to be drawn by and large from classes of our population which are identified in some presumptive way as intrinsically defective or deviant. The problem lies not in the defective genes of these individuals, but rather in the social bias of concepts which are used to identify such individuals as somehow different and inferior. We are endlessly doing studies on such classes of people rather than looking at the social context which draws them into such institutions.

HOOK: In answer to Prof. Chorover, I specifically stated that my definition of the term "deviance" was purely an operational one and that this was not to imply that anyone in a security setting was there appropriately, or conversely.

As to the question of whether there is a meaningful correlation,

I think this is really a question of what you mean by "meaningful".
Prof. Beckwith and others have argued that the correlation is due
to malnutrition - or other adverse socioeconomic circumstances -
and therefore a purported association with any other factors is
not "meaningful". But this is to define that term in accord with
their ideological viewpoint.

As to the question of obscuring the sources of the problems,
let me give you a counterexample of the kind of obscuring that
has arisen in this controversy. I quote from the March 11th,
Boston Phoenix in which a member of the same group that had criticized the Harvard study was quoted as saying the following about
this research: "...(Such) research makes the ghetto and campus
riots appear not to have been externally caused; that is, caused
by either lousy economic opportunities or by rats biting children.
Rather, this research, done by Harvard doctors, makes the riots
appear to be the fault of a few abnormal genes." If anything
illustrates geneticophobia or irrational views about the matter,
I submit that that statement does. (By the way, this came from a
Ph.D. in Biology.) The views of people who raise these issues
become so polarized that statements like this are made.

Furthermore, I suspect that the thrust of those people who
argue about consequences of the XYY studies and the imprinting on
the public mind of inevitable fatalistic association are simply
misreading the public view. The results of the street corner poll
suggest that.

DERSHOWITZ: I think what we have heard this afternoon is an
example of the polarity and the extremism, really, on both sides.
On the one hand, we have those who would prevent experiments from
going forward because they think nothing good will be achieved.
(I do not want to use the word "good" for positive, I want to use
it neutrally.) Nothing scientifically validatable will be accomplished, but moreover, if something validatable would be accomplished, that would be even worse. We do not want to allow experiments
on XYY because firstly, they won't tell us anything, and secondly,
God forbid if they do tell us something, you know what that is
going to be. On the other hand, we hear those who say we want to
do our own experiments without any governmental control whatsoever.
I think it is clear to me that both of these points of view are
mistaken, but the critical issue is not that. The critical issue
to me is which is worse, which kind of society is more dangerous
to live in. A society in which there are those, whether they be
well motivated academics or governmental people, or social scientists, who have the power to say this experiment shall not be
conducted - its evil potentials are greater than its beneficial
production. Is that worse than a society which is like our society and says the government shall be able to dictate and determine which experiments will be funded and encouraged?

I may surprise some of you who know my political views. I
think my political views generally are very closely associated
with Prof. Beckwith's, and generally tend to be on the liberal
left side of most issues. But here I fundamentally disagree
with his conclusion. I think it is a far worse society that pre-
vents experimentation for fear of the consequences and results.
Again, I am trying to distinguish out my views as politician from
my views as an academic. It is critically important to let the
chips fall where they may, even if they fall in dangerous, unpleasant, and even counterproductive places. If the government is
allowed to determine where research is done, that's bad, but
it is not fatal. There are always alternative sources of experimentation.

Yes, you can answer, not in our complex society. All experimentation really does have to be funded. Well, not quite. A lot
of the great experiments in the past and I am sure many of the
great experiments in the future will be conducted without government funding. It will be harder, it will be much more difficult,
it will take many more years, but it is not an outright ban.

What I fear most for example, are the experiences in the Free
University of Berlin - which is no longer free for the carrying
out of important social, political and scientific experiments,
because the left wing has captured that university in large part.
This should teach us that we should be more afraid of prevention
than of other kinds of control. So the message I would like to
come away with from this general discussion is let the chips fall
where they may, let the experiments be conducted, let Prof. Shockley
do his thing (not to make any comparisons) let Prof. Walzer to
his thing, let Prof. Beckwith do his thing, let everybody experiment
whichever way they want. Let the government fund one kind or another, let there be private funds available if possible for other
kinds of experimentation. But Brandeis, when he talked about the
marketplace of ideas, could also have been talking about the
marketplace of experimentation. I think prohibition should be prohibited, if anything should be prohibited. We should simply tolerate
and try to make the best of a bad situation when the government
tries to tell us in which direction our research is to go forward.

A. FALEK: Emory University, Atlanta: Presentations this morning have revolved about up to date controversial issues in genetic
studies of the fetus, what types of responses have been employed,
and discouraging reports, at least from the human geneticist point
of view, on the outcomes of these responses. It was also pointed
out that the courts have been inconsistent in their findings and
the law emerges as a result of a political process. Each time
human geneticists have tried to acquiesce and adapt to new requirements to meet the desires made by others, further demands are
introduced. It should finally be realized that these seem to be

attempts to fill a bottomless well. Recently the physicians in
California with regard to increasing cost of malpractice demonstrated that the legislature does respond to forceful action.
Therefore, I should like to hear some comments from this distinguished group of speakers on what types of forceful action
they would suggest be taken to support research in this field of
medical science?

LEDERBERG: Rather than seeing the XYY argument as one between genetic fatality, fatalism, determinism, and environmental
manipulation or growth of an individual, one might perhaps alternatively take a look at the problem of XYY with the following
structure. We might ask what are the moral reasons, arguments or
issues present, and then what ethical approach can reach a morally
satisfactory goal. We might ask, as an example, if in fact it is
a moral goal to allocate liberties to individuals who have
different genotypes, if these genotypes in fact do have a difference
in predictable anti-social behavior. Should this unfold correctly,
we might ask if it is morally defensible or correct, and we'll
get a yes or no answer to that question. If we take a look at the
spectrum of genotypes, XX, XY, and XYY, is there some sort of
incorrigeability criterion for the pertinancy to life imprisonment
or preventive detention for such individuals. This might show that
women with an XX might be allowed five crimes in their lifetime
before they are considered to be incorrigible, that XY men might
be allowed the usual three crimes, and that an XYY, by virtue of
an additional propensity, might be allowed no crime before we decide on taking a preventive measure. The question is whether this
allocation of threshhold is morally defensible or not?

We have heard arguments on the prospective studies. We might
ask instead to compare prospective studies, which have introduced
new elements of concern, with retrospective studies which have been
available to us, and which we might perfect by adding to the
collection thereof, to see if in fact either of these two possible
approaches are ethically satisfactory. I think if we do that, we
might find that we would be content to live with the data that we
can get from retrospective studies on the frequency of the XYY
genotype and associated anti-social behavior which we might obtain
from voluntary or from institutional karyotyping, rather than going
to the prospective studies which have the scientific invalidity
that was raised by the Beckwith group and the impossibility of obtaining the correct control. In any event, we might approach the
general problem, and many of the other problems here, by first
asking if the goal as stated is a morally acceptable one or not.
And then which of the various alternatives are ethically and scientifically valid?

HAMERTON: I had not intended to intervene in the discussion
of the XYY male; however, my own study has been referred to and I
felt, therefore, that I would like to indicate my views. We
heard an excellent review of the XYY controversy from Prof. Hook
and a discussion from Prof. Dershowitz as to whether the XYY
karyotype should be "predictive" or "excusatory" of criminality,
either of which I am sure all serious workers in this field would
deplore at the present state of our knowledge, just as we would
deplore the labeling of all such individuals as potential criminals.
Prof. Beckwith tells us that all newborn and other studies aimed
at identifying a newborn sample of XYY males and their subsequent
follow-up should cease, and he and his colleagues have done their
best to bring about this end.

Prof. Beckwith further questions the political motivation of
the investigators, and of the funding agencies concerned with this
work, and feels that the research for genetic factors predisposing
to abnormal behavior of individuals with abnormal sex chromosome
complements (XXY, XYY, XXX, XXYY) will obscure the more important
social problems. He takes this stand despite the fact that no
serious investigator is suggesting a purely genetic or purely
environmental cause to behavioral problems, but rather the possibility of a genotype-environmental interaction. The facts about
this condition, ably reviewed by Prof. Hook yesterday, may be
summarized as follows: 27 XYY babies have been identified in
about 30,000 newborn males studied in the various parts of the
world, an incidence of just under 1:1,000 male births. As Prof.
Hook showed, the incidence in penal settings is about four times
this level (1:225), while in certain mental/penal settings the
incidence is much higher (3-4%). The high frequency of the "double
Y" karyotype (XXYY and XYY) in the United Kingdom studies in Broad-
moore, Rampton, and Carstairs may be accounted for by the unique
nature of these maximum security mental/penal hospitals, rarely duplicated elsewhere in the world, and the specialized nature of their
clientele. The original and careful observations of the Edinburgh
and Sheffield groups about the XYY karyotype have been colored by
sensational and inaccurate reporting in the lay press. Such misleading phrases as the 'criminal chromosome' have undoubtedly
affected the whole discussion of this condition and made the collection of careful and unbiased observations difficult, if not
impossible.

To stop all newborn and other population studies and follow-up
as Prof. Beckwith would have us do, because of an unfortunate historical accident and so prevent the identification and careful follow-up
of randomly ascertained XYY males seems to me at least to be not only
counterproductive, but positively unhelpful. We need to determine
if possible - and it may not be possible - what environmental factors
lead to behavioral problems in males who may have some predisposition
to such problems as the result of sex chromosome anomalies. We also

need information on mortality and morbidity in these conditions, and for this we need to identify the XYY male in adult populations in addition to our work with newborns. Only in this way can a sufficiently large sample be obtained for a properly designed and careful follow-up .

This is, of course, most difficult to do in the emotionally charged atmosphere surrounding the question, and I suggest that Prof. Beckwith's approach that nothing should be done is unhelpful and even harmful and will undoubtedly hinder the solution to these complex behavioral problems that I am sure we all desire.

ROSENBERG: Prof. Beckwith indicated that as a result of the controversy concerning the Boston XYY study, that such screening has been stopped in Boston and possibly elsewhere. I think that in the company of lawyers it is appropriate to talk about precedents since that is in fact what many people in the law do, and it would be equally appropriate for us to do it in medicine. Let us take the clock back a few years, relate our discussion to phenylketonuria, and ask what would have happened if we followed the history of PKU as a disease - and as a disease to be screened for. It was in the 1930's and 1940's that Jervis and Foley identified phenylketones in the urine of children who were retarded. It was not so long thereafter that the enzymatic lesion responsible for the appearance of phenylalanine and phenylketones was found by Jervis working in New York state. A few years later it was clearly determined that this genetic disease was due to an enzymatic deficiency and could be modified by a diet low in phenylalanine, an observation made in Europe and the United States in the late 1950's. Only after all that experience were screening programs developed to find out whether the mental retardation produced by this disease could be lessened or prevented by the institution of a diet.

Prof. Beckwith, my question to you is this. Would it have been perceived in the 1940's and 1950's as an invasion of privacy to study those individuals with mental retardation and phenylketones in their urine? Since there was no suitable control group, (it would have been very difficult to administer large amounts of phenylketones to those individuals or to normal individuals to see whether they also became retarded) it seems to me quite likely that the field of endeavor related to this particular prototype of an inherited disease whose consequences can be prevented postnatally, would have been lost. What then are the parameters in our current understanding of phenylketonuria which in a sense may be extrapolated to some of the current controversy about the XYY syndrome?

BECKWITH: In the case of phenylketonuria there is from 30 years or so of research rather well defined biochemical characteristics which were associated with a particular syndrome. In the case of the XYY male this is just not the case. Again, from the review of research which just started 10 years ago (starting in 1965 with Jacobs' report), we have no information on any syndrome associated with XYY males. There does seem to be an increased frequency of XYY males in certain kinds of institutions, but no syndrome is associated with these XYY males when compared to XY males. So it is a very, very different situation to extrapolate from PKU screening to XYY screening where we had a very definite biochemical characteristic associated with a very definite syndrome. Hence to screen for XYY males among newborns in addition to telling parents of the XYY characteristic, I think it is a very dangerous thing. It is not the first time I have heard the connection raised between PKU and XYY. I find it really an extremely frightening extrapolation. Many of us have been concerned about genetic screening programs not per se, but because most of them have been used for the most part to benefit people, although some have had some negative implications. But the fact is that under present social conditions they are potentially the opening wedge for eugenic programs with much more serious implications. To start to extend the reasoning behind a PKU screening program to an XYY program I think very much illustrates this problem. That is to extend it from a well defined biochemical problem to behavioral problems I think gets much more into social and political issues and, therefore, into the general area of the potential for eugenics programs in this country.

I feel obligated also to go over some other points because clearly there's been a lot of criticism of our position on the XYY issue and we in turn have had very little opportunity to respond to these here. The issue of whether there are dangers to the children in these studies has been emphasized by most people working in the field itself. In fact Prof. Hook said to me over the phone some time ago that if his child were XYY, he would not want to know it. The process we went through was to present our criticisms of this study. We felt the risks outweighed the benefits and the informed consent procedures were not adequate to the committee at Harvard. A majority of the first committee that considered this at Harvard actually voted that the risks of the study outweighed the benefits. Despite that, the chairman of the committee chose to lie to the faculty and to lie to the press about the decision of the committee and this affected and colored the whole development of the situation since then. I feel that the way the issue has been presented here in fact is as though it is just a bunch of nuts criticizing something, whereas in fact I think there is very strong support for our criticism of this study, even among many of the workers in the field.

Finally, I'd like to make a few comments about the structure of this meeting itself. I'm really very disturbed at the fact that for the most part, almost entirely, the people who have had the

opportunity to speak at this meeting are people with careers and
self-interest in screening, either in the process of screening itself or legal aspects of screening, and that those who are critical
of some aspects of it have had very little opportunity to offer
their criticisms, and in fact very little opportunity for the floor.
I have talked with people at this meeting who are very concerned
with programs they are involved in and about funding for some of
the programs. They have had very little opportunity to speak
from the floor on these issues.

    MILUNSKY: I would just simply have to point out that there is
a random selection here and there has certainly been ample time
for people of every particular persuasion to approach the microphone. In fact no one has actually been turned back from any
microphone.

    HOOK: I will respond to a few of the points touched upon by
Prof. Beckwith. The study in Boston was not a broad spectrum
complete screening of all newborns by government fiat. It was a
research procedure done in a single hospital. Parents had the option either to participate or not to participate. Admittedly, there
were problems with the original informed consent procedure. But
as I understand it women are now coming in and asking for the procedure to be done on their infants as a consequence of publicity
given to the research because of the criticism. Perhaps they want
to be reassured their child is not affected or, if there is an
abnormality, to watch their child more closely. There is very
strong irony in that the adverse publicity may have alerted the
parents to the possibility of the newborn test being available.

    Again regarding the streetcorner poll of women of child-bearing
age in Albany last week, none of the women who were aware of the
XYY or "criminal chromosome" stated that they thought every affected
child must inevitably become a criminal. And they all said if their
child was affected, they would want to be told.

    The tenor of Prof. Beckwith's discussions has been that the
newborn study of the XYY genotype is the thin edge of the wedge of
all kinds of unpleasant social control programs. Knowledge does
accumulate in a step by step way and often we take one step backwards for every two forward. But to stand where we are right now
in our current status of uncertainty and predict such an inevitable
future, is to use a very cloudy and one-sided ideological crystal
ball.

    STEINBERG: It has been mentioned several times today that the
XYY frequency in people in institutions is not much greater than
the XYY frequency of people in the general population. The reason
for this is that relatively few of the XYY individuals born wind
up in institutions. The latter conclusion is based on the fact

that the frequency of XYY at birth is higher than the frequency
of XYY in institutions. But the interesting datum that is missing
is that we know nothing about the frequency of XYY among adult
males in the general population. We do not know what happens to
XYY males between birth and adulthood. If their death rate turns
out to be higher than what it is for XY males, then the frequency
of individuals in institutions may turn out to be very much higher
than we suspect relative to the number that survived to be put in
the institutions. I do not say that this is true. I simply would
indicate that the argument saying that relatively few entered
institutions is based on an absence of data.

BECKWITH: In response to Prof. Steinberg's comments, there has
been some population screening in Europe and in general the frequency of XYY males does turn out to be more of the same order
of the frequency among newborns.

LAPPE: I don't think I have the good answer that Prof. Rosenberg was asking for in regard to the comparison of PKU and XYY
screening, but I think I can make some morally and perhaps scientifically relevant discriminations between the two. In the case of
PKU screening at least to a non-medical geneticist, it seems fairly
clear for whose benefit the screen is intended. In the case of
the XYY screen, a much broader question of benefit is raised since
it may not be merely the individual who will benefit by any therapies
that potentially could be instituted, but a very clear impression
that the intention of the screen is to aid the society at large.

I am sure Prof. Rosenberg knows quite well that in the case of
PKU there is a known ideology and prognosis which was terribly
grim at the time. There was reasonable expectation of benefit.
Proxy consent, therefore, could be considered acceptable. But for
XYY we have neither an understanding of proximal cause of the defect
or the syndrome if there is such, and no reasonable reason to use
compulsory screening when you have an individual who will be able
to give his consent at maturity.

DAVIS: I would question Dr. Lappe's argument that screening
for XYY is morally unjustifiable because the sole aim is to try to
do something for society and not to help an individual. From the
many studies reviewed by Borgaonkar and Shah, as well as by Prof.
Hook, it is clear the frequency of XYY in mental penal institutions
is 10 to 20 times that in a variety of general populations, and this
simply cannot be brushed aside as a myth. That association has some
cause. We don't understand at all the developmental consequences
of XYY. A statement made by Prof. Steinberg is perfectly correct:
we don't know what fraction of these subjects might die before they
become adults. We are not going to find out by saying let's not
look at it. Prof. Beckwith's remark that the Harvard study and
other studies of XYY have been stopped seems to me to be a cause

for wearing black crepe at a meeting of this sort, rather than
for considering it as a triumph for the individual. If individuals
go to jail, whatever the social cause may be, and if we can acquire
information that will help keep them out of the trouble that sends
them to jail, it seems to me we are helping those individuals as
well as society.

I would also question the notion that anything financed by the
National Institute of Mental Health and its Center for Crime and
Delinquency is automatically concerned with helping society and not
with helping individuals. No matter how angry we may be at police
brutality or at the persistence of social inequities that contribute to crime and delinquency, it seems to me a fantastic political
distortion to suggest that research aimed at protecting society
from crime is necessarily aimed against the interests of individuals.

LEDERBERG: I want to point out the application of a little
common sense and good science to the excellent point made by Prof.
Steinberg. Differential viability of the XYY is possible. A
very simple approach to ask if this does occur is to screen the
dead. There is no ethical question of self-fulfilling prophecy
in obtaining tissues of the dead and asking whether or not this is
an XYY person. I know in Massachusetts this may be a problem.
But if we accept data from jurisdictions other than Massachusetts
we might come to the conclusion that there is or is not a differential viability. In fact, if there is a differential viability
seen in a pronounced increase in the frequency of XYY in the dead
as compared to the newborns, then we have the additional possibility
of correlating that increased differential loss of viability with
the symptom of their death, leading perhaps to a further understanding
of the biochemical or health ramifications of these chromosomal
variations.

Genetic Counseling—
Mass Population Screening
for Homozygotes and Heterozygotes

MEDICOLEGAL ASPECTS OF GENETIC COUNSELING

Kurt Hirschhorn

Division of Medical Genetics of the Mount Sinai School

of Medicine of the City University of New York

When I was asked to prepare a paper on potential situations in genetic counseling which may result in questions of malpractice, I felt a bit like the unarmed Christian martyr who was told to enter the Roman arena in order to fight a group of lions with large teeth. The current attitudes in the United States encouraging such suits, while reducing protection, make me quite hesitant to engage in an exercise designed to sharpen those teeth. I will therefore largely refrain from listing too many specific problems and will rather address myself to the general principles involved. Although many of the issues concern the procedures of amniocentesis and screening, these will not be dealt with in my paper, but are being considered by other speakers. I am not an expert on legal matters and therefore wish to express my gratitude to Mr. Roger Dworkin of the University of Washington for bringing several of these matters to my attention.

As in all other cases of negligence, one must consider both acts of omission and commission by the counselor. In many respects, potential negligence in genetic counseling falls into the categories considered in other medical malpractice suits. The most important of these is the case where counseling is based on a wrong diagnosis made by the counselor or, in the special situation considered here, counseling based on the acceptance by the counselor of a wrong diagnosis made elsewhere without an attempt to confirm this diagnosis. The latter problem is especially relevant to the increasing reliance on non-medical individuals such as the Ph.D. geneticist or genetic associates for the actual performance of genetic counseling. The results of such wrong diagnoses may include the birth of an abnormal child, the risk for whom could have been predicted prior to the pregnancy or in time to consider prenatal diagnosis.

Alternatively, an unnecessary abortion of a fetus not at risk
may result from the belief of the parents that they are carriers
of a genetic disease, particularly one not diagnosable prenatally.
For example, if a child dies of a neurologic disease, wrongly
believed to be a case of Werdnig-Hoffmann syndrome, a disease
inherited in autosomal recessive manner, and counseling is first
given during the subsequent pregnancy, the couple may be unwilling
to take the 25% risk of another abnormal child and may decide to
abort. If later information derived from the autopsy findings
results in the conclusion that the child was not affected by this
disease, but rather was affected by a non-genetic neurologic
degenerative process, the aborted fetus was in fact not at risk.
An even more difficult but similar situation derives from the
failure of the geneticist to differentiate between autosomal
recessive inheritance and a spontaneous mutation for a dominantly
inherited syndrome. If one falsely diagnoses a syndrome to
represent a dominant mutant, a future pregnancy may result in an
abnormal child, while if the error consists of a diagnosis of
recessive inheritance, a fetus not at risk may be aborted or
the family may wrongly decide to refrain from future pregnancies.
The latter decision may result in unnecessary voluntary sterilization. Alternatively, such a family eventually proven not to be
at risk may opt for artificial insemination which under the best of
circumstances is a difficult medicolegal matter. If done unnecessarily, the problems are greatly multiplied. The latter two
procedures, sterilization and artificial insemination, even if done
on the basis of a correct diagnosis may lead to potential actions
if alternative options were not completely explained or understood
during the counseling session. I cannot stress enough the importance of a clear and complete letter to the family after the
counseling session for the purpose of avoiding confusion as best as
possible. It is of course clear that such a letter in the case of
wrong advice may reasonably be expected to be used in evidence.

Among the many possible examples of negligence by omission are
the failure to discuss all possible options and their potential
consequences, the failure to make as sure as possible the understanding of risk by the family and a number of other omissions which
could be construed to represent failure to provide treatment, in
the language of the standard medical malpractice suit. Included in
this category may be the failure to advise prenatal diagnosis or
to warn families at risk that future children should be tested at
birth when therapy is available for the disease in question but
must be begun early in life, as is the case in galactosemia or
phenylketonuria.

It is well accepted that the birth and care of a defective
child can result in severe psychological problems in the parents
which can probably be exacerbated by the stress encountered during
genetic counseling and by the facts learned at such a session.

Certainly, the confirmation that one or both parents carries the
genetic material resulting in the abnormal offspring, could
potentially trigger a severe and even self-destructive reaction of
guilt and other emotions. One could then ask whether failure of
recognition of this risk or failure to follow the family with this
problem in mind, even to the extent of asking for psychiatric
consultation, may represent an act of omission. An important
example is the increase in marital problems observed in such
families which can result in a cessation of sexual intercourse
or even in divorce. I believe that the obligation of the counselor
to concern himself with these matters is currently not clear.

What appears to be even less clear is who has the right to
sue and who can be sued. The major aspect of this question relates to the rights of a child to sue for what has been called
wrongful life. A recent study (1) concerns itself with injuries
to unborn children. Physical injury before birth is almost certainly cause for an action by the child. Determination by the
geneticist that a potential teratogen was responsible for a malformation may also result in such action. These rights are probably
not those of the fetus but require that an affected child must be
born alive. The action, however, for wrongful life appears somewhat
illogical in that the child would be able to claim that it would
have been better if it never had been born. If suits of this
nature are brought, there are a group of potential defendants including for example, the physician prescribing the teratogen. Action
against the genetic counselor or the parents would seem to be
for wrongful life and therefore not very likely to be adjudicated
against these individuals. On the other hand, suits by the parents
themselves or by normal or abnormal children in the family for
damages resulting from dilution of parental attention are certainly
possible.

Another aspect to be considered is the potentially staggering
level of the damage awards that can be envisioned. In an analagous
ruling (2), a pharmacist negligently filled a prescription for
oral contraceptives with tranquilizers. When this couple subsequently had a normal child they recovered medical and hospital
expenses, lost wages, costs of rearing the child until majority and
damages for pain and anxiety minus an amount representing the benefit to the parents of having a normal child. The implications of
this ruling for genetic counseling are frightening, where the costs
of rearing a defective child would be enormous and life-long and
the benefit to the parents essentially non-existent. Again, to
this may be added an award for sibs for the loss of their share of
parental affection and money and for the affected child himself.
Although as mentioned before, suits for wrongful life may not be
valid but with the current emphasis on quality rather than mere
existence of life the possibility for the success of such a suit
increases.

Another legal issue surrounding genetic counseling concerns the question of who may give such counseling. This is relevant to the standards the counselor must meet to avoid being negligent. I am not certain whether the current discussions regarding the possible licensing of genetic counselors are helpful in this matter. It is not certain whether the establishment of strict criteria for such qualifications would aid in defining negligence or whether the present system in which essentially anyone can call themselves a genetic counselor dilutes the level of responsibility.

Finally, I would like to draw attention to two potential situations which in my mind are typical of the medicolegal dilemmas faced by the genetic counselor. Both cases represent situations where you are damned if you do and damned if you don't. The first of these relates to the accidental discovery of non-paternity during a family study. It is generally recognized that between 5 and 20% of children are not the offspring of the supposed father. Let us look at the case of a family with a child with an autosomal recessive inborn error, for example Tay-Sach disease, who come for counseling prior to another pregnancy. Heterozygote testing of the parents reveals the father to be normal and subsequent genetic marker studies exclude his paternity of the affected child. The couple knows about the ability to diagnose the disease prenatally and the father requests a discussion of this option. On the one hand, the statement that he is not at risk for fathering an affected child requires a statement of the reason for this conclusion and invades the mother's privacy if she does not want to reveal her past infidelity. On the other hand, the promise to perform an amniocentesis in a future pregnancy is based upon false information and involves an unnecessary risk. In the first instance, the mother could sue for invasion of privacy and both parents could involve the counselor in a messy divorce proceeding. In the second instance, if the amniocentesis results in damage or spontaneous abortion of the fetus, the mother could eventually sue for an unnecessary procedure. If the father subsequently discovers the truth of the matter, I am certain that there is a variety of reasons for action by him.

The second example may represent an even more difficult quandary. Suppose that a family comes for counseling after the birth of their second boy with Hemophilia-A, an X-linked recessive disorder. The mother is therefore a proven carrier of the gene and a variety of her female relatives may be at greater or lesser risk for having an affected son. During the proper procedure of obtaining a pedigree, such potential carriers are identified. The family is made aware of which individuals are at risk and of the advisability of contacting, testing and counseling these relatives of the mother. For reasons of past family difficulties, the mother refuses to contact these relatives and declines permission for such contact to be made by the counselor. If on the one hand the counselor takes it upon himself to search out these individuals, the mother again has a case for invasion of privacy. If on the other hand, he accedes to the wishes of the mother and the following year, one of these relatives has a son affected with hemophilia, a potential problem exists. This relative is probably quite aware of the existence of the disease in the original family and is quite likely to seek genetic counseling. The second counselor would quite properly inform her of the fact that she could have been appropriately tested and counseled prior to this pregnancy based upon the information obtained from the first family. The possibility exists that she could sue for damages, both her relative and the first counselor, the latter either for negligence or even potentially with reference to public health procedures requiring the identification, testing and treatment of individuals exposed to certain infectious diseases. Although the rationale for comparing infectious diseases with inherited diseases may on the surface seem unwarranted, a change in the public attitude may be occurring as demonstrated by the change of name of the former Communicable Disease Center to the Center for Disease Control and their involvement in the epidemiology of genetic defects.

I have not attempted to give any answers to the many questions relating to medicolegal aspects of genetic counseling, nor do I believe that these answers are available. As in all these situations, court rulings will determine practice. The degree to which the questions I have raised are leading to a defensive posture by the counselor no doubt varies from clinic to clinic and individual to individual. Since the obligations of the counselor in this field would seem to be ambiguous in many cases as shown by the last two examples, it is difficult to make specific recommendations. It is my hope that the members of the legal profession can clarify at least some of these questions so that those doing genetic counseling can perform this important service without expending an undue amount of concern regarding the legal consequences of their actions.

ACKNOWLEDGEMENT

Supported in part by grants GM19443 and HD02552 from the NIH and a genetics service grant from the National Foundation C-155. Dr. Hirschhorn is a Career Scientist of the Health Research Council of the City of New York (I-513).

REFERENCES

1. Report of the Law Commission, #60. HM Stationery Office, London, 1974.

2. Troppi v. Scarf, 31 Mich. App 240, 187 N.W. 2d 511 (1971).

PROBLEMS OF INFORMED CONSENT AND CONFIDENTIALITY IN GENETIC

COUNSELING

George J. Annas

Center for Law and Health Sciences

Boston University School of Law

It is the premise of this paper that all persons who are given genetic counseling should be provided with complete and accurate information concerning the procedures used, the results obtained, the alternatives available, and the reasonably expected risks and problems associated with each such alternative. This premise is based primarily on the right of citizens to self-autonomy, and upon a definition of genetic counseling that has as its primary purpose the "explaining of predicted recurrence risks, with the relevant scientific basis, and describing available reproductive options to families with genetic problems" (1). To further the patient's interest in both autonomy and privacy, no information obtained in genetic screening or counseling should be disclosed to any third party without the patient's informed consent.

While these conclusions may appear to be entirely non-controversial, a number of specific instances will be discussed in which various commentators have suggested that material information be concealed from patients, or that confidential information be disclosed without the patient's consent. This paper will assume either that the person providing genetic counseling is a physician, or that the non-physician counselor should be held to the same legal and ethical standard as a physician-counselor.

THE CONTEXT OF GENETIC COUNSELING AND INFORMATION CONVEYANCE

At the outset it is instructive to briefly review the literature on genetic counseling. While there are more than a dozen studies assessing the information gained by patients and their changes in reproductive habits as a result of this information, no study reports explicitly on the nature or type of genetic counseling that is actually being provided to patients. Rather, the studies to date have taken genetic counseling as a constant, and proceeded as if only the patients and their conditions varied in any meaningful way (2).

The thrust of these studies, and other medical statements on the subject, is that informed consent is an ideal that probably cannot be attained in the real world because patients are unable to understand complex medical information (3). Stated this way the argument is another of the "blaming the victim" type. Here the patient is blamed for the possible short comings of the counselor. For example, in their study of counseling for phenyl-ketonuria (PKU), Sibinga and Friedman begin with the observation that"(t)he communication of medical information from physicians to parents is often complicated by the parents' insufficient ability to understand the information or by their tendency to distort it." Only about 20% of the parents counseled about PKU in their study gave answers that indicated an understanding of the disorder. How could this be explained? The authors' hypothesis was that the better educated the parents the better their understanding would be. However, they found that "parents with greater education were no less inaccurate or distortion prone than those with less education" (4). No mention is given at all of the possibility that the reason only 20% of the parents studied understood the disease, independent of their education, was that the physicians doing the counseling were doing a poor job of communicating information!

Another study was based on the premise that the way to assess whether information provided had been properly understood was to follow up actual changes in reproductive patterns (5), i.e., the premise was not that individuals should be given enough information to make their own decisions, but rather that they should be given information in such a way that it would have a predetermined effect on their behavior. Similarly, Leonard and her co-workers regarded genetic counseling as a failure if not followed up with what they considered to be appropriate changes in reproductive practices (6). Their study did at least acknowledge, however, that the physician's personal qualities and ability to communicate might have some influence on patient knowledge.

The goal of imposing the beliefs of the counselor on the patient being "counseled" is nowhere so blatantly stated as in an article by Fort and his Tennessee co-workers on the counseling of young women with sickle cell anemia. Their conclusion from a finding of a 6% maternal mortality rate and a 20% infant mortality rate was that permitting a woman with sickle cell disease to undergo pregnancy could not be justified. In their words, "We advocate primary sterilization, abortion if conception occurs, and sterilization for those that have completed pregnancies. Patients with

sickle cell disease should be unhesitatingly thus counseled" (7).
While the authors might argue that such "counseling" is for the
patient's own good, what is really at stake is an attempt by a
group of physicians with specific beliefs, which could be viewed
by some as racist or even genocidal, to impose those beliefs on a
defined population of patients. What is being advocated is not
counseling, but propaganda.

IMPLICATIONS OF PRACTICE TO INFORMED CONSENT

These examples highlight two important questions regarding
informed consent to genetic counseling: 1. Is it a realistic
goal?; and 2. Should counseling be directive? The answer to the
first question must be that we don't know, since no studies have
yet been done on the question of how physicians and other genetic
counselors actually convey information to patients. From what we
know in other contexts, however, it is certain that no communication
will be effective unless a sincere effort is made to communicate
in language that is understandable to the patient. A recent study
has shown, for example, that even in cases where a consent form
was signed which described the procedure to be performed as
experimental, 40% of women in the study on the effects of various
drugs designed to induce labor did not know they were in an experimental study at the time the drug was administered (8). In another
context, a recent study by the American Civil Liberties Union
indicated that many women continue to be sterilized without their
informed consent in spite of HEW regulations which mandate express
informed consent guidelines. Some, for example, have signed consent forms written in English, although they were unable to read
in this language (9).

Rather than accept without question the argument of many
physicians that informed consent is a non-obtainable ideal in real
life (10), one should place primary responsibility on physicians
to come up with a way to make informed consent a reality, or demonstrate to the satisfaction of the courts that the doctrine is
unworkable. My own view is that if physicians cannot effectively
communicate with patients, their entire mode of dealing with patients is open to serious question, any consent obtained is by
definition not informed, and decision-making remains entirely in the
physician's hands. Moreover, what few studies do exist indicate
not that informed consent is unworkable, but rather that even in
the clinical setting patients are able to deal with complex risk
information and make decisions based on it (11).

Pearn has applied related risk data directly to the genetic
counseling setting. In his paper on subjective interpretation of
risks offered in genetic counseling, he notes, for example, that
most of us accept a 1 in 100 chance of winning a prize at a carnival,

but reject the 1 in 6 chance of losing our lives by playing Russian roulette. In one case what we stand to lose is a dime, in the other, our life. The conclusion is that odds themselves are relevant only when one knows the consequences that follow from the event occurring or not occurring. In the genetic counseling situation this implies, according to Pearn, "that parents can assess specific genetic risks only if they are informed of the sequelae and all their implications ..." (12).

Pearn goes on to note as an example that parents may be willing to take the risk of a genetic disease if the affected child is likely to be stillborn or die in early infancy, but would be less likely to take the risk of having a defective child that would require a lifetime of constant care. This, of course, implies that the more information parents have, the more likely they are to make a final decision consistent with their own values. As a policy matter, physicians should be charged with developing communication skills, and not be permitted to "blame" patients for their inability to comprehend medical information. Those who cannot communicate effectively should not counsel.

The second question is easier: should counseling be directive? Until the day we are willing to forbid by legislation all reproduction by carriers of certain genetic defects, all women over 35, all women with sickle cell disease, or any other similar category of individuals (and I hope this day will never come), counselors should expend all of their efforts toward getting information across in understandable language, and none of their efforts toward attempting to impose their own preferences on their patients.

The entire purpose of the doctrine of informed consent is to permit the individual to make up his or her own mind regarding a proposed course of action - and to give him or her the objective information that may be material to the decision. No matter how irrational the decision of an individual to have a child may seem to be, it must be the individual's or couple's decision, not the counselor's! As Harper and James put it:

The very foundation of the doctrine of informed consent
is every man's right to forego treatment or even cure
if it entails what for him are intolerable consequences
or risks, however warped or perverted his sense of values
may be in the eyes of the medical profession, or even of the
community, so long as any distortion falls short of what
the law regards as incompetency. Individual freedom here
is guaranteed only if people are given the right to make
choices which would generally be regarded as foolish (13).
(emphasis supplied)

PROBLEMS OF INFORMED CONSENT IN PREGNANCY COUNSELING

An initial question that deserves comment is, under what circumstances does a physician have a legal duty to refer his patient to a specialist for the performance of amniocentesis (intrauterine testing of the fetus for certain genetic defects)? The general rule is that referral to a specialist is required when the physician knew or should have known that this particular pregnancy was beyond his own competence (14). If the plaintiff was able to establish that her age or medical history indicated that amniocentesis should at least have been considered, then the physician could be held liable for the birth of a defective fetus if it could be shown that amniocentesis would have detected the defect and led to an abortion (15). The physician should not be permitted to argue that he or she made an independent judgment that amniocentesis was not appropriate and therefore did not discuss it with the patient - the decision must be the patient's, not the doctor's. Further, no therapeutic privilege should protect the physician from nondisclosure in these circumstances since he is not treating the condition, but actually preventing the mother from making an informed decision concerning abortion, currently the only available "treatment" to prevent most genetic diseases.

A more novel, but not inconceivable, approach would hold the physician negligent for not routinely either performing amniocentesis on all pregnant women with potentially affected fetuses, or routinely referring them for such testing, even if such routine testing is not the standard of practice. The rationale would follow that enunciated in the recent case of Helling v. Carey (16). There the Supreme Court of the state of Washington held that an ophthalmologist was negligent because he did not routinely perform a pressure test designed to detect glaucoma, even though the use of such a test was not standard medical practice among specialists and the incidence of glaucoma in patients the age of the plaintiff was approximately 1 in 25,000. The major rationale the court used was that the diagnostic test was safe, inexpensive, simple, and accurate, and could prevent or at least arrest blindness if routinely performed (17). Therefore, the court reasoned that the public was entitled to the benefit of the test, and its non-use was itself evidence of negligence. A minority of the court would have found against the physician on the basis of strict liability on the theory that while they may not have been personally culpable, they were in the best financial position to bear the loss and obtain insurance for such statistically predictable missed diagnoses (17).

Since amniocentesis presently is relatively expensive, not easy, not 100% accurate, and carries some risks to both the mother and fetus, the analogy may not presently be persuasive. However, as techniques improve in terms of accuracy and safety, one can envision application of this analogy to permit recovery for the

birth of a defective child. A court would not have to go this far,
however, to find a physician liable for not disclosing to an at-
risk patient the existence of this diagnostic test. One possible
rationale could be to find that the physician was treating the
patient throughout the pregnancy and birth without her informed
consent because he had withheld from her a vital piece of material
information - the existence of a test to determine whether or not
her fetus was affected by some specific defect (18).

What remedy should a patient have for non-disclosure of this
type of information? In a famous 1967 case the New Jersey Supreme
Court held that even though a physician did not tell a pregnant
woman that she had rubella, she could not sue him for the birth of
a defective infant because the court could not measure the damages
(19). Specifically, the court was unable to determine how much a
defective child was worth as opposed to no child at all, which would
have been the result of an abortion. This case has been properly
criticized for concentrating on the wrong issues (20), and a
recent Texas case concerning a similar set of circumstances came to
a more reasonable conclusion. In that case the Texas court said it
was not necessary to determine the value of a life with a defective
body as opposed to no life at all. Instead, one could sue the
negligent physician not for the amount of money it takes to raise
a child, but for the amount of additional money the parents must
spend solely because of the physical defects of the child. The
decision to permit the parents to sue was based on the physician's
failure to inform her of the potential risk to her fetus. In the
words of the court:

> It is impossible for us to justify a policy which at once
> deprives the parents of information by which they could
> elect to terminate the pregnancy likely to produce a
> child with a defective body, a policy which in effect
> requires that the deficient embryo be carried to full
> gestation until the deficient child is born, and which
> policy then denies recovery from the tortfeasor of costs
> of treating and caring for the defects of the child (21).

Any woman who employs a physician for prenatal care should
have a right to have the physician fully inform her of any reason
he has to believe that the fetus might be defective, and to
further inform her of the existence of diagnostic tests that might
identify precise genetic defects (22). The physician incurs this
duty of disclosure because it is precisely this kind of information
that the woman employed the physician to learn in the first place,
i.e., to learn all she could to help her have a healthy child. If
the physician fails to disclose this information, the physician
may be treating the patient under false pretenses, and accordingly
her consent to that treatment may be invalid. The physician does
not guarantee a healthy child, but the reasonable expectation of the

patient is that she will be appraised of any information the
physician has that the child might be defective, and of the alternative ways to proceed, so that she can determine what to do.

Another set of problems arises after a diagnostic test is
performed (the explanation of the risks, alternatives and success
rates of the procedure itself is essentially no different than any
other consent question to a diagnostic procedure and so is not
dealt with here) (23). Specifically, must the physician disclose
to the patient all of the information learned from the test, or can
he or she disclose only that information directly related to the
suspected defect? The most common example discussed in the literature is the case in which amniocentesis is done because Down's
syndrome is suspected. The fetus is found not to be affected with
Down's, but does have the XYY karyotype. Must the parents be
informed of this finding when the general view in the scientific
literature is that this "defect" may not have any serious consequences. For example, on the issue of criminality, there is no
evidence that XYY males are more prone to commit crime than individuals over 6 feet tall (24). My view is that since XYY is looked
upon as a defect by many, and since it may be material to the
parents' decision to terminate the pregnancy, they must be told.
They should, of course, receive a thorough explanation about what
is currently known of the XYY genotype so that they can intelligently
proceed, but there seems to be no acceptable legal rationale for
not telling them in the absence of a prior agreement with them that
this type of information would not be disclosed. Indeed, even if
there exists a chromosomal abnormality that is considered immaterial
by the counselor, the parents should be informed since its existence may be material to their decision to continue or terminate
the pregnancy.

An analogous question arises concerning the sex of the child.
Must the parents be told this? Since the law allows the pregnant
woman to elect an abortion for any reason during the second trimester, she could, of course, elect one for the reason that she
only wanted a girl. It would seem that since the purpose of the
test was to find genetic "defects", and since sex itself is not
generally thought of as a defect, the physician should have no
affirmative duty to disclose this information. However, if the
parents ask,there does not seem to be any legal justification for
withholding this information from them (22).

GENETIC COUNSELING OF THE INDIVIDUAL OF REPRODUCTIVE AGE

The adult or adolescent may be counseled for one of a number
of reasons. Most likely, however, it will be because of an at-risk
pregnancy (previously discussed), because he or she participated in
a genetic screening program that detected a certain condition, or

because he or she had a child that was found to be genetically
defective. These latter two cases can be dealt with together.

No one should, of course, be screened without his or her
prior, fully informed consent. Since the genetic basis of disease
is not well understood by the population, special efforts to make
the implications of a positive finding known to the individual
prior to screening must be made. The potential hazards of stigmatization, loss of employment or insurance, and family discord
should all be openly emphasized, as well as the possibilities of
a false-positive or false-negative finding. The procedure should
be fully explained to the individual, and the individual should be
granted complete access to all his or her medical records regarding
the test and its interpretation. The individual should also have
the right to refuse to permit any person other than his or her
physician or the person in charge of the screening program to see
or copy these records without his or her prior written permission,
unless there is no way the third party with a legitimate interest
in the data could identify the patient from the record. As in
amniocentesis, it seems apparent that the subject of the screening
process has the right to all information obtained, unless he or
she has made a voluntary and informed prior agreement restricting
access to the findings (3).

The much more difficult question that arises in this context
is the right or duty of the physician-counselor to inform potentially
affected relatives of their findings. If one of the parents is
found to be a carrier of a serious genetic disease, can the physician inform potentially affected relatives? For example, if the
mother is found to be a carrier of the Lesch-Nyhan syndrome through
an affected son, can the physician inform the mother's sisters (25)?
Empirically, there is some indication that little communication
actually goes on between affected parents and their relatives.
Assuming that the affected parents refuse to give the physician
permission to notify their relatives who might also be affected,
what should the physician do? The remedy of a suit for breach of
confidence is inadequate protection for the patient since it of
necessity involves public disclosure of the information the patient
desires to be kept secret. Therefore the doctrine of informed
consent prior to counseling (and screening), and again prior to
disclosure to third parties, may help create an atmosphere that
encourages strict observance of confidentiality since the informed
patient will probably not consent to screening and counseling in
the first place if provisions for data confidentiality are known
and perceived as being inadequate.

There is a long line of cases that permits a physician to
disclose the diagnosis of a contagious disease to all who need to
know this information in order to protect themselves from contracting
the disease (26). Statutes have also been enacted that require

physicians to disclose confidential medical information to public
authorities under certain circumstances, e.g., some contagious
diseases, gunshot wounds, child abuse, etc., under the police
power of the state to protect the health and safety of its citizens
(29). In such cases the physician has an affirmative duty to
disclose what would otherwise be confidential medical information.
While none of these seem to directly apply to the genetic counseling
situation, a recent California case has indicated that the duty of
a physician to warn potentially affected third parties of confidential medical information may be very broad indeed.

In enunciating a general rule based on a case in which a
psychologist failed to warn a woman that his patient had threatened
to kill her (the woman was, in fact, murdered by the patient), the
court said: "Where a doctor ... in the exercise of his professional
skill and knowledge, determines, or should determine, that a
warning is essential to avert danger arising from the medical or
psychological condition of his patient, he incurs a legal obligation to give that warning" (27). The basis for this far-reaching
and arguably unprecedented decision was the court's belief that
we live in an "interdependent" and "risk-infested" society, and
that members of such a society cannot tolerate being exposed to
additional risks that physicians could eliminate by a simple act of
communication (26).

It would be stretching this decision considerably to find a
duty on the part of a genetic counselor to warn other family
members that their _offspring_ might be in danger because of a gene
the family member _might_ be carrying. However, in view of the
public policy enunciated by this and other courts, a strong argument can certainly be made that such a disclosure would be _permiss-
ible_, even if not required. In the face of this type of uncertainty
in the law, and given the fact that this situation can easily be
anticipated as counseling becomes more widespread, it would seem
appropriate that this be the subject of legislation (22). The
policy of routine disclosure or of strict nondisclosure would be
dictated by the view that the legislature took of the primary purpose of screening and counseling - the promotion of individual
autonomy in making procreative decisions, or the minimization of
certain genetic defects in the species. Unless and until such
legislation is enacted, it is extremely important that the
genetic counselor make clear, both verbally and in writing, the
policy that he or she follows so that the patient can refuse to
be screened or counseled if he or she is not in agreement with the
policy. Such a policy is, of course, also necessary in deciding
whether or not to obtain a complete listing of blood relatives as
a routine part of the medical history.

The possibility of a central registry of genetic defects
raises analogous problems of privacy and confidentiality, but with

even more potential for abuse. The issues are similar to those involved in any centralized system of medical records keeping. First, any such system should be used to store identifiable patient data only with the fully informed authorization of the patient. Second, all information should be available for inspection and correction by the patient. Third, the information should be stored in such a way that gross data on incidence and prevalence can be made available to researchers and policy-makers without identifying any individual patient. Finally, access to the information by unauthorized third parties (i.e. parties not authorized by the patient) should be strictly guarded against, with the central registry liable in tort for the foreseeable consequences of giving out information without authorization (28).

SUMMARY AND CONCLUSION

In summary, it is a proper burden to put on the genetic counselor to fully inform the patient of all the implications of all of the medical and genetic findings. If there are specific reasons why the counselor believes disclosure of some information is not proper (e.g., sex of fetus following amniocentesis) these should be made known to the patient in advance of counseling or screening and be incorporated into an informed consent form signed by the patient so that the patient can either agree to the conditions or seek advice elsewhere. Secondly, in view of the uncertainty of the legal rights and obligations of the counselor with regard to disclosure of information to third parties and central registries, it is improper to place a burden of informing potentially affected relatives on the counselor in the absence of specific legislation requiring such disclosures. Moreover, while counselors should be permitted to attempt to persuade patients to permit them to make disclosures of this information to relatives, they themselves should not make any disclosures to third parties without the patient's express and informed consent.

Any policy that promotes either the withholding of genetic information from the patient, or the dissemination of such information without the patient's consent, will not only violate the legal rights of patients, but will also serve to destroy the public's confidence in genetic counseling and discourage individuals from voluntarily participating in both screening and counseling. Conversely, aggressive policies that have as their goals the provision of complete information to prospective patients, and the maintenance of strict confidentiality of medical information, will serve to promote both patient rights and public confidence in genetic screening and counseling services and encourage the voluntary participation of the at-risk public.

REFERENCES

1. Hsia, Y.E., Parental reactions to genetic counseling, Contemp. Obstet. Gynecol. 4:99 (1974).

2. Scotch, N.A., Sorenson, J.R. and Swazey, J.P., "An Evaluation of Birth Defects and Genetic Services/Programs Supported by the National Foundation - March of Dimes." This two year proposal was submitted in November 1974 and funded in March 1975. Dept. of Socio-Medical Sciences, Boston University School of Medicine (unpublished funding proposal).

3. National Academy of Sciences, "Genetic Screening: Procedural Guidance and Recommendations," Nat. Acad. Sci., Washington, D.C. (1975) p. 28.

4. Sibinga, M.S. and Friedman, C.J., Complexities of parental understanding of phenylketonuria, Pediatrics 48:216 (1971).

5. Emery, A.E.H., Watt, M.S. and Clack, E., Social effects of genetic counseling, Brit. Med. J. 1:724 (1973).

6. Leonard, C.O., Chase, G.A. and Childs, B., Genetic counseling: a consumer's view, New Eng. J. Med. 287:433 (1972).

7. Fort, A.T., Morrison, J.C., Berreras, L. et al, Counseling the patient with sickle cell disease about reproduction: pregnancy outcome does not justify the maternal risk!, Amer. J. Obstet. Gynecol. 111:324 (1971).

8. Gray, B., Human Subjects in Medical Experimentation, John Wiley & Sons, New York (1975).

9. Krauss, E., Hospital Survey on Sterilization Policies", American Civil Liberties Union, New York (1975).

10. E.g., Ingelfinger, F., Informed (but uneducated) consent, New Eng. J. Med. 287:465, (1972).

11. Alfidi, Informed consent, in Meaney, et al., Complications and Legal Implications of Radiologic Special Procedures", Mosby, St. Louis (1973); and Alfidi, Informed consent: a study of patient reaction, J.A.M.A. 216:1325 (1971).

12. Pearn, J.H., Patients' subjective interpretation of risks offered in genetic counseling, J. Med. Genet. 10:129 (1973).

13. Harper and James, The Law of Torts (1968 Supp.) sec. 171.1, p. 61.

14. Annas, G.J., The Rights of Hospital Patients, ch. VIII, Consultation, referral and abandonment, Avon Books, New York (1975).

15. Waltz, J.R. and Thigpen, C.R., Genetic screening and counseling: legal and ethical implications, Northwestern U. L. Rev. 68:696, 757 (1974).

16. 83 Wash. 2d 514, 519 P.2d 981 (1974).

17. Annas, G.J., The case of the simple, harmless, inexpensive, conclusive, diagnostic test, Orthopaedic Rev. 4:67 (1975).

18. Milunsky, A. and Reilly, P., The "New" Genetics: Emerging medico-legal issues in the prenatal diagnosis of hereditary disorders, Amer. J. Law Med. 1:71 (1975).

19. Glietman v. Cosgrove, 49 N.J. 22, 227 A.2d 689 (1967).

20. Capron, A.M., Informed decision-making in genetic counseling: a dissent to the "wrongful life" debate, Indiana L. J. 1971: 581, p. 595.

21. Jacobs v. Theimer, 519 S.W. 2d 846, 849 (Texas, 1975).

22. cf. J.M. Friedman, Legal implications of amniocentesis, U. Pa. L. Rev. 123:92, 146 (1974).

23. Annas, G.J., The Rights of Hospital Patients, ch. VI, Informed consent to treatment, Avon Books, New York (1975).

24. National Institute of Mental Health, Report on the XYY Chromosomal Abnormality, U.S. Gov. Printing Office, Washington, D.C. (PHS Pub. No. 2103) (1970).

25. Milunsky, A., The Prenatal Diagnosis of Hereditary Disorders. Charles C. Thomas, Springfield (1973) p. 159.

26. Annas, G.J., Law and psychiatry: when must the doctor warn others of the potential dangerousness of his patient's conditions? Medicolegal News 3:1 (1975).

27. Tarasoff v. Regents of U. of Cal., 118 Cal. Rptr. 129, 529 F.2d 553 (1974).

28. Annas, G.J., The Rights of Hospital Patients, ch. XI, Confidentiality and privacy, Avon Books, New York (1975).

DISCUSSION

Papers of Profs. K. Hirschhorn and G.J. Annas
<u>Principal Discussants</u>: Profs. S.S. Gellis and S.J. Reiser
<u>Moderator</u>: Prof. A. Milunsky

GELLIS: Today physicians are increasingly faced with malpractice suits. Prof. Hirschhorn has been given time to touch upon a
few of the potential problems which beset the genetic counselor and
I shall not try in the few minutes alloted to me to offer additional
examples. Instead, I wish to concentrate on a small section of his
paper. He stated "In many respects potential negligence in genetic
counseling falls into the categories considered in other medical
malpractice suits. The most important of these is the case where
counseling is based on a wrong diagnosis made by the counselor or,
in the special situation considered here, counseling based on the
acceptance by the counselor of a wrong diagnosis made elsewhere
without an attempt to confirm this diagnosis. The latter problem
is especially relevant to the increasing reliance on non-medical
individuals such as Ph.D. geneticist or genetic associates for the
actual performance of genetic counseling." It is this area of his
paper upon which I wish to enlarge.

Physicians are being swamped with schemes to enable them to
expand or extend their services. We are told that not only are
there too few physicians but that we are over-specialized and over-
concentrated in suburbia with too few in rural areas and ghettos.
I'll not get too deeply into this argument but the scene has been
set for the expanders -- nurse practitioners, aides, corpsmen,
and genetic counselors. Increasingly these new associates are
taking over roles formerly played by physicians and are actively
seeking certification, and licensure, of which the ultimate goal
is operation independent of the physician and the result of which
will be the legal inability of the physician to train in his own
way paramedical personnel responsible to him medicolegally. If
this interpretation led to increased and improved health services
to the public, one could hardly demur, but I doubt that this will
be the case.

Let us take the genetic counselor. There are programs in the
United States which give two years of human genetic training to
college graduates. Following such training, the counselor then
is recommended to serve in a Birth Defects Center or with a
Health Department. How can such individuals possibly function for
a family? Counseling cannot consist of working out a family tree
and then discussing the inheritance pattern of a particular birth
defect. For a physician skilled in diagnosis of inherited disorders
to hand genetic counseling over to another individual less skilled
than he is, is inconceivable. Prof. Hirschhorn has clearly indicated the multiplicity of physical, emotional and financial problems

which plague the parents who have a child with major inherited
defect. Only the physician who has seen the total impact of a
defective child on a family can possibly lay before the parents
the future of the child and other children to come. To assign the
task of counseling to incompletely trained individuals is to me
the very height of malpractice. The physician who assumes responsibility for determining whether or not a condition is due to a
teratogen, or is inherited or is a mutant takes on enormous responsibility, both moral and legal, and he has no moral or legal
right to assign the task of counseling to anyone else. This field
is now so complex that the physician with usual training is at
risk if he attempts to determine how a condition is inherited.
This role should be played by an expert birth defects center. If
a physician today encounters an infant with a significant heart
murmur he is at risk if he has not sought out expert opinion on
the infant's heart. Similarly he must obtain expert opinion on
potential inheritance of multiple defects or syndromes. In the
same way, the physician is at great risk within a medical center
if he assigns counseling to someone less skilled than himself.

This, then, is a plea to terminate non-physician expanders
within the field of genetic counseling, not only on the grounds
of medico-legal risk but on the need to offer to a family the
highest skills in interpretation, advice and understanding.

REISER: Discussion over informed consent has been central to
the development of medical ethics in the period since the end of
World War II when the subject had its modern renaissance. In
this early phase, physicians and society became concerned over
subjects participating in human experimentation from whom informed
consent had not been obtained. Informed consent is so crucial
because it focuses on the exchange of knowledge between doctor
and patient. The exchange of knowledge that is an act at the
heart of medical practice. How much and how should knowledge be
disclosed and taught to patients? And in this context, informed
consent touches on an issue central to the bond between one human-
being and another, and to the maintenance of human society. That
is whether truth will inform the relationship between doctor and
patient.

Informed consent is often discussed as a special problem of
different parts of medical work, e.g. in genetic screening or in
human experimentation. These specialized medical procedures are
discussed as if they had special problems in connection with informed consent such that physicians practicing other medical specialties do not encounter. There is no need to think of informed
consent as if it affected centrally only certain parts of medical
work. Informed consent broadly considered as a component of the
transfer of knowledge between doctor and patient is a general aspect of the art of medicine. We see much agonizing about informed

consent today because we have been poorly educated in the method
and art of informing patients about the essence, not the technical
detail of the procedures we perform on them or knowledge we have
about them. And we pass on this ignorance to our medical students.

Truth telling is compatible with kindness as well as virtue,
and part of the special training of physicians should be how to
convey difficult to bear knowledge to patients. Prof. Annas declared
that facts found by a physician that are in dispute scientifically
or even considered by the physician as immaterial to the case,
should be disclosed to the patient. This point of view raises a
severe problem. Is there information learned in medicine and concerning our patients that we do not inform him of? This is a
difficult question. The doctor is wedded, as all people, to uphold
the virtue of truth telling in his relationship, yet he is also
bound to shield the patient from needless suffering. How does the
doctor weigh in the balance these two codes in relationship to
data? My yardstick would be the doctor's judgment about the certainty of ramifications he has about a given fact. Facts can be
introduced into medicine which are tentative. Physicians may have
not yet made up their mind about their meaning. These facts the
doctor need not disclose, for he himself is not confident of their
meaning. Therefore to disclose them would lead to unwarranted
suffering. With such facts he might properly follow such patients
closely about whom he has such knowledge, until the implications
of the facts he has learned about the patient are clarified
scientifically. But all facts about which medical opinion has
agreed are real and correct, must be conveyed to patients.

R.L. KAUFMAN: St. Louis Children's Hospital: I think that
many of our legal colleagues have some confusion about some of the
informed consent problems which have really gone very far afield
and also as to what we should or shouldn't do. For example, should
a pregnant woman be told that it is safer to her health to terminate a pregnancy by first trimester abortion than to continue the
pregnancy? Just as an example of informed consent, should someone
be told that despite the risks of the pill, it is more effective
than the rhythm method? These are the kinds of questions that
come farther afield into what we do not normally deal with, but
that people perhaps in some ways may.

From a practical point of view, women over 35 years of age have
a 1 in 300 risk of having a child with Down's syndrome. Any
woman in this age category who wants to have an amniocentesis should
be able to have it. Yet I wonder how many Boston physicians tell
their Boston Irish Catholic patients that they have a 1 in 300
chance of having a child with a neural tube defect which can be
detected in 90% of the cases by amniocentesis and alpha-fetoprotein
determination? To what effect not doing so would be considered not
good medical practice?

MILUNSKY: Perhaps I can give you one figure. In a
survey of cases we have found that the risk of chromosomal abnormality in women 35-39 appears to be of the order of 1 in 70.
This figure, of course, would be much higher than most people
would expect for that particular age bracket. I emphasize that
this is not the risk for Down's syndrome, but the risk for chromosomal abnormality related to advanced maternal age, which I believe
is a more sensible way of looking at that age bracket than simply
tailoring your remark to Down's syndrome.

In Boston I suppose physicians might mention the risk of
neural tube defects to their Irish Catholic patients. I am not
too sure to what avail.

CAPRON: Prof. Hirschhorn suggested that it was "illogical" to
allow suit for a person who would not have been born, the so-called
action for wrongful life. I have suggested in another publication*
that if the action is conceived as one of wrongful life, there is
at least a good argument that can be made that it is hard to value
what that wrongful life is. I do not think it is right to say that
it is illogical that a life cannot be worth living. That is rather
a value judgment.

I would suggest that that is the kind of statement about which
people can come to reasonable differing opinions. A better approach,
it seems to me, is to regard this as a matter of parental decision
making. I prefer that parents should become informed decision-
makers rather than simply give informed consent. In fact, their
choice is to make a decision not simply a consenting to go forward.
If that is the case, then parents are in a position when they go
for counseling to have information conveyed to them on the basis of
which they would then be free to make a decision. If that information is withheld from them and a child is born with a defect of
which the counselor knew, I don't think it is right to say the child
is suing for wrongful life. Both the child and the parents are
suing because the parents, who are recognized by the law and by society in general as the people who have the power to make the decision, were deprived of the opportunity to make the decision by
physician's judgment to withhold the information for what he thought
were good reasons.

Prof. Hirschhorn, I also do not think that it is a damned if
you do, damned if you don't example you gave, of the Tay-Sachs
case. This need not pose such a hard problem because it may be
that the physician's first response can be to tell the woman (if
she hasn't already figured out that the testing of her husband will
reveal that he was not the father), that that is indeed what the

* Capron, A.M., Legal rights and moral rights, in "Ethical Issues in
Human Genetics", B. Hilton, D. Callahan, M. Harris, P. Condliffe, and
B. Berkley (eds.), p. 221, Plenum Press, New York (1973).

test has revealed. Since it is a medical procedure on her, namely amniocentesis, which he is proposing to do, he need not do it, since the father (her actual husband) is not a carrier, if she is willing to reveal to her husband that the test is not being done for that reason. If she would rather deal with that in a separate manner with her husband and she wishes to undergo the test, I suppose she can do so. She has consented to the procedure and she is liable for her medical bills and can pay them, though she is going through a charade, that is between her and her husband for their marital harmony.

One final comment on Prof. Gellis' remarks. I would agree with him that nobody would want to see us move to a situation where medical or other professional decisions or functions are allocated to inadequately trained people. The question, however, is who are the people who are correctly trained to provide certain services. It may be that physicians are not best trained to provide certain services. Your suggesting that the physician is in the position of knowing most about the family and most about the child, may be correct for some physicians but may not be correct for others. It may be correct for some genetic consultants or counselors, who are trained in other methods and other programs. We may see this as a cooperative approach with the person with the best training and the most ability providing the service, whatever his or her professional training happens to be.

R. MARX: Vermont: As a Ph.D. trained geneticist who has been involved in non-directive genetic counseling, I am struck by the amount of time that is involved in a good counseling session with the family. I am wondering if the fact that a physician is highly trained and very busy and does not have large amounts of time to spend with individual patients leads to uninformed consent.

HIRSCHHORN: In reply to Prof. Capron, in terms of the wrongful life aspect, I completely agree with you and in fact did in the paper. I was not talking about the concept of wrongful life, with which I fully agree. It is the action for wrongful life that I was concerned about being illogical. In other words, a legal action for wrongful life as being an illogical pursuit. Perhaps I am wrong. But as far as the concept is concerned, I fully agree with your point of view.

In terms of the Tay-Sachs family with the paternity problem, I think one step was not really considered in your answer. It may be acceptable for the woman to go through that charade, but the problem is that the procedure is being performed with a known risk. In other words, you may now abort or potentially damage this fetus by means of going through a charade. I think that is an actionable situation.

ROSENBERG: Prof. Annas argued that because there are so many studies in the literature which indicate that there is a low rate of knowledge transmission from counselor to counselee, that this therefore, in some way means that counselors are not very confident of the value of informing for consent. I do not understand this argument at all. I think I have read most of the same literature. There are also some papers which say that when counseling is appropriately done (as the paper by Emery from Scotland), that people in fact do understand what they have been counseled for and they do retain the information. In no case do I think that people who do genetic counseling argue that because people do not understand everything that they have heard that this means that we do not have an obligation to try to the best of our ability to continue to do that informing for consent. It is a statement of our failure. It is not a statement of haughtiness in any sense. Therefore, I do not think it should be perceived either as a point in the argument about who should be doing genetic counseling. It would be, I think, a real error of this meeting if we find ourselves embroiled in the discussion are physicians the only people to do genetic counseling, or should it be better done by people who are not physicians because they have more time to spend. That seems unproductive to me.

DAVIS: It seems to me that the existence of this meeting, and of similar meetings elsewhere in recent times, is due to the confluence of two different developments: a rapid increase in our knowledge of human genetics, and a period in history that emphasizes, more than any preceding period, individual rights balanced against those of society. The latter development has created a good deal of uneasiness about the right of a professional to impose his judgment on patients or to exercise discretion in withholding information.

I raise this point because Mr. Annas questioned whether the genetic counseling ever has the right to counsel, whether he shouldn't be simply a consultant. He noted the hypothetical case of a pregnant woman with sickle cell anemia who is predicted to have a 20% chance of dying and a 6% chance of losing her baby, and he suggested that the counselor would be going far beyond his legitimate responsibilities if he were to do more than simply present the figures to the woman and let her make up her own mind.

It seems to me that society has a serious interest in the question of what people do with the information that modern genetics makes available. In a case of this sort the genetic counselor may have a better basis for judging what is in the interest of the patient, and of society, than the patient. If, for example, this woman had a baby that would be left motherless, her decision would place a large burden on others; and while the physician cannot require her to seek abortion or sterilization, one might argue that he is evading a responsibility in simply presenting facts and not

offering advice. Considering that societies have been willing to
interfere with personal choices to the extent of banning polygamy,
incest, or even cousin marriages, I suspect that eventually our
accumulation of genetic knowledge will lead to restrictions on the
kinds of risks pregnant women will be allowed to take. But before
we reach the stage of legislation it seems to me that the physician
might be expected to take into account society's interest in
avoiding predictable burdens.

GELLIS: I am pointing out that the physicians who should be
diagnosing inherited defects are not the ordinary practicing physicians. This is now a highly technical, difficult specialty all in
itself. It is for this reason that there are birth defect centers
throughout the country. The ordinary trained practicing physician
is in a very weak position to diagnose genetic disease and give
genetic counseling on a great variety of disorders with which he
is confronted. Moreover, the physician trained in diagnosis of
birth defects should not consider his job finished when he has
made the diagnosis. This to me is comparable to the physician who
makes the diagnosis of infectious disease and then hands the treatment over to a microbiologist. You may argue perhaps that he
should. I am arguing that he should not. To properly diagnose and
help a family with a child with an inherited disorder calls for a
complete job by the physician.

I am sure you do not measure the success of genetic counseling
by the subsequent outcome. This has to be the final decision of
the patient. There is no point in testing genetic counseling by
just looking at outcome. On the other hand, I think the physician
has to do more than state the risks and give the facts to the patient. The physician must know what the family and the patient are
confronted with for the rest of their lives.

Only if you have been involved in the care of a patient who is
totally disabled can you really try to describe it all. You may
not be successful even then advising a family what lies ahead in
terms of urinary tract problems, motor problems, gastrointestinal
problems, and intellectual and emotional problems, associated for
example with myelomeningocele. I do not think therefore, that this
is the area one hands over to a person who may be highly skilled
in drawing up family trees, tracing inherited defects and in pro-
nouncing the statistical risk of inheritance. This can only be
done if one has been deeply immersed in what the specific problem
means to a family. I doubt very much that an individual with a
Ph.D. in human genetics is in such a position. I do grant that it
is possible to reach this point, but I think it takes a lot of time.
It is not difficult in a single disorder, such as Down's syndrome,
because there are many such patients. However, if you talk about
many other defects which are relatively rare, no paramedical, no
genetic counselor, without thorough training in the physical,

mental and emotional aspects of these disorders can, I believe, give proper help and advice, and the patients cannot be left with just making the final decision. A great part of health care and of medicine consists of advising the family what to do. A family which has not had any experience has to be helped.

EISENBERG: I think it is worth putting this in a somewhat broader context. What troubles me is that the emphasis on malpractice law is not the same as guaranteeing or increasing the likelihood of good medical practice. In fact, each of us wishes in his relationship with his own physician for something very different from what malpractice law is bringing into effect, namely the physician looking at the patient as a possible adversary and the patient looking at the physician in the same sense. There is an inordinate difference between the number of entered and successful malpractice suits in the United States and England. Yet I do not think anyone would argue that malpractice is much greater in the United States than it is in England based on that assessment of the law. What it seems to me we need to be concerned with is getting good information to patients, providing social support for those who are the victims of misfortune so that they don't suffer anymore than is unavoidable biologically. From this we should separate the question of punishing the physician who may be guilty of poor practice, who should have his license suspended or be sent to jail (or whatever the appropriate remedy is), rather than seeing the whole thing as somehow equated in pecuniary terms.

We have had the situation, which many of you may have noticed in the New York Times recently, in which a verdict was entered against a physician in the case of a young woman who was blind from retrolental fibroplasia. She was an underweight newborn at the time the oxygen was administered. When the physician administered the oxygen, it was the best medical treatment anyone knew how to provide. It was a year later that the discovery was made that oxygen may be causally related to the subsequent blindness. Yet the court or the jury on the basis of their sympathy for this young woman and her misfortune adjudicated the physician as responsible for something which under no reasonable sense could he be guilty of since his practice was in fact complete.

If you look at the kinds of questions Prof. Hirschhorn raises as potential problems in the future of genetic counseling, one sees the extension into what ought to be a relationship between two people out to help each other, of the notion of the adversary relationship right from the start. I am afraid that what we are doing is putting into law and into our own thinking about the problem a reflection of the general alienation that exists in this society, which I doubt is going to be solved by legal formalisms and by refinements of malpractice law. What we need is good practice and we ought to consider what is going to be effective in

getting good practice. I doubt that malpractice insurance bears
on that one way or the other.

The other good we would like to preserve is the protection of
people who are victimized from suffering alone from their misfortune,
whether it is an unpreventable anesthetic death or one that came
about because the anesthetist hooked up the gases incorrectly.
The death or the suffering is just as tragic and if social reimbursement ought to occur, it ought to occur equally for both individuals.
If the anesthetist hooked him up wrong, then you ought to take him
out of practice and not simply sue him.

HIRSCHHORN: I would like to respond to Prof. Davis' question,
"what is counseling?" Is it only giving information or is it
or should it in fact contain some direction? I think the error
comes from conceiving of giving information only from the statistical
point of view. As I tried to indicate in my paper, counseling, if
it is to be proper treatment in the standard medico-legal sense,
should not only include the risks, but a statement of the consequences of each option. The moment those consequences are spelled
out, it is then up to the family to interpret them. I do not think
that one needs to express the bias regarding the options any more
than by statement of the consequences of these options.

FALEK: I would like to talk about genetic counseling and the
counselees. There is some evidence based on the psychological
aspects of phases in the coping reaction of counselees, that it is
important for those offering genetic counseling to be aware of when
genetic counseling will be effective. Most genetic counseling has
been offered shortly after diagnosis when counselees cannot accept
this information.

BECKWITH: I wanted to respond and add some further comments
on Prof. Hook's statement. I was somewhat surprised when he played
down the dangers of informing parents that their children have XYY
genotypes. There has been a major discussion in the whole area of
the XYY screening newborns. I am surprised because in fact in
Prof. Hook's review article he did mention the dangers. In the
review article by Borgaonkar and Shah (the most recent review
article) these dangers are also mentioned. Prof. Walzer himself
in his research protocol has personally agonized over the possible
problems of possibly telling parents that it may cause psychological
harm to the children and to the family. As a result of this I
think many of us feel that it will be impossible to obtain meaningful scientific data from these studies. In addition, potential
harm may be done to the individual. I believe that as a result
of these discussions and of the airing of the issue here in Boston,
we know that the screening of newborn males for the XYY karyotype
has stopped as of May 1st in the hospital in Boston and it is our
understanding that this has stopped in other hospitals around the

country and the only place where it is being done today is in
Winnipeg, Manitoba.

HAMERTON: We are no longer screening newborns in Winnipeg,
and have not been doing so since September 30, 1973. Not because
of the controversy that has arisen here, but simply in order to
allow us to continue with the follow-up of those patients that
we found. The question of whether or not to inform the parents
of an XYY or of other sex chromosome abnormality has been one,
I think that all of us involved in newborn screening have agonized
about. We took the decision at the beginning of our study with
the agreement and approval of our local ethics committee not to
inform the parents, but to inform the physician, and we are now
reviewing whether that was the correct decision to take or not.

LAPPE: Just a point of possible clarification about the legal
origins of consanguinity laws. It was not my understanding that
at least the majority of the state laws in this country evolved in
response to eugenic processes. Rather that they were expressions
of a particular cultural tradition that we wanted to enforce, particularly as a significant number of these laws recognize non-blood
relationships as well as blood relationships as precluding marriage.

PROBLEMS IN GENETIC SCREENING WHICH CONFRONT THE LAW

Harvey L. Levy

State Laboratory Institute, Massachusetts Dept. Public Health; Neurology Service and the Joseph P. Kennedy, Jr. Laboratories, Massachusetts General Hospital, Department of Neurology, Harvard Medical School

Before outlining those aspects of genetic screening that may confront established and accepted modes of medical behavior as well as actual laws, it is important to review genetic screening as it is currently practiced and as it has arisen. This discussion will be confined to that screening for genetic disorders conducted routinely either on a specific age group (such as newborns) within an entire population or on a certain ethnic segment of a population. In fact, it is this type of "wholesale" testing that is usually considered to be genetic screening rather than the original type of selective testing for genetic disorders that is confined to small groups of individuals, such as those in schools for the mentally retarded or those who are admitted to hospitals.

Genetic screening began as a result of the development of a simple test that allowed for the detection of phenylketonuria (PKU) in newborns. This test, a bacterial assay, is the brainchild of Professor Robert Guthrie of Buffalo and is widely known eponymically as the Guthrie test (1). The great value of the test is that a disorder such as PKU, which causes mental retardation, can be detected in the neonate when it presents as a biochemical abnormality and before brain damage has occurred. Treatment begun at this early age will prevent mental retardation in contrast to the poor results if treatment is begun when the signs of brain disease have become clinically manifest (2). Thus, this first Guthrie test has served as a prototype for virtually all genetic screening -- biochemical detection before the onset of clinical signs and thus early therapeutic intervention (3).

The greatest value of the Guthrie test, however, is not the simplicity of the assay itself but the type of specimen utilized.

For the first time, one did not need to obtain a specimen from an
infant via a relatively elaborate method such as venipuncture.
One only needed to puncture the heel and squeeze a few drops of
blood into filter paper. This paper could then be easily and
inexpensively mailed to a central laboratory for testing. Equally
important was the fact that only a fraction of each specimen was
necessary for the test, with much additional blood remaining for
further testing. This latter fact was well recognized by Guthrie,
who set about modifying his original assay to make it applicable to
the detection of genetic disorders in addition to PKU. Guthrie
has subsequently devoted his life to the establishment of these
assays for genetic screening over the United States and in other
parts of the world (4).

Table I lists those bacterial assays that were developed by
Guthrie and his group in the early and mid-1960's and subsequently.
Based on the encouraging early results of these assays and the
availability of the blood specimens, two other important and in-
genious techniques were developed. One was the Efron method of
paper chromatography (5) which utilized a filter paper blood or
urine specimen to detect any one of several inborn errors of
metabolism (6). The other was the Beutler enzyme spot screening
test (7) which utilizes the filter paper blood specimen to detect
galactose-1-phosphate uridyl transferase, the enzyme missing in
galactosemia. Based on the Beutler principle spot tests for glu-
cose-6-phosphate dehydrogenase (G-6-PD) deficiency (8), hereditary
angioneurotic edema (9), and a whole host of other red blood cell
enzymes or serum factors have been made available. By application
to thin-layer chromatography, hemoglobin abnormalities such as

Table I. Bacterial Assays Developed by the Guthrie Group

	Assay	Disorder(s)
1961	Phenylalanine	PKU
1963	Galactose*	Galactosemias
1964	Leucine	MSUD
1965	Methionine	Homocystinuria
1968	Tyrosine	Tyrosinemia
1970	Histidine	Histidinemia

*Based on a principle discovered by Dr. K. Paigen of Buffalo

sickle cell disease can be detected (10). If a small amount of serum
is obtained, even from a finger puncture, the carrier state for Tay-
Sachs disease can be ascertained (11). In actuality, there are
probably few biochemical disorders now detectable in blood or urine
that could not be screening for within entire populations if we so
desired. In Massachusetts we are now receiving three specimens on
every infant and testing these specimens in such a manner that we
can probably detect any one of 30 or more genetic disorders (Table
II).

Where does all of this leave us in relation to the law and
"accepted" medical practice? For certain, it leaves all of us --
physicians, nurses, administrators, technicians -- in a very
difficult position. For one thing, there are virtually no laws for
most disorders now being screened. And the laws that exist are
ambiguous. For instance, in 45 states it is mandatory that a test
for phenylketonuria (PKU) be performed on every newborn baby (12).
But who is responsible? In Massachusetts the law names the physician
as the one who must see that this test is performed. But the
attending physician does not perform the test. The specimen is
probably obtained by a nurse or technician, is sent through the
mails to the State Laboratory Institute, an arm of the Department of
Public Health, and tested there by several technicians who are under
my direction. Thus, in a real sense we are all responsible, including the President of the United States or at least the Postmaster
General, who directs the mail service. I suppose an error could
conceivably be traced to one person but records are rarely so
carefully kept.

In several states, including Massachusetts, several tests
are performed on the blood specimen that is mandated only for PKU
testing. Is it illegal to perform a second or third or fourth test
on a specimen sent only for the first test, if these additional
tests would enable disorders to be diagnosed that might be just as
important to the individual as is the mandated disorder? To even
begin to answer this, I suppose we need to know the answer to an
even more basic question, i.e. who does the blood specimen belong
to? To the baby, that's for sure but perhaps also to the parents
since they must answer for the baby. But it is also in the hands
of the laboratory who is responsible for it, so does it not in a
sense belong here as well? And if the laboratory is an arm of
the State, as it is in most instances, does the State own a share
also?

These are not frivolous questions. Hardly a week goes by
that I am not approached by someone who wants to come to our laboratory and use the specimens in evaluating a new test for a genetic
disorder. Some go further and ask us to send the specimens to
another laboratory, perhaps even out of Massachusetts, for testing.
Thus, the question -- can the specimens we and others are responsible

Table II. Specimens and Disorders Sought in the Massachusetts Metabolic
           Disorders Screening Program

SPECIMEN*	DISORDERS
Birth – Cord Blood	Galactosemia
	Maternal PKU
2-4 Days – Newborn Blood	PKU
	MSUD
	Homocystinuria
	Tyrosinosis
	Galactosemias
3-4 Weeks – Urine	Amino Acid Disorders
	Histidinemia
	Organic Acid Disorders
	Disulfidurias
	Glucosurias

*All are filter paper specimens

for be used for research, even when that research may lead to the development of an important and practical test? Can we use these specimens even in our own laboratory for that purpose?

Two additional potential confrontations should be mentioned. One is that of regionalization. In the future genetic screening will be conducted on a regional rather than a statewide basis. Already the Oregon Public Health Laboratories test the blood specimens of newborns from Montana as well as Oregon. Will this mean that each state within any region will have to frame identically worded laws? Or will laws be necessary? Suppose an error is made but the undetermined source of the error could be either at the hospital or physician in one state or at the laboratory in another state? If litigation ensues, would this be in a federal court? The second potential confrontation involves the concept of malpractice. Genetic screening has done more to uncover and spread knowledge of genetic disorders among the lay and the medical community than all other methods combined. As a result physicians are now called upon to diagnose and treat disorders that they had not even heard of until suddenly faced with the patient. Will a mistake or poor result in such an instance constitute malpractice, even in regard to a disease that is understood by only a handful of physicians in the world?

I would suggest that the legal questions raised by genetic screening constitute some of the most difficult to answer yet important questions in medicine today. They must be answered and the sooner, the better.

REFERENCES

1. Guthrie, R. and Susi, A., A simple phenylalanine method for detecting phenylketonuria in large populations of newborn infants, Pediatrics 32:338 (1963).

2. Levy, H.L., Genetic screening, in "Advances in Human Genetics" (Harris, H. and Hirschhorn, K., eds.), Vol. 4, pp. 1-104, 389-394, Plenum Press, New York (1973).

3. Smith, I. and Wolff, O.H., Natural history of phenylketonuria and influence of early treatment, Lancet 2:540 (1974).

4. Guthrie, R., Mass screening for genetic disease, Hospital Practice, June 1972, pp. 93-100.

5. Efron, M.L., Young, D., Moser, H.W. et al, A simple chromatographic screening test for the detection of disorders of amino acid metabolism, New Eng. J. Med. 270:1378 (1964).

6. Levy, H.L., Shih, V.E., Madigan, P.M. et al, Results of a
    screening method for free amino acids. I. Whole blood, II.
    Urine, Clin. Biochem. 1:200, 208 (1968).

7. Beutler, E. and Blauda, M.C., A simple spot screening test for
    galactosemia, J. Lab. Clin. Med. 68:137 (1966).

8. Beutler, E., A series of new screening procedures for pyruvate
    kinase deficiency, glucose-6-phosphate dehydrogenase deficiency,
    and glutathione reductase deficiency, Blood 28:553 (1966).

9. Murphey, W.H., Patchen, L. and Guthrie, R., Screening tests
    for argininosuccinic aciduria, orotic aciduria, and other
    inherited enzyme deficiencies using dried blood specimens,
    Biochem. Genet. 6:51 (1972).

10. Garrick, M.D., Dembure, P., and Guthrie, R., Sickle-cell anemia
    and other hemoglobinopathies, New Eng. J. Med. 288:1265 (1973).

11. Kaback, M.M. and Zeiger, R.S., Heterozygote detection in Tay-
    Sachs disease: a prototype community screening program in the
    prevention of recessive genetic disorders in "Sphingolipids,
    Sphingolipidoses and Allied Disorders"(Volk, B.W. and Aronson,
    S.M., Eds.), p. 613, Plenum Press, New York (1972).

12. United States Department of Health, Education, and Welfare,
    Public Health Service, Health Services and Mental Health
    Administration (Maternal and Child Health Service).
    State Laws Pertaining to Phenylketonuria as of November 1970,
    U.S. Government Printing Office, Washington (1971).

THE LIABILITY OF PHYSICIANS AND ASSOCIATED PERSONNEL

FOR MALPRACTICE IN GENETIC SCREENING

Jon R. Waltz

Northwestern University School of Law

INTRODUCTION

The topic to be discussed in this paper is narrowly defined: the potential malpractice liability of physicians and personnel associated with them in the conduct of genetic screening. The paper's title is perhaps inappropriately contracted, since a measure of potential legal liability in the screening context arises from doctrinal bases other than the principles of medical malpractice. Topic titles to the contrary notwithstanding, those additional principles will not be ignored in the discussion that follows.

On the other hand, it apparently -- and appropriately -- falls to someone else to address the quite possibly more subtle and complex potential for malpractice liability inhering in the conduct, both by physicians and nonphysicians, of the counseling that may, indeed ordinarily should, follow genetic screening. The close relationship between the screening and counseling functions makes some overlapping inevitable but the effort here will be to restrict discussion to the screening phase.

The dimensions of the problem are not made less ominous by the circumstance that they remain vague. Two movements, one essentially medical and one essentially legal, are on a convergent course. There is on one set of tracks the rapidly accelerating movement to more elaborate and inclusive programs aimed at detecting persons who are "at risk" for developing or transmitting diseases and disabilities that are genetic or at least genetic-related. And there is the stunning upsurge in medical malpractice and closely related litigation in the courts. A collision can be predicted, although its precise magnitude cannot be, unless the problems are defined and safeguards carefully constructed and as carefully implemented by those concerned, directly and indirectly, with the genetic screening function.

The discussion that follows is intended not as a definitive legal treatise but as a helpful communication in straightforward, reasonably jargon-free language, from one interested group (those concerned with the legal system) to another (those who participate in genetic screening). What is contemplated is a brief catalog of the interfaces between genetic screening programs and the law.

THE SOURCES OF LEGAL REGULATION OF GENETIC SCREENING

The actual conduct of genetic screening, as such, is not regulated either by state or federal statutes. And the only general statutory provisions that have a significant impact on the screening process are those that restrict the practice of medicine to physicians and persons under their direct supervision. Since genetic screening involves physical intervention for diagnostic purposes, these medical practice acts are applicable. Furthermore, some special state statutes dictate that physical examinations of public school children be conducted only by persons licensed to practice medicine "in all its branches," an injunction -- under attack in some states -- which appears to have been aimed primarily at chiropractors. Aside from these two forms of statutory control, it is the common law -- judge-made law rather than legislator-made law -- that will act as a regulator of the genetic screener, at least until more specific legislative regulatory schemes are devised.

The common law principles most likely to be encountered in a genetic screening context are those governing --

    (1) Medical malpractice (i.e., professional negligence), including incorrect diagnosis;

    (2) Failure to obtain informed consent to the screening procedure;

    (3) Failure to disclose the results of screening; and

    (4) Unauthorized disclosure of screening results to persons other than the screenee.

MEDICAL MALPRACTICE

The procedures employed in genetic testing are sufficiently uncomplicated that malpractice claims of the traditional sort, based on a negligence theory which will be described in some detail below, are not likely to be frequent or of very serious magnitude. There is a limit to how much can go wrong during a simple blood test to determine whether a person has the recessive trait for such

diseases as sickle cell anemia or Tay-Sachs (1). Mistaken diagnosis
is not likely to occur with significant frequency; based on blood
test results, physicians can give prospective parents fairly precise
odds on the likelihood of the birth of a defective child (2). It
must be granted, however, that the relatively new post-conceptional
screening method called amniocentesis is more complicated; the
compensating factor is that it permits even more definite prognoses
for some genetic diseases (3). Amniocentesis involves the direct
examination of fetal cells. Amniotic fluid is withdrawn from the
amniotic sac. This can be accomplished transabdominally or trans-
vaginally with a needle inserted through the uterine wall. The
procedure involves some risk. Fetal risks include fetal puncture,
abortion, and induced abnormalities. Maternal risks include infection, hemorrhage, and sensitization (4).

When we speak without special qualification of medical malpractice, we are talking about the liability of a physician and
associated personnel for money damages for negligence or other
improper conduct toward his patient or, occasionally, third persons
(5). Like lawyers and other professionals, the physician is liable
in damages for negligent or unauthorized actions done within the
ambit of his/her professional functions.

Lawyers categorize the claims of patients against a physician
as being either for breach of contract or for the commission of a
"tort." (6). The contract theory, not likely to be encountered
with any frequency in the genetic screening context, can be based
on either an express or an implied agreement between the physician
and the patient. The tort theory is based on the existence of a
legal duty of care owed by the physician to the patient. In general,
the common law (judge-made law, as distinguished from legislatively
enacted statutes) requires that a physician and those acting with
him possess that degree of skill ordinarily possessed by average,
reputable practitioners of the same school of practice and that
he/she exercise ordinary care in applying that skill when dealing
with a patient (7). Most lawsuits against physicians and those
under their supervision are based on this negligence (tort) theory.
Recovery of money damages in a negligence action flows from the
physician's failure to adhere to the applicable standard of care,
coupled with resulting injury to the patient. Money damages can
be awarded by a court for pain and suffering as well as for actual
expenses incurred by the patient as a consequence of the asserted
professional negligence.

To be somewhat more specific, a valid tort claim against a
physician has three elements. First is the duty toward the patient
which the law imposes on the physician and those associated with him
in the health care delivery process. "Duty" can be translated as
"standard of care." Second is the specific conduct on the physician's
part which, in the law's view, violated his duty to his patient.

The physician's conduct will be measured against the standard of
care applicable to him. Third is the causal connection between
the physician's actions and the damage alleged by the patient. A
litigant cannot recover damages for arguably negligent conduct
that produced no injury whatever (except perhaps where the conduct
can be shown to have been willful and motivated by some indefensible
purpose). This is because damages for simple negligence are ordinarily intended to be compensatory, not punitive.

To run the sequence of tort elements backward, there must be
1. damage to the patient, caused by 2. conduct of the physician
that fell below 3. the standard of care governing the physician.

To comprehend the standard of care applicable to medical personnel functioning in a genetic screening context, one has only to
substitute the word "screenee" for the word "patient" in the foregoing formulations.

It is easy, in this generalized way, to state the physician's
legal duty to the patient or screenee. The broad and flexible
common law rule laid down by the courts has left it pretty much to
physicians themselves to set their own standard of performance.
That is, a physician is expected to do what reputable practitioners
of his school of medicine would do in a particular type of case.
He is not expected to be the best-trained, most highly skilled
physician in his locale; otherwise all other physicians would have
to be considered substandard. But he must possess skill and
judgment conforming to the average. And the level of his skill
and judgment is not evaluated in terms of the fee he receives.
Except in certain emergency situations not pertinent here, it is
wholly irrelevant to a malpractice action whether the defendant
was being compensated for the professional services about which
complaint is made (8). This, of course, is a consideration relevant
to most voluntary genetic screening programs, under which the
screenee is not expected to make compensation for the screening
service.

The standard of care applicable to physicians is, as a generali-
zation, understandable enough. Standing alone, however, it will
not assist lay jurors in deciding most medical malpractice cases
because they cannot determine, intelligently, whether the defendant's conduct fell below the standard. The quality of the
defendant physician's conduct, gauged by the generalized standard,
is the crux of a malpractice case. Except as to a few self-evident
situations, lay jurors are unequipped to determine whether a physician's professional actions violated the generalized standard,
and they will not be permitted to speculate. Thus in all but the
most self-evident cases the plaintiff patient (screenee) must give
meaning to the standard of care by presenting expert medical witnesses who are competent to characterize the defendant's conduct as

having been negligent (9).

Only two fact-situations that can be expected to be encountered in the genetic screening context are likely to give rise to occasional malpractice claims grounded upon the principles outlined above.   1. There may be infrequent and usually petty claims stemming from assertedly negligent use of hypodermic needles in withdrawing samples of blood or amniotic fluid.   2. And there may be occasional claims arising from mistaken diagnoses.

Negligent or Otherwise Improper Use of Hypodermic Needles. Typical of malpractice actions stemming from the use of hypodermic needles are those for damages caused by --

(1) The negligent breaking of the needle;
(2) Failure to sterilize the needle;
(3) Failure to sterilize the place of insertion; and
(4) Injection into an improper place (veins, arteries, muscles, nerves, etc.).

Tort liability for the breaking of a hypodermic needle is fairly uncommon even in the field of anesthesiology. What has been needed by successful plaintiffs is positive proof of negligence, buttressed by expert medical testimony that a hypodermic needle does not ordinarily break in the absence of negligent use. Most of the decided cases have involved anesthetists; none thus far have involved genetic screeners. Wiley v. Wharton (10) is a more or less typical case, showing how courts react to claims of this sort. It involved an anesthetist who broke off a hypodermic needle in a patient's spine. There was expert medical testimony that if a needle is properly inserted in the spine it can be thrust, with little exercise of force, through soft tissues to its proper destination. The evidence also was that the person making the injection should be able to tell, by the "feel" of the needle, whether it is passing through soft tissue or bone. Finally, there was X-ray evidence that the needle had been driven into the bone to some extent. The court concluded that the breaking of the needle, coupled with its location outside the channel of soft tissues and against the bone, presented a submissible case of negligence, requiring an explanation from the anesthetist.

Liability for Mistaken Diagnosis. Just as a screener may be held liable for failure or refusal to disclose genetic test results, the screener may be liable for damages resulting from a mistaken diagnosis resulting from his negligent failure to conduct or interpret the test properly. The prospect is an especially serious one when the counseling factor is added. If a screener were to induce a person to have an abortion or to be sterilized on the basis of his mistaken diagnosis, damages could be substantial. If the screener erroneously advised a couple that there existed no

genetic impediment to their having children, the birth to the
couple of a child with a genetic defect which the screener should
have detected,could render him liable for all medical and special
expenses relating to the child's genetic difficulty. The screener
might also be held liable to the child on a "wrongful life"
theory (11).

In a related type of case, courts have held that physicians
may be liable for negligence in the performance of sterilization
operations which result in unwanted pregnancies, even when the
child is normal and healthy. Troppi v. Scarf (12), a recent
judicial straw in the wind, was an action against a pharmacist
for the negligent filling of a birth control prescription. The
parents alleged that the pharmacist's negligence in substituting
a tranquilizer for the desired birth control pills resulted in an
unwanted pregnancy and the subsequent birth of a normal child. The
complaint alleged four items of damage: 1. the mother's lost
wages; 2. medical and hospital expenses; 3. the pain and anxiety
of pregnancy and childbirth; and 4. the economic costs of rearing
the child. The trial judge dismissed the complaint, saying that
whatever damage the plaintiffs may have suffered was "more than
offset by the benefit to them of having a healthy child," but an
appellate court reversed the lower court, holding that the basic
conditions of tort liability were present: a pharmacist is held
to a high standard of care in filling prescriptions; the defendant
pharmacist's conduct constituted a clear breach of duty; the possibility that the plaintiff woman might become pregnant was a foreseeable consequence of the defendant's failure to fill the prescription properly; and, as a consequence of this failure, the
plaintiffs suffered measurable damages. The reviewing court rejected the notion that the birth of a healthy child always confers
an overriding benefit but held that the benefits of an unplanned
child may be weighed against all the elements of the damages
claimed. The court also considered the suggestion that parents
seeking damages for the birth of an unwanted child are under a
duty to mitigate their damages by obtaining an abortion or placing
the child for adoption but rejected this argument by noting that
"a living child almost universally gives rise to emotional and
spiritual bonds which few parents can bring themselves to break"
(13).

The reasoning of the Troppi decision has applicability to
instances of negligence in genetic screening. If a mistaken
diagnosis is caused by a screener's negligence and results in the
birth of a defective child, the basic elements of a tort action
are present. The screener's failure to use appropriate skill and
care constitutes a breach of his duty to the screenees. It is
reasonably foreseeable that his negligence will result in the birth
of a genetically defective child, and if a defective child does in
fact result from the breach, "reasonably ascertainable" damages may

ensue in the form of medical and other special expenses relating to the child's condition and the mental anguish of the parents (14).

The most difficult of the tort elements to establish would, of course, be causation. It would have to be demonstrated that the defective child was the proximate result of the screener's negligence and, to establish this fact, the parents would have to prove that if the screener had not been negligent but had properly informed them of the possibility of a genetically defective child, they would not have had the child. In a case in which the child had already been conceived before the screening was conducted, the plaintiff mother would have to convince the court that she would have procured a lawful abortion had she known the true facts (15). If the screener's negligence were pre-conceptional, the plaintiff would have to show that she would have taken steps to avoid pregnancy or that if she did become pregnant she would have had the pregnancy lawfully terminated unless additional tests showed that the fetus would not be afflicted with the defective genetic condition. Under the Troppi court's reasoning, however, if the plaintiff became pregnant in reliance on the screener's assurances and later discovered that the child might be defective, she would not be obligated to "mitigate" her damages by having an abortion (15).

In addition to a recovery by parents for a screener's negligence, some decisions indicate that the siblings of the defective child might have a right to damages. In Coleman v. Garrison (17), a negligent sterilization resulted in an unwanted pregnancy and a suit was brought by the husband and wife and their first four children for the birth of a fifth defective child. In denying the defendant's motion to dismiss, the trial court stated that by seeking sterilization, the Colemans had attempted to maintain "a certain standard of living, a certain amount of love and affection, and a certain amount of parental protection" for their first four children. The court said that the addition of a fifth child would upset the portion previously allotted to each existing child and added that if this change could be measured economically, it should be compensable in damages. In Custodio v. Bauer (18), another negligent sterilization case, the court noted that the mother, as a result of the subsequent birth, "must spread her society, comfort, care, protection and support over a larger group," and added that compensation should be awarded so that "the new arrival will not deprive the other members of the family of what was planned as their just share of the family income" (19). A child with a serious genetic disease or defect would probably require more in the way of time, concern and financial resources than would a normal child, and under the theory expressed in Coleman and Custodio, the child's siblings might be permitted to recover for the corresponding loss.

Improper counseling because of a mistaken diagnosis could

generate damages more difficult to ascertain. If, relying
on a doctor's prognosis, a person had an abortion or was sterilized
and later discovered that the operation was unnecessary, he or she
might recover substantial damages as a result of being deprived of
the ability to reproduce. Although some items of damage, such as
the loss of a particular child through abortion or the inability
to have children, would be difficult to measure monetarily, the
general policy in favor of estimating such damages to compensate
the person injured and to discourage negligence and wrongdoing
would support a right to recover. Considerable damages might also
be allowed to compensate the couple for the expense of the abortion
or sterilization operation, for any physical or mental pain and
suffering, and for any special medical expenses related to the
procedure. Furthermore, liability in this sort of situation might
arise if a screener convinced one spouse that it would be unwise to
have children. Courts have held that procreation is one of the
basic functions of marriage (20), and, if the couple were divorced
because one partner, relying on a screener's mistaken diagnosis,
refused to have children, the doctor might be held liable for the
result. Even if the couple were not divorced but suffered
considerable marital strain because of the screener's mistake,
there might be grounds for an action for damages under the theories
of loss of consortium, tortious interference with the marital relationship or alienation of affection (21).

Another problem, closely related to the field of professional
negligence but nonetheless different, is encountered when a
practitioner employs unimpeachable practices but does so without
the informed consent of the patient or someone authorized to speak
for the patient. In this situation, the patient may be in a position to recover damages even though the defendant was in no way
negligent. This problem, involving the scope of a physician's
duty to inform the patient regarding the possible outcome of a proposed test or procedure, is considered by Prof. Annas (see page 104).
and will also be discussed in lesser detail below.

                              INFORMED CONSENT

There has been heated debate in the medical and legal communities generally concerning the validity and appropriate scope of the
so-called informed consent concept (22). In 1972 a private entity,
the Research Group on ethical, social, and legal issues in genetic
counseling and genetic engineering of the Institute of Society,
Ethics and the Life Sciences published an article about ethical and
social issues in genetic screening (23). This article brought the
controversy home to the field of genetic screening by stating unequivocally that:

Screening should be conducted only with the informed

consent of those tested or of the parents or legal representatives of minors...In addition to obtaining signed
consent documents, it is the program director's obligation
to assure that knowledgeable consent is obtained from all
those screened, and to review the consent procedure for
its effectiveness (24).

Thereafter the Research Group commenced to "wonder if the...
informed consent requirement had been so strict as to be unattainable in practice" (25). But after some further study of the matter,
the Group declined to soften its earlier pronouncement. Instead
it published an "amplification" of the original statement:

> This statement of obligation is made with awareness of
> the difficulties of direct person-to-person application of
> informed consent procedures, since screening usually in-
> volves working with large groups. As a practical approach
> to the ideal of individualized person-to-person informed
> consent, we suggest the use of an informed consent ques-
> tionnaire..., which is adaptable to the purposes of in-
> dividual screening programs. This consent sheet of ques-
> tions could be used singly or added to the prescreening
> informational materials, if any are used in the program.
> In addition, we recommend that the program director or
> his designee review the answers to the informed consent
> questionnaire before each individual is tested, in order
> to complete the education of potential screenees who remain
> confused about important aspects of the genetic screening
> program.

> We argue that heterozygote screening is a new and not-
> yet evaluated medical procedure, with unknown sociopsych-
> ologic risks, and should therefore be treated as a re-
> search procedure as far as consent is concerned (26).

On a legalistic level as well as on a practical level, the
application of the informed consent concept to large-scale genetic
screening programs continues to be debatable. Assuming, as I
shall, the existence of a relationship that is at least akin to
that of physician-patient, the informed consent concept separates
into two elements: 1. the physician or associated personnel
must disclose certain information about risks collateral to a
proposed procedure, and 2. he must not proceed without having
secured consent to the risks that have been, or should have been,
disclosed (27). The information element of informed consent concerns the scope of the duty to disclose risks collateral to a
contemplated procedure (28). This duty becomes relevant when the
patient neither knows nor could be expected to know of particular
collateral risks. There is no duty to disclose collateral risks
that ought to be known to everyone (29) or that are in fact known

to the patient, perhaps because of prior experience with the
contemplated procedure (30).

    Furthermore, a physician probably need not disclose every
risk that could be disclosed, if only because of the time that
would be consumed in describing every remote risk (31). Less
than total disclosure will satisfy the law's demands. The sometimes hard question is, how <u>much</u> less in any given context?

    Without impinging too extensively on the terrain of other
contributors to this volume, let me say that the fundamental task
is to determine what risks are <u>material</u> and therefore to be disclosed to the patient in the absence of any privilege to withhold
(32). And in the usual physician-patient context, the materiality
of a risk must be determined in the first instance by the physician.
He must first know how much impact a risk must have on the patient's judgment before its disclosure is dictated. The ideal rule
would require that a risk be disclosed when the patient would
attach importance to it, alone or in combination with other risks,
in making the decision whether or not to consent to the contemplated
procedure. But neither a physician nor those associated with him
can be required to know the inner workings of every patient's
mind. The physician and others can, however, be required to
exercise a sense of how the average person would probably react.
In resolving the materiality issue the physician and those working
with him can apply the standard of the reasonable person who finds
himself/herself in the position of the patient.

    A risk is thus material when a reasonable person, in what the
physician knows or should know to be the patient's position, would
likely attach significance to the risk or cluster of risks in deciding whether or not to undergo the proposed procedure. And I am
inclined to think that a basic consideration underlying the materiality of all collateral risks of any procedure is the extent of
the particular procedure's prior use, since it is reasonable to
require that more be disclosed about an innovative procedure than a
customary one. Beyond this, the basic factors to be considered are
the nature of the overall risk, its severity, and the likelihood of
occurrence. Each factor must be weighed in combination with the
others to determine whether a particular risk is material and therefore subject to disclosure in the absence of a supportable claim of
privilege.

    I have thus far been speaking rather generally about a physi-
cian's duty to obtain informed consent. Again speaking generally,
the risks ordinarily associated with a requirement of informed
consent to a medical procedure have been serious physical ones.
There is not much physical risk/medical risk involved in genetic
screening. For example, the risk from taking blood is minimal.
Most screeners seem to agree that the real risks in genetic

screening are psychological, such as the anxiety over possible
stigmatization that may be produced (33). Returning to a purely
legalistic level, the realization of such psychological risks has
not in times past lent itself to claims for substantial money
damages. Still, on other than a purely legalistic level one must
agree with the suggestion that obtaining informed consent (the
emphasis is on informed, since voluntary screening programs are
obviously consensual) is a worthwhile aim (34).

     This much can be suggested. The screener should inform those
tested of the nature and purpose of genetic screening. Moreover,
because of the possible psychological effects of unfavorable test
results, persons tested should be made aware that the tests could
disclose that their children might be born with serious genetic
defects. The screener should also point out that the screening is
completely voluntary and confidential and that it is not a prerequisite to any other services or programs. In cases of more
complicated genetic tests, such as amniocentesis, the screener
should fully apprise the screenee of significant collateral risks
to her and to her unborn child including sensitization, abortion,
puncture, and induced abnormalities. They should be described in
clear and understandable language (35).

FAILURE OR REFUSAL TO DISCLOSE SCREENING RESULTS

     Somewhat akin to the problem of faulty diagnosis is the problem
of failure or refusal by the screener to disclose the results of
screening to the screenee or to those responsible for the welfare
of a screenee. Genetic screeners will ordinarily be under a duty
to disclose the results of their efforts, especially when test
results are unfavorable (36). This is so because there usually will
have been either an explicit or implicit promise to make disclosure;
indeed, the promise of disclosure will commonly have provided the
motivation for volunteering to be tested (37). It is a duty that
usually devolves upon physicians (38). Although the traditional
physician-patient relationship will not invariably be involved in
the genetic screening situation, analogy to the law governing
physicians continues to be apt.

     The relationship of physician and patient ought to be one of
trust and confidence, based on the notion that physicians will
employ their expertise in the best interests of the patient. So
should the relationship between screener -- be he physician or non-
physician -- and screenee. Thus the relationship carries with it
an obligation to reveal to the patient anything which it would
be in his best interests to know.

     A screener may be liable in damages for failure to convey to
screenees information, based on genetic test results, that a child

might be born defective (39). In situations involving the birth
to the screenees of a defective child, legal actions might be
brought against the screener by the parents, siblings, or by the
child himself under the controversial theory of "wrongful life"
previously mentioned (40).

CONFIDENTIALITY

A genetic screener may incur tort liability for an unauthorized
disclosure of confidential information about a screenee and might
be liable for breach of contract as well (41). A suit for breach
of contract would be based on terms of secrecy implicit in the
relationship between screener and screenee or in the medical profession's code of ethics and the Hippocratic Oath (42). The theory
on which breach of confidence suits are usually based, however, is
the tort theory of invasion of privacy. There are a number of
grounds for such an action (43) and, while no physician-patient
privilege existed at common law, some courts have held that the
unauthorized disclosure of confidential information obtained as a
result of a physician-patient relationship is against public policy
and therefore an actionable wrong (44). This theory of action has
been based on state licensing statutes, on statutory physician-
patient privileges relating to courtroom disclosures of information,
and on the medical profession's code of ethics (45).

Two types of confidentiality problems could arise in the
genetic screening situation. One relates to the disclosure by a
physician of specific information about a particular individual to
a third person; the other involves dissemination of statistical
information for research purposes which incidentally reveals the
identity of, and confidential information about, a person tested.
Caution should of course be taken in the revelation of any data
for statistical or scientific purposes to assure that the identity
of those tested is concealed (46). There have also been reports of
serious stigmatization resulting from disclosures of information
obtained from sickle cell anemia screening tests. Many people fear
that positive indications may result in loss of employment or
difficulty in obtaining insurance. Without consent, there is no
justification for a physician revealing genetic test results to
an employer or to an insurance company. In all but a few unusual
cases, the fact that a person is a carrier of a genetic disease
should have no effect on his employment or on the procurement of
insurance. In those rare cases in which such information might
be relevant, the physician alone should not decide the issue of
disclosure; many people would be dissuaded from participating in
screening programs if they had to worry about whether the results
would be disclosed. Because of widespread misunderstanding
relating to genetic disease, test data should not be disclosed to
anyone but the person tested (or his parents, if he is a minor)

unless the individual has given his specific consent to wider
dissemination.

There are several defenses to an action for invasion of privacy. One of these is consent (47). If a patient has knowingly
authorized the physician to disclose information, he cannot complain about the disclosure. A second defense is compulsion of law
(48). Some states require that physicians and others report certain diseases or medical conditions and one cannot be held liable
for disclosing information which one is legally obligated to report
(49). If the results of genetic screening tests were to become
legally reportable, persons tested would have no cause of action
against a screener for disclosing this information to the proper
governmental authority. A screener would still be liable, however,
for making a disclosure to anyone else. Another line of defense
is disclosure for the purpose of protecting the general health and
welfare (50) or for the good of the patient himself (51), but
since genetic diseases are not communicable and since the mass tests
now planned would usually reveal carrier status and not the presence
of an actual disease, this defense would probably have little
application to the genetic screening situation.

Another theory under which a screener might be liable for
statements about a patient's condition is that of defamation (52),
but, unlike the situations already mentioned, a suit for defamation
is based on the making of a false communication (53). If a screener
falsely reported unfavorable information about an individual undergoing genetic screening, he could be held liable in tort. It is
unlikely that such a cause of action would often arise in connection
with genetic screening programs, however, since screeners are
hardly likely to make untrue declarations about the persons whom they
test. It is more probable that such an action would arise from a
statement made in good faith which proves to have been mistaken.
Mistake is not a defense to defamation (54), but some courts have
refused to hold physicians liable in such a situation when some
interest that the court deems desirable might have been advanced by
the disclosure (55). The one absolute defense to a defamation
action, of course, is truth (56), but although the statement be true
a physician could still be legally liable for an invasion of privacy
as a result of an unauthorized disclosure of confidential information.

CONCLUSION

From this discussion it should be evident that the risks of
malpractice liability to the genetic screener are unquestionably
fewer than they are to practitioners in such high-risk fields as
orthopaedic surgery, plastic surgery, and anesthesiology. Still,
risks there are, partly because of judges' misunderstanding or
over-intellectualization of such concepts as informed consent.

What is needed to avoid the potentially disastrous collision mentioned at the outset of this paper is foresight, comprehension, and planning by everyone concerned with genetic screening and counseling. This is what Milunsky and Reilly have said:

> Sadly, law reform often occurs only after the infliction of substantial harm to an individual, family, or group, and sufficient legal measures seem to be instituted only after the occurrence of tragedy. Clear recognition of the issues confronting law and genetics should lead to anticipatory operative guidelines with or without corrective legislation (57).

Milunsky and Reilly are right.

REFERENCES

1. Fletcher, J., Roblin, R. and Powledge, T. cite six genetic
    screening program directors for the statement that "the risk
    involved in taking the blood sample for testing (is) negli-
    gible." in"Ethical, Social and Legal Dimensions of Screening
    for Human Genetic Disease." Miami: Symposia Specialists,
    1974, p. 140.

2. Waltz, J. and Thigpen, C., Genetic screening and counseling:
    the legal and ethical issues, Northwestern Univ. Law Rev.
    69:696:700,(1973).

3. Waltz, J. and Thigpen, C., Genetic screening and counseling:
    the legal and ethical issues, Northwestern Univ. Law Rev.
    69:696:700, 744,(1973).

4. See Milunsky, A. and Reilly, P., The "new" genetics: emerging
    medicolegal issues in the prenatal diagnosis of hereditary
    disorders, Amer. J. Law Med. 1:71,(1975).

5. Waltz, J. and Inbau, F., Medical Jurisprudence. New York,
    Macmillan Company, 1971, p. 38 et seq.

6. The lawyers' term "tort" has an evil connotation. It comes
    from the Latin tortus, meaning twisted or crooked. Courts
    employ the word tort as a label to identify almost any wrongful
    act, other than a breach of contract, for which a civil action --
    as distinguished from a criminal charge -- can be maintained.

7. See, e.g., Loudon v. Scott, 58 Mont. 645, 194 Pac. 488 (1920),
    Pike v. Honsinger, 49 N.E. 760 (Ct. App. N.Y. 1898).

8. See e.g., Fortner v. Koch, 272 Mich. 273, 261 N.W. 762 (1935),
    Ritchey v. West, 23 Ill. 385 (S. Ct. Ill. 1860).

9. Waltz, J. and Inbau, F., Medical Jurisprudence. New York,
    Macmillan Company, 1971, p. 54-74.

10. 68 Ohio App. 345, 41 N.E. 2d 255 (1941).

11. This controversial concept is analyzed as length in Waltz, J.
    and Thigpen, C.: Genetic screening and counseling: the legal
    and ethical issues, Northwestern Univ. Law Rev. 69:696:759
    et seq.,(1973).

12. 31 Mich. App. 240, 187 N.W. 2d 511 (1971).

13. 31 Mich. App. at 257, 187 N.W. 2d at 519. The court added:
    If the negligence of a tortfeasor results in conception of

a child by a woman whose emotional and mental makeup
is inconsistent with aborting or placing the child for
adoption, then, under the principle that the tortfeasor
takes the injured party as he finds him, the tortfeasor
cannot complain that the damages that will be assessed
against him are greater than those that would be determined if he had negligently caused the conception of a
child by a woman who was willing to abort or place the
child for adoption. 31 Mich. App. at 260, 187 N.W. 2d at
520.

14. In some states a plaintiff cannot recover for mental suffering alone, unaccompanied by any physical injury. See, e.g.
Bishop v. Byrne, 265 F. Supp. 460, 465 (S.D. W. Va. 1967).

15. Since the United States Supreme Court's decision in Roe v.
Wade, 410 U.S. 113 (1973), it would not be difficult to
demonstrate that a lawful abortion could have been obtained.

16. In Troppi v. Scarf, 31 Mich. App. 240, 260, 187 N.W. 2d 511,
520 (1971), the court said: While the reasonableness of a
plaintiff's efforts to mitigate is ordinarily to be decided
by the trier of fact, we are persuaded to rule, as a matter
of law, that no mother, wed or unwed, can reasonably be expected to abort (even if legal) or place her child for
adoption.

17. 281 A. 2d 616 (Del. Super. 1971), appeal dismissed sub nom.,
Wilmington Medical Center, Inc. v. Garrison, 298 A. 2d 320
(1972).

18. 251 Cal. App. 2d 303, 59 Cal. Rptr, 463 (1967).

19. 251 Cal. App. 2d at 323, 59 Cal. Rptr. at 476.

20. See, e.g., Kreyling v. Kreyling, 20 N.J. Misc. 52, 23 A. 2d
800 (1942); Shaheen v. Knight, 11 Pa. D. & C. 2d 41 (Lycoming
1957). Cf. Jones v. Jones, 186 Md. 371, 46 A. 2d 617 (1946).

21. See Prosser, W. , Torts. St. Paul: West Publishing Company,
4th Ed. 1971, § 124.

22. For an extensive discussion of the informed consent concept,
consult Waltz, J. and Scheuneman, T.   Informed consent to
therapy, Northwestern Univ. L. Rev. 64:628,(1970)

23. Genetics Research Group, Ethical and social issues in screening for genetic disease, New Eng. J. Med. 286:1129,(1972).

24. Ibid.

25. Fletcher, J., Roblin, R. and Powledge, T., Ethical, Social
    and Legal Dimensions of Screening for Human Genetic Disease,
    Miami: Symposia Specialists, 1974, p. 138.

26. Id. at p. 143.

27. Waltz, J. and Scheuneman, T., Informed consent to therapy,
    Northwestern Univ. Law Rev. 64:628:630,(1969).

28. Ibid.

29. See, e.g., Roberts v. Young, 369 Mich. 133, 119 N.W. 2d 627
    (1963); Starnes v. Taylor, 272 N.C. 386, 158 S.E. 2d 339 (1968).

30. See, e.g., Yeates v. Harms, 193 Kans. 320, 393 P. 2d 982
    (1964).

31. There is a temptation to give the informed consent concept a
    narrow application so that physicians and others can spend more
    time delivering health care services and less time informing
    patients of potential risks. The point would seem to be, howev-
    er, that required disclosure of all risks would be prohibitive
    but that disclosure which will enable the patient to make an
    intelligent dicision is part of the physician's duty. See
    Waltz, J. and Scheuneman, T., Informed consent to therapy,
    Northwestern Univ. Law Rev. 64:628:635:n.23,(1969). For the
    proposition that a mini-course in medical science is not
    required, see Cobbs v. Grant, 104 Cal. Rptr. 505, 502
    P. 2d 1 (1972).

32. The leading case is Canterbury v. Spence, 464 F. 2d 772
    (D.C. Cir.), cert. denied, 409 U.S. 1064 (1972), which in turn
    draws heavily on Waltz, J. and Scheuneman, T., Informed consent
    to therapy, Northwestern Univ. L. Rev. 64:628, (1969).

33. Two knowledgeable commentators have said, "The indications
    for amniocentesis, the inherent risks of the procedure, and
    the reservations which may attend any results provided should
    be discussed with both parents prior to initiation of this
    procedure" (authors'emphasis). Milunsky, A. and Reilly, P.,
    The "new" genetics: emerging medicolegal issues in the prenatal
    diagnosis of hereditary disorders, Amer. J. Law Med. 1:71, (1975).

34. Ibid. It is sometimes suggested that informed consent can be
    effectively obtained through oral information-disclosure.
    See, e.g., Note: Informed consent -- a proposed standard for
    medical disclosure, New York Univ. Law Rev. 48:548, (1973).
    For the genetic screener's protection, however, signed consent
    forms or questionnaires are preferable. The form or questionn-
    aire should reveal the substance of the information imparted

and that the form and level of disclosure was geared to the
needs and capacities of the particular screenee.

A sample informed consent questionnaire can be found in
Fletcher, J., Roblin, R. and Powledge, T., Informed consent
in genetic screening programs, in"Ethical, Social and Legal
Dimensions of Screening for Human Genetic Disease." Miami:
Symposia Specialists, 1974, pp. 143-144.

35. Prof. Capron has said, "...in genetic counseling the parents
    have a legal right to be fully informed decisionmakers
    about whether to have a child; and, likewise, the genetic
    counselor has the duty to convey to those he advises a clear
    and comprehensible picture of the options open to them, the
    relative risks and benefits, and the foreseeable consequences
    of each option, to the best of his ability." Capron, A.,
    Informed decisionmaking in genetic counseling: a dissent to
    the "wrongful life" debate, Indiana Law J. 48:581:582, (1973).

36. See Green, H. and Capron, A., Issues of law and public policy
    in genetic screening, in"Ethical, Social and Legal Dimensions
    of Screening for Human Genetic Disease." Miami: Symposia
    Specialists, 1974, pp. 59-62.

37. See, e.g., Stafford v. Shultz, 42 Cal. 2d 767, 270 P. 2d
    1 (1954).

38. See Waltz, J. and Thigpen, C., Genetic screening and counsel-
    ing: the legal and ethical issues, Northwestern Univ. Law Rev.
    68:696:757, (1973).

39. Two similar cases with opposite rulings at the trial court
    level deal with the parents' right to recover for a physi-
    cian's failure to inform them that their child might be born
    with a disability. However, both cases rejected any right of
    recovery by the child itself. Gleitman v. Cosgrove, 49 N.J.
    22, 227 A. 2d 689 (1967) (no right of action); Stewart v.
    Long Island College Hospital, 58 Misc. 2d 432, 296 N.Y.S. 2d
    41 (S.Ct. 1968), modified, 35 App. Div. 2d 531, 313 N.Y.S. 2d
    502 (1970), aff'd., 30 N.Y.S. 2d 695, 283 N.E. 2d 616, 332
    N.Y.S. 2d 640 (1972) (right of action upheld).

40. See, e.g., Hammonds v. Aetna Casulty & Surety Co., 237 F. Supp.
    96 (N.D. Ohio 1965); Horne v. Patton, 291 Ala. 701, 287 So. 2d
    1973); Clark v. Geraci, 29 Misc. 2d 791, 208 N.Y.S. 2d 564 (1960)

41. Cf. Quarles v. Sutherland, 215 Tenn. 651, 389 S.W. 2d 249 (1965)
    For a fuller discussion, see Note: Action for breach of medical
    secrecy outside the courtroom, Univ. of Cincinnati Law Rev.
    36:103, 1967.

42. Id. at p. 104.

43. For a discussion of the various branches of the right of
     privacy, see Waltz, J. and Inbau, F.: Medical Jurisprudence.
     New York, Macmillan Company, 1971, pp. 270-274.

44. See, e.g., Hammonds v. Aetna Casualty & Surety Co., 237 F.
     Supp. 96 (N.D. Ohio 1965).

45. See Clark v. Geraci, 29 Misc. 2d 791, 208 N.Y.S. 2d 564
     (1960).

46. See Waltz, J. and Thigpen, C., Genetic screening and counsel-
     ing: the legal and ethical issues, Northwestern Univ. Law Rev.
     69:731, (1973).

47. See Waltz, J. and Inbau, F., Medical Jurisprudence. New York,
     Macmillan Company, 1971, pp. 278-280.

48. See, e.g., Boyd v. Winn, 286 Ky. 173, 150 S.W. 2d 648 (1941).

49. For a catalog of specific state statutes, see Note: Medical
     practice and the right to privacy, Minnesota Law Rev. 43:
     953,(1959).

50. See, e.g., Collins v. Howard, 156 F. Supp. 322 (S.D. Ga. 1957);
     Simonsen v. Swenson, 104 Neb. 224, 177 N.W. 831 (1920).

51. See, e.g., Kenney v. Gurley, 208 Ala. 623, 95 So. 34 (1923).

52. The term "defamation" refers to the torts of libel and slander.
     For a general discussion of physicians' liability for de-
     famation, see Waltz, J. and Inbau, F., Medical Jurisprudence.
     New York, Macmillan Company, 1971, pp. 262-269.

53. See, e.g., Berry v. Moench, 8 Utah 2d 191, 331 P. 2d 814 (1958).

54. See Waltz, J. and Inbau, F., Medical Jurisprudence. New York,
     Macmillan Company, 1971, p. 267.

55. See, e.g., Kenney v. Gurley, 208 Ala. 623, 95 So. 34 (1923).

56. Although truth is a defense, a physician may bear the burden of
     proving that his statements are actually true. See Bingham v.
     Gaynor, 203 N.Y. 27, 96 N.E. 84 (1911).

57. Milunsky, A. and Reilly, P., The "new" genetics: emerging
     medicolegal issues in the prenatal diagnosis of hereditary
     disorders, Amer. J. Law Med. 1:71, (1975).

STATE SUPPORTED MASS GENETIC SCREENING PROGRAMS

Philip Reilly

University of Texas Graduate School of Biomedical

Sciences

INTRODUCTION

This presentation is to briefly survey the development of laws which mandated (1) neonatal screening for human genetic disease and (2) adult screening for genetic traits. Extended discussion of the genesis of the phenylketonuria (1) (PKU) and sickle cell trait (2-4) screening laws are available. I will also discuss in more detail recent expansion of government supported mass genetic screening in the United States. Much of this information was obtained through a mail survey of the state public health departments that I made during February of 1975. My purpose here is to be descriptive; I leave analysis of the important constitutional questions raised by mass genetic screening for another time (5,6).

MASS NEONATAL SCREENING FOR GENETIC DISEASE

Phenylketonuria Legislation

Although limited neonatal screening for PKU was initiated in the United States and Great Britain during the 1950's, it was not until Guthrie perfected an automated bacterial inhibition assay test in 1961 (7), that a truly comprehensive and effective program could be implemented. The Guthrie test satisfied the two critical requirements of high accuracy and low cost. This fact combined with the relatively high frequency of PKU (1:11, 500) and the impressive results obtained through early invocation of a low-phenylalanine diet set the stage for a very rapid expansion of screening for this disorder.

With the assistance of the Children's Bureau of the Department
of Health, Education and Welfare a large scale pilot program was
set up in Massachusetts in 1962. The results were very encouraging
and interest in mass neonatal screening grew (8). Although the
Massachusetts experience suggested that a state public health department could develop an effective program on its own initiative,
PKU screening soon received quite unusual legislative attention.
Massachusetts enacted the first PKU screening law in 1963; three
more states adopted similar laws the following year. By the end
of 1965 more than 20 states had followed suit. Today 43 states
have PKU screening laws (9); in other jurisdictions active testing
programs proceed without statutory support.

The phenomenology of the PKU screening laws remains unexplained.
Some investigators suggested that the small budgetary outlay required for a state PKU testing program, combined with the unquestionable benefits of a plan to reduce mental retardation, provided
special interest groups with a powerful lobbying weapon (10). Although there is some evidence that a few members of the medical
research community became zealous advocates of screening, it seems
that much of the lobbying was done by members of the various state
associations for retarded children. The National Association for
Retarded Children (NARC) first announced its support of mandatory
PKU screening in October of 1963. That support continued unabated
despite the attack on PKU screening laws launched by the American
Academy of Pediatrics and organized medicine in general. Recent
investigations of the genesis of PKU laws have concluded that state
organizations followed NARC's lead, but that a carefully structured
game plan was never developed (11).

A content analysis of the PKU screening laws uncovers several
interesting facts. First, it was the spectre of mental retardation,
not phenylketonuria per se, that impressed the state legislators.
In at least twenty jurisdictions provision was made for testing for
"other" preventable diseases which could lead to retardation. Two
states (Kentucky and Maine) did not even include the word phenylketonuria in the statutory language! Thus in at least 22 states
it is possible to interpret the original PKU law as a general mandate for mass neonatal screening for genetic disease. Second, it
is clear that although the vast majority of the statutes compel
neonatal screening, the mandatory language was chosen to emphasize
the importance of testing rather than to threaten those who did not
wish to comply. Twenty-eight states permit parents to object to
the test on religious grounds; a few others allow objection for non-
religious reasons (1, 12). It is, however, unusual for parents to
be informed of their right to refuse a PKU test on their child.
Only a few states suggest that a non-compliant parent might be
penalized; I know of no such incident. In reality it is the behavior
of the medical community that is directed by these statutes. An
attending physician or a hospital that failed to administer a PKU

test to a child who was affected might face a malpractice suit.

Most PKU laws left the details of program administration up to the public health departments. A few states, particularly those that wrote their laws after criticism of PKU screening had begun, developed more comprehensive legislation. There are five areas that one might reasonably expect a carefully drafted program to have considered: quality control of testing, treatment of affected neonates, counseling of the families of children with PKU, public education, and the storage of genetic information acquired by screening. The state legislators quite correctly deferred to experts within the public health departments on the question of testing methodology. However, a requirement that all tests be performed by one facility would probably have improved PKU screening efforts (13). Interestingly, no state required that affected children be placed on a low phenylalanine diet. It is of course difficult to imagine a parent who would refuse to comply with the therapeutic regimen. Child welfare laws would probably enable state public health officials to act on behalf of an infant that they knew was not receiving the proper diet. To my knowledge no state gave any statutory consideration to genetic counseling for the families of affected children. Presumably, the importance of the diet was made clear. Perhaps the very effectiveness of dietary controls obviated the need for counseling. A minority of states (at least nine) did mandate programs of public education. A very few state laws created PKU registries; a much larger number of state health departments developed some follow-up system without enabling legislation. The current problem of maternal PKU illustrates the need for information storage and retrieval systems.

In the mid-sixties sharp criticism of mass PKU screening developed. Among the more voluble critics was Dr. Samuel Bessman who faulted the programs on scientific and political grounds. He felt that infants diagnosed as false positives ran a risk of injury from invocation of the special low-phenylalanine diet. Further, he argued correctly that high serum phenylalanine titres could be caused by conditions other than homozygous PKU. Finally he feared that the marriage of medicine and law could result in dangerously rigid views of a disease entity (14, 15).

The PKU screening controversy provides interesting material with which to study the role of statutory law as a tool of public health policy (an in-depth study is available elsewhere) (1). It is instructive that the complex technical and social problems raised by PKU screening remain unresolved after fifteen years. At a recent meeting of the National Academy of Sciences Committee on Inborn Errors of Metabolism much attention was devoted to this problem (16).

Mass population screening for PKU is now an established part

of public health care in the United States. More than 8,000,000
infants have been tested; about 550 persons homozygous for PKU
have been ascertained and, presumably, have been saved from mental
retardation (17). Mass screening for PKU has been shown to satisfy
cost-benefit analysis (18) and testing will, unquestionably,
continue. The future of PKU laws is somewhat less certain. Because PKU screening has succeeded in several states and many countries without specific enabling legislation (17), it may be that in
time the laws will be repealed. One can expect that a more general statutory approach to mass neonatal screening will evolve.
Currently, Maryland, which has created a Commission on Hereditary
Disorders (19), is considering the repeal of its old PKU statute.
PKU screening legislation has offered an important precedent for
state activity in mass neonatal screening.

Recent Developments in Neonatal Screening Programs

1. New Programs. During the 1960's Guthrie continued his
pioneering work in the development of microbiological assays for
screening inborn errors of metabolism. By 1968 tests for maple-
syrup-urine disease, histidinemia, homocystinuria, hyperlysinemia,
tyrosinemia and galactosemia were ready for use in mass testing
programs. In addition to these tests, enzyme assays, fluorometry,
thin layer chromatography, column chromatography and protein electrophoresis offer methodologies for screening a number of other genetic
disorders. The Massachusetts Metabolic Disorders program was the
first to implement many of the Guthrie tests thus validating multiphasic approach to neonatal testing (17).

By 1974, largely as a consequence of the sickle cell trait
testing controversy (vide infra) various medical, ethical, social
and legal problems raised by mass genetic screening had been given
considerable attention (20).

Yet few people seemed to know exactly what kind of programs
were under way in the various states. Because mass population
screening techniques had been developed for a variety of genetic
diseases, I decided to survey their use in the United States. In
February of 1975 I mailed a simple questionnaire to the public
health departments in the fifty states and the District of Columbia
to discover: (1) what genetic conditions were screened for, (2)
whether statutory law or public health department policy guided
local screening programs, and (3) what, if any, screening programs
were being planned. Thirty-four states replied to the initial
mailing; seven more replied to a follow-up conducted in March. Information about programs within five of the remaining 12 jurisdictions was acquired from secondary sources (statutory code books
and medical literature), yielding some data on 46 of the 51 (21).

The first set of three questions was designed to find out what disorders other than PKU were being screened for in neonates. Table I lists six specific human genetic diseases, their frequency in the general population, and the states that have initiated programs for them. The responses from a few states were too vague to permit a description of the precise disorders which they screened. Alaska indicated that it planned to screen for "aminoacidurias" in 1975. Rhode Island mentioned that it screened for maple-syrup-urine disease, galactosemia and "other aminoacidurias." The Massachusetts Metabolic Disorders program screens for many more inborn errors than are listed on the chart.

The states seemed about evenly divided in the use of specific enabling legislation or public health department policy to support expanded neonatal screening. Alaska, Maryland, Montana, New York, Louisiana and Mississippi cited statutory law; Alabama, Ohio, Oregon and Rhode Island noted a health department policy.

One set of questions was intended to probe for state interest in expanding neonatal genetic screening programs. Sixteen states indicated a general interest in expanding current programs; 12 of these states have no current newborn screening programs other than those for PKU. The answers to the questions suggested a moderately strong interest across the nation in the expansion of this public health service. One interesting point was the frequency with which public health officials referred to plans to develop programs with local medical schools. This may indicate that the initiative of the research physician is crucial to expanding screening efforts.

Among the most common genetic disorders which can be identified in the infant are the sex chromosome aneuploidies. Approximately 1:1,000 males is born with Klinefelter's syndrome (XXY), about 1:700 males is born with the XYY syndrome; 1:1,000 females is born with the XXX syndrome and 1:5,000 females is born with Turner's syndrome (XO). For every child born with PKU there are perhaps 30 infants born with one of these disorders. Sex chromatin analysis offers a relatively low cost, efficient method for screening infants for the XXY, XXX and XO syndromes. Neonatal karyotyping or Y-body fluorescence screening would also permit identification of persons with the XYY syndrome.

Because of the immense socio-ethical problems raised by XYY screening pursuant to research programs, it is doubtful that any state is prepared to engage in that activity. However, recent medical evidence suggests that persons with Turner's syndrome (22) or Klinefelter's syndrome (23) might benefit from early diagnosis and hormone therapy. Because of the high frequency of these disorders, the potential for therapeutic benefits and the relative ease of detection, I asked the states if they planned to develop programs for routine neonatal chromosome studies. Eight states

Table 1: Current State Programs in Mass Neonatal
Screening (other than PKU)

	Adenosine Deaminase Deficiency (?)	Galactosemia (1:75,000) b	Homocystinuria (1:220,000)b	Sickle Cell Anemia (1:500) a,b	Maple-Syrup-Urine Disease (1:200,000)b	Tyrosinemia (1:1,000,000)b (?)	Histidinemia (1:24,000)b
Alabama				X			
Alaska a					X		
Connecticut		X					
Georgia				X			
Kentucky				X			
Louisiana				X			
Maryland					X		
Massachusetts d		X	X		X	X	X
Mississippi				X			
Montana		X	X		X	X	
New York	X	X	X	X	X		X
Ohio		X	X				
Oregon		X	X		X	X	
Rhode Island e			X		X		

a = American blacks
b = estimated frequency
c = plans to expand screening for aminoacidurias in 1975
d = screens for many disorders not listed in this table
e = screens for "some aminoacidurias"

Eight states expressed a general interest in such a program; five mentioned that karyotyping is done on a selective basis (to confirm a diagnosis). However, no state appears ready to routinely study the chromosomes of newborns.

There was a tremendous range of response to my inquiries about non-statutory programs of genetic disease control. I will mention two of the more interesting programs, those in Tennessee and Ohio. The Tennessee program, although state-wide in scope, is not operated by the public health department. The Birth Defects Prevention Clinic of Vanderbilt University School of Medicine has begun a concerted effort to provide prenatal chromosome diagnosis to all women over the age of 35. Because I think it represents a unique development I quote the entire text of a letter sent to many physicians in Tennessee (24).

> The incidence of Down's syndrome (Mongolism) is 1 in 200 for the pregnant woman who is between 35 and 39 years of age, whereas the incidence increases to 1 in 50 for the pregnant woman who is between 40 and 45 years of age. Our clinic is prepared to offer you the assurance that your gravid patient doesn't suffer this tragedy. Pre-amniocentesis ultrasound evaluation, amniocentesis, and chromosome analysis will be performed without charge on all patients referred for consultation. A detailed report and interpretation describing the genetic diagnosis will be conveyed to their original physician for further care.

It is interesting to speculate why a state-wide antenatal screening program is offered by a local medical school rather than the state health authorities. A relatively small number of abortions were performed in Tennessee in 1973 (25). That state is among those that have read the Supreme Court abortion decision conservatively; recent legislation probably has had a restrictive effect on the availability of abortions (26). Perhaps because the legislature has taken a critical approach to liberalized abortion, the state health officials are hesitant to sponsor diagnostic programs which rely on the availability of therapeutic abortion.

The Ohio Department of Health has compiled a most impressive "State Plan for Genetic Services" which represents one component of a comprehensive maternal and child health program. "It is meant not only to consolidate piecemeal efforts but to expand services for the population at risk in the entire state. It is meant to adhere to high standards of quality and to move forthrightly ahead as experience accumulates and according to the dictates of changing circumstances." The Ohio plan makes a strong argument for the need for genetic services. It cites inability to

cure many genetic disorders, their high prevalence, and the spiraling costs of care of the affected. The report notes "it is not
uncommon also, for families with two or three children with genetic
disorders to report that, had they known the risks, they would
have opted for adoption." A positive cost-benefit analysis of
PKU screening is offered and it suggests that expansion of screening activities would improve the health care budget (27).

The objectives of the Ohio plan are: (1) identify newborns
affected with genetic diseases, (2) identify those who are in
mental institutions because of a genetic disease and counsel their
parents and siblings as indicated, (3) identify those people coming
to ambulatory mental care facilities...who have a genetic disease
and counsel their parents and siblings as indicated, (4) provide
public information on a continuing basis, (5) provide continuing
education in genetics to physicians in private practice, (6) provide continuing education to allied health professionals, (7) insure that families who encounter unusual problems in keeping their
children on prescribed regimens are provided assistance. Further,
the Ohio Department of Health has strongly favored a regional
approach to the provision of genetic screening and counseling services. A single state laboratory will perform all genetic screening tests; genetic counseling will be available at three genetic
centers spaced nicely throughout the state (at three medical schools).

Finally, the Ohio program has adopted a laudable set of
principles of operation:

1. The decision to bear children must remain the free choice
    and responsibility of the parents concerned.
2. The objectives must be realistic and attainable and must
    promote quality of life and increased potential for each
    individual. They must be clearly defined at the outset.
3. Priority must be given to conditions of highest inci-
    dence and/or greatest severity which are preventable or
    treatable.
4. Screening must be incorporated into a general program of
    prevention and remediation that is primarily service, not
    research-oriented.
5. A state program must be reviewed not less than every two
    years to consider changing medical knowledge and insure
    full public representation and protection. The program must
    prove to the public that its benefits outweigh the costs
    and/or physical and emotional risks.
6. A single administrative and coordinating agency must in-
    sure integration of findings and services provided, keep-
    ing in perspective all developmental needs of the child--
    physical, mental, social and emotional--as well as those
    of his family.
7. At least one appropriate provider/consumer voluntary group

must be identified or created for political action aimed at increased funding and the assurance of a full range of quality genetic services for every child.

8. Cooperative linkages must exist between screening programs and medical centers.
9. Participating professional institutions must be totally supportive of the program's service emphasis.
10. Criteria for standards of service delivery, especially for laboratory procedures and counseling, must be developed.
11. All patient information must be afforded the same confidentiality as any other medical records (27).

2. <u>New Laws</u>. During the past two or three years several states have enacted laws which implement greatly expanded programs of neonatal screening for genetic disease.

<u>Nebraska (28)</u>: In July of 1972 the State of Nebraska created a birth defects prevention program. It recognizes that a congenital anomaly is not only a tragedy for the child and the family, but also "a matter of vital concern to the public health." The law establishes a registry to investigate "the causes, mortality, methods of prevention, treatment and cure of birth defects and allied diseases." It empowers public health officials to carry on programs of professional education about birth defects and to "conduct and support clinical counseling services in medical facilities." It requires that birth defects and allied diseases be reported by persons in attendance at births (within 40 days of an infant's birth) to the public health department. The confidentiality of this data is guaranteed; it has also been made inadmissible in evidence.

The comprehensive birth defects information collected by the state registry is sent to the Center for Disease Control in Atlanta where it is subjected to computer analysis. Presumably, Nebraska now has a sensitive method for ascertaining a sudden increase in birth defects. A teratological agent should be identified with great rapidity. Pursuant to this new law the Nebraska Department of Health has initiated a formal <u>in utero</u> detection project for Down's syndrome. Already efforts have been made to alert all physicians in the state to the maternal age-associated risks of chromosomal disorders (29). Amniocentesis and fetal cell culture studies were provided free by the state to women at high risk for bearing a child with birth defects. Thus, the state of Nebraska now operates an antenatal screening program similar to that recently started in Tennessee.

<u>Montana (30)</u>: In 1973 Montana enacted a law to require that persons in charge of facilities where children are born or responsible for the registration of births have "administered tests designed to detect inborn metabolic errors as shall be required to be administered under rules adopted by the department." A single lab-

oratory will perform tests on the serum or urine of every newborn
in the state for a host of disorders. Currently the intent is
to use paper chromatography to measure unusual levels of leucine,
isoleucine, valine, tyrosine, glutamine, arginine, histidine,
glycine, cystine, homocystine and argininosuccinic acid. Tests
for galactosemia, the mucopolysaccharidoses and congenital hypo-
thyroidism are also planned (31).

The Montana law is compulsory; no provision for a religious
exemption is made. It is sensitive to the need to provide families
of affected children with adequate genetic counseling. Further it
authorizes the hospital in which testing is done to provide medical
services and assistance as needed by the affected individuals.

New York (32):   In June of 1974 the state of New York enacted
an amendment to its PKU testing law. The new law declares:

> "It shall be the duty of (1) the administrative officer
> or other person in charge of each institution caring for
> infants 28 days or less of age and (2) the person re-
> quired...to register the birth of a child, to cause to
> have administered to every such infant or child in its or
> his care a test for PKU, homozygous sickle cell disease,
> branched-chain ketonuria, galactosemia, homocystinuria,
> adenosine deaminase deficiency, histidinemia and such
> other diseases and conditions as may from time to time be
> designated by the commissioner in accordance with rules
> or regulations prescribed by the commissioner. Test-
> ing and the recording of the results of such tests shall
> be performed at such times and in such manner as may be
> prescribed by the commissioner."

It is interesting to speculate on the number of diagnoses of
the six enumerated disorders that will be made in New York during
one year. Perhaps 100 children will be born with sickle cell
disease; about ten will be born with PKU and perhaps seven with
histidinemia. Two or three children will be born with galactosemia
and adenosine deaminase deficiency; perhaps one each with branched-
chain ketonuria and homocystinuria. How did these last three
disorders receive special attention in a public health law? Automated genetic screening can be applied quite efficiently to very
large populations. Indeed, the appropriation made in support of
the New York program is a miniscule 250 thousand dollars. Multiple
screenings for genetic disease provide economies of scale. It takes
relatively minor expansion of facilities and manpower to add a
disorder or two to a screening program. Even the discovery of one
child with genetic disease that might otherwise have gone undetected
could save thousands of dollars of medical costs and institutional
care as well as a human life. Just as with PKU legislation the
appeal of ostensibly low cost preventive medicine and averting

tragic, albeit rare disease has proven persuasive.

But if genetic disease control is the purpose of state screening laws why then is the program so incomplete? There is for example
no provision made for the delivery of competent genetic counseling
services to "at risk" couples. No attention is given to the possibility of identifying and counseling persons heterozygous for
these disorders who may through an unlucky mating choice bear
children with a disorder. From the memorandum offered in support
of the bill it is apparent that the importance of counseling is
understood by its proponents. They stated: "early detection is
important for genetic counseling and expectant medical management"
(33). The decision not to specifically provide for counseling services in the law probably reflected concerns for the continuing
abortion controversy and the appeal of very low budget requirements.
A second omission in the New York law is its failure to consider the
need for a mechanism to guarantee that neonates recording positive
tests be so informed at an appropriate later date.

Maryland (19): In 1973 Maryland created a "Commission on
Hereditary Disorders." This extremely comprehensive law (five
printed pages) is a far cry from the one sentence PKU screening
laws passed in a number of states a decade ago. The turbulent
sickle cell anemia controversy had sensitized many public health
officials to the problem of discrimination against the screenee.
Writing with the aid of political scientists, ethicists and clini-
cian-researchers, the legislators tried very hard to draft a law
that would maximize the efforts to reduce genetic disease while
guaranteeing that the rights of individuals be protected (3).

Essentially an 11-member blue ribbon commission is created to
oversee all state efforts to detect and manage hereditary disorders.
It is empowered to engage in programs of public education, develop
a genetics registry, monitor the efficacy of state screening efforts,
and investigate discrimination against persons because of their
genotypes. The legislature has commanded by what principles the
commission shall operate. Among the more important are those that
require prior public and expert review of a screening decision;
that every individual over 18 and the parents of children under 18
be informed of the purpose of a test and given an opportunity to
refuse its administration; "that no program require mandatory participation, restriction of childbearing, or be a prerequisite for
eligibility for, or receipt of any other service or assistance...";
"that counseling services for hereditary disorders be available to
all persons involved in screening programs, that such counseling be
non-directive, and that such counseling emphasize informing the
client and not require restriction of childbearing."

The Maryland law may be a prototype for a comprehensive legislative solution to mass genetic screening. It represents a quite

different approach from the disease-specific law enacted in New
York. It would be difficult to fault the Maryland law on ethical
grounds; a couple of poorly drafted sentences do raise unnecessary
ambiguities. For example the law commands that "carriers not be
stigmatized." Why were not affected persons protected by such a
clause? However, exact compliance with the law could skyrocket
the costs of mass genetic screening. To secure the informed consent of each individual for every genetic test would require a lot
of counseling hours. Where, how and when will such discussions
occur?

Bills Before State Legislatures in 1975: Only three of the
41 states that responded to my questionnaire mentioned that new
genetic screening laws were under consideration. Arizona is considering a mandatory law for PKU screening (in the same year that
Maryland is debating the repeal of the old PKU law)!

In the state of Washington two different bills are under review. House Bill No. 780 would amend the PKU screening law to
"promote screening tests and counseling programs for persons susceptible to sickle cell disease or sickle cell trait." Such a law,
if enacted,would apparently cover neonatal screening for sickle
cell disease. Senate Bill No. 2225 is most interesting. With the
exception of one very minor deletion the bill is a copy of the
Maryland laws.

On February 19, 1975 Assembly Bill 412 was introduced in the
Wisconsin legislature. It creates a Council on Infant Health Screening to be composed of five members (at least three of whom are
experts in this field) who will serve for staggered six year terms.
That group is charged with performing feasibility studies for future
mandatory screening for congenital abnormalities. The bill requires
a truly extraordinary number of blood and urine tests to be performed
on infants. These include blood tests for "PKU, histidinemia, homocystinuria, galactosemia, branched-chain ketonuria, adenosine deaminase deficiency and homozygous sickle cell disease." The urine
tests would include "argininosuccinic acidemia, citrullinemia,
hyperglycinemia, hyperlysinemia, cystinuria, Hartnup disease, imino-
glycinuria and Fanconi (renal) syndrome."

Future Laws and Future Problems: It seems reasonable to predict that whether pursuant to public health policy or state law,
multiphasic neonatal screening activities have entered a period of
log phase growth. A sort of screening imperative seems to be at
work. A confluence of forces in the biomedical research community,
industry and government as well as consumer interest may continue
to push for the expansion of mass testing for genetic disease (12,20).

Three new kinds of mass screening for human genetic disease
may be anticipated in the future. First, it may become possible to

perform antenatal diagnoses upon the fetus by screening the serum
or urine of the woman. Diagnosis of anencephaly and spina bifida
have already been made based upon maternal serum levels of alpha-
fetoprotein (34). If a host of disorders could be diagnosed in
this manner a strong impetus to use this technique could develop.
Second, antenatal diagnosis by amniocentesis (and later with amnio-
scopy) especially for target populations (i.e., women over 35) is
already on the edge of foreseeability. Third, neonatal karyotyping
certainly could be supported with a cost-benefit argument if it
becomes possible to semi-automate cell culture and diagnoses of
metaphase chromosomes. As new therapies for persons with sex
aneuploidies are developed this kind of screening will appear
quite valuable.

Antenatal screening, particularly for untreatable disorders,
focuses the question of abortion as the key method of genetic
disease control. How would our society react to a law that required antenatal diagnosis, but left the decision about termination
of pregnancy up to each woman? Some persons would adopt the position that a responsible citizen may be forced to know certain
information; others would see such screening as unacceptably coercive. The prospect of antenatal screening forces us to rethink
the clause in the Nebraska law that suggests that the birth of
children with severe defects is a public as well as a private
concern (28). How important will the costs of care of such children be to a discussion of state supported antenatal screening? The
cost benefit argument for amniocentesis of women over 35 may be
much more impressive than that for PKU!

At least two major issues will have to be resolved as mass
neonatal screening increases. First, there must be adequate
genetic counseling to the parents and, when appropriate, to the
affected person. The current problem of maternal PKU argues that
homozygous females must be counseled of that fact fifteen years
after diagnoses. This suggests the second problem. Comprehensive,
well-protected systems of information storage and retrieval must be
developed. Genetic data should be available to the screenee, but
safeguarded from misuse by third parties.

MASS SCREENING FOR GENETIC TRAITS

Sickle Cell Anemia Legislation

Mass neonatal screening to find presymptomatic individuals
with serious genetic disease does not represent a radical departure
from other programs of preventive medicine (e.g., venereal disease
testing, glaucoma tonimetry screening). The test is performed in
an attempt to identify and treat affected persons before they suffer

irreversible damage.

A large number of genetic diseases are at the moment recalcitrant to therapy. A quick scan of the <u>Birth Defects Atlas and
Compendium</u> (35) indicates that genetic counseling is considered to
be the primary means of controlling many of these diseases. The
efficacy of genetic counseling is a function of when persons or
couples "at risk" for bearing children with severe genetic disease
are ascertained. Today, most individuals first learn of their
risk after the birth of an affected child.

For a few autosomal recessive disorders it is now possible to
use a mass screening approach to detect persons who are carriers.
If by chance two healthy carriers marry, they face a 1:4 risk that
their children will be affected with genetic disease. Thus it makes
sense to identify carriers before they have children (ideally,
before they marry). It is reasonable to expect that the detection
and counseling of all carriers would lead to a reduction of births
of children with this disorder. Retrospective studies of three
decades of screening for thalassemia in Italy lend some support to
this expectation (36). In America during the past four years mass
screening of healthy persons has been conducted to detect carriers
of two serious diseases: Tay-Sachs and sickle cell anemia. The
Tay-Sachs screening programs have been conducted without overt
government intervention. For that reason (and because they are
well documented (37)) I will focus on state supported screening
for sickle cell trait.

Early Sickle Cell Anemia Laws

Although it is possible to document certain events which must
have figured in the sudden expansion of sickle cell screening laws,
their evolution remains shrouded. Unlike PKU screening a major
technological breakthrough did not immediately precede the enactment of new laws; the methods had been available for many years.
An important contribution was made by Dr. Robert Scott; articles
published by him in 1970 called the attention of the medical profession to the real importance of the disease as a community health
problem (38, 39). His review of NIH grant support of childhood
disorders and charitable efforts by voluntary organizations drove
home the point that sickle cell anemia was a neglected disease.

The civil rights movement of the 1960's had coalesced the
black vote and led to an impressive increase in the number of
black officeholders in the various states. The low cost of sickle
cell screening programs, their obvious appeal as a means to reduce
genetic disease,and the political dividends that many elected
officials felt might be earned from supporting a screening law
ensured success at the state levels. Similar forces were at work

on the federal plane. In early 1971 President Nixon promised to
increase federal support for research and treatment of sickle cell
anemia four-fold (to six million dollars). In the same year
Senators Kennedy and Tunney began hearings on a national sickle
cell law that would result eventually in a gigantic funding increase
(115 million dollars over three years) (12). Between 1970 and
1972 12 states and the District of Columbia enacted sickle cell
screening laws. Usually these bills were introduced by black
legislators and voted in unanimously and without debate. In retrospect it is clear that the haste with which these laws were drafted
and passed contributed substantially to the acrimonious controversy
that soon engulfed screening practices.

    The first major criticism of the sickle cell screening was
caused by the ethnicity of the disorder. From a cost-benefit
perspective it obviously made sense to screen only blacks for sickle
cell trait. But the laws (as are most public health measures) were
written in compulsory language; the requirement that only a certain
class of persons submit to a test raised a difficult equal protection
problem. The semantic gymnastics that some states performed to try
to avoid this problem are illustrative. For example New York required persons "not of the Caucasian, Indian or Oriental races"
to be tested for sickle cell trait prior to obtaining a marriage
license. In a separate law New York required urban, but not rural
school children to be screened (of course most New York blacks are
urban dwellers). A number of states tried to avoid this problem
by delegating the power to screen appropriate persons to public
health officials (12).

    A second major criticism of the state laws was their scientific
inaccuracy. In some jurisdictions compulsory pre-marital sickle
cell screening laws were added as amendments to venereal disease
testing statutes. This may have indicated confusion as to the
manner in which sickle cell trait was transmitted; certainly, it
could have had a stigmatizing effect. Virginia for a short time
required that all prisoners be screened for sickle cell trait.
Assuming that this population is unlikely to be involved in childbearing and recognizing the immense problems raised by the XYY
controversy, it is best to avoid programs which may associate a
behavioral profile with a genotype. The title of a Georgia law
read "Education-Immunization for Sickle Cell Anemia Required for
Admission to Public Schools" - a patently absurd suggestion.
Routinely, state laws confused sickle cell trait with sickle cell
disease (4).

    A third major criticism of the laws was based on their omis-
sions. Provisions for confidentiality of test results, free
counseling services to persons with the trait, general programs of
public education about genetic disease, and guidelines to insure
quality control at screening facilities were not considered. No

guarantee of financial support for care of affected persons was
made (40). During late 1971 and 1972 criticism of the state
sickle cell statutes became widespread. Dr. James Bowman was perhaps the most articulate critic of the laws. His efforts sensitized the medical profession and the black community to the dangers
of discrimination implicit in compulsory mass screening. The
critique of the laws had a substantial effect on the drafting of
the federal statute (41).

Federal Legislation

In May, 1972 Congress passed the "National Sickle Cell Anemia
Control Act" which allocated 115 million dollars to a three year
program of screening, research and treatment of sickle cell anemia;
85 million dollars was devoted to screening, counseling and education efforts, 30 million dollars was earmarked for research into
development of programs and basic science efforts (42).

The federal law clearly reflected the demands of critics of
early sickle cell detection programs. Designed as a grant-in-aid
program to be shared with complying state and private groups, it
required that participation in any funded program be "wholly voluntary." "Strict confidentiality" was to surround all screening
test results. Wherever possible, "appropriate community representation" in sickle cell screening and counseling programs was to be
secured. This provision reflected the criticism that white medical
and health professionals were cornering control of a black disease.
Logically, it would make more sense to utilize black genetic counselors and paraprofessionals in community screening programs.

The law paid special consideration to the priorities that
screening programs developed with federal money would embrace. It
demanded that grant applications provide

> assurances satisfactory to the Secretary that (A) the
> screening and counseling services to be provided under the
> program for which the application is made will be directed
> first to those persons who are entering their child-
> producing years, and secondly to children under the age
> of seven, and (B) appropriate arrangements have been
> made to provide counseling to persons found to have
> sickle cell anemia or the sickle cell trait.

This section illustrates the dual focus of the law: to provide
information that will permit enlightened childbearing decisions and
to identify at the earliest possible time persons not yet manifest-
ing sickle cell disease to improve their health care. Finally, the
law authorized the Public Health Service to provide "voluntary
sickle cell anemia screening, counseling, and treatment...to any

person...and...include appropriate publicity of the availability
and voluntary nature of such programs"(12).

Shortly after passage of the federal sickle cell anemia law,
Congress voted favorably on its second genetic disease legislation.
The National Cooley's Anemia Control Act allocated 11 million
dollars to a comprehensive attack on this little known genetic
disease (43). Cooley's anemia (thalassemia), a blood disorder also
caused by an autosomal recessive disease, appears with high frequency in persons of Mediterranean extraction.

The money allocated over 3 years followed the pattern of the
preceding sickle cell law. A larger percentage was devoted to
research efforts, yet more than/half the appropriation was earmarked
for education, screening, and counseling about the disease. Some
persons were critical of this decision. Because there are fewer
carriers to detect (about 200,000 as opposed to two million who
have the sickle cell allele), screening programs could be expected
to identify many fewer at-risk marriages. In the wake of successful
passage of the Cooley's anemia law, a similar bill designed to attack
Tay-Sachs disease was introduced, but not enacted.

New Sickle Cell Laws

The National Sickle Cell Anemia Control Act has had two predictable results. The offer of substantial sums of money to voluntary state and local programs designed to screen for sickle cell
anemia has helped to stimulate the amendment of some of the early
compulsory state laws. The second effect of the federal legislation
is that more states, heretofore without genetic screening laws, are
writing such legislation. Properly written laws guarantee any state
a share of the federal pie, as long as it lasts.

In late 1972 South Carolina enacted a "sickle cell anemia
education and prevention program" that includes provisions for
voluntary testing of "black citizens in the reproductive ages",
counseling of carriers "for the purpose of preventing sickle cell
anemia in the future offspring", referral of affected persons for
treatment and a program of public education "to eradicate the stigma
of this malady."

In 1973, Massachusetts greatly expanded the coverage of its
original screening law. It reads in part: "The state department
of public health shall furnish necessary laboratory and testing
facilities for a voluntary screening program for sickle cell anemia
or for the sickle cell trait and for such genetically linked diseases as may from time to time be determined by the commissioner of
public health such as Tay-Sachs disease, Cooley's anemia, and hemophilia...." None of the listed diseases is presently curable.

Carrier detection would be the most likely objective of any program developed pursuant to this mandate. By furnishing "laboratory and testing facilities" for the use of localized screening projects, Massachusetts is validating the concept that persons (particularly groups at special risk) will welcome the opportunity to discover any hidden heterozygosity for a deleterious allele.

An interesting outgrowth of the Massachusetts law might be the first governmental delineation of what constitutes adequate genetic counseling credentials. The state commissioner of health has been delegated the power to determine what "post screening counseling service" would be "appropriate or practical." Few persons are professional genetic counselors. Rigid criteria could freeze community counseling efforts, yet loose criteria foster inadequate counseling.

Of more significant concern is the obvious effect that federal legislation had on stimulating states that had not written genetic screening laws to create such programs. Only a few months after passage of the National Sickle Cell Anemia Control Act, Ohio passed a law that substantially complied with the principles announced by the federal law. Unlike earlier programs that had mandated screening a target group at a specific time, the Ohio law merely directed the health commissioner to "encourage and assist in the development of programs of education and research pertaining to the causes, detection, and treatment of sickle cell disease and provide for rehabilitation and counseling of persons possessing the trait of or affected with this disease." Section C of the new Ohio law indicates that it was a direct response to the offer of federal money. The health director is to "accept and administer grants from the federal government." This is the first section of its kind in any of the laws. Despite its efforts to satisfy the federal statute, the failure of the Ohio law to embrace confidentiality of test results will certainly be noticed by grant administrators.

Kansas and New Mexico passed sickle cell screening laws in early 1973. Both became effective on July 1 of that year. The Kansas law provides for a statewide program for "blood tests for sickle cell trait and the disease sickle cell anemia." Free counseling services are to be given to persons screened. Voluntarism, the principal federal prerequisite, is not mentioned in the law. Provision is made for confidentiality of test results. In fact, Kansas has become the first state to deter invasion of test confidentiality by making that a criminal misdemeanor.

The New Mexico law also appears to be a response to the federal law, but, as written, it certainly fails to comply. Its decision to launch a public education program about "the nature and inheritance of sickle cell trait, and sickle cell anemia," is laudable, but what is needed is general education about human genetics. Special attention to a single disorder will inevitably cloud its meaning to the lay person. However, the main objection to the state law is that it commands the health and social services board to provide by regulation for "the testing of all school age children who may be susceptible to sickle cell trait and sickle cell anemia." The language must be interpreted as a mandatory screening program.

The new North Carolina legislation sets up a "Council on Sickle Cell Syndrome." The Council is to investigate the problems associated with screening, particularly discrimination against persons with sickle cell syndrome and to suggest further legislation after experience with pilot programs. North Carolina will furnish testing and counseling services to all persons requesting their utilization. The North Carolina law contains several unique provisions. It defines sickle cell syndrome to include "sickle cell thalassemia, and variants" as well as sickle cell trait and disease, thus expanding its disease coverage. It requires that counselors be trained according to "criteria established by recognized authorities in the field of human genetics." Like the Massachusetts law, this statutory language may require the formulation of licensing requirements for genetic counselors. The North Carolina law also requires that voluntary mass screening be preceded by a 60-day period of public education.

During 1974 laws intended to establish voluntary programs of screening for sickle cell anemia were under review in California, Florida, Georgia, Indiana, and Iowa. Indiana did approve a sickle cell anemia grant program last year (1974). Two hundred thousand dollars were allocated to fund the project; an 11 member commission was established to oversee and administer the program which is aimed at the "prevention, care, and treatment of sickle cell anemia or for educational programs concerning the disease...." In 1975 Iowa enacted a new voluntary sickle cell screening law also. To the best of my knowledge 17 states (listed on Table 2) now have sickle cell testing laws most of which are voluntary.

At least during its first year of existence, the federal sickle cell screening law prompted a good deal of legislative activity. To the extent that these new state laws represent a more sensitive consideration of problems implicit in heterozygote screening, they are an improvement. However, it may be that sickle cell anemia now has a distorted image. Perhaps a generalized genetic screening law authorizing voluntary programs of carrier detection for those disorders for which there is a diagnostic technology combined with a program of general public education would alert persons to the extent of genetic disease without twisting the importance of any particular disorder.

An omnibus federal law intended to "establish a national

Table 2: Sickle Cell Anemia Screening Laws
Provisions

State	Voluntary	Preschool testing	Premarital testing	Other testing	Confidential	Counseling	Public Education	Citation
Arizona	X	X	X	X				36-797.41(1973 Supp.)
California		X	X					Health & Safety 325 (1974)
Georgia	X		X			X		53-216 (1974)
					X	X		88-1201.1 (1973 Supp.)
Illinois		X						122 & 27-8(1974 Supp.)
Indiana			X			X		31-1-1-7 (1973)
		X						20-8.-1-7-14 (1973 Supp.)
Iowa								(CH 141, 1975)
Kansas	X				X	X		65-1, 105.(1973 Supp.)
Kentucky			X	X		X		402.310 (1973)
Louisiana	X			X				17:170 (1974 Supp.)
	X	X						40:1299.1(1974 Supp.)
Massachusetts		X					X	76 & 15A (1974 Supp.)
	X				X	X	X	76 & 15B (1974 Supp.)
Mississippi		X					X	41-24-1 (1973 Supp.)
New Mexico		X					X	12.3.45. (1973 Supp.)
New York		X						Ed.Law 903, 904 (1974)
			X					Dom. Re. Law 13aa (1974)
North Carolina	X				X	X	X	& 143 B-188.(1974)
Ohio	X					X	X	3701.13.1 (1974 Supp.)
South Carolina	X					X	X	32-562 (1973 Supp.)
Virginia	X				X	X	X	32-112. 20 (1973 Supp.)

program to provide for basic and applied research, research training, testing, counseling, information and education programs with respect to genetic diseases has been drafted at the request of Senator Javits by representatives of the National Genetics Foundation. It is intended to replace the inefficient disease specific approach currently in use. This bill may receive Congressional attention in 1976.

Current State Health Department Support of

Screening for Genetic Traits

Part of my survey of health departments was intended to discover state support of screening for genetic traits not enabled by law. It is interesting to compare my results with those of another survey conducted in January of 1973. Twenty-two states queried in 1973 favored pre-marital screening for sickle cell trait. When asked to predict the future role of mass genetic screening 20 states responded that it would be very important and 24 states characterized it as moderately important; only five states described it as not important (44). Exactly two years later 28 (of 41 respondents) indicated that they actively supported screening for sickle cell trait. During the same period the number of state sickle cell screening laws rose from 14 to 17. Three states (Connecticut, Oklahoma and North Carolina) mentioned support for testing of other hemoglobin traits (Cooley's anemia). Three states (Connecticut, Nebraska and Virginia) acknowledged support of Tay-Sachs screening programs. Support may be manifested as financial aid or providing laboratory facilities.

One interesting program is underway at the federal level. Job Corps, a manpower training program operated by the Labor Department, aids persons between 16 and 21 years old. Since April, 1972 free hemoglobin screening has been made available to its enrollees (more than 70% of whom are black or Puerto Rican). The test is voluntary and education and counseling are offered to persons identified as carriers. Apparently, there is some tendency to counsel carriers not to engage in strenuous labor (45).

I expect that state support of voluntary screening for genetic traits will parallel technological developments. The next major government effort will probably be stimulated by refinement of an assay to detect persons heterozygous for cystic fibrosis. Further into the future one can anticipate screening for carriers who may be placed at a health risk in unusual environments. Evidence for the correlation of lung cancer with inducibility of aryl hydrocarbon hydroxylase is illustrative (46). In Sweden mass screening for alpha-1-antitrypsin heterozygotes is already being performed. These persons may be at elevated risks for respiratory disease (47). A

variety of correlations may be discovered between HL-A haplotypes
or other markers and increased risk of various diseases. With
time public health arguments may be developed to favor massive
efforts in these areas (48). The nature of the state intervention
will in part be a function of perceptions of the public health
burden.

ACKNOWLEDGMENTS

Supported by U.S. Public Health Grant #GM 19513

REFERENCES

1. Swazey, J.P., Phenylketonuria: a case study in biomedical legislation, J. Urban Law 48:883 (1971).

2. Keck, J., Sickle cell legislation: beneficence or the new ghetto hustle?, J. Fam. Law 13:278 (1974).

3. Powledge, T.M., Genetic screening as a political and social development, in "Ethical, Social and Legal Dimensions of Screening for Human Genetic Disease," D. Bergsma (ed.) p. 25, Stratton Intercontinental Medical Book Corporation, New York (1974).

4. Reilly, P., Sickle cell anemia legislation, J. Leg. Med. 1(4): 36 (1973).

5. Green, H.P. and Capron, A.M., Issues of law and public policy in genetic screening, in "Ethical, Social and Legal Dimensions of Screening for Human Genetic Disease," D. Bergsma (ed.), p. 57, Stratton Intercontinental Medical Book Corporation, New York (1974).

6. Waltz, J. and Thigpen, C., Genetic screening and counseling: the legal and ethical issues, Northwestern U. Law Rev. 68: 696 (1973).

7. Guthrie, R., Blood screening for phenylketonuria, J.A.M.A. 178:863 (1961).

8. MacCready, R., Remarks made at the National Academy of Sciences meeting on genetic screening, March 21, 1975.

9. U.S. Department of Health, Education and Welfare, "State Laws Pertaining to Phenylketonuria as of November 1970," Government Printing Office, Washington, D.C. (1971).

10. Bessman, S. and Swazey, J., PKU-a study of biomedical legislation, in "Human Aspects of Biomedical Innovation," E.Mendlesohn, J. Swazey and I. Taviss (eds.), p. 49, Harvard University Press, Cambridge, Mass. (1971).

11. Capron, A., Lecture delivered at the National Academy of Sciences meeting on genetic screening on March 21, 1975.

12. Reilly, P., Genetic screening legislation, in "Advances in Human Genetics," H. Harris and K. Hirschhorn (eds.), Vol. 5, p. 319, Plenum Press, New York (1975).

13. Holtzman, N.A., Screening for phenylketonuria and its problems,

in "Birth Defects," A. Motulsky and W. Lenz (eds.),p. 263, American Elsevier, New York (1974).

14. Bessman, S., PKU laws - a model for the future?, Amer. Med. Dig. (March, 1966).

15. Bessman, S., Legislation and advances in medical knowledge - acceleration or inhibition?, J. Pediat. 69:334 (1966).

16. National Academy of Sciences - Committee on Inborn Errors of Metabolism, "Genetic Screening: Programs, Principles and Research," National Academy of Sciences, Washington, D.C. (1975).

17. Levy, H., Genetic screening, in "Advances in Human Genetics," H. Harris and K. Hirschhorn (eds.),Vol. 4, p. 1, Plenum Press, New York (1973).

18. Massachusetts Department of Public Health, Cost-benefit analysis of newborn screening for metabolic disorders, New Eng. J. Med. 291:1414 (1974).

19. Maryland Code Ann. Art. 43, Sect. 814 et. seq. (1973).

20. Bergsma, D. (ed.), "Ethical, Social and Legal Dimensions of Screening for Human Genetic Disease," Stratton Intercontinental Medical Book Corporation, New York (1974).

21. Reilly, P., Recent developments in state supported mass neonatal screening, Amer. J. Pub. Health (1975) (submitted).

22. Mellman, W., Chromosomal screening of human populations: a bioethical prospectus, in "Ethical, Social and Legal Dimensions of Screening for Human Genetic Disease," D. Bergsma (ed.)p. 123, Stratton Intercontinental Medical Book Corporation, New York (1974).

23. Caldwell, P. and Smith, D., The XXY (Klinefelter's) syndrome in childhood: detection and treatment, J. Pediat. 80:250 (1972).

24. A copy of the letter was sent to me by the Tennessee Department of Public Health in March, 1975.

25. Weinstock, E., Tietze, C., Jaffe, F.S. and Dryfros, J.G., Legal abortions in the United States since the 1973 supreme court decisions, Fam. Plan. Persp. 7(1):23 (1975).

26. A review of state abortion laws enacted since January, 1973, Fam. Plan./Pop. Reporter 3(5):88 (1974).

27. Ohio Department of Health, State plan for genetic services, unpublished (1974).

28. Neb. Rev. Stat. 71-645 et seq. (1973).

29. Eisen, J., Nebraska's prenatal diagnostic program, Nebraska Med. J. 60(2):13 (1974).

30. Mont. Rev. Stat. 69-6711 (1973).

31. Pallister, P., Montana, Personal communication.

32. New York Public Health Law 2500-a (McKinney's 1974 Supp.).

33. New York Senate Bill S.7005 Support Memorandum, January 9, 1974.

34. Brock, D., Bolton, A. and Scrimgeour, J., Prenatal diagnosis of spina bifida and anencephaly through maternal plasma alpha-fetoprotein measurement, Lancet 1:767 (1974).

35. Bergsma, D. (ed.), "Birth Defects Atlas and Compendium," Williams and Wilkins Company, Baltimore (1973).

36. Silvestrioni, E. and Bianco, I., Screening for microcytemia in Italy: analysis of data collected over the past 30 years, Amer. J. Hum. Genet. 27:198 (1975).

37. Kaback, M. and O'Brien, J., Tay-Sachs: prototype for prevention of genetic disease, Hosp. Prac. 8:107 (1973).

38. Scott, R.B., Health care priority and sickle cell anemia, J.A.M.A. 214:731 (1970).

39. Scott, R.B., Sickle cell anemia - prevalence and low priority, New Eng. J. Med. 282:164 (1970).

40. Lappe, M., Gustafson, J. and Roblin, R., Ethical and social problems in screening for genetic disease, New Eng. J. Med. 286:1132 (1972).

41. Sinnette, C. and Smith, J. (eds.), "Legislative and Socio-economic Aspects of Sickle Cell Disease," Harlem Hospital Center - Columbia University, New York (1973).

42. 86 Stat. 136.

43. 86 Stat. 650.

44. Rutkow, I. and Lipton, J., Some negative aspects of state health departments' policies related to screening for sickle

cell anemia, <u>Amer. J. Pub. Health</u> 89:217 (1974).

45. Fielding, J., Batalden, P., Tolbert, G. et al, A coordinated
     sickle cell program for economically disadvantaged adolescents,
     <u>Amer. J. Pub. Health</u> 88:427 (1974).

46. Kellermann, G., Shaw, C.R. and Luyten-Kellermann, M.,
     Aryl hydrocarbon hydroxylase inducibility and bronchogenic
     carcinoma, <u>New Eng. J. Med.</u> 289:934 (1973).

47. Laurell, C.-B., and Sveger, T., Mass screening of newborn
     Swedish infants for α-1-antitrypsin deficiency, <u>Amer. J. Hum.
     Genet.</u> 27:213 (1975).

48. Lappe, M. and Roblin, R., Newborn genetic screening as a
     concept in health care delivery: a critique, <u>in</u> "Ethical,
     Social and Legal Dimensions of Screening for Human Genetic
     Disease," D. Bergsma (ed.)p. 1, Stratton Intercontinental
     Medical Book Corporation, New York (1974).

DISCUSSION

Papers of Profs. H.L. Levy, J.R. Waltz and P. Reilly
<u>Principal Discussant</u>: Prof. R.W. Erbe
<u>Moderator</u>: Prof. A. Milunsky

ERBE: I find myself spread a little thin to try to cover the
broad range of points that have been made. Prof. Reilly has told
us that there are many laws. Prof. Levy has told us there is much
screening, and Prof. Waltz has told us that it is all very simple.
I find that perhaps there are two major themes here that are intertwined, and which perhaps can be taken apart a little to help
clarify the discussion that I hope will follow. I think we are
mixing the discussion of screening for individuals who we would call
"affected" and talking in that regard about what constitutes genetic
disease.

The second theme that I think we are talking about is heterozygote screening with the possibility of changing childbearing plans
in those individuals who are not affected by the disease, and who
do not have a direct medical stake themselves in the outcome of the
screening. I must confess personally that I would like to have
heard more discussion of the latter, as to the problems surrounding
heterozygote screening, because I think the physician in his or her
role as a screener is in a very different position from the physician
in his or her role as a therapist, however that is construed.

Prof. Levy really talked about screening for the purposes of
treatment, and I think that that is quite different. Prof. Reilly
indicated that even when treatment enters into a formal legal mandate, there can be real problems. Prof. Levy also spoke about laws
that facilitate the availability of testing, and which largely do
not contain information about what should be done to follow-up on
the results of that testing.

I would point out for the non-geneticists that screening for
carriers is primarily the screening for autosomal recessive, and
X-linked recessive disorders. It is more loosely designed for
autosomal dominant disorders (such as familial hypercholesterolemia)
which might affect as much as ½ percent of the general population
and for which there may be no established treatment at the present
time.

Speaking about the pre-symptomatic autosomal dominants, or
screening to identify these before the medical consequences of
carrying that gene become apparent, or in addition screening for
those with mild manifestations of a more severe disease (e.g. looking
for cafe au lait spots), geneticists recognize the fundamental reason for carrier state screening. It is that genetic counseling,
however complex it may be, following the birth of the first affected

child which is of exceedingly limited effectiveness, if one defines effectiveness in terms of reduction of the frequency of individuals having a particular disease. Such genetic counseling can certainly promote understanding and correct diagnosis and so forth. The geneticist in the past two years has become a kind of an activist entering into carrier state screening and attempting to identify such carriers prior to the birth of the first affected child in order to convey the counseling in a setting where the parents may not have any familiarity with the disease in question. This has raised some very real difficulties. My concern is that the experience which we have gained in the past five years from the only two major programs existing in the area of heterozygote screening has given us somewhat divergent results. In the Tay-Sachs screening program, some tens of thousands of individuals and couples have been screened to identify perhaps a dozen and a half couples at risk, who then subsequently have made heavy use of prenatal diagnostic techniques and in general have considered this to be a valuable effort. The other major program is that for sickle cell trait and related hemoglobinopathy carriers and which is the most extensive screening carried out to date with many tens of thousands of individuals screened and no prenatal diagnosis available at present. I think the conclusions to date perhaps point up some important contrasts.

I doubt that medical geneticists can really define effectiveness in the context of the heterozygote screening programs. Prof. Waltz referred to the nature and purpose of these programs, and I think it is very difficult for medical geneticists to come to grips fundamentally with what the definitions of those terms are. The evaluation of almost any of the most meaningful aspects of heterozygote screening programs has proved to medical geneticists to be much more difficult than was originally envisioned. To date it is not yet clear that in the much more extensive hemoglobinopathy programs, that there is what would generally be considered to be a net benefit to those for whom the program is directed.

I would submit, that many complexities surround these kinds of questions in the area of heterozygote screening. While I am glad to hear Prof. Waltz say it is unlikely that malpractice claims will be registered in this area, I think that the fundamental concern of the screeners is to do what is right in terms of the screenees, more so than what is deemed correct in terms of legal standards. However, until the field of medical genetics can decide what the goals of these screening and counseling programs are and what constitutes effectiveness, I think the law will have a difficult time setting valid guidelines and standards. I think in this regard I agree with Prof. Reilly's final comments. Genetic counselors would however, welcome good advice and counsel from lawyers and any other segment of society.

D. DEYE: Mayo Medical School, Rochester, Minnesota: I
greatly appreciated Prof. Levy's commentary earlier on and I
had the impression that he in a way left us hanging. He asked all
the right questions, but as a real world person involved in day to
day pragmatic problems, did not give his cogent commentary to
possible answers. I would like to address one scattering of
specific questions to Prof. Levy and then one generalized extra-
polative question to anyone who feels moved to respond.

What about using samples which come for the most part unsolicited
from the patient or mothers for research purposes. How have you
personally responded to such requests and what are your personal
feelings regarding uses of samples so routinely collected on all
new citizens? What of informing the local doctor and/or patient of
the results of tests which were not in fact solicited? The crux of
much of the screening problem concerns a model form for record
keeping. How can you keep records of screening to insure these three
things: 1) confidentiality; 2) information availability to the
local doctrs; and 3) statistical (that is not individually identified) information availability for research purposes?

LEVY: I left you hanging for one good reason, and that is I
don't have the answers. I suppose I came here as much to give you
a bit of information and to find answers as much as anything else.
Your second question dealt with the current policy in relation to
using specimens for research purposes. We do use them for that
purpose, if one includes as research the use in terms of the development of new tests as well as the modification of existing tests.
I think many state laboratories do, either within their own laboratory or within ancillary groups. We feel as if we have a basic
responsibility to the patient and the physician to tell him about
any unsolicited test results, and thereby inform the patient of
results of all tests. Quite frankly, you have asked a loaded
question. May a laboratory legitimately withhold information if
indeed the director of that laboratory feels that that information
is not going to be beneficial to the patient, is going to be irrelevant to the patient's medical condition, and even may induce new
anxiety. We are in the process of doing a study which we hope will
answer at least the question as to how much anxiety we are indeed
inducing in patients by giving them information about basically
medically irrelevant diseases or observations. Our preliminary
indications are that we do induce anxiety, although less than we
had anticipated prior to doing the study. But the dilemma is
focussed on whether we may withhold information legally, ethically
and morally? Should we withhold certain bits of information because in itself it may be damaging to the patient.

As far as the record keeping question is concerned - records
are kept. Prof. Waltz alluded to the fact that he felt from my
presentation that all was very simple and that one never made mis-

takes or one need not make mistakes because testing is simple.
Actually testing is simple, and I meant that sincerely. But the
logistics of the testing are exceedingly complicated. In Massachusetts, we dealt with 71,000 babies this year on almost all of
whom we have received three specimens. This adds up to over
210,000 specimens. There is a terrific problem handling this
number of specimens, keeping the results in order and making sure
we know the results are reasonably filed so we can recover them.
The specimens must be reasonably filed so that hopefully at some
future date if a mistake were implied, we could recover the specimen and retest it.

WALTZ: I am not at all certain that I am competent to respond
to all three aspects of the question, but maybe if I can have a
moment to respond to several of these, it will be responsive to that
one in part. If I may step back for just a second in connection
with Prof. Reilly. I think I may have suffered from a communication
defect. You may recall that Prof. Reilly referred to the fact
that there are numerous statutes. There are, of course, numerous
statutes that provide for screening. My suggestion was that there
are none as of the last reading that regulate methodology. I
believe that is the correct remark.

If you look for standards of care, it can be found only in
common law. Lest anyone suggest that I dodge either artfully or
otherwise, may I mention to you that in my profession we do not
read papers. We paraphrase them and then publish them, with the
consequence that what you will get in due time is a 20 page paper
with 53 footnotes which will in turn lead you to our 140 page
article entitled, "Genetic Screening and Counseling -- The Legal and
Ethical Problems."* If you take a look at that, I think you may
be persuaded that if we restrict ourselves to the topic suggested -
the application of the law of malpractice - that the problems are
not likely to be large in your area except perhaps in the area
of refused or mistaken diagnoses.

The question that Mr. Deye raised has one aspect as to which I
think I am competent. I have to avoid getting into scientific areas
but you see we lawyers separate out principle and follow through.
The principles here are quite simple. Principles of malpractice,
for example, are quite simple and seem to pose no large and looming
problems except in a few relatively rare situations. The proof

---

*Waltz, J. and Thigpen, C., Genetic screening and counseling: The
legal and ethical issues, Northwestern Univ. Law Rev. 69:731,
1973.

problems are more difficult, and that takes us back to record-keeping. I am not sufficiently knowledgeable to describe how Prof. Levy's record-keeping might be conducted in order to avoid proof problems, but perhaps I can be permitted to refer to the informed consent situation. I illustrate the point by suggesting that the principles of informed consent in this or any other relevant area are not hugely complicated once understood, but the proof problems are terrible as a consequence of the poor record-keeping that one encounters. I suppose you will think I am making a strange remark in this post-Watergate era. But I would think if one were being very cautious in connection with information disclosure, one would tape the exchange. Otherwise, I the lawyer, am confronted by the doctor who says there is no problem here because, "I told her." And it comes as a real revelation when the lawyer says to the doctor, "I will tell you she will testify that you did not." She is under oath and you are under oath, and it becomes what is referred to as a 'who do you believe case.' As people in Boston probably know as well as in any other city, when a case involving scientific matters becomes a 'who do you believe case' for 12 lay jurors, and there are no records or tapes to demonstrate that in fact the information was disclosed, the physician can be in very serious trouble.

MILUNSKY: Prof. Waltz, all of us would like to know how you think we can get informed consent in screening.

WALTZ: That, of course, is to me a vexing question. I want to be clear that I am hard-pressed to comprehend what serious risks are involved in any given situation. I would simply have to be advised because I tend to think of the simplest situation on the question, as Prof. Erbe suggested.

All you can do from a legal standpoint is assess if there is any significant information that must be disclosed. If the answer to that is yes, the legalistic question, too, is who is authorized at law to provide the consent. I would suppose in most of the situations you speak of, it would be a living parent. At least at that point you are confronting an adult who can perhaps read intelligently the drafted questionnaire or other literature, and in some effective way indicate some comprehension and consent. If it is done in writing, the writing itself will probably speak to its comprehensibility, its lack of intense jargon, and so forth.

J.A. GOLD: Attorney General's Office, Pennsylvania: Prof. Waltz you made two assumptions. First that the genetic screening program would be voluntary and second that the relationship involved would be akin to that of doctor-patient. I have two related questions.

First, under what circumstances would those assumptions not

apply? Second, how would their not applying affect the issues you discussed?

WALTZ: The reason I engaged in the initial assumption was to avoid legal questions having to do with the validity of mandatory or compulsory programs which would be far, far beyond my assigned topic. I also engaged in that assumption because, as you know perfectly well, if I engaged in the other assumption, it would have significant impact on the informed consent issue. Informed consent in the face of a mandatory program is quite Alice in Wonderlandish. I have very real problems with mandatory programs. Prof. Reilly alluded to the nature of some of those early mandatory programs. Those were the reasons I engaged in the assumption. Informed consent discussion would be rendered virtually irrelevant in the face of an involuntary or mandatory program. That is why I said the emphasis is on informed because one is assuming a consensual situation.

CAPRON: I do not know if Prof. Waltz would agree, but as I hear it you are telling the genetic counselors here that there may be no novel problems and no large problems of medical malpractice in the sense of interesting legal issues. I do not think they should be lulled into the feeling there is no large amount of litigation that could arise. That, of course, will depend upon the care with which procedures are carried out, the kind of potential areas of negligence that you identify, the harm that could potentially be done and whether that would be something for which people would seek compensation.

My main comment is on Prof. Levy's remarks. I hear you coming to this group and asking in effect for legal advice. I wonder why, and if you have sought from the Attorney General in Massachusetts a reading of your need for additional statutory amendments. When you talked to the Committee on Inborn Errors of Metabolism in the National Academy of Sciences a couple of years ago, I think it was pointed out at that time we were in an interesting situation in Massachusetts where we have a law that permits mandatory screening only for phenylketonuria, and the only excellent laboratory in the state has taken the stand of using the sample for these other tests, which now gives you some pause. California by contrast has a very broadly drafted statute and yet after a year or so abandoned its testing of additional inborn errors of metabolism on the basis that they were not cost-beneficial. So California and a number of other states that permit it, do not do it. Massachusetts, which by law does not permit it, does it. This is relevant to the Attorney General and the legislature. Prof. Waltz suggests, if the legislature reaches a judgment that mandatory screening is appropriate, we no longer are necessarily in the realm of informed consent.

Certainly, there is one question the legislature could confront.

Is there such a great likelihood that we do not want to make people take this risk unless they are willing to do so. If they were to reach the judgment that the risks are indeed small (and I applaud your attempt to find out about those social and psychological risks which are so often discussed and about which we know so little beyond speculation, stigmatization, etc.), then perhaps the legislature could reach the judgment that it is worthwhile making people undergo the tests. Until they do so, however, I would question whether you ought not to take the precautionary step of informing people that the blood sample is being taken as required by law to test for phenylketonuria, and that you ask their permission for the use of that sample for additional tests.

This would require, however, that women be informed of the test before the little heel prick is done on their children. Prof. Reilly mentioned that in some 20 states there are provisions for an objection exercised by the parents on religious or other grounds to the test. Yes a study that we did at the National Academy of Sciences indicated that in most states the first thing a parent, whether a religious objector or otherwise, would ever know of the test, is when they say "what is this little band-aid doing on my child's foot?" It is possible to tell the parents - we did a test and you will get something in the mail. In those states that do a little better process of informing parents, a booklet may be given to them to read suggesting they not worry unless they hear from the laboratory. Some states do not even have a booklet. So I suggest to you that it would be appropriate to go to a legal body other than this one (as fine as the legal advice is you are going to get here), and get advice from someone who is in effect your counsel on this matter, and seek further legislation if you feel that you are making use of the test results in the way that is not authorized by law.

MAHONEY: Prof. Waltz talked about the problem of unauthorized disclosure of genetic information. This is a problem which often vexes genetic counselors of what to do when there are lateral relatives who would benefit from genetic information found in a screened person. The caution that he gave us is that the law today recognizes confidentiality and the right of privacy almost in an absolute way and that consent obtained prior to the fact or compulsion of the law to transgress confidentiality constitutes a proper defense.

I agree that both of these provide ways for us to give information to other persons who may benefit from it. I also would suggest, though, that there are counterbalancing claims against the right of privacy that may have or deserve expression in law, such as that mentioned by Prof. Eisenberg this morning. Instead of assuming an adversary's position within families, perhaps we should be moving towards a position that encouraged help towards other

family members and sharing of genetic information? Perhaps a
field or concept of family law could be developed in which the
family was a unit of confidentiality rather than the individual.
In such a case there would be no assumption of privacy of genetic
information within the family, but instead the presumption that
this information would be shared. I wondered if Prof. Waltz might
comment upon that kind of an evolution in law.

WALTZ: That is very interesting. Most of the law that would
appear to be applicable is by analogy. But in the field of de-
fammation there is an immunity to the transmitter of information
if the transmission would be to the advantage of the person to whom
the information pertains. I would think that would be applicable
in the situation that you raised, that is if it is potentially to
the advantage of the screenee to have the information transmitted
to someone beyond the immediate family cluster, the law would probably recognize an immunity.

I tend to think of these things in a practical way. Nobody
likes to be told that their problems are simple, but the fact of
the matter is many of these problems are rendered simple in consequence of the fact there is simply no damage, with the consequence
that lawyers, for example, contemplate the splendid lawsuit that
might result in the recovery of 6 cents or nominal damages.

In partial response, I simply ask you what would be the prayer
for damage in a lawsuit arising out of a situation you raised where
in fact the transmission advantages the screenee? The real
problem, of course, and one that surely is simply solved, is the
unauthorized disclosure to, for example, an employer, who ignorant
of the significance of the trait fires an employee. There is damage.
I think perhaps by a slightly different route, however, the law is
beginning to give credence to the sensible sort of approach that
you suggested.

MAHONEY: I might point out to Prof. Waltz that the example
that he just gave could certainly give rise to claim for damages
if sharing one's genetic information with a close relative did
reveal your own carrier state and an employer acted against that
information. I can see the reasons why confidentiality and privacy
are closely guarded, but I can also see very justifiable reasons
why we should be trying to move towards sharing of information.

HIRSCHHORN: I am a little disturbed by something that I think
may be a straw man that has been talked about now several times
this afternoon. As Prof. Capron has said, the Massachusetts law
mandates phenylketonuria screening. As far as I know, it does not
forbid anything else in terms of what is being done. I would like
to draw the analogy of the individual who comes into the hospital
for one reason or another and from whom a blood sample is taken.

The sample is automatically sent to a laboratory which has a 12-channel autoanalyzer. Out of that 12-channel analysis arrives a high uric acid value and the person is diagnosed as having gout, for which he is given appropriate therapy to prevent renal disease. I do not see the difference between that and devising additional tests that are automatically done on a blood sample for which there is a mandated reason, and a good health reason, namely discovery of phenylketonuria. If additional information of benefit to that individual was derived from that sample, I can certainly see no objection. I am probably naive from a realistic point of view, but it just does not make any sense.

REILLY: I wanted to comment about an earlier remark by Prof. Waltz. He mentioned that there were not to his knowledge any genetic screening laws that spoke to methodology, and that he had a problem with communication between us. Firstly, I think there are such laws, and I would refer to the Maryland law. Of course, I could not be certain about his meaning of the word "methodology." Secondly, I would like to emphasize that there is a fundamental mistake if you end your examination of the growth of genetic screening policy in this country with a statutory code book. You have to look at policies of the Public Health Department first of all in broad language. Often the laws delegate authority and properly so, to the Public Health Department. Ohio sent me a 22 page single typed list of methodologies that it has created pursuant to general public health law. So I think we have to look more than at the tip of the iceberg into this question when trying to perceive policy developments.

CAPRON: It seemed to me, Prof. Mahoney, that you were suggesting an encouragement to people to regard their larger family as the proper recipient of this information. I do not think anyone would argue with that. That is a matter of public education and communication, and it seems perfectly appropriate for a physician to state his views to people. We have talked a lot about consultands and I think this is an unrealistic view. Of course physicians can have views and may express them to their patients as to what course of action would be beneficial to the relatives and the like. The hard case is faced when the relative says, "Look, I haven't seen Aunt Sadie for 20 years. She is the black sheep of the family. We don't like her." Or, "I'm the black sheep of the family more likely, I have been kicked out, I have no desire to let them know anything else about me that will further make them think there is anything wrong with me. If Aunt Said develops multiple polyposis of the colon and dies, so much the better."

Unless and until the physician is authorized by a statutory change or until a court would go as far as you do, I think a physician skates on thin ice conveying that information. It may be, to take the case that Prof. Waltz put, that there will be no harm done.

But there are certainly going to be situations in which there is harm done. The conveyance of private information may be in itself cause of a dignitary harm, which some juries may find sufficient evidence on which to give a judgment. I do not think you can take only the easy case in which there would be no harm. You have to take the cases where there would be harm. At the present there is no basis that I know of for saying privacy extends to the whole extended family, aunts, uncles, cousins, or any collateral relative that shows up on the pedigree. That could be changed by statute, but, Prof. Mahoney, I do not think you should look toward the common law for the quickest way of having that change come about.

J.R. PAUL, JR.: Moseley Diagnostic Clinic, South Carolina: Several people have talked about harm that can come to someone in the family. The person whose relative has a trait may be harmed because some other individual would not want their children to go out with these other black children. I want to talk about the subject of sickle cell disease. Prof. Erbe mentioned sickle cell screening had not really accomplished any good. I think that the screening for sickle cell disease has been motivated mostly by political considerations and not out of any thought that some good can come to people because they have been screened and found to have the trait or some other hemoglobinopathy trait. The dominant condition, of course, is entirely different. The point is that when we have screening that is being done for political reasons, perhaps learned societies should come out against this kind of screening until it can be shown that some good can come to the person who has been identified as a carrier. I believe that a great deal of harm can come to these people by being stigmatized and be being told that they have this bad disease. I have seen many people who have sickle cell trait who believe that this causes them to have certain symptoms and illnesses, and also the problem about whether they should marry or even let their child go with someone from this family.

Genetics and Family Law

ARTIFICIAL INSEMINATION BY DONOR - STATUS AND PROBLEMS

Donald P. Goldstein

Harvard Medical School; Children's Hospital Medical
Center, and the New England Trophoblastic Disease
Center, Boston Hospital for Women

Research, both basic and applied, has led to significant
progress in the therapy of female infertility. The treatment of
male infertility, on the other hand, has been discouragingly slow.
Until recently, couples with infertility secondary to oligospermia
(too few sperm) or azospermia (absence of sperm) relied principally
on adoption to establish their families. In the last decade,
however, newly accepted sociological and moral attitudes and legal
statutes concerning abortion and contraception have led to decreasing numbers of infants available for adoption and a marked increase
in the number of requests for donor insemination. This increase is
also due in part to the knowledge that the service is available from
more and more physicians and clinics, and to the growing success
rate and greater social acceptance of the procedure.

Since approximately 15% of all married couples are infertile
with the male partner responsible approximately 40% of the time -
donor insemination has become a major technique employed in the
therapy of couples with infertility secondary to azospermia and
oligospermia.

The increasing importance of this therapy and the continuing
legal discussion over the rights of the issues of pregnancies thus
conceived has necessitated including a discussion of the problem
in this symposium.

INDICATIONS

AID (artificial insemination donor), or heterologous insemination, is employed in the treatment of infertility when the husband's

sperm count is too poor by virtue of numbers and/or motility to permit natural insemination to occur, or successful AIH (artificial insemination husband), homologous insemination. In rare instances the problem is a mechanical one where the husband is unable to ejaculate because of a neurologic, anatomic or psychological disorder. Donor insemination has also proven to be extremely useful in certain dominant (e.g. myotonic muscular dystrophy) or recessive (e.g. Tay-Sachs disease) genetic disorders where the husband carries a mutant gene and the offspring have a high risk of being affected.

Many couples with oligospermia, where the count is very low but some viable sperm are present, may wish to undergo husband insemination for several months before donor insemination is performed even though the chances of pregnancy are slight. The goal here is to exhaust all possibilities of producing a child who has the husband's genetic endowment. When AIH fails, or where azospermia is present, donor insemination is ultimately employed.

EVALUATION OF PARTICIPANTS AND COUNSELING

Prior to the initial donor insemination the three individuals involved, the donor, the husband, and the recipient must be carefully evaluated. Most of our donors are medical students or house officers of known intellectual capacity and excellent health. Ideally their employment should not restrict their availability for on-call insemination, even on weekends. Donor family histories are reviewed in an effort to decrease the risk of transmission of genetic and familial disease. General physical features such as habitus, complexion, and hair and eye color are matched to the recipient parents. Blood type is determined. All donors must be of known fertility or have had at least three normal semen analyses. Spot checks on semen quality and compatibility may be made 15-20 minutes after insemination by microscopic examination of the cervical mucous. Anonymity of the donors is maintained and a code system enables us to use the same donor for subsequent insemination treatments.

All couples for donor insemination are interviewed together and the insemination procedure and methods of donor selection are discussed. Opportunities for adoption are also reviewed. Counseling by clergy, a trained psychologist, or even a psychiatrist is obtained if desired by the couple or recommended by the physician, particularly if there is a question of ambivalence toward the procedure or marital instability. Ideally the physician who performs the procedure should assume this responsibility. At least he should have the training and experience to evaluate the couples' understanding of the procedure. The social, psychological, and legal ramifications of producing a child by this method should be carefully explained.

The principle obstacle is usually the husband's unwillingness

to accept his infertility. He may interpret it as sexual inferiority. Such misunderstanding can lead to impotence, premature ejacu-
lation, and other forms of poor sexual performance. If, however,
the husband can clearly differentiate between fertility and potency,
the physician is usually on safe ground in performing AID. In the
event of confusion over this distinction, the father must be carefully counseled. He needs to understand that "being a father" means
rearing a child, not contributing genetic material to its conception.
Usually if a couple can accept the idea of adopting a child of
completely unknown parentage, it should be relatively easy for them
to accept the concept that artificial insemination really involves
adoption of only one set of genes instead of two. However, if there
is any reluctance, the procedure should be abandoned. As a general
rule only more sophisticated couples tend to inquire about donor
insemination. Those most likely to suffer emotional consequences
usually screen themselves out. It is remarkable considering the
thousands of babies conceived through AID - that in only a few instances has the child's paternity been an issue in marital break-
downs. Even when there are divorces, paternity rarely enters the
picture.

     After the couple understands the issues involved in having a
child via artificial insemination, a document is signed by both
husband and wife absolving the donor of responsibility for paternity.
The doctor is also absolved of any responsibility for birth defects
or abnormalities of labor and delivery. The couple is furthermore
assured of complete secrecy. Donors and their wives waive all
rights to the resulting children. They also waive the right to
legal action to find out the identity of the recipients.

                              TECHNIQUES

     Following these preliminary steps, a systematic infertility
evaluation is undertaken to identify any area of female pathology,
for it is unwise to undertake insemination treatments unless the
physician is assured of probable success. Blood type of the female
is determined. Demonstration of normal ovulation, tubal patency,
and absence of any uterine or tubal pathology are essential. If
these are normal donor insemination may be initiated. Otherwise
the infertility evaluation should be continued and appropriate
therapy given before artificial insemination is commenced. The day
of ovulation is usually determined by basal body temperature chart.
Insemination is initiated one to two days prior to the anticipated
ovulation and repeated at two day intervals until the basal body
temperature has shifted to a luteal elevation which indicates that
ovulation has occurred. The semen specimen is collected by mas-
turbation into a clean container within two hours of the scheduled
insemination or obtained from a sperm bank where it has been preserved frozen under controlled conditions. Even under the best

conditions this decreases the chance of pregnancy by 15%. There
are a number of techniques used to provide optimal insemination.
Most commonly the semen specimen is injected into the cervix and
upper vagina and the patient is required to remain in the treatment position for about 30 minutes, after which a pack is inserted
and left in for eight hours. We prefer to use a specially designed
cervical cup which is first applied, and then kept in place with a
pack. The sperm specimen is then injected via a syringe into the
small caliber catheter and the cup left in place for four hours.
The advantages of this method are the complete mobility of the
patient immediately after treatment without loss of the specimen
and maximal exposure of the cervix to the specimen. The total
procedure takes about 10 minutes.

RESULTS

The overall success rate with AID is approximately 80-85%.
The success rate during the first month is very low - perhaps
because of the patient's apprehension. It is not unusual to see
a normally ovulating women become anovulatory when she first
comes for her first insemination treatment. The maximum success
rate occurs during the third month. On occasion, we have continued artificial insemination for as long as a year. Pregnancies
after six months effort, however, are rare and may imply that the
patient has an occult infertility problem. It is usually difficult
to tell why all attempts at insemination sometimes fail since every
candidate goes through a basic infertility investigation and any
abnormalities are corrected. Thus, if conception has not occurred
by the third month, the patient is required to undergo a more
intensive examination that includes inhospital endoscopic examination of the pelvic organs. Even so, persistent failures in 15-20%
of patients are rarely explained.

The congenital abnormality rate among children born as a
result of donor insemination is somewhat lower than that for the
general population. This is perhaps because half of the child's
genetic make-up comes from men who have previously produced only
normal children. Another factor is the greater likelihood that
fertilization occurs at the optimal time of the cycle - just after
ovulation. Yet many patients still feel a vague concern that the
sperm manipulation required of artificial insemination carries
more risk than coitus. We usually tell patient- that there is no
difference in the abnormality rate for the two approaches. If a
defective child is born, they are less likely to feel guilt or to
blame the physician for giving false expectations.

DISCUSSION

Artificial insemination has been practiced since the late 18th century. Initially insemination was limited to the use of husband's semen but in 1890 Robert Dickerson secretly began the practice of donor insemination. Due primarily to moral and legal attitudes careful data and records are limited. During the first half of the 20th century demand and acceptance of donor insemination increased very slowly. A careful report in 1960 estimated that up to that time only 10,000 births in the U.S. had resulted from donor insemination. In the past ten years, however, the demand for this treatment has increased dramatically.

The legal aspects of donor insemination are at best unclear and must be carefully examined as the procedure gains greater application. A few instances of litigation have occurred during the past two decades. However, most could have been avoided by appropriate counseling and evaluation of the applicants. The following steps are recommended to avoid litigation: 1) obtain written consent of the wife, including permission for the physician to use his best judgement regarding donor selection; 2) obtain written consent of the husband; and 3) obtain written consent of the donor for unrestricted use of his semen. Many physicians today insist that consent should also be obtained from the donor's wife. Even though these steps are taken they do not replace the necessity for careful consultation between the couple and the physician involved.

Donor insemination is a very simple procedure and successful therapy for couples who are childless due to a male factor Success depends upon accurate timing, careful evaluation of female factors, and a high degree of patient cooperation. In those couples with a normal female the conception rate approaches that observed in the general population. The spontaneous abortion rate, however, is somewhat higher. We are perplexed, however, with the failure of conception in 15-20% of patients in whom no female infertility pathology can be identified. We cannot overemphasize the need for careful evaluation of the female partner. All too often this is neglected. Early diagnosis and treatment of female factors decreases the interval from consultation to conception and avoids fruitless insemination of an abnormal female. There still remains a significant number of eligible couples who are reluctant to pursue donor insemination. Motivation seems to be much greater when both partners have an infertility problem.

Many physicians have been reluctant to incorporate donor insemination into their infertility practice. In addition to fear of legal problems several factors may be involved in this decision. The ability of a woman to spontaneously ovulate erratically frequently makes scheduling of the insemination difficult to fit into

a busy schedule. Furthermore, a group of donors may be difficult
to organize, and screening donors is a time-consuming task. Utilization of fresh semen demands a larger use of donors and university and military communities have an obvious advantage for
obtaining an adequate donor pool. Although the experience with
frozen semen is limited, further utilization of this technique
is necessary if donor insemination is to become more generally
available.

CONCLUSION

Artificial insemination is an important tool in controlling
human reproduction. By choosing sperm from selected donors, doctors have taken the first step toward the awesome responsibility
of control of genetic characteristics. The proliferation of
sperm preservation banks and the advent of ovum preservation and
in vitro human fertilization will enable the physician to offer
increasingly wider options to patients. However, such control
over human reproduction will significantly increase the social
responsibility and social accountability of the physician. Many
physicians have expressed a reluctance to be placed in such a unique role. We will have to increasingly address ourselves to the
ethical, moral, and social consequences of our actions as well
as to the medical factors involved.

LEGAL ASPECTS OF ARTIFICIAL INSEMINATION BY DONOR AND PATERNITY TESTING

Joseph M. Healey, Jr.

Harvard Medical School

INTRODUCTION

My presentation involves two interesting biomedical technologies with a great deal of significance to everyone concerned
about reproductive decision-making, the concept of parenthood,
and the rights and responsibilities which originate in and about
the family as a social institution. Though these topics have
tended to attract the attention of physicians, lawyers, genetic
counselors, ethicists, philosophers and theologians, they are
indisputedly of great importance to society as a whole as we try
to develop coherent, intelligent and humane social policies in
these areas.

The use of Artificial Insemination with Third Party Sperm (AID)
suggests a variety of scenarios concerning asexual reproduction,
genetic manipulation and genetic engineering, all of which will
unavoidably affect the concept of the family in our society. Our
legal system has tended to concentrate not so much on these implications as it has upon the effect of AID upon the marital relationship, the legal identity of a child conceived by AID and
the recognition of AID as acceptable medical practice.

I would like to begin by focussing upon some of the ways in
which the Anglo-American legal system has treated AID. Several
courts have considered the procedure and its implications; several
American states have legislation dealing with it. We will find
that there still remains a great number of unanswered questions.
Though answers to these questions will not come easily, it is
important for all of us to try to understand the unfinished agenda
which we will face during the next several years.

In a similar fashion, the use of blood tests in paternity identification (BTFP) or more accurately, for exclusionary purposes, suggests the unresolved, perhaps unresolvable, broad-based tension between "truth" and "information" obtained from scientific testing and the traditional reluctance of the legal system to be compelled to follow such evidence. The limits of time and topic will prevent wandering too far off into the variety of situations in which this tension exists, but it is important to recognize that the tension is present in a great number of medico-legal contexts and to recognize this discussion tonight as only part of something much larger.

The closest thing to a consistent national policy in either AID or BTFP is found in the recommendations of the National Conference of Commissioners on Uniform State Laws. This Conference is an official national body composed of three representatives from each state designated by the respective governor who recommend "uniform legislation" to the respective states (1). The commissioners have promulgated several laws involving issues in family law, in particular the use of blood testing for paternity identification purposes. The most recent example is the Uniform Parentage Act (2) and we will look more closely at some of its provisions in subsequent discussion.

ARTIFICIAL INSEMINATION BY THIRD PARTY DONOR SPERM

The fundamental question presented by AID confronted by our system of laws, has been the legal identity of a child conceived by third party donor sperm and the effect of this identity upon the donor of sperm, the mother, her husband, the physician, and the institution providing the insemination. By effect I mean both the nature of the respective rights and duties of the parties and the potential liability, both civil and criminal, of the parties.

Several aspects of this question must be considered: 1) What is the legal identity of the offspring? 2) Who may perform this procedure? 3) What type of consent is required? 4) What parameters exist for the selection of a donor? 5) What basis of potential liability exists?

1) Legal Identity of the Child

Our Anglo-American legal system has placed a great deal of value upon the legal identity of a child and a wide variety of rights and duties are derived from this identify (3). For almost its entire history, our system of law has preferred, indeed exclusively recognized the marital union and family as the appropriate context for the conception, delivery, and upbringing of a child (4).

Traditionally this preference has been expressed by determining the legal identity of a child according to the concepts of "legitimacy" (5) and "illegitimacy" (6).

In the Anglo-American Common Law System, the concept of legitimacy as applied to offspring, is a very significant concept. Legitimate children possess the power to inherit from both father and mother, since the husband of the wife is the biological father of this child. Legitimate children have the right to claim the necessities of life from their biological parents. Likewise the parents of their legitimate offspring are accorded significant areas of decision-making affecting the rearing of their children. Any severing of the parent-child relationship must conform to the requirements of such criteria as child custody acts (7).

Illegitimacy has been regarded with much less favor. Blackstone described the bleak position of an illegitimate child at common law:

> The incapacity of a bastard contains principally in
> this, that he cannot be heir to anyone, neither can
> he have heirs, but of his own body; for, being nullius
> filius, he is therefore of kin to nobody; and has no
> ancestor from whom any inheritable blood can be derived
> (8).

Though recent cases have tended to break down both legal and social barriers between "legitimate" and "illegitimate" offspring (9), it nonetheless remains important to understand the effect of such distinctions since the common law prejudice remains in some areas. This is of particular relevance in the AID situation since the husband of the mother is not the biological father of the child, and the question of legitimacy remains an issue of primary importance.

2) The Provider of AID

Significant medico-legal discussion has been generated by "scope of practice" problems, in deciding whether a specific act is the practice of medicine and must be restricted to physicians (10). Traditional arguments for legal mechanisms such as medical practice acts and personnel licensure are based upon concern for the public health, safety, and welfare (11). There has been a strong movement to allow non-physician providers, arguably equally competent in a given situation, to perform some tasks for which a physician may not be needed. AID raises the question of whether the use of AID is restricted to physicians. The potential for genetic engineering in AID makes the question of who may perform AID all the more important.

3) The Donor of Sperm

In a similar manner, the question of who will serve as the
donor of sperm has implications beyond strictly medical concerns.
Dr. Goldstein has presented a representative example of how the
donation process is handled (though not everyone screens as
carefully as he suggests). The social and political implications
of the donation process raise interesting problems which also derive from the potential use of AID in genetic engineering.

4) Informed Consent and AID

One of the more controversial evolutions within legal medicine
over the past 20 years involves the role of consent in medical
treatment. The emerging consumer orientation toward requiring
disclosures of what a reasonable consumer needs in order to make
an intelligent decision (as opposed to the traditional standard of
what a reasonable physician would disclose in the same or similar
circumstances) has created a great deal of confusion in medical
practice (12). A major problem in AID involves determining what
"informed, voluntary, and competent" consent means in the AID
setting.

5) Sources of Liability

Potential liability in AID is similar to potential liability
in other areas of legal medicine and family law. Most of the
cases litigated to this point have involved separation, divorce
and paternity proceedings. As of this writing, there have been no
reported cases based upon either medical malpractice or the theory
of "wrongful life." However, it is not difficult to imagine such
theories as the basis of future litigation.

In answering these questions, we will find that the Anglo-
American legal system has concentrated upon the legal identity
of the child and has considered to a limited extent the problems
of who may perform the procedure and the role of consent. It is
important to remember, while seeking answers to our questions
that the Anglo-American Common Law system has not always looked
with favor upon AID. Consider this quote from a 1921 Canadian
Court:

> That no authority can be found declaring directly or
> indirectly that "artificial insemination" would constitute
> adultery is not to be wondered at. This is probably the
> first time in history that such a suggestion has been
> put forward in a Court of Justice. But can anyone read
> the Mosaic law against those sins which, whether adultery

or otherwise, in any way affect the sanctity of the
reproductive functions of the people of Israel, without being convinced that, had such a thing as "artificial insemination" entered the mind of the lawgiver,
it would have been regarded with the utmost horror and
detestation as an invasion of the most sacred of the
marital rights of husband and wife, and have been
the subject of severest penalties?

"In my judgment the essence of the offence of adultery
consists not in the moral turpitude of the act of sexual
intercourse, but in the voluntary surrender to another
person of the reproductive powers or faculties of the
guilty person; and any submission of those powers to
the service or enjoyment of any person other than the
husband or the wife comes within the definition of
"adultery."

The fact that it has been held that anything short
of actual sexual intercourse, not matter how indecent or
improper the act may be, does not constitute adultery,
really tends to strengthen my view that it is not the
moral turpitude that is involved, but the invasion of
the reproductive function. So long as nothing takes
place which can by any possibility affect that function,
there can be no adultery; so that, unless and until there
is actual sexual intercourse, there can be no adultery.
But to argue, from that, that adultery necessarily begins
and ends there is utterly fallacious. Sexual intercourse
is adulterous because in the case of the woman it involves
the possibility of introducing into the family of the
husband a false strain of blood. Any act on the part of
the wife which does that would, therefore, be adulterous.
That such a thing could be accomplished in any other than
the natural manner probably never entered the heads of
those who considered the question before (13).

It is important to keep in mind also, that the response of
the law has been uneven, inconsistent and sometimes contradictory.
These factors make it very difficult to predict with any amount
of certainty how any specific case will be handled.

There are three main sources that exist for finding answers
to our questions: a) Court Cases;   b) State Legislatures; and
c) Proposed Uniform Legislation.

A) Court Cases. Issues involved in AID in Court Cases
generally arise in paternity, separation or divorce proceedings.
It should come as no surprise to those who have some understanding
of our common law heritage, that these courts have tended to

consider the problems raised by AID a further extension of traditional problems in family law. The above mentioned Canadian court
was concerned about adulterous behavior (14). Other courts have
been concerned about the legitimacy of children conceived by AID (15).
Other courts have been concerned about the duties and obligations
of the husband of the mother of the child conceived by AID (16).
As you can see, court treatment of AID has been unsystematic and
has yielded conflicting positions, once even within the same state
(17)!

    B) State Legislatures. In order to confront the lack of a
clearly enunciated social policy, several states have passed legislation directly dealing with AID. To my knowledge, seven states
have enacted legislation: Georgia (18), Oklahoma (19), Kansas (20),
California (21), Arkansas (22), North Carolina (23), and Maryland (24)
Two statutes contain explicit recognition of the legality of performing AID (Oklahoma and Kansas). In the remaining seven states such
recognition appears to be implicit. Who can perform AID? Only
two states have answered this question directly. Georgia and Oklahoma allow those licensed to practice medicine to perform AID. Six
states have some provision requiring written consent: Oklahoma (husband and wife); Kansas (husband and wife); California (husband);
Georgia (husband and wife); Arkansas (husband) and North Carolina
(husband and wife). In Georgia, Oklahoma, Kansas, California, Arkansas, and North Carolina, the child has been recognized specifically as either legitimate or entitled to the same rights as a
natural child.

    The statutes of Oklahoma and Georgia are good examples of ex-
isting state legislation:

    Oklahoma:
    1) Who may perform
    2) Legitimacy

Section 551. Authorization

The technique of Heterologous Artificial Insemination may
be performed in this state by persons duly authorized to
practice medicine at the request and with the consent in
writing of the husband and wife desiring the utilization of
such technique for the purpose of conceiving a child or
children.

Section 552. Status of Child

Any child or children born as the result thereof shall be
considered at law in all respects the same as a naturally
conceived legitimate child of the husband and wife so
requesting and consenting to the use of such technique.

Section 553. Persons Authorized-Consent

No person shall perform the technique of Heterologous
Artificial Insemination unless currently licensed to practice
medicine in this State, and then only at the request and with
the written consent of the husband and wife desiring the
utilization of such technique. The said consent shall be
executed and acknowledged by both the husband and wife and
the person who is to perform the technique, and the judge
having jurisdiction over adoption of children, and an original thereof shall be filed under the same rules as adoption
papers. The written consent so filed shall not be open to
the general public, and the information contained therein
may be released only to the persons executing such consent,
or to persons having a legitimate interest therein as evi-
denced by a specific court order.

Georgia:
  1) Legitimacy
  2) Who may perform
  3) Civil Liability
  4) Criminal Liability

a) All children born within wedlock, or within the usual
period of gestation thereafter, who have been conceived by
the means of artificial insemination, are irrebuttably
presumed legitimate if both the husband and wife consent
in writing to the use and administration of artificial
insemination.

b) Physicians and surgeons licensed to practice medicine
in accordance with and under the provisions of Chapter 84-9
shall be the only persons authorized to administer or perform
artificial insemination upon any female human being. Any
other person or persons who shall attempt to administer or
perform, or who shall actually administer or perform, artificial insemination upon any female human being shall be guilty
of a felony, and on conviction therefor shall be punished by
imprisonment in the penitentiary for not less than one year
nor more than five years.

c) Any physician or surgeon who shall obtain written
authorization signed by both the husband and wife authorizing
him to perform or administer artificial insemination shall be
relieved of civil liability to the husband and wife or to any
child conceived by artificial insemination for the result or
results of said artificial insemination: provided, however,
the written authorization provided for herein shall not relieve
any physician or surgeon from any civil liability arising from
his or her own negligent administration or performance of

artificial insemination.

Some mention should be made of one other state statute.
As the American legal system struggles with how best to
define what is meant by the rights of children, it is worth
noting that the state of North Carolina has expressed its
policy toward artificial insemination in a section which is
entitled "The Rights of Children":

Section 49 A-1.   Status of Child Born as a Result of
                   Artificial Insemination

Any child or children born as the result of heterologous artificial insemination shall be considered at law in all respects the
same as a naturally conceived legitimate child of the husband and
wife requesting and consenting in writing to the use of such
technique.

(C) Uniform Legislation. The Uniform Parentage Act has a
section specifically dealing with AID:

Section 5 Artificial Insemination

a) If, under the supervision of a licensed physician and
with the consent of her husband, a wife is inseminated artificially with semen donated by a man not her husband, the
husband is treated in law as if he were the natural father
of a child thereby conceived. The husband's consent must
be in writing and signed by him and his wife. The physician shall certify their signatures and the date of insemination, and file the husband's consent with the (State
Department of Health), where it shall be kept confidential
and in a sealed file. However, the physician's failure to do
so does not affect the father and child relationship. All
papers and records pertaining to the insemination, whether
part of the permanent record of a court or of a file held by
the supervising physician or elsewhere, are subject to inspection only upon an order of the court for good cause shown.

b) The donor of semen provided to a licensed physician for
use in artificial insemination of a married woman other than
the donor's wife is treated in law as if he were not the natural father of a child thereby conceived.

In order to determine how any legal question about AID would
be answered, it is important first to determine whether the specific
state has dealt with the procedure and the problems derived from it.
In those states in which no legal policy has been enunciated, it
is by no means clear how the courts or legislature if confronted by
such problems would solve them. One would hope that the approach
suggested in the Uniform Parentage Act would guide the thinking of
those resolving the problems. But there is no guarantee that such

would be the case. And as all of us realize, there is a high degree
of unpredictability in the resolution of medico-legal problems.

⌐A wide variety of questions has not yet been raised or resolved in the legal context: 1. Who may be inseminated? An unmarried woman? A married woman without the consent of her husband?
A woman before the age of majority? 2. Does anyone have a right to
be inseminated? Can a physician/provider be compelled to provide
AID?⌐ (These questions are part of a broader social policy question
- is there a right to be fertile?) 3. Some have suggested that not
enough is known about the freezing of sperm and its possible effects
on increasing the risk of malformation and deformity. Is the use
of frozen sperm subject to the regulations governing human experimentation?

In summary, it should be clear that we know much less about AID
that we should, in order to advise those who ask about the legal
implications of their involvement with this technology. It is also
true, however, that we know more about the law's approach to AID,
then we do about most other aspects of genetics and the law. The
tone of caution which underlies this presentation may be exaggerated,
but it is not, I believe unnecessary. The issues involved in AID
have enormous consequences for institutions and values which the law
has long protected. It will take a good deal of time and discussion
before such issues have been resolved.

BLOOD TESTING FOR PATERNITY

I have left to Dr. Konugres, the task of presenting the complex
scientific aspects of B.T.F.P. Briefly stated, Mendel's Laws of
hereditary characteristics as applied to antigen-antibody reaction
make it possible, in some situations to arrive at a conclusion that
a certain person is not the biological parent of a child. This is
what I meant by an earlier reference to its exclusionary importance.
The process cannot identify a given person positively as the biological parent of the child. It can, however, operate to exclude a
given person. Its use is particularly important when there is a conflict in testimony between the man and woman with respect to the
parentage of a child. By taking a look at one of the classic
cases in this field, Houghton v. Houghton (25), we can see how this
process works.

The Houghton case involved a rather complicated divorce proceeding. Among the major issues was the parentage of a child born
to the wife seeking divorce. Both parties agreed to allow blood
tests of themselves and of the child. Blood was drawn from each of
the three in the presence of the doctor and the samples were labeled
in his presence. Tests on the three specimens were made by qualified medical technologists under the supervision and direction of

the physician by separate technologists. On the following day the
tests were repeated, each by a different technologist than the one
who had analyzed the particular specimen the day before. The
results of the two series of tests were identical.

Tests were made under two systems of each person's blood: the
Rh system and the MN system. The physician made out a report, admitted into evidence, which contained the following conclusions:

(1) Rh system: There are 6 antigens in the Rh system.
These are usually written, C, D, and E, and c, d, and e.
All persons have 6 Rh antigens and these occur in three
pairs. There is a pair of "C's", a pair of "D's", and a
pair of "E's". Each pair may be any combination, i.e., CC,
cc, or Cc. One of the antigens in each of the pairs comes
from the father and one from the mother. In the above case,
Mary Jane Houghton has e antigen and no E antigen, and her
formula for this particular antigen pair must be ee. James
Richard Houghton has e antigen and no E antigen, and his
formula for this antigen pair must also be ee. Sandra Kay
Houghton has e antigen and E antigen. Her formula for
this pair, therefore, would have to be eE. Since neither
Mary or James have the E antigen, it must have come from
another source.

(2) In the MN system: The MN system is composed of a pair
of antigens which occur in the following combinations: MM,
NN, or MN. In the above typing, Mary Jane Houghton is positive
for M and positive for N. Her formula is MN. James Richard
Houghton is negative for M and positive for N. His formula
is NN. Sandra Kay Houghton is positive for M and negative
for N. Her formula is, therefore, MM. One of the M's in
Sandra Kay's formula could have been inherited from the
mother, Mary Jane Houghton. However, the other M could not
have been inherited from James Richard Houghton, since he does
not possess this factor. It would, therefore, have to come
from another source.

The above findings would exclude James Richard Houghton as
father of the infant, Sandra Kay Houghton (26).

As in the example of AID, the first step is to ascertain the
approach of the individual state in which the use of B.T.F.P. is
sought. There are two significant levels to this question:

1) What weight is to be given to evidence which is clear
    and conclusive on the issue of paternity?
2) What weight is to be given to evidence upon which there
    is disagreement or which is not conclusive?

States vary in their approaches (27). Some allow the introduction of evidence of an inconclusive or disputed nature (28).
Others require that such evidence be conclusive (establish a definite exclusion (29)). In evaluating evidence which is admissible,
three different approaches have emerged:

1) Evidence from blood testing to exclude paternity should be
   afforded only such weight as other evidence (e.g. the
   testimony of the parties themselves (30)).
2) Evidence from blood testing to exclude paternity should be
   afforded greater weight than other evidence but shall not
   be conclusive on the issue (31).
3) Evidence from blood testing to exclude paternity should
   be conclusive and determinative on the issue provided
   there are no defects in the testing method itself (32).

As in the case of AID attempts have been made to make more consistent the existing laws in the area through uniform laws: The
Uniform Illegitimacy Act in 1922; the Uniform Act on Blood Tests to
Determine Paternity in 1952; the Uniform Act on Paternity in 1960;
and the Uniform Parentage Act in 1974.

The Uniform Parentage Act states in part:

Section 11. (Blood Tests.)

(a) The court may, and upon the request of a party shall,
     require the child, mother, or alleged father to submit to
     blood tests. The tests shall be performed by an expert
     qualified as an examiner of blood types, appointed by the
     court.

(b) The court, upon reasonable request by a party, shall order
     that independent tests be performed by other experts
     qualified as examiner of blood types.

(c) In all cases, the court shall determine the number and
     qualifications of the experts.

Section 12. (Evidence Relating to Paternity.)

Evidence relating to paternity may include:

1) evidence of sexual intercourse between the mother and
    alleged father at any possible time of conception;

2) an expert's opinion concerning the statistical probability
    of the alleged father's paternity based upon the duration
    of the mother's pregnancy;

3) blood test results weighted in accordance with evidence,
    if available, of the statistical probability of the
    alleged father's paternity;

4) medical or anthropological evidence relating to the
    alleged father's paternity of the child based on tests
    performed by experts. If a man has been identified
    as a possible father of the child, the court may, and
    upon the request of a party shall, require the child,
    the mother, and the man to submit to appropriate tests;
    and

5) all other evidence relevant to the issue of paternity of
    the child.

A recent case decided by the Supreme Court of North Carolina
(State v. Camp. (33)) dealt with the weight to be given regarding
properly administered blood test that shows nonpaternity. The
trial court instructed the jury that blood tests are not conclusive
on the issue of nonpaternity but that the results of such tests are
to be considered along with all the other evidence in determining
the issue of paternity. The Court of Appeals awarded a new trial,
saying that the instruction as given was erroneous, and that the
court should have charged that under the law of genetics and heredity a man and woman of blood group "O" cannot possibly have a child
of blood group "A", and that if they believed the testimony of the
doctor and believed that the tests were properly administered, it
would be their duty to return a verdict of not guilty.

In North Carolina, when paternity is at issue, there is statutory authority for ordering blood tests for mother, child and alleged
father (34) and "the results of such blood grouping tests shall be
admitted in evidence when offered by a duly licensed practicing
physician or other qualified person" (35). There is no statutory
provision dealing with the weight to be given such evidence.

The court expressed its belief in the reliability and significance of such evidence. However, the court looked to the legislature as the appropriate forum to establish this social policy.

Perhaps the General Assembly should provide that the results
of such tests showing nonpaternity should be conclusive. However, when public policy requires a change in a constitution-
ally-valid statute, it is the duty of the Legislature and not
the courts to make that change. 2 Strong, N.C. Index 2d,
Constitutional Law & 10 (1967); Clark's v. West, 268 N.C. 527,
151 S.E.2d 5 (1966); Insurance Co. v. Bynum, 267 N.C. 289, 148
S.E.2d 114 (1966); Fisher v. Motor Co., 249 N.C. 617, 107, S.E.
2d 94 (1959)....As long as (the legislative body) does not
exceed its powers, the courts are not concerned with the motives

wisdom, or expediency which prompt its actions. These are not questions for the court but for the legislative branch of the government. State v. Warren, 252 N.C. 690, 114 S.E. 2d 660; Ferguson v. Riddle, 233 N.C. 54, 62 S.E.2d 525; State v. Harris, 216 N.C. 746, 6 S.E.2d 854. Clark's v. West, supra. 'The legislative, executive, and supreme judicial powers of State government shall be forever separate and distinct from each other.   Article I, section 6, North Carolina Constitution.

For the above reasons, we adhere to the interpretation of the statute as set out in State v. Fowler, supra, and leave to the General Assembly the question of the weight to be given such blood-grouping tests. (36)

The Supreme Court reversed the Court of Appeals and reinstated the lower court opinion.

The Uniform Parentage Act and the Camp case are invitations to state legislatures to develop a coherent social policy toward B.T.F.P. One can only hope that legislatures will avail themselves of opportunities like these.

CONCLUSION

Though at first glance the two subjects of my presentation may seem unrelated, a closer look should indicate that they both give us an opportunity to examine five extremely important components of our societal policy in establishing parameters for reproductive decision-making:

1) The concept of the family in our society, especially the role of the single parent.
2) The process of deriving rights and duties in the parent-child relationship from the legal identity of the child.
3) The desire to afford extensive privacy in reproductive decision-making. (An extremely significant contemporary concept in Supreme Court decisions concerning contraception and abortion.)
4) The newly evolving area of the "rights of children".
5A) The general response of our Anglo-American Common Law System to new technologies affecting institutions as significant to our concept of society as the family.
 B) The manner in which our legal system accepts and uses information of apparent evidentiary value obtained from scientific testing.

In confronting the many unanswered questions I have raised, we as a society must make important decisions about these components. The decisions we will make unavoidably will shape the society in

which we live. My only hope is that we will bring to this task
the cooperative spirit which is essential for resolving significant
social policy issues.

REFERENCES

1. For a description of the National Commissioners and their work
    in the field of organ transplantation, c.f. Curran, W., The
    uniform anatomical gift act, New Eng. J. Med. 280:36 (1969).

2. c.f. Krause, H., The uniform parentage act, Fam. Law Quart.
    8:2

3. c.f. Krause, H., Illegitimacy: Law & Social Policy (1971) and
    Clark, H., The Law of Domestic Relations (1968).

4. Though developments in the area of adoption with respect to
    the single parent are important to keep in mind. c.f. Clark,
    op. cit., p. 641.

5. "Lawful birth, the condition of being born in wedlock, the
    opposite of illegitimacy or bastardy." (Black's Law Dictionary).

6. "The condition before the law or the social STATUS of a bastard;
    the state or condition of one whose parents were not inter-
    married at the time of his birth.(Black's Law Dictionary).

7. c.f. Katz, S., When Parents Fail: The Law's Response to Family
    Breakdown. (1972).

8. 1. Blackstone, W., Commentaries on the Law of England 459.

9. For example, Levy v. Louisiana 391 U.S. 68 (1968).
                  Weber v. Aetna Casualty & Security Company
                  406 U.S. 164 (1972)

10. c.f. Curran, W. and Shapiro, E., Law, medicine and forensic
    science, 517-524.

11. c.f. Grad, F., Public Health Law Manual, 53-75.

12. c.f. Annas, G., The Rights of Hospital Patients, Chapter VI,
    "Informed Consent to Treatment."

13. Orford v. Orford, 58 Dominion Law Reports, 251, 255 (1921).

14. Ibid.

15. Doornbos v. Doornbos (23 U.S. Law Week 2308 (1954)
    Anonymous v. Anonymous (246 NYS 2n 835 (1964)*
    Gursky v. Gursky (242 NYS 2n 406 (1963)*

16. Strnad v. Strnad 78 NYS 2d 590 (1948)*
    People v. Sorenson 68 Cal 2d 280 (1968)
    In the Matter of the Adoption of Anonymous, 345 NYS 2d 430
    (1973)*

17. Compare The New York Cases included in notes 15 & 16 (*).

18. Georgia Code 74-101.1.

19. Oklahoma Statutes, Title 10, 551 to 553.

20. Kansas Statutes, Sections 23-128; 23-129; 23-130.

21. California Civil Code Section 216; California Penal Code
    Section 270.

22. Arkansas Statutes 61-141.

23. North Carolina General Statutes, Section 49A-1.

24. Maryland Code, Article 43, Section 55%.

25. 137 N.W. 2d 861 (1965).

26. 137 N.W. 2d 861, 865-6.

27. c.f. Schatkin, Disputed Paternity Proceedings.

28. c.f. New Hampshire: "If the experts disagree in their findings
    Revised Statutes   or conclusions, the question shall be
    Annotated 522:4   submitted upon all the evidence."

29. E.G. - Alabama: "The result of the tests shall be receivable
                          in evidence in the trial of the case, but
                          only in cases where definite exclusion is
                          established."
    Alabama Code Title 27, Section 12(5)

30. c.f. Berry v. Chaplin, 74 Cal. app. 2d 652.

31. c.f. Beck v. Beck 153 Colo 90.

32. Kentucky: "If the court finds that the conclusions of all the
              experts, as disclosed by the evidence based upon the
              tests are that the alleged father is not the father

> of the child, the question of paternity shall be re-
>   solved accordingly."

Kentucky Revised Statutes
406.111

33. 286 W.C. 148, 209 S.E. 2d 754, 1974.

34. North Carolina General Statutes 49-7.

35. North Carolina General Statutes 8-50.1.

36. 209 S.E. 2d 754, 757.

THE CURRENT STATUS OF PATERNITY TESTING

Angelyn A. Konugres

Boston Hospital for Women; Harvard Medical School

Blood consists of four components: erythrocytes, leukocytes, platelets, and plasma. Each blood component exhibits individual differences demonstrable by either immunologic or physico-chemical methods. These individual differences in the molecular structures of blood constituents are governed by genes or chromosomes and are generally known as allotypes, phenotypes, or simply types. Types which are genetically related have been assigned to the same system. The number of systems and specificities currently being used by some laboratories in paternity testing are listed in Table I.

Specificities and groups have also been demonstrated in platelets and hemoglobin. However, they are not being regularly used for paternity testing and are not listed. Table II lists the chances of exclusion of paternity by 24 blood group systems.

Table I. Blood Properties Used in Paternity Testing

Blood Components	Systems		Specificities	
	# Known	# Used	# Known	# Used
Erythrocyte antigens	14	9	260+	24+
Erythrocyte enzymes	12	6	55	11
Plasma protein	13	7	90+	13
Leukocyte antigens	1	1	24	21

219

Progress in the field of immunohematology has been rapid in the past 15 years. Today more than 250 red cell antigens have been recognized. The variety and number of reliable antisera has also increased substantially and has therefore added to the number of red cell antigens which can be used in paternity testing.

The finding and description of the serum protein groups and red cell enzyme polymorphisms has added a new dimension to blood grouping in that now we are no longer limited to the red cell membrane. Some of the serum group systems are even more discriminating than some of the red blood cell groups in making distinctions between humans. The accurate distinction between human beings on the basis of blood groups has become almost a surety and at present is only surpassed by finger printing.

A character that is to be used in paternity evaluation (testing and interpretation) must be simply inherited, its mode of inheritance must be known, and it must be fully developed at birth or soon thereafter and remain unchanged throughout life. The blood groups, assuming proper testing and interpretation, fit these criteria.

Extensive blood grouping of large numbers of families has shown that the antigens of human blood behave predictably and statistics have been accumulated which allow precise calculations concerning the genes which control the inheritance of blood group antigens (1-6).

INHERITANCE OF BLOOD GROUP SYSTEMS

Blood group genes have been shown to be inherited in pairs according to the Mendelian Law, one from each parent. Homozygosity is when both members of the pair are identical, such as AA, KK, Fy^aFy^a. Heterozygosity is when they are different such as OA, Kk, Fy^aFy^b.

Determination of zygosity can be shown in somatic cells in one of the following ways:

1. using a pair of antisera for "allelic" antigens, such as anti-K and anti-k;
2. using comparative titration and scoring technique (7, 8);
3. by the number and location of stained bands separated by electrophoresis;
4. by testing other members in the family.

Paternity testing is done by testing the blood of the alleged father, the child and the mother.

There are three types of exclusions at present in disputed paternity.

Table II.   Chances of Exclusion of Paternity by 24 Blood
Group Systems

| Systems | Chances of Exclusion in % | |
	Each System	Cumulative
1. A-B-0	20	20
2. M-N-S	32	45.6
3. Rh-Hr	29	61.4
4. Kell	4	62.9
5. Duffy	18.4	69.7
6. Kidd	18.7	75.4
7. Lutheran	3.6	76.3
8. P	4	77.2
9. Xg^a	5	78.3
10. Se	4	(I) = 79.2
11. AcP_1	25	25
12. PGM_1	14.5	35.9
13. ADA	5.8	39.6
14. AK	3.3	41.6
15. PGD	2.1	42.8
16. GPT	18.6	(II) = 55.5
17. Gm	20	20
18. Inv	5.7	24.6
19. Hp	18	38.1
20. Gc	16	48
21. C3	13.8	55.2
22. Ag^x	14.3	61.6
23. Tf	1	(III) = 62
24. HL-A	76	(IV) = 76

Grand Cumulative

    I + II = 90.33%   I + III = 92.1%
    I + IV = 95%   I + II + III = 96.3%
    I + II + III + IV = 99.12%

1. Direct exclusion is based on the presence or absence of blood
factors determined by direct examinations:
      a). The child has a blood factor (e.g. C^W) which is not
           present in one or both parents:

           Putative father C^W negative   (exclusion)
           Mother C^W negative
           Child C^W positive

The mother and alleged father both lack the Rh factor C^W; (they are C^W negative.) The child has the antigen C^W; (it is C^W positive.) If it is conceded that the woman is the actual mother, the true father of this child is C^W positive, not C^W negative.

    b). The child lacks a factor that the putative father would have to contribute to his offspring:

Putative father	AB	(exclusion)
Mother	O	
Child	O	

2. Indirect exclusion is based on the inference of homozygous genotypes:
    a). The child has a gene in presumed homozygous state (e.g. KK) which is not present in both parents:

Putative father	kk	(exclusion)
Mother	Kk	
Child	KK	

    b). The child lacks a gene (e.g. K) for which the father is homozygous:

Putative father	KK
Mother	kk
Child	kk

3. A third case of exclusion concerns the linkage between blood groups. Certain of the blood group antigens are determined by closely linked genes which have been shown to segregate almost always in close association. The possibility of exclusion exists when it can be shown from other children of the same couple how the linked antigens are being passed on. This is not a consideration in most paternity cases, but does occur in paternity allegations surrounding divorce suits.

    An exclusion based on linkage in the MNSs system:

	Father		Mother	
	MNSs		MSs	
	Ms·NS		MS·Ms	
Children	#1	#2	#3	#4
	MS·NS	MS·NS	Ms·Ms	Ms·Ns

    In this mating it can be seen from the first three offspring that, so far as the father is concerned, M is transmitted packaged with s, and N with S. Therefore, the MNSs group of the fourth child is such that if the putative father is not excluded, another man must be the father of the first three children. The fourth child has Ms which it obviously received from the mother and must then have received Ns from its father. The alleged father in this case, however, could not have contributed Ns and is therefore not the actual father.

Red Cell Antigen blood group systems that can be employed in paternity testing in addition to ABO, Rh-Hr, MNSs are Kell, Lutheran, Kidd, P and Xg^a: (Anti Xg^a can only exclude men from the paternity of female children. An Xg (a+) man cannot have an Xg(a-) daughter and an Xg(a-) man cannot have an Xg(a+) daughter if the mother is Xg(a-) (1).

Most people's red cells have at least one antigen in each of these systems; however, red blood cells which lack both antigens in the Kell, Lutheran, Duffy and Kidd as well as the S system have been observed in some individuals. These so-called "minus-minus" phenotypes will be discussed later; however, they must be given consideration in the interpretation of exclusion in disputed paternity.

Good, potent antisera for some of these blood factors are not readily available nor are all laboratory personnel familiar with this testing. Therefore, the use of any of the blood groups in problems of parentage, whether legal cases or not, should be done by an expert constantly engaged in such work (2, 9, 10).

INTERPRETATION OF RESULTS

Exceptions to the rules of inheritance are unusual, but errors in interpretation of data can lead to incorrect conclusions. Some problems that may be encountered are as follows:

A. Specificity of reagents. There is probably no such thing as a pure grouping reagent; thus it is important that appropriate quality control measures be used.
B. Physiologic variation. Before interpreting test results one must know if the characteristic is developed in the individual being tested. For example, since the A₁ antigen may not be fully developed at birth, one must be cautious in reporting results on a child less than a year old. The I and i and Lewis antigens should not be used in paternity testing. Other physiologic variations include acquired antigens, effect of disease states on antigens, etc.
C. Genetic variations. An unexpected result in testing a family could be the result of a mutation or a crossing over of closely linked alleles. However, these phenomena are so rare as not to cause a problem. Other phenomena which

may produce unexpected results are chromosomal abnormalities
including aneuploidy, translocation, etc. These usually
are associated with congenital malformations that could be
a tip-off when doing paternity testing and might indicate
that karyotyping should be done (paternity exclusion or
inclusion might be established by the karyotype). One must
also consider the possibility of gene deletions, chimeras
and mosaicism.

D. Specific problems in various blood groups. Exceptions to
    previously well-established blood grouping principles do
    exist and as time goes on, we undoubtedly will recognize
    even more exceptions. Assuming all the antisera are potent
    and specific, there are some "apparent exceptions."

    1. ABO

        a. The Bombay phenotype (O_h). Individuals homozygous
            for the gene h, i.e. hh lack the expected A or B
            antigen which can be found in offspring that are
            heterozygous Hh. However, this blood type is easily
            recognized if the serum of all people involved is
            tested with known A, B and O red blood cells. The
            Bombay phenotype has anti-A, -B and -H in its serum
            and thus will react with normal O cells. Testing
            results are as follows:

Reagent Cell	Serum Bombay	Normal O	Cells Bombay	Normal O	Reagent
A	+++	+++	-	-	Anti-A
B	+++	+++	-	-	Anti-B
O	+++	-	-	-	Anti-AB
			-	+	Anti-H

        b. Weak variants of A & B. A variety of weak antigens
            exist that can only be detected by lack of an ex-
            pected agglutinin, using anti-A, B(O), testing
            secretions, or doing absorption and elution studies.

        c. AB/O individuals. A rare situation in which A & B
            occur on one chromosome.

    2. Rh-Hr.

        The usefulness of the Rh-Hr groups depends on the anti-
        sera available (11). If only anti-D is used, it con-
        tributes very little. The only exclusion is that of
        an Rh_O (D) positive child from a supposed mating of two
        Rh_O (D) negatives (dd x dd) and the frequency of this
        mating is only about 2%. Using anti-C, -D, -E, -c, -e,

-Cw and V, the Rh-Hr system is of great value.

a. Deletion phenomena such as -D-, Rh null, etc.,
    must be considered when anomalous results occur.
    Usually deletion phenotypes can be detected by
    quantitative studies since the D antigen is stronger
    than normal.

b. Depression of antigens may give false results when
    weak antisera are used, e.g. $\bar{\bar{R}}$ ^{N} and (C)D(e) indi-
    viduals appear as -D- but the D is not enhanced.

c. Variations in antigens which will not react with
    supposedly specific antisera, e.g. in Negroes,
    V(ce^s) or VS(e^s) positive individuals will give
    weak or negative reactions with anti-hr" (e). These
    should be tested for by the more sensitive ficin
    technique. Exclusion of paternity in the Negro as
    far as the variants of the Rh e and C antigens are
    concerned must be very carefully evaluated.

3. MNSs

The MNSs is one of the most, if not the most, informa-
tive of all the blood group systems.

a. M^g (12), a very rare antigen which can be detected
    with anti-M^g; but an M^{g}N person will appear as NN
    when using only anti-M & N. Similarly an M^{g}M in-
    dividual tests as MM.

Example in the MN groups when one parent is M-negative
tive, N-positive; the child is N-positive.

	Anti-M	N	M^g	Phenotype	Genotype
Father	0	E	+	N	M^{g}N
Mother	+	0	0	M	MM
Child	+	0	+	M	M^{g}M

Thus, an apparent exclusion on the basis of MM
typing prior to the discovery of the M^g factor becomes invalid if both child and father are M^g positive. The M^g blood type is very rare (1 in 44,000).
This then would not be an exclusion but, on the
contrary, would almost prove paternity. In all MN
exclusions the blood should be tested for the M^g
factor.

b. M^k - similar to M^g but no anti-M^k exists.

      c. S^u - either an allele of S, s, or an inhibitor that suppresses S, s; common in Negroes; responsible for absence of S or s.

4. Minus-Minus Phenotypes

      a. Absence of antigenic expression can result from suppression, deletion, inversion or translocation, an amorph, or because of an antigen present for which the defining antibody has not been found. Examples include p, Lu(a-b-, K_0, JK(a-b-), Fy(a-b-). The possibility of these rare so-called "minus-minus" phenotypes must be given consideration in interpretation of exclusion in disputed paternities, on the second principle (i.e. a child must not lack a factor which the father must pass on).

ERYTHROCYTE ENZYMES IN PATERNITY TESTING (13-18)

Hopkinson's demonstration that hemolysates of human erythrocytes contained a polymorphic enzyme system, red cell acid phosphatase, introduced a new group of markers (Table III) for investigation of populations and families. To be useful in paternity testing, an enzyme system must:

1. be discriminating; i.e. it must exist in a population with variation between unrelated individuals;
2. have a well-documented inheritance pattern;
3. be stable enough so that reproducible results can be obtained on testings;
4. be well-developed at the time the test is performed.

Red cell acid phosphatase, of which the function is unknown, has five genetic variants which exist as codominant alleles at one autosomal locus. The variants p^A, p^B, p^C, p^R, and p^D identified on starch gel in family studies have so far not shown any deviation from normal Mendelian inheritance patterns.

Phosphoglucomutase (PGM). The genetic variants are controlled by three separate loci which are not closely linked. Family studies and mother-child pairing indicate that the isoenzymes of each loci exist as codominant alleles and follow simple Mendelian inheritance.

Glutamic pyruvic transaminase (GPT), an aminotransferase, has six codominant alleles at a single locus. This enzyme has great potential in paternity studies but its use depends on testing fresh specimens because of its instability.

Glucose-6-phosphate dehydrogenase (G6PD) is a useful poly-

Table III. Population Data - Red Cell Enzymes (5)

Population	Number Tested	Phenotype Distribution			Gene Frequencies	
Adenosine Deaminase (ADA)		1-1	2-1	2-1	ADA^1	ADA^2
Caucasian						
Seattle	168	152	16	0	0.95	0.05
Negro						
Seattle	186	178	6	0	0.98	0.02
Adenylate Kinase (AK)		1-1	2-1	2-2	AK^1	AK^2
Caucasian						
Seattle	172	163	9	0	0.9738	0.0262
Chicago	1311	1193	118	0	0.9529	0.0471
Ann Arbor	254	240	14	0	0.9724	0.0276
Negro						
Seattle	223	220	3	0	0.9939	0.0061
Chicago	1062	1049	13	0	0.9933	0.0067
Ann Arbor	139	135	4	0	0.9856	0.0144
6 Phosphogluconate Dehydrogenase (6-PGD)		AA	AC	CC	PGD^A	PGD^C
Caucasian						
Chicago	600	554	45	1	0.961	0.039
Chicago	58	57	1	0	0.983	0.017
Buffalo	1377	1313	62	2	0.976	0.024
Seattle	647	623	24	0	0.981	0.019
Negro						
Chicago	416	385	31	0	0.961	0.039
Chicago	296	278	18	0	0.970	0.030
Buffalo	1224	1141	83	2	0.965	0.035
Seattle	507	452	52	3	0.961	0.039

Table III(continued)

Population	Number Tested	Phenotype Distribution			Gene Frequencies	
		1-1	2-1	2-2	PGM_1^1	PGM_1^2
Phosphoglucomutase (PGM)						
Caucasian						
Seattle	429	287	116	26	0.752	0.228
San Francisco	271	164	94	13	0.777	0.223
Negro						
Seattle	654	428	202	24	0.809	0.191
San Francisco	284	184	89	11	0.805	0.195
Ann Arbor	202	143	53	6	0.841	0.169
					PGM_2^1	PGM_2^2
Caucasian						
Seattle	508	508	0	0	1.00	0.0
San Francisco	271	271	0	0	1.00	0.0
Negro						
Seattle	653	649	4	0	0.996	0.004
San Francisco	284	282	2	0	0.996	0.004
Ann Arbor	202	201	1	0	0.997	0.003

Population	Number Tested	Phenotype Distribution								
		AA	AB	BB	AC	BC	CC	RA	RB	BD
Acid Phosphatase (P)										
Caucasian										
Seattle	193	33	76	61	13	10	0	0	0	0
Negro										
Ann Arbor	224	12	50	160	2	0	0	0	1	0
Texas	294	11	100	166	1	7	0	1	1	2

Table III(continued)

Population		p^A	p^B	p^C	p^R	p^D
			Gene Frequencies			
Acid Phosphatase (P)						
Caucasian						
Seattle		0.394	0.547	0.059	0.0	0.0
Negro						
Ann Arbor		0.17	0.82	0.01	0.0	0.0
Texas		0.21	0.76	0.76	0.012	0.003

morphism when testing Negroes or individuals of Mediterranean origin. This enzyme is X-linked so interpretation is only valid on female children.

Hemoglobin, though not an enzyme, is a polymorphic protein fround in erythrocyte hemolysates. The decision whether or not to look for a variant hemoglobin depends on the race of the individuals being studied and the age of the child. It is obvious that when 99+ percent of a Caucasian population is HbA, the likelihood of discriminating between putative fathers is nil while if one studies Negroes having an incidence of HbS of 8-11% the chance of obtaining useful information is excellent. The age of the child is important when using Hb, since Hb-F may be present for several months after birth.

SERUM PROTEINS IN PATERNITY TESTING

The first serum protein polymorphism was observed in 1955 by Smithies, studying starch gel electrophoresis of haptoglobin (19). The existence of polymorphisms among serum proteins (Table IV) makes them potentially useful in establishing non-paternity. These characteristics, like blood group factors, vary in frequency depending on the ethnic origin of the individual being tested. Interpretation of protein studies depends on a knowledge of their genetics, physiologic function, anthropologic distribution, and the variation that occurs due to the method used (16, 20-23).

Many serum proteins have variant forms but often these occur with such low frequency that they are not useful discriminators or are useful only in specific ethnic groups. Included in this group are albumin, ceruloplasmin, and transferrin. For example, there are at least eight variant forms of albumin, however, in Caucasian populations variants occur with a frequency of less than 1 in 10,000 and would be of little use in routine paternity testing (24). In certain Amerindian populations such variants have a much higher frequency (albumin Mexico is seen in 7.3% of Pimas, albumin Naskapi in 4% of Ojibwas) and are useful markers.

Ceruloplasmin, the copper-binding protein, has little variance in Caucasians but shows polymorphism in about 4% of Negroes and therefore can be useful in some instances.

Transferrin, the iron-binding beta globulin, is also of use in certain Amerindian groups and in Negroes but is of little value in Caucasians.

The two serum proteins which we routinely use in paternity testing because of their widespread variance are Gc and Haptoglobin. Group specific component (Gc) exhibits three distinct phenotypes.

Table IV. Population Data - Serum Proteins (5)

Group Specific Component (Gc)

Population	Number Tested	Phenotype Distribution			Gene Frequencies	
		1-1	2-1	2-2	Gc^1	Gc^2
Caucasian New York	86	47	35	6	0.74	0.26
Negro New York	120	97	22	1	0.90	0.10

Ceruloplasmin (Cp)

Population	Number Tested	Phenotype Distribution					Gene Frequencies		
		AA	AB	BB	AC	BC	CpA	CpB	CpC
Caucasian United States	334	0	4	330	0	0	0.006	0.994	0.0
Negro United States	576	2	56	514	1	3	0.053	0.944	0.003

Haptoglobin (Hp)

Population	Number Tested	Phenotype Distribution					Gene Frequencies		
		1-1	2-1	2-2	2-1M	2-2M	Hp^1	Hp^2	Hp^{2M}
Caucasian Seattle	409	54	206	149	0	0	0.394	0.616	0.0
Negro Seattle	1657	472	641	307	181	56	0.552	0.349	0.199

Transferrin (Tf)

Population	Number Tested	Phenotype Distribution					Gene Frequencies		
		DD	CD	CC	CB	BB	TfD	TfC	TfB
Caucasian Canadian	425	0	0	420	5	0	0.0	0.98	0.02
United States	471	0	0	465	6	0	0.0	0.98	0.02
Negro New York	99	1	9	89	0	0	0.101	0.899	0.0
California	48	0	6	42	0	0	0.125	0.875	0.0

In U.S. Caucasians, the Gc^1 allele has a frequency of about 0.7 and the Gc^2 allele about 0.3. In U.S. Negroes, the frequency of Gc^1 increases to about 0.9 and Gc^2 drops to 0.1. In both cases, the distribution of the three phenotypes, 1-1, 1-2, 2-2, is large enough to provide a useful marker.

Another serum protein is the alpha-2 glycoprotein - haptoglobin (Hp). This highly polymorphic protein has the property of forming complexes with hemoglobin.

Gm and Inv; -Gm factors are due to peptide variations of the heavy chain portion of the IgG molecule. Inv factors are due to differences in the structure of the kappa light chains of the Ig molecules. These two systems of allotypic markers are not linked. Two other systems involving the Ig molecules have also been described - the Am marker which is linked to Gm and the Isf marker which is inherited independently.

At the present time about 18 well-defined Gm factors and 3 Inv factors have been described (25-28). The Gm factors are not distributed at random, but occur in defined combinations which vary by race. These gene complexes have been called phenogroups, allogroups or haplotypes. (Most authorities now use this latter term which is also used to designate the combinations of HL-A factors inherited as units.) Table V shows the common haplotypes and their approximately frequencies for Caucasians, Negroes and Orientals. The data used are from several sources. The frequency of Inv(1) positive individuals is also variable between races with 10-20% of Caucasians, 50% of Negroes and 60% of Orientals being positive.

The age of the individuals tested is also of importance. Children under 4-6 months of age have predominantly maternal IgG, and therefore the Gm phenotype obtained may reflect the presence of maternal IgG.

HL-A ANTIGENS IN PATERNITY TESTING

HL-A is potentially of great usefulness in paternity testing since there are at least eight LA factors and 13 Four factors; thus more than 104 haplotypes are possible with about 8000 genotypes and 4000 phenotypes (29-32). There is a relatively low frequency of each allele in populations studied to date and a marked difference between populations of different ethnic background.

There are many methods for determining HL-A antigens. Most utilize either agglutination of leukocytes, cytotoxicity of lymphocytes, or complement fixation by platelets. In doing these tests,

Table V. Common Gm Haplotypes and Frequencies in Various Populations

Gm Haplotypes			Caucasian	Negro	Orientals	
IgG_3	IgG_1	IgG_2			Japanese	Chinese
-b1Pab5 Ray b3b0	f--	n+	0.52	0.00	0.00	0.00
-b1Pab5 Ray b3b0	f--	n-	0.17	0.00	0.00	0.00
g-Pa- Ray --	za-	n-	0.20	0.00	0.47	0.23
g-Pa- Ray --	zax	n-	0.10	0.00	0.17	0.09
-b1Pab5 Ray b3b0	za-	n-	<0.01	0.55	<0.01	<0.01
-b1Pa-c5 c3b0	za-	n-	<0.01	0.25	0.00	0.00
-b1Pab5 Ray c3b0	za-	n-	0.00	0.08	0.00	0.00
--sb5 Ray b3b0	za-	n-	0.00	0.12	0.00	0.00
--stb5 Ray b3b0	za-	n-	<0.01	0.00	0.28	0.06
-b1Pab5 Ray b3b0	fa-	n+	0.00	0.00	0.08	0.62

one is dependent on utilizing fresh samples with intact white
cells (platelet CF is an exception) and the availability of well-
defined antisera. This latter factor is a major limitation of HL-A
typing in paternity studies.

ESTIMATION OF THE LIKELIHOOD OF PATERNITY

Biostatistics are not required when there is a positive evidence for exclusion of paternity. However, using biostatistics
it is possible to determine the confidence of a non-exclusion and
to assess the likelihood of paternity.

The confidence of a non-exclusion depends on the number of
genetic markers used in the testing, the frequency of those genetic
markers, and the genetic pattern of a given mother-child combination.
In general, a 95% or greater confidence is considered as statistically significant. Although such a high value may be achieved by
using a large number of genetic markers, it is impractical at least
at the present time; the use of selected genetic markers and the
consideration of the genetic pattern of a given mother-child combination may improve such a confidence. In order to accomplish
this goal, one must be familiarized with the chances of exclusion
by each blood group specificity or system (A) and by the genetic
pattern of a given mother-child combination (B).

The likelihood of paternity can never be entirely certain.
However, if the child and the alleged father share one or several
genetic markers and the chance of their being such a coincidence
is less than one in one thousand or even in a million; the man
admits his involvement and a positive assignment of paternity can
be made. The likelihood of paternity is being used in many European
countries. Again, in most cases, the chances are much greater
than one in one thousand but can be evaluated. The estimation of
likelihood can be based on the genetic pattern of a given mother-
child combination (B) alone or in conjunction with a comparison
between a random man and the alleged father (C).

Three applications of biostatistics in parentage problems are
as follows:

A)   For estimation of the chances of exclusion of paternity by
     each blood group specificity of system or a combination
     of several systems;
B)   For estimation of the chances of plausibility or exclusion
     of paternity for a given mother-child genetic pattern;
C)   As in B, except the blood group pattern of the alleged
     father is taken into consideration.

Many complicated and useful mathematical schemes have been

developed to calculate the likelihood that an accused male is in fact the father of the child in question. Unfortunately many of these mathematical formulas are given without mentioning the logic behind them nor giving an actual example, and are difficult to follow. Dr. Chang Lee has developed a very simplified approach which is easy to follow (33).

Evidence concerning the possibility that the putative father is the real father is not admissible in the court of law. However, as in the following case it is possible to calculate the probability of paternity and to show that the chances are so small of the putative father not being the actual father, that he can in all probability be considered the actual father.

	A	B	C	D	E	c	e	M	N	S	s	Fy^a	Jk^a	Jk^b	Kp^a
Father	0	+	0	+	+	+	+	+	+	+	+	+	+	+	+
Mother	0	0	0	0	0	+	+	+	0	0	+	0	+	+	0
Child	0	+	0	+	+	+	+	+	+	+	+	+	0	+	+

The blood types of mother and child being what they are, only .01% (1 in every 10,000) men have blood types such that they could father this child. This constitutes very strong evidence, though not proof, that this man is actually the father of this child.

Although this type of evidence might be given in an advisory opinion and it might at present even be used to assure the father that he is indeed responsible, it has not yet become an established legal precedent. However it should be acceptable as evidence (weighty evidence at that) and in the future may figure more prominently in court than it has in the past.

Using these techniques of applied genetics, paternity testing has already become an integral part of affiliation litigations in Massachusetts (34). The laws of Massachusetts (Massachusetts Blood Grouping Test statute: G.L. (Ter. Ed.) c. 273, & 12A, enacted by St. 1954, c. 232) state the court shall order the mother, her child and the defendant to submit to blood grouping tests to determine whether or not the defendant can be excluded as being the father of the child. The results of such tests shall be admissible as evidence only in cases where definite paternal exclusion has been established. If one of the parties refuses to comply with the order of the court, this is also admissible evidence in court. This appears to be just, because the court is limiting the admissibility of evidence to those cases where there is a positive exclusion, as it is not yet possible to definitely identify the putative father as the actual father.

REFERENCES

1. Race, R.R. and Sanger, R., Blood groups in man, ed. 1-5,
    F.A. Davis, Philadelphia, (1968).

2. Sussman, L.N., "Blood Grouping Tests. Medico-Legal Uses,"
    Charles C. Thomas, Springfield (1968).

3. Konugres, A.A. and Polesky, H.F., Use of blood groups in pat-
    ernity testing, in "Paternity Testing," Amer. Soc. Clin. Pathol.,
    H.F. Polesky (ed.), Chicago (1975), p. 1.

4. Schatkin, S.B., "Disputed Paternity Proceedings," 4th Ed.,
    M. Bender, New York (1967).

5. Polesky, H.F., "Paternity Testing," Amer. Soc. Clin. Pathol,
    Chicago (1975).

6. Weiner, A.S., "Blood Groups and Transfusion," 3rd ed., Charles
    C. Thomas, Springfield (1943).

7. Sussman, L.N., Titration and scoring in disputed parentage.
    Transfusion 5:248 (1965).

8. Polesky, H.F., Pitfalls in paternity testing. Laboratory
    Medicine, in "Paternity Testing," Amer. Soc. Clin. Pathol.,p. 28,
    H.F. Polesky (ed.), Chicago (1975).

9. Weiner, A.S., Problems and pitfalls in blood grouping tests for
    non-parentage. 1. Distribution of the blood groups. Amer. J.
    Clin. Pathol. 41:9 (1969).

10. Weiner, A.S., Problems and pitfalls in blood grouping tests for
    disputed parentage. III. Chances of proving non-paternity by
    blood grouping tests when the putative father is dead. Acta
    Genet. Med. Gemmellol 18:285 (1969).

11. Boyd, W.C., Compact tubular presentation of mother-child-alleged
    father combinations which establish non-paternity in the Rh blood
    group system, Vox. Sang. (OS) 5:99 (1955).

12. Allen, F.H., Corcoran, P.A., Kenton, H.B. et al, Mg, a new blood
    group antigen in the MNS system. Vox. Sang. 3:81 (1958).

13. Hopkinson, D.A., Spencer, N. and Harris, H., Red cell acid
    phosphatase variants: a new human polymorphism, Nature 199:969
    (1963).

14. Harris, H., Enzyme polymorphisms in man, Proc. Roy. Soc. Lond.
    164:298 (1966).

15. Fuhrman, W., and Lichte, K.H., Human red cell acid phosphatase polymorphism: a study on gene frequency and forensic use of the system in cases of disputed paternity. Humangenetik 3:121 (1966).

16. Giblett, E.R.,"Genetic Markers in Human Blood," F.A. Davis, Philadelphia (1969).

17. Monn, E., Application of the phosphoglucomutase (PGM) system of human red cells in paternity cases. Vox. Sang. 16:211 (1969).

18. Broman, P., Grundin, R. and Lins, P.E., The red cell acid phosphatase polymorphism in Sweden: gene frequencies and application to disputed paternity. Acta Genet. Med. Gemollol.20:77 (1971).

19. Smithies, O., Zone electrophoresis in starch gels; group variations in the serum proteins of normal human adults, Biochem. J. 61:629 (1955).

20. Allison, A.C. and Blumberg, B.S., An isoprecipitation reaction distinguishing human serum protein types, Lancet 1:634 (1961).

21. Butler, R., Isoantigenicity of human plasma proteins, in "Bibliotheca Haematologica" No. 31, S. Karger, Basel (1969).

22. Prokop, O., Human Blood and Serum Groups, Wiley Interscience, 1969.

23. Schultz, H.E. and Hermans, J.F.,"Molecular Biology of Human Proteins," Vol. 1., Elsevier, Amsterdam (1966) p. 173.

24. Weitkamp, L.R., An electrophoretic comparison of human serum albumin variants: Eight distinguishable types. Human Heredity 19:159, 1969.

25. Bulletin of the World Health Organization, 35:953 (1966).

26. Steinberg, A.G., Globulin polymorphisms in man. Ann. Rev. Genet. 3:25 (1969).

27. Grubb, R., "The Genetic Markers of Human Immunoglobulins," Springer-Verla , New York (1970).

28. Ellis, F.R., Camp, F.R. and Litwin, S.D., "Application of Gm Typing to Paternity Exclusion," AABB 23rd Ann. Meet., San Francisco (1970).

29. Allen, F., Corcoran, P.A., Kenton, H.B. et al, Joint report of Fourth International Histocompatibility Workshop, in

"Histocompatibility Testing," P.I. Terasaki (ed.), Munksgaard, Copenhagen, p. 17 (1970).

30. Kissmeyer-Nielsen, F., Genetics of the HL-A system in a seminar on histocompatibility testing. Amer. Assoc. Blood Banks, p. 7-20 (1970).

31. Walford, R.L., A seminar on histocompatibility testing, Amer. Assoc. Blood Banks, p. 37 (1970).

32. Histocompatibility Testing 1972. Munksgaard.

33. Lee, C.L., Estimation of the likelihood of paternity, in "Paternity Testing," Amer. Soc. Clin. Pathol., p. 28, H.F. Polesky (ed.), Chicago (1975).

34. Lombard, J.F., Family law, adoption, paternity and blood tests, Massachusetts Practice, 1:part 2, (1967).

DISCUSSION

Papers of Prof. D.P. Goldstein, Mr. J.M. Healey, and Dr. A. Konugres
Moderator: Prof. G.J. Annas

R. MARKS: University of California: It seems to me that Prof. Goldstein goes further than assuring that there will be no negative diseases or negative genetic characteristics passed on to the off-spring. Is that a correct assumption on my part?

GOLDSTEIN: We do make every effort to screen our donor, as much as possible. We do not go to any extraordinary measures. We take a family history and prefer to have donors who have fathered normal children as a sign of some genetic stability.

MARKS: Men who are all admitted to medical school?

GOLDSTEIN: No. That happens to be a selection based on our availability and on the availability of people with whom we deal. One might choose even law school if we were in that type of environment.

MARKS: What I am suggesting is that there was a shift from the discussion this morning. We were talking about therapeutic or preventive medicine and approaching the possibilities at least of social engineering. I wonder if randomly selected children are not in part what the American family has coming and do not deserve, rather than in the sense of having children that will live up to their hopes. I mean I am getting into some deeper philosophical issues, but you frighten me slightly.

GOLDSTEIN: No, I don't think any attempt is made to carry out any type of selection on the basis of which you outlined. The job as a physician is to get the woman pregnant in the most expeditious way possible, and that may include donor insemination. But our selection of donors is because of their availability and we just try to match the donor to the husband rather than the wife, which I feel is more appropriate. There is, I am sure, a certain selectivity, but it is not a conscious one in the sense that we do not try to breed an unusually fine child. We are trying to really just achieve pregnancy in that individual patient.

STEINBERG: One of the things that has worried me about artificial insemination by donor is the possibility of half-sib mating because the donor is anonymous and the family is anonymous. What efforts are made to take a migratory donor so that his children (because you have mentioned selection of donors who have one or two normal children of their own) and the children sired through artificial insemination with his sperm are not apt to marry?

GOLDSTEIN: We do not take any precautions. You cannot with
the type of world we are living in where people are moving around
so extensively. It is impossible to do that. I do not think the
possibility you raised is practical, or really in probability
very likely either.

M. LEVINE: Harbor General Hospital, Torrance, California:
Mr. Healey, you briefly alluded to the problem of AID without a
husband's consent. What actually would be the legal rights or
the legal responsibilities of that husband should his wife go and
have AID without his consent and then deliver?

HEALEY: There has never been a case dealing with that exact
problem. Some of those annulment cases involved situations where
a legal bond between husband and wife still existed, but there was
a separation. Those situations dealt more with the concept of AID
itself than it did with the husband's responsibility. I do not
really know what you would do with that particular problem. They
certainly could say the husband had no obligation at all in that
situation or they could say that if this pregnancy occurred in a
marriage, a strong assumption of legitimacy should carry and,
therefore, the child shall carry the rights of all other children.

GOLDSTEIN: In a situation like that I'd say the physician
would be considered to have done a very poor job, because it is
very important to have AID a couple-based experience. I would
personally be very hesitant to perform AID in any woman where the
husband was not participating to some extent by sharing the responsibility.

SHAW: Would you consider inseminating a single female?

GOLDSTEIN. This is a very different world and I think the
women have rights that they never had before, and particularly the
single girl. I think it is entirely possible that a single woman
might wish to be inseminated, although I think the natural route
might be preferable.

M. STEELE: University of Pittsburgh, Pennsylvania: Mr.
Healey, I learned with some horror that I practice in a state that
does not have one of those nice statutes. Since I could suggest
several instances of AID could you not leave me hanging here about
what exactly in Pennsylvania or other states is the legality of
AID? What is the status of the children when parents are married?

HEALEY: Without any legislation or any court determination,
it remains an open issue before the law. Certainly we hope that
as each state deals with the problem they will follow what other
states have done, and affirm legitimacy of such a child, and also
to recognize AID as medical practice and something that can be

performed by the licensed physician within the state. But I really
do not know. Has there been an attempt in your state to have such
a law passed? Has it been defeated?

STEELE: I am not aware at all. Do you suggest we just go
along as we are and suggest it when it seems to be appropriate?

HEALEY: My preference is never to leave such issues open to
the court's determination when it is possible to have the legislature deal with them. Nobody expected for example, that Dr. Edelin's
case would ever turn out the way that it did.

P. SIERSMA: Western Massachusetts Family Planning Council:
I am aware of several single women who are desirous of having
children. They are not married and not involved in relationships
with men. Due to the prejudice of the medical community around us,
(some of which has been reflected on the panel) there is a considerable black market of underground sperm donors desiring to be kept
anonymous, and whose anonimity is desired by the women concerned.
What is the legal status of the woman seeking this kind of practice?
Can she be in some sense brought before the law for practicing
medicine outside the law? What are the rights of the child in this
case to knowledge of its genetic heritage? Is the mother to be held
for concealing information directly relative to the child's life
and happiness?

HEALEY: Firstly, no one has a legal right to tell a physician
to provide any sort of health care service. Hence, it cannot be
said that any woman has a right, single or otherwise, to be inseminated. Secondly, with respect to status of a woman, did you say
she came from Oklahoma?

SIERSMA: No, Western Massachusetts.

HEALEY: I have been handed a card in the interim that in Oklahoma single women have been inseminated, but no cases have occurred
so far. I do not know. Again, in the absence of any formulation
by either the state legislature or by the court, their status is in
limbo. With respect to children, we talked a little earlier today
about the whole concept of wrongful life suits. To my knowledge,
none has ever been brought in an AID case, but certainly there is
potential there as there is in any reproductive situation.

P. LEVINE: Ortho Research Foundation, New Jersey: The remark
was made that in artificial insemination the donor should be matched
to that of the husband. That could lead to serious consequences.
Suppose the woman is Rh negative and she has previously had a
transfusion. It would be very dangerous to use an Rh positive
donor. One must use an Rh negative donor. In the case of a Group
O woman whose husband is a Group A, if you use a Group A donor, you

run the risk of inducing AO hemolytic disease of the newborn.
So in all cases the rule should be to match the donor to that of
the mother.

The other point I want to indicate is that the blood test as
done in the United States does not do justice to the individual.
This is my conclusion after years of personal experience and
knowledge of what is being done in the European institutes for
medico-legal work. They have expertise to handle all of these
numerous differences because a number of disciplines are involved,
whereas not one institution in the U.S. has experts in all these
areas. I am aware of the fact that there is something being done
to employ other genetic markers, but this is only a very poor
beginning. What we have to do is encourage the organization of
Institutes of Forensic Medicine.

L. SCHACHT: Minnesota Department of Health: Dr. Konugres
talked about paternity exclusion. In our experience we do have a
percentage in which maternity has been excluded. Have you run into
this, where the mother is not the mother of the child?

KONUGRES: There must be another explanation for this. You
would have to look closer at your findings and you'd have to take
into consideration some of the minor blood types, and I'd be glad to
discuss this with you further. There are some apparent genetic
exceptions, but they are in fact, not exceptions. You have to do
further testing.

SCHACHT: No, these have been done! We sent them to Dr.
Levine and he substantiated these. What we have done is to trace
these to mix-ups in the hospital. We have traced this down to the
hospital where on the day the child was born there were four
mothers all with the same last name! We have about five such
similar cases.

KONUGRES: Then I think the hospital record has to be looked at.

GENETIC COUNSELING FOR COUPLES WHO ARE FIRST COUSINS

Lewis B. Holmes

Harvard Medical School and Genetics Clinic

Massachusetts General Hospital, Boston

It is general knowledge that parents should not be related to each other. This is based in part on hearsay information which suggests that related parents are more likely than unrelated couples to have mentally retarded offspring. The legislatures in most states in the United States have passed laws which prohibit marriage between first cousins (1). Consanguinity is rare in the United States; less than 1 in 1,000 couples are first cousins. Yet, each year several couples who are first cousins come to our Genetics Clinic for information about their risks of having abnormal or handicapped children. These consultations have prompted us to review the data available for defining the magnitude of the risk faced by these couples. While several studies have been conducted on the effects of inbreeding (2), it is difficult to translate this data to information useful to these couples. The information available can be summarized as follows:

First, every person has several rare lethal recessive genes. As one can prove the presence of only a few of these genes by testing healthy persons, parents usually learn that each is a "carrier" or heterozygous for the same rare harmful recessive gene only after having a homozygous, affected child.

Second, all healthy couples have a 3 to 4% chance each child will have a serious birth defect. About 2% of newborns are found in the first week of life to have a congenital malformation that is considered serious because of either its surgical or cosmetic complications (3). Additional handicapping problems, such as malformations, hearing loss, slow development, seizures and the like, become evident in subsequent years.

Third, parents who have common ancestors are much more likely to have a rare lethal or harmful recessive gene in common. The co-efficient of consanguinity for the children of parents who are first cousins is 1/16, meaning the chance the child is homozygous for one of four genes present in his or her two grandparents. This is illustrated in Figure 1. The boy in generation IV has a 1/8 probability he has inherited gene A from his father (the chance he inherited the gene from his father is 1/2 X the chance his father inherited the gene from his grandmother is 1/2 X the chance his grandmother inherited the gene from her father is 1/2(or 1/2 X 1/2 X 1/2 = 1/8); this boy also has a 1/8 probability he inherited gene A from his mother. Therefore, the chance he has inherited the same abnormal autosomal recessive gene from both parents is 1/64 (or 1/8 X 1/8). The boy has a similar chance of inheriting the other 3 alleles B, C and D at the same genetic locus, which means his risk of being homozygous for one allele at this locus is 1/16 (or 1/64 + 1/64 + 1/64 + 1/64).

Fourth, the critical question for parents who are first cousins is how much does their risk exceed the baseline risk of 3 to 4% that each child will have a serious birth defect. We have found

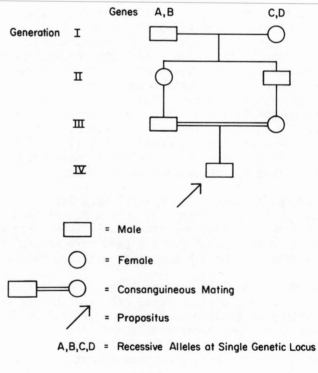

Figure 1

two studies which help answer this question (4, 5). The study of 218 children born of first cousins in a north Sweden isolate showed a higher incidence of genetic disorders than was found in a control sample (4) (Table I). Nineteen percent of the children of parents who were first cousins had a genetic disorder or mental deficiency in comparison to 8% among controls. However, the conditions listed are so heterogeneous it would be difficult to obtain convincing uniformity in the evaluation of "controls".

Table I

EMPIRIC RISKS - OFFSPRING OF PARENTS WHO ARE FIRST COUSINS

I. North Swedish Isolate (Annals Hum. Genet. 21:191, 1957)

	Cousin Children	Control Children
Genetic Disorders (including 6 with schizophrenia)	16/218 (7%)	8/165 (5%)
Mental Deficiency	9	2
Other	16	3
	41/218 (19%)	13/165 (8%)

II. Japanese Newborns 1948-1954 (Amer. J. Hum. Genet. 10:398, 1958)

Major Congenital Defects: 1.02% Non-consang. Parents

1.42 Consang. Parents

The study of major congenital malformations among Japanese newborns from 1948 to 1954 showed that the incidence was 1.42% among newborns of consanguineous parents in comparison to 1.02% for newborns of non-consanguineous parents.

Fifth, we hope that more data will soon be available to use for counseling consanguineous couples. At the present time we explain the nature of their theoretical risk and discuss the data that is available. We indicate their risk that each child will have a serious birth defect maybe as high as 6 to 8%. We stress the need for more precise data. In our experience most couples are surprised the risks are so low and are reassured by this information.

REFERENCES

1. Farrow, M.G. and Juberg, R.C., Genetics and laws prohibiting marriage in the United States. J.A.M.A. 209:534 (1969).

2. Fraser, G.R. and Mayo, O., Genetical load in man, Humangenetik 23:83 (1974).

3. Holmes, L.B., Inborn errors of morphogenesis. A review of localized hereditary malformations. New Eng. J. Med. 291: 763 (1974).

4. Book, J.A., Genetical investigations in a North Swedish population. Ann. Hum. Genet. 21:191 (1957).

5. Neel, J.V., A study of major congenital defects in Japanese infants. Amer. J. Hum. Genet. 10:398 (1958).

STATE CHANNELING OF GENE FLOW BY REGULATION OF MARRIAGE AND PROCREATION

Seymour Lederberg

Division of Biological and Medical Sciences

Brown University, Rhode Island

GENETIC CHANNELING

The genetic makeup of an individual is dependent on the genotypes of the germ cells from whose fusion he arose. The number of
different genes we carry in each cell is unknown, but is roughly
estimated at between 10,000 and 100,000. Each gene may have more
than one form called an allele so that we refer arbitrarily to a
standard or wild-type allele and variant allele of a given gene.
Our body or somatic cells generally have two representatives of
each gene, one on each member of a chromosome pair. A person
whose alleles for a given gene differ from each other is termed
heterozygous for that gene, whereas when the alleles are the same,
the person is termed homozygous wild-type or variant. This simple
picture is marred by two exceptions: male humans having only one
X chromosome have only one representation of the genes of that
chromosome, and in either sex some genes may be duplicated extensively.

Our genes, both wild-type and variant, taken collectively,
make up our gene pool. In large populations, the frequency of the
different alleles of a given gene is determined by mutation from
one allelic form to another, by the relative viability of gametes
and zygotes bearing a given allelic form, and by the differential
viability through sexual maturity which a given allele will allow
by any differential in reproductive behavior among bearers of
different alleles. The frequency of different alleles is not only
modified by these physiological and psychological sources of selection, but also by political, cultural, and economic factors which
imports and exports genes from one set of selection conditions to
another through migration of people. Finally, gene frequency is

247

further affected by sampling processes which become important
when the number of individuals who can mate is reduced by geograph-
ical, social or behavioral restraints.

Assortative matings occur when parents are sorted and mated
according to their genetic or phenotypic similarity. The effect
is to increase the frequency of the homozygous genotypes at the
expense of the heterozygous genotype. Inbreeding among related
individuals is an example of genetic assortative mating. Here,
homozygosity at all gene sites is favored. When assortative
mating is based on similar phenotypes, such as pigmentation or
extreme height, those genes responsible for these traits and closely linked ones progress to homozygosity. Political, legal, and
societal factors which reduce or channel the mating opportunities
for people with a given phenotype or genotype will create assortative mating systems among the remaining individuals.

STATE AUTHORITY TO CONTROL GENETIC CHANNELING BY REGULATING
MARRIAGE

Economic, social, property, moral, and medical interests in
the marital relation have elicited corresponding legislative regulation, some of which have collateral consequences to gene flow
from one generation to the next. The origin of state authority
in this area is its police power, derived from the Tenth Amendment
to the Bill of Rights of the United States Constitution (1). Legal
commentators have pointed out the infrequency of Supreme Court
review of state regulation of matrimony and of the restrictions of
classes of people who may marry (2, 3).

In Reynolds v. United States (4), the Supreme Court upheld
the power of Congress to prohibit the practice of bigamy in the
Territories over an appeal to the constitutional guarantee of
religious freedom. Speaking for the Court, Justice Waite gave an
account of the odious status of polygamy from early England on
and capped this with allusions to the importance of marriage (5).
Marriage, provided it was not bigamous, was again extolled in
Murphy v. Ramsey (6), where the Court coupled its support for
disenfranchisement of a bigamist in the Territory of Utah with
the pronouncement that

For certainly no legislation can be supposed more whole-
some and necessary in the founding of a free, self-
governing commonwealth, fit to take rank as one of the coordinate States of the Union, than that which seeks to
establish it on the basis of the idea of the family,
as consisting in and springing from the union for life
of one man and one woman in the holy estate of matrimony;
the sure foundation of all that is stable and noble in
our civilization, the best guaranty of that reverent

morality which is the source of all beneficent progress
in social and political improvement. And to this end,
no means are more directly and immediately suitable than
those provided by this Act, which endeavors to withdraw
all political influence from those who are practically
hostile to its attainment (7).

More specific identification of the breadth of legislative
regulatory authority over marriage was developed in Maynard v.
Hill (8) when the Supreme Court in upholding the authority of a
legislature to grant divorce to a husband without notice of
application or knowledge of the legislative divorce given to
the wife, went on to affirm that:

Marriage, as creating the most important relation in
life, as having more to do with the morals and civilization of a people than any other institution, has always
been subject to the control of the Legislature. That
body prescribes the age at which parties may contract
to marry, the procedure or form essential to constitute
marriage, the duties and obligations it creates, its effects
upon the property rights of both, present and prospective,
and the acts which may constitute grounds for its dissolu-
tion (9).

AFFIRMATION OF STATE AUTHORITY TO REGULATE PROCREATION

Early in this century a Supreme Court decision emerged with
profound impact on the authority of the State to regulate the
ability of an individual to establish a family. The Court in
Jacobson v. Massachusetts (10) dealt with a challenge to the constitutionality of a state compulsory vaccination statute which
provided that the board of health of a city or town, if necessary
for the public health or safety, shall require vaccination or
revaccination of all the inhabitants; a fine of $5 was applied for
noncompliance, but children who were deemed by a physician to be
unfit for vaccination were excepted. The purpose of the compulsory
vaccination was to reduce the incidence of cases of smallpox
which would be an infectious hazard to the public at large. Curiously, individuals who acquiesced to the vaccination would themselves be protected so the real penalty to the dissenting individual (as compared to the statutory penalty of $5) would be his
failure to develop immune resistance to the disease. Upholding
the authority of the State, Justice Harlan affirmed for the Court
that:

The authority of the state to enact this statute is to
be referred to what is commonly called the police power,--
a power which the state did not surrender when becoming a

member of the Union under the Constitution. Although
this court has refrained from any attempt to define the
limits of that power, yet it has distinctly recognized
the authority of a state to enact quarantine laws and
"health laws of every description;" indeed, all laws that
relate to matters completely within its territory and
which do not by their necessary operation affect the
people of other states. According to settled principles,
the police power of a state must be held to embrace, at
least, such reasonable regulations established directly
by legislative enactment as will protect the public
health and the public safety (11). And further
the defendant insists... that a compulsory vaccination
law is unreasonable, arbitrary, and oppressive, and,
therefore, hostile to the inherent right of every freeman
to care for his own body and health in such way as to
him seems best; and that the execution of such a law
against one who objects to vaccination, no matter for
what reason, is nothing short of an assault upon his person. But the liberty secured by the Constitution of the
United States to every person within its jurisdiction
does not import an absolute right in each person to be,
at all times and in all circumstances, wholly freed from
restraint. There are manifold restraints to which every
person is necessarily subject for the common good. On
any other basis organized society could not exist with
safety to its members. Society based on the rule that
each one is a law unto himself would soon be confronted
with disorder and anarchy. Real liberty for all could not
exist under the operation of a principle which recognizes
the right of each individual person to use his own, whether
in respect of his person or his property, regardless of
the injury that may be done to others. This court has
more than once recognized it as a fundamental principle
that "persons and property are subjected to all kinds of
restraints and burdens in order to secure the general
comfort, health, and prosperity of the state; of the
perfect right of the legislature to do which no question
ever was, or upon acknowledged general principles ever
can be, made, so far as natural persons are concerned (12).

Speaking of the conflict between individual rights and the
interests of the public, the Court noted further that:

There is, of course, a sphere within which the individual may assert the supremacy of his own will, and rightfully dispute the authority of any human government,--
especially of any free government existing under a written
constitution -- to interfere with the exercise of that will.
But it is equally true that in every well-ordered society

charged with the duty of conserving the safety of its
members the rights of the individual in respect of
his liberty may at times, under the pressure of great
dangers, be subjected to such restraint, to be enforced
by reasonable regulations, as the safety of the general
public may demand (13).

Inasmuch as the State interest identified in Jacobson v.
Massachusetts lay in minimizing the transmission to other individuals of agents which create hazard to their health, we might
expect this decision to have importance for the constitutionality
of eugenic or population control measures designed to prevent by
compulsory sexual sterilization or birth control, the transmission
of deleterious genes to offspring.

The first sterilization law in contemporary Western society
was passed in 1907 in Indiana. During the subsequent 30 years,
sterilization laws proliferated in a number of states in parallel
to the social trend to couple genetic theory to political isola-
tionism, American nativism and racism (14-17). Many of these
statutes were challenged for violation of the equal protection
law clauses or of the due process clause of Section 1 of the
Fourteenth Amendment to the United States Constitution (18). Thus,
the Supreme Court of Michigan determined that the equal protection
clause was violated by one of the sections of a sterilization law
which applied only to "those of the feeble-minded class who are
unable to support any children they might have, and whose children
probably will become public charges thereof (19).

Shortly thereafter the Virginia Supreme Court of Appeals ruled
in the case of Buck v. Bell that a statute providing for the
sterilization of mentally defective inmates of state hospitals
upon order of an impartial board after reasonable notice to all
parties interested and an opportunity for a hearing, met the constitutional requirements of procedural due process and equal protection of law (20). The earlier Jacobson v. Massachusetts decision was drawn on by the Virginia Court to rationalize the use
of reasonable regulations to protect the public health, the
other purported aim of the statute being to protect the mentally
defective from themselves. On review of this judgement by the
United States Supreme Court (21), Justice Holmes affirmed the
constitutionality of the Virginia statute. Procedural due process
was held available by initial notice, hearings, written notice,
opportunity for appeals to a county circuit court and then to the
State Supreme Court of Appeals. Limitation of the law to inmates
of institutions was found acceptable with the aphorism "the law
does all that is needed when it does all that it can, indicates a
policy, applies it to all within the lines, and seeks to bring
within the lines all similarly situated so far and so fast as its
means allow"(22). Justice Holmes saw the main question as one of

substantive due process which was met by a minimal rational basis
for a claimed interest of the state to promote the health of the
patient and the welfare of society. Justice Holmes considered
sterilizations as "lesser sacrifices often not felt to be such
by those concerned in order to prevent our being swamped with
incompetence" (23), and cited the Jacobson case, drawn on earlier
by the Virginia Supreme Court, as providing the principle to
cover cutting the Fallopian tubes. However, instead of an analysis
of the extension of this principle, from Jacobson to Buck v. Bell,
we were told, "Three generations of imbeciles are enough" (24).
Now, although there is question whether there were three generations
of imbeciles, in that the mental capacity of Carrie Buck, her
mother, and especially her daughter, were incorrectly presented,
there is no question that the impatience of Justice Holmes sufficed
to sustain the constitutionality of a statute authorizing sterilization of a mentally defective person who by the laws of heredity
is the probable potential parent of socially inadequate offspring
likewise afflicted (25). In short, an individual in one generation,
bearing a poorly quantified mental shortcoming whose probability
of inheritance is even more poorly defined was accepted as a proper
subject of this statute.

CONSTITUTIONAL PROTECTION OF THE RIGHT TO MARRIAGE AND THE RIGHT TO PROCREATION

The case on involuntary sterilization to reach the Supreme
Court after Buck v. Bell dealt with an Oklahoma statute providing
for sterilization of habitual criminals (26). The statute applied
to persons convicted of larceny but specifically exempted persons
convicted of embezzlement, although the crimes are often intrinsically the same in nature and in punishment. Justice Douglas,
speaking for the Court, ruled that the State act violated the
equal protection clause and pointedly raised the constitutional
significance of marriage and procreation to require strict scrutiny
of classification, not mere rationality:

> We are dealing here with legislation which involves one
> of the basic civil rights of man. Marriage and procreation
> are fundamental to the very existence and survival of the
> race. The power to sterilize, if exercised, may have
> subtle, far-reaching and devastating effects. In evil
> or reckless hands it can cause races or types which are
> inimical to the dominant group to wither and disappear.
> There is no redemption for the individual whom the law
> touches. Any experiment which the State conducts is to
> his irreparable injury. He is forever deprived of a basic
> liberty. We mention these matters not to re-examine the
> scope of the police power of the States. We advert to them
> merely in emphasis of our view that strict scrutiny of the

classification which a State makes in a sterilization
law is essential, less unwittingly or otherwise, invidious discriminations are made against groups or types
of individuals in violation of the constitution guaranty
of just and equal laws... When the law lays an unequal
hand on those who have committed intrinsically the same
quality of offense and sterilizes one and not the other,
it has made as invidious a discrimination as if it had
selected a particular race or nationality for oppressive
treatment (27).

However, Buck v. Bell's upholding of the sterilization of the
class of feeble-minded who are institutionalized was cited with
approval as meeting equal protection (28). Moreover, although
marriage and procreation have become identified as basic civil
rights, the Court did not offer a decision on the substantive
due process issue of whether the State has a compelling interest
to invade these liberties. Chief Justice Stone concurred in the
result, but thought the real question was:

whether the wholesale condemnation of a class to such
an invasion of personal liberty, without opportunity to
any individual to show that his is not the type of case
which would justify resort to it, satisfies the demands
of due process (29).

Justice Stone went on to affirm the constitutionality of
eugenic sterilization when procedural due process is met:

Undoubtedly, a state may, after appropriate inquiry,
constitutionally interfere with the personal liberty of
the individual to prevent the transmission by inheritance
of his socially infurious tendencies (30).
And so, while the state may protect itself from the
demonstrably inheritable tendencies of the individual
which are injurious to society, the most elementary
notions of due process would seem to require it to take
appropriate steps to safeguard the liberty of the individual by affording him, before he is condemned to an
irreparable injury in his person, some opportunity to show
that he is without such inheritable tendencies (31).

Justice Jackson concurred in the Court holding, because of
the shortcomings in equal protection created by the statute's
classification and for the inadequacies of the statute's procedural due process, and then suggested another set of questions
which, however, remain to this day unresolved:

I also think the present plan to sterilize the individual
in pursuit of a eugenic plan to eliminate from the race

characteristics that are only vaguely identified and
which in our present state of knowledge are uncertain as
to transmissibility presents other constitutional questions
of gravity. This Court has sustained such an experiment
with respect to an imbecile, a person with definite
and observable characteristics, where the condition had
persisted through three generations and afforded grounds
for the belief that it was transmissible and would continue to manifest itself in generations to come (32).

Considering Justice Jackson's citation of Buck v. Bell,
pursuit of substantive due process at that time might have voided
statutes authorizing sterilization of criminals per se, but there
is no suggestion that higher rationality would be needed or have
failed to support eugenic sterilization.

Subsequently, the Court in Griswold v. Connecticut overthrew
a State statute which made the use of contraceptives a criminal
offense (33). This itself has enormous implications for gene
flow and already has made serious impact on family planning and
mean family size. A majority of the Court reached its decision,
not directly by the Fourteenth Amendment's due process clause,
but by developing the principle of a zone of privacy as penumbra
to the various guarantees in the First, Third, Fourth, Fifth,
and Ninth Amendments to the Bill of Rights (34). Justice Douglas
held for the Court's majority opinion on a relationship within
the zone of privacy:

> ...a law which, in forbidding the use of contraceptives
> rather than regulating their manufacture or sale, seeks
> to achieve its goals by means having a maximum destruc-
> tive impact upon that relationship. Such a law cannot
> stand in light of the familiar principle, so often
> applied by this Court, that a "governmental purpose to
> control or prevent activities constitutionally subject
> to state regulation may not be achieved by means which
> sweep unnecessarily broadly and thereby invade the area
> of protected freedoms (35).

Justice Goldberg, Chief Justice Warren, and Justice Brennan
joined in concurrence, but spoke to the Ninth Amendment as
extended to the states by the Fourteenth, as the origin of the
fundamental right of privacy in a marriage relation:

> The entire fabric of the Constitution and the purposes
> that clearly underlie its specific guarantees demonstrate
> that the rights to marital privacy and to marry and raise
> a family are of similar order and magnitude as the
> fundamental rights specifically protected... as the
> Ninth Amendment expressly recognizes, there are funda-

mental personal rights such as this one, which are
protected from abridgement by the Government though
not specifically mentioned in the Constitution (36).

The question of whether this zone of marital privacy was
conserved to the married or available to the unmarried, and whether
the privacy right is an absolute protection of one's body was met in
the Eisenstadt v. Baird (37) and the Roe v. Wade (38) cases, respectively. The Court in Eisenstadt held that a state violated the
Equal Protection of Law Clause for fundamental rights by providing
dissimilar treatment in a statute which prohibited distribution of
contraceptives except by prescription to married persons, an invidious discrimination against unmarried persons.

Justice Brennan held for the Court:

If the right of privacy means anything, it is the right
of the individual, married or single, to be free from
unwarranted governmental intrusion into matters so
fundamentally affecting a person as the decision whether
to bear or beget a child (39).

A limit to the use of privacy was revealed in the Roe v. Wade
abortion decision at the point where the Court in an opinion given by
Justice Blackmun, determined that there is a time in pregnancy
that:

a state may properly assert important interests in safeguarding health, in maintaining medical standards, and
in protecting potential life. The privacy right involved,
therefore, cannot be said to be absolute. In fact, it is
not clear to us that the claim asserted by some amici that
one has an unlimited right to do with one's body as one pleases
bears a close relationship to the right of privacy previously
articulated in the Court's decisions. The Court has refused
to recognize an unlimited right of this kind in the past (40).

Jacobson v. Massachusetts and Buck v. Bell are the only
citations affirmed here.

Justice Blackmun went on to say:

We therefore conclude that the right of personal privacy
includes the abortion decision but that this right is
not unqualified and must be considered against important
state interests in regulation (41).

Were these words merely parenthetical dicta? If so, regulation

by a state of the third trimester of pregnancy would need other
justification. Moreover, Justice Douglas in a separate concurring
opinion repeated and detailed this limitation on privacy:

> The state has interests to protect. Vaccinations to
> prevent epidemics are one example, as Jacobson holds.
> The Court held that compulsory sterilization of im-
> beciles afflicted with heredity forms of insanity or
> imbecility is another. Buck v. Bell, 224 US 200, 71 L Ed
> 1000, 47 SCt S84 (42).

We are left with Court holdings which say that a State has
shown no overriding and compelling interest to prevent contraception, but that state compulsory eugenic sterilization passes
the strict scrutiny of the Court given to state infringements
on personal liberty as fundamental as privacy.

One further case illuminates for us the limitation on a
state's ability to regulate the entry into marriage. A Virginia
statutory scheme for miscegenation prohibited marriage between a
white person and a colored person (defining such persons in terms
of the proportion of Caucasian, Negro, and American Indian "blood")
(43). Richard Loving, a white, and Mildred Jeter, a Negro
woman, had married in the District of Columbia pursuant to its
law and returned to Virginia. They were indicted and convicted
for violation of the ban on interracial marriages. A series of
appeals led to the upholding of their conviction in the Virginia
Supreme Court. The higher court held that the Virginia miscegenation statutes violated the Fourteenth Amendment and reversed the
state conviction of the Lovings. Justice Warren gave the Court
opinion:

> We have consistently denied the constitutionality of
> measures which restrict the rights of citizens on
> account of race. There can be no doubt that restricting
> the freedom to marry solely because of racial classifica-
> tions violates the central meaning of the Equal Protection
> Clause (44).

and affirmed an earlier principle taken curiously from a case
upholding compulsory curfew for Americans of Japanese ancestry:

> "Distinctions between citizens solely because of their
> ancestry" are odious to a free people whose insti-
> tutions are founded upon the doctrine of equality'
> (45).

In this context it is worth noting a dissent by Justice Jackson in
a similar case, cited in Loving v. Virginia, involving the exclusion from a West Coast military area of all persons of Japanese

ancestry (and not of any other enemy alien ancestry).

> Now, if any fundamental assumption underlies our
> system, it is that guilt is personal and not inheritable.
> Even if all of one's antecedents had been convicted of
> treason, the Constitution forbids its penalties to be
> visited upon him, for it provides that no attainder
> of treason shall work corruption of blood, or forfeiture
> except during the life of the person attainted (46).

This would have sufficed to bury miscegenation, but the
Court in Loving v. Virginia went on to extend the breadth of
their ruling:

> These statutes also deprive the Lovings of liberty
> without due process of law in violation of the Due
> Process Clause of the Fourteenth Amendment. The freedom
> to marry has long been recognized as one of the vital
> personal rights essential to the orderly pursuit of
> happiness by free men. Marriage is one of the basic
> civil rights of man, fundamental to our very existence
> and survival. Skinner v. Oklahoma, 316 U.S. 535, 541
> (1942). See also Maynard v. Hill, 125 U.S. 190 (1888).
> To deny this fundamental freedom on so unsupportable a
> basis as the racial classifications embodied in these
> statutes, classifications so directly subversive of the
> principle of equality at the heart of the Fourteenth
> Amendment, is surely to deprive all the State's citizens
> of liberty without due process of law. The Fourteenth
> Amendment requires that the freedom of choice to marry
> not be restricted by invidious racial discriminations.
> Under our Constitution, the freedom to marry, or not
> marry, a person of another race resides with the
> individual and cannot be infringed by the State (47).

RESTRICTIONS ON MARRIAGE WHICH RELATE TO GENETIC CONSIDERATIONS

Restrictions on marriages between relatives in Western
societies, have their origins in biblical and ecclessiastic codes.
One may find in them elements of taboo from Oedipus, and economic
and political pressure to add extrafamily allies to a small social
group, pressures to avoid intrafamily jealousy and friction,
protection for young females, and attempts to prevent confusion
over inheritance. What is outwardly a rational argument for
their existence, namely the concern for dire genetic consequences,
fails to stand of closer analysis. Codes going back to
Leviticus XVIII ban consanguineous unions for the same reasons that they ban unions for affinity wherein a genetic relationship is no closer than in the population at large.

It is at best mischievous, and as we shall see, more likely
perilous to premise the existence of eugenic concerns as the
rationale for such laws. This is not to deny the higher risk
of genetic defects in the offspring of consanguineous union. If
an individual is heterozygous for a rare autosomal recessive
deleterious gene, then a parent, or child, or sib has roughly the
probability of 0.5 of also being heterozygous for that gene. The
offspring of unions between the individual and a parent, child, or
sib would have the probability of 0.125 of being homozygous for
that recessive genetic defect. The analogous risk of defective
offspring of uncle-niece and aunt-nephew unions is 0.0625 and
that for first cousin unions is 0.031. The difference between
the frequency of mortality or genetic defect for the children of
first-cousin marriages and for the children of non-consanguineous
marriages can tell us how often we are heterozygous for a lethal
or detrimental gene. Data of this type indicate that on the
average we carry one to two genes for serious defective physical
and mental traits. If stillbirth to early adult death is considered, we have between three to five different lethal gene
equivalents; spontaneous abortion and premature adult death add
to this number (48). This frequency of genetic burden which is
distributed amongst all of us should give us pause. The genetic
burden is mutational in its primal origin and therefore may be
assumed to have a random distribution, although some social groups
may be more prone to have one specific gene burden. For example,
American whites are much more likely than American blacks or
Japanese to carry the gene for cystic fibrosis, whereas American
blacks have a higher incidence of the HbS gene for sickle cell
hemoglobin. An average burden of five lethal genes means that
less than 1% of a population achieves a state free of lethal genes,
and even then their offspring risk new mutation or inheritance of
lethal genes from the other parent. What then is the interaction
between this burden and the law?

The assorted laws on incestuous marriage have been conven-
iently collated by Drinan (49) and by Farrow and Juberg (50).
Since these laws restrict the fundamental right to marry, they
can survive only if they meet a strict scrutiny test of equal protection and of due process as a result of the Loving v. Virginia
and the Griswold v. Connecticut decisions. But each state has its
own version of what the compelling interest is and how it can be
most narrowly met; Oklahoma is the only state to limit second-
cousin marriages but recognizes as valid marriages of first or
second cousins in another state authorizing such marriage. Twenty
states do not prohibit first cousin marriages. These include many
of the original Atlantic states as well as Alabama, Alaska, California, Colorado, Hawaii, New Mexico, Tennessee, and Texas. The
citizens of these states are not known to have unsolveable social,
moral, or health problems as a result of the absence of a state
law banning cousin marriages. It is likely that such restrictions

by other states would be held invalid as infringing on the fundamental right to marry for no necessary compelling reason.

Stronger social arguments can be made for the prohibitions
on marriages between a person and his parent, child, or sib,
which are uniformly abhorred. There is no need for a genetic
reason for the latter ban, and I would be apprehensive over the
precedent of a legal classification based on risks of 0.125 of
defective offspring. To survive an equal protection test, such a
genetic classification would have to be extended to unions between
two known recessive heterozygotes where the risk of defective
offspring is 0.25 and serve to prevent or void them. This is not
gene-genocide, since recessive genes will be protected in unions
between heterozygote and normal people, and the frequency of the
recessive gene would rise to a higher equilibrium level. But
whose welfare would be enhanced by such a measure? Not the
general welfare from a eugenic view, since the frequency of the
deleterious gene will rise in future generations. Not the heterozygote person since his marital choice has been reduced, and his
marital privacy grossly invaded by a compulsory genetic screening
program required to identify and recall the heterozygote of an
ascertainable deleterious gene. Not the general public, since
except perhaps for those 1% of us in the null distribution, we are
all heterozygous for some lethal and deleterious genes. Most of
this gene burden is not yet identifiable in screening, so that
the traits chosen now for examination would create for a class of
individuals a premature and undeserved stigma based on their ancestry. Unlike the determination of an infectious disease, the identification of a heterozygote gene is not something an individual
can treat or dissociate from. The situation is similar to the
Korematsu case where Justice Jackson noted:

> But here is an attempt to make an otherwise innocent
> act a crime merely because this prisoner is the son
> of parents as to whom he had no choice and belongs to
> a race from which there is no way to resign (51).

Absent the 1944 need for wartime powers, there is now no
pretense of a compelling interest to disadvantage an ancestry-
dependent class. It would appear to be more rewarding to remove
all genetic rationalization from consanguineous laws and to rely
on our readings of Sophocles for the guidelines which may foster
intrafamily tranquillity. This would allow us to offer voluntary
genetic screening programs for young adults and others who might
benefit from an opportunity for early diagnosis or family planning
as they see fit.

REGULATION OF MARRIAGE OF THE MENTALLY DEFECTIVE AS A BARRIER TO
THEIR GENE FLOW

At present restrictions on the marriage of the mentally
infirm, may be based on:

1. Their incompetence to appreciate their responsibilities
    under the marriage contract, or
2. The protection of the infirm from others who might
    abuse a marital relation as servitude, or
3. As an indirect means of inhibiting the procreation of
    individuals whose offspring may need protection from
    potentially inadequate parental guidance, or
4. As an indirect means of inhibiting the procreation of
    individuals whose mental defectiveness may be inherited.

At a minimum these restrictions should be accompanied by the
procedural due process which provides for individual hearing and
review by disinterested boards, and opportunity for judicial
appeals. All of the restrictions suffer from the imprecision of
the definition of the mental disability and from our inability to
distinguish the different degrees of its severity and impact on a
marital relation. An American Bar Foundation study showed that
seven states did not proscribe the mentally disabled from marrying
(52). Incompetence to consent to a civil contract is the sole
basis for proscription by six other states (53); the remainder use
different variations of "unsound mind" and combinations of the
terms, feeble-minded, idiots, lunatic, imbecile, mental deficiency,
mentally retarded, mentally ill, insane, and hereditary epilepsy.
Extending an analysis by Drinan (54), we note that since some
states meet any presumed need to police the marital state without
disqualifying statutes, then the other states with such laws should
be able to repeal them without loss to the general welfare and
with gain to individual liberties. Moreover, the statutes are
overbroad if concern for the potential offspring is an issue, since
all but six states (55) make no concession in their disqualification
for individuals who wish to marry without bearing children, and
two of these, Nebraska and North Carolina, require sterilization.
Finally, if concern for offspring is an issue, equal protection
of the law is hardly satisfied inasmuch as child support laws are
relied on to correct for inadequate guardianship by mentally
sound parents, whereas disqualification for marriage is used to
correct for possible shortcomings by the mentally infirm. I am
pursuaded that an alternative of creating requirements for competency as a parental guardian for all marriage applicants would
only create equal invasion by the law of a fundamental right.
Therefore, the better law may be the withdrawal of all restrictions
other than competence of an individual to enter a civil contract.

EUGENIC REGULATION OF PROCREATION BY THE MENTALLY DEFECTIVE

Two alternative challenges to involuntary eugenic sterilization may be raised. One would question whether less onerous
means can achieve compelling state interest. Considering the
different contraceptive technology now available, it is reasonable
to expect that reversible contraceptive drugs and birth control
devices could be authorized instead of surgery for mentally
defective women. Since for mentally defective people it is mainly
the pregnant woman who has the problem of child care and support,
this approach meets the therapeutic concerns of the burden of
pregnancy to the mentally defective parent. It meets the social
concerns for a child of unfit parenthood. It meets the State's
needs to minimize costs for welfare and child care. If there is
eugenic merit in preventing procreation by the mentally infirm,
then that too is obtained. Moreover, the reversibility of contraceptive programs would allow for greater normalization of the
woman should her mental condition improve. Since voluntary birth
control is available to a female partner of a mentally defective
male, the present asymmetry of available contraceptive technology
is not a barrier to this scheme.

The second challenge to involuntary sterilization focuses
on the classification used to meet a state interest in heritable
inadequacy. It would ask that the identification of heritability
of a genetic disorder be given the strict scrutiny needed for
justifying an invasion of procreative rights.

Although it is not necessarily clear what level of social
inadequacy is meant by the terms of a given statute, there are
several instructive surveys of familial inheritance patterns of
mental shortcomings wherein the latter are defined by intelligence
tests and adaptive behaviour. The terms "mildly retarded,"
"educable," "high grade," "feeble-minded," and "dull" are generally
used for individuals whose IQ range is about 50-80. This range
encompasses the great majority of the retarded and is frequently
associated with a polygenic etiology. The terms "moderately
retarded," "trainable," and "imbecile" are applied to individuals
in the IQ range of about 36-60 and are often associated with
severe single gene defects.

However, although these assessments are moderately predictive
of achievement in school, they leave us the controversial problem
of distinguishing between the determinants of mental ability
which are biologically inherent or culturally acquired. Considering the difficulty in making reliable metric observations needed
for determining the mental qualities of individuals, and the
sampling biases encountered in working with human populations,
estimates of inheritability risk for non-cultural retardation are
understandably suspect.

Different American and British surveys find that between
12 and 40% of the children born to a mentally defective parent
were themselves defective, using an IQ level of between 60-80
as the distinguishing criterion (56-59). However, the average
child of retarded parents tended to be brighter than the parents,
a situation known as regression to the mean. In one group of
studies, the average IQ of the offspring was about 90, with 11%
of the children having an IQ over 110 (60). This data can be
used to stress the view that retardates beget retardates, or to
emphasize the opposite view that up to 7/8 of their children are
not retarded. A cup that is part-empty is also part-filled.

Studies differ on the category of parents responsible for
most retarded children. In Penrose's Colchester survey of 2,465
ascertained parents of retarded children, 8% (195) were imbecile
or feeble-minded, 14% (351) were dull or borderline, and 78% (1919)
were normal or superior (61). In the Reed study of 468 ascertained
parents of retarded children, 41% (193) were retarded and 59% (275)
were normal (62). The Reeds estimate the empiric risk of birth
of a retarded first child to two normal parents to be between 0.5
and 3.6%, depending on the status of sibs of the parents (63). The
risk rises to 13% for the next child if such a couple has had a
retarded first child, as compared to 20% for a union between a
normal and retarded parent similarly situated (64).

Population surveys such as these teach us that the major
contribution to the retarded individuals of the next generation
comes from the normal individuals of the present (65). The few
per cent of the people who are now retarded are a minority who
are classified aside for an invasion of rights not applied to the
rest of the people who share their bearing of deleterious genes.
Involuntary sterilization schemes with a eugenic goal deny equal
protection to this minority class because they are under-inclusive
of the non-symptomatic carrier of deleterious genes. Here, the
interchangeability found acceptable by Holmes for inmates and
outmates in Buck v. Bell (66) cannot occur since sterilization does
not convert a retardate into a normal carrier, and it would confirm
our gravest concern if it were thought that normal carriers may
be involuntarily treated in the reciprocal way.

Finally, if a state is interested in eugenic goals, it may
be constitutionally more appropriate for it to focus its public
health police powers, affirmed in Jacobson v. Massachusetts, to
minimize the exposure of its people to mutagenic agents which
induce the prime genetic defect. The next interface between
genetics and law may concern the mutagen screening programs which
monitor and evaluate these agents and the regulatory principles
which seek to minimize their harm (67). The state will be a far
more effective custodian of the gene pool for the next generation
if it shifts its emphasis from regulating mutants to regulating
mutagens.

REFERENCES

1. United States Constitution, Amendment 10. The powers not
    delegated to the United States by the Constitution, nor
    prohibited by it to the States, are reserved to the States
    respectively, or to the people.

2. Foote, C., Levy, R.J. and Sander, F.E.A., "Cases and Materials
    on Family Law," Little, Brown & Company, Boston (1966).

3. Drinan, R.F., The Loving decisions and the freedom to marry,
    Ohio State Law J. 29:358 (1968).

4. Reynolds v. United States, 98 U.S. 145 (1878).

5. Ibid at p. 165.

6. Murphy V. Ramsey, 114 U.S. 15 (1884).

7. Ibid at p. 45.

8. Maynard v. Hill, 125 U.S. 190 (1887).

9. Ibid at p. 205.

10. Jacobson v. Massachusetts, 197 U.S. 11 (1905).

11. Ibid at pp. 25-26.

12. Ibid at p. 26.

13. Ibid at p. 29.

14. O'Hara, J.B. and Sanks, T.H., Eugenic sterilization, Georgetown
    Law J. 45:20 (1956).

15. Robitscher, J., "Eugenic Sterilization," Charles C. Thomas,
    Springfield (1973).

16. Ludmerer, K.M., "Genetics and American Society," Johns
    Hopkins University Press, Baltimore (1972).

17. Haller, M.H., "Eugenics," Rutgers University Press, New
    Brunswick (1963).

18. Amendment 14. Section 1. All persons born or naturalized

in the United States, and subject to the jurisdiction thereof,
are citizens of the United States and of the State wherein
they reside. No State shall make or enforce any law which
shall abridge the privileges of immunities of citizens of
the United States; nor shall any State deprive any person of
life, liberty, or property, without due process of law; nor
deny to any person within its jurisdiction the equal protection
of the laws.

19. Smith v. Command, 231 Mich. 409 (1925).

20. Buck v. Bell, 143 Va. 310 (1925).

21. Buck v. Bell, 274 U.S. 200 (1927).

22. Ibid at p. 208.

23. Ibid at p. 207.

24. Ibid at p. 207.

25. Ibid at p. 207.

26. Skinner v. Oklahoma, 316 U.S. 535 (1942).

27. Ibid at p. 541.

28. Ibid at p. 540 and p. 542.

29. Ibid at p. 544.

30. Ibid at p. 544.

31. Ibid at p. 545.

32. Ibid at p. 546.

33. Griswold v. Connecticut, 381 U.S. 479 (1965).

34. Ibid at pp. 482-486.

35. Ibid at p. 485, and see NAACP v. Alabama, 377 U.S. 288
     (1964).

36. Ibid at p. 495 and p. 496.

37. Eisenstadt v. Baird, 405 U.S. 438 (1972).

38. Roe v. Wade, 410 U.S. 113 (1973).

STATE REGULATION OF MARRIAGE AND PROCREATION

39. See 37 Supra at p. 453.

40. See 38 supra at p. 154.

41. See 38 supra at p. 154.

42. See 38 supra and Doe v. Bolton, 410 U.S. 179 at p. 215.

43. Loving v. Virginia, 388 U.S. 1 (1966).

44. Ibid at p. 11 and p. 12.

45. Ibid at p. 11 and at Hirabayashi v. United States, 320
    U.S. at p. 100 (1943).

46. Korematsu v. United States, 323 U.S. at p. 243 (1944).

47. See 43 supra at p. 12.

48. Morton, N.E., Crow, J.F. and Muller, H.J., An estimate of the
    mutational damage in man from data on consanguineous marriages,
    Proc. Nat. Acad. Sci. (U.S.) 42:855 (1956).

49. See 3 supra, Appendices A, B, and C.

50. Farrow, M.G. and Juberg, R.C., Genetics and laws prohibiting
    marriage in the United States, J. Amer. Med. Assoc. 209:
    534 (1969).

51. See 46 supra at p. 243.

52. Brakel, S.J. and Rock, R.S. (eds.), "The Mentally Disabled
    and the Law," revised edition, The University of Chicago Press,
    Chicago (1971). The eight states are Alabama, Arizona,
    Connecticut, Florida, Louisiana, South Dakota, and Texas.

53. Arkansas, Colorado, New Mexico, New York, Nevada, and
    Oklahoma.

54. See 3 supra at p. 372.

55. Kansas, Nebraska, North Carolina, North Dakota, Virginia,
    and Washington.

56. Scally, B.G., A survey of mentally defective parents and their
    offspring, in "Human Genetics," Proceedings of the Fourth
    International Congress of Human Genetics, Paris, 1971,
    pp. 258-262, Excerpta Medica, Amsterdam (1972).

57. Shaw, C.H. and Wright, C.H., The married mental defective,
     Lancet 1:273 (1960).

58. Reed, E.W. and Reed, S.C., "Mental Retardation: A Family
     Study," W.B. Saunders C₀mpany, Philadelphia (1965).
     A value of 14.3% retarded children is given at p. 39 in
     Table 27.

59. Penrose, L.S., "The Biology of Mental Defect," Grune and
     Stratton, New York (1949).

60. See 58 supra at p. 40, Table 28.

61. See 59 supra at p. 274, Appendix 10 for a tabulation of the
     Colchester Survey, 1938.

62. See 58 supra at p. 34, Table 20.

63. See 58 supra at p. 56, Table 40.

64. See 58 supra at p. 56, Table 41.

65. See 58 and 59 supra.

66. See 21 supra at p. 208.

67. Drake, J.W., Abrahamson, S., et al, Environmental mutagenic
     hazards, Science 187:503 (1975).

VOLUNTARY STERILIZATION OF THE MENTALLY RETARDED

Charles H. Baron

Boston College Law School

It may be that the era of explicit compulsory sterilization is slowly drawing to a close. The effort to purify the American gene pool through sterilization of misfits which began in earnest at the turn of the Century seems to be losing much of its political base. Of course, the United States Supreme Court's favorable holding as to the constitutionality of the compulsory sterilization of Carrie Buck on the ground that"(t)hree generations of imbeciles are enough" (1) has never been explicitly overruled. But compelling arguments have been made (2) that the case would not be decided the same way today under the strict equal protection and due process standards which have been developed in the areas of marriage and procreation in the 50 years since the decision in Buck v. Bell. Moreover, the last 50 years have also seen a significant change in scientific opinion regarding the degree of threat which reproduction by "misfits" poses to our society (3, 4). As a result, one author has claimed in a recent article that "(w)hile ethical and psychological assessments of sterilization may differ, few would deny that the operation should be performed only upon those who knowingly consent to it" (2).

But, if explicitly compulsory sterilization is losing favor, the same certainly cannot be said for sterilization in general. Voluntary sterilization is becoming the birth control method of choice for a growing number of males and females in the United States. In March of 1975, the Association for Voluntary Sterilization reported that it believed the total number of sterilized adults in the United States had reached close to seven million. The number sterilized in 1974 alone was estimated at 1.3 million, an increase of 42% over the number sterilized in 1973 and of 210% over those in 1969 (5). A popular women's magazine reported in

1973 that voluntary sterilization had become the favored form of contraception among married women between the ages of 30 and 44, and second only to "the pill" among women of all ages (6). And the Association for Voluntary Sterilization reported in March, 1975 that vasectomy had become the second most common operation performed on men, surpassed only by circumcision (5).

In light of the growing popularity of sterilization as a method of birth control, the question now arises of the extent to which sterilization should be made available on a "voluntary" basis to those persons who would have been the subjects of compulsory sterilization in the past. The developing acceptance of the notion of "normalization" of the retarded - a recognition of a right on the part of retarded persons to live, where feasible, in the community instead of in institutions or the homes of parents or guardians (7, 8) - gives timely importance to this question. On the one hand, is it fair to deny to retarded individuals a method of birth control which has become so popular among the rest of the community? On the other hand, to what extent can we allow sterilization of individuals who are generally under the control of others and whose competence to protect themselves is doubtful if we are opposed to sterilization which is other than truly voluntary? Clearly, any procedure which allows sterilization of individuals on the basis of consent of persons other than the individual, or on the basis of a consent which is suspect as to its truly uncoerced nature, leaves open the door to a form of compulsory sterilization which differs from the older form only in the fact that its compulsory nature is covert.

The problems inherent in providing sterilization options to the mentally retarded are nicely illustrated by the 1968 Nebraska case of In Re Cavitt (9). There, a 35 year-old woman with an I.Q. of 71 was offered the opportunity to be released from a state home on the condition that she submit to sterilization. This was done under the authority of a 1943 Nebraska statute (10) which provided:

> It shall be the duty of the board of examiners to make a psychiatric and physical examination of these patients and, if after a careful examination, such board of examiners finds that such patient is mentally deficient, in the opinion of the board of examiners, is apparently capable of bearing or begetting offspring, and, based on their psychiatric and medical findings as a result of this examination, it is the opinion of the board of examiners that such patient should be sterilized, as a condition prerequisite to the parole or discharge, then such patient shall not be paroled or discharged, as the case may be, unless said patient be made sterile...

The determination of the board of examiners that Mrs. Cavitt should
be sterilized as a condition of release was appealed by her guardian
ad litem to the Nebraska district court which set aside the board's
order on the ground that the 1943 statute was unconstitutional in
that it did not lay down sufficient standards for the board in
determining whether or not sterilization should be required. The
state took an appeal to the Nebraska Supreme Court.

The Supreme Court reversed the district court in a very unusual way. Despite the fact that four of the seven justices of the
court believed the statute to be unconstitutional, the remaining
three judges were able to write an opinion upholding the statute
because the Nebraska Constitution requires a majority of five
justices to strike down a statute on constitutional grounds. In
that opinion, the court admitted that the predecessor to the 1943
statute had been more explicit in requiring a finding by the board
that "children born or begotten by such inmate would inherit
a tendency to feeblemindedness, insanity, degeneracy...that such
children would probably become a social menace and that procreation
by such inmate would be harmful to society..." The removal of such
language, the court observed, was a result of the fact that "advances in medical science have dispelled the theory that all mental
defectives produce mental defectives and all normal persons do not.
Such is not the case of unexplainable reasons which has (sic) brought
about a change of thinking in the medical profession." The more
general discretion provided by the 1943 statute was constitutional,
the court believed, where, as in this case, the board had considered
the probable effect upon the inmate of having children (additional to
the eight she had already had by her common-law husband before breaking up with him and being institutionalized), "her minimal capacity
to handle the responsibilities of parenthood, the possibility of
producing mentally defective children, and the probability that
added responsibilties of parenthood would in all likelihood handicap
her potential rehabilitation." The court seemed to think it was
relevant as well that the support of the eight children was being
carried largely by public aid.

In its opinion denying a motion for rehearing, (11) the court
implied that it thought the case involved an instance of voluntary
sterilization. Although it noted the fact that Mrs. Cavitt had
expressed the desire to have more children, the court argued that
"(t)he order does not require her sterilization. It does provide,
in accordance with the statute, that she shall not be released
unless she is sterilized. The choice is hers."

Clearly, there are grave problems with suggesting that the
Cavitt case involves an instance of voluntary sterilization. Mrs.
Cavitt explicitly stated her desire for more children. Moreover,
even if she had consented to the sterilization, her consent would
be suspect. Her I.Q. of 71 raises questions about her ability to

decide in an informed and intelligent way what would actually be in her best interests. And the fact that her consent would be given in the face of a requirement to remain institutionalized if she refused to consent - a situation which may confront many retarded persons who are eligible for "normalization" - makes it clear that her choice would not be a free one.

However, one could argue that actual consent of the patient, given freely and upon an informed basis, is not the crucial determinant of whether sterilization is "voluntary" when one is dealing with retarded individuals. Even John Stuart Mill, who believed that the requirement of individual consent to state action was justified by the fact that even "the most ordinary man or woman" is the best judge of what is in his own best interests, recognized an exception for "(t)hose who are still in a state to require being taken care of by others..." (12). If we agree with Mill that the requirement of consent is a means to the end of attempting to insure that the best interests of individual citizens are achieved where those citizens are sufficiently mature to be presumed to be the best judges of what is in their best interests, then we may be justified, where that presumption no longer holds, in making at least some decisions for individuals on the basis of what is, in fact, in their best interests. This is, of course, the role which parents and guardians are normally required by the law to play in making "proxy consent" decisions for their children and wards.

As an example, let us consider the hypothetical case of a moderately or severely retarded woman in her twenties who is being considered for release from an institution into the "community" - perhaps a supervised "village" of mentally retarded individuals. It is possible, in some cases, that a decision in favor of sterilization before release would be justified on the ground that it was actually in her own best interests. Suppose that she suffers from a physical condition that creates a serious risk to her health from pregnancy or delivery. Suppose that there is strong evidence that she would not be able to cope with or be happy about having a family. If her mental limitations make it unlikely that she will be able to follow effectively the regimen involved in the use of a diaphragm or birth control pills, and if the use of an intrauterine device is contraindicated, it could be argued that sterilization is indicated in her own interest.

As mentioned above the Cavitt court did consider, among other things, the effect that having more children would have on Gloria Cavitt's welfare in light of the problems she already had in taking care of her existing eight children. But the court did not limit its consideration to the question of what was in Mrs. Cavitt's best interests. It considered as well the interest of other members of society in excluding the possibility of defective children being born to her and preventing the addition of children to the public aid rolls. Where such considerations are part of the standard for determining whether a person should be sterilized, no pretense can be made that the sterilization is "voluntary" in any sense. We do not as yet tell members of society who are considered competent to make their own decisions that they may not decide to have additional children because we are fearful that the children may be defective, or that they will have to be supported by public aid. If such competent individuals believe that having additional offspring is in their own interests, they may have them whatever the impact may be upon the rest of society. Hence, a decision not to have children made for a person who is considered incompetent to make that decision for himself can be considered "voluntary" only if it is based solely upon those factors which the individual would clearly consider determinative if he were competent to make the decision for himself - i.e., those factors which relate to the impact of the children upon his own happiness. As Rawls put it:

> Paternalistic decisions are to be guided
> by the individual's own settled preferences and interests
> insofar as they are not irrational, or failing a know-
> ledge of these, by the theory of primary goods ... We
> try to get for him the things he presumably wants, what-
> ever else he wants (13).

If we are to speak, therefore, of "voluntary" sterilization for the mentally retarded, it can only be in those cases where sterilization is justified as being in the best interests of the retarded individual.

But who is to determine whether the best interests of a particular retarded individual are promoted by sterilization? The natural candidates would seem to be the parents or guardians of the retarded individuals. After all, they are provided with the legal power to make other decisions for their children or wards on the presumption that they are generally able and motivated to make such decisions solely on the basis of what is in the best interests of the child or ward. However, there are reasons for doubting whether that presumption can be indulged here. As one author has pointed out:

> In the sterilization context,... parents
> or guardians often have interests that conflict with
> those of the retarded child. The parents of a re-
> tarded child may have understandable fears that the
> grandchild will also be retarded. Moreover, the
> parents may perceive a danger of their retarded child
> proving to be an unfit parent, and might wish to avoid
> the risk of shouldering responsibilities of grand-
> children--either normal or retarded--in that event (2).

Hence, the parents or guardians may face a conflict between their own interests and those of the child or ward and thus not be motivated to act solely in the best interests of the child.

In situations of this sort, where the presumption that parents will give "proxy consent" solely on the basis of what is in the best interests of the child seems unjustified, there has been a discernible trend in the United States toward court review of parental decisions and judicial determination of what course of action is actually indicated in order to promote the child's best interests. Particularly in the area of consent to medical treatment, the courts have increasingly exercised their parens patriae power in this way. Most of the cases involve parents who had refused treatment for their children on religious grounds (14). Where the life of the child was at stake, the courts have always mandated the operation despite parental veto (15). But they have also overridden refusal to consent by parents in cases involving vaccination, removal of tonsils and adenoids, and other conditions which have not been immediately life-threatening (16). On the other hand, courts have acceded to parental refusal in cases concerning medical treatment for rickets, a disfigured arm, a speech impediment, and a spinal fusion operation (17), but in each such case the court found that the advisability of the treatment was reasonably open to question and that the parents sincerely believed that the medical treatment was not in the best interests of the child.

In another area more closely related to that of proxy consent to sterilization, the courts have exercised parens patriae power where the parents have consented to operations. Where minors or incompetents are asked to donate organs or tissue to siblings or other recipients, a number of courts have required prior judicial approval of the donation (18). This has been done explicitly on the ground that, as in the case of sterilization, the parents are faced with a conflict of interest. Since the parents are naturally concerned with the welfare of the recipient whose health depends upon the donation, the general presumption that they are consenting only because they believe the transplant operation to be in the best interests of the donor child cannot be indulged.

The reasons which have motivated the courts to take on the proxy consent power in the above-mentioned cases would seem to apply with equal force in the area of "voluntary sterilization" of the mentally retarded. Since there must be grave doubt that the parents or guardians will be motivated to consent to sterilization only where it is justified as in the best interests of the child or ward, the decision should not be left solely to them. And although some authors have suggested that the decision should be left to the person to be sterilized - at least in cases where the mentally retarded person is only mildly retarded (2) - there are reasons to doubt whether that is the best course. The

decision to undergo sterilization is a complicated and extraordinarily important one which some authors have suggested (19)
is beyond the competence of many normally intelligent people.
Certainly, an individual who is thought to require the supervision
of his parents or guardian in making much less drastic or complicated decisions in his life should not be thought competent
to make this decision without some supervision. But this is not
to say that the opinion of the candidate for sterilization is to
be ignored. Although the consent of the candidate should not be
considered alone to be   sufficient basis for sterilization, it
should certainly be considered important evidence, along with such
other evidence as is available, that the sterilization is in fact
in his best interests. If, as Mill suggests, the most ordinary
individual is the best judge of what is in his own best interests,
then the closer that the candidate comes to the level of intelligence of a fully competent person the more weight should be given
to his consent as evidence of what is in his best interests - at
least where the court is satisfied that the consent has been given
free from illegitimate influence and on the basis of full information.

Of course, giving over to the courts the power to consent to
sterilization for retarded individuals is no guarantee that sterilization for retarded individuals is no guarantee that sterilization will be allowed only in those cases where sterilization is in
the best interests of the individual. Even if the courts were
restricted by law to authorizing sterilization only in those cases
where the best interests of the retarded person were promoted
thereby - as they presently are not - procedures would need to be
assured by means of which the courts would be presented with all
and only that evidence which was relevant to the best interests
question. Most important in that regard is the necessity for providing advocates before the court who are charged with the responsibility for developing the strongest evidence and arguments for
and against the proposition that sterilization is in the best
interests of the candidate. If we assume that the position in
favor of sterilization will be effectively advocated by counsel
for the parent, guardian, or state agency proposing sterilization,
then the most pressing problem is to make sure that some advocate
is appointed to aggressively represent the position opposed to
sterilization. This can be done by the traditional device of
appointing an attorney as guardian ad litem for the person to be
sterilized with the role of developing the best arguments and evidence against sterilization. Without advocates on both sides of
the issue to develop the record, the court is too likely to face
the mental set and path-of-least-resistance pitfalls pointed out
in a 1958 report of a commission on professional responsibility
which stated:

   (F)ailure generally attends the attempt to dispense
with the distinct roles traditionally implied in adjudi-

cation. What generally occurs in practice is that at
some early point a familiar pattern will seem to emerge
from the evidence; an accustomed label is waiting for
the case and, without awaiting further proofs, this label
is promptly assigned to it (20).

Hence, the effort to insure that sterilization of the mentally
retarded be done only on a "voluntary" basis - in the sense that
it is in the best interests of the subject - requires appropriate
advocacy of the positions for and against sterilization on that
ground before the court.

    Unfortunately, the present relationship of the courts to the
sterilization of the mentally retarded bears little similarity to
the relationship which has been proposed. Of the 26 states having
statutes providing for sterilization of the retarded, at least 22
permit sterilization to be authorized on an involuntary basis. In
those states the courts clearly have the power to allow sterilization on grounds other than its tendency to promote the best interests of the person to be sterilized. On the other hand, in those
states where there are no statutes providing for sterilization of
the mentally retarded, a minor trend seems to be developing in
which the courts are concluding that they have no jurisdiction to
authorize sterilization in the absence of an explicit legislative
mandate to do so (21, 22, 24). In light of the fact that the courts,
as we have noted, will normally exercise the state's parens patriae
power to give or deny proxy consent for other kinds of medical treatment where there is some question about the exercise of that power
by the individual to be treated and by his parents or guardian, the
four courts, which have found there to be no jurisdiction to authorize
sterilization, have apparently done so on the ground that there is a
significant difference in degree of gravity between sterilization
and other kinds of medical treatment. As one court has put it:

    The courts are not faced in this case with a prayer for
    a judgment authorizing ordinary medical treatment, or
    radical surgery necessary to preserve the life of a child;
    we are faced with a request for sanction by the state of
    what no doubt is a routine operation which would irre-
    versibly deny to a human being a fundamental right, the right
    to bear or beget a child. Jurisdiction of the juvenile
    court to exercise the awesome power of denying that right
    may not be inferred from the general language of the
    sections of the code to which we have referred. Such
    jurisdiction may be conferred only by specific statute (22).

    However, it is very difficult to assess the extent to which
court authorization of sterilization is being granted in states
which have no sterilization statutes since the vast majority of
such decisions are likely to go unreported, especially where no

guardian ad litem is appointed who might take an appeal from a decision to sterilize. In an Ohio case, the only reported decision
(23) in which a court has held itself empowered to authorize sterilization of a retarded individual in the absence of statute, the
judge based his decision in part upon an unpublished memorandum
opinion of the Circuit Court of Baltimore, Maryland. And a later
federal case (24) was brought against the same Ohio judge for
having ordered the sterilization of another individual in a case
which had gone unreported. The federal court determined, by the
way, that the Ohio judge did not in fact have jurisdiction to order
sterilization and therefore might well be subject to personal liability for having ordered the sterilization. In passing, the court
noted the fact that the judge had failed to appoint a guardian ad
litem for the incompetent, but did not reach the argument that this
in itself deprived the judge of jurisdiction since the court believed that the absence of an Ohio statute explicitly giving jurisdiction to order sterilization was a sufficient ground for its decision.

     Obviously, what is needed in this area is legislation in each
of the states making clear that the courts have the sole legal power to authorize sterilization of the mentally retarded in all and
only those cases where it has been shown through a full adversary
hearing that such sterilization is in the best interests of the
mentally retarded individual. As some evidence of the fact that
an effort is afoot to have such legislation passed, I have attached
as Appendix A to this paper a bill which was introduced into the
present session of the Florida legislature for the purpose of
assuring that sterilization of the mentally retarded would be done
only on a "voluntary" basis. Essentially, the bill provides that
mentally retarded persons shall not be sterilized unless they in
fact consent and are either found by a court to be competent to
consent or a court determines that the sterilization is in the best
interests of the incompetent. The bill also provides that the person to be sterilized must be represented by counsel at all stages
of the court proceeding.

     Although the bill is a vast improvement over legislation
which presently exists, it seems to me that it has problems, including some fundamental ones. First, the bill permits a court to
authorize sterilization upon finding that the mentally retarded
individual is competent to make the decision. As has been argued
above, the decision to be sterilized is such a grave and medically
complicated decision that it should not be authorized in the case of
a mentally retarded individual without some court review of the
question of whether it is in fact in his best interests. Of course,
the consent of a mildly retarded person should have great probative
value of what is in the best interests of the individual, but it
should not be determinative. Second, in any situation where the
mentally retarded individual himself requests sterilization, the

draft requires that there be counsel only to represent the petitioner and does not attempt to insure that in every case there should
be advocates both for and against the position that sterilization
is in the best interests of the mentally retarded individual. In
order to make sure that the court renders its decision on a fully
developed record, it is crucial to require that the procedure
involve advocates prepared to present the best evidence and arguments on both sides of the question. Third, it makes the whole
question of whether a court procedure is needed to sterilize, depend
upon whether a Florida physician has refused to perform sterilization because he had "reason to believe that a person seeking sterilization ... is legally impaired ..." Presumably the statute
does not prevent any Florida guardian or parent from obtaining sterilization in the first instance from an out-of-state physician and
it places no obligation upon the guardian or parent to inform a
a Florida doctor of grounds for believing the child or ward to be
mentally impaired or incompetent.

It is to be hoped that the interest in voluntary sterilization
of the mentally retarded displayed by the legislature of Florida,
which previously had no statutes authorizing sterilization, will
be manifested as well by legislatures in all other states.* A first
step toward insuring that such sterilization is voluntary is that
of prescribing a substantive standard which allows sterilization
only where the procedure is justified as in the best interests of
the mentally retarded individual. But it is crucial for the state
legislatures to recognize that such a substantive standard is not
self-effectuating. Without procedures that are designed to make as
certain as is humanly possible that the standard is applied to all
and only those cases where sterilization is in fact in the retarded
person's best interests, the substantive standard is likely to become a pious platitude and "voluntary" sterilization of the mentally
retarded will become only a masquerade for the continuation of the
outmoded policies of compulsory sterilization.

APPENDIX A

A bill to be entitled

An act relating to sterilization; providing legislative

---

* The bill was defeated in the Florida legislature in part because
supporters of voluntary sterilization believed the "best interests"
standard to be too open to abuse because of its vagueness. The
author believes that this is, of course, a serious problem but that
its remedy must come from the provision of adequate procedural
safeguards and not by a retreat to less "consensual" substantive
standards.

intent; providing definitions; prohibiting the performance of a sterilization on certain persons without a court order; providing court procedures for certain persons seeking a sterilization; providing a procedure for a determination of the best interests of a person for whom a sterilization is sought; providing for appeal as a matter of right from a court order; providing for confidentiality of court records; providing limitations; providing penalties; providing for the awarding of court costs; providing an effective date.

Be It Enacted by the Legislature of the State of Florida:

Section 1. Legislative intent.-- The legislature finds and declares that sterilization procedures are irreversible and as such represent permanent and highly significant consequences for the patient involved. Although it is not the intent of the legislature to infringe on the physician-patient relationship or to treat sterilization procedures differently than other surgical procedures, the legislature recognizes that certain legal safeguards are necessary to prevent indiscriminate and unnecessary sterilization. The legislature intends through the enactment of this act to provide legal procedures designed to protect the rights, privileges, and welfare of minors or legally incompetent or mentally impaired citizens.

Section 2. Definitions.-- As used in this act, unless the context clearly requires otherwise:

(1) "Sterilization" means any surgical or medical procedure performed in order to render a person permanently incapable of reproduction. Sterilization does not refer to procedures which must be performed for distinct and urgent medical reasons, and which may have the unavoidable secondary effect of rendering the individual infertile.

(2) "Parent" means the natural or adoptive mother or father of a person.

(3) "Guardian" means the legal guardian of a person.

(4) "Mentally impaired" means an incapability to understand the nature and consequences of sterilization or to give free and intelligent consent to sterilization.

(5) "Disinterested expert" means an appropriately licensed or certified professional not employed by the state, not associated with an institution engaged in custodial care of the petitioner, and

not personally related to the petitioner.

(6) "Physician" means any person licensed or authorized to practice medicine under chapter 458 or 459, Florida Statutes.

(7) "Psychologist" means any person licensed to practice psychology under chapter 490, Florida Statutes.

(8) "Court" means the circuit court.

(9) "Legally incompetent" means any person who has been adjudicated incompetent by a court of competent jurisdiction and who has not been relieved of such status.

Section 3. Sterilization authorized by court.--

(1) WHEN COURT ORDER REQUIRED.-- When a physician has reason to believe that a person seeking sterilization is under the age of majority and is not married, or is legally incompetent or mentally impaired, the physician shall not perform a sterilization procedure except upon order of the court.

(2) COURT PROCEEDINGS.--

(a) When the performance of a sterilization has been refused by a physician as required in subsection (1), the person seeking a sterilization, or the parent, spouse, or legal guardian of any such person subject to the jurisdiction of the court who desires a sterilization for such person, shall file a petition for sterilization with the court. The circuit court of the county in which the person for whom a sterilization is sought is a resident shall have sole jurisdiction and authority to order that a sterilization procedure may or may not be performed when the person is:

1. Legally incompetent;
2. Under the age of majority and not married; or
3. Believed, by the person's physician, parent, spouse, or legal guardian, to be mentally impaired.

(b) The petition shall be executed under oath and shall set forth:

1. Name, age, and residence of the person for whom a sterilization is sought.
2. Names and residences of any parents, spouse, or legal guardian of such person.
3. Such person's mental condition, if appropriate.
4. A statement of the reasons for which sterilization is sought.
5. If voluntary sterilization is sought, a statement that

competency to consent is the only issue for court determination.

(c) Copies of the petition and notices of the time and place
for a hearing on the petition shall be served on the person for
whom the sterilization is sought and his parents, spouse, or legal
guardian not less than 20 days before the scheduled hearing. If
any of said individuals are not residents of the state, notice
may be served by registered mail. If the residence of any of the
foregoing is unknown, an affidavit to that effect shall be filed
in lieu of service.

(d) A full hearing on the petition shall be held as soon as
practicable after the petition is filed. The person for whom a
sterilization is sought shall be physically present throughout
the entire proceeding, unless waived by the person for whom a
sterilization is sought or his attorney. The person for whom a
sterilization is sought shall be represented by counsel, and provided the right and opportunity to be confronted with and to cross-
examine all adverse witnesses. Counsel may not be waived. In
the event that such person cannot afford counsel, the court shall
appoint an attorney not less than 20 days before the scheduled
hearing. A court-appointed or otherwise provided attorney shall
represent the rights and legal interests of such person. An attorney appointed pursuant to this act shall be entitled to a reasonable
fee to be determined by the circuit judge and paid by the county
in which the person for whom sterilization is sought resides. All
stages of the hearing shall be reported. In all cases, the court
shall issue written findings to support its decision and the basis
for such findings.

(e) Appeal of a final order in a cort proceeding shall be by
right in accordance with Article V of the State Constitution and
the Florida Appellate Rules. Pendency of an appeal pursuant to this
act shall stay proceedings until a final determination is made.

(3) PROCEDURE TO DETERMINE COMPETENCY TO CONSENT.--

(a) If there is reason to believe that a person for whom a
sterilization is sought who is over the age of majority lacks the
competency to consent to a sterilization, the court, upon the filing
of the petition, shall immediately fix a time for a hearing to
determine the person's competency to consent to sterilization. For
this purpose, the court shall appoint no fewer than two disinterested
experts experienced in the field of mental retardation or mental
health, including at least one licensed psychologist or psychiatrist,
to examine the person and to testify at the hearing as to his competency. Other evidence regarding the person's mental condition may
be introduced at the hearing by any party.

(b) The burden of proof beyond a reasonable doubt shall be on the party seeking to establish the incompetency of the person for whom a sterilization is sought.

(c) If the court determines that the person is competent to consent, the court shall order that a sterilization may be performed on such person if, in fact, such person does consent. If the court determines that the person is incompetent to consent to be sterilized, a sterilization shall not be performed unless, pursuant to the provisions of subsection (4), the court determines that sterilization is in the best interest of the person.

(4) DETERMINATION OF BEST INTEREST OF THE PERSON.--

(a) If a person is under the age of majority and not married, or has been found legally incompetent pursuant to the provisions of subsection (3), or is mentally impaired, the court shall upon petition immediately fix a time for a hearing to determine the person's mental and physical condition and to determine whether sterilization is in the best interest of the person. The court shall appoint no fewer than three disinterested experts, including at least one licensed physician and one licensed psychologist or psychiatrist with experience related to the condition of the person as alleged in the petition to examine the person and to testify at the hearing as to the person's mental and physical condition. The court shall hear and consider evidence as to the positive or negative psychological and physical effects of a sterilization. Any other evidence regarding the person's mental and physical condition may be introduced at the hearing.

(b) Sterilization is in the best interest of the person if clearly necessary to preserve his or her health.

(c) The burden of proof beyond a reasonable doubt shall be on the party seeking to establish that a sterilization is in the best interests of the person for whom the sterilization is sought.

(d) If the court determines that a sterilization is in the best interest of the person and that less drastic alternative methods of contraception have proven to be unworkable or inapplicable to the needs of the person, the court shall order that a sterilization may be performed. If the court determines that a sterilization is not in the best interest of the person, the petition for sterilization shall be dismissed.

(5) CONFIDENTIALITY OF PROCEEDINGS AND RECORDS.--

(a) All court proceedings as provided in this section shall be confidential and closed to the public unless requested to be open to the public by the person for whom sterilization is sought or his attorney.

(b) Records of such court proceedings shall not be open to inspection by the public, unless so requested by the person for whom sterilization is sought or his attorney. On special order of the circuit judge, appropriate disclosure may be made for use in connection with the treatment of the person for whom sterilization is sought or for purposes of scientific research relating to sterilization; however, such disclosure for research purposes shall only be made on condition that the person shall not be identified.

Section 4. Limitations.--

(1) Consent to sterilization shall not be made a condition for release from any institution nor shall it be made a condition for the exercise of any right, privilege or freedom, nor shall it be made a condition for receiving any form of public assistance, nor as a prerequisite for any other service. The person must be free from constraints and from express or implied inducements or contingencies.

(2) The fact that a person of any age has not been sterilized or has not sought sterilization shall not be a ground for confinement in any institution.

(3) Nothing in this act shall require any hospital or any person to participate in any sterilization, nor shall any hospital or any person be civilly or criminally liable for refusing to participate in any sterilization.

(4) The guarantees and limitations provided in this section shall be given orally to individuals seeking sterilization. These guarantees and limitations must also appear prominently at the top of the consent document.

Section 5. Penalties.--

(1) Anyone knowingly or willfully violating the provisions of subsection (1) of section 3 is guilty of a felony of the third degree, punishable as provided in s. 775.082, s. 775.083, or s. 775,084, Florida Statutes.

(2) Anyone knowingly or willfully falsifying a petition for sterilization or otherwise aiding or procuring the performance of an unlawful sterilization is guilty of a misdemeanor of the first degree, punishable as provided in s. 775.082 or s. 775.083, Florida Statutes.

Section 6. If any section of this act, of any part thereof, is adjudged by any court of competent jurisdiction to be invalid, such judgment shall not affect, impair, or invalidate the remainder of any other section or part thereof.

Section 7. The court after considering the financial resources of the parties concerned and the source of initial action, shall assess court costs.

Section 8. This act shall take effect October 1, 1975.

ACKNOWLEDGMENTS

The author wishes to thank Donald Freedman, Margot Botsford, Garrick Cole, and Fay Saber for their contributions to the development of this paper.

REFERENCES

1. Buck v. Bell, 274 U.S. 200 (1927).

2. Murdock, C.W., Sterilization of the retarded: A problem or a solution? Calif. L. Rev. 62:917 (1974).

3. American Neurological Association, Committee for the Investigation of Eugenical Sterilization, Report (1936).

4. Ferster, E.Z., Eliminating the unfit - Is sterilization the answer? Ohio St. L. J. 27:591 (1966).

5. Association for Voluntary Sterilization, A.V.S. News, March 1975.

6. Good Housekeeping, the growing use of sterilization for birth control, May 1973.

7. Nirje, B., The normalization principle and its human management implications, in "Changing Patterns in Residential Services for the Mentally Retarded", R. Kugel and W. Wolfensberger (eds.), p. 179-195, President's Committee on Mental Retardation, Washington, D.C. (1969).

8. Wolfensberger, W., "The Principle of Normalization in Human Services", National Institute of Mental Retardation, Toronto, Canada (1972).

9. In re Cavitt, 182 Neb. 712, 157 N.W. 2d 171 (1968), rehearing denied, 183 Neb. 243, 159 N.W. 2d 566 (1968), appeal denied, 396 U.S. 996 (1969).

10. Nebraska Statutes Ann., Chapter 83, Section 504, R.R.S. 1943.

11. In re Cavitt, 183 Neb. 243, 159 N.W. 2d 566 (1968).

12. Mill, J.S., On liberty, in "The Utilitarians", pp. 475-600,
     Dolphin Books, New York (1961).

13. Rawls, J., "A Theory of Justice" p. 249, Harvard University
     Press, Cambridge (1971).

14. See, for example, Jehovah's Witnesses v. King County Hosp.,
     278 F. Supp. 188 (D.D.C. 1967); In re Karwath, 199 N.W. 2d
     147 (Iowa 1972); In re Sampson, 29 N.Y. 2d 900, 278 N.E. 2d
     918, 328 N.Y.S. 2d 686 (1972).

15. People ex rel. Wallace v. La Brenz, 411 Ill. 618, 404 N.E.
     2d 769, certiorari denied, 344 U.S. 824 (1952); State v.
     Perricone, 37 N.J. 463, 181 A.2d 751, certiorari denied,
     371 U.S. 890 (1962); Hoener v. Bertinato, 67 N.J. Super.517,
     171 A.2d 140 (Juv. & Dom. Rel. Ct. 1961); Application of
     Brooklyn Hosp., 45 Misc. 2d 914, 258 N.Y.S. 2d 621 (Sup. Ct.
     1965); Heinemann's Appeal, 96 Pa. 112 (1880); Mitchell v. Davis,
     205 S.W. 2d 812 (Tex. Civ. App. 1947).

16. Mannis v. State ex rel. DeWitt School Dist. No. 1, 240 Ark.
     42, 398 S.W. 2d 206 (1966) (vaccination); In re Karwath, 199
     N.W. 2d 147 (Iowa 1972) (removal of tonsils and adenoids);
     In re Sampson, 29 N.Y. 2d 900, 278 N.E. 2d 918, 328 N.Y.S. 2d
     686 (1972) (disfigurement); In re Carstairs, 115 N.Y.S. 2d
     314 (N.Y. Dom. Rel. Ct. 1952) (emotional illness); In re
     Rotkowitz, 175 Misc. 948, 25 N.Y.S. 624 (N.Y. Dom. Rel. Ct.
     1941) (deformity of foot resulting from polio); In re Weintraub,
     166 Pa. Super. 342, 71 A.2d 823 (1950) (emotional illness).

17. In re Tuttendario, 21 Pa. Dist. 561 (Dist. Ct. 1911) (Rickets);
     In re Hudson, 13 Wash. 2d 673, 126 P.2d 765 (1942) (disfigured
     arm); In re Seiferth, 309 N.Y. 80, 127 N.E. 2d 820 (1955) (cleft
     palate and hare lip); In re Frank, 41 Wash. 2d 294, 248 P.2d
     553 (1952) (Speech impediment); In re Green, 448 Pa. 338, 292
     A.2d 287 (1972) (spinal fusion operation).

18. The cases are collected and commented upon in Baron, C.H.,
     Botsford, M. and Cole, G.F., Live organ and tissue transplants
     from minor donors in Massachusetts, B.U.L. Rev. 55:159 (1975).

19. For example, Health Policy Advisory Center, Sterilization:
     Women fit to be tied, Health PAC Bulletin 62 (January/February):
     1 (1975).

20. Report of the Joint Conference on Professional Responsibility
     of the Joint Conference of the American Bar Association and
     the Association of American Law Schools, A.B.A.J. 44:1159 (1958).

21. In re Kemp, 118 Cal. Rep. 64 (ct. App. 1974); Frazier v. Levi,
     440 S.W. 2d 393 (Tex. Ct. Civ. App. 1969); Holmes v. Powers,
     439 S.W. 2d 579 (Ky. 1969).

22. In re M.K.R., 515 S.W. 2d 467 (Mo. 1974).

23. In re Simpson, 180 N.E. 2d 206 (Ohio Prob. Ct. 1962).

24. Wade v. Bethesda Hosp., 337 F. Supp. 671 (S.D. Ohio 1971).

DISCUSSION

Papers of Profs. L.B. Holmes, S. Lederberg, and C.H. Baron
Moderator: Prof. G.J. Annas

DEYE: There is the recurring question of the interests of the individual versus that of the society. Always when discussing things genetic, partially I imagine because of ghosts of Nazi "eugenics," we always say that the right of the individual is paramount and the questions of the interests of society are always skirted. In what conditions in our culture here are the interests of society allowed to supercede those of the individual? One obvious thing that comes to mind is incarceration. When an individual has transgressed society's rules, his rights are thought no longer to supercede that of society's. Another one less well recognized perhaps is universal military service to the country. Here an individual's rights or freedom are abrogated, albeit temporarily, for society's good.

I heard some participants in this discussion earlier today say we were prisoners of Jefferson and Mills and that the individual in our culture is everything and society's interests are really not allowed to be considered on the individual plane. I would like to just give one example of where things like this become hazy as culture becomes tighter in terms of competition for foodstuffs. Last summer I was in Lagos, Nigeria, listening to a fellow who is in charge of the birth control program in Bombay. He was telling us of the "non-coercive" setting up of a vasectomy program in where participants were given transistor radios that were readily exchangeable in the black market. A person also has to pose the question as to whether a sub-dermal deposit of a timed-release contraceptive might not be more humane than indefinite long-term incarceration, say for example, in a mental institution. The universal contraceptive idea that is recurring in science fiction literature also can be appropriately mentioned where the person is automatically impotent from something for example, he drinks in the water, and you need a birth license showing ability to care for your offspring in order to reproduce. You also have the cultural enforcement of the traditional contraceptive mode of abstinence very well practiced today in China. I think these things have to be at least entertained as topics for discussion.

H. ROLLE: E. Lindeman MHC, Boston: I support Prof. Lederberg's statement that the criteria for sterilization should be whether the person is competent to enter a civil contract or not. Firstly, many mildly retarded or borderline retarded people are able to enter civil contracts. Secondly, the psychological testing just is not accurate enought to really distinguish one from the other. Often mistakes are made. A number of mildly retarded people have become successful parents with adequate support or else have been able to reach voluntary decisions to become sterilized, either to avoid having any children, or else to limit the family size when the difficulty of being a parent is explained to them. So I would really modify that statement and say that before you decide that all retarded people or that no retarded person should be able to decide for themselves, that competency should really be determined.

BARON: It is a very close question whether in the case of mildly retarded individuals you ought to make a determination of competency or whether you ought to say as long as they are border-line, we ought to make a de novo determination as to whether it is in the individual's best interests. The reason why I have trouble with it is because I think it is somewhat denigrating. I am sure this is one of the things that is motivating you - to tell some-body that he/she cannot make that decision for him- or herself. On the other hand, I am worried about the problems of informed consent with somebody whose mental capacity is even suspect. As a result, to protect that individual, there is at least an argument to be made that an independent determination should be made as to whether it is in the individual's best interests.

In that proceeding to decide whether or not sterilization is in the individual's best interests, I think the opinion of that individual ought to be extraordinarily powerful evidence, and the more mildly retarded or the more intelligent the individual is, the more probative value that opinion should have. So that if you have a mildly retarded individual, it ought to be very difficult to overcome the evidentiary value of that individual's consent or lack of consent. But I think it is a very close question.

ANNAS: Both Profs. Baron and Lederberg have made a number of inroads into the compulsory sterilization statutes. Both thought they could not stand constitutional challenge today. Do you feel that the Supreme Court, given another case like Buck v. Bell, would come out differently than it did in the 1920's?

LEDERBERG: Professor Baron, please pick an answer, I will disagree.

BARON: I think it is very likely that the Supreme Court would come out differently, the reason being both procedural due process and equal protection. The court has imposed very heavy burdens on the state to prove that such legislation is needed or rational where marriage or procreation is involved. As a result, I think it would be very tough for that kind of legislation to survive a constitutional test today.

LEDERBERG: That sounds like the court in 1972 in the Eisenstadt v. Baer case, speaking very highly of the rights of the individual, married or single, to be free from unwarranted governmental intrusion into matters so fundamentally affecting a person, as the decision whether to bear or beget a child. This looks very good as the end therefore of the state regulation of procreation. The next year, of course, we see the climax of this in the Roe v. Wade case. But let us look at the Roe v. Wade case and the very important point where after agreeing that a woman has a right to abort a fetus during the first two trimesters, the court then goes on and points out why the state has a right to be involved in the third trimester. In the Supreme Court decision of Roe v. Wade, Justice Blackmun, who determined there is a time in pregnancy that a state may properly assert important interests in safeguarding health and maintaining medical standards in protecting potential life, stated that "The privacy right involved therefore cannot be said to be absolute. The court has refused to recognize unlimited rights of this kind in the past," citing as the only citation Jacobson v. Massachusetts and Buck v. Bell. Justice Blackmun goes on to say, "We therefore conclude that the right of personal privacy includes the abortion decision, but that this right is not unqualified and must be considered against important state interests and regulation." Without referring to the state's ability to intervene relying on Buck v. Bell and Jacobson v. Massachusetts, we would not have found a way to give the state back the right to interfere in the third trimester.

There is a concurrence by Justice Douglas, a rather liberal member of the court. We might otherwise have said perhaps the words by Justice Blackmun were parenthetical dicta. But Justice Douglas says the state has interests to protect. Vaccination to prevent epidemics is one example, as Jacobson holds. The court reminded us that compulsory sterilization of imbeciles afflicted with hereditary forms of insanity is another as in Buck v. Bell.

T. MYERS: Children's Hospital, Omaha: Nebraska has taken it on the chin a little bit. I thought I should let you know there is before the unicameral legislature in Nebraska at the present time a bill to liberalize our laws to permit first cousin marriages to people over the age of 60 years.

RIGHTS AND RESPONSIBILITIES OF THE INSURER

John L. Thompson and Wendy M. Greenfield

Blue Shield of Massachusetts

Although I am a lawyer, I am here today in my capacity as
President of Blue Shield of Massachusetts. For the benefit of
this discussion, the terms have changed from "law" and "ethics"
to "rights and responsibilities." Although I am honored to have
been invited to participate with you in your deliberations on
these issues, I must make clear that I am not expert in the field
of genetics and genetic diseases. In my professional capacity,
contact with that field of science and medicine has been extremely
limited. And, that, I gather, is <u>really</u> why I am here with you
today.

Two major issues, I understand, have prompted my appearance
here today. First, there were questions regarding how Blue Cross
and Blue Shield handle the hereditary aspects of genetic disease
as well as the expression of genetic problems in our subscribers.
Second, there have been numerous questions regarding Blue Cross-
Blue Shield coverage of genetic counseling and genetic screening
procedures.

The first set of questions, which turn largely on patient
privacy and right-to-know issues, is fairly simple to deal with.
Blue Cross and Blue Shield generally neither know nor care about
possible or diagnosed genetic traits in our subscriber population.
Group subscribers are invariably fully covered regardless of their
genetic makeup. While non-group subscribers are required to file
a health statement prior to acceptance, the questions, and any
subsequent specific waivers of liability, relate to active conditions recently or currently under medical treatment rather than
to genetic carrier status.

Consider the logical and practical difficulties of doing otherwise. First, it would have to be determined what genetic problems we should be concerned with, or, more to the point, how to decide. Should we deal only with those genetic diseases for which screening procedures are reasonably accurate and inexpensive? We would thus penalize only those with diseases which have especially interested geneticists or which tend to be concentrated in one segment of the population. Should we exclude that disease by waiver for someone who is asymptomatic but carries the trait? Should we set ourselves up as genetic counselors, examining the genetic makeup of married subscribers and determining the extent of risk to unborn (and as yet unconsidered) children? Should we exclude further children of families into which one genetically flawed child has already been born? At what risk level should we cut off? At Carter's high risk level, 1 in 10 (1)? Some arbitrary figure? And how do we find out? Do we penalize only those sophisticated enough to have found out themselves? Or do we institute routine screening procedures? If we consider screening, we must consider the cost in relation to the savings likely to be derived. We would have to weigh the cost of screening and of administering some system for gathering, collating, and analyzing data against the cost of covering the roughly 5% of U.S. babies born with some congenital defects. We would also have to account for those we would miss in any case since they generally are the result of unpredictable nondisjunctional or other events (e.g., some chromosome anomalies such as Turner's syndrome, Klinefelter's syndrome, XXX, XXY, and a majority of Down's syndrome) (2).

Even assuming we could be 100% accurate and fully account for all defects, the ethical issue would still remain. By determining in advance whether we should cover certain genetic risks, we would not only be engaging in the practice of medicine and interfering with the rights of the patient family, but also we would be going into the eugenics business. I do not believe that an insurer either has or should have that right.

The second set of questions requires a rather more concrete explanation than the essentially ethical and methodological monologue I just completed. You all want to know -- and rightly so -- what we cover, what we do not cover, and why. Let me begin with whose and what we do cover.

First, for adults, in cases where the onset of a genetic disease symptom occurs in later life (e.g. Huntingtons chorea) and while the patient is covered under Blue Cross Blue Shield, the coverage is precisely the same as for any other medical condition. If it falls into the category of prolonged illness under our Master Medical Contract, deductibles and coinsurance would be waived for many services such as office visits. Under the extended

benefits portion of Master Medical such services normally require
them.

In cases where onset is prior to non-group enrollment in Blue
Cross-Blue Shield, a waiver of liability can be required exempting
that specific condition from coverage permanently or for a limited
period. Group members, as I stated earlier, are exempt from
health statement requirements.

Any newborn in a family with family coverage in force is
automatically covered by Blue Cross Blue Shield at birth. Under
Master Medical, the vast majority of our contracts, congenital
defects requiring immediate and intensive treatment are specified
in our subscriber contract as covered conditions. In addition, we
are developing a rider which will classify certain congenital
anomalies, congenital megacolon, cleft plate, and harelips, among
others, prolonged illness conditions and therefore eligible for
certain benefits without deductibles or copayments.

That is who we cover. Now for the what.

Blue Cross and Blue Shield generally cover all medically necessary hospitalizations and disease or symptom related medical
care in any location. Visits to physician's offices and certain
other services are subject to deductibles and coinsurance except
in prolonged illness situations which I mentioned before. Although
we do not cover genetic counseling, we do cover most of the diagnostic tests and procedures used in the analysis of genetic risk--
blood tests, buccal smears, and amniocentesis, among others. Should
a couple decide, as a result of genetic analysis and counseling, to
abort the definitely or probably defective fetus, claims for the
abortion procedure would be paid under our medical necessity
guidelines. As I mentioned earlier, the genetically defective newborn's services are fully covered.

Yet we do not cover genetic counseling or geneticists as a
specialty grouping. I was asked specifically to deal with our
perception of these facts. Let us consider two groupings of problems surrounding the questions. In the first grouping, delivery
mode issues, I will be speaking strictly as a local Blue Shield
representative. In the second, preventive medicine, I will be
reflecting the philosophy of Blue Shield at local and national
levels.

While numerous physician and doctoral geneticists no doubt
work and study in Boston, most are apparently involved in research
and almost all are apparently employed by the four Boston hospitals
which have genetic clinics: Massachusetts General, New England
Medical Center, Boston Hospital for Women, and Boston City. Of
the ten physician clinical geneticists we found, none is in private

practice. Most, in addition, specialize in pediatrics or internal medicine with a dual specialty in genetics.

Two items here are crucial to Blue Shield's reimbursement philosophy. The first is the research aspect of genetics. The second is the apparent mode of service delivery at present.

Blue Shield, and also for that matter, Blue Cross, does not consider it the responsibility of an insurer to support research efforts--although we agree, of course, that research is necessary and beneficial. The question of who should fund it is another issue. In the case of genetics, apparently the largest single source of private funding is the National Foundation-March of Dimes. A recent Gallup poll, reviewed at the National Health Forum in March, showed overwhelming support for the idea that funding research is a national role as opposed to a state, local or third party role. We agree.

This is not to say that we should not cover those procedures within the research effort that we normally cover. A prime example of this sort of split funding is the research now being carried out in Boston on daughters born to mothers who took diethylstilbestrol during pregnancy. While Blue Shield covers the diagnostic procedures and treatments that we normally cover, the remainder is funded through a federal grant. Incidentally, participation in the entire project reportedly costs the patient nothing.

On the second point, current delivery mode, we must point out that apparently virtually all of the activity in the field of genetics is hospital-based. The work being done requires extensive laboratory back-up which is generally not available to solo practitioners in the field. As a case in point, we checked our billings for procedures we do cover and for which we could be billed. We found that, for example, out of all the amniocentesis procedures done in the Commonwealth in 1974, Blue Shield paid for 316. Most were apparently done through hospitals and their associated clinics and billed to Blue Cross in the cost base of the hospital. That is, they were done and analyzed in hospitals by salaried personnel. Because of the Blue Cross reimbursement method, however, it is impossible to determine exactly how many were paid for in this way.

Now let me return, for a moment, to what I gather is the major issue--our perception of genetic counseling as a preventive service and our treatment of preventive services in general.

That genetic counseling is a preventive service is not at issue. Carter reported that of 169 families seeking counseling, 150 came because of the birth of one or more abnormal children and 18 because one of the parents was abnormal. No reason was given

for the additional 1 family (3). The desire is to determine the
risk of producing a defective child or an additional abnormal
child. Should the couple then decide to do so, they may prevent
conception, or, if a fetus in utero is shown to be defective or
probably defective, choose to abort the fetus. Should they choose
to conceive, in utero testing showing a normal or probably normal
fetus may make them decide to carry it to term.

Carter also reported on the results of his genetic counseling.
Of 129 families judged to have high risk of recurrence, 33% decided to have further children. Sixty-two subsequent children
were produced, 14 of whom were affected in the same way as the
index patient. Of 177 low risk families, 75% had 154 additional
children only 3 of whom were affected (4). If the results of
this study are typical, slightly over 30% of all families who receive genetic counseling disregard stated risk levels.

Essentially, the genetic counseling procedure is wholly
discretionary at this point in time and the expenditure can be
anticipated by those involved. Any action or inaction taken subsequent to counseling is also discretionary. In general, Blue
Shield does not cover services that are purely discretionary and
not, in current insurance terminology, "medically necessary."

There are a number of reasons for this position. First, and
basic to our position, is the fact that services that can be anticipated and are discretionary are not insurance risks. The purpose
of prepaid health insurance has traditionally been to provide for
unexpected occurrences. Annual physicals, routine well-baby care
and other such services, including genetic counseling, are in no
sense unexpected services causing unanticipated costs.

Second, offering genetic counseling to all our subscribers
would rapidly move that service from the highly selective base upon
which it is now provided toward large scale screening processes.
In other words, care, to a great extent chases dollars. The best
example is mammography which, while a useful procedure for older
women, is reportedly relatively ineffective for younger women.
Some clinics and physicians are, however, routinely screening all
females over 15 years of age. The shift in scale raises the same
issue I discussed before in terms of the cost/benefit of screening
prospective parents and/or fetuses.

I should note that preventive services in general are now
coming under more careful scrutiny from all quarters. At one time
we looked into the possibilities of offering multiphasic screening,
for example, and found the yield too low to be cost-effective.
Physicians are now beginning to question the value of annual physicals for everyone in terms of the cost and the drain they create
on physician time.

The efficacy, in terms of results, of certain screening procedures is also being questioned. Most recently, for example,
oncologists and others have raised questions regarding the value
of Pap. smears on a yearly or semi-annual basis. This was previously an article of faith. Questions are being raised about the
competence levels of those taking the smear and effects of improper
procedure on results. Questions are also being asked regarding
the value of the smears in terms of patient outcomes. Relating
these issues to Carter's reported results, then, we must note that
30% of families who sought counseling and presumably paid for it
disregarded the indications of the data. Fourteen affected children were produced despite the fact that results accorded with
predictions in both groups having children and all of those births
could have been prevented.

In sum, then, we do not now cover and we do not anticipate
expanding our benefit programs to include such preventive services
under our regular contracts. This position is based on our concern
over the appropriateness of covering such a risk and the essential
financial issue of whether genetic counseling would be cost-effective if applied to the population as a whole. In assessing this
latter point, I would urge you to do so in the perspective of financial priorities that must be applied to a whole array of different yet beneficial services that are not currently covered by prepaid insurance. While genetic counseling is not covered, we will,
of course, continue to cover diagnostic and therapeutic procedures
which provide the backbone of genetic analysis and treatment of
genetically controlled conditions.

REFERENCES

1. Carter, C.O., Prospects in genetic counselling, in "Modern
    Trends in Human Genetics", A.E.H. Emery (ed.), Butterworth's,
    London, p. 341 (1970).

2. Ibid, p. 342.

3. Murray, R.F., Jr., Genetic counseling in clinical medicine,
    in "Genetics in Medical Practice", M. Bartalos(ed.),
    Lippincott, Philadelphia, p. 149 (1968).

4. Carter, op. cit., p. 341.

DISCUSSION

Paper of Mr. J.L. Thompson
Principal Discussant: Prof. G.W. Melcher
Moderator: Prof. A.G. Steinberg

MELCHER: My job is trying to finance the delivery of good health services. You have got all kinds of new products coming out and for some reason or other, I cannot seem to get either the doctors to use them or the public to accept them. I can tell you as far as many of us are concerned in the financing area, we are not going to sit around forever and simply be conduits for money. The old way that Blue Cross-Blue Shield (though I am not speaking for them) and all of us as insurers have operated has been to allow the marketplace to dictate. I think those days are rapidly drawing to a close.

If we had perhaps been far more aggressive in trying to meet some of the solutions than we have been, perhaps some of our present problems in financing would not be taking place. You have sitting around you remarkable examples of how intervention and some pressure here or there can bring about not only better quality services but in many instances more economical as well as better service.

Your experiment here in Boston in taking a group of hemophiliacs and making them smarter than the doctors or at least as smart as the doctors who treated them and gave them a new way to live. Practically speaking, look at the dollars saved. All the way through medicine we can find many examples.

I personally feel that the largest area of preventive health services is in the genetic area. The fact that we have not brought it out and not learned ways to use it all is another matter. I don't think that we are going to sit by quietly and let the traditional ways of financing health services continue in this particular area.

At least I will speak for one company which is independent and represents some 3 million insured. I am under a mandate from my board of directors not to do that. I think others will begin to follow once they see some of the ways.

CAPRON: Is the rationale for not covering genetic counseling that people do not always follow the advice? Indeed you cited Carter's study showing that 30% do not. I wonder how far you carry this rationale. For instance, a patient who is told the medically advised treatment for a certain disease and who then declines to take that treatment. Would there be any question about paying? I wonder if we can carry this over one step further and look to the future.

There is often in these discussions of screening and counseling a parade of things about the government mandating amniocentesis and abortion. It seems reasonable to me to look to the future and ask what the insurance companies are going to do. I wonder if there is now in your policies anything that would lead you to a conclusion to the following question. Assume that you now exclude people for whom it is possible to detect a pre-existing disease or you at least make them waive coverage of that disease. Assume that it is possible to screen for a certain condition in the heterozygous state and you discover a man and wife are both carriers for a condition and their offspring have a one in four risk of being affected.

Would you consider it at all improper to write into your coverage that they would have to agree to an amniocentesis and then to an abortion if they were to have a child that would be born with a serious defect that would amount to large medical costs, e.g. Tay-Sachs disease? Would this be within the range of things that would be presently acceptable under your procedures?

THOMPSON: Frankly, I admit it is really not very easy to stand up before this particular audience and argue with great persuasiveness as to the cost-benefit relationships. That is not an attractive argument that nevertheless has to be made at times, but it is not one that is very enjoyable. It is particularly difficult when you deal with the unfortunate results of some of that philosophy in our society which says you do have to make those kinds of decisions. So I don't stand here really as an advocate of providing all this on the basis of dollars. That really isn't my point. I have the practical problem that faces me, and I guess people like me in this country whether they are in private business or whether they exist in government, that somewhere in society we have to make those kinds of difficult decisions we hope rationally and humanely.

In regard to your specific question, I really can't imagine under any set of circumstances a Blue Shield plan, particularly in Massachusetts, having any kind of agreement that required somebody to have an abortion if the result turned out a particular way. I really don't think that is my business, to be very honest with you.

I think the way you present it is a very practical way of perhaps approaching it from the standpoint of some other jurisdiction, but it really isn't practical here in Massachusetts. I'm not entirely sure where we go, to reach the broader thrust of your question, because really there's been very little pressure in this particular area. Although there are 400 here today, there really is very little demonstrated interest from either the insured population, from governmental entities, or from employers particularly in this particular area. Certainly the meeting of this par-

ticular type adds to that body of knowledge on the part of the
public at large, employers, labor unions, and others who are decision makers to a certain degree in regard to health insurance
and respond to pressures from within the different groups.

I don't mean pressure in an unsavory aspect at all. I use
it in the sense also of education by groups as to what the needs
of the people really are. So far other particular specialties
have obviously enjoyed a priority that geneticists have not. Maybe
that's a challenge that you have discussed in other parts of your
program.

G. OAKLEY: Center for Disease Control, Atlanta, Georgia:
I wondered if you would address yourself to two hypothetical situations. One is a woman who is 35 and requests a chromosome test
and then says, "How about doing all the other tests, specifically
alpha-fetoprotein." You say to her, "At your age you are not at
an increased risk and it isn't cost-benefit to pay for that."

The other analogy,which is the converse of that,is a 25 year-
old woman who has had a previous child with a neural tube defect.
She asks for amniocentesis to have the alpha-fetoprotein done,
and says, "By the way, can you tell me whether my child is going
to have Down's syndrome or not?" In both those situations you say,
"My policy is only to do the tests for which you are at high risk."
What sort of medico-legal liability may you incur?

THOMPSON: I don't perceive any legal liability upon a carrier
because he limits the particular service for which he pays. But
I assure you in the operation of Blue Shield in Massachusetts, and
I am sure elsewhere in the country, we do not have people within the
institution themselves making those kinds of determinations. All of
the screening guidelines that we use are developed by the appropriate specialty. It would seem to me unreasonable for somebody who
works for me being given a series of tests, making some determination on a cost-benefit relationship. They don't. They do it on
the basis the physician believes it was medically necessary under
the guidelines that his specialty supports. I think those are
different issues.

OAKLEY: What would be the medico-legal position of the counsel-
or who said he would only ask for the test the patient was at high
risk for, even though the patient asked for the other test.

THOMPSON: It would seem to me if the body of scientific knowledge supported the determination that there should have been additional tests and he doesn't do it because of insurance considerations or something like that, the man travels at his peril.

OAKLEY: I think the point is that for the other things they requested, the family is at no greater risk than anyone else in the population.

Research and Experimentation—
In Vitro Fertilization—
Clonal Man

THE SOCIAL CONTROL OF SCIENCE

Arthur G. Steinberg

Department of Biology, Case Western Reserve University, Cleveland; Medical Advisory Board, National Genetics Foundation, New York

The expression, "Social Control of Science" means different things to different people. My interpretation is that any form of control of either goal directed (i.g. applied) or non-goal directed (i.e. basic) science exerted by individuals or groups other than the scientists responsible for the initiation and prosecution of the experiments is social control of science. Governmental, religious, cultural (i.e. Zeitgeist), sociological and financial controls are, under this definition, forms of social control of science. Reflection will show that "control" need not be disadvantageous, it may be benign, or beneficial, and even necessary.

As I have defined the term, social control of science has existed as long as scientific activity has existed. I suppose the best known early case is the action of the Church in the 16th century to compel Galileo to retract his support of Copernicus' hypothesis that the earth revolves about a stationary sun. A much earlier case prescribing the application of a "genetic" finding is described in the Talmud (1). It states that a woman must not circumcise a third son if two earlier born sons bled to death after circumcision. In addition to being an early record of social control of the application of a genetic finding, this is also probably the first recognition of hemophilia and of sex-linkage!

We are all too aware of the infamous social control of biological science practiced by the Nazis. The supression of genetics by the Soviets and other Communist countries is not so well known (see (2) for review). It is important to note that in each instance of suppression, the suppressor suffered more in the long run than did the suppressed or abused science. The correlation is perfect; regardless of possible short term gains, suppression or abuse leads

301

to negative return for the suppressor or the abuser. This does
not mean by any stretch of the imagination, that social control
of science should not exist. It is my conviction that it not only
should exist, but that it must exist. It is no accident, as I
said earlier, that social control of science has existed for as long
as scientific activity has existed.

The question, therefore, is "How can social control of science
best serve humanity?" Unfortunately, humanity is divided into many
nations with different cultural values, and with different kinds of
socio-economic development. This makes the question as posed above
too broad to be meaningful. I say this because I do not believe in
absolutes (and here I part with many, if not most ethicists) and
because I am certain that I do not understand the cultures of countries other than the U.S. well enough to discuss the problem in the
context of their societies. The question becomes manageable for
me when rephrased as, "How can social control of science in the U.S.
best serve the American people?" I recognize the danger in this,
namely, that what is best for the American people may not be the
best for humanity as a whole, but my limitations compel this
approach.

Although the American Colonies were agricultural, with essentially no science at the time of the founding of the U.S., the
framers of the Constitution recognized that science should be encouraged. We find in Article I, section 8 of the Constitution,
that Congress shall have the power, "To promote the progress of
science and useful arts by securing for limited times to authors
and inventors the exclusive right to their writings and discoveries."
Relatively early in our history (1863), Congress established the
National Academy of Sciences (N.A.S.). The origin of the National
Institutes of Health (N.I.H.) may be traced to the founding of the
Marine Hospital Service in 1798 or, for those who would like a more
restricted definition to 1879, when a National Board of Health
was created with an organized medical research effort (3). An
interesting variety of controls of science has been exercised
during recent times.

A major, goal directed medical research program arose, because a popular President of the U.S. had suffered paralytic polio-
myelitis. Millions of dollars were raised by well designed publicity campaigns to fight a frightening, but relatively minor
disease - minor in the sense of frequency of morbidity and mortality. It probably was the perceived necessity for publicity that
led to the rapid introduction of the Salk vaccine and to the death
of several children, rather than waiting for the safer Sabin vaccine
which has replaced it. If it were not for a particularly inept
burglary, we might have seen the establishment of a crash program
for the study of phlebitis.

The potential dangers of publicity in science as contrasted to informing the public were well expressed by J.D. Bernal (4) in 1937 as follows:

"The expenditure on science in the United States is colossal. The position of the scientist cannot fail to be influenced by the existing values outside science, particularly those of the struggle for success and the importance of publicity. Although the better of the American scientists are free from these influences, it is quite clear, from the quality of the bulk of the work published in America, that they are not without an effect. ...in America there is a suspicion that the position of a man may depend on the bulk of his published work." Bernal continues, however, to say, "The advertisement side of research, however, is by no means uniformly bad for science. ...in America research has an advertisement value both to the firm and to the university which undertakes it. This enables a good deal of purely scientific work, whose direct utility value would be small, to be done. On the other hand, it places an undoubted emphasis on branches of science which have high publicity value, ...to the detriment of other equally important branches of science."

The use of publicity to raise funds has spread from volunteer non-profit organizations, to universities, and to individual investigators. This has led to exaggerated claims for the potential use of a too little explored "new" discovery and to distortion of the relative worth of faculty to the University. Preference too often being given to the spectacular rather than to the sound.

It has been claimed that, the competition for funds and for status has led in recent years to outright fraud in one instance, strongly suspected fraud in a second instance, and to a change in the relationship of scientists to each other, from one of openness and trust to one of secretiveness and competition. This changed relation is nicely summed up by a remark made to me a few years ago by a colleague working in the field of microbiology. When I told her that it was my practice to send my manuscripts to various colleagues for review before I submitted them for publication, she replied, "You must have most unusual colleagues. I would not dare to do that!"

I am old enough to know that such an attitude did not exist before the Second World War, when the need for funds and the competition for "fame" was less intense than it is today. Nevertheless, I am aware of two additional cases of fraud that occurred prior to our present day of "big" science. Hence, there is some uncertainty concerning a cause and effect relationship between "big" science and fraud.

The recent cases of fraud have led to some peculiar statements

from those who should know better. Consider the following from a
letter to the editor of Science (5): The writer referred to the
two recent cases and complained that there is, "...little or no
public access to the facts or involvements with the issues." He
went on to ask, "Why should research scientists be any less accountable to the public for the consequences of their misconduct than
are physicians, lawyers, or politicians?" His reason appears to
be that, "One false lead can cost science (and society) years of
potentially constructive work." I note that he offers no examples
and I sympathize with his omission, because I cannot think of any
either. I wonder who would decide between honest errors and forged
data, before tests to check the result have been done. Erroneous
data are soon revealed to be erroneous, because they cannot be
obtained by others. Such data are no threat to science. Science
has always experienced false leads. One must hope that it always
will experience false leads, because this will indicate that science has remained free, and of equal importance because testing
false leads provides data and guidelines to correct paths. Not
only is the writer's logic poor, but so also is his knowledge of the
history of genetics. I will not bore you with the details of his
distortion of the origin of the Lysenko affair (2).

     The falsity of Lysenko's work was known to the scientists who
participated in the debate at the Lenin Academy of Agricultural
Sciences of the U.S.S.R. which took place from 31 July through 7
August 1948 (2). They expressed their views with vigor and offered
data to show his errors. All this changed after Lysenko reported
(page 605) as follows on the morning of 27 August 1948.

     "Comrades, before I pass to my concluding remarks I
     consider it my duty to make the following statement.
     "The question is asked in one of the notes handed
     to me, What is the attitude of the Central Committee
     of the Party to my report? I answer: The Central Comm-
     ittee of the Party examined my report and approved it.
     (Stormy applause. Ovation. All rise.)"

It was not Lysenko's false data that led to the supression of
genetics. It was his political maneuvers in a dictatorial state.
The danger to science stems not from investigators' errors, nor
from outright forgeries. It stems from interference by the state
or other powers. I remind you, however, that while none of the
false data published by Lysenko and his followers harmed science,
the governmental control of "truth" in science did immense harm
to scientists and to science in the U.S.S.R.

     The author of the letter stated that, "These events (the two
forgeries) are so troubling...that they call out for action."
Loss of position, loss of standing in the field, effective disbarment from research positions, widespread publicity are not action

enough for our author. I wonder what he had in mind for these
people, that would do more to protect science. I fear the author
of that letter far more than I do the forgers of data. Forgers of
data are easily found out and their harm, if any, quickly circum-
scribed. The harmful course advocated by the writer of the letter
would affect all of science in unforeseen, but certainly deleterious ways for many, many years. We are beginning to experience
the effects of an example of such control of the application of
science resulting from a recent criminal trial in Boston (6)
and from a Massachusetts law designed to regulate experimentation
on human fetuses (7).

The pursuit of science has always required funds. As scientific experimentation became and becomes more complex and more dependent upon elaborate equipment, the requirement for funds has and
will increase. These funds come from sources other than the scientist - primarily and increasingly from the Federal Government.
In 1961 the Federal Government disbursed 574 million dollars for
Medical Research and Development (MRD), exclusive of funds for
training and construction. These constituted 55% of all such funds
spent by all sources in the U.S. By 1964 the government was providing 63% of the funds for MRD. It is estimated that the proportion was 63% in 1973 also (8).

Virtually all funds for training in the biomedical sciences
come from the Federal Government and most of these are from the
N.I.H. The funds increased from $9,404,000 in 1950 to $263,873,000
in 1966. They dropped abruptly to about $185,000,000 in 1967 and
remained there through 1972. In 1973, the funds plunged to $141,
184,000 and there was and is havoc in the medical schools and the
biological divisions of graduate schools. These abrupt shifts in
funding, instituted for reasons having little or nothing to do
with needs of science or of society (9) (If its needs can ever be
evaluated separately from those of the science.) constitute a
major threat to the orderly development of a reservoir of scientific talent. The shifts in the funds available for research have not
been so great. While funding for MRD has increased steadily, in
terms of constant (1970) dollars (8), funds for research projects
have not done so, because increasing proportions of the total funds
have been devoted to contract research and to program projects and
centers. Funds for contracts changed from none, budgeted prior to
1971,to about 17% of the funds obligated for research in Fiscal
Year (FY) 1974 and of the estimated obligation of such funds in FY
1975 (8). Funds granted for contract work are not subject to peer
review.

J.A. Shannon (9), (Director of the N.I.H. from 1955-1968),
has succinctly summarized the impact of this shifting program on
the biomedical sciences and has underscored the destructive impact
of placing program decision making at organizational levels defi-

cient in evident scientific and professional competence. Neither
Dr. Shannon, nor any other competent person maintains that reduction in federal funding is never justified. The argument is that
changes should be made on the basis of studies which involve persons with an adequate technical and administrative competence and
which have an adequate public information base. Changes should not
be made simply on the advice of the Office of Management and Budget, or of other financial, or political administrators.

Use of science for immediate gains and without regard for its
possible long range effects has caused great hardships and has placed
us in our current dilemma of excessive population growth, imbalance
of food production and distribution, and of wealth, not only between nations, but also within nations. Even well intentioned application of biomedical science without adequate attention to foreseeable consequences may do great harm.

Seaborg (10) discussing primarily the non-biomedical sciences,
has indicated that the failure to correlate knowledge has permitted
errors contributing to increased pollution, crime, violence and
social unrest. I believe this holds for the biomedical sciences
also. An example is application of modern medical care in a developing country without providing food for the inevitable increase
in population.

Since I know genetics best, let me illustrate my points with
examples from this field. The basic principles of Mendelian genetics and of sex-linkage and linkage were well established by the
end of the second decade of this century. The genetics of multi-
factorial characters was still to be studied. There was essentially
no detailed knowledge of the relation between the genotype and the
phenotype. Similarly, there was little knowledge concerning the
interaction between the genotype and the environment to modify the
phenotype, though geneticists appreciated the importance of the
environment. Ignorance did not prevent an attempt to apply genetics,
in the form of eugenics, to solving various sociological problems.
(See Ludmiller (11) for review). There followed a series of laws
in several states making sterilization of certain persons mandatory
or permissable to improve the genetics of the species - at least in
the U.S. The ultimate result of this premature, ignorant, and prejudiced application of genetics to man was a revulsion toward eugenics and by extension toward human genetics. Human genetics was
taught, so far as I know, only at Ohio State University and its
advocate, a competent and ultimately highly respected geneticist,
has told many stories of his ostracism. This peculiar form of
social control should warn us not to rush to apply poorly understood techniques, regardless of how well intentioned we may be.

The actions of Jensen, Herrnstein, Shockley and others indicate
that we have not yet shaken free of haste to apply poorly understood

genetic concepts to society. The distortion of genetics and its misuse by the Nazis made the study of the genetics of human races difficult for a period after the Second World War. Even today, because of racism in this country there are voices raised, fortunately weak ones, decrying genetic studies of simply inherited characters among various races.

Controls on science by society fall into broad categories of legal, economic, and peer; the last, in the sense of approbation or disapprobation. Prior to the second world war most funds for research came from the institution in which the work was done or from volunteer foundations such as Rockefeller or Carnegie. Private foundations have, through the distribution of vast sums of money, influenced areas of research and application. The intense interest of a major foundation in population control has greatly increased investigation in that area, just as the early support of the Eugenics Station at Cold Spring Harbor inspired activity in that area. Scientists obey the principle in the advice said to have been given many years ago by a father to his daughter, "Thee shall not marry for money, but go thee where the money is."

It is important to know how the foundations determine what areas of research to support, just as it is important to know how decisions concerning science are arrived at in government. I have no profound knowledge of either area. I am aware, of course, that the foundations and the government consult with scientists and others before deciding on programs, but I am not cognizant of the weight given by the foundations to the advice of the scientists, nor am I cognizant of how they are chosen.

Within the guidelines laid down by Congress, the N.I.H., using the peer review system, has performed excellently in distributing funds for research and for fellowships. As I have indicated, an increasing proportion of N.I.H. funds is being assigned to contract research. This is a dangerous trend, because contract research is not subjected to the rigorous peer review system and because the base for ideas for research is restricted to a relatively small group of administrators at the N.I.H., rather than being extended to the entire scientific community.

During the Eisenhower administration, under the so-called Mc-Carthy influence, many research grants were summarily terminated for political reasons without a hearing or an explanation, and many investigators were black-listed. These investigators were ineligible for grant support or for service on study sections, or for service as consultants to the N.I.H. Although eligibility for grant support was reinstated for these investigators by the end of the Eisenhower administration, the black-list was not abandoned until about five years ago. During the Nixon reign we have seen the illegal impounding of funds for many programs including those of the N.I.H. and the intrusion of politics into appointments of officials administering the Institutes. The latter aspect of the Nixon program which President Ford seems to be continuing, threatens grave dangers for the biomedical sciences of the U.S., because their support is primarily from the N.I.H. It seems redundant to say that damage to the biomedical sciences means damage to the health of the population of the U.S.

Control of science at a state or city level varies greatly, but is usually on a smaller scale than the Federal Programs. We have had some unfortunate examples of poor control. Thus, various state and city governments, under pressure from religious groups are regulating what shall be taught concerning evolution and thus indirectly influencing research in that area. We have laws controlling the application of science and this is as it should be. We must, however, be very careful about how these laws are enforced. In Boston a physician has been convicted of manslaughter allegedly because he did not allow a legally aborted fetus to be born alive, and still other physicians are under indictment for grave robbery for using tissue from a dead fetus for experimental purposes.

Haste and extreme measures seem to be characteristic of our nation. Our legislators and federal administrators, anxious to correct abuses, pass laws or institute procedures without adequate consideration of their possible harmful effects. Thus, the highly laudable program of informed consent is so inadequately defined that blood, urine, and fecal samples remaining after their use for diagnosis may not be used for research purposes without obtaining permission from each patient to do so.

The most commendable program to protect humans and vertebrates from abuse in experimentation has led to an ever increasing accumulation of paper work and waste of man-hours. To be more specific, at my University the "Protocol of Human Experimentation" must be approved by the Department Chairman, a Department Committee, and a University Clinical Research COmmittee. Twenty-three people were involved in the review of the 18 required copies of the protocol of an ongoing project that I recently submitted. Only the manufacturers of paper and of duplicating equipment can applaud such a program.

Shameful abuses have occurred, and they should not recur, but I know of no data indicating the incidence of these abuses. Nor do I know of studies to determine simpler methods than the one now used to prevent such abuse.

The use of financial supportive programs to change medical school curricula and to influence hiring practices throughout the university were underscored in a recent editorial in Science (14). These uses of supportive programs have been introduced recently

or are planned for introduction. I do not doubt the good intentions
of those advocating the programs, but I wonder if they have considered the possible damage such actions may have by eroding the independence of American universities from political control.

The forms of social control of biomedical science required
for research and for the application of the fruits of research
are, it seems to me, quite different. The best form of control of
research is that exerted by the scientists themselves in collabor-
ation with informed laymen with broad knowledge of the nation.
Excellent examples are the recent "Academy Forum" (18, 19 February
1975) on "Experiments and Research with Humans: Values in Conflict"
sponsored by the National Academy of Sciences, and the position
taken by the "Committee on Recombinant DNA Molecules Assembly of
Life Sciences," National Research Council, National Academy of
Sciences (12) which led to the conference at Asilomar (13). Self
appointed groups of ethicists, sociologists and others, who are
not practicing and highly competent scientists, and who issue unqualified statements on what should be done, do no good at best
and may do considerable harm.

The applications of biomedical science must be controlled by
various actions of society, including legislation, not only because application often, if not always, involves profit for someone,
but also because application without adequate planning may cause
considerable harm. Such controls, however, must allow for some
degree of flexibility and experts as well as informed laymen must
be involved, not only in drafting of the regulations, but also
in their enforcement. Let me dare to say to our legal colleagues
that I do not believe that our ordinary jury system is the proper
method for deciding whether regulations governing the application
of highly technical procedures have been violated. I believe this
applies to medical malpractice suits as well as to legal prosecutions. Such matters should be weighed by jurors with sufficient
knowledge to be able to understand the technical problems central
to the issue.

In summary, biomedical research should be subjected to social
control. Such research is best controlled by biomedical scientists
working with informed laymen. A model is the N.I.H. peer review
system combined with the Institute Advisory Councils. The latter
being composed of scientist administrators, and informed laymen.
Applications of biomedical science require legislation, but this
should be instituted with the aid of experts and informed laymen,
and enforcement should involve juries composed of individuals with
adequate knowledge to be able to understand the technical matters
at issue.

REFERENCES

1. Nashim, I. and Yebamoth, I., "The Talmud," pp. 440,
   Soncino Press (1936).

2. Medvedev, Z.A., "The Rise and Fall of T.D. Lysenko," pp. 284,
   Columbia University Press, New York (1969), and "The Situation
   in Biological Sciences," Proc. Lenin Acad. Agricultural Sci.
   U.S.S.R., July 21-August 7, 1948, pp. 636, International
   Publishers, New York (1949).

3. Department of Health, Education and Welfare, "N.I.H. Almanac,"
   DHEW Publication No. (NIH) 74-5 (1974).

4. Bernal, J.D., "The Social Function of Science," p. 206, 482,
   The Macmillan Company, New York (1939).

5. Lappé, M., Accountability in science, Science 187:(February
   28, 1975).

6. Wade, N., Genetics: Conference sets strict controls to replace
   moratorium, Science 187:931 (1975).

7. Culliton, B., Fetal research (III): The impact of a Massachusetts law, Science 187:1175 (1975).

8. U.S. Department of Health, Education and Welfare, "Basic Data
   Relating to the National Institutes of Health," W.T. Carrigan,
   (ed.) (1975).

9. Shannon, J.A., Federal and academic relationships: The biomedical
   sciences, Proc. Nat. Acad. Sci. 71:3309 (1974).

10. Seaborg, G., Science, technology and the citizen, in "The Place
    of Value in a World of Facts", A. Tiselius and S. Nilsson (eds.)
    Proc. 14th Nobel Symp., Wiley-Interscience, New York (1969).

11. Ludmerer, K.M., "Genetics and American Society," p. 222, The
    Johns Hopkins University Press, Baltimore, Maryland (1972).

12. Berg, P., Baltimore, D., Boyer, H.W. et al, Potential biohazards
    of recombinant DNA molecules, Proc. Nat. Acad. Sci. 71:2593
    (1974).

13. New York Times, "World Biologists Tighten Rules on 'Genetic
    Engineering' Work," (February 27, 1975).

14. Brewster, K., Coercive power of the federal purse, Science
    188:105 (1975).

DISCUSSION

Paper of Prof. A.G. Steinberg
Principal Discussant: Prof. B.D. Davis
Moderator: Prof. L.E. Rosenberg

DAVIS: Prof. Steinberg has pointed out that some degree of
public control over science has been both traditional and inevitable.
If society pays the bill it has to decide among competing demands
for its funds. But to a very large extent the public has been willing to leave decisions about the relative value of various projects,
and about their moral justifiability, in the hands of the scientific
community, since technical considerations usually loom large in
these decisions. Moreover, the public has accepted the view that
the interest of scientists in advancing knowledge generally coincides
with the interests of society, and that the biases and self-interest
of individual scientists are best detected and corrected for by their
peers. Hence legislators, guided by scientist administrators, have
generally determined only how much money to appropriate and have
left the apportionment and the mechanisms of distribution entirely
up to peer groups.

The last few years, however, have seen an increasing demand
for public input into these decisions. The abruptness of this development, and the accompanying criticisms of the scientific community
have come as a surprise. Yet some such reaction can be now seen as
inevitable, as science has become more visible and expensive, as it
continues to generate novel ethical problems, and as we belatedly
recognize that the technological applications of science yield not
only benefits but also environmental and social costs. The reaction
was intensified, and perhaps precipitated, by several other social
developments that coincided with it: the recognition that technological advances present costs and dangers as well as benefits, widespread mistrust of social institutions, heightened concern with the
rights of individuals, and antagonism to a vaguely defined elitism.
This last development inevitably extended to science, since that
enterprise must emphasize respect for intellectual excellence and
for objective standards.

The reaction of the scientific community has been one of dismay.
It is natural that a group accustomed to self-regulation will resist
and resent efforts to introduce external sources of restraint.
This is particularly true of the biomedical sciences, proud of their
humanitarian goals and accustomed to trust in the judgment of physicians. Yet we must recognize that the change in the public attitude
is no passing fad, and we cannot expect to return to the earlier
pattern. Moreover, few would deny that the new pressures have had
some tangible benefits. For even though the record would no doubt
show that most medical investigators have been responsible and con-
scientious in trying to balance the interest of the subjects of res-

311

earch and those of society, they have acted largely on the unexamined traditions of an earlier, more stratified society. Hence recognition of the need for informed consent where real risk is involved, and recognition of the need for research review committees in hospitals, represent real gains.

Nevertheless, I have deep apprehension, like many of my colleagues, at the prospect of overreactions, and a loss of perspective, that will have serious consequences.   This is not a distant specter. As current examples we have the recent ban on fetal researc and even limitations on the study of waste materials from a patient. In a particularly ironical twist, a cell biologist at MIT, using the byproducts of circumcision as a convenient source of cells from a young individual, found his supply cut off because the surgeon did not wish to get tangled up with the problem of obtaining adequately informed consent!

The danger of foolish restrictions on research seems especially great in the medical area, for several reasons. First, in the field of medical ethics it is particularly easy to arouse an emotional reaction by presenting a onesided, simplistic analysis of a complex problem: the XYY story is a recent example. Second, the widespread dissatisfaction of the public with the quality, availability, and economics of medical care is easily projected upon the highly visible teaching and research centers. Third, the problems of biomedical research have attracted the attention of public interest lawyers, who bring with them the familiar adversary process. Hence instead of the traditions of scientific discussion, in which each participant is expected to try to consider all the evidence, we find unpleasant, polarized exchanges between prosecutors and defendants. This atmosphere was conspicuous in a recent National Academy of Sciences Forum on the ethics of medical research, and the results did not seem very constructive.

The ancient adversary tradition of the law may conceivably be the best way to resolve questions of guilt, where the crime is well defined, but it is hardly the best way for society to decide what is licit or illicit in medical research. The greatest danger is that the attacks by public interest groups will lead not simply to closer regulation by governmental agencies concerned with science, but to direct intervention by legislators, who are quick to seize on issues that catch the public fancy. In areas involving complex technical considerations, not well understood by the public, the result is likely to be premature, heavy-handed legislation, such as the laws passed in many states a few years ago requiring screening for the sickle-cell gene. In this case the laws did not persist very long, for they resulted in direct public actions whose harmful consequences were easily recognized. However, equally foolish legislation restricting scientific research might last much longer, for sins of omission are much less visible than sins of comission.

Genetics is particularly vulnerable to politically based attacks, such as that of Lysenko in the Soviet Union in the 1930's. One would think that the disastrous effect of that development on Soviet biology and agriculture, for 30 years, would warn us. Nevertheless, we see parallel arguments being used in this country today to oppose the field of behavioral genetics. Indeed, this is obviously the reason for the attack on the study of XYY children, rather than on many larger and more disturbing problems in medicine. Fear of genetics has roots in the past, in various premature extrapolations from Darwin's theory to human society, by the nineteenth century Social Darwinists and eugenicists. Moreover, over a long period distorted genetic concepts were used to provide alleged scientific support for racism, whether of the American or the Nazi variety. Finally, in recent years anxiety over genetics has been generated by the fear that current developments will lead to genetic engineering of human personalities.

To assign to modern genetics the reactionary social role played by its primitive precursors is no more rational than it would be to identify modern medicine with phlebotomy. I would suggest that geneticists try to neutralize this negative image by emphasizing the positive social contributions of human genetics, present and potential. Three points seem especially important. First, gene therapy (i.e., the replacement of single defective genes) is still so far off that it is not profitable to guess at the date, but its achievement would be an enormous triumph. Current apprehension over such research is a sad indication of the low threshold of public anxiety about genetics, for even if we achieve the cure of monogenic defects we would still be a very long way from a predictable modification of behavioral traits, because these are highly polygenic. Second, in our desire to eliminate social inequities it is an error to confuse social equality and biological equality, and to consider the recognition of genetic diversity as an enemy. On the contrary, social equality is an idea that rests on a moral foundation, and it should not be jeopardized by resting it on the foundation of shaky assumptions about biological equality. Moreover, genetic diversity is an enormous cultural resource, and its recognition can help us to improve the environment in the different ways that will optimize the self-fulfillment of genetically different individuals. Finally, genetics has an enormous contribution to make to solving the problem of racism. This destructive attitude was based on a Platonic, typological concept of races as entities whose members all share the same characteristics. Modern genetics and evolutionary theory, however, have led to the recognition that races (i.e., populations within a species that have long been separated reproductively) differ only statistically in their genetic composition. This biological knowledge provides powerful support for the modern social pressures to eliminate race discrimination; for it replaces earlier myths about racial superiority and inferiority by the recognition that assignment of an individual to one or another race does not define any of his behavioral potentials.

It is my impression that many geneticists are responding to the present political climate by bending with environmentalists, and with the attacks on behavioral genetics. I would suggest that we can perform a more useful service by helping the public to understand the need to recognize the realities of genetic diversity, and to define and build social equality in a manner that does not conflict with that reality.

LAPPE: It was polite of Prof. Steinberg not to identify me as the author, though I am, of that letter to "Science." I would like to expand on a few points. I in fact, did allude to the potential cost of basic research, and in a subsequent paragraph alluded to Lysenkoism as the example which was not, I admit, readily apparent, because the editors of "Science" took out, in what was a long letter, a long exposition of the real costs of not having science be self-correcting as it is in its ideal form.

As most of you are well aware, the very best geneticists in Russia, like Vavilov, were suppressed by the perpetuation of an ideal which was not allowed to be self-correcting, and it was this central point which was my issue in this letter. Today the question of accountability in science as it applies to basic research is a terribly knotty one. We walk on a tightrope between science when it is at its best, that is, science that is unregulated in pure research has given us often the most fruitful results. Yet a greater feeling on the part of the public that it should be involved in decisions that influence its own life does not seem to me entirely unreasonable.

We juxtapose a problem of researchers who come to have vested interests in sustaining their own hypotheses and do not follow a Popperian method of rejecting their hypotheses and testing them scrupulously. There is a problem and a prospect for misuse of science and the whole purpose of the letter was to raise this issue for further discussion.

(Dr. Lappe's letter Science 28 Feb. 1975 is reproduced here in full -Editor)

ACCOUNTABILITY IN SCIENCE

The recent disclosure of yet another possible breach in the integrity of scientific research raises some hard questions about the public's right to oversee the conduct of science. Both in the Summerlin affair of last April, in which a Sloan-Kettering cancer researcher was given a psychiatric leave after tampering with skin-graft data, and in the current case at Harvard, in which a student is suspected of forging experimental results, the research in question was supported both directly and indirectly through public funds. Yet the actions which have been taken to date have involved internal "housecleaning" with little or no public access to the facts or involvement with the issues. Why should research scientists be any less accountable to the public for the consequences of their misconduct than are physicians, lawyers, or politicians?

Some maintain that scientists should be sequestered from malpractice or malfeasance by virtue of the impersonal and indirect nature of their work. Behind such a proposition lies the false assumption that scientific data, in contrast to the surgeon's scalpel, "never hurts anyone. After all," the argument goes, "it's the use that's made of science that deserves our scrutiny, not basic research. But ethical judgment is needed at the basic research level as well. Those who practice it know that the nature of the scientific enterprise itself hinges on the scrupulous integrity of its practitioners. Scientific accountability begins at the research bench. One false lead can cost science (and society) years of potentially constructive work.

It is no accident that the current disturbing events are occurring in transplantation immunology, a field still in its infancy. Transplantation immunology may now be in the same inchoate and explosively expansive stage that genetics was in in the Lysenko era of 25 years ago. When "normal" science, as Thomas Kuhn (1) described it, begins to falter, as new data repudiate old hypotheses, then basic research takes on new meanings -- and basic researchers, new responsibilities. Immunologists today are struggling for coherent theories to incorporate seemingly divergent data. They are met at every turn by paradoxes and anomalies. The immune system can seemingly be turned to good or evil by a quirk of happenstance. Clinicians do not know how to predict when an immune response to a virus may cause a disease or cure it; or if they generate an immune reaction, whether it will stimulate cancer growth or retard it. Reproductive biologists are met with paradoxical success in the survival of the immunologically discrepant fetus and remain ignorant of the adaptive role of the mother's immune response.

Historians of science would recognize in these perturbing uncertainties a scientific field in flux, an old paradigm collapsing, and tentative new models proliferating. It is at just such a time that a field becomes most vulnerable to chicanery and deceit. Total objectivity becomes difficult for even the most scrupulous practitioner. Often it is impossible for the average scientist to distinguish between a vagary of chance to be noted and placed aside and a potential breakthrough result which could unlock a logjam of inexplicable data. Others, like Newton and Mendel before them, consciously or unconsciously suppress variations in their data which "do not fit" in order to sustain the hypothesis they believe to be the right one. All of these perturbations of conduct and reasoning need not occur in the "perfect" practice of the scientific method, with its insistence on blind observation and reproducibility. But human foible, ambition, and the urgency to straighten things out often suppress the ideal.

A science in revolution fairly invites scientific entrepreneurs to ply their new hypotheses. It is these people who are simultaneously the most valuable and the most dangerous among the dramatis personae of the morality play of scientific discovery. One extra bit of egoism, one iota of self-aggrandizement and the play can become a tragedy. The stakes are enormous, the tensions great. Some are keen to take up the challenge; others succumb to what Lawrence Kubie (2) described as "the neurotic distortion of the creative process." There are those who have the courage to promulgate seemingly rash hypotheses selflessly, willingly taking responsibility for their actions by setting about to refute their own ideological progeny. This is when science is at its best.

Then there are those for whom the fragility of the times calls forth an opportunism that leads to a contamination of the free marketplace of ideas with forged data or rigged experiments. This happened in the Summerlin affair. These events are so troubling and potentially so damaging to the conduct of science that they call out for action.

It is a disservice to science and society alike to treat such events as isolated and idiosyncratic. My experience as a transplantation immunologist at three major laboratories in this country strongly suggests that Summerlin-like observations are the rule, not the exception. Indeed, as Karl Popper has emphasized, the vitality of a science may depend on the number and richness of falsifiable hypotheses available as grist for the scientific mill. However, the proliferation of false (rather than falsifiable) hypotheses may also be a sinister symptom of the heightened stakes for scientific success in research areas, such as cancer or immunology, in which public expectations have been grossly inflated. Scientists in fast-breaking areas and "normal" science alike ought now to take seriously the implication of misconduct on the part of their colleagues. Some laboratories have already instituted internal checks to verify novel results. But such checks themselves are likely to have a chilling effect on innovative research. The line must be strictly drawn between proffering serious hypotheses, simple speculation, and outright fabrication. Somehow, the recognition must be engendered in scientist and citizen that the scientist who intentionally forges or misrepresents basic research data is no simple miscreant or neurotic. Such persons misuse the public trust as well as public funds and should not be shielded behind a veil of "psychiatric illness" or bureaucratic maneuvering. Scientists must be willing to look at the systems which create these perturbations -- both in society and in their own enterprise -- and begin to undertake a searching analysis of their roots.

REFERENCES

1. Kuhn, T., "The Structure of Scientific Revolutions," Ed. 2,
    University of Chicago Press, Chicago (1970).

2. Kubie, L., "The Neurotic Distortion of the Creative Process,"
    Farrar, Straus & Giroux, New York (1961).

STEINBERG: In the original manuscript I did discuss Dr. Lappé's
reference to Lysenko and also pointed out some errors in interpretation. It was not lack of knowledge of the error of Lysenko that
led to the suppression of genetics in the Soviet Union. It was an
oppressive state. If Dr. Lappé will read the original debates, he
will recognize that the opposition to Lysenko was expressed until
Lysenko said Stalin has endorsed my position. Then they all retract-
ed, and this is in the official transcript of the debate. The error
was exposed, it was known, it was known before Lysenko's work was
done, because Lysenko was not original. He built on older work
which had been shown to be false.

The point at issue is not the forging scientist, it is a free
government that you need. What Dr. Lappé is advocating is restriction of freedom of expression among scientists. When you pass laws
involving prosecution, you get into the situation that we now have
in Boston, and his advocacy would go much further than that. I
maintain that it is necessary to maintain a free exchange of ideas
and we need nothing beyond that.

LAPPÉ: In no place did I make the claims for suppressing science or basic research alluded to by Prof. Steinberg.

P.M. TOCCI: Univ. Miami School Med.: I think forums such as this
will help society settle some of the questions that have been posed
lately. I want to congratulate the society and the foundation for
sponsoring this kind of forum. However, I feel something funny
happened on the way to the forum. This is a National Symposium and
I am surprised to see so many XX persons in the audience, but only
one speaker. It has been pointed out that these XX's are different
from us XY's and that perhaps their views may be different on some
of these subjects and I for one would like to hear them.

In speaking about genetics and the law, I also do not see how
we can fully discuss that issue without hearing from some Blacks
who have had to deal with the legislation on sickle cell anemia. I
also would like to know how we can fully discuss carrier screening of
mass populations without hearing from people who have had to deal
with these issues in the last three or four years on a daily basis.

MILUNSKY: This meeting was called to explore the interface

between genetics and the law. The invited speakers have well
recognized expertise in all the fields you mention, and more.

J.E. TROSKO: Michigan State University, East Lansing: Any
society that hopes to direct its future via democracy must rely obviously on an informed electorate. If a society such as ours
chooses technological means to achieve its end, then we are going
to know we have an inherent dilemma. There is no human way that
each member of this technological society can be informed on the
plethora of technological and value alternatives which will be posed.
It seems to me to afford technology the full rights of jurisprudence
or of the economic laissez faire principle, as we do to human-
beings, will surely lead to major disasters. That is, if we assume
technologies are innocent until proven guilty, we are going to be
in much trouble, which we are already. We have to switch that around.
We have to now assume technologies guilty until proven innocent.
In order to deal with the potential consequences of the use or misuse of science and technology, there are those who wish to cut off
the creation of knowledge and technology. We need more knowledge
rather than less. Then where and how do we solve these dilemmas?
It seems to me the first time technological societies must seriously
entertain technological assessment, because in essence we are all
living experiments and if we want to use more knowledge rather than
less, we must control for the first time not so much the creation
of knowledge, but the use of that knowledge.

EXPERIMENTATION AND HUMAN GENETICS: PROBLEMS OF "CONSENT"

Alexander M. Capron

University of Pennsylvania Law School

As in all fields of medicine, the modern practice of human genetics is closely linked with experimentation. Genetics research sometimes involves patients who are offered new and as yet unproven means of therapy or diagnosis that are intended to benefit the patients, such as the levodopa challenge which is being explored as a test to detect Huntington's chorea (1) and which has raised such a storm of controversy (2-4). The experimentation may also take the form of a procedure not intended to benefit its subjects, as for example routine mass screening of newborn infants to provide population data on chromosome aneuploidy, without any intention of following up detection with medical intervention (5). Needless to say, research on genetics poses all the problems and provokes the same argumentation as has occurred concerning other types of human experimentation, which is reflected in an ever-growing body of literature (6-11). The involvement of the fetus in much of this research heightens interest and concern in this period when fetal experimentation is getting so much attention from the National Commission for the Protection of Human Subjects (12, 13) on down (14-16). Rather than attempt to address, in what would have to be a very cursory fashion, all the issues of "genetic experimentation," I have chosen to concentrate on a type of intervention that raises problems which commentators often acknowledge but seldom (if ever) seem to dispose of.

THIRD PARTY PERMISSION - CONTINUING THE DIALOGUE

In every field there are a few very simple questions which are highly embarrassing because the debate which forever arises around them leads only to perpetual

319

failure and seems consistently to make fools of the
most expert (17).

Erickson's good-natured but devastating remark unfortunately provides a very accurate description of a number of basic
issues in medical jurisprudence, including some of interest to
this symposium on Genetics and the Law.

One such problem is experimentation with subjects who are regarded as being incapable, by reason of formal legal incapacity
or actual physical impediment, of giving their own consent to participate in research. I choose to focus on this topic because
it is one that arises often in clinical genetics and which is frequently concerned with the fetus, the neonate or the child. Although this is a topic which is commonly broached in discussions
of "informed consent," I do not find that a useful rubric. I suggest that we speak instead of "third party permission" or some
similar title, because the things which make this a difficult topic
are not primarily those which are of concern when one is talking
about a person's agreement to permit him or herself to be used in
an experiment (11).

What, then, are the questions for a lawyer considering such
third party permission? They seem to me to fall into two groups.
First, who has the authority and competence, and under what circumstances, to determine that someone else lacks the competence, and
hence the authority, to make decisions about his or her own life,
particularly about medical care and research? Second, who has the
authority and competence to make decisions for a person determined
to be unable to do so for him or herself? The first question is seldom addressed because the answer is usually taken for granted - it
is assumed that we all know who is incompetent, don't we? Yet once
one probes a little into the subject and asks questions about the
propriety of guardians making decisions for their wards, one has to
go back to square one and ask questions about the way in which the
wards lost control over their own lives in the first place. Was it
because of a judge's ruling, supported by testimony of a psychiatrist perhaps? Or because the legislature has ruled that all un-
emancipated fourteen year-olds are incompetent? Questions of this
type about competence and authority are coming more to the fore
because of recent interest in the rights of the mentally disturbed
and disabled.

As necessary and important as consideration of such issues
I intend here to address the second question and the issues which
it raises. A few years ago, in a talk on drug experiments in children (18), I first took on the question of who should have the power
to allow someone else to be used in research, and why. Two theses
were advanced there. First, that the overly broad way in which the
problem of pediatric experimentation is usually presented complicates

it unnecessarily; the issues can be better focused if decision-
making follows what I termed "a model of successive limited approx-
imations," in which there is a narrowing down in turn of the
perceived need for research, of the risks to be encountered, of the
participants, and of the damages that are left on the shoulders
of those who may still be injured. The second thesis was that there
are other methods of selecting incompetent subjects for research
besides parental "informed consent" which better serve some of our
objectives. Today I would like to continue the dialogue on this
subject, in which others have joined (19-21) by seeing what analogies one can find in the law for the exercise of authority by one
person for another and by looking for the indicia of competence
which justify the exercise of that authority.

WELL-BEING AND CONSENT

The aim of the law concerning medical intervention with incompetents would appear to be largely the promotion of well-being.
This aim is served in part by malpractice law, which provides
redress for negligently created harm. But for the incompetent,
that may not exhaust the legal protection of well-being, as it
usually would for the competent person; for the latter, who has
chosen to seek some self-defined benefit by exposing himself to the
risk of non-negligent injuries, there is no derogation of his leg-
ally-protected well-being by the actual occurrence of such injuries.
The fact that the incompetent has, by definition, not chosen to
permit any intervention could mean that even those which do him
no physical harm are still violations of his well-being. But if
this were the case, then no one would ever dare intervene to help
him; where such interventions are physically helpful, one finds in
fact that claims seldom if ever arise,* and the context in which
the law is most likely to confront our "very simple" but "highly
embarrassing" question is when an incompetent is attempting to
collect damages for harm caused by a non-negligent intervenor+
(a term used to encompass the person conducting all types of
medical interventions, whether therapeutic or experimental). The
question thus comes down to: What can be asserted as an adequate
defense in such actions?

---

* They would be most likely to occur in an action by the interven-
or to collect from the incompetent on his bill for services rendered.

+ This may arise, as a matter of litigation strategy and so forth,
as one count in an action that also alleges other counts of negligence on the part of the intervenor.

"Implied" Consent

Three responses to this query have been recognized: Implied consent, beneficial intent, and proxy consent. It is the third which is of most interest to us, but a few words are in order about the first two. The usual meaning of implied consent is that social customs or the apparent compliance of a person with another's course of conduct provide sufficient grounds for reliance that the person consents, although he has not manifested his willingness in so many words (22). In the medical context, the term is used without distinction, as though it meant the same thing, while in fact its use there is different and even more fictitious; when a person is in need of emergency medical care but is unable to consent (by reason of unconsciousness, for example), his or her consent is said to be "implied" because it is reasonable to assume that he or she would agree to the treatment if he or she were competent and understood the situation. A better term would be "inferred consent," since the focus of legal concern is on the reasonableness of the conclusion the intervenor drew from the situation, not whether the injured person acted in such a way as to imply that he or she consented (since no such actions are ever actually involved).

Beneficial Intent

The defense of beneficial intent, which would in effect extend inferred consent to the non-emergency situation, has been suggested by commentators but finds little support in case law. Daube posed the issue nicely when he objected to the concept that an operation is only "justified or legalized by consent or its equivalent." Rather than viewing an intervention as a "lawful infliction of harm," it should, Daube says, "be treated as a positive, beneficent, admirable action from the outset" (23). An extension of this concept, from those interventions intended to be beneficial to the patient (therapy) to those intended to gain knowledge but not harm the patient (low-risk experiments) is obvious.* The result would be to give medical personnel a privilege to proceed not only in the case of emergency care (where "beneficial intent" would avoid the fictitious idea of an unconscious patient having "consented," implied or otherwise) but in therapy and low-risk experiments with incompetents generally and, indeed, even with competent patients. In fact, it is only in the case of the latter group that one finds any common law support for the idea; courts which have recognized a "therapeutic privilege"+ seem to be allowing the beneficial intent

---

*Daube himself did not have such an extension in mind; quite the opposite, since he called experimentation "a class apart."

+The concept of therapeutic privilege seems to have been more or less created out of whole cloth by Dr. Hubert W. Smith (24); although often mentioned in dictum, it is seldom invoked as a ground for a

of the physician to excuse the lack of disclosure that his patient would need in order to give "informed" consent. Neither the notion of "beneficial intent," nor its extension to "nonharmful intent," has much that is likely to recommend it to the judiciary, which has shown increased concern lately with protecting patients' autonomy and self-determination in both private (28-30) and public law contexts (31).

Proxy Consent -- Inaccurate Terminology

Thus, the focus of a discussion of medical interventions with incompetents, particularly in genetic experimentation, will be on the third defense, proxy consent. Two prefatory observations are needed here. First, we may assume that the question at hand is whether the intervenor is protected from liability by the proxy's consent; the liability of the proxy (either to the competent or as an indemnifier of the intervenor) -- a separate, albeit closely related issue -- seems seldom to arise (perhaps for reasons of practicality and of intrafamilial immunity, rather than for any reasons of principle) and will not be treated here. Second, just as I have already objected to the word "consent" for its misleading connotation of self-choice in matters medical, so too the term "proxy" falsely suggests notions of express agency or deputization. The term "proxy consent" will nonetheless be used here as a starting point, because of its general use in the literature. The discussion of legal analogies and their underlying philosophical justifications will, I hope, suggest how other phrases better describe the third party permission* with which we are here concerned.

LEGAL ANALOGIES

In making reference, as I have, to a notion of legal analogies, I do not mean that one will find any hard and fast legal rules which will determine conduct in genetics research. Rather, I expect that by looking at choices which one person is enabled by the law to make for another, we may discover contexts in which the interests and

---

holding (25, 26) and has been widely criticized. See (27) and (11) at p. 412.

*It may bear emphasis that the term "permission" is intended to convey an authority to withhold as well as to give approval for the intervention. Like "consent" it is capable of the connotation that only agreement with the choice offered by the biomedical professional is acceptable, from which refusals are then erroneously seen, as Goldstein has written, "as a justification for challenging the capacity of the citizen to decide what is best for himself." (75 at p. 691).

relationships are analogous to the ones which concerns us. It is
fair to assume that the purposes of rules on third party permission in the biomedical context are the same as those being served by the law in analogous areas -- which are to permit choices
to be made while protecting incompetents from undue harm -- although
some differences in the purposes will be noted as our study progresses. We may also uncover some of the assumptions which lie
behind the choices which the typical proxies -- parents -- are permitted to make. Indeed, among our legal analogies are examples of
the three major explanations for allowing third party permission:
first, that the person giving permission is able to express the
choices which the incompetent would in fact have made because of
individualized, subjective knowledge of the incompetent; second,
that the person giving permission will make an objectively reasonable choice which comes close to being what the incompetent, as
a reasonable person, would want or which will at the least serve
the incompetent's interests; or third, that the interests of the
third party and those of the incompetent are so close that in choosing his or her own interests the third party will choose very much
as the incompetent would. A fourth explanation for parental power
over children -- that the children are akin to the parents' other
property -- need not be discussed here, since it does not illustrate the phenomenon of A choosing for B. If B is akin to property, one would not usually think of B having independent interests
which needed to be protected by self-choice or its substitute.

Subjective Rules

The first justification for "proxy consent" is probably the primary one which would suggest itself to most people thinking about
parents (or other general guardians) making choices for children.
Parents are not expected to be mind-readers, in the sense of clair-
voyants, but it is generally thought that they know their children
well enough to discern what the latter would choose were they able
to do so. Thus, it is interesting to discover that examples of
this situation are scanty in the law. And even these depend on
prior actions of the incompetent, such as in the doctrine of substitute judgment from the law of trusts, or on express delegation,
such as in the attorney-client relationship.

Substitute Judgment. Suppose that a person with a substantial
estate becomes incompetent to manage his or her own affairs, and
that a trustee is appointed by a court to administer the property.
It is obvious that the trustee is authorized to pay, on behalf of
the incompetent, any amounts lawfully owed for the support and
care of the incompetent and any other people whom the incompetent
is obliged to support. But what of a cousin, or a charity, to
whom the incompetent had given money in the past, without legal
necessity of doing so? May the trustee make gifts to such a person?

What about a person of whom the incompetent has always been very
fond but who only recently became needy, so that there is no
pattern of past gifts from the incompetent? The answer given by
the law to the question of whether such gifts are proper has been
a guarded "yes." The trustee may petition the court of which the
incompetent is a ward for permission to act as the incompetent would
have were he or she capable of acting (32). The request will be
approved to the extent that it can be met out of excess income which
will not be necessary now, or in the future, to meet the needs of
the incompetent. The subjective nature of the doctrine is thus
hemmed in by objective limitations. In setting a standard of reasonable conduct, the law assumes that no person would give away
his property so as to endanger him or herself: a petition will be
disapproved if it derogates from the fiduciary's primary duty,
which is to preserve the incompetent's estate. Within those limits,
the doctrine has been treated as subjective by the courts (33, 34)
because an attempt is made to act as the incompetent person would.

The doctrine of substitute judgment will thus clearly be of
limited value in devising a rule about third party permission for
genetic interventions. First, in the hands of most courts the
doctrine is taken to require some individualized evidence about
what the incompetent would have done; in the case of a fetus or a
young child a judgment on this point would be speculative. Second,
the doctrine is concerned with the donation of property to a specific person; by contrast, in the medical situation, the patient-
subject's body is being given to unspecified people (the potential
beneficiaries of the knowledge gained) or to "science," as an abstract entity. Third, the limitation that only the excess may be
given may render the entire analogy in opposite since it is hard
to know what "excess" is in a biomedical context, unless it means
that only non-harmful interventions are permissible.

Attorney-Client Relationship. A second example to the attorney-client relationship provides some further insight, but is also
not fully comparable. An attorney possesses broad powers to make
choices on behalf of his or her client. At the very least, since
clients typically lack expertise in the law, the choice of which
legal instruments will be used falls to the lawyer. But it is
still necessary for the attorney, as a fiduciary, to disclose the
options to the client and for the client to decide which among
the various goals he wants to pursue. For reasons both of ethics
and self-interest (35), the lawyer should not attempt to make the
basic substantive choices. The powers of the attorney, which can
effect the client's person as well as his property, are closer to
those of the "proxy" in biomedical intervention than those of most
of our other analogies. Yet, while an attorney's power to speak
for and bind his client (36) is premised on the attorney's thinking
as his client actually would, the basis for the presumption is that
the client has instructed his attorney, as he would any agent, how

to carry out his affairs. The client is protected by the attorney's
professionalism which dictates, among other things, that the
attorney's own interests not be in conflict with those of the
client.

Objective Rules

If the hallmark of the subjective rules is that the decision-
maker be personally familiar with the wishes and values of the incompetent person, one would expect in the case of objective rules
to discover that anyone who behaves reasonably according to defined standards could be the decision-maker. This is well illustrated by the law concerning guardians ad litem (also called "next
friends" in some cases) for infant parties to legal actions.

Guardians ad litem. Under the rules developed by the common
law, any adult can act as a guardian, "regardless of his lack of
kinship to the infant" in question (37).

Subject to the broad supervision of the court (of which the
infant becomes a ward for purposes of the litigation), the guardian ad litem hires an attorney and makes decisions with the attorney
just as a party would make for him or herself about the conduct
of litigation. The guardian must "acquaint himself with all of
the rights of the infant" whom he is supposed to be protecting
and "not do any act which will prejudicially affect" those rights
(38). If the choices made by the guardian later prove to be
detrimental to the infant, the latter is not bound by them (once
he or she reaches maturity) unless they were approved as reasonable
by the court. This rule, which governs the interests that infants
have in real estate, as beneficiaries under a will, and so forth,
comes particularly into play in determining whether decisions made
about a lawsuit amount to binding waivers of the infants' rights.
Thus, the judgment rendered by the court, in a case in which a
child was represented by a guardian is as valid against the child
as it would be if the child had been competent to represent him or
herself, but a guardian's election of which remedy to pursue (a
decision made without judicial supervision) will not bind the
child (39). The law opts for uncertainty -- which is generally
disfavored because of its disruptive effect on property and commercial transactions -- in order to give maximum protection to the
interests of those who cannot make decisions for themselves. A
second safeguard is the requirement that the guardian be completely
free of any conflicting entanglements which might make him adverse
to the interests of the ward.

"Best Interests" Doctrine. A second objective rule (although
one with subjective undertones) is the rather vague and elastic
doctrine of "best interests" which is invoked in two ways by courts

in disputes concerning the care and custody of children. Its
first use is in determining who should have decision-making authority for the children in question. Here "best interests" is
arrayed against the competing and more traditional view that unless
the natural parents are affirmatively shown to be unfit they are
entitled to make all decisions about their children, as about any
other item of property. A natural parent is, for example, typically
permitted to withhold consent to a child's adoption by another adult
even if there are good reasons to believe that the child would be
better off with the adoptive parents; the parent's choice must actually be contrary to the child's interests before it will be overridden (40). Such a presumption in favor of the natural parents
has been upheld by the Supreme Court (41). In the context of neglect proceedings and the like, similar rules determine whether the
state, as <u>parens patriae</u>, should interfere with parents' authority.
Sometimes the result of such "best interests" decisions is to deprive parents of control over their children, although in recent
years the judiciary "has been noticeably more reticent in checking
parental discretion than in limiting the power of the state" (42).
For the state to interfere there must typically be parental conduct which falls below the very minimum acceptable in the community.

In addition to those cases in which parents have been found
unfit*, judges are also faced with cases in which the natural parents, or others with a strong claim, dispute amongst themselves
over the custody of a child. In both circumstances it will thus
fall to the judiciary to make decisions concerning the care and
custody of children (44), which leads to the second use of the
term "best interests." Although courts may take into account the
wishes of older and more mature children, they are left to their
own discretion as to what disposition would best serve the child's
welfare. Since there is no requirement that the decision reflect
individualized knowledge about what is actually best suited for a
particular child, the doctrine seems to rest on an objective standard of what a reasonable person would find appropriate for the ordinary child; in application, this may amount to a highly <u>subject-
ive</u> decision, but subjective in the sense that it reflects the values
and beliefs of the judiciary not those of its individual wards.
Moreover, by custom and by statute, the "best interests of the
child" are taken to include the wishes of its parents and of children's agency officials who are responsible for it, not just factors
relating to the health and competence of its prospective custodians
or the quality of the relationship it may already have developed
_____
*The choice by a natural parent of an alternative which is against
the "best interests" of his or her child has in rare instances been
found to be "unreasonable," so as to collapse the first stage question of "who can best decide?" into the second one, "what decision is best?" (43).

with such custodians. As Goldstein, Freud and Solnit (45) conclude,
"many decisions are 'in-name-only' for the best interests of the
specific child" and are fashioned rather "to meet the needs and
wishes of competing adult claimants or to protect the general
policies of a child care or other administrative agency."*

   The safeguards built into "best interests" judgments are sur-
prisingly few, considering that the personal health and well-being
of the incompetent, not merely his or her property, are at stake.
What protection there is derives largely from the impartiality of
the judiciary and from the full development of the relevant issues
by counsel in the litigation, although the child is seldom represented separately.

Identity of Interests

   The final set of analogous legal rules to be canvassed is
that which is premised on an identity of interest between the
person who makes the decisions and the one who is affected by them.
The premise that such an identity exists is taken to be an element
in most justifications of the common practice of leaving decisions
about children to their parents. Of course, identity of interests
does not tell the whole story, any more than the previous two rationales. But in common-sense terms parents are "in the same boat"
with their children; risks which the latter experience will have
direct and probably unavoidable effects -- physical, psychological
and financial -- on the former. Thus, there may be something to
be learned from such examples as the doctrine of virtual representation in the law of trusts, the rules governing class actions,
and what is called "third party consent" to searches and seizures
by police officers. Since these doctrines relate to joint or
similar interests in property, however, care must be taken in ex-
trapolating them to biomedical interventions. As close as two
individuals may be it is hard to say that one has the same interest
in the other's physical integrity as the second person has; the

---

*Goldstein, Freud and Solnit suggest instead that decisions about
children should provide "the least detrimental available alternative," by which they intend, quite rightly, to remind the decision-
maker that the child in question is already a victim of his environment and is greatly at risk if prompt action is not taken. Yet a
"least detriment" suggests that the guiding principle would be to
choose the alternative which minimizes harm, while the authors describe their objective as maximizing the child's opportunity for being wanted and for having a continuous relationship with a "psychological" parent. In their understandable determination to avoid
the sorry connotations the term "best interests" has come to have,
they were led to drop a phrase which accurately describes just what
they have in mind, namely "best interests of the child."

parallel may be closer if the first person (who is giving the permission) is also willing to permit the procedure to be performed
his or her own body.

Virtual Representation. To be bound in a legal action, as some
of the illustrations in previous sections may already have made
apparent, a person has to take some part in that action either personally or through a representative. Usually, a representative
must be appointed by the person (or by the court, such as a guardian
ad litem) and be given the authority to act as the person's agent
in the litigation. But in certain circumstances an incompetent
person without an actual representative may nonetheless be bound
by the outcome of the legal action if another party to the action
stood in the same legal position vis-a-vis the questions at issue;
this person is called the virtual representative of the incompetent.
Typically, it will be the sibling of an unborn child who bore the
same relationship to the testator or the grantor of a trust; by
pursuing his or her own selfish interests the virtual representative
also promotes those of brothers and sisters yet unborn.

Beyond the threshold requirement of identity of interests, the
law of virtual representation erects few protections. The sole
basis for finding that a person's interests were not sufficiently
represented is affirmative proof that the virtual representative
acted in hostility to the absent beneficiary's interests. As the
American Law Institute restated the accepted rule: "Evidence as to
either the inactivity of the representative or the inadequacy of
his conduct is material only as it conduces to establish the hostility of the conduct of the representative to the interest of the
person represented" (46).

Class Actions. More rigorous requirements have been established
for maintenance of class actions because of the profound effect
which the actions of the litigant can have on the rights and obligations of absent and otherwise unrelated persons.* In class act-

_____

*The rules on standing, by requiring a party to have a "concrete
adverseness" (47) and precluding the assertion of a "generalized
grievance" (48) shared by a large class of citizens, are closely
related to those on class actions. Since the rights of others may
be affected, the rules about standing not only look for a party
who identifies with the legal questions in issue but who will also
(or in consequence) be a vigorous advocate. This is the sort of
question which arose in the challenges to contraceptive and abortion
statutes, in which physicians were sometimes found to lack, and
sometimes found to have, the requisite standing to assert the interests of their patients. To have standing a person must allege
such a personal stake in the outcome of a controversy with the
defendant as to justify the exercise of the court's remedial powers
on his or her behalf (49). This requirement derives both from

tions, the named party's decisions and the court's judgment are binding on all members of the class (51), so that it is necessary that what he has at stake be significant enough that he will pursue the case with the proper vigor and that he have the capability to undertake a massive and complicated lawsuit. Furthermore, his interests must be nearly identical with those of the whole class in order that the self-interested choices he makes as a litigant will truly represent the interests of the class. Although the notion of one party appearing in court on behalf of a larger group, in order to avoid repetitious litigation, is not a new one, it has taken on increased importance recently and became the subject of a complex provision of the <u>Federal Rules of Civil Procedure</u>. Rule 23 provides that the named parties must "fairly and adequately represent the interests of the class." "Fairness" has been interpreted by the courts to require that they have the same interests (52), or alternatively have no interests which are antagonistic to those of the class (53)*, or both (56), and "adequacy" means that they (and their attorneys) be qualified to conduct the litigation (57).

Although not strictly analogous, the rules on class actions serve to remind us of the importance which the law attaches to having safeguards which will limit the harm one person can do to another, even when their legal positions seem coincident. In class actions only property is at stake, while in medical jurisprudence life and health may be endangered, so greater care should be involved in designating any representative. On the other hand, requirements of notice to members of the class, which are among the most difficult aspects of Rule 23, would be much simpler in the medical context; the persons for whom permission is to be given will usually be few in number and easily accessible -- although, if they are incompetent, "notice" may be meaningless.

<u>Search and Seizure</u>. "Third party consent" to search and seizure, our third example of rules relating to an identity of interests, probably provides the least useful analogy for several reasons.

the limitation on federal court's jurisdiction in Article III of the Constitution to adjudicating a "case or controversy," and from the judiciary's own "prudential limitations" on the exercise of its authority (50).

*Another aspect of this rule -- that the party have no conflict of interest with the class -- is most often invoked when the party is also the attorney prosecuting the action; potential conflict may obviously arise between seeking the largest possible recovery for the class and bringing the litigation to a swift conclusion with a highly remunerative fee (54). A similar problem arises when the person desiring to represent the class is involved in other, non-class litigation with the opposing party (55).

First, there is no unanimity among the courts on the basis for regarding a third party's consent to the search of the defendant's premises as a valid exception to the Fourth Amendment's requirement of a search warrant from a judicial officer. The Supreme Court initially suggested that the proper grounds for third party permission would be express agency (58) a view which has been explicitly followed by many courts and which has much to recommend it (59). Since such agency is lacking in the medical setting with an incompetent (incompetence terminates an existing agency) the same problems are presented as with the comparison to the attorney-client relationship. Subsequent opinions of the Court, however, have approved third party consent for searches based on the mutual relationship between the parties and the premises: if the user of a duffel bag (60) or the occupant of a building (61, 62) gives permission for a search, the items seized are admissable against joint users or occupants. Since the evidence can be used against all those with joint authority, there is an identity of interest to validate the nondefendant, third party's consent.

Even if the latter view is taken, however, further more basic problems remain with this analogy. On the one hand, the search and seizure cases may set rules which are too high since the interests involved enjoy constitutional protection. The courts and commentators who object to the joint control theory do so, at least in part, because the defendant's Fourth Amendment rights are private (63) and can only be waived "knowingly" (64). While an express authorization to an agent to permit officials of the state to inspect one's premises might meet this standard, merely sharing control over those premises with someone else does not amount to a waiver of the right to refuse a warrantless search. Although one's interests in being protected against unauthorized bodily invasions -- for example, a "search and seizure" of fluid on which to conduct genetic studies (65) -- is undeniably greater than the interest in privacy of property, the consequently greater limitations on intervention would not be relevant where the party conducting the interventions were nongovernmental.

The third and final objection, which cuts the other way, is that the purposes to be served by rules in the medical and search areas are so divergent that the rules developed for the latter would not adequately protect an incompetent party being subjected to a medical procedure. The question before the court in search and seizure cases is whether evidence, otherwise admissible against the defendant, should be suppressed because it was improperly obtained, and the intent in the court's suppressing it is to deter unconstitutional police conduct. Thus, evidence might be admissible even when the person giving permission for the search was not authorized to do so if it had been reasonable for the police who seized the items to have believed that he or she was a proper person to give permission. All of search and seizure law, but particularly the joint control (i.e. identity of interests) theory, is therefore of doubtful help in the biomedical context, where the question is not the reasonableness of official conduct but the designation of a proper party to give permission for intervention with an incompetent.

CONCLUSION

The differing purposes and origins of the law in the various areas which we have surveyed make it difficult or perhaps impossible to construct a unified theory of third party permission. Nonetheless, the effort is not wasted if it at least reminds us that rules developed outside medical jurisprudence may prove useful in our attempt to answer such "highly embarrassing" questions as the one posed by "proxy consent."

Our journey through the land of analogies has suggested a number of procedural and substantive safeguards which might reasonably be taken as requirements for third party permission. First and foremost, there should be no conflict of interest between the decision-maker and the incompetent person for whom permission is being given. It was just such a conflict which led to the perceived need for judicial review in the various twin and sibling transplant cases (11, pp. 423-29). Similarly, the parens patriae theory which is the basis for the "best interests" decisions of judges also underlies those "exceptional situations" (66) where the conflict of interests between parent and child are extreme enough to justify a finding of "neglect" because of a decision about medical care made by the parents. This is most likely to arise in the case of a religious objection to life-saving medical care (67, 68), rather than a willingness to submit a child to a risky and unnecessary intervention. But in a leading case, which upheld the conviction of a Jehovah's Witness for allowing her nine year-old niece to sell the sect's literature publicly in violation of a state statute, the Supreme Court declared that parents are not free "to make martyrs of their children before they have reached the age of full and legal discretion when they can make that choice for themselves" (69). The unwillingness of courts to go beyond ordering treatment which is needed to keep the child's condition from being a "substantial threat to society" (70) indicates, however, that the "best interests of the child" may not be too well protected. Even when the focus is on the child's well-being, the idea that this is a matter for simple factual determination as some cases have held (71) is dubious.

Second, in borrowing from the various areas of the law, one may wish to incorporate both the "subjectivity" about what a particular person would want to do (as in the "substitute judgment" doctrine) and the "objectivity" which is derivable from a neutral party's judgment about what is reasonable under the circumstances. These twin objectives could be achieved through a two-stage procedure in which initial screening is done by parents, who are not likely to be neutral but who should be well informed about their children's idiosyncrasies as well as their family's ability to deal with any adverse consequences to the child which result from the choice made, and then a second screening is performed by a neutral and professionally oriented person.

Third, the law which is based on identity of interests (but also some of the examples, such as guardians ad litem, of substituting judgment) teaches the importance of a capable and vigorous advocate* of the incompetent's interests who maintains control of decision-making throughout the intervention. Just as it is well understood in the law of informed consent for competent parties that a right to withdraw at any time should be effectuated to the extent possible, so too the third party who has given permission should retain the right to withdraw it and the duty to remain vigilant in supervising the intervention and protecting the incompetent's interests (72).

A fourth possible procedural protection for the interests of the incompetent emerges -- albeit less clearly -- from our analogies, particularly the law of guardians ad litem. As was noted, a guardian cannot waive any interest or right of the ward to the latter's detriment. One way to surmount the barrier to action which this could create -- the one adopted in the transplant cases -- is to seek judicial approval of the guardian's decision, which thereby becomes binding on the ward. But if the interests are sufficiently important -- such as protecting one's body from harmful invasions -- and if it is recognized that many of the choice points leading up to the final decision will, in fact, never get real judicial security, greater protection could be assured if the guardian's permission did not bind the ward. Clearly, this would purchase greater protection for the incompetent at a high price of uncertainty for the guardian and the biomedical personnel conducting the procedure.+ To make it reasonable, it would clearly have to be limited in some measure. For example, recovery could be allowed for non-negligent injuries (negligent injuries already being recoverable, even with valid permission) but not for the harm of an "unconsented touching"

---

* The lowest formal requirements, which occur in the case of virtual representation, can only be justified by the complete identity of interests and the close familial relationship between the representative and the represented.

+ Their understandable anxiety might be reduced if insurance were available, although the long period before liability might attach would make this very difficult insurance to write.

itself (i.e. assault and battery). It would also seem advisable to limit the application of the practice to non-beneficial interventions, such as research, and perhaps especially to cases of sibling transplants. The question for the persons deciding to go ahead in such cases would then be: Are we sure enough of the probable outcome (no real harm to the incompetent but great benefit to someone else or to science) that it is highly unlikely that the incompetent party will, upon achieving majority, have any reason to want to sue us rather than feeling grateful that he or she was not prevented from helping someone else just because of being too young to give consent personally? The probability of suit would be further diminished if the incompetent party were assured (through an insurance mechanism) of full, immediate medical and rehabilitative care for any untoward results of the intervention, without necessity of waiting until he or she comes of age to sue, although suit at that time (to collect for any additional expenses and for the pain and suffering associated with the injury) would not be precluded.

A final procedural device derivable from our analogies would place greater emphasis on determining the wishes of the incompetent. At the outset we excluded from consideration the standards or procedures for determining competency. If we assume that these might permit differentiation among classes of those found to be incapable of consenting for themselves then there can also be variations in the rules about third party permission. Dissenting in a recent case involving a dispute between the state and parents, who objected on religious grounds to their children being compelled to attend secondary schools, Justice Douglas argued that children who are "mature enough to express potentially conflicting desires" from those of their parents should have their views "canvassed" (73). In the case of pediatric procedures, for example, this might indicate that a third party would have authority to decide for or against participation of children up to the age of 8 to 10, at which point they could be found to be "mature enough" to agree or decline to participate,* although third party permission would also still be required until the age of consent (which is now 18 years in a majority of American jurisdictions).

The primary substantive safeguard, which is supported by only some of our comparative study of legal doctrines, is that a biomedical intervention ought not to be permitted if it creates anything more than the most minimal risk. This conclusion, which is

---

*In the Seiferth case (68), the trial judge indicated that he would have been willing to order the operation on the cleft palate if the question had arisen before the fourteen year-old patient, who was opposed to the surgery, had acquired convictions of his own.

similar to that reached by some ethicists (19, 74), is derived from
the doctrine of substitute judgment, under which all gifts from the
estate of an incompetent must be made from any surplus not needed
for support and may not endanger the corpus. By analogy, this
rule would apply only to nonbeneficial interventions, not to therapeutic ones.* Although this discussion took genetic experimentation
as its starting point, we have not had to distinguish the questions
raised by third party permission for therapy versus research when
examining our analogies, since the reasoning has for the most part
been applicable to both settings. Nevertheless, it is experimentation which raises the issue for most people, and parents' decision to expose their child to even risky surgery would not be
criticized where it is reasonable to expect that the child will
derive a needed benefit from the intervention. Moreover, even
though the same question about whether the parents are the proper
decision-makers ought to apply to therapy as it does to research,
tradition, convenience and ideology (that is, the belief that state
interference with private choice should be kept to a minimum) coal-
esce to support parental authority over decisions about treatment
for their children.

For the geneticist desiring to conduct newborn karyotype screening or faced with a pregnant thalassemia carrier (married to another
carrier) who wants a still-experimental form of prenatal diagnosis
performed, the problem of "proxy consent" is very real and immediate.
If ethicists or lawyers are going to be helpful to the geneticist,
however, they will have to insist upon the luxury of first engaging
in discussions which may seem highly academic and which do not yield
answers in time for the immediate case. Eventually, through many
types of reasoning, we may be able to arrive at an analysis of the
problem which suggests a solution. One means of possibly reaching
that goal, which is to broaden our horizons to other examples of
one person being enabled by the law to make choices for another,
has been attempted here. While there are many differences between
those other situations and the one at hand, they have sufficient
points in common that the principles which guide their operation

---

*Only the doctrine of substitute judgment takes as its starting
point the assumption that steps may be authorized which are not
intended to benefit the incompetent person. In the case of all the
other legal rules surveyed, the assumption is that the person giving
permission will act so as to benefit the incompetent, and then safeguards (of varying rigor) are established to reduce the probability
that this assumption will prove erroneous. If one is talking, then,
of nonbeneficial (research) interventions, these rules would be
applicable if they are taken to teach that interventions are permissible only when they involve virtually no risk; they might be
taken as completely inapplicable if emphasis is placed instead on
the fact that they all involve an intent to benefit the incompetent.

may prove useful in answering our "simple, but highly embarrassing question" (76).

ACKNOWLEDGMENTS

Supported in part by GM 20138, National Institutes of Health.

REFERENCES

1. Klawans, H.L., Paulson, G.W., Ringel, S.P. et al, Use of L-dopa in the detection of presymptomatic Huntington's chorea, New Eng. J. Med. 286:1332 (1972).

2. Gaylin, W., Genetic screening: The ethics of knowing, New Eng. J. Med. 286:1361 (1972).

3. Hemphill, M., Pretesting for Huntington's disease, Hastings Center Report 3(3):12 (1973).

4. Freemon, F.R., Pretesting for Huntington's disease, Hastings Center Report 3(4):13 (1973).

5. Committee for the Study of Inborn Errors of Metabolism, National Research Council, "Genetic Screening: Programs, Principles, and Research," National Academy of Sciences, Washington, D.C. (1975).

6. Katz, J. with the assistance of Capron, A.M. and Glass, E.S., "Experimentation with Human Beings," Russell Sage Foundation, New York (1972).

7. Beecher, H.K., "Research and the Individual: Human Studies," Little, Brown & Company, Boston (1970).

8. Fried, C., "Medical Experimentation: Personal Integrity and Social Policy," American Elsevier, New York (1974).

9. Gray, B.H., "Human Subjects in Medical Experimentation," John Wiley & Sons, New York (1975).

10. Barber, B., Lally, J.J., Makarushka, J.L. et al, "Research on Human Subjects: Problems of Social Control in Medical Experimentation," Russell Sage Foundation, New York (1973).

11. Capron, A.M., Informed consent in catastrophic disease research and treatment, U. Pa. L. Rev. 123:340 (1974).

12. National Research Act, Public Law No. 93, §§ 202(b) & 213 (July 12, 1974).

13. The National Commission and Fetal Research, Hastings Center Report 5(3):11 (1975) (excerpts from eight memoranda on fetal experimentation submitted to the National Commission for the Protection of Human Subjects plus the Commission's report).

14. Powledge, T.M., Fetal experimentation: Trying to sort out the issues, Hastings Center Report 5(2):8 (1975).

15. Gaylin, W. and Lappe, M., Fetal politics: The debate on experimenting with the unborn, Atlantic 235(10):66 (1975).

16. Culliton, B.J., Fetal research, I: The case history of a Massachusetts law, II: The nature of a Massachusetts law, III: The impact of a Massachusetts law, Science 187:237, 411 and 1175 (1975).

17. Erikson, E., "Childhood and Society," p. 23, W.W. Norton & Company, New York (2nd ed., 1963).

18. Capron, A.M., Legal considerations affecting clinical pharmacological studies in children, Clin. Res. 21:141 (1972).

19. McCormick, R.A., Proxy consent in the experimentation situation, Persp. Biol. Med. 2:20 (1974).

20. Lowe, C.U., Alexander, D. and Mishkin, B., Nontherapeutic research on children, J. Pediat. 84:469 (1974).

21. Ramsey, P., "The Ethics of Fetal Research," pp. 89-99, Yale University Press, New Haven (1975).

22. Prosser, W.L., "Handbook of the Law of Torts," pp. 101-03, West Publishing Company, St. Paul, Minn. (4th ed., 1971).

23. Daube, D., Transplantation: Acceptability of procedures and the required legal sanctions, in "Ethics in Medical Progress" G.E.W. Wolstenholme and M. O'Connor (eds.), p. 193, Little, Brown & Company, Boston (1966).

24. Smith, H.W., Therapeutic privilege to withhold specific diagnosis from patient sick with serious or fatal illness, Tenn. L. Rev. 19:349 (1946).

25. Patrick v. Sedwick, 391 P.2d 453 (Alas. 1964).

26. Nishi v. Hartwell, 52 Haw. 188, 473 P.2d 116 (1970).

27.   Shantis, A.J., Informed consent: Some problems revisited,
      Neb. L. Rev. 51:527 (1972).

28.   Canterbury v. Spence, 464 F.2d 772 (D.C. Cir.), cert. denied,
      409 U.S. 1064 (1972).

29.   Cobbs v. Grant, 8 Cal. 3d 229, 502 P.2d 1, 104 Cal. Rptr. 505
      (1972).

30.   Wilkinson v. Vesey, 110 R.I. 606, 295 A.2d 676 (1972).

31.   Roe v. Wade, 410 U.S. 113 (1973).

32.   Engel, R.M., Making gifts from the estate of an incompetent:
      The substitution of judgment doctrine, Wake Forest L. Rev. 9:
      199 (1973).

33.   City Bank Farmers Trust Co. v. McGowan, 323 U.S. 594 (1945).

34.   In re Guardianship of Brice, 233 Iowa 183, 8 N.W. 2d 576 (1943).

35.   Rosenthal, D.E., "Lawyer and Client: Who's in Charge?"
      Russell Sage Foundation, New York (1974).

36.   Link v. Wabash Railroad Co., 370 U.S. 626 (1962).

37.   Kleinfeld, A.J., The balance of power among infants, their
      parents and the state, Family L. Q. 4:320 (1970).

38.   See, e.g., Lee v. Gucker, 186 N.Y.S. 2d 700, 702 (Sup. Ct. 1959)

39.   See, e.g., Williams v. Briggs, 502 P. 2d 245 (Ore. 1972).

40.   Malpass v. Morgan: Determining when a parent's consent to an
      adoption is withheld contrary to the best interests of the
      child, Va. L. Rev. 60:718 (1974).

41.   Armstrong v. Manzo, 380 U.S. 545 (1965).

42.   Ellis, J.W., Volunteering children: Parental commitment of
      minors to mental institutions, Calif. L. Rev. 62: 840 (1974).

43.   See, e.g., Re W (an infant), (1970) 3 All E.R. 990, rev'd
      (1971) 2 All E.R. 49 (Ct. App.), reinstated (1971) 2 All E.R.
      55 (House of Lords).

44.   Note, The custody question and child neglect rehearings, U.
      Chi. L. Rev. 35:478 (1968).

45.   Goldstein, J., Freud, A. and Solnit, A.J., "Beyond the Best

Interests of the Child," p. 54, Free Press, New York (1973).

46. "Restatement, Property" § 185, at p. 747 (comment), American Law Institute Publishers, St. Paul, Minn. (1936).

47. Flast v. Cohen, 392 U.S. 83, 99 (1963).

48. Schlesinger v. Reservists Comm. to Stop the War, 418 U.S. 208, 217 (1974).

49. Baker v. Carr, 369 U.S. I86, 204 (1962).

50. Warth v. Seldin, 43 U.S. L.W. 4906, 4908 (1975).

51. See, e.g., Hansberry v. Lee, 311 U.S. 32 (1940).

52. See, e.g., Hettinger v. Glass Speciality Co., 59 F.R.D. 286 (N.D.Ill. 1973).

53. See, e.g., Williams v. Sheet Metal Workers, Local 19, 59 F.R.D. 49 (E.D. Pa. 1973).

54. Graybeal v. American Savings & Loan Assoc., 59 F.R.D. 7 (D.D.C. 1973).

55. duPont v. Wyly, 61 F.R.D. 615 (D.Del. 1973).

56. See, e.g., Shulman v. Ritzenberg, 47 F.R.D. 202 (D.D.C. 1969).

57. Comment, The importance of being adequate: Due process requirements in class actions under federal rule 23, U. Pa. L. Rev. 123:1217 (1975).

58. Stoner v. California, 376 U.S. 483 (1964).

59. Recent cases, Harv. L. Rev. 79:1513 (1966).

60. Frazier v. Cupp, 394 U.S. 731 (1969).

61. United States v. Stone, 471 F.2d 170 (7th Cir. 1972).

62. United States v. Matlock, 415 U.S. 164 (1974).

63. Boyd v. United States, 116 U.S. 616 (1886).

64. See, e.g., People v. Flowers, 23 Mich. App. 523, 179 N.W. 2d 56 (1970).

65. Friedman, J.M., Legal implications of amniocentesis, U. Pa. L. Rev. 123:92 (1974).

66. Foster, H.H., Jr., "A Bill of Rights for Children," p. 68,
     Charles C. Thomas, Springfield, Ill.(1974).

67. People ex rel. Wallace v. Labrenz, 411 Ill. 618, 104 N.E.2d
     769 (1952).

68. In re Seiferth, 309 N.Y.80, 127 N.E.2d 820 (1955).

69. Prince v. Massachusetts, 321 U.S. 158, 170 (1944).

70. In re Green, 448 Pa. 338, 343, 292 A.2d 387, 389 (1972).

71. In re Sampson, 65 Misc.2d 658 (Fam. Ct., Ulster Co., 1970).

72. Cf. Massachusetts General Hospital, "Human Studies: Guiding
     Principles and Procedures," pp. 6, 8, 11, Massachusetts
     General Hospital, Boston (2d ed., 1970).

73. Wisconsin v. Yoder, 406 U.S. 205, 242 (1972). (Douglas, J.,
     dissenting).

74. O'Donnell, T.J., Informed consent, J.A.M.A. 227:73 (1974).

75. Goldstein, J., For Lasswell, H., Some reflections on human
     dignity, entrapment, informed consent, and the plea bargain,
     Yale L. J. 84:683 (1975).

76. The author is indebted to his colleagues in the Behavior Cont-
     rol Research Group at the Institute of Society, Ethics and
     the Life Sciences, with whom he has scrutinized the topic of
     "proxy consent," and to the students in his 1974-75 seminar
     on Law and the Life Sciences, particularly Nadine Asner,
     Nancy Bregstein, Duncan Grant and Charles MacKay, whose dis-
     cussion of these issues provoked his thinking about them.

DISCUSSION

Paper of Prof. A.M. Capron
Principal Discussant: Prof. S.L. Chorover
Moderator: Prof. L.E. Rosenberg

CHOROVER: In keeping with the overall topic of this conference,
'Genetics and the Law,' my remarks are concerned with the relationship between science and society. More specifically, I want to
comment briefly on what I take to be a salient, and much-neglected
aspect of the relationship between the bio-behavioral sciences (including both genetics and psychology) and the problems of human
society (including problems of law and justice).

Let me begin by stating, in the form of four brief sentences,
an idea that has been expressed by various participants in this
conference and which repeatedly arises in similar contexts:
1) We live in a time of great social turmoil surrounded by problems
which urgently demand solution; 2) Among the more serious of our
problems are those which derive from human behavior; 3) The bio-
behavioral sciences provide tools and techniques for effecting
changes in human behavior; 4) We should use the instruments of
science and technology to solve our problems by improving the ways
in which people behave. Put in a nutshell, the idea in question
comes down to this: the bio-behavioral sciences, including genetics
and psychology, have a proper and crucial role to play in solving
social problems.

It is not my intention to deny the obvious; namely, that modern
natural science is an extraordinarily powerful system for unraveling
the mysteries of nature, for obtaining reliable and trustworthy
knowledge of the universe and its contents, and for developing
tools and techniques capable of transforming the world in which we
live. I do want to point out, however, that proposals to put science to work solving social problems represent a departure from the
idea that science is (or ought to be) the disinterested pursuit of
knowledge 'for its own sake.' I do not mean to suggest that there
is anything wrong in this. On the contrary, science has been and
remains something very far removed from the abstract, disinterested,
morally neutral enterprise which myths of long standing hold it to
be. Proposals to put science to work in the domain of practical
affairs have been a constant accompaniment of modern civilization
at least since the time when Francis Bacon uttered his oft-quoted
remark that 'knowledge is power.' Accordingly, the gist of my
remarks may be summarized by saying that proposals to put science
to work solving social problems are proposals to exercise power in
the pursuit of certain objectives. That being accepted, it remains
to be said that questions about the exercise of power are political
questions. 'Real politics,' as Benjamin Disraeli once observed, 'is
the possession and distribution of power.'

341

Were there time to do so, I would argue at some length that attempts to claim logical and moral neutrality for the bio-behavioral sciences are attempts to foster a pernicious myth. Now a myth, as the dictionary says, is more than just a traditional or legendary story of doubtful authenticity. It is, 'an unproved collective belief that is accepted uncritically and is used to justify a social institution.' My point is that the myth of scientific neutrality is often used to buttress prevailing social arrangements in precisely this way. And it is used in this way whenever the weight of ostensibly objective scientific evidence is brought to bear upon social problems in ways that tend to reinforce the status quo.

Now, it ought to be self-evident that the applications of science and technology are not invariably desireable or beneficial in their effects. It is therefore naive (or worse) to pretend that the effective solution of pressing social problems is ensured by applying to them the tools and techniques of bio-behavioral science. In a world in which knowledge and skills may be used for either constructive or destructive purposes, it clearly behooves scientists and technologists to reflect upon the consequences to which our work is liable to lead. My own opinion is that the arsenal of tools and techniques that has already been developed in the field of bio-behavioral science is being deployed in pursuit of social objectives and that the objectives deserve a far more careful and critical examination than they usually receive.

In the brief time available, I cannot do more than suggest the kind of examination I have in mind. But let me give an example in outline with respect to the problem of crime. Crime is a pressing social problem. It is a problem in which both bio-behavioral scientists and public officials have shown increasing interest in recent years. Now a crime, as the dictionary tells us, is an action or instance of negligence that is deemed injurious to the public welfare or morals or to the interests of the state and is legally prohibited. I suspect that both scientists and public officials who address themselves to 'the crime problem' understand that it is a controversial issue because of differences of opinion that exist within our society regarding the justifiability and propriety of various acts. The point is an obvious one that crime is defined and dealt with in terms of prevailing norms and values. Our attitudes toward stealing may serve as an illustrative case in point. I know of a Black man from Alabama who attempted to steal a car in Boston five years ago. He was arrested, jailed, tried, convicted, labeled as a felon, and is presently serving a 35 year sentence in Walpole prison in Massachusetts. I also know of a white man from California who attempted to steal a whole country three years ago. He was allowed to resign his position and flown home at government expense, given a splendid pension, pardoned without trial, given a third of a million dollars to ease his relocation and is presently spending his time on a sunny beach writing his memoirs for personal profit.

The man in Walpole prison has been examined by psychologists, psychiatrists, and geneticists who are 'studying' his behavioral history, chromosomal makeup and biochemical constitution, ostensibly in order to learn something about the factors which cause criminal behavior and to bring it under control. For a time he was sent to a Federal prison in Missouri to participate in a behavior modification program aimed at inducing adjustment in particularly 'recalcitrant' prisoners. Throughout this process, those who have been concerned with his behavior have been receiving financial support for their efforts from public agencies concerned with 'mental health' and 'law enforcement.'

At work here is the assumption that crime arises primarily from genetic variance and that social troubles arise primarily from the disordered or defective behavior of certain individuals or groups. At work here also are two classes of people who tend to share that assumption: first, there are the 'investigators'; people engaged in these fields of science, including psychologists, geneticists and other mental health professionals. Second, there are the administrators of our public institutions, and over them, the public officials who enjoy the amenities of power in society and are essentially deemed to be responsible for managing our affairs. They, too are inclined to perceive the sources of turmoil as lying outside of the social arrangements over which they preside. The relationship between those two classes of people is complex, but there is insufficient time now to explore it further.

The point is not that a conspiracy exists, but rather that a positive feedback loop exists between the scientists who perceive the root causes of crime as lying in defective histories of reinforcement or in deranged neurobiology, on the one hand, and the public agencies which manage what is euphemistically called the 'war on crime' on the other hand. Money, to put it bluntly, plays a major role in shaping what passes for science today. What passes for biobehavioral science today is neither more nor less than that which is legitimated by financial support. The image of the selfless scientist earnestly pursuing knowledge for its own sake is appealing, but its occurrence is rare and as an ideal it pales before the reality of grantsmanship in which one is driven by the need for professional survival to seek money wherever it can be found. My point is that the existence of this positive feedback loop legitimates the use of behavioral and genetic control technology as a means of dealing with social problems. Scientists can, in their choice and formulation of projects become so interest-bound that they are simply no longer able to see certain facts which would undermine their self-image of scientific neutrality. And, with politicians, scientists may exploit the alleged 'objectivity' of

their work to create the impression that something rational and
humane is being done to deal with social problems. The net result
is that the existing social arrangements are left undisturbed.

Social problems (intelligence and deviance) are controversial
precisely because each of us regards them from perspectives already
colored by our beliefs, interests and experiences. That our society is rife with disagreements over moral and ethical values and
that there is much jostling over the propriety of dissident and
deviant forms of behavior is an important fact of contemporary
life. To pretend that the disagreements can be resolved and the
jostling controlled by the tools and techniques of psychotechnology
is to ignore the systematic nature of social reality and to confuse
power with wisdom.

Let me conclude by drawing to your attention the profound importance of definitions as determinants of social reality. I have
been arguing that it is wrong to define social problems in terms of
individual disorders because such definitions foreclose the possibility of addressing the problems in more proper social terms. I
have suggested that the tendency to define social problems in this
way serves the professional interests of bio-behavioral scientists
and public officials at the same time. Let me be more explicit:
The way in which a problem is defined determines what will not be
done about it (and not just what will be). Some 300 years ago, an
otherwise gloomy social philosopher, Thomas Hobbes, made what will
be my concluding point: the ultimate source of social stability,
he said, is the power to give names and to enforce definitions.

Science and the state are today the great definers, and the
relationship between them is such as to serve the status quo. The
former (science) provides the definitions of behavior disorders
and deviance which the latter uses to reinforce prevailing patterns
of social control. The question is not whether behavior is genetically controlled or how best to bring certain aspects of behavior
under genetic control; whether we are talking about IQ, deviance,
drug 'therapy,' or behavior modification. The fundamental question,
which we avoid at our peril is this: who holds the power in society
and toward what ends is that power used to exercise social control?
The existence of that question is what makes all discussions of
genetics and the law, political discussions. And, if politics is
the field in which some people exercise their power over others, all
proposals to put bio-behavioral science to work 'solving social
problems' will continue to be proposals to enable one group of
people to exercise power over another, with science and technology
merely serving as the chosen instruments of power.

R. MARKS: University of California School of Law, Berkeley:
The discussion on consent of children for experimentation leaves
out one critical aspect. Let us assume for the moment they lack

capacity to fully accept the responsibility of their own choices, (and that is an assumption that I would quarrel with, namely the question of how much capacity an incompetent really has) and suggest that there is another element present. That is, I will state parents alone cannot provide sufficient consent to experimentation on their children for operations. The reason for it is the other element. That is a child and a person in a mental institution has a personality, a set of privacy interests, and a right probably, even as a very young child, to be a participant in their own destiny, even though somebody else may be going surety, like a court or like parents. A child has a right to be consulted with respect to the procedures that are going to be used and have some sense of participation. I grant you we have major institutions, like compulsory education, that go against that paradigm, but when considering experimentation on children one ought to rethink the whole concept of the role of children in our society.

CAPRON: Just to clarify what I said, I regard the first question as extremely important. That is the question of how a person is determined to be incompetent and what does it mean to be incompetent? What are you left with? I would indeed think that at a fairly early age one would want to say that a child has some sort of a veto power even if you would not feel comfortable going ahead on their sole consent. I do not quarrel with that at all.

I want to address the second question of from whom in addition to the child, would what I call permission and not consent, be obtained. It does not at all exclude the child or the child's interest from being voiced by the child or the other incompetent. The question of incompetence is being raised most clearly in the courts concerning mental patients, although I am sure this will occur in the children's area more often in the future.

DAVIS: Prof. Capron has been talking mostly about consent for genetic experimentation or for gene therapy, which is still far off. I'd like to discuss the question of whether we should need consent for acquiring knowledge of prognostic value: something we can do right now, with an increasing variety of tests that are themselves harmless. The XYY issue raises this problem in an acute form, and I don't think it has been formulated quite clearly enough.

Doctors have traditionally been free, and have even been obligated to look for information that may help to look ahead into the patient's health problems. If you go into a hospital for a lump and the doctor takes a blood pressure, surely you are not going to sue him because he gives you the disquieting information that you have high blood pressure, or anything else discovered in the course of a general examination. Indeed, if he does not look for these other things he is usually a pretty poor doctor.

So I think it is widely accepted that physicians look for anything they can find in a patient that may help them not only to
treat the cause of the presenting symptom, but also to make a
prognosis with respect to the patient's health. I can understand,
then, how the question of risk might not have been raised with Prof.
Walzer undertook his study some eight years ago, for it was then
taken for granted that if we have a new technique, which allows us
to detect chromosomal abnormalities of possible prognostic value,
the subject could only benefit from a research program that made
that technique available. Now we realize that this approach
overlooked the psychological risks that may arise if the information
creates anxiety: but it is not clear that this risk is large enough,
if sensitively handled, to outweigh the potential benefits. You
also create anxiety if you do tests that reveal a high level of
lipids in the patient's blood, leading to the prediction that he is
likely to develop atherosclerosis at an early age. Can he sue the
doctor and say, "I didn't want that information?"

It seems to me the general question of risks involved in
obtaining valid information of prognostic significance is one that
should be addressed here.

H. JACKSON: New England Medical Center, Boston: Prof. Capron
we have been talking a lot about XYY individuals. What about those
genotypic males with XX? The specific question I have concerns
such an individual who enlists in the army. He is not fully aware
of his specific karyotype. He writes to the authorities requesting
that he obtain his records from his physician. The physician does
not oblige. What are the consequences?

CAPRON: I do not think that is a question I addressed. It is
not a question of incompetence. I think it does go to this question
Prof. Davis has raised, and I will speak to that. In the situation
which he described (but I'm not sure in the situation you described),
the patient in a relationship with a doctor gives what I was referring to as inferred, or what one calls implied consent, to all
the steps that are naturally involved in the care of the patient.
The patient has, in other words, entered into a relationship in
which the doctor and patient have a common assumption.

In the case of screening as part of a mass procedure, I'm not
sure that that assumption is proper or that it exists. If it is
in effect mandated by the state, or army physical, the information
probably then should be disclosed. The question is disclosure in
what context? Are there adequate means available to inform the
person of what the significance of that disclosure is, particularly
if it is going to have a medical impact on him, or if there is
any danger involved.

JACKSON: In the same context suppose we encourage adult screening and phenotypic males with XX karyotypes are determined. What would the results of such individuals be? Would there be increased incidence of suicide, etc.?

CAPRON: I am in no position to answer that. I have no idea if there would be an increased incidence of suicide. Once again, that is a question of the context in which the information is conveyed.

C. CANN: Harvard School of Public Health, Boston: I wanted to make a point to Prof. Davis on one aspect that has not been raised in this conference. Although Prof. Walzer's study has been going on for some eight years, informed consent was not obtained from the parents until about two years ago. I think that is a very important issue, and one which I think people should understand as to why the controversy started.

R. GREENSTEIN: University of Connecticut Medical School, Farmington: I felt that you were talking about some organized way of identifying a method of legitimizing permission or consent by incompetent individuals. What role might an institutional committee, like a human experimentation committee, have in relationship to obtaining this consent? Would you think perhaps that this is not in the best interests of the patient, but in the interests of the experiment?

CAPRON: If we look to the examples which I have found in other areas of the law, I am not quite sure that the committee is the best analogy. The reason is that it is doubtful that the committee will have much individual knowledge of the child - how well that child can cope with exposure to the experiment, how well the parents, if they are the ones who are really going to get the information that came out of the experiment, can cope with it, etc. It may be that some committee could serve the role of reviewing parental consent. This has been the practice in a number of kidney transplant cases and has been criticized by some of the commentators as an undue insertion of the court's authority into the parental decision-making. That is to say the court has looked at the decision.

What I find objectionable about those decisions, including a recent one here in Massachusetts in the Farinelli case, is mostly what the court does. The court decides whether the experiment, or in those cases the kidney transplant, or bone marrow transplant, is within the range of what the court would allow if it were the court's child, rather than deciding that the parents have been conscientous and gone through a legitimate decision-making process.

That just seems to me to substitute something like a committee, that does not have familiarity with the child, for the parents. I would like to try to identify the parents or someone else who can rigorously exercise that other interested judgment about the value of the experiment and the risks.

GREENSTEIN: I raise that point because the tendency for human experimentation committees through federal guidelines is to begin to identify sub-groups of those committees, which will become autonomous to such committees and, therefore, follow the effects of research on the subject, both prior to and after the results of the experimentation.

R.L. INGRAHAM: San Jose State University, California: I would like a response from someone with a legal background to a couple of paragraphs that appeared in a case before the Supreme Court of California concerning a controversy involving the hiring of females to tend a bar. Our Supreme Court decided that there could be regulations against them. These two paragraphs, I think, may have some bearing upon what Prof. Davis said.

I cannot see that XYY is really comparable to high blood pressure. They referred here to suspect classifications. Sex, like race and lineage, is an immutable trait, a status to which the class members are locked by the accident of birth. What differentiates sex from non-suspect statuses such as intelligence and physical disability, and aligns it with the recognized suspect classifications, is the characteristic frequently bears no relation to ability to perform or contribute to society. The result is that the whole class is relegated to an inferior legal status without regard to the capabilities or characteristics of the individual member. Where the relationship between the characteristic and evil to be prevented is so tenuous, courts must look closely at classifications based on that characteristic lest outdated social stereotypes result in invidious laws or practices.

In light of our recent knowledge of XYY and sophistication of the public, I wonder if we really have a problem of a different dimension than something like high blood pressure. I'd like to have any comments on the thinking of the Supreme Court in California.

CAPRON: It is important to notice from your discussion that there is not merely a definition of something as a condition, whether it be XX, XY, XXY, etc., but an action taken upon that. It would certainly raise some questions, not only as to sexual identification, but racial identification (which is the more historic suspect classification) as to where action is to be taken on the basis of an in-born racially and sexually identified characteristic. Thus far the sorts of things we are talking about are all highly speculative. At the point at which they become a little closer in hand, I think that quotation and the law which lies behind it will come into play.

DAVIS: I think that the comment just made would be thoroughly
pertinent if one were to discover an XYY case and then publish the
information. But as I understand it, the studies have exerted
all possible effort to keep the information private, known only to
the family and the physician. Hence it is not a matter of public
classification.

ON LEGISLATING FETAL RESEARCH

Charles U. Lowe

National Commission on the Protection of Human Subjects,
National Institutes of Health, Department of Health,
Education and Welfare, Bethesda

Although the title of this symposium is "Genetics and the
Law," I must hasten to advise you that I am neither a geneticist
nor a lawyer. I assume, therefore, that my presence on this platform reflects a special privilege that has been mine; that is, to
observe at rather close quarters the legislating of fetal research,
a process with a history confined to the last four years.

Let me point out quickly that as a non-lawyer, I perceive
two distinct aspects of such legislative activity. One is legislation in the sense of controlling what people do with their own
lives; the second, which in fact has taken place, has to do with
telling the federal government what it may do with public money.
These are two quite different elements of the law. Nevertheless,
I suspect that the interplay between these two elements reflects
the fact that we are a nation or a civilization ill-equipped to
deal with certain human problems through the legal processes currently established. Consequently we bumble a bit, try to find our
way through hit or miss, and ultimately achieve a compromise which,
if not satisfactory to all, is at least offensive to the fewest
in our nation.

The present discussion traces the history of the involvement
of the federal government, and in particular an agency of the
government, the National Institutes of Health, in legislating
fetal research. The history in a general way goes back to the
Nuremberg trials, when there was a deep concern about the rights
of individuals involved in biomedical and behavioral research. The
resulting Nuremberg Code and later, the Declaration of Helsinki,
were followed in 1966 by proclamation by the Surgeon General of
the U.S. Public Health Service, Dr. Stewart, of a code of ethics

to govern all funding of biomedical research by the Department of Health, Education, and Welfare. These guidelines primarily affected funds from the National Institutes of Health rather than other elements in the Department. The Stewart code was modified in 1971 and remained in effect as guidelines until 1974, when in slightly altered form the guidelines were formally adopted as federal regulations.

There is an important distinction in the federal system between guidelines and regulations. Guidelines in this case simply set forth the rules governing the awarding of federal funds for the conduct of research. In contrast, the violation of a regulation has the effect of a violation of the law; thus publishing regulations means in effect that a new statute exists in the area of administrative law.

In the regulations of the Department published in May, 1974, virtually no attention was paid to the special groups; that is, to those individuals such as children, the institutionalized mentally infirm, prisoners, and the fetus, who due to diminished civil rights or other reasons are unable to give fully informed consent.

From this point the tale takes on certain elements of a Baroque symphony. There are points and counterpoints, there are themes which emerge and then disappear, there is cacaphony in the background, there is no real conductor of the music, and instrumentalists often take off on their own, probably in part simply through exuberance in relation to the issue, but frequently ending up far from the original theme.

During this period when the Department was converting its guidelines to regulations, there was increasing concern in the nation for the protection of individuals with diminished civil rights. Certain other factors also emerged on the public scene which impacted upon the popular concern for the protection of subjects involved in biomedical and behavioral research. Perhaps the most potent of these came from the revelations of the Tuskegee experiment, an undertaking which was many years old, but surfaced to public attention only in 1972. A second event which comes closer to the issue at hand was the decision of the Supreme Court in Roe v. Wade in 1973 which made the decision as to whether or not she would carry a fetus to term a matter between a woman and her physician through the second trimester of pregnancy.

To many it appeared that the legitimatizing of abortion in a sense was making available abortion on demand, one consequence of which would be providing a large number of fetuses for research. (I might add parenthetically that at least to the limits of my own review of the issue there seems to be very little evidence that the total number of abortions conducted in this country has substantially

changed as a result of the Supreme Court's decision. What has
occurred is the shifting from criminal abortions to medical abortions, with a concomitant major decrease in the number of injuries
to women who were obtaining criminal abortions and who now receive
abortions conducted under aseptic circumstances and with all the
care attendant to surgical procedures.)

In any case, these two events made it seem imperative that
protection be offered to the fetus if it were to be involved in
biomedical research. What made the issue even more important was
the realization among pediatricians and physicians caring for the
fetus or the pregnant woman that the future of medicine lay in the
understanding of normal processes. Therefore, there was a tremendous increase in interest in studying the fetus both in utero and
ex utero, in order to make pregnancies safer. This interest was
heightened by the fact that our nation, one of the most advanced
in the world, found itself still with a rather appallingly high
infant mortality rate. Consequently investigators turned more
frequently to the fetus as a research subject, and requests for
funds from tne NIH to support such research concomitantly increased.

At the time these events occurred in the United States, the
British were also concerned with the problems of research on the
fetus. The genesis of their concern was in part related to the
abortion issue as in this country, but there were two specific
elements which emerged in Great Britain which had not surfaced here.
One was the emergence of an apparent traffic in fetuses, with physicians buying fetuses for the purpose of research; the second, some
highly publicized attempts to maintain the nonviable fetus ex utero
in some kind of suspended animation. These revelations appeared to
affront the moral sense of the British public. As a result, the
Peel Commission was established, and issued its report, attempting
to set a code of ethics for fetal research for the British Isles
and provide physicians and investigators with some understanding of
what the community considered acceptable. It is interesting that
the principal recommendation of the report is that each hospital
or aggregate of hospitals should have the right to make decisions
on what was ethically permissible and not permissible with respect
to fetal research.

In 1972, Dr. Robert Marston, then Director of the National
Institutes of Health, decided that the guidelines at that point
extant in guiding or advising grantees on what research practices
would and would not be supported by funds from the National Institutes of Health failed to offer sufficient protection to those individuals with diminished civil rights who lacked the ability to
give truly informed consent as a sine qua non for participation in
biomedical research. Consequently he directed NIH staff to begin
to develop revised guidelines which would lead to increased protection for these subjects. Early in 1973, approximately four

months after Dr. Marston initiated these activities, the Acting
Secretary of the Department of Health, Education, and Welfare himself became aware of the need for regulations to protect these
special subjects. The activity, although continuing at the NIH,
was eventually taken over by the staff of the Secretary, and culminated in a series of recommended regulations.

In November of 1973 there resulted a publication in the Federal
Register of a document which proposed practices, regulations, limits, and methods for protection of these special subjects, including
the fetus, and requested public comment. The public did respond
generously and with some enthusiasm, pointing out both strengths
and weaknesses, but in general recognizing the need for these protections. I would judge that there was a general note of public
satisfaction that the federal government had finally moved into
this area, using its regulatory mechanism to provide guidelines
and control fetal research. Taking into account the public comments, there was published in the Federal Register in August 1974
a notice of proposed rulemaking which would begin to control fetal
research.

All this time the counterpoint alluded to earlier was being
played by Congress, which had become deeply involved in the issue
of fetal research. While one would have to conclude that part of
the concern of the Congress stemmed from the putative purpose, that
is, control of fetal research, there also seemed to be an overlay
of concern about the whole problem of abortion on request. A
whole series of bills introduced in Congress, some as amendments
to major pieces of legislation and some as self-standing bills,
seemed to have the intention of prohibiting fetal research, hoping
that the net effect would be a reduction in the number of abortions
performed in this country. Somehow certain legislators seemed to
become convinced that fetal research encouraged abortion, and that
curtailing fetal research would diminish the number of abortions.
Fuel for the legislative fire was provided by publicity of a single
fetal research project conducted by an American investigator in
Finland, in which heads were removed from dead aborted fetuses for
isolated perfusion studies. This research, in combination with the
temper of the times, resulted in the passage of a notable piece
of legislation affecting fetal research, the National Research Act.

This bill was signed into law on July 12, 1974. It did a
number of things, two of which particularly pertain to fetal research. In the first place, it established under the Secretary of
the Department of Health, Education, and Welfare, a National Commission for the Protection of Human Subjects of Biomedical and Behavioral Research, charged with reviewing a whole series of ethical
issues, but particularly those relating to individuals with some
diminution of civil rights. Second, it dealt with the question
of fetal research by placing a ban on such research for a specific

period of time, and by requiring the Commission to review the nature and extent of research on the fetus, the purposes for which it had been undertaken, and alternative means for achieving these purposes. The Commission then was to advise the Secretary on the need for fetal research and the circumstances, if any, under which research on the live human fetus could be conducted or supported.

Having so charged the Commission, the law then provided that the ban on fetal research would be lifted when the Commission had acted. In a generous mood, the Congress offered the Commission a period of four months in which to meet this obligation. This proved to be an overwhelmingly demanding charge. Nevertheless, on May 21 the recommendations of the Commission will in fact be presented to the Secretary, a bit tardy, but all things considered not so tardy as to be embarrassing to anyone concerned.

Analysis of the simultaneous performance of point and counter-point reveals a number of problems that have emerged in trying to deal with fetal research through the legislative pathway rather than the regulatory or guideline pathway. Many of these problems relate to language and the meaning of words. Most important is the definition of life. The law imposed a ban on research on the living fetus, but medical specialists, theorists, philosophers, and scientists have found themselves in a bind as they attempt to reduce a definition of life to a structure which permits enforcement of the law. In addition, there have been misunderstandings about the meaning of the law per se in terms of what kinds of research was prohibited.

Many of the laws proposed before the Congress failed to realize that the fetus spent a period of nine months of vulnerability in the uterus and, therefore, did not address research on the pregnant woman. Confusion, however, was not limited to the legislative community. Some of the most powerful and ambitious proponents of fetal research in the biomedical research community seemed to confuse the difference between living cells and a living fetus and incorrectly argued that a great deal of research which had been successful and helpful to the nation's people would have been prohibited if the Congressional ban on fetal research had in fact existed five, ten or fifteen years ago. Further ambiguities arose in interpreting the legislation. The fetal research ban states: "Until the Commission has made its recommendations to the Secretary pursuant to section 202(b), the Secretary may not conduct or support research in the United States or abroad on a living human fetus, before or after the induced abortion of such fetus, unless such research is done for the purpose of assuring the survival of such fetus." Clearly this says that the ban is on the Secretary, and that he is prevented from funding research. It says nothing about a government-wide ban; it concerns only the funding of research by the Secretary, DHEW. Second, it does not speak to any research

except that related to abortion. And third, it does permit any
research which is intended to preserve the life of the fetus.

Publication in the Federal Register announcing imposition of
the ban by the Secretary of Health, Education, and Welfare, and
advice concerning the ban published in the periodical "Science,"
from the Assistant Secretary for Health unfortunately did not
clarify the limited nature of the ban. In both instances these
publications seemed to have the net effect of sustaining indefinitely
the ban, which the Congress identified as being lifted at the time
the Commission made its report to the Secretary. Further, the biomedical public in fact misinterpreted the ban as a total ban, a
government-wide ban, and a ban which prohibited any manipulation of
the fetus.

Many more examples of such problems could be cited, but some
general observations may be made in conclusion. An issue as complex as fetal research may not lend itself comfortably to legislative action. The questions are complex, the language is technical
and specific, and even specialists in the area have difficulty
dealing with the meaning of words. Nonetheless, it is of interest
to note that the net result of the federal legislation, the recommendations of the Commission, differs only slightly from the recommendations in the regulatory approach proposed by the Secretary.
What remains at issue is whether this result will be accepted by
the public.

DISCUSSION

Paper of Dr. C.U. Lowe
Principal Discussant: Prof. M.J. Mahoney
Moderator: Prof. L.E. Rosenberg

MAHONEY: Dr. Lowe has told us what happened at the federal
level when legislators attempted to control or to tell us how to
govern a very complex area. Most of you know what happened in
Boston. A law was read in much wider context than the legislators
had meant it to be. Much research was stopped which in retrospect
the legislators had no intent to stop. I think these are two
very graphic illustrations of what happens within complex scientific areas when we allow or when the public requires legislators
to step into the area. I have watched closely and participated
to some degree in the formulation of policy with regard to fetal
research that is now evolving in state legislatures, specifically
in Connecticut, as well as in the federal government. There are
two observations that seem particularly pertinent to me.

Firstly, the process has become increasingly politicized and
requires analysis and understanding in that context. But also
there is ample opportunity, I believe, to successfully work within
the political process if we are adequately prepared. The National
Commission for the Protection of Human Subjects and the moratorium
on fetal research which Dr. Lowe just summarized for us, came of
political compromise after there was sufficient pressure built
up throughout the nation, specifically in Congress, to require it.

The idea of a national ethics review had been proposed at least
a decade before that and it had prominent senatorial backing.
Appointment to the national commission also had considerable political input, this to the dismay of several of our scientific societies. Knowledge of the political process, especially of its
many hidden agendas that are operative, and of the sources and
execution of power, are imperative for the understanding of these
issues. Within this process, I believe, scientists can work very
effectively, admitting that the political arena is not our chosen
home, that we are not fully comfortable there, and that we require
help to know how to proceed effectively. We have allies in law and
in politics who can provide this help and we should be seeking
close bonds with them.

My own experience finds that many legislators and other interested laymen remain open and desirous of information on recent arguments. Although the prestige of the physician and the scientist
has been significantly eroded, it remains visible and strong. One
thing that legislators do require is assurance that there is a
constituency in support of a given position. Unfortunately, short-
term goals are usually foremost in the politician's hierarchy. Our

political process is highly vulnerable to control by a well organized and vocal minority. Whenever there is neither opportunity nor time for sufficient education and debate, a situation which ofttimes results in the kind of legislation which we have faced.

How to accomplish this education I submit, must be a major and continuing goal, not yet successfully addressed. One route is to form our own vocal and powerful minority lobby by enlisting allies from special health consumer groups and from those who share economic benefits with the research community, and to some extent this has always been done and it continues to be done. I do not believe this will be sufficient in today's social climate. It further seems to me to be less satisfactory in obtaining continuing and stable public support. To create an informed public is extremely difficult and our vocabulary and dialogue require modification to accomplish it. It further requires help from community leaders, clergy, teachers, and others who want to learn and are willing to help - and there are many of these.

A forum like this one and the press coverage attendant to it do not accomplish this kind of education, and at best only begin the process. In fact, even within this kind of a meeting, some degree of rhetoric here refuses to acknowledge underlying assumption or paradigms as common. I believe we must carefully identify these and illuminate them. I further suggest that we must recognize a wider educational goal as a legitimate and for some of us a full-time obligation, that we find effective ways to accomplish the goal, and that we pursue it enthusiastically.

IN VITRO FERTILIZATION - A LEGAL PERSPECTIVE

Philip Reilly

University of Texas Graduate School of Biomedical

Sciences

HUMAN IN VITRO FERTILIZATION - THE STATE OF THE ART (1)

The birth of a child via in vitro fertilization (I.V.F.) requires 1. aspiration of a pre-ovulatory oocyte; 2. fertilization
of the egg by sperm in culture media; 3. normal cleavage to the
blastula stage; 4. transfer and implantation into a human uterus
and 5. a normal gestation. Although the first efforts to fertilize human ova in vitro were made several decades ago, only recently
have such experiments succeeded (2). Three major problems have
been resolved within the past few years. First, for a long time it
was thought that extracorporeal fertilization could only be accomplished with sperm that had been "capacitated" in the female tract.
However, studies with hamsters revealed that epididymal sperm could
fertilize eggs cultured in tubal or follicular secretions (3). Further investigations led to the development of a culture medium
that closely matched the uterine environment (4). Fertilization of
mammalian eggs in vitro is now accomplished routinely (5). A second
major advance has involved the perfection of the post-fertilization
environment. If implantation is to be successful, then preimplan-
tation development must proceed normally and embryo transfer (E.T.)
technology must be perfected. Much research has been devoted to
the problem of cleavage (the early divisions of the zygote) and to
the development of transfer surgery (6). Finally, the clinical
application of I.V.F. requires the timed harvest of oocytes. Recently it has become possible to control follicular development and
oocyte maturation by the use of purified human menopausal and human
chorionic gonadotrophins. These oocytes can now be harvested by
laparoscopic aspiration, a simpler and safer technique than lapar-
otomy (7).

The transfer of an 8-celled embryo into a human uterus is relatively simple. The blastula, riding in a drop of culture media, is placed inside a thin plastic tube which is then threaded through a cannula which has been passed through the cervical canal into the uterus. Positive pressure forces the embryo out of the tube into the womb (8).

As many as 2% of women suffer from occluded oviducts. I.V.F. and E.T. offer a means to circumvent infertility for those who wish to be pregnant. Scientists have been ready to attempt embryo transfer for more than five years (9). The last major obstacle to success involves the problem of implantation. Edwards has reported that E.T. has been unsuccessful in 8 patients. However, he and other researchers are sanguine about the future. At least one report of a pregnancy achieved after I.V.F. and E.T. has appeared. Apparently, the pregnancy, which was monitored by hormone assays, aborted spontaneously (8). In 1974 Bevis, an obstetrician at Leeds University in England, announced that he was aware of three healthy children who had been born via I.V.F. within the last 2 years. He refused, ostensibly to protect the privacy of the persons involved, to divulge any details. Wide skepticism greeted his remarks. It seems clear, however, that the birth of a child by this technique is imminent. It is not unrealistic to expect that considerable pressure could develop to make I.V.F. available to infertile women after the first few births are documented.

THE ETHICAL DEBATES

Behavior which is morally correct is often not compelled by the law. No man is required to be a good Samaritan; a champion swimmer is under no legal duty to plunge into a river to save a child. By the same token from no legal "is" can a moral "ought" be drawn (10). Ideally, we can work to create a world in which moral suasion is coequal with legal command. It is particularly appropriate when examining a problem about which there is no black letter law to scrutinize the ethical analyses that have been undertaken. From a review of the quite substantial and fascinating ethical literature there emerge 3 major questions about the use of human I.V.F. Space demands that we be content with only a brief enumeration of them.

1. Is I.V.F. a non-human form of reproduction and therefore absolutely immoral? This question is asked by ethical a priorists. Ramsey, a Princeton theologian, has offered perhaps its most celebrated analysis in his book Fabricated Man (11). Proceeding from basic Christian premises (however personally formulated) he concluded that this was not a morally permissible form of procreation. It is quite possible that a technological advance which erodes the conjugal basis of marriage does pose a threat to society.

However, given the myriad other pressures operating upon the marriage institution,the threat of I.V.F. appears minuscule. It is
important to note that Ramsey also refutes the use of I.V.F. with
an analysis that draws only on medical ethics. He argues that
because infertility is not a disease I.V.F. treats desires instead
of illnesses and thus cannot be medically justified (12, 13).

    2. Does in vitro fertilization constitute unethical exper-
imentation upon human beings? This is really 2 questions. The
larger theoretical question asks whether the woman, the husband
and the physician have the right to attempt to achieve pregnancy
in this manner. There is an unknown burden of risk associated
with I.V.F. and blastocyst transfer. Naturally, a substantial
number of fertilized human eggs will be sacrificed pursuant to
perfecting the technology. Some of the first fetuses produced
by I.V.F. (these pregnancies will be monitored) may be aborted because of malformation. An 8-celled human blastocyst cannot exercise the choice to run this risk. Is that a sufficient moral reason to interdict a woman's search for fertility? Perhaps the most
persuasive arguments against this sort of ethical stance are those
that point to the extraordinarily high natural rate of conceptus
failures (estimates range as high as 80%). Does any embryo ever
consent to its conception? Should this fact argue against conception generally? The experimentation question also focuses on the
protocols actually used by the investigators who have attempted
embryo transfers on infertile women. Critics generally perceive
an injudicious haste to use human material. They frequently cite
the need for primate studies, very few of which have been conducted.
At least one scientist, Kass, has voiced serious reservations about
the adequacy of the understanding of those women who have agreed
to participate in these studies. He fears that they may not realize how small a chance they have of achieving a successful pregnancy (14).

    3. Is in vitro fertilization a paradigm for our semiconscious
collective urge to dehumanize ourselves? This formulation particularly argues a dichotomy between man and technology. It is especially wary of haste in application of scientific knowledge. Carried
to its extreme it envisions a non-human type catapulted out of
our culture into the future. On a more immediate level one can
appreciate the argument which fits nicely into concern over data
banks, wire taps, and psychosurgery.

    Not all ethicists have concluded that human I.V.F. should be
interdicted (for this or any other reason). For example, Fletcher,
the father of situation ethics, has asserted a strong defense of
the practice. He looks to the result of a medical procedure and
weighs that against the detriments perceived. He is primarily
concerned with actual human needs, not abstract human rights.
He concludes that this need to bear children justifies a woman's

choice to undergo I.V.F. (15). Other ethicists have developed
theories of informed consent that might support the right of a
woman to participate in I.V.F. (16).

THE IDEA OF A MORATORIUM

During the past three years four major areas of the biomedical
sciences have been subjected to intense scrutiny (both from within
and without the professional community) to determine whether certain research and clinical activities should be interdicted or
harnessed with social controls not recently experienced in America.
In 1971 a major controversy developed around mass population
screening for sickle cell trait. Sporadic, but serious, discrimination leveled against persons because of genotype fueled the
attack against sloppily written compulsory testing laws. Social
criticism was an important force in the drafting of a comprehensive
federal sickle cell program premised on voluntarism and confidentiality (17). The fetal research debate was an immediate outgrowth
of the Supreme Court decisions which extended the privacy right to
cover the abortion decision during the first two trimesters (18).
Anti-abortion forces turned their attention to exposing allegedly
ghoulish research practices; this highly effective campaign culminated in a nationwide moratorium on fetal research conducted with
federal funds (19). In 1974 and 1975 a somewhat more esoteric
scientific debate led to a temporary, self-imposed moratorium on
certain experiments with "recombinant DNA" (20). The remote risks
that a dramatic health hazard could be created by such studies
culminated in more sophisticated laboratory containment procedures.
Criticism of mass genetic screening has focussed primarily on the
risk of stigmatizing individuals; the fetal research debate centers
on the definition of personhood; the genetic engineering issue was
simply a question of regulating a health hazard.

The practice of human I.V.F. and embryo transfer has generated
the most sustained discussion of and the most frequent demands for
a moratorium on clinical application. Ironically, Edwards,in whose
laboratory much of this research has been conducted, was among the
first to publicly consider the question of social regulation of
such clinical investigations. With good reason he expressed the
fear that if the gap between scientific achievements and societal
allegiances grew too wide research would be hobbled:

What is to be feared is that if the biologists do not
invent a method of taking counsel of mankind, society will
thrust its advice on biologists and other scientists and
probably in a manner or form seriously hampering to
science (21).

Shortly thereafter the first major argument for "a profession-

wide self-imposed moratorium on attempts to produce human children
by means of I.V.F. and E.T. (and by other new procedures), <u>at least</u>
until such time as the safety of the procedure can be assessed
and assured" (14) was made by Kass. A few weeks later Lappe'
suggested a "moratorium on experiments leading directly to human
egg implantations" and the establishment of an international review body to oversee such research (22). Several months later
another call was made for a temporary halt to human I.V.F. (23).
Edwards had correctly anticipated sharp ethical criticism of his
work, but he had misjudged the source. Most of the moratorium
requests were generated by scientists who were motivated by a
genuine concern that clinical use of human E.T. was premature and,
therefore, unethical and dangerous.

The controversy about studies of human I.V.F. ripened just as
the federal government was becoming deeply concerned about protocols for clinical research on human beings. On October 9, 1973
the Department of Health, Education and Welfare published its first
comprehensive "proposed rules" for treatment of human subjects in
experimental situations. Recognizing the complexity of the ethics
of human experimentation, it followed in November with a working
draft that detailed review procedures and special classes of subjects. One of these was: "the products of I.V.F." At that time it
tentatively advocated I.V.F. in sub-human primates prior to human
studies. It also firmly stated that "no implantation of human ova
fertilized in the laboratory should be attempted until guidelines
are developed governing the responsibilities of the donor and recipient parents and of research institutions and personnel" (24).
The possibility of a formal moratorium on government funding for
embryo transplant research had emerged. The formal adoption of
rules to govern human experimentation was made on May 30, 1974,
but at that time no protocols were published concerning I.V.F. A
few weeks later President Nixon signed into law a bill which created
a National Commission for the Protection of Human Subjects of Biomedical and Behavioral Research. Among other things this law
forbade the Secretary of H.E.W. to "conduct or support research in
the United States or abroad on a living human fetus, before or
after the induced abortion of such fetus, unless such research is
done for the purpose of assuring the survival of such fetus" (19).

A PRELIMINARY NOTE ON GOVERNMENT CONTROL OF HUMAN EMBRYO TRANSFER

Should the state forbid human I.V.F. and E.T.? There are at
least three distinct rationales that our society can use to justify
decisions to curtail behavior. First, implicit in any social contract is that a society must be free to insure its survival. This
notion permits conscription in time of war; it also may validate
compulsory vaccination to avoid large scale epidemics. Second

a society has both the right and the duty to make laws to protect
citizens from harm caused by others. This extends beyond the interdiction of clearly immoral acts such as murder to include the regulation of automobile speeds on public thoroughfares. Third, society claims a limited right to protect individuals from self inflicted physical or moral harm. Although it is possible to argue
that laws requiring motocyclists to wear helmets are designed to
protect other citizens from the hazard caused by unconscious persons lying in the roads, the real intent of such rules is to keep
people alive and healthy. Laws that regulate individual morality
are the most difficult to justify (and to enforce); yet our society
is permeated with them.

Consider the most likely use of human I.V.F.: removal of ova
from a woman with blocked oviducts, test-tube fertilization with her
husband's sperm, and transfer of a cleaving blastocyst to her uterus. Do any of the three enumerated rationales justify denying
this clinical procedure to infertile women? I think we all would
agree that the rationale of security survival is not applicable.
The second rationale (citizen protection) could be applicable,
but under current Constitutional law it is not. If the protections
of the Constitution were extended to a fertilized ovum and if the
state could somehow prove that embryos created by test-tube fertilization were burdened with a greater risk of spontaneous abortion
or deformed birth than were embryos conceived by sexual intercourse
then it might be possible to support the interdiction of the clinical practice. However, as long as a fetus is not a person within
the meaning of the Fourteenth Amendment, as long as women have a
right not to conceive and a right to destroy fetal life, a fortiori
they must have a right to conceive by whatever means they choose.
If the state truly wished to protect human embryos from malformation
it should turn its attention to the many situations in which the
fetus is known to be at increased risk for congenital injuries (Rh
incompatibility, maternal age greater than 35, and persons or
couples known to be at risk for genetic disease transmission).

Wearing the cloak of parens patriae the state could argue that
its duty to protect citizens from physical and moral injury justifies forbidding human E.T. The argument built upon the risk of
physical injury to the woman is easily refuted. The morbidity associated with laparoscopic removal of human ova and intra-cervical embryo transfer must be very low. Logically, if the state were to
act on this basis it would have to deny the general right to elec-
tive surgery without prior risk-benefit review. It would also be
extremely difficult to justify interdiction of embryo transfer on
moral grounds. First, the procedure would be done privately; it
would not be offensive to the public eye. Second, it would be
next to impossible to argue that clinical efforts to achieve conception and birth of a healthy child is immoral. Those who would
argue that it is the means not the ends of I.V.F. that are immoral

face the formidable task of proving that this "immorality" is not
religiously defined. Although the Arkansas "monkey" law (designed
to block the inculcation of Darwinian thought) did not contain any
explicit reference to the Christian religion the Supreme Court
still managed to see it as an effort "to blot out a particular theory
because of its supposed conflict with the Biblical account" (25).
Besides the fact that a law which forbade the clinical use of I.V.F.
would be incompatible with current Constitutional doctrine, it would
also probably be quite difficult to enforce.

The state may choose to regulate a technology for the benefit
of those affected by it. The limits of reasonable state action to
guarantee quality control to the practice of human I.V.F. will be
determined by the dual concerns of maternal and fetal health.
Following the logic of Roe v. Wade it would seem that the state
may make rules relating to the preservation and protection of maternal health during ova harvest and E.T. Because the procedures
are intended to produce a healthy infant, the state may properly
develop guidelines to protect the blastocyst during its stay in the
laboratory. Of course the woman must retain control over the fate
of the test-tube embryo; she may refuse to have it transferred and
she may exercise her right to abort it.

Precise suggestions for regulating I.V.F. technology are beyond
the scope of this paper. I would like, however, to mention two
areas that I think would benefit from carefully structured guidelines. Assuming that I.V.F. becomes a major component of fertility
therapy or genetic disease prophylaxis, ova banks may be developed.
If E.T. becomes a routine procedure, some women may choose to store
several ova in a gamete repository and undergo tubal ligation.
There are already a growing number of commercial sperm banks in
this country, a large proportion of their clientele are men who
plan to undergo vasectomies and who wish to have a kind of fertility
insurance (26). Many women (especially those who suffer side effects
from various contraceptive practices) might also be eager to use a
system of "fertility on demand." Sperm and ova banks should be
required to meet high standards of storage safeguards. One of the
many problems that needs resolution is what happens to the gametes
of an individual who defaults on the annual storage fee. A second
area that should be regulated is that of donor selection. As we
shall discuss more fully, the fertilized ovum implanted into a
woman's uterus need not be descended from her ovary. This female
counterpart to artificial insemination by donor and A.I.D. itself
raise some complex questions of relationship and liability that
should be answered. For example should a free market economy in
human ova be allowed to develop? Can a vendor warrant the fitness
of her gametes? The legal history of artificial insemination suggests that these will be real-world questions sooner or later (27).

EMBRYO TRANSFER: A CLARIFICATION OF LEGAL RELATIONSHIPS

In the following discussion I have assumed that the state will
not interdict the clinical use of human embryo transfer. Although
it is possible to read the Griswold (28) - Eisenstadt (29) - Roe
(18) trilogy more narrowly, I argue here that they have created a
general (but not absolute (30)) right of reproductive autonomy.
That is, the right of a woman to seek clinical treatment of infertility is superior to the state's interest in protecting her physical or moral health or the physical health of an embryo that she
plans to carry. This assumption, admittedly, solves the ethical
problems by avoiding them. Absolutist ethics are not compatible
with our social structure; all moral problems are to some extent
arbitrarily (politically) resolved. With some awareness of the
intellectual weakness of legal positivism (as manifested by my
reliance on Roe v. Wade) let me review some of the potential uses
of human E.T.and the legal duties of the parties involved.

There are three clinical situations which will eventually require delimitation by legal or quasi-legal mechanisms. These are:

(1) Aspiration of an oocyte from a woman with occluded oviducts, fertilization in vitro with the sperm of her husband and
subsequent transfer of the blastocyst to her womb.
(2) Aspiration of an oocyte from a donor woman, fertilization
in vitro with the sperm of a husband and subsequent transfer of the
blastocyst to the womb of his (donee) wife.
(3) Aspiration of an oocyte from a woman, fertilization in
vitro with the sperm of her husband and subsequent transfer to the
womb of another woman (the surrogate or uterine mother) who will
carry the child to term and return it to the genetic parents after
its birth.

The legal status of the pre-implantation blastocyst should
also be defined so that clinicians and laboratory personnel will
be aware of their duties. Finally, the legal relationship between children born via I.V.F. and the physician (and laboratory)
who mediated the pregnancy, the gamete donor and the parents
(that is the couple who desire to be parents) must be defined.
Because these last two issues are common to all clinical use of
I.V.F., we begin there.

What is the legal status of the human blastocyst after test-
tube fertilization, but prior to uterine transfer? Does the clinician in charge of an in vitro fertilization have a special duty of
care in regard to the blastocyst? If a third party damages the
blastocyst may he be sued for negligence? A court may soon be
asked to resolve these and related questions. In the summer of
1974 Shettles, a well known reproductive physiologist, agreed to
attempt an in vitro fertilization and embryo transfer with the

gametes of a married infertile couple. The oocytes were successfully aspirated and apparently a test-tube fertilization occurred.
At about that time this clinical research came to the attention of
the chairman of the Columbia University Medical School Department
of Obstetrics (Shettles was a member of this department also).
Believing that this procedure was in conflict with federal regulations on human research, the chairman destroyed the contents of
the test-tube. This caused a minor furor. Shettles left Columbia
Medical School after 27 years of employment. The couple who were
hoping to be parents have sued the chairman for 1.5 million dollars
because he "maliciously destroyed" the test-tube culture (31).

How would the courts react to this lawsuit? Prior to implantation it may be appropriate to consider a blastocyst the "property"
of the couple. However, ample damages could still be awarded for
the destruction of the blastocyst if it was found that an intentional tort had occurred. A large damage award would indicate that
although a blastocyst clearly is not a "legal" person, the special
interest of the germ cell donors suffuses it with a great value,
one that any reasonable person would be expected to anticipate. It
seems quite proper to hold the clinician and laboratory to special
standard of care in regard to I.V.F. Perhaps invocation of a doctrine of strict liability would be warranted.

What of the defective child born after an I.V.F.? I have
great difficulty in prognosticating a right of action against the
physician. Assuming that appropriate consents had been secured
and that fetal monitoring had been employed, a negligence action
would be exceedingly difficult to bring. How would plaintiff ever
succeed in demonstrating the causal connection between the mode of
conception and the birth defect? All conceptuses face a high statistical risk of defects; indeed, a very large percentage abort
spontaneously. Nor does the much discussed "tort of wrongful life"
offer a theory of action here (32). Crucial to the five lawsuits
that have used this theory has been the failure of a physician to
communicate a known risk of birth defects to the pregnant women.
Presumably prior to I.V.F. the woman and her husband would be informed of risks ad nauseam.

1. The vast majority of candidates for I.V.F. will be women
with occluded oviducts who are physically competent to carry a
fetus to term if conception did occur. No biological third party
would be involved in these in vitro fertilizations. Clearly a
child born via such a technique would not be burdened with metaphysical doubts of his ancestry; biological and legal parenthood
would coincide. This is the female counterpart of artificial insemination by husband.

There are two legal problems involved with simple I.V.F.

First, for some years (until an undefined threshold of experience is crossed) human I.V.F. will be considered an experimental technique. Risk to the test-tube blastocyst is not easily quantified, but few people would dispute the probability that many blastocysts will fail to implant, that some will abort and that some will come to term as deformed children. This focuses the legal question. May two persons consent to the use of their gametes to attempt to achieve a test-tube conception which will then be transferred to the womb of the female in an effort to achieve pregnancy? The key word here is consent, the key question is whether the interest of the potential conceptus has any legal effect on the power of the two potential parents to consent. When a couple agrees to achieve pregnancy in this manner are they merely exercising their fundamental right to control their bodies? Or are the interests of a third party involved? Is the couple also engaging in a kind of "proxy" consent on behalf of the fetus they wish to acquire?

This distinction has an important legal consequence. Although the legal nature of proxy consent is not well-defined, it appears that an individual may only consent to actions which benefit the person on behalf of whom consent is exercised (33). Assuming for the moment that there is a third party (the conceptus) involved in in vitro fertilization, then the risks implicit in that procedure become important. As I have already mentioned, it would be possible for the state to argue that if there was a substantially larger risk of spontaneous abortions or deformed births via I.V.F. than in natural pregnancy the couple could not select this reproduction. Presumably the state would act to protect the interests of these lives not yet in being and interdict the use of I.V.F. A second rationale which could support statutory restriction of the clinical use of I.V.F. would become operative if there appeared to be such substantial risk of birth defects that the state could reasonably suspect that a number of such children would wind up in public institutions.

The main legal argument supporting the decision of a couple to consent to I.V.F. and blastocyst transfer may be found in the emerging constitutional doctrine of fundamental interests. If a woman has the unqualified right to terminate her pregnancy during the first trimester, a fortiori she has the right to choose an unusual mode of conception regardless of the risk of spontaneous abortion. An interdiction of clinical I.V.F. would destroy the possibility of pregnancy for women with fallopian tube dysgenesis (assuming the oviducts are not amenable to surgical reconstruction). Such an action would be in direct conflict with case law that asserts the right of persons to control reproductive decision making. Hopefully, in a short time I.V.F. will be a low risk laboratory technique helping many couples to have children. When I.V.F. ceases to be experimental the interest of the state in controlling its use will be correspondingly diminished.

A second legal problem involves the relationship of the physician to the couple who choose I.V.F. and the child born via that technique. As long as the wife and the husband have been made fully aware of the known risks with laparoscopy (to aspirate oocytes), hormone administration and laparoscopy (to accomplish blastocyst transfer); the completely unknown odds of achieving pregnancy and the unquantifiable chance that a defective child could be born, I can find no unusual legal liability carried by the clinician. As always he is held to a certain standard of care in the actual performance of the techniques, but this is not altered because of its unusual purpose.

2. A much smaller number of women will be capable of carrying a fetus to term, but unable or unwilling to supply an egg. This would include women with primary ovarian dysgenesis (such as Turner's syndrome), older infertile women, known carriers of x-linked genetic disease and persons at risk for late onset dominant disorders. Eventually, a small number of women may wish to mother children who are the product of ova harvested from donors that they perceive to be genetically superior.

Ovum donation (O.D.) is the female counterpart to artificial insemination by donor. However, for two reasons it is in practice qualitatively different. First, unlike sperm donation or blood donation, oocyte donation requires a surgical intervention which presupposes physical discomfort and risk. For the immediate future it will be possible to secure needed oocytes from women undergoing surgery for other reasons, but it is important to realize that this source limits the size of the donor pool and consequently, the latitude of choice which the donee couples can exercise. Surgical patients may not be able to supply sufficient oocytes. This situation suggests the possibility that a rather exotic commodities market could develop in human eggs. The sad experience with commercial blood donation in America, especially when compared to non-commercial practices in Great Britain, should caution us about the use of money incentives in tissue donation programs (34).

A second important difference that argues a need to regulate the practice of O.D. is that it will be much more difficult to maintain donor anonymity than it has been for A.I.D. conceptions. The need for surgical oocyte harvest, a clinical preference for an immediate effort to achieve I.V.F., and the necessity of hormonally preparing the donee for implantation suggest that the parties involved will be attending the same fertility clinic at about the same time. This will to some extent increase the possibility that the ovum donor will later be able to contact the child conceived with her germ cell. Although this risk is no doubt small, the possibility that such a contact could disrupt a family may urge that the ovum donor be forbidden to know the recipient of her gift. But, what about the child? Does he have a "right" to ascertain his genetic heritage? In Scotland for example, adopted children have been guaranteed by law the right to trace their biological origins (35). Perhaps all children should have this right. This is one of the problems that could be settled by legislative fiat.

3. Some women may be physically incapable of carrying a fetus to term. Cardiac disorders, partial paralysis, a history of miscarriages or a variety of other medical disorders may suggest that women who wish to be genetic parents enlist the aid of surrogate mothers. Please do not think this is fanciful. A colleague of mine has already received an inquiry from a woman who has had a partial hysterectomy and wishes to have a child arising from the gametes of her and her husband. It does not appear that adoption offers a meaningful alternative to those women who cannot bear their own children. The dramatic shortage in young, racially matched babies has already stimulated the development of a black market where couples often pay over $10,000 to procure an infant (36). Of course surrogate motherhood could also be used by female lawyers or doctors busy running an active practice, movie stars and models concerned about the effects of pregnancy on their careers and any older woman disturbed by the increased risk of maternal morbidity with age. Young, healthy, proven child bearers might be willing to carry another woman's blastocyst to term if an appropriate fee were paid.

It is interesting to speculate whether the state might choose to permit surrogate motherhood to women physically incapable of childbirth, but forbid it to women who choose to avoid gestation for professional reasons. Among the very few legal commentaries on this question is that of a French scholar who argues in favor of such distinction:

> Of course, the application of embryo transfer should be subservient to therapeutic considerations: any other motivation coquetry, ambition or pursuit of a career where aesthetics are essential - should exclude such action. The publicity roused by these latter applications is enough to remind us that solutions which are therapeutically acceptable can become scandalous when there is no medical justification for them (37).

I disagree. First, I believe women may have decidedly valid non-medical reasons for engaging the services of surrogate mothers. Would the writer condemn the busy woman doctor who leaves her infant with a nanny? Second, women should have the legal right (whether it be motivated by altruism or economics) to carry any blastula to term for any reason they wish. (Much as I am in favor of the reduction of genetic disease I have yet to be convinced that compulsory abortion can be justified.) To distinguish physical from non-physical reasons for using surrogate motherhood is an unacceptable form of value imposition.

I suppose that the state could forbid the use of surrogate motherhood on the grounds that it violated a child's right to a "normal" birth. This argument may receive some support from laws that forbid extramarital intercourse (written in part to curb the births of illegitimate children). However, if the state did interdict surrogate motherhood for this reason, it would be burdened with the exceedingly difficult task of proving that children born in this manner would face an unusual risk of stigmatization. This rationale supports a kind of morality legislation that the courts have become skeptical of where personal freedoms are infringed.

Given the unquestionable physical and psychical burden implicit in pregnancy it is most probable that "uterine" mothers would be well paid for their services. (In a random survey of ten adult women I found that the average suggested fee was $15,000.) Rather unique and complicated contractual problems are raised by the practice of surrogate motherhood. In the best interests of all parties particularly the child born in this manner, it is quite appropriate that the state regulate the activity. Extensive discussion of the contractual problems associated with surrogate motherhood is too premature to be warranted. However, let us briefly raise some of the more obvious question that would demand resolution if such a contract were to be made.

Let us assume that a woman, Mary, contracts with a couple, Mr. & Mrs. Jones, to carry their fetus to term. Must Harold, the husband of Mary, be a party to this agreement? May the couple place reasonable restrictions on the habits, the medical care or the diet of Mary? Could Mary, for example, be restricted to a certain weekly intake of alcohol or prohibited from smoking? Could she be reasonably made to undergo amniocentesis (to monitor fetal abnormalities)? Could the Jones' require that she undergo an abortion if there were good indications of substantial fetal deformity? Could they request Mary to submit to an abortion for non-medical reasons (because they had decided to terminate their marriage)? Could they restrict Mary's right to seek an abortion subject to certain medical indications? Would the Jones' be liable for extraordinary medical costs incurred by complications of the pregnancy?

What if a defective child is born? If the defect could be associated with environmental factors that Mary negligently allowed to influence the gestation would she be liable for extraordinary medical and social costs incurred on behalf of the child? Would the child have a right of action against her for negligence - as he might against any other tortfeasor? What if Mary refused to release the child to its genetic parents? Could they compel the release of the child into their custody? How would they enforce

their rights? Would Mary be equitably stopped from claiming parenthood? If the Jones decided they no longer wished to be parents
and Mary refused a request to abort could they extinguish their
legal relationship with the child? If the couple died, should Mary
have a first right to adopt the child? Should the interests of the
next of kin of the couple be considered? Could Mary under any circumstances be compelled to care for the child?

Should the state require that contracts of surrogate motherhood
be in writing, that specified insurance agreements be included in
the contract, that liquidated damage provisions be included? Should
surrogate mothers be regulated by the state? Must they be proven
child-bearers? May their function as surrogates be limited to a
specific number of gestations? Should they be bonded? Must they
satisfy certain age and health requirements? These are only the
more obvious questions that may require resolution.

Serious discussion of statutory regulation of novel reproductive
technologies is not yet warranted. However, a working draft of a
"Uniform Embryo Transfer Act" would not be premature. I would like
to suggest five guidelines that may provide part of the skeleton of
such a model law:

1. Legal interdiction of the clinical use of human I.V.F. is
inappropriate. Such a law would certainly infringe a fundamental
interest of infertile women - their right to bear children. It
might also infringe the first amendment rights of clinician researchers by improperly restricting their freedom of inquiry. Finally,
such a law could be quite difficult to enforce.
2. The donor of a human egg should have absolutely no legal
interest in a child born from that egg, nor should the child have
any legal interest in the donor. Interest in the integrity of the
family of which the child is a member offers an overriding rationale
for this rule.
3. Ova donation should be structured to minimize the introduction of market incentives. Because discomfort and risk is involved women should be discouraged from undergoing unnecessary surgery. Every effort should be made to collect oocytes from women
undergoing appropriate surgery for other reasons. The altruism of
that group or female relatives of infertile women should be encouraged.
4. The parents of a child born to a surrogate mother are its
genetic parents. The surrogate should have absolutely no legal
interest in the child, not the child in its surrogate. The name
of the surrogate should not appear on the birth certificate, nor
should it be recorded on any other document. The best interests of
the child require the utmost concern for confidentiality.
5. Surrogate motherhood should be regulated in such a way as
to guarantee the best interest of the developing fetus. The state
may make reasonable rules as to who is permitted to serve as a ut-

erine mother. Approved women could be licensed. It might be correct to limit the practice to women who have completed their own families but who have had no more than two pregnancies. It may exclude women for a wide range of health reasons (cigarette smoking?). It may decide that a uterine mother who capriciously aborts a fetus will be permanently barred from further third party pregnancies (and perhaps subject to other sanctions). It may restrict the right of the genetic parents to request an abortion to circumstances where fetal disorders have been diagnosed. These are but a few of the detailed rules that may be necessary to the orderly use of this technology (38).

ACKNOWLEDGMENTS

Supported by U.S. Public Health Service Grant #GM 19513

REFERENCES

1. Edwards, R.G., Studies on human conception, Amer. J. Obstet. Gynecol. 117:587 (1973).

2. Edwards, R.G., Donahue, R.P., Baramki, T.A., et al, Preliminary attempts to fertilize human oocytes matured in vitro, Amer. J. Obstet. Gynecol. 96:192 (1966).

3. Yanagimachi, R. and Chang, M.C., In vitro fertilization of golden hamster ova, J. Exp. Zool. 156:361 (1964).

4. Edwards, R.G., Bavister, B.D. and Steptoe, P.C., Early stages of fertilization in vitro of human oocytes matured in vitro, Nature 221:632 (1969).

5. Edwards, R.G., Fertilization of human eggs in vitro: morals, ethics and the law, Quart. Rev. of Biol. 49:3 (1974).

6. Edwards, R.G., Steptoe, P.C. and Purdy, J.M., Fertilization and cleavage in vitro of preovulator human oocytes, Nature 227:1307 (1970).

7. Steptoe, P.C. and Edwards, R.G., Laparoscopic recovery of pre-ovulatory human oocytes after priming of ovaries with gonado-trophins, Lancet 1:683 (1970).

8. de Kretzer, D., Dennis, P., Hudson, B. et al, Transfer of a human zygote, Lancet 2:728 (1973).

9. Shettles, L.B., Human blastocyst grown in vitro in ovulation cervical mucus, Nature 229:343 (1971).

10. Ramsey, P., "The Ethics of Fetal Research" p. 47, Yale University Press, New Haven (1975).

11. Ramsey, P., "Fabricated Man", Yale University Press, New Haven (1972).

12. Ramsey, P., Shall we "reproduce"? I. The medical ethics of in vitro fertilization, J.A.M.A. 220:1346 (1972).

13. Ramsey, P., Shall we "reproduce"? II. Rejoinders and future forecast, J.A.M.A. 220:1480 (1972).

14. Kass, L., Babies by means of in vitro fertilization: unethical experiments on the unborn?, New Eng. J. Med. 285:1174 (1971).

15. Fletcher, J., "The Ethics of Genetic Control" pp. 92-95, Anchor, Garden City, New York (1974).

16. McCormack, R.A., Proxy consent in the experimentation situation, Persp. Biol. Med. 18:2 (1974).

17. "National Sickle Cell Anemia Control Act" P.L. 92-294, 86 Stat. 106 (1972).

18. Roe v. Wade 410 U.S. 113 (1973).

19. P.L. 93-348, 88 Stat. 348 (1974).

20. Wade, N., Genetic manipulation: temporary embargo proposed on research, Science 185:333 (1974).

21. Edwards, R.G. and Sharpe, D.J., Social values and research in human embryology, Nature 231:87 (1971).

22. Lappe, M., Risk-taking for the unborn, Hastings Center Report 2(1):1 (1972).

23. Editorial, Genetic engineering: reprise, J.A.M.A. 220:1356 (1972).

24. Federal Register 38:221 (Nov. 16, 1973), amended Federal Register 39:105 (May 30, 1974).

25. Epperson v. Arkansas 393 U.S. 97 (1968).

26. Frankel, M., "The Public Policy Dimensions of Artificial Insemination and Human Semen Cryobanking," Monograph No. 18, Program of Policy Studies in Science and Technology, George Washington University, Washington, D.C. (1973).

27. Smith, J., Through a test-tube darkly: artificial insemination and the law, Mich. L. Rev. 67:127 (1968).

28. Griswold v. Connecticut 381 U.S. 479 (1965).

29. Eisenstadt v. Barid 405 U.S. 438 (1972).

30. Dandridge v. Williams 397 U.S. 471 (1968).

31. Couple charge doctor thwarted implantation, New York Times p. 39, Vol. 6, August 20 (1974).

32. Tedeschi, L., Tort liability for wrongful life, Israel L. Rev. 1:513 (1966).

33. Bonner v. Moran 126 F. Supp. 121 (1941).

34. Titmuss, R., "The Gift Relationship," Pantheon Books, New York (1971).

35. Stone, O., English law in relation to A.I.D. and embryo transfer, in "Law and Ethics of A.I.D. and Embryo Transfer", G. Wolstenholme (ed.), p. 69, Associated Scientific Publishers, Amsterdam (1973).

36. Levy, M., The baby peddlers, Philadelphia, p. 76, March (1975).

37. Revillard, M., Legal aspects of artificial insemination and embryo transfer in French domestic law and private international law, in "Law and Ethics of A.I.D. and Embryo Transfer" G. Wolstenholme (ed.) p. 87, Associated Scientific Publishers, Amsterdam (1973).

38. Oakley, M.A.B., Test tube babies: proposal for legal regulation of human conception and prenatal development, Family Law Quart. 8(4):385 (1974).

LAW AND CLONING - THE STATE AS REGULATOR OF GENE FUNCTION

Seymour Lederberg

Division of Biological and Medical Sciences

Brown University, Rhode Island

THE BIOLOGY OF CLONING

Cloning is the asexual reproduction of cells from a single parent so that the genetic constitution of the progeny cells is the same as that of the parent cell. The process is widespread throughout the microbial and plant world, lower animals, and in the natural growth and regeneration of the tissues of adult higher animals. We, ourselves, are the clones derived from a parental zygote, the formation of the latter being the only sexual step in going from two germ cells to the one zygote cell to the 10^{14} cells that we are.

For some microbes and for all higher forms of life, cloned cells although genetically like the parent cell and each other, take on separate specialized activities -- they make different biological products, they associate with other cells selectively and they share different roles in organizing a multicellular stage of life. This remarkable differentiation of cloned cells to make biological man is followed by cultural development to form the social person. In this sense, cloned man has been fabricated since his genesis. The processes of biological differentiation which lead to our adult selves have been at the core of scientific inquiry for millenia and are still not understood.

One of the forms taken by such inquiry was to question whether differentiation of the clone from a zygote involved the irreversible loss of genetic potentialities at some early embryonic stage to form separate lines of progeny cells increasingly committed to spe-

cific functions. This would explain the unilateral direction of
differentiation despite the appearance of continuity of the same
genotype. Germ cell lines of course would be spared this irreversible loss.

The question was approached experimentally by injecting the
nucleus from a cell from the embryonic stage of the leopard frog,
Rana pipiens, into a frog egg whose own nucleus had been removed.
Some of the eggs treated in this manner went on to develop into
normal post-neurula embryos (1). Improved versions of the nuclear
transplant technique promoted unrestricted normal development to
the adult stage in several species of Amphibia and Insecta (2-4).
Overall, the basic conclusion to emerge is that the genetic totipotency of a differentiated cell can be conserved, since nuclei of
adult differentiated tissues remain competent to direct complete
development of an enucleated egg into a normal, fertile adult.
Irreversible changes or losses of genes are not the cause of dif-
ferention and need not arise from it.

The transplanted nucleus has an informational function. Its
genes provide the coded directions for making nucleic acid messages
which are translated into proteins. In the differentiated somatic
cell only selected genetic regions were functioning; the remainder
either were repressed by complexing with a controlling molecule,
or were inactive because of the absence of a molecular signal.
Enucleation of the egg destroys its resident genetic information
but leaves the cell's biosynthetic capacity to work with the
chromosomes and genes of a nucleus should these be reintroduced.

Somatic cells in culture can fuse and coordinate the biosynthetic programs directed by the two coexisting sets of genes.
Therefore, in principle, any biological obstacle to using enucleated
eggs of one species as the incubator for the nucleus of another
would depend primarily on whether cytoplasmic signals left in the
heterologous egg were adequate to initiate use of the new nucleus.
As activation of the transplanted nucleus proceeded, the egg's
newly made biosynthetic apparatus would be increasingly derived from
the transplant. The same cell fusion technique may provide a means
for transferring somatic nuclei to mammalian eggs whose small size
makes them technically difficult to manipulate (5).

The genetic totipotency of somatic plant nuclei has been demonstrated directly using single dissociated plant cells from car-
rots and tobacco (6). Normal somatic animals cells have not yet
been shown to be capable of the same dedifferentiation and activation without transfer to an egg cell. However, transfer studies
with animal cell nuclei may be expected to lead to our ability to
promote directly such regulation changes involving gene function.

ISSUES ARISING WHEN CLONING IS APPLIED TO GENE REGULATION
DURING DEVELOPMENT

Even as the original observations on nuclear transfer grew
out of interest in fundamental questions of biology, the same
motivations relate to the ongoing development of this work on the
factors which regulate the expression of different components of
our genome. Inasmuch as the principles at work pervade the phenomena of cancer, human embryological development and genetic
disorders, nuclear transplant techniques will be increasingly employed in basic research concerning such health problems.

One particular medical application relates to the host acceptability of tissue and organ transplants. There is a greater medical need of human transplantable organs than can be supplied from
donors of any source. The search for the technology to create synthetic replacement parts can be complemented by a search for the
biological regulatory controls which can be manipulated to allow
organ regeneration in vitro from organ samples, or if dedifferentiation is needed, to allow embryonic organs to develop in vitro.
If these are derived from the person in whom they are ultimately
reintroduced, the antigenic identity of host and organ would be
expected to prevent immune rejections of the implant.

A major ethical issue that arises here stems from the extent
of embryonic development that is needed prior to isolating an
embryonic organ or tissue. Current federal guidelines (7) for the
protection of human subjects, pursuant to the National Research
Act (8), regulate experimentation on the human conceptus when it
has been implanted in the donor of the ovum. At root are concerns
for the sanctity that human fetal life shares with human persons,
the impossibility for obtaining consent from a human fetus for experimentation, and pressures for minimizing incentives for abortion
and for maximizing the ability of a woman to reverse a decision to
schedule an abortion.

Present guidelines which refer to a human ovum fertilized by
a human sperm appear not to apply to a human ovum which has received
a somatic nucleus by injection or cell fusion, and they surely do
not apply to a human somatic cell activated without involvement of
a human ovum; nor do they apply to any use of ova other than human
fertilized by any sperm. To expedite discussion of the applicability of research guidelines, the term "clonus" is proposed for the
early division products of the activation of a somatic nucleus irrespective of the cell which is its host. Clonus is the asexual
homolog of conceptus.

The versions of the clonus described here are studied in vitro
and so have no substantial relevance to a woman's decision on abortion even as the donor of an enucleated egg. Therefore, this

leaves to an Ethical Advisory Board and human experimentation consent committee (9) the issue of the disposition of the clonus and
cell lines derived from it. Since the focus of the studies would
be on embryonic differentiation, the Board will presumably also
see parallel attempts to develop for the human clonus and in vitro
conceptus an in vitro attachment and metabolic exchange surface
comparable to the collagen layer successfully used for substantial
development of the mouse embryo (10). The first question facing
the Board will be whether the clonus is classed as a tissue or organ culture or as a conceptus. If classed as the latter, is the
study of the factors which promote its attachment and development
on surfaces in vitro the same as a study of implantation? If so,
is such a study therapeutic because it is constructive to the development of that clonus, or non-therapeutic because for any variable
under study some subjects may receive non-optimal treatment?

The present guidelines apply restrictive protections to the
conceptus, whatever the nature of the conception process, upon
implantation into "the donor of the ovum" (11). Presumably, protection upon implantation in the uterus of any woman will be a
preferred future reading of the rules. With anticipated advances
in mammalian organ and embryo culture, cultivation of the clonus
or conceptus in vitro may be able to be sustained longer. If the
stage of development achievable in vitro is comparable to a post-
implantation stage in vivo, then a difficult question arises -- is
it the continuous in vitro history or the developmental maturity
which will determine if the embryo warrants the protection of due
process? Compounding this is our ignorance of whether prolonged
cultivation in vitro increases the probability of subsequent successful transfer to a uterus, or whether the probability of such
integration diminishes as the embryo's complexity progresses.

ISSUES ARISING WHEN CLONING IS APPLIED AS AN ALTERNATIVE TO
ARTIFICIAL INSEMINATION, ADOPTION, AND CONCEPTION

At present the socially acceptable alternatives for a male-
sterile infertile couple to develop a family are by adoption or
artificial insemination. Adoption poses the disadvantage of absence of the prenatal and neonatal emotional experiences for the
couple, the concern for psychological trauma should the natural
parents attempt to reassert their relationship, the absence of a
genetic contribution to the next generation, and the limited availability of children from backgrounds acceptable to the couple.
Artificial insemination by donor sperm (A.I.D.) has none of these
disadvantages, but can have serious legal consequences.

Although some jurisdictions have statutes establishing the
legitimacy of a child conceived by A.I.D. (12), case law differs
widely in court holdings. A child conceived by A.I.D. consented

to by the husband was considered illegitimate by New York trial
courts,(13, 14) although other jurisdictions held such a child
to be "lawfully begotten" (15). An extreme position taken earlier
by Canadian (16) and British (17) courts was that A.I.D. was adultery. It would appear that for an infertile couple, implanting a
clonus drawn from the enucleated egg of the woman and a somatic
nucleus of either parent would avoid the possible stigma of adultery
for them and illegitimacy for their children. They would acquire
none of the disadvantages of adoption or A.I.D., and each parent's
genes would have an opportunity to be transmitted to their offspring.
Parenthetically, we note that any desired sex ratio among their
children could be obtained.

Without yielding my own preferences for a less complicated
mode of procreation, I cannot fault this option. The couple will
be 25-35 years older than the children, so resemblances will appear
strong but not identical. If the family elects to have one boy and
one girl, the two will be dissimilar; if not, the family presumably
risks psychological trauma of unknown severity.

An action by a child for "wrongful life" (18) might arise as
a result of the mental distress and emotional suffering encountered
as a cloned person, but the holding in Williams v. State denied
recovery for being born under one set of circumstances or parents
rather than to another (19).

Now, until we learn how to coordinate the pace of the divisions
of the transplanted somatic nucleus with the biosynthetic abilities
of the enucleated host ovum, the clonus risks chromosomal aneuploidy.
Implantation itself represents an enormous technological barrier
whose overcoming has yet to be reliably documented (20). Presumably,
an abnormal clonus or embryo has a high probability of spontaneous
abortion since this is the customary fate of a chromosomally abnormal conceptus (21). We can assist this natural screening by amniocentesis in the 14th-16th week of gestation on the assumption that
the couple is at higher than average risk for chromosomal errors.

Should a defective child be brought to term, there is the
possibility of tort liability by the investigator for prenatal
injury (22, 23), if it could be shown that the trauma was initiated
after the clonus was formed and was caused by negligence of a duty
owed by the investigator. This possibility makes an amniocentesis
diagnosis by the investigator virtually mandatory.

A state may choose to regulate and prohibit development of a
cloned cell to a human. The Massachusetts statute (24) on fetal research might not apply if the procedures used to learn the optimum
conditions for development were accepted as diagnostic or remedial
procedures to determine or preserve the life or health of that fetus.

Counter to this type of statute would be the due process appeal that the state was invading the couple's right to privacy and to procreate (25), that the state was in effect affecting involuntary birth control on the male partner by prohibiting his only way to transmit his genes to children, and that the interest of the state to interfere with experimental procedures in development of the clonus was irrational rather than compelling since absent optimum experimental conditions the clonus would not develop normally.

If cloning is allowable for the infertile family, the application of the equal protection of law suggests that it could not be denied per se to the fertile family, and it makes no sense for public policy to encourage a vasectomy in order to qualify for access to cloning technology. Any family which desired to continue the genotype of one of the parents, or of another person, might elect to clone offspring. A "socially desirable" genotype which would otherwise be reassorted on subsequent sexual reproduction could be thereby protected. Genetic variability in our population would be maintained through ongoing mutation and parallel sexual reproduction with selected genotypes conserved for the next generations to obtain the "tempered clonality" proposed by Joshua Lederberg (26). The choice of mode of procreation could still be a personal decision influenced as always by the social pressures which modify autonomous perception of desirability and rationality. Overall, however, the motivation for this pathway for a fertile family is dubious because of the alternate modes of procreation available.

ISSUES ARISING WHEN CLONING IS APPLIED TO CREATE HOMOGENEOUS CHANNELED SOCIAL GROUPS

The gravest concern over cloning comes from its possible use to create large classes of identical people selected for some genetically determined set of characteristics (27-34). Presumably, excellence in specialized talents and occupations would be the phenotypic criteria used for the classification, and therefore socio-economic castes would emerge as in Huxley's Brave New World.

It has been suggested that the nobility clauses (35) of the Constitution may be construed to bar the granting of special privilege to socially prestigious cloned classes (36). The Thirteenth Amendment (37) prohibiting slavery and involuntary servitude has been proposed to cover cloning since a "genetic bondage" which diminishes autonomy is deliberately designed to reduce the option of choices which create individuality (38). The constraints on nobility would deny a governmentally imposed differential on the access to the technology of cloning, and that on servitude would bar a public policy which coerced cloning of an individual.

However, there is a stage in the formation of socio-economic

strata which is more benignly amenable to governmental regulation.
To now, a cloned person has been considered as operatively identical
to the parent and to similarly derived sibs. Attention has focused
on the replication of like behavioural and intellectual traits.
Yet, this decade has seen profound doubts arise over the extent to
which genetic endowments and environmental experience create
differentials in these attributes. An alphabet caste system requires a structured cultural cloning to convert genetic opportunity
into people behaving in a replicate manner. Without such an imposition of identical nurture, the rigid definition of an individual
fails, and he remains free to choose his own development.

The real danger of stratification of our society then comes
from the unequal access to cultural experiences which now quite
effectively channel us independently of our genetic makeup. To
escape this danger we need to affirm the position espoused by the
Supreme Court in Meyer v. Nebraska that the Spartan model of education and training does "violence to both letter and spirit of the
Constitution" (39). The governmental policy most likely to prevent
cloning technology from being misused to create castes, can do this
with least risk to our welfare, not by limiting research or procreative instruments, but by truly providing people with opportunities for diversity in education, professional training, employment,
and cultural experience.

REFERENCES

1. Briggs, R. and King, T.J., Transplantation of living nuclei
    from blastula cells into enucleated frog's eggs, Proc. Nat. Acad.
    Sci. 38:455 (1952).

2. Gurdon, J.G., Adult frogs derived from the nuclei of single
    somatic cells, Develop. Biol. 4:256 (1962).

3. King, T.J., Nuclear transplantation in amphibia, in "Methods in
    Cell Physiology", D.M. Prescott (ed.), Vol. II, pp.1-34,
    Academic Press, New York (1966).

4. Gurdon, J.B., "The Control of Gene Expression in Animal
    Development," Harvard University Press, Cambridge (1974).

5. Graham, C.F., Virus assisted fusion of embryonic cells,
    Karoninska Symp. Reprod. Endocrin. 3:154 (1971).

6. Steward, F.C., From cultured cells to whole plants: The
    induction and control of their growth and differentiation,
    Proc. Roy. Soc. B 175:1 (1970).

7. Federal Register 38:27382, October 9, 1973; 38:31738, November

16, 1973; 39:18,914, May 30, 1974; 39:30648, August 23, 1974.

8. PL:93-348 National Research Service Award Act of 1974, Title
II - Protection of Human Subjects of Biomedical and Behavioural
Research.

9. See, supra note 7.

10. Hsu, Y.-C., Differentiation in vitro of mouse embryos to the
stage of early somite, Develop. Biol. 33:403 (1973).

11. See, supra note 7.

12. Sagall, E., Artificial Insemination, Trial Magazine, January/
February:59 (1973).

13. Gursky v. Gursky, 242 N.Y.S. 2d 406 (Superior Court 1963).

14. Anonymous v. Anonymous,246 N.Y.S. 2d 886 (Superior Court 1964).

15. People v. Sorenson, 66 Cal Reporter 7, 437 P.2d 499 (1968).

16. Oxford v. Oxford, 58 Dom. Law Reports 251 (Ontario Sup. Ct.
1921).

17. Russel v. Russel,A.C. 687 at p. 148 (1924).

18. Zepeda v. Zepeda,41 Ill. App. 2d 240, 190 N.E. 2d 890 (App.
Ct., First Dist., 1963).

19. Williams v. State,18 N.Y. 2d 481, 276 N.Y.S. 2d 885 (Ct. of
Appeals, 1966).

20. DeKretzer, D., Dennis, P., Hudson, B. et al, Transfer of a
human zygote, Lancet 2:728 (1973).

21. Hamerton, J.L., "Human Cytogenetics" Vol. II at pp. 388-389,
Academic Press, New York (1971).

22. Smith v. Brennan,31 N.J. 353, 157 A. 2d 497 (Supreme Ct. 1960).

23. Sylvia v. Gobeille,101 RI 76, 222 A. 2d 222 (Supreme Ct. 1966).

24. Mass. Gen. Laws, Chapter 112, Section.12J.

25. See chapter by S. Lederberg in this volume, p.
(Case history on privacy and procreation is developed in this
companion paper.)

26. Lederberg, J., Experimental genetics and human evolution,

Amer. Natural. 100:519 (1966).

27. Id.

28. Fletcher, J., Ethical aspects of genetic controls, New Eng.
    J. Med. 285:776 (1971).

29. Fletcher, J., "The Ethics of Genetic control," Anchor Press/
    Doubleday, Company, Garden City, New York (1974).

30. Kass, L., New beginnings in life, in "The New Genetics and the
    Future of Man," M. Hamilton (ed.), Eerdmans Publishing Company,
    Grand Rapids, Michigan (1972).

31. Kindegran, C.P., State power over human fertility and individual
    liberty, Hastings Law J. 23:1401 (1972).

32. Pizzulli, F.C., Asexual reproduction and genetic engineering:
    A constitutional assessment of the technology of cloning,
    So. Calif. Law Rev. 47:476 (1974).

33. Ramsey, P.,"Fabricated Man," Yale University Press, New Haven,
    Connecticut (1970).

34. Tribe, L.H., "Channeling Technology Through Law," The Brockton
    Press, Chicago, Illinois (1973).

35. U.S. Constitution, Article I, Section 9, Clause 8. No Title
    of Nobility shall be granted by the United States: And no
    Person holding any Office of Profit or Trust under them, shall,
    without the Consent of the Congress, accept of any present,
    Emolument, Office, or Title, of any Rival whatever, from any
    King, Prince or Foreign State.

    Article I, Section 10, Clause 1. No State Shall enter into
    any Treaty, Alliance, or Confederation; grant Letters of Marque
    and Reprisal; coin Money; emit Bills of Credit; make any Thing
    but gold and silver Coin a Tender in Payment of Debts; pass any
    Bill of Attainder, ex post facto Law, a Law impairing the Ob-
    ligation of Contracts, or grant any Title of Nobility.

36. See, supra 32, at p. 579.

37. U.S. Constitution - Amendment 13, Section 1. Neither slavery
    nor involuntary servitude, except as a punishment for crime
    whereof the party shall have been duly convicted, shall exist
    within the United States, or any place subject to their juris-
    diction.

    U.S. Constitution - Amendment 13, Section 2. Congress shall have power to enforce this article by appropriate legislation.

38. See,_supra_ 32 at p. 517.

39. _Meyer v. Nebraska_, 262 U.S. 390, at p. 402 (1923).

THE PSYCHOPATHOLOGY OF CLONAL MAN

Leon Eisenberg

Department of Psychiatry, Harvard Medical School and

Children's Hospital Medical Center, Boston

My title was assigned, not chosen. I bow reluctantly to the authority of the Chairperson in addressing myself to it, for I fancy I hear in the distance the laughter of the gods at our hubris in speculating on the psychopathology of clonal man, a creature who is likely never to exist. More to the point, I wince at the knowing smiles of those in this audience who consider it all too appropriate for a psychiatrist to discuss non-disease in non-man, given their view of how remote at best psychiatry is from reality. Gods and audience aside, the title foreshadows a conclusion I am not at all certain is correct. The psychopathology, if there be any, may be more in our preoccupation with the appari- tion than in the possibility of its realization. But that is a theme I will return to later.

I will not attempt to discuss the methodological barriers and technical impediments to human cloning, except to note that I read the record to suggest that its final accomplishment, should it be sought, lies in the more remote future than the popular literature suggests. As we know, it has proved possible to use microdissection to remove the nucleus of a toad intestinal cell, transfer that somatic nucleus to an enucleated ovum, and induce the development of a mature toad identical with the original donor (1-3). The experiment is not easy to replicate and is not uniformly successful. Defining the conditions for success in higher organisms presents formidable problems. But we can state that a solution exists in principle -- much like the Chinese mathematician who, observing his house on fire and noting water in a nearby pool, decided that he could return to his studies, now that the fire had been extinguished in principle.

     Should cloning prove possible and were it to be practiced on a
wide scale, its most disasterous consequences would be biological
rather than ethical; its most predictable outcome would be a
sharp and cumulative restriction in the diversity of the gene pool
of the human population. That restriction could compromise the
viability of the human species in the face of environmental vicissitudes. There are, it is true, extant species, with a high degree
of genetic homogeneity, delicately adapted to a narrow ecological
niche. But if that niche is perturbed, by change in the physical
environment or invasion by a predator, extinction is the likely
outcome. Indeed, serious concerns have been expressed (4) that
the ever more selective cultivation of grain seeds chosen for high
yield under modern conditions of agriculture have led to the widespread adoption of a narrow range of genotypes which make world-
wide grain production highly vulnerable to the appearance of new
blights, unpredictable changes in climatic conditions and the like;
indeed, steps are underway to create seed banks which will contain
representatives of diverse species in the event such catastrophies
should occur (5). It is evident that precisely the same risks would
hold for man were he to opt for replication by cloning rather than
by sexual reproduction whose very biological virtue is its constant
enhancement of diversity.

     Further we face a dilemma in the task of selection of the
"ideal" types to be perpetuated. The choice of those to be cloned
could only be made on the basis of characteristics which have led
to outcomes considered desirable under the environmental conditions
that had existed during the decades in which those individuals had
matured.

     Put aside, for the moment, the difficult value choices in-
volved in selecting these paragons, whether we emphasize intelligence, achievement orientation, cooperativeness, empathy, artistic
ability, what have you, or some combinations thereof. Let us
assume we could agree on the traits to be valued, however dubious
that assumption may be. By definition, the "genetic potential"
for those traits will have existed in the individuals who exhibit
them. But the translation of that genetic potentiality into the
visible phenotypes occurred in a complex interaction with the physical and social environment that coincided with their evolution.
Having identified him or her accurately as the carrier of the genotype, we must acknowledge that we know so little of the salient
aspects of the coterminus environment that we cannot specify, except in the grossest fashion, what environment we would have to
provide, both intra- and extra-uterine, to assure ourselves that
the adult outcome would be phenotypically identical with the ideal
type we seek to replicate.

     Let us make a further dubious assumption: Let us say that
we know enough about that environment to provide it or that our

genotype is relatively impervious to deviations from it. None-theless, the phenotype so admirably suited to the world in which it came to maturity may not be nearly as adaptive, and may even be maladaptive, for a world a generation hence. Not only is the en-vironment not static, but one of man's most alarming traits is his extraordinary impact on his physical and social ecology. Clon-ing would condemn us ever to plan the future on the basis of an outdated past (for we cannot identify the successful phenotype sooner than early adulthood) and leaves us utterly unable to anti-cipate the fitness of the chosen genotype for the generation hence when it will have ripened into its phenotype. Those who propose human cloning misconceive the process of epigenesis.

For the student of biology, cloning is a powerful and instruc-tive laboratory enterprise that can contribute a deeper under-standing of the mechanisms of development. The range or norm of reaction of the genotype is a measure of its multivariate charac-teristics in dynamic interrelationship to the environment. That norm is estimated from the manifestations of the phenotype in a wide variety of environments. In general, the more varied those environments, the more diversity we observe in the phenotypic mani-festations. In human populations, there exists an extraordinary range of latent variability. Dissimilar genotypes produce remark-ably similar phenotypes under "average" conditions. The differences become manifest under "extraordinary" conditions when unusual stresses overbalance the homeostatic mechanisms which buffer the system successfully against smaller perturbations.

Thus, for identity in phenotypic outcome, we require identity in genotype (assured by cloning) and identity in environmental interactions. At the most trivial level, I would anticipate less similarity even in physical appearance between cell donor and cloned recipient than the range evident between monozygotic twins. Intra-uterine growth conditions are critical factors in the outcome of pregnancy; these can vary significantly even for the uniovular twins who share a common uterus because of inequalities in placen-tation and fetal-maternal circulation (6, 7). A greater difference must be anticipated between the developmental circumstances for both donor and "clonee" who will have been born from different unteri.

Let us, however, assume, once again to force the argument, that the conditions for the cloned infant have been identical with those of his or her "grandmother" so that at birth he or she is a replica of the infant his "father" or her "mother" was at birth. Thus, within the limits of precision of developmental maturation, the initial wiring of the central nervous system and its dispositions of response to internal and external stimuli will be the same.

Nonetheless, the further evolution of that neonatal central

nervous system is highly dependent upon the precise quality,
quantity and timing of its nutritional, intellectual and emotional
"alimentation" (8, 9). The very structure of the brain as well as
the function of the mind emerges from the interaction between
maturation and experience (10). The density of the cell and
fiber structure of the human brain, its inaccessibility to detailed
pre-mortem examination and the limitations of neurobiological techniques restrict demonstration of the anatomical hypothesis to experiments in lower animals.

Let me exemplify the point briefly. The work of Hubel and
Wiesel has revealed the remarkable organizational sophistication
and functional complexity of the neonatal visual system in the
kitten prior to the opening of its eyes (11, 12). Some 80% of
the cells in the striate cortex are bilaterally innervated at birth;
that is, they can be driven by either eye. Yet, if one eye is
deprived of patterned vision (even though light is admitted through
a translucent goggle) for several weeks, while the other eye is
free to see, the restricted eye looses its capacity to drive most
of the previously binocular striate cells (and there is significant
cell shrinkage in the intermediate way stations) (13, 14). If both
eyes are so treated, unilateral "capture" does not occur and the
striate cells remain accessible to each when normal opportunities
for visual experience are restored (15). If you will, the genetically coded wiring diagram, present at birth, having evolved
during gestation, is fashioned into its final circuitry by the
patterns of stimulation falling upon it. An equivalent phenomenon
is demonstrable in man. Adults with congenital astigmatism resulting from lenticular asymmetries, are no longer able to attain normal
visual acuity in the meridians of prior error, even when precise
beams of light are focused directly onto the retina by the use of
special optical devices (16). Abnormal input during the early years
of developement has permanently modified the receptive fields and
synaptic properties of retina and brain. The impact of sensory deprivation on both brain and behavior (8, 17) is one side of the
coin; the other is provided by studies of environments constructed
to emphasize physical and social complexity (18, 19). In general,
the "richer" the environment, the greater the complexity of dendritic branching and synaptic junctions and the more efficient the
learning in novel situations (18). At the same time, it should be
noted that the variance is partialled into litter set, set-environ-
ment interactions and environmental conditions, all as important
variables (20).

If I pause to stress actual molding of brain cytoarchetectonics,
it is only to underline the profundity of the impact of experience
in shaping the evolution of genotype into phenotype. Further to
the point, the elaborate human psychological traits whose cultivation
we seek are polygenic rather than monogenic in character; similar
outcomes may result from quite different genomes interacting with

variable social and cognitive environments. To produce another Mozart, we would need not only Wolfgang's genome, but mother Mozart's uterus, father Leopold's lessons, his friends and theirs, the state of music in 18th century Austria, papa Hydn's patronage and on and on, in ever widening circles. Without the genome, the rest would not have sufficed; there was, after all, only one Wolfgang Amadeus Mozart. But we have no right to make the converse assumption: that his genome, cultivated in another world at another time, would have resulted in an equally creative contemporary musical genius. Given that a particular strain of wheat yields quite different harvests under different conditions of climate, soil, cultivation and the like, what permits us to assume that so much more complex a genome as the human would yield its desired crop of operas, symphonies and chamber music under different circumstances of nurture?

I have thus far identified three objections to cloning: its devastating impact on the diversity of the human gene pool, were it to be widely adopted; its inevitable selection for traits successful in the past and not necessarily adaptive for an unpredictable future; and the vulnerability of the phenotype it might produce, given the poorly understood and uncontrollable vicissitudes of the environment it will encounter. These seem to me to be the fundamental objections to human cloning.

The cloned zygote -- one cultivated in vitro until it could be implanted in utero -- would in other respects be no different from one produced by joining father's sperm (or donor's sperm) and mother's ovum in vitro to overcome infertility. Such procedures carry hazards of maldevelopment which must give us pause, but so do other methods for overcoming infertility, as, for example, the multiple ovulations produced by clomiphene, sometimes with tragic outcome; yet these are risks infertile couples have been willing to take. I will acknowledge that a cloned child and its parents (say, the father as nuclear donor and the mother as contributor of ovum and uterine housing) might be in for a difficult time if they harbored unrealistic expectations of genetic determinism but so do biological parents who hold false beliefs about "hereditary taint" in the family. If the donor of the nucleus were not a family member, the relationship between the rearing parents and the child would not differ genetically from that in extra-familial adoption, except insofar as they would have chosen the donor and would "know" more about their child's heritage; I have already indicated how little predictive value that knowledge would have. It may well be true that Darwinian evolution has selected for sexual and parenting behaviors such that they enhance the likelihood of gene transmission (21). With the elaboration of consciousness and culture in the human community, parental and filial commitment can be just as complete in the absence of genetic commonalities.

There are two additional issues that relate to my topic; they can be dismissed in a word. I am simply unable to imagine the possibility of a "test tube" baby (that is, one brought to via- bility in an artificial uterus) nor can I conceive of what would justify the attempt. As to the notion of a "borrowed" or "rented" uterus, I consider the proposal beneath contempt: women are not brood mares or sows.

To return to my initial comments, the "psychopathology of clonal man" is to be found not so much in this extraterrestrial creature but in the metaphysical cloud that surrounds it. Human cloning is wrong because it is biological nonsense; to elevate it into a profound ethical issue is sheer casuistry. Pseudo-biology provides a platform for pseudo-ethics and distracts attention from real and present injustice. It has become fashionable to engage in specu- lation about despotic governments which might employ the "technology" of cloning by selecting donors to create docile populations. It is instructive to recall the passage in Plato's <u>Republic</u> in which Socrates puts forth a falsehood useful for the state: "Citizens, we shall say to them in our tale, you are brothers yet god has framed you differently. Some of you have the power to command, and in the composition of these he has mingled gold, wherefore also they have the greatest honor. Others he has made of silver to be auxiliaries. And others again who are to be husbandmen and craftsmen he has composed of brass and iron, and the species will generally be preserved in the children." Shall we believe that, by restraining mad scientists from perfecting cloning, we will avoid such bestiality? Rulers and slaves were already present in ancient Athens. The awesome power of the state quite suffices to stratify society into castes and classes. The division of mankind into master races and inferior subspecies and the belief that both breed true is as ancient as human history and as current as the riots over busing school children that tear apart Boston. Pre- occupation with the psychological status of the clonal homunculus provides safe and genteel occupations for those better employed in the struggle against the violations of the rights of real women and men.

To a generation reared in the shadow of nuclear catastrophe, it needs no acknowledging that the fruits of applied science are sometimes bitter and the aftertaste long delayed. Man's ambivalence about knowing is an ancient theme. Greek mythology abounds in minatory legends of man's punishment for daring to steal fire from the gods, for fashioning wings to fly, for venturing into the realms of the dead. Western religions tradition tells us man was cast out of Paradise for having eaten from the tree of knowledge. Faust must sell his soul to the devil in his quest for wisdom and immor- tality. Legends and dogma delayed but finally could not halt the power of the new science. Grudgingly, the goods coveted by all were reinterpreted as signs of God's bounty though with caveats that there were limits we dare not transcend. As our age discovers that we sometimes transmute gold into dross in the technological imperative to do what can be done without weighing its cost, old doctrines re-emerge in new guise. Because science is incomplete, reason imperfect and both are traduced by the power of the state, some would have us abandon science and reason in favor of mysticism, hermetics and transcendental rapture. Particularly is this so when the new biology confronts the greatest wonder of all: the nature of life itself.

Indeed, we should consider, with reason, evidence and compassion, what we are about to do before we attempt it. Virtuosity is not its own justification when human values are at stake. But I reject categorically the proposal that we turn back at the edge of greater understanding of the biology of life which can increase man's dominion over himself. In what sense is in vitro cultivation of the beginnings of wanted life any more "unnatural" than contraception and abortion to prevent unwanted progeny? Some condemn them all. I confess myself utterly unable to understand the "ethics" that condemn contraception and abortion as abominations without blinking at the sight of women crippled by back alley surgery, of infants abandoned and children starving (22). It is no less natural that we now possess the means to prevent famine, did we have the moral commitment to do so, than that once we were its hapless victims. It is no more natural that we beggar ourselves by overpopulation than that we learn to plan parenthood. Because God or nature joined the sexual act with procreation, are we to be forbidden to put them asunder by artificial insemination or fertilization in vitro? I find the logic as persuasive as the proposition that penicillin violates our moral convenant because God or nature intended the pneumococcus no less than man.

It is not knowledge, but ignorance that assures misery. It is not science, but its employment for inhuman purposes that threatens our survival.

The fundamental ethical questions of science are political questions: Who shall control its products? For what purposes shall they be employed?

The "psychopathology" in discussions of clonal man lies in the substitution of biological myths about genetic determinism in place of moral concern for the social realities of caste and class.

REFERENCES

1. Briggs, R. and King, T.J., Transplantation of living nuclei from blastula cells into enucleated frogs' eggs, Proc. Nat. Acad. Sci. (USA) 38:455 (1952).

2. Gurdon, J.B., Adult frogs derived from the nuclei of single somatic cells, Develop. Biol. 4:256 (1962).

3. Gurdon, J.B., Transplanted nuclei and cell differentiation, Scient. Amer. 219:24 (1968).

4. Harlan, J.R., Our vanishing genetic resources, Science 188: 618 (1975).

5. "Genetic Vulnerability of Major Crops," National Academy of Sciences, Washington, D.C. (1972).

6. Benirschke, K., Multiple births, in "Pediatrics" H.L. Barnett, (ed.), pp. 117-124, Appleton-Century-Crofts, New York (1972).

7. Storrs, E. and Williams, R.J., A study of monozygous quadruplet armadillos in relation to mammalian inheritance, Proc. Nat. Acad. Sci. 60:910 (1968).

8. Horn, G., Rose, S.P.R. and Bateson, P.P.G., Experience and plasticity in the central nervous system, Science 181:506 (1973).

9. Eisenberg, L., The human nature of human nature, Science 176: 123 (1972).

10. Aronson, L.R., Tobach, E., Lehrman, D.S. et al (eds.), "Selected Writings of T.C. Schneirla," Freeman, San Francisco (1972).

11. Hubel, D.H. and Wiesel, T.N., Receptive fields, binocular interaction and functional architecture in the cat's visual cortex, J. Physiol. 160:106 (1962).

12. Hubel, D.H. and Wiesel, T.N., Receptive fields of cells in striate cortex of very young, visually inexperienced kittens, J. Neurophysiol. 26:994 (1963).

13. Wiesel, T.N. and Hubel, D.H., Single cell responses in striate cortex of kittens deprived of vision in one eye, J. Neurophysiol. 26:1003 (1963).

14. Wiesel, T.N. and Hubel, D.H., Effects of visual deprivation on morphology and physiology of cells in the cat's lateral geniculate body, J. Neurophysiol. 26:978 (1963).

15. Wiesel, T.N. and Hubel, D.H., Comparison of the effects of unilateral and bilateral eye closure on cortical unit responses in kittens, J. Neurophysiol. 28:1029 (1965).

16. Freeman, R.D., Mitchell, D.E. and Millodot, M., A neural effect

of partial visual deprivation in humans, Science 175:1384 (1972).

17. Riesen, A.H., Sensory deprivation, in "Progress in Physiological Psychology" I, E. Stellar and J.M. Sprague (eds.), pp. 117-147, Academic Press, New York (1966).

18. Greenough, W.T., Experiential modification of the developing brain, Amer. Scient. 63:37 (1975).

19. Globus, A., Rosenzweig, M.R., Bennett, E.L. et al, Effects of differential experience on dendritic spine counts in rat cerebral cortex, J. Comp. Physiol. Psychol. 82:175 (1973).

20. Greenough, W.T. and Volkmar, F.R., Patterns of dendritic branching in occipital cortex of rats reared in complex environments, Exp. Neurol.40:491 (1973).

21. Trivers, R.L., Parental investment and sexual selection, in "Sexual Selection and the Descent of Man 1871-1971," B. Campbell (ed.), pp. 136-179, Aldine-Atherton, Chicago (1972).

22. Eisenberg, L., Acting amidst ambiguity: the ethics of intervention, J. Child. Psychol. Psychiat. 16:93 (1975).

DISCUSSION

Papers of Profs. P. Reilly, S. Lederberg and L. Eisenberg
Principal Discussant: Prof. M.W. Wartofsky
Moderator: Prof. L.E. Rosenberg

WARTOFSKY: Prof. Reilly's paper raises a number of profound conceptual questions. The most profound one concerns the rights and responsibilities, moral or legal, which come under consideration in the case of in vitro fertilization (IVF). He raises two counterposed contexts. First, that of the reproductive rights of parents, particularly of women to conceive and bear children by whatever means. Second, that of the rights of the conceptus. That is a more complex issue than that of fetal rights, since what is at issue is not to question the rights of the fetus after the first trimester, but more radically the rights of the oocytes as potential persons if successfully aspirated, preserved, transplanted, and carried to term.

Two sorts of arguments appear in Prof. Reilly's excellent survey and discussion of the state of the art and of the moral and legal issues raised by IVF. Firstly, the claims made of what he characterizes as absolute morality, that is of non-prudential, context-free, categorical, moral standards (what ethical theorists call theontological efforts). Second, consideration of the prudential, pragmatic and situational sort where moral judgments depend on the consequences of social effects of the practice in some conducts of general good or social welfare.

Let me however, introduce a different question at the outset. Why is the issue of IVF like those of fetal research, abortion, artificial insemination, ovum donation and so forth? Why are these issues so fraught with moral as well as legal concerns? Certainly it is a life and death question in a rather plain and uncomplicated sense. It concerns conception under unusual conditions - the problem of preserving a successfully fertilized ovum during an initial period of extrauterine existence through the risks of implantation. But I'd like to suggest that IVF stirs up a more deeply traumatic and indeed tragic consciousness. What is at issue is human mortality, the self-definition, self-conception of our own humanity. Why? Because both birth and death seem to mark the limits of the conditional criterion of every person or human being, that is a freedom; freedom to choose, concept, refuse, risk, in short the capacity to exercise one's will, to be an agent in one's own affairs and in one's own destiny.

Birth and death mark two absolute limits of such freedom, and birth even more clearly so. To choose to be born is beyond us. It is in the hands of others or of a nature which won't yield to our own determinations. The arguments over the rights of the conceptus

397

seem to me thoroughly abstract since what is really involved is not the rights of the conceptus, but rather the rights and responsibilities of the conceptors and the related rights and responsibilities of those who in the case of IVF come to play a role in the coming into being and preservation of the conceptus until it is implanted.

Though we may be struck with some defect, substantial and metaphysical dread in the face of our own incapacity to choose whether or not to be born, we manage to overcome this dread by transferring it to the one context in human life we are able to control, in the choice of conception in our control over bringing others into life as our offspring.

This choice becomes, therefore, a fundamental human right historically. It wasn't always so. As a right it has its ground in the social and historical determination of human values. It becomes an enlightened society as a right of the parent and not of the state. Therefore, it is not a right that is established by law, but rather a moral right requiring protection of the law, as for example, the rights of conscience, right against self-incrimination and so forth, in which the law recognizes a moral claim, but is not itself the ground for it.

IVF is a particularly poignant case in this regard. It concerns the rights of the woman as a parent. It concerns her choice to reproduce by means other than the usual mode of sexual reproduction. It is no different in principle from artificial insemination and yet because it involves extrauterine insemination and formation of the blastula prior to implantation, the issues has somehow been conceived differently. Why? I suggest because of the consideration which reflects the social value particularly of an historical sort, that such freedom to conceive by IVF means potentially that the marital context of coitus and reproduction are threatened and so is the traditional concept of the family.

Apart from what is a cogent precise medical question, which Prof. Reilly addresses in his paper, there is a deeper question. IVF could conceivably free a woman from the marital condition of reproduction, could make the woman the sole identifiable genetic parent of the child, and, therefore, raises the same issue which would be raised by artificial insemination by an anonymous donor sperm or by polyandry, the problem of matriarchy.

It is interesting that every account of IVF speaks of fertilization by the husband, whether the wife's oocytes or the donor's oocytes. Ovarian rights are justified ultimately by the conjugal rights of the husband and by the context of the traditional family. This is not a rhetorical but a real question. Has the issue been raised in the same way with respect to artificial insemination?

Do sperm banks require that only the husband's sperm be used? Donor sperm presumably are the same status as the donor ovum. Have all the same issues been raised concerning possible regulation of cigarette smoking, alcohol drinking, prior successful fertilizations of male donors that have been raised with respect to female donors?

First issue I would raise, therefore, concerns that of the equality of the rights of reproduction in IVF and in AID. Second, there is a prudential consideration which has profound moral implications. Prof. Reilly remarks on the dangers of rather exotic commodity markets in human eggs and also uses the agricultural production metaphor, at the time of harvest of oocytes in talking about clinical conditions of IVF. He also talks about the question of dehumanization which some critics of IVF allege are marking a dichotomy between human technological reproduction.

There is a two-sided issue here. First, whether IVF as a medical technology somehow replaces natural human reproduction in some metaphysically or ethically repugnant way. Second, whether IVF can become like blood donation and child adoption, another arena of the commodification of the human and transformation of human use values into exchange values in the marketplace.

I separate these two aspects but I would argue differently on each one and I will conclude with this. First, human reproduction ceased being natural and became technological as soon as the societal introduction of kinship relations imposed consideration of social technique and social organization on mating. Medical intervention is no more technological in principle than is kinship, courtship, marriage, or the aid of midwives or obstetricians in delivery. All of these are social technologies which separate us all from our animal ancestry.

Yet technology is not inherently denying the production of children by reproduction, the planting of seed, the harvesting of a crop, the use of products. All these production metaphors remind us that human social technology with regard to childbearing have very historical uses, many of them exploited ones. The historical factors that child breeding in slave societies, in feudal agrarian capitalist societies has often used the product and even the act of conception for social purposes other than the good of the fetus and without any respect for the rights of the parents.

Finally, it seems to me that Prof. Reilly raises all the right questions concerning practical and legal concerns over protection of parents, fetus, child, and so forth, and gives reasonable views. But IVF bears on a deeper human anxiety about identity and mortality and also on the conflict between the requirement of a traditional social morality concerning the family and the freedom of the individual to reproduce by any means benevolent to the parents and the child.

MARX: I'd like to address my question to Prof. Reilly. Having had two uncomplicated pregnancies, I am interested in the rights of the surrogate mother. Would this be a paid job? If the surrogate mother decides to keep the child, what would be the answer here? If she claims that the implant aborted and the child was really her own? And what about restitution for complications due to pregnancy, such as liver damage, pre-diabetes?

REILLY: Let me assure you that I addressed all those questions in the printed paper. I will just allude to them briefly now, and I might take this occasion to respond to one sentence in Prof. Eisenberg's paper. I consider the discussion of or the designation of surrogate motherhood as beneath contempt and to be a completely paternalistic kind of position, which I disagree with strongly. I think that it is possible to introduce reasonable regulations here - surrogate motherhood could be a paid job. I would hope to foster altruism here. I am assuming that at least at the outset there would not be a great rush for this particular technology.

Recently in Texas we received a letter from a young woman who has had a partial hysterectomy, but could provide her own ova and wants very much to have a child with her genetic contribution. She asked whether she could utilize a near relative who might operate altruistically, but suggested she'd be willing to pay a reasonable amount. We discussed some of the issues about payment. I did a little survey of single and married women and they suggested that a reasonable fee would be $10,000. I think that the free market economy might drop that down a little. I see, by the way, nothing wrong with giving a woman another job opportunity here. No one's forcing her to do it and being a disciple of Adam Smith, I am not particularly perturbed by it. We live in a society where if it is perfectly all right to have women work as maids in our society for $2.25 an hour. Therefore, I don't see anything wrong with paying them a lot more for perhaps easier work.

R. LEBEL, S.J.: Graduate Theological Union in Berkeley, California: I want to emphasize that my question to Dr. Lowe is not rhetorical. It is a real search for information which I think is valuable to be exposed here. I'd like to know what the statistical information and analyses are on which you based your statement early in your paper that currently we are probably not experiencing more abortions in this country than we had before the change in the legal situation? I think it would be good if you exposed the sources of those statistics so we could spread them around.

LOWE: There have been several surveys and at least on in New York City, which purports to provide the information I gave you.

Arthur Campbell in an update of a chapter that he wrote on abortion has made the same statement. Center for Population Research in the National Institutes of Health have provided the same general information. The problem with validating this is the fact that the number of illegal abortions in the past are virtually impossible to document and the number that continue today is also difficult to document.

LEBEL: Prof. Reilly, one of the presuppositions which I think Prof. Wartofsky has already begun to explore in your paper was the question of the right to bear children. And this is as much a reply to what Prof. Wartofsky said as it is a reply to my question. Would you please just explore briefly what your philosophical and legal justification would be for establishing a right of an infertile woman or, for that matter, infertile man to have children. I am especially vexed by this question because I don't know how to approach it without getting tied up in the kind of natural law philosophy that has already been attacked a moment ago by Prof. Eisenberg, and which even us Catholics are trying to get away from.

REILLY: From the legal perspective I can answer it quite simply. It is an argument, if you will, a fortiori. If the Supreme Court in this country has determined that a woman has a right to destroy a fetus, I think a fortiori she has the right to get pregnant and to use whatever reasonable means are available to achieve that status. That is a legal positivism, if you will. From a philosophical perspective, what I would do would be to really express myself in this regard as a disciple of some of the attitudes that Joseph Fletcher has expressed. If it in fact is a basic human need to have a family, to bear children, then I think that it is basic human right to utilize technology that will accomplish that if it is available. I would note parenthetically that Fletcher has also said, and by no means does he pay obeisance to inconsistency, that having children is not necessarily a fundamental aspect of humanhood and that an infertile person is certainly a complete human person. But the concept of human needs is where I stand on this issue and I certainly don't have anything more about it to say than that.

CAPRON: I would take issue as a lawyer with Prof. Reilly that there is a legal right to have children as such. I don't think you can reason from the Supreme Court's declaration that a woman has a right to control her own body when she is at risk (and the Supreme Court emphasized the greater risk of carrying a fetus to term than not carrying the fetus) to a right to have children as such. I think that is a very much open question and the cases on contraception and abortion do not settle it. Moreover, once we move beyond law to a question of policy, it seems to me to be an open question of whether we should encourage in our society the extreme concern we have for childbearing and for children in the sense that

everybody needs to have a family to the point at which I think
it was in Prof. Lederberg's paper, where he referred to the right
of the genes to be expressed in the next generation.

This then leads us, or leads Prof. Lederberg at least, to make
reference to protecting a good genotype by having a clone of that
genotype made. I doubt if that means protecting it from the deleterious effect that the spouse might have on that genotype.

MARKS: In connection with dependant children, Dr. Sprague
and Dr. Goldstein have produced a very good book in which the major
thesis indicated a substantial difference between psychological
and natural parenting. I wonder if any of you would care to
comment not on the 21st century and cloning, but what these procedures do with respect to natural and psychological parenting.

EISENBERG: It is true in my own clinical experience that I
have encountered some men who have found it extremely difficult
to serve as a father of a child produced by artificial insemination.
The fact that that occurs I'm not sure settles the question as to
psychological difficulties since we have no epidemiologic data to
answer whether that occurs with greater frequency than the problem
of natural fathers assuming parental responsibilities for the
children cultivated in natural circumstances.

People do erect barriers because of false conceptions about
what is natural and what is unnatural. But what is natural or
unnatural as defined by the state of medical art and biological
science at a given time in history and by the set of values people
gather from their culture. What I find distressing in the themes
that recur during this conference and which reflect those that
exist in our society is that our alienation one from the other is
making it impossible to assume that anyone acts in good faith
toward anyone else, including the parents toward their children.

When we talk, as the lawyers have in some circumstances,
about restricting the rights of parents to make decisions that
may seem warranted, since we know that some parents make very unwise
decisions for their children and some parents even batter, abuse,
and kill their children. But for those exceptions to be taken as
the basis for structuring law seems to me to be highly dubious,
because if we define the relationship between parent and child
as one that under ordinary circumstances requires the intervention
of the state, the treatment may be much worse than the disease.

LEDERBERG: I am in complete agreement with Prof. Eisenberg on
his fine analysis of the failure of our ability to impose a cultural
cloning on a genetic cloning situation to recreate the presumptive
Mozart, etc. I don't think it will work. I think thinking that it
will work is nonsense. I stated this by pointing out that without

imposing identical nature, the individual remains free to choose
its own development. Nor do I think cloning is desirable.

However, I felt that the place to protect ourselves against
its undesirability is to insure that we, regardless of our genotype,
have access to a variety of cultural experiences. I do differ with
him without saying I am pessimistic or optimistic on how soon in
fact we will arrive face to face with the ethical issues that we
are met with when cloning technology is vastly improved. I think
it won't come through technology derived from working on ova. I
think it will come about through the billions spent on cancer
research. Fundamental to cancer research is the question of what
dictates repression of individual sets of genes and chromosomes.
What turns some on and what turns some off. We know already from
hybridization of human cells that unusual gene expressions emerge.
These tend on the one hand sometimes to be gene expressions not
usually seen in the cultured human cell, but often reminiscent of
a differentiated cell function.

In any event, without understanding the basis for the new
expressions, we find genomes, in part or in toto, unexpectedly
turn on when they have not been turned on before as a result of
hybridization. I can't but imagine after the billions of dollars
spent in this direction, either accidentally or deliberately, that
a way will not be found of turning on the somatic cell nuclei
in culture into something which can now grow into a blastocyst.

Then the technology of cloning and in vitro fertilization
can take over. I don't think this is the next century.

ROSENBERG: You don't? I guess we disagree on that. I'd be
terribly surprised if it was!

Eugenics, Ethics,
Law, and Society

BIOLOGICAL ROOTS OF ETHICAL PRINCIPLES

Salvadore E. Luria

Department of Biology, Center for Cancer Research

Massachusetts Institute of Technology

In his exciting if controversial book "Chance and Necessity," Jacques Monod suggested that an important source of ethical values was what he called the "Ethics of Knowledge," that is, the commitment to the scientific exploration of natural phenomena. This suggestion was made within the intellectual framework of an existential ethics that denies the existence of absolute, ultimate values. In this framework, values are not given but chosen, partly consciously, partly unconsciously, and are adhered to or modified or abandoned in the continuing effort of each individual to create a moral identity -- what we may call a moral self. In this light, the ethics of knowledge is the commitment to face factual reality as intelligently as possible -- essentially, the value of intellectual integrity.

Monod's formulation has given rise to several kinds of misunderstandings. On the one hand, the ethics of knowledge has been interpreted by some as the proposal of an absolute set of values, like the revelation of the decalogue or the promulgation of a penal code. It has been seen as a claim of the priority of scientific knowledge over other types of human activities which also serve as sources of values. As such, the idea of an ethics of knowledge has been criticized as a manifestation of a scientific elitism.

More dangerously, the ethics of knowledge is often embraced by some who interpret it as the right to pursue the quest for knowledge whenever one so wishes, irrespective of consequences. We are all familiar with the abuses of this principle in a variety of areas, from pointless research on phony subjects to research in controversial fields of social and medical science.

Thus, for example, the believers in extrasensory perception or telepathy insist on their right to be funded for their meaningless research on non-existent phenomena in their field of unreality. More seriously, it was sufficient for some self-styled educational geneticist to assert that the lower mean I.Q. scores of black youngsters are genetically determined, for a whole pack of racists and intellectual profiteers to generate a bandwagon of so-called genetic research on race differences in intelligence. The right-to-knowledge becomes the analogue of the right-to-life: The right to affect and possibly blight the life of others for the satisfaction of being proved right. If one points out that before drawing conclusions from measurements of I.Q. tests one should know what it is that the tests measure, and whether genetic analysis can be done on such data, one is accused of wanting to suppress the pursuit of knowledge. More important still, the expectation that doing and advertising this kind of "research" will have serious social consequences, irrespective of its findings, is discounted as irrelevant by the champions of the right-to-know.

Another example is the XYY story. Initial observations of a significantly high incidence of this chromosomal anomaly among prison inmates quickly become incorporated into sordid tales of a "crime chromosome." Despite solid evidence contrary to the existence of a correlation between crime and the extra Y, research projects have proliferated, some probably innocuous, others scientifically meaningless, others medically and socially questionable, because their performance can create medical problems where none was present. The right-to-know attracts research funds.

What is wrong with the claim of an unfettered right-to-know, whether in the social or the medical research field? I believe that the main pitfall is the failure to balance the right-to-know value, that is, the ethics of knowledge, with what I shall call the ethics of innocence. What I mean by the ethics of innocence can best be stated metaphorically by the words that Dostoeviski put in the mouth of Ivan Karamazov: "If the suffering of children serves to complete the sum of suffering necessary for the acquisition of truth, I affirm that truth is not worth such a price."

What this means is simply that morality does not exist in a vacuum, and that human pursuits should always be judged in terms of what their consequences are for other human beings. Values are only norms for human interaction. If the ethics of knowledge urges us to strive to add new knowledge to the intellectual patrimony of mankind, the ethics of innocence prescribes that we must refrain from doing anything that has a foreseeable chance to cause suffering. The principle of not inflicting damage or unnecessary pain onto patients or experimental subjects is well established in medical practice and research. But the issues raised by biological

research in the social science field are more subtle. Damage can
be done indirectly, through the functioning of social forces and
institutions.

If a single person, black or white or yellow, should suffer
because of the social consequences of the right claimed by Jensen
or Hernstein to find out what a 15-point mean difference in I.Q.
really means, then I would say, let us forsake that knowledge.
That truth is not worth such price.

If a single XYY child or its parents should have their life
blighted or anguished because of the wish of some psychiatrist to
know the true facts about the psychological effects of the XYY
pattern, again I would say, that truth is not worth such price.
Knowledge gained at such price is not like the diagnostic knowledge gained by a physician through the inevitable infliction of
some pain to a patient under treatment, or by a researcher through
experimentation on informed human volunteers.

The ethics of knowledge and the ethics of innocence are
two complementary aspects of morality. Both are expressions of the
unique biological destiny of humankind. The development of the
human brain and the acquisition of consciousness in the course of
evolution have given to us human beings the power to organize and
transmit knowledge, as well as the power to identify ourselves
with the feelings and the sufferings of other human beings. They
have forced upon us the need to know and the need to be innocent,
both of them biologically rooted values. We cannot legitimately
follow either one and ignore the other.

One more point may be worth emphasizing. Whenever the right-
to-know is claimed to supersede the obligation of innocence, we
should suspect behind that claim some form of obscurantism and
oppression -- that is, the denial of innocence. Behind the I.Q.
propaganda are lined the forces of that racism that is unfortunately
embedded in the cultural and legal tradition of America. Fifty
years ago, the powers of genetics were enlisted by the forces of
social oppression to prove that pellagra, then prevalent among the
southern poor, was a syndrome of the genetically inferior rather
than a nutritional deficiency of the exploited. Now genetics is
once more being invoked -- fortunately not by any competent geneticist -- in the service of racial prejudice.

In a similar way, behind the XYY fuss there looms the crime-
oriented paradigm of the law-enforcement agencies, a paradigm that
has already succeeded in making a criminal of every addict and
would like to make every social deviant or political rebel into a
genetically programmed criminal.

To preserve the values that we cherish, in science as in

medicine, we must be careful never to become, consciously or unwittingly, the instruments of forces that would subordinate those
values for selfish or misguided goals of their own. Ethics of
knowledge and ethics of innocence must never become dissociated,
lest either one without the other becomes a vehicle for ignorance
or a tool of oppression.

ON THE NECESSITY OF LEGISLATING MORALITY FOR GENETIC DECISIONS

Daniel Callahan

Institute of Society, Ethics, and the Life Sciences

Hastings Center, Hastings-on-Hudson, New York

The initial question I want to touch on is whether genetic disease should be of governmental concern. The specific thesis I then want to argue is that, to the extent governmental concern takes the form of mandating tests or screening, to that extent its action can be construed as an instance of the legislation of morality. Since the "legislation of morality" is popularly considered to be wrong in our society, a choice will then have to be made. Either we abandon the notion that the legislation of morality is in all instances a wrongful governmental act; or we declare -- to preserve the purity of the distinction between public policy and private morality -- that the government should stay entirely out of the area of genetic disease, at least out of it to the extent of passing no mandatory laws of any kind bearing on the control of genetic disease. I realize that by no means all members of our society, or of our legislatures, believe that the legislation of morality is necessarily bad; they may have no particular problem with my line of reasoning. My special challenge will be to those who want to uphold a strict separation of law and morality while at the same time pressing for greater governmental intervention into procreative decisions which give promise of maintaining or increasing the present individual and societal burden of genetic disease. Just whose foot the shoe I am going to fashion will fit will have to be left to those prepared to try it on.

It is not difficult to discover why many think genetic disease should be of concern to government. Genetic disease is ordinarily a burden on the afflicted individual, on their families, and in many instances on society as a whole. In those respects, it is like anything else we call a disease; it is a form of illness and illness is, by definition, a condition we ordinarily judge to be harmful, and all the more so as the burden of the illness increases. Our government, with full public support, long ago decided that in order to promote the general welfare it should be concerned with the prevention and treatment of disease. It is thus perfectly reasonable that it should now take an interest in genetic disease. The only thing that hindered governmental concern with genetic disease in earlier times was a lack of scientific knowledge about such disease and an almost total inability to do anything about it. Now, with such knowledge in hand, and some means both to prevent and treat genetic disease, it can take its legitimate place among the full array of health conditions of concern to the government. In sum, given the individual and social burden of genetic disease, it is not difficult to make the case of why and whether it should be of concern to the government; up to that point the reasoning is conventional and generally acceptable.

Naturally, along the way a number of moral judgments have been made, but most of them so hidden in the conventionality of the logical chain that they are hardly noticed. It was essentially a moral judgement that led our society in the first place to decide that government had an obligation to concern itself with the general welfare, and that health was a part of the general welfare. Once it decided that genetic health was a legitimate part of a more general concern with health, obligations of government toward genetic health could then be easily encompassed as part of a well-established moral obligation on the part of government. While it could not necessarily be said that the outcome of this chain of moral reasoning is tantamount to the "legislation of morality" -- if by that term is meant the imposition of a moral system or set of moral convictions -- it certainly reflects the power of a set of moral claims, i.e., all those claims that government has an obligation to be concerned with the health of its citizens.

The question of to what extent, and in what ways, the government should concern itself with genetic disease takes us into deeper waters. I will assume, for the purpose of this paper, that no "legislation of morality" is involved when government restricts its concern for genetic disease to support of scientific research, to the establishment of medical and public education programs, and to the provision of voluntary genetic counseling and screening programs. Note that I said my assumption would be "for the purpose of this paper." We should know enough by now to realize how often in our society supposedly value-free and voluntary programs of research, education and provision of services can hide a multitude of tacit moral assumptions and convictions and can, with more or less sublety, serve to promote a whole set of quite precise moral values. There is no reason to piously assume that is less likely to happen in the area of "voluntary" genetics programs than in any other kind of "voluntary" programs. But I will not pursue that problem here, other than to note that it is a far more serious problem than most people committed to a voluntaristic philosophy seem to realize.

My focus here will be on proposals to governmentally mandate counseling and screening programs. These proposals have taken the form, at the most innocuous level, of mandatory educational programs to inform the public of the nature of genetic disease. At another level, it has been proposed (and in some places legislated) that certain groups of people be required to undergo mandatory genetic screening, either upon entering school or entering marriage or entering the armed forces. At still another level, it has been proposed that, once technically feasible, all people be mandatorily screened at some point for whatever conditions it is scientifically possible to detect. (Somewhere in-between those two stages, and raising rather different issues, are proposals to make screening a part of "standard medical practice," thus avoiding the problem of legislation but at the same time gaining the power of high medical sanction, which is probably more powerful than legislation anyway. I am particularly thinking of proposals to employ amniocentesis upon all women over the age of 35 or 40 as a standard part of prenatal maternal care (1). Finally, one can find proposals here and there that would forbid some people from marrying at all, or from having children at all. If this is not said outright, it is a direct implication of language which denies that people have a right to bring defective, burdensome children into the world, or can make any claim upon public assistance if they knowingly do so. If it can be argued that people do not have rights of that kind, and argued moreover that the exercise of any claimed rights poses a threat to the common good, then it is only a small step to concluding that government has an obligation to stop them.

Proposals for mandatory public education on genetic disease raise all the general problems associated with mandatory education on any subject, and I will pass over them here. More critical are those proposals that would mandate some action on the part of individuals, either the undergoing of certain examinations or, in the extreme, straight government intervention that would interdict certain forms of behavior. My contention is that to propose either form of governmental action is, in direct effect, to propose the legislation of morality; and that the enactment by legislation of such proposals would be nothing less than the legislation of morality.

Two preliminary steps are necessary to establish my case. First, I would like to present a very brief history of the course of the argument over population growth in recent decades, pointing out certain interesting twists and turns in the different stages of that argument. Some clear analogies to the ongoing debate on genetics will appear. Second, and no less briefly, I would like to take us back to Mill and some of his contentions about govern-

mental coercion, moving on quickly to the problem of the legislation
of morality as it emerged in the aftermath of his work.

Although a concern with population growth can be dated back to
Malthus' Essay on Population (1798), his cry of alarm was not taken
up during the nineteenth and much of the early twentieth century.
Instead, spurred by the work of Sanger and others, family planning
programs aimed at maximizing individual procreative choice became
the dominant reformist movement in the early decades of the twentieth century. But it was a movement which encountered considerable
and often bitter religious and governmental resistance. For decades,
the family planning movement struggled to get the right to family
planning accepted as a genuine human right, sanctioned and supported
not only by society in general but also by government in particular.
By the 1950's it was a movement that had triumphed, at least in
most of the world's developed countries. The UN Declaration of
Human Rights, which explicitly recognized a right to family planning,
was as good a signal as any of the extent of the triumph.

In essence, the family planning movement had argued that procreative decisions on the size of families, and the spacing of
children, are an inherently private matter. Two implications
followed: negatively, no government had the right to interfere in
any way, by law or policy, in individual procreative decisions;
and positively, that governments had the obligation to maximize
freedom of choice by providing information and education on family
planning and, where necessary, by actually supplying those services
and contraceptive devices which would actually allow freedom of
individual choice to be maximized. And so it came to pass in many
places, most notably the United States.

During the '40's and '50's however, a fresh concern with world
population growth began to develop, fueled by concern with rapid
population growth in the developing countries. Spurred by data
indicating that people would willingly reduce family size if given
access to effective contraceptives, there seemed at first to be
a perfect fit between the goal of reducing world population growth
and the goal of maximizing individual freedom of procreative choice;
no one used the term "invisible hand" but it was lurking in the
background.

By the 1960's, however, considerable skepticism began to appear.
First, despite a couple of decades of work promoting family planning,
there was little evidence of any significant drop in birth rates in
most countries; India was the classic example. Second, doubts began to be expressed about whether, in fact, even if the programs
worked and people did choose the family size they wanted, that family size would actually be sufficient to deal with the world population problem. What if couples voluntarily chose to have an average family size of four children, rather than the ideal size of 2.1

necessary in the long run to achieve stability (2)?   Third, with
that possibility in mind, the next step was for some to begin proposing that realism required an exploration of ways in which governments might effectively, with the good of societies rather than
the desires of individuals in mind, intervene to put pressure on
people to have families whose size would be compatible in the end
with a zero population growth. Berelson, in a much-cited article
with a much-cited title, summed up and analyzed that trend in his
article "Beyond Family Planning" (3).

      That trend, which led to a debate which still continues, rested
on a perception which flew directly in the face of the assumption
of the earlier family planning movement. The early assumption was
that the sum total of freely chosen procreative decisions would
either have no harmful social consequences or, more hopefully,
some indirect beneficial social consequences. The later perception,
spurring proposals to move "beyond family planning" cast doubt on
that assumption; indeed, it was prone to deny it altogether. Unless one is in every sense a true believer in the promotion of the
general welfare by a policy of laissez-faire, as much in procreation
as in economic policy, there is no reason whatever to assume there
can be no conflict between the aggregate of individual choices and
what is good for society as a whole. It was finally seen by many
in the population field that the sum total of private, free procreative choices has enormous social consequences. All those "free"
choices can add up to thousands of babies. Coming full circle,
it was then argued in effect that, in the area of procreation, nothing was more important than to break down the earlier individual-
istic conviction that procreation was a matter of private morality
only. In an era of dangerously rapid population growth, what could
be more naive? Both the course of realism and of morality now
require that matters of family size be seen as legitimate areas for
governmental intervention, even coercive intervention if necessary.

      I have cited the stages of the population debate to draw
some direct analogies with what seems to me the emergent, and quite
similar, course of the genetics debate. The latter also began
with an early stress on the freedom of couples to make a rational,
voluntary choice about whether to bear a defective child. No one,
particularly the government, was going to tell anyone whether or
not they should bear a defective child. The important point was to
provide people with information and services, so that if they freely chose not to have a defective child, then they might be able
fully to exercise that choice. That was the first step. But the
second step was just around the corner. Some people might not exercise their new freedom "responsibly," they might in fact knowingly
or negligently bring defective children into the world. But would
that not be wrong? Wrong to the child, wrong to other family members and, maybe most of all, wrong to society, which would have to
bear the social and economic costs of such children? I believe

there is enough scattered evidence to indicate that some people are already taking just that step. In brief, they are saying that private procreative choices on the quality of children are anything but private in their social impact, that decisions bearing on the procreation of defective children are issues of public interest and not only private morality. It is only a small hop, skip and jump to the conclusion that government has every right to intervene in procreative decisions bearing on the genetic quality of children, a right, that is, to protect society as a whole from the consequences of irresponsible private decisions.

I want to say at this point that I do not mean to pass a moral judgment on the trends I have noted both in the field of population and genetics. I personally believe there is much to be said for the moral validity of that trend. I do not believe in an absolute and unlimited "right to procreate," either for quantity or quality of children. However, that is a complicated issue which I must skirt here. At the moment, all I want to do is call attention to the chronology and logical chain of reasoning which led to similar trends in population and genetics. They have both seen a breaking down of the cherished distinction between public policy and private morality, they both lead in the direction of the "legislation of morality," and they both rest on the perception that private acts can have public consequences.

Mill is a good point of departure for a consideration of the "legislation of morality." He and many of his followers have been the strongest advocates of a sharp distinction between public policy and private morality. Mill was particularly concerned with making a distinction between those acts that do, and those acts that do not harm others, for it is precisely that distinction which will allow us to set limits to government coercion. Mill's essay On Liberty (1859) was designed, he said, to "assert one very simple principle...That principle is, that the sole end for which mankind are warranted, individually or collectively, in interfering with the liberty of action of any of their number, is self-protection. That the only purpose for which power can rightfully be exercised over any member of a civilized community, against his will, is to prevent harm to others" (4).

In the eyes of many commentators, Mill himself could not hold on as tightly as he would have liked to his "simple principle." Even harm to oneself could have at least some indirectly harmful consequences for others. More importantly for my purposes, however, others have tried to hold on to the "simple principle" in order to maintain the distinction between private morality and public policy, and to affirm the illegitimacy of government attempting to legislate morality. The late Herbert Packer, one of the major exponents of the concept of "crime without victims" in recent times, thought that Mill's "simple principle" still has some validity. It helps to en-

sure that "a given form of conduct is not being subject to the
criminal sanction purely or even primarily because it is thought
to be immoral. It forces an inquiry into precisely what bad
effects are feared if the conduct in question is not suppressed
by criminal law" (5). Packer was trying to work with a distinction between that which is immoral and that which has bad effects;
the latter can be prohibited by law while the former cannot. An
implication of that position, spelled out by Henkin and others, is
that legislation must have a public purpose only; it cannot be
used to sanction or support private morality.

Yet as Golding has noted, it is difficult if not impossible
to maintain this distinction, either in theory or practice (6).
An obvious difficulty is that it is hard to conceive of a "public
purpose" which does not rest on some moral value. What else, for
instance, are we to call the values of "life, liberty and the pursuit of happiness" mentioned in the Preamble to the Constitution,
values which are part of the American "public purpose." Moreover,
it is exceedingly difficult to even imagine an example of a moral
act which is intrinsically private in nature. We can imagine acts
which, at given times and in given places, would seem to have no
public consequences. But it is impossible to imagine any which
would always be intrinsically private regardless of circumstance.
Surely, it was thought by the early advocates of family planning,
what could be more private and of less consequence to the public
that the decisions of an individual couple as to how many children
they should have? Surely people had an absolute right to make such
decisions, without interference from governments, churches or anyone else.

Just as surely of course -- once the population crisis was
discerned -- it was seen as self-evident that the private procreative choices of individuals can have in aggregate enormous social
consequences. What area could be more fit for government intervention and a limitation on individual rights? Knowing what we
do about the economic and social burden of Down's syndrome, what
area could be more fit for governmental intervention than the de-
ision of parents as to whether knowingly bring a child with that
condition into the world?

Now it might be claimed that none of the proposals that would
require people to be screened for genetic disease as a condition
for entry into school, marriage or the military have in mind any
kind of "legislation of morality." It might be claimed that only
a "public purpose" would be served. But what could that possibly
mean? Is there any public purpose which does not rest on some
moral convictions about what is good for human beings and society?
Even arguments from the economic burden of genetic disease make
some important moral assumptions: that economic considerations are
pertinent to the general welfare, that certain kinds of economic

burdens imposed by individuals (e.g. the genetically defective) are burdens which it is unjust to impose upon society. Both a moral theory of what is good for societies and a theory of justice come into play. If it is proposed on that basis to impose legal sanctions on those who would bear defective children, then that would clearly be an instance of the "legislation of morality." Worse still, since we know that society is now and will probably for the foreseeable future be divided on how government should treat potential parents of defective children, we will be legislating a sectarian morality, that is, the morality of those who propose and if they are successful get enacted into law such proposals.

Matters are made even worse when we realize that the most common arguments in favor of mandating screening programs, or even more coercive measures, rarely restrict themselves to pointing out the social benefits of screening. They ordinarily also invoke the harm done to a defective child by allowing such a child to be either conceived or born, as well as the potential harm done to other family members. The motive of protection of the child-to-be is clearly paternalistic, and "paternalism" as a motive has been traditionally classified as part of the genus called "legislating morality" (even though Mill himself had to give in a bit on that point). In any event, we are immediately into the area of morality -- and a very "private" morality at that because of the notorious differences of opinion on the subject -- the moment we begin talking about what is good for the welfare of children and families.

The modest conclusion of this essay is that any proposals to mandate behavior out of concern for genetic disease, whether in the mild form of mandating screening only, or the more extreme form of placing restrictions on the behavior of those at risk for bearing defective children, is a clear-cut case of "legislating morality." But I would not want to leave matters at that. Since I believe it impossible in any area of legislation to avoid "legislating morality" and in most cases impossible to avoid legislating the "private morality" of some group or other, we might as well go directly to the moral issues at stake, bring them into the open, make our moral choices, and vote accordingly.

If we choose to allow voluntary programs of genetic counseling and screening only, we will be choosing the familiar morality of giving priority to individual freedom in a hierarchy of moral values. It is a subtle but nonetheless real fallacy to assume that a political choice in favor of permissiveness and freedom represents no "legislation of morality." As a society we now certainly know better in the case of civil rights, having decisively rejected the libertarian argument of racists that giving them freedom of choice would not interfere with the right of others to make a different choice. Any society which allows freedom of choice on any subject over against those who conscientiously believe that matter should not be left to free choice is "legislating morality." Should it sound too paradoxical to say that a society which does not legislate at all on a given subject is "legislating morality," then let me try an alternative formulation. If a society's social policy is, in a given case, not to legislate on a matter because of a division of opinion or for whatever other reason, it can surely be said that the decision to go in the direction of free choice is a policy decision; and that is close enough for me to the notion of "legislating morality" that I am quite willing to give up the term -- but the reality will be the same.

If, then, morality will be legislated whether our society moves in the direction of maximum freedom of individual choice concerning the bearing of defective children, or in the direction of establishing some mandatory requirements, which morality should we choose? I will not try to answer that question here. I will only conclude by asserting that it is the question which must now be answered, and that we will delude ourselves if we think we can evade it by drawing a distinction between private morality and public law or policy.

REFERENCES

1. Stein, Z., Screening programme for prevention of Down's syndrome, Lancet 1:305 (1973).

2. Davis, K., Population policy: Will current programs succeed? Science 158:730 (1967).

3. Berelson, B., Beyond family planning,"Studies in Family Planning" No. 38 (1969).

4. Mill, J.S.,"On Liberty", Chicago: Gateway Edition, p. 13 (1955).

5. Packer, H., "The Limits of the Ciminal Sanction," Stanford University Press, p. 267 (1968).

6. Golding, M.P., "Philosophy of Law, Prentics-Hall, Englewood Cliffs, New Jersey, p. 59 (1975).

WHY SHOULDN'T WE HAVE A EUGENIC POLICY?

Marc Lappé

Institute of Society, Ethics and the Life Sciences

Hastings Center, Hastings-on-Hudson, New York

We civilized men ... do our utmost to check the process
of elimination; we build asylums ... we institute poor
laws ....   There is reason to believe that vaccination
has preserved thousands, who from a weak constitution
would formerly have succumbed to small pox. Thus the
weak members of civilized society propagate their kind.
No one who has attended to the breeding of domestic animals will doubt that this must be highly injurious to
the race of man. It is surprising how soon want of care,
or care wrongly directed leads to the degeneration of a
domesticated race; but excepting in the case of man
himself, hardly anyone is so ignorant as to allow his
worst animals to breed.

> Charles Darwin, The Descent of
> Man and Selection in Relation to
> Sex, 1871

The aim of eugenics is the improvement of the species
by decreasing the propagation of the physically and
mentally handicapped (negative eugenics) and by increasing that of the "more desirable" types (positive
eugenics). It is, in other words, the application to
man of the methods developed by breeders for improving
their stocks by artificial selection.

> L.L. Cavalli-Sforza and W.F. Bodmer,
> The Genetics of Human Populations,
> 1971

RATIONALES AND DEFINITIONS OF EUGENICS

It is remarkable to me that the century which has elapsed since Darwin's pronouncement in <u>The Descent of Man</u> has brought forth no better analogy for the practice of human genetics than the breeding of animals. Another reflection of this curious persistence can be found today in the human application of the self-same equations for heritability developed by Lerner and Dempster in the 1940's for poultry breeding (1). No matter that the metric traits used by Lerner and Dempster are not analogous to I.Q. scores, or that the confounding of genetic estimates by interactional components greatly reduces the potency of the equations (2). The assumption remains that <u>somewhere</u> underneath that labyrinth of culturally distorted behaviors and attributes, lurks the animal known as <u>Homo sapiens sapiens</u>.

HISTORICAL OVERVIEW

But to treat eugenic policy merely as a problem in approximating for man what has been done to dogs, is to trivialize a much broader problem in human affairs. Eugenics today has less to do with breeding than it does with the policies which flow from the presumptive demonstration of the factual basis for human inequalities based on ascertainments of genetically based characteristics. No one has to look beyond the present I.Q./heredity conflict to appreciate that the greatest threat of eugenic concepts today is not what they promise to do with people as breeders, but what these formulations portend for them in their day-to-day lives. Contemporary history has been rife with examples of the misappropriation of eugenic concepts to legitimate class or racial barriers or distinctions (cf 3, 4). The question for our time, is whether or not we have passed into an age where reason acts to buffer the scientific imperative to apply "factual" data to human affairs without consideration of their political and social ramifications.

At first inspection, there appears to be little doubt that the contemporary wellspring of bona fide knowledge of genetic differences between persons genuinely challenges social policies based on the presumption of equality. But <u>biological</u> inequality does not reduce the validity of social programs predicated on a basis of equality. The deservedness of all persons for equal treatment under the law, or the one-person, one-vote doctrine are each examples of a normative egalitarian decision.

In a previous publication, I emphasized what I considered to be most problematic about eugenic policy: However an eugenic program is to be instituted, it must not only systematically violate radical egalitarianism; it must do so in a way which penalizes the least advantaged (5). This seemingly insurmountable stumbling

block need not be so. Other societies, imagined and real, have
incorporated eugenic concepts in ways which cannot be easily dismissed on moral grounds. For these societies, the critical question rests in differentiating between the causes of class status.
To oversimplify the question, are persons who are well-to-do, tall,
healthy, and long-lived generally so because of their genetic makeup or the happenstance of their birth from parents who could provide the social conditions for their flourishing? Walzer has made
the critical observation that a central concept among those who
would preserve our present class system is the idea "that the present division of wealth and power corresponds to some deeper reality of human life" (6). One such "deeper reality" that has surfaced in the writings of proponents of the status quo is genetic
differences. The real risk of eugenic concepts lies in their ability
to serve as an apology for the existence of inequitable institutions unjustified by the demonstration of inequalities. (Where inequalities exist, I generally agree with Rawls (7) that they are
to be rectified in favor of the least well-off.)

Wherever there has been a society which has sought to achieve
the greatest efficiency through differential distribution of
labor and skills, I suspect there would eventually have emerged a
eugenic rationale to justify its existence. In Plato's mythical
Republic, the excellence of the "guardian class" was presumed to be
hereditary, to be perpetuated by eugenic breeding practices authorized by the state. The moral order of the state, in this model,
permitted the subordination of the notion of equality where reproduction was concerned, since the characteristics of the guardians
could theoretically only be perpetuated efficiently by a eugenic
means. The justification for such a system is linked to the pri-
macy of the prerogatives of the state.

PRIMACY OF THE STATE

Such a claim can be found among the writings of early eugen-
ists in this country. For example, Davenport justified his eugenical views in Hereditary in Relation to Eugenics (c. 1911) by
declaring that

> The commonwealth is greater than any individual in it.
> Hence the rights of society over the life, the repro-
> duction, the behavior and the traits of the individuals
> that compose it are, in all matters that concern the life
> and proper progress of society, limitless, and society
> may take life, may sterilize, may segregate so as to
> prevent marriage, may restrict liberty in a hundred
> ways (8).

The justifications given for supporting the prerogatives of
the state in regulating the lives of its members have fluctuated
over the centuries. In our country, the scope of the exercise of
police powers to regulate public health has been substantial. As
Reilly notes,

> Despite clear theoretical limitations on the exercise
> of the public health power, the state traditionally
> has had little difficulty in justifying compulsory
> requirements under its rubric. Indeed, since the days
> of the first quarantine laws, compulsion has been common
> to laws in this field (9).

Reilly cites substantial precedent for the legal acceptability of
some of the principles of eugenics in the United States.

This paper, however, is concerned with the moral acceptability
of eugenic ideas. The cogency of the reasons for justifying state
intervention are to be assessed on the basis of their moral weight,
not their legality. At root, one of the strongest reasons to
question the moral validity of eugenic concepts is the potential
loss of human autonomy. In part, this risk is embedded in the
association of genetic concepts with biologic determinism. By
fostering the belief that human behavioral characteristics are
genetically determined (to any degree), genetic determinism threatens to erode traditional views of responsibility. The current
attempt to define the possible association of an XYY genotype with
behavioral deviancy has already been misused in this regard (cf 10).

INDIA AS AN EXAMPLE

When a whole society adopts a eugenic ideological base, as
happened in India at the time of the writing of the Mahabarata
(2nd century B.C.), the erosion of moral values can become pronounced. In Hindu society, as in Plato's Republic, rights and
social standing were distributed according to a formula of deservedness based on status in   eugenically-perpetuated classes.
Although since expanded to over two thousand sub-groups, the classic caste system in India identified four levels of society: the
Brahmans, or priests; the Kshatriyas, or warriors; the Vaisyas, or
peasants; and the Sudras, or untouchables.

According to the Laws of Manu, the oldest and most authoritative Hindu book of law, the Brahman is to be afforded extraordinary rights and prerogatives, purely on the basis of his genetic affiliation with an enlightened group through which he has
"accrued merit" in his previous lives (11). The moral justification for gross inequalities in receipt of social goods was predicated on the belief that the moral order of society as a whole de-

pended on the integrity of caste lineages. Intermarriage between castes was considered an appalling sin which threatened the integrity of the entire social fabric. The society-wide conviction in the truth of this statement was underscored in recent times by Gandhi's own reluctance to do away entirely with the caste system, except to break the onus attached to the untouchables.

Because the Hindu society represents the only "natural" experiment undertaken in which eugenic measures were in fact put into practice over a protracted period (the Oneida colony in New York was much more limited in its objectives and duration, for example), it serves as a foil against which to posit the fundamental paradox of any eugenic system: Can a society which institutionalizes human inequality encourage the development of social values which recognize human autonomy and liberty? Can moral responsibility be exercised in a community of persons with intrinsic dissimilarities in rights, duties and obligations?

The possibility that eugenic programs/ideologies play havoc with the concept of moral responsibility was recognized by writers in Hindu society. Indeed, the most widely read morality tale in the world today, the Bhagavad Gita, centers on the struggle of a member of the warrior caste to throw off the burden of determinism which compels him to fight against members of his own family. For some, the outcome of that tale in which the God Krishna overrules the warrior's attempt at moral assertion by persuading him that his duties are inborn and therefore he is blameless, counted as a heavy indictment of the moral concomitants to a caste system (12).

JUSTIFYING EUGENIC POLICY

To satisfy a minimal definition of justification, the acceptance or rejection of eugenic policies have to be based on more than one criterion. In the past I have argued that a eugenic program should meet at least the following requisites to be acceptable: 1) scientific validity (for example a demonstration of sufficient genetic variation to allow for selection of the attribute in question); 2) moral acceptability, i.e., a demonstration that the attribute(s) chosen for selection are rightly considered "socially desirable"; 3) ethical acceptability, i.e., a demonstration that the programs needed to institute a eugenic program do not compromise individual rights and liberties previously sanctioned by public policy and the law (cf. 13). Here, the best way to proceed would be to attempt to reject the two critical hypotheses which together vindicate the moral acceptability of eugenic ideals and techniques. If we are unable to reject these hypotheses, then the sole determinant for deciding whether or not to institute such policies will rest with second order assessments of eugenic policies.

The two hypotheses can be stated as follows:

1. There are no morally relevant reasons for instituting a
    eugenic program in the United States; and
2. The procedures required to effect such a program, were it
    undertaken, are morally unacceptable.

The first hypothesis can be refuted by noting that good moral reasons for instituting eugenic programs exist. Eugenic programs
theoretically would allow moral action through the exercise of
intergenerational responsibility, the reduction of human suffering,
and the improvement of the human species. Similarly, the second
hypothesis can be rejected by noting, as I did in a previous paper,
that purely demographic mechanisms exist for modifying population
characteristics of a eugenic nature. Were these to be undertaken
voluntarily (e.g., restriction of age at childbearing to an optimal
level), a eugenic program could be instituted which could meet
modest objectives over the short run (5). Thus, in spite of the
existence of a spate of morally questionable techniques, such as
procreative incentives in the form of negative tax strategies,
artificial insemination with donor semen, eugenic sterilization,
or proscription of reproduction on the basis of carrier status,
there are a family of techniques which do not in and of themselves
violate ethical norms of society.

Are we left with any further basis to evaluate eugenic programs? Even if acceptable for reasons which are internal to its
structure, the benefits of such a program must be weighed against
the aggregate weight of the indirect costs which its implementation
might incur. These potential second-order costs fall into three
categories: moral, political, and scientific.

If demonstrable, the potential moral cost of diminishing
human responsibility (by substituting a genetic model for a social
one in explaining human behavior, for instance) could be prohibit-
ive. More realistically, the institution of eugenic policies might
discriminate against the disadvantaged (cf. 5). Politically, eugenic policies could reinforce social institutions which were intrinsically unjust. Programs to effect eugenic ends might penalize
the less well off, if we take seriously the view of otherwise
competent scientists that the principal eugenic problem lies in
the slums of major cities.

For example, Julian Huxley writes that

the marked differential increase of lower-income groups,
classes, and communities during the last hundred years
cannot possibly be eugenic in its effect. The extremely
high fertility of the so-called problem group in the

slums of many industrial cities is certainly anti-
eugenic (14).

To my understanding, there is no basis in fact for this statement.
Scientifically, presumptive "eugenic" programs could have the reverse effect, increasing the frequency of certain deleterious
genes, or reducing the overall fitness of the population by reducing genetic variability. For example, the selection for intelligence based on I.Q. scores might concomitantly select for
undesirable genes as would be the case were the gene predisposing
for retinoblastoma, a rare eye tumor, found to be closely linked
to genes related to high I.Q. scoring (15). Certainly, human
geneticists like Dobzhansky have been loathe to accept the notion
that we currently have enough information to act reasonably intelligently in any eugenics program. Dobzhansky stated in 1965 that

> It seems scarcely credible that a serious scientist
> can see no need for more detailed knowledge of human
> genetics than is now available to embark on a program
> of genetic improvement of mankind (16).

MODELS OF EUGENICS IN SOCIETY

A final test for the acceptability of eugenic programs would
be an exercise in which we tried to imagine vividly what a society
which incorporated eugenic stratagems would be like. The arguments
for a eugenic society might include this kind of rationale:

> Given human genetic diversity, it is inevitable that some bio-
> logical inequalities among individuals for socially relevant
> traits will exist. Recognizing and acting on these inequalities
> on the "best" would allow a political system to make more rapid
> economic and social progress than it could if it ignored these
> differences. Cavalli-Sforza and Bodmer recognize

> > that some genotypes can do very well in certain environ-
> > ments, while they do less well, or worse than average in
> > others. It would be a terrible waste to force a potential
> > Bach to become a bricklayer or an engineer, or a potential
> > Einstein to be an accountant (17).

The present economic system could be seen as mirroring our hypothetical eugenic program: Both include a mechanism which can discriminate among "opportunities" such that those aspects of the
system which are subject to improvement can be selected and "capi-
talized" upon. In an eugenic society, the aim is rapid improvement
of stocks of individuals with desirable qualities, so that the
gains made each generation can be reinvested through gametic or mate
selection into the next generation.

A eugenic society simply operates with a conscious metaphysic that recognizes the importance of genotypes over phenotypes. Phenotypes are seen as resulting from interactions between genes and cultures and are hence much less stable and accurate than genotypes as predictors of the quality of future members of society. But could we also not envision a society in which eugenic concepts and policies play an insignificant role -- where individual differences were not subject to economic or genetic capitalization. Genetic differences here would be seen as just as real, but would be denied the moral relevance afforded to other principles, such as liberty and equality of opportunity.

Such a society would likely be less "efficient," both economically and genetically, than would our first model. But opting for "efficiency" in such circumstances is itself a moral decision which carries social costs. For example, under the guise of efficiency it might be expedient to reduce programs which would aid the mentally or physically handicapped. Under some circumstances, a less efficient society might be a more moral one.

The Chinese, for example, have a maxim which calls for raising the material welfare of the entire population -- but only on an egalitarian basis. In the analysis of economist Gurley, to the Chinese, "development is not worth much unless everyone rises together. No one is to be left behind, either economically or socially" (18).

Such a program is likely to be inefficient, and in economic terms, leads to slower improvement than in a capitalist system. In genetic terms, it carries with it the possibility of no net improvement over time. But until we know what such "improvement" might consist of, we cannot take this outcome as disqualifying.

CONCLUSIONS

The United States is not China, and we could not reasonably expect to adopt a completely egalitarian policy and leave the present system intact. But this is no reason for rejecting the moral desirability of such a system, in principle. The practical question for the present which is begged by all discussions of eugenics and intergenerational responsibility,is how ought we to integrate a growing knowledge of human genetic diversity and variability into intragenerational public policy. Responsibilities to those alive now are generally taken to take precedence over responsibilities to generations in the future (19).

I take no comfort from the sometimes heralded finding that there has been a reversal of the presumptive dysgenic effect of larger family sizes in the lower socioeconomic classes. That such a transition itself could be taken to be "eugenic" (cf. 14) bespeaks a narrowness of social view and shallowness of scientific understanding of the complexities of expression of human traits and attributes.

To greet the differential decline of fertility among lower class members of our society as a harbinger of eugenic reform is to risk endorsement of repressive social forces which themselves might be the primary factor in the decline of fertility in the underprivileged. Further, asking for genetic tests of normalcy or social deservedness sets a dangerous precedent. For here, as in the more egregious uses of eugenic justifications for social and political programs, choosing to give weight to a person's genetic worth may mean that we will fail to acknowledge his human worth altogether.

REFERENCES

1. Lerner, I.M., "Genetic Homeostasis," Dover Publications, New York (1970).

2. Layzer, D., Heritability analyses of IQ scores: science or numerology? Science 183:1259 (1974).

3. Haller, M.H., "Eugenics," Rutgers University Press, New Brunswick, New Jersey (1963).

4. Lappé, M., Reflections on the 'cost' of doing science, "Annals of the New York Academy of Sciences (in press).

5. Lappé, M., Can eugenic policy be just? in "The Prevention of Genetic Disease and Mental Retardation," A. Milunsky (ed.), W.B. Saunders Company, Philadelphia, p. 456 (1975).

6. Walzer, M., In defense of equality, Dissent 20:399 (1973).

7. Rawls, J., "A Theory of Justice," Harvard University Press (Belknap), Cambridge (1972).

8. Davenport, C.B., "Heredity in Relation to Eugenics," Henry Holt & Company, New York, p. 267 (1911).

9. Reilly, P., The role of law in the prevention of genetic disease, in "The Prevention of Genetic Disease and Mental Retardation", A. Milunsky (ed.), W.B. Saunders Company, Philadelphia, p. 422 (1975).

10. Gardner, L.I. and Neu, R.L., Evidence linking an extra Y chromosome to sociopathic behavior, Arch. Gen. Psychiat. 26:220 (1972).

11. Zaehner, R.C., "Hinduism," Oxford University Press, London, p. 144 (1962).

12. Gandhi, M.K., "Autobiography -- The Story of My Experiments with Truth," 2nd edition, Ahmedabad Press, New Delhi (1940).

13. Lappe, M., Moral obligations and the fallacies of genetic control, Theological Studies 33:411 (1972).

14. Huxley, J., Eugenics in evoluntionary perspective, Persp. Biol. Med. Winter (1963). Reprinted in The Eugenics Review 54:123 (1962).

15. Eldridge, R., O'Meara, K. and Kitchin, D., Superior intelligence in sighted retinablastoma patients and their families, J. Med. Genet. 9:331 (1972).

16. Dobzhansky, T., Letter to the editor, Scient. Amer. p. 8, (March 1965).

17. Cavalli-Sforza, L.L. and Bodmer, W.F., "The Genetics of Human Populations," W.H. Freeman and Company, San Francisco (1971).

18. Gurley, J., Capitalist and Maoist economic development, Monthly Review p. 15 (February 1971).

19. Golding, M., Our obligations to future generations, UCLA Law Rev. 15:443 (1968).

DISCUSSION

Papers of Prof. S.E. Luria and Drs. S. Callahan and M. Lappé
Moderator: Prof. A.G. Steinberg

E.C. JENKINS: New York State Institute for Basic Research in
Mental Retardation, Staten Island: Prof. Luria, concerning the
ethics of knowledge being balanced by the ethics of innocence -
I take that infliction of suffering by the type of experiments that
are being done - could you define the limits? Are there any limits
to suffering? If there is any suffering at all involved, should
the experiment be discontinued or stopped? Secondly, since grave
differences have been before us and apparently been very poorly
designed in the experiments thus far done, should we drop this or
should someone properly conduct an experiment to finally resolve
this issue.

LURIA: To the first question, it seems to me that the matter
has to be judged in any case between the balance between the certain
or the likely damage and the likely good. The likely damage can
often be measured in terms of social or medical evaluation. The
likely good is often a little bit more difficult to evaluate. But
I suspect in every case one has to have a sensible balance between
the two.

The second question referred to studies on race differences. I
have previously written about my philosophy. Suppose, as a biologist, I were to sit down and write a paper to the effect that
some sort of strange bird had appeared in Boston with three legs.
I do not believe that ornithologists should feel obligated to waste
their time to study non-existent birds. It seems to me the burden
of proof of somebody who claims that something is important is on
the people who make the claims. On the other hand, I do believe
that IQ studies do not fall into that category. IQ falls into the
category of a phenomenon which certainly does exist and I do believe one has to balance the danger of studying this phenomenon with
lots of hullabaloo and the advantages of not studying it and risking
the idea that maybe black people will continue to have lower IQ's.
My tendency would be to abolish the IQ tests altogether. I think
they are a fraud.

R. PARKER: California Institute of Technology, Pasadena: Your
talk left me with one question. Who makes the decisions to balance?
Who balances both sides and who makes the decisions. The scientists
or the geneticists alone do it in conjunction with society? How
are those decisions made?

LURIA: Are you asking me who makes them or who should make them?

PARKER: Who should make them?

LURIA: I think these decisions should not be made by those who make decisions for others, except in the legal sense that you make decisions to prohibit or discourage things that do recognizable harm. That would be my thinking, but I'm not a lawyer.

DAVIS: The general thrust of Prof. Luria's remarks has been so inspiring that I am uncomfortable at raising any questions. On the other hand, Prof. Luria made some statements that seem to me to deserve a little more inquiry, even though the subject of XYY has already had much consideration in earlier sessions.

You made the statement, I believe, that there is solid evidence against any correlation between XYY and criminal behavior. Now, I don't know what correlation means to you, but there seems to be general agreement on a 10 to 20-fold enrichment for XYY in mental-penal institutions, and that would seem to me to be a real correlation. The difficulty is that that finding has led to conclusions going far beyond the correlation: to a lot of nonsense in the press, and to a widespread public misconception that the XYY karyotype has a serious, deterministic consequence. I am sure you and I agree that it would be very desirable to clear up that misconception. We then face the problem of how to do so; and it seems to me that you may be discouraging the necessary studies by your dramatic statement that if one person's life might be blighted, it is not worth getting the knowledge to please the curiosity of some investigator. Would you not agree that there is more at stake than the curiosity of an investigator, and that we have an obligation in the field of genetics to try to clarify public misconceptions? Can you recommend any way of doing it other than an extensive study of the facts about XYY?

LURIA: I agree with the general principle, but I would correct two things. The first one is certainly there is evidence contrary to the existence of a correlation between crime, not between being in a criminal-penal institution. I am not convinced that that is a good way to measure this problem. I think that according to an article that I have read in the "Psychological Bulletin," there is no evidence for the correlation between crime and XYY persons not in penal institutions. I think Prof. Chorover may know more about the subject.

As far as the other matter, I do believe, I was not referring to any special study because I unfortunately have nothing to do with Harvard Medical School. I was not present for any discussion, and I really don't know. I don't want to refer to any study. I do believe, however, that studies which are done in such a way that the individual (especially the children) and the families are provided with information which can create emotional disturbance are not good studies, and as such I would not justify them. If I were on a committee at MIT, I certainly would vote strongly against such a study.

CHOROVER: I'd like to respond briefly to the two previous questions of Prof. Luria. One was the question about who makes decisions and how they ought to be made. It seems to me that the first thing that ought to be taken away from this meeting is a collective awareness that decisions are made and that they are made by a process within society. The question is for us to examine in detail how these decisions are made and to come to some reasoned judgments about how they ought to be made.

The second point relates to the general question which Prof. Davis raised and my response is intended to refer not only to the prohibited subject of XYY. It is very common, for scientists to "deplore" public misunderstanding of what is supposed to be a scientific question when that question comes into the public arena of discussion. Precisely that kind of objection has been raised repeatedly within the intelligence testing community. 'How deplorable', we are repeatedly told, 'that the public does not understand what IQ tests test.' The protest against 'misunderstanding' usually takes the form of insisting that IQ tests are intended to measure IQ not 'intelligence.' The intelligence quotient (or so the argument goes) is not the same thing as intelligence. But it ought to be understood, both with respect to the notion of innate criminality and the notion of native intelligence, that although the authorities are quick to deplore the so-called misinterpretation on the part of the public of what the data are supposed to mean, the fundamental appeal to significance that is made by them when seeking public support for the work they do is predicated on the notion in the first instance that what IQ really is about is how smart people are.

If you read the manuals describing IQ tests, you will find the term "IQ" and "intelligence" as you and I understand it used perfectly interchangeably. When you read the authoritative documents of the people who deplore the misunderstanding of the prohibited subject of XYY, you will very quickly understand that what is supposed to be understood as the significance of that work is its relevance to the problem of 'criminality.' There is no 'public misunderstanding' -- protests to the contrary notwithstanding.

AUTHORIZING DEATH FOR ANOMALOUS NEWBORNS

Robert A. Burt

University of Michigan Law School

I.

Medical technologies that sustain life for otherwise doomed newborns bring special tensions in their wake. These technologies -- fervently welcomed in most cases -- also can prolong life for tragically deformed and limited infants, and this fact presses forward an old question: if, through medical science, life is within our power to maintain, does that mean there are times when we can choose to withhold life?

It may seem ironic that the question of willfully destroying life appears in harness with power to give life. But there is inescapable logic to this complementarity since power to give life necessarily implies capacity to deny it. We may choose never knowingly to exercise life-denying power, but we cannot choose not to think about the fact of that potential power (1).

The new possibilities of fetal genetic screening through amniocentesis emphasize this tension. For the most part, developmental anomalies currently detectably by amniocentesis cannot be corrected (2). This advance in health science offers only one stark choice: either accept that the child-to-be-born will be significantly "defective" or destroy that child, the fetus. The Supreme Court's recent proclamation that the abortion choice, at least in early pregnancy, is the exclusive province of the pregnant woman and her physician (3) fits comfortably with the underlying ethos of this developing technology -- that human choice through medical science can and should control what the gods, uncontrolled and unknowable fate, previously dictated.

The Supreme Court's decision has, I think, dramatically changed the context of current debate about withholding treatment from anomalous newborns. Though the Court was careful to withhold "personhood" from the fetus only in the earliest months of pregnancy, the Court's conclusive resolution of this fervently disputed issue in favor of the mother's rights -- and in utter derogation of any competing rights for the potential newborn -- has already had significant generative impact beyond early pregnancy. In the immediate wake of this decision, pediatricians have been emboldened publicly to proclaim that they regularly withhold treatment from anomalous newborns and, even more significantly, to demand explicit social approbation of these practices.

Duff and Campbell broke the "public and professional silence (as they put it) on a major social taboo" (4). They forthrightly stated that, in the Yale-New Haven Hospital Special-Care Nursery, "discontinuance or withdrawal of treatment" was the special care some gravely deformed babies received. Specifically, this conscious collaborative decision between parents and physicians was the immediate cause of death for 14 percent of the newborns who died (i.e. 43 of 299 deaths) in this nursery between January 1970 and June 1972 (5). In describing the plight of many severely deformed newborns and their families, Duff and Campbell stated that "both treatment and nontreatment constitute unsatisfactory dilemmas for everyone" and they conclude that "if working out these dilemmas in ways such as those we suggest (that is, nontreatment for some) is in violation of the law, we believe the law should be changed" (6).

The recent criminal conviction of Dr. Kenneth Edelin in Boston, for death of a fetus following an apparently lawful abortion, will no doubt prompt many pediatric physicians toward more fervent espousal of Duff and Campbell's proposal that the law must be changed. In a recent article Robertson has amply documented that in the practices described by Duff and Campbell, both parents and physicians are violating a number of criminal law proscriptions in virtually every state (7). Robertson suggests that, for the future, the law in this matter can take one of two directions. Either, he says, "present criminal sanctions should be enforced more fully, or legislation permitting nontreatment should be enacted" (8).

There is another alternative, however, for which I would opt: that is, no change in existing laws, so that decisions to terminate treatment by parents and physicians would continue to carry risks of criminal liability, and that risk would materialize -- as in the Boston case -- occasionally and more or less unpredictably depending on varying policies of local prosecutors, randomly selected local jurors and sentencing judges.

I know that such a soluation will not satisfy physicians who seek social validation of the more problematic aspects of their

professional role as life-dispensers, or those who seek to be freed
from the shadow cast by the Edelin prosecution. But, for reasons
that I will try to develop in this paper, I believe that explicit
and generalized community validation of the physician's death-
dispensing role should be withheld and that the shadow of possible
criminal liability for both parents and physicians should fall
starkly across the path toward decision for withholding treatment
from any anomalous newborn.

Let me anticipate one aspect of my argument here. I do not
think it likely that the Edelin prosecution will lead to a substantial increase in criminal actions for the deaths of anomalous
newborns identified by Duff and Campbell. There would be at least
one reason for this. Newspaper accounts of the Edelin case have
suggested that photographs of the aborted fetus were most strongly
persuasive for the jury in its decision to convict. Photographs of
many of the babies described by Duff and Campbell would undoubtedly
inspire much less than singleminded revulsion at the parents' and
physicians' decisions.

But it seems clear that, unlike in the past, some prosecutions
in some places would occur for these deaths (9). The new forces
massing in outraged reaction to the Supreme Court's abortion decision will probably lead to this result. I would predict throughout the country only a few prosecutions, fewer convictions and
even fewer prison terms in response to the practices discussed by
Duff and Campbell. I personally would not urge more, though my
position in this matter would not give protection against more.

Though I expect some prosecutions of parents and doctors, I
should make clear that I expect treatment will continue to be
withheld from many anomalous newborns for which no criminal liability for parents or physicians will result. As the Duff and Campbell
article makes clear by implication, this is the current tacit legal
arrangement. There is no necessary reason to be surprised at this
situation. Unreported and unsolved crimes are, after all, reasonably common. But for most crimes, complete detection and law enforcement seems at least an acceptable, if always unattainable,
goal. This is not so, I think, for the crimes involved here. I
am prepared, if not to applaud, at least to accept the continued
regime of many ignored law violations when treatment is withheld
from newborns considered anomalous by parents and physicians.

Why, then, am I unwilling to agree with Duff and Campbell that
if their conduct is not invariably to be condemned under the law, it
should be explicitly approved by the law? The basic reason for my
ambivalent stance was given classic formulation almost a century
ago, in a case on which generations of law students have begun
their introduction to the principles and purposes of the criminal
law. In Regina v. Dudley and Stephens, decided in 1884, the de-

fendants were seamen who had been shipwrecked, lost at sea for
20 days and without food for seven days. Finally the defendants
killed a young boy -- a boy who was already, more certainly than
the others, dying of diseases beyond exposure and hunger -- and
the defendants then survived by eating the dead boy's flesh. Lord
Coleridge, the trial judge, refused to accept the defendants' contention that their conduct should be excused under the criminal law.
The judge said this -- which is the heart of the matter for me here:

> It must not be supposed that in refusing to admit
> temptation to be an excuse for crime it is forgotten how
> terrible the temptation was; how awful the suffering;
> how hard in such trials to keep the judgment straight
> and the conduct pure. We are often compelled to set up
> standards we cannot reach ourselves, and to lay down
> rules which we could not ourselves satisfy (10).

Such a position may seem hypocritical, particularly to the
parents and doctors who are bound up in the care of the obviously
and tragically deformed infant. But this double standard -- this
hypocrisy, if it is that -- is necessary to protect us all as
caretakers.

Let me illustrate this by taking a lawyer's prerogative for
a moment, to pose the "next hard case" following those described
by Duff and Campbell. This "next hard case" will come inevitably
from recent developments in fetal diagnosis through amniocentesis.
Assume a pregnant woman over 35 who early in pregnancy asks her physician to perform an amniocentesis to assure that she is not carrying a child with Down syndrome. "If the child will have Down
syndrome" the woman says, "I will abort the fetus now, as is my
constitutional right proclaimed by the Supreme Court." The physician performs amniocentesis and assures the woman that she is not
carrying a Down syndrome baby. But the doctor's diagnosis was in
error; a baby with Down syndrome is born. For this woman, has the
moment of choice irrevocably passed? Is choice restored to her if
-- but only if -- by some turn of fate, the newborn with Down syndrome is suffering from a condition requiring surgery to permit its
survival? This occurred in a widely publicized case at Johns
Hopkins Hospital a few years ago. Parents of a newborn with Down
syndrome refused permission for routine surgery for an intestinal
blockage which, if uncorrected, would lead the baby to starve to
death. After the parents refused, the Johns Hopkins physicians
permitted the baby to die (11).

In the case I have hypothesized, it is easy to construct a
reasoned argument that the physician's error was the cause of the
baby's life, and that error should now be corrected, in justice
to the mother -- and she well might argue that her Supreme Court-
given rights have been infringed. Now consider a lawyer's further

refinement: should the error be corrected only if the doctor was
at fault in his diagnosis, if he was negligent; should, that
is, the question of authorizing death for this newborn be decided
as an aspect of a malpractice suit? Further, if there is a claim
of justice to the mother's position -- and I think there is such a
claim, whatever its weight -- is there not also a claim for mothers
of babies with Down syndrome who have not had equal access to amniocentesis because of their poverty, their race, their ignorance, or
whatever?

This kind of argumentation has a coolly rational quality.
This is inevitably the tone of the discourse that will be carried
out if we enact statutes to govern when treatment may be withheld
from defective newborns, statutes specifying criteria and providing
that judges or hospital review boards with lay and professional
membership should apply these specified criteria. Some might
argue that the examples I was giving were absurd -- that no legislature, no judge, no physician would agree to permitting the death
of an otherwise healthy Down syndrome newborn, that the line between
passive and active euthanasia would never be so breached, and that
withholding treatment from a baby with an intestinal blockage is
radically different from withholding food from a baby already
equipped to digest it.

All this may be so. Nonetheless, it is striking in itself
that we are today seriously debating the propriety of terminating
the lives of some anomalous newborns. A generation ago proposals
for authorizing voluntary euthanasia for terminally ill adults
were met, in part, by assertions that such practices would lead to
euthanasia for defective newborns. Proponents of voluntary euthanasia rejected this argument, in effect, as implausible and wholly
fanciful (12). But it is not accidental that social validation of
willful decisions to withhold life cannot easily be confined. The
reasons for an expansive tendency in these matters are suggested,
first of all, by the cool tone of the discourse I have sketched in
posing these "next hard cases."

Even when we try to draw criteria to authorize withholding
treatment from newborns in a much narrower compass, the same cool-
ness is evident. Robertson, for example, envisions one possible
criterion for withholding treatment: "profoundly retarded, nonam-
bulatory hydrocephalics who are blind and deaf ..." (13). One is
then tempted to ask, what about those only blind? only deaf? and
so on. There is, in short, a bloodless quality about specifying
these criteria in such a visible, articulated way -- a bloodless
quality which begins to obscure the fact that we are engaged in a
very bloody business. We are defining which human beings are
"persons" whose continued life must be cherished and which humans
we are entitled to turn into "non-persons" first by conceptually
removing them from humankind and then acting on that conceptuali-

zation to -- what should the word be? -- "kill" them, "abort" them, "withhold treatment" from them.

We all bear heavy costs, I think, when we engage in this kind of conceptualization. I can only speculate about those costs, their causes and their consequences. (This question should be more closely and systematically researched by students of social psychology.) But my speculations stem from this -- that formal, visibly articulated rules clearly invite those who witness their formulation and application to participate vicariously in those processes. In that vicarious participation, all of us identify, in different degrees and with different conscious awareness, with both the regulated (here the newborn) and the regulators (parents, doctors, judges, special panel). We are led to ask ourselves a variety of questions, trying both to feel what the immediate participants are feeling, and to evaluate the justice of their claims -- questions like, "If I were blind, deaf and profoundly retarded, would my life still be worth living to me?" or "If I were the parent of such a child, would I want not to continue as that parent to that child?"

As we watch, and vicariously participate in, these definitional processes -- asking ourselves, as the question is asked, "Is that a child worth saving?" "Is that a parent worth being?" -- we are defining ourselves as children, as parents, as human beings in our various roles and perspectives. If we say "that blind, deaf, retarded child cannot live, that parent need not remain a parent," I think we are also saying "the part of me that can approximate what it feels like to be blind, deaf, retarded, is a 'dead part,' a part that I am willing to extrude from my definition of myself. That part need not be parented, need not be cared for."

When we find ourselves authorizing death for the deformed, we must also vicariously harden our hearts to the deformities we all feel, circumscribing the range of abnormality we are willing to accept in ourselves. As we do this to ourselves -- as we vicariously authorize terrible punishments (death, that is) for deformities we were earlier willing to tolerate, we are pushing along in barely perceptible steps the internal psychological processes which permit us one day rationally, coolly, bloodlessly, to consider what today seems wildly beyond possibility.

II.

Another aspect must also be considered -- the plight of parents who choose to bear and nurture abnormal children and the plight of the children themselves, in a regime where the children's death would have been validated. We can see this plight by looking further through the eyes of the current regulators, to watch them and us grapple with the implications of insisting for the present that these deformed babies must live. Such an insistence can, I have suggested, represent an empathic identification with the deformed child and a corresponding tolerance and even caretaking acceptance of those parts of ourselves that feel monstrous and deformed. But that posture is hard to maintain consistently and continuously. There are many ways, besides inflicting actual death, of making someone into a "non-person," of "cutting him dead."

Social banishment is one such way. And that is precisely the fate we as a society now provide for vast numbers of deformed children and their families. The most visible aspect of that banishment is our extensive network of state institutions for the mentally retarded. Warehouses for human beings is, if anything, an understated depiction of many, perhaps most, of these large-scale, geographically isolated institutions (14). Our collective willingness as a society to forbid killing these children but then to banish them to a living death in these institutions does not connote an unambivalent identification and loving tolerance of the deformed among us and within us.

The medical profession has actively colluded in these double-faced dealings with deformed children. The institutions for the retarded have been typically administered and staffed, at least at the most publicly visible strata of the administrative hierarchy, by medical doctors, physicians or psychiatrists. The institutions are bureaucratically placed in most states in the Department of Health or of Mental Health. The publicly stated rationale for the existence of these institutions is that these children need special care which the health sciences can provide. The reality of the institutions is that they have offered only custodial, not remedial, services, and that even these custodial services have not been adequate to guard against nightmarish brutality and neglect.

Our public institutions for the mentally retarded epitomize the double-edged role in this society of the medical profession, to which I alluded at the beginning of this paper. The doctors' hallowed role is to heal the sick and thus be custodian of life. The dark underside of this role is to keep sickness away, to take custody of deformities among the living.

From this perspective, current proposals to give physicians explicit authority to end the lives of defective newborns would carry forward the logic of our current policies excluding deformed children from our community. There would be some irony in this. In recent years, those working with the mentally retarded have documented the destructive inappropriateness of institutional placement for most children consigned there, and federal courts in particular have been led by intense advocacy efforts to look directly at our socially-sanctioned brutality in these institutions (15).

All seem agreed, at least in principle, that the proper remedy is to insist on community life for retarded children, to press every effort toward keeping such children living with their families and to provide the families with extensive community support toward realizing the fullest potential for these children (16).

Proposals to authorize withholding treatment from defective newborns cut against the force of social commitment to this course. If there is a socially sanctioned mechanism for ending the lives of deformed infants -- whether that sanction extends to the parents and physicians alone or requires some external approval of their decision -- the question will be insistently posed for every obviously deformed child and his parents: why was this child permitted to live? In individual cases, of course, there will be reasons given, distinctions offered between this child's condition and the others. But this is the cool logic that asks cold-hearted questions and invites us to turn away from all monstrous deformity.

New advances in fetal diagnosis will add a special twist to this attitude. When amniocentesis or its refinements become a regular aspect of obstetric practice, and is extended beyond overage mothers to the general child-bearing population, every Down syndrome child will present these special stigmatizing questions. Every parent of such a child will hear in redoubled intensity the implicit question that each now confronts: why have you inflicted this "monstrosity" on our pleasant and tidy community?

Intensification of this kind of social attitude, in response to new medical technologies to control birth, is regrettably inevitable. The only effective safeguard against intensifying this attitude is to abandon these new diagnostic techniques and efforts through them to increase rational control of our child-bearing futures. Such abandonment of a new technology seems, however, inappropriately self-denying. Our instinctive unwillingness to forego the technology comes, I think, from our deep-rooted communal conviction that mastery of natural forces, through our technology, can be the highest achievement of our rational self-control.

There is truth to this conviction -- much truth but not too much truth. Costs come with each advance in technology. I have suggested earlier in this paper that, for the life-controlling medical technologies, every increment in capacity for rational self-control brings with it corresponding redefinitions of our identities, our subjective sense of what parts of ourselves are tolerably out of control. Because our technologies change the ways in which we look at ourselves, and thus change the context in which our basic values are formulated, it is critical that these changes themselves are brought into high visibility. Otherwise, our claim that human technology increases our capacity for rational self-control is a hollow boast. We can control our technology only if we understand clearly how that technology can act to control us, can take life on its own terms (17).

Ultimately, the proposals for new social mechanisms to regulate whether treatment may be withheld from defective newborns must be evaluated in this broader perspective. That is, do these proposals help us as a society to look clearly at the ways in which these new technological developments themselves are shaping our value perspectives? I am not suggesting that our values must not change in response to these technologies. That would be like the proverbial King Canute commanding the rising tide to recede. I am suggesting, however, that any socially-sanctioned mechanism for responding to these technologies must adequately highlight the fact that they place values in question and that -- at least from our contemporary perspective -- substantial costs will be incurred by altering those values.

Current proposals for giving authority to parents and physicians to withhold treatment obscure these costs. Whether this authority is given outright to parents and physicians, or whether it is made available only on a case-by-case basis by a judicial or panel decision, the same fundamental obscuring will occur -- that is, explicit legitimacy will be given today to actions which, today, still leave most of us deeply uneasy. When treatment is withheld from a defective newborn, its clear advance authorization by socially-sanctioned mechanisms will force us all to be cool and bloodless though the act itself still triggers feelings that are hot and bloody.

III.

The discussion thus far has put greatest stress on the inhumane implications of authorizing death for anomalous newborns. This is, however, only one side of the contemporary argument. There is another side to the argument, that pulls us toward that authorization. That is the aspect Duff and Campbell most recently have brought into public visibility -- that there are terribly, tragically deformed newborns whose lives can be prolonged only by persistent and extensive medical efforts, and whose lives are grievous, even unbearable, burdens to their parents and siblings. The doctors charged with treating these infants, and collaborating closely with their families, must feel how cruel their caretaking efforts appear.

Consider, for example, the terrible plight of the family and child suffering from Tay-Sachs disease, a genetically transmitted disorder peculiarly prevalent among Jews of Eastern European origins (18). This disease is now reliably detectable by amniocentesis during early pregnancy. Neurological damage from the disease

occurs even in the fetus during pregnancy, but the first obvious
symptoms appear in the infant between three and six months.
Neurological deterioration -- leading to blindness, loss of any
motor function, and ultimately insensate existence -- occurs invariably after this, leading in all recorded cases to death by four
to six years of age. There is no known treatment for this disease.
Parents and family are thus condemned to watch as their
child progressively, hopelessly, declines into a vegetative state.
Beginning at an early stage of the disorder, the infant's life can
only be sustained by intensive efforts and increasingly full-time
hospitalization.

I have suggested that authorizing the death of defective
newborns can have stark dehumanizing implications for all of
us. But ignoring the suffering of the parents and other relatives
of such infants can be equally dehumanizing for us. The law must
respond to the reality of this suffering while not obscuring the
full implications of the actions which seeks justification in this
suffering.

The true enormity of these actions to withhold life from newborns, viewed from our contemporary perspective, will remain in
high visibility only if advance social authorization is withheld,
and only if the parents and physicians who wish to take this action
are willing to accept some significant risk that they will suffer by
such action. Their suffering will come in increasing intensity if
criminal prosecution is instituted, if a jury finds them guilty of
unconscionable conduct and if a judge imposes sanctions on them
accordingly. In deciding whether to withhold treatment from the
newborn, the parents and physicians will be led to balance the
suffering imposed on them by the continued life of the child against
the suffering likely from their decision to end the child's life.

This gives no guarantee that every newborn will be kept alive,
no matter what. But choosing this social mechanism for regulating
the decision to withhold treatment does guarantee that the decision-
makers will have powerful incentive to favor the child's continuing
life, to uphold what one court has called "our felt intuition ...
(that even a blind, deaf and dumb infant) would almost surely
choose life with defects as against no life at all" (19). Some
current proposals for law change call for child advocacy by an
attorney, for example, appointed to present the newborn's perspective to a judge empowered to authorize withholding treatment. But
no imaginable formal mechanism for child advocacy could so starkly
press home directly on the decision-maker, as possible criminal
liability, the proposition that ending the child's life may inflict
unjustifiable suffering on him.

IV.

It may seem harsh, particularly to physicians themselves,
that the risk of criminal liability should attach equally to parents and physicians. The doctors, it might be argued, should not
be forced to run the risk of imprisonment for advice or decisions
which laymen later judge to be mistaken. As Robertson has pointed
out, criminal liability can come to the physician if he advises
parents that treatment should be withheld or if, in face of such a
decision by parents, the physician fails to report that decision
to legal authorities before the child's life is ended (20).
Further, because criminal liability will fall only occasionally
and even haphazardly, it may seem even more harsh that doctors
under this regime will be forced to act with great uncertainty
about their ultimate legal status.

But harsh as this legal regime may be for physicians who are
regularly involved in the tragic dilemmas presented by defective
newborns, the possibility of criminal liability for the physician
should remain. All of medical practice does not present these
stark choices between life and death, so much as a matter of course.
Physicians who attend birth -- and particularly those who practice
in the "special-care nurseries" for gravely threatened newborns --
have chosen to emphasize, in their daily practice, the most intense
and even magic-laden aspect of the physician's social role as custodian of life. Because these decisions, dispensing life and by
necessary implication dispensing death, press against our most
basic communal identities, I think it proper that the society impose
an extraordinary burden of care-taking on these physicians.

The possibility of criminal liability should force these physicians to give of themselves, to identify both with the family and
with the newborn child as if the suffering of each were the physicians' own. Professional norms demand that all physicians care for
their patients in this empathic way. But for these stark "special
care" decisions, it seems important and correct that these general
professional norms be reinforced by an added element, that the physician must know if he accepts the withholding of treatment -- if,
that is, he acts on the death-dispensing facet of his professional
role -- he may himself suffer for it.

I am not a physician. I see these matters in my professional
perspective as a lawyer and in my personal perspective as a patient
of physicians. These perspectives have played their roles in my
request here, to physicians, that they accept some of their patients'
suffering as their own, and that they care for us in that way. Many
people have spoken of the physician's god-like role in our society
as if that were a pejorative depiction. But it is not simply that.
That role points to an implicit aspect of the time-honored injunction, "physician, heal thyself" -- that he must feel pain, as his

patients do.

Maintaining the current legal regime will undoubtedly prompt most physicians in most cases to favor prolonging life. But this bias would not, in practical effect, be absolute. A doctor may come to believe that the suffering of those for whom he cares is so great that death is the best care he can offer. In all decency, he and we should come to this decision reluctantly. This legal regime would ensure that much.

I am not suggesting that existing values must not change or that no self-respecting physician would ever or should ever with-hold treatment from a newborn. Rather, I am suggesting that if we are evolving toward new values in this matter, we must do so gradually, hesitantly, and looking backward to what we have been, as often as we look forward to imagine what we will become. Our contemporary values here have been pushed into flux, in significant part, by the Supreme Court's decision in the abortion case. In that case, I think, the Court fell into the fallacy of believing that because a legal-appearing question could be asked, a legal answer should be given. The Court thus disregarded its special function for withholding definitive resolution of fundamental social ethics questions to permit passionately held, irreconcilable views to work toward accommodation over time (21).

The Court, however, has acted. The question whether a poten-tial newborn, early in pregnancy, has an ethical/legal "right to life" has been definitively resolved. The very conclusiveness of that current resolution makes it imperative that legal institutions withhold similarly definitive resolution of questions -- such as the anomalous newborn's "right to life" -- pushed into visibility in the wake of that Court decision. Existing mechanisms for criminal lia-bility are most sensitively attuned to this task. Those mechanisms force physicians and parents to justify withholding treatment only after they have come to this decision unguided, and provide only limited precedential force to any individual justification accepted by any particular prosecutor, jury or judge in a particular time and place. From a multiplicity of these transactions -- parents and physicians deciding, prosecutors, juries, and judges reviewing those decisions -- we will incrementally come toward a new social ethos or repeatedly reassert our old ethos, which will hopefully accommodate the best of what we are and want to be.

Many, I know, will be unpersuaded by my arguments for the virtues of less-than-full enforcement of the criminal law. Clarity in substance and predictability in application is a highly prized value of the legal system and, in particular, of the criminal laws. Actual practice in the criminal justice system frequently falls short of these ideals, but most critics do not applaud these short-comings as I have here. Current examples of these criticisms come

to mind regarding informal police practices in deciding whether to
enforce criminal law proscriptions generally, prosecutorial discretion in plea-bargaining generally, and judicial discretion in
sentencing generally (22).

It can be argued that the competing values drawn into question
by the current relatively haphazard regime in these areas are
neither so incommensurate nor so fundamental as the values in conflict in deciding between life and death for newborn infants. But
for those who remain unpersuaded and committed to the overarching
value of certainty in the criminal law, let me rephrase my argument.
To accept the relatively haphazard application of the criminal laws
regarding treatment of newborns, it is not necessary to agree with
my jurisprudence of the high value of uncertainty. It is enough
to see that certainty of application would require us either to
press enforcement to end all purposeful withholding of treatment
for newborns or to establish that someone in this society has clear
authority to end some infants' lives. I have suggested earlier in
this paper that either stark position involves unacceptable costs.
From this perspective, I would argue that the "middle ground" of
formal criminal law proscription but only occasional application is
not so much a good in itself but rather a position reached as the
best choice among bad choices. Uncertainty, from this perspective,
is not a virtue but a necessity.

V.

I take some professional and personal comfort in ending this
presentation by invoking a case in point decided by a great judge
from our immediate past. Judge Hand, in 1947, was asked to decide
whether an immigrant named Louis Repouille could become a citizen
of this country (23). Our naturalization statute required the
judge to certify that the prospective citizen had conducted himself
as a person "of good moral character" during the five years preceding his citizenship application. Four years before filing his
application, Repouille had deliberately killed his 13 year-old son
by chloroform. Judge Hand explained:

> His reason for this tragic deed was that the child had
> "suffered from birth from a brain injury which destined
> him to be an idiot and a physical monstrosity malformed
> in all four limbs." The child was blind, mute, and
> deformed. He had to be fed; the movements of his bladder
> and bowels were involuntary, and his entire life was
> spent in a small crib. Repouille had four other children
> at the time towards whom he has always been a dutiful and
> responsible parent (24).

The government opposed citizenship for Repouille, contending

that his act demonstrated he was not a person "of good moral
character." Judge Hand acknowledged that Repouille's act violated
the criminal law. He had, in fact, been convicted of manslaughter,
though the jury recommended "utmost clemency" and the trial judge
placed him on probation without imprisonment. But Judge Hand refused to conclude that Repouille's act was immoral simply because
it violated the criminal law. The judge stated:

> Many people -- probably most people -- do
> not make it a final ethical test of conduct that
> it shall not violate law; few of us exact of our-
> selves or of others the unflinching obedience of a
> Socrates (25).

Nonetheless, Judge Hand refused to find that Repouille's act
was moral. The question of euthanasia, he said, in effect, is
deeply unsettling and unsettled in this society. As judges, Hand
concluded, we are "left at large." Accordingly "the outcome
must needs be tentative; and not much is gained by discussion"
(26). Thus the judge was willing neither to condemn Repouille's
act as immoral nor to condone it as moral.

But still he was required to decide the case; would Repouille
qualify or not as a citizen? Judge Hand found relieved refuge in
the terms of the naturalization statute, that proof must be offered
for the moral character of the applicant only during the preceding
five years. Repouille had asked to become a citizen four years
after killing his son. But when Judge Hand decided the case, this
five year statutory period had elapsed. Hand explicitly invited
Repouille to submit a new citizenship petition, which would not
require any formal state judgement regarding the morality of his
act. And thus, Hand concluded, "the pitiable event, now long
passed, will not prevent Repouille from taking his place among us as
a citizen" (27).

The passage of time, and the naturalization statute's reliance
on the healing qualities of time, permitted Judge Hand to carry out
this basic ethical precept in considering euthanasia of grossly
deformed children -- that "the outcome must needs be tentative;
and not much is gained by discussion." I would amend his statement
only slightly -- that much may be gained by continued discussion
over time, but no amount of contemporary discussion will bring us
to a comfortably definitive resolution today on this question.
Only the passage of time, and debate by many people in many forums
with many differing perspectives will ultimately move us toward
resolution or, perhaps, toward accepting continued irresolution.

This time-consuming process does not diminish current anxieties,
and in its course many people will undoubtedly suffer grievously.
From their individual perspectives, many will feel or appear arbi-

trarily and unjustly victimized -- whether they are parents forced
to accept and nurture a child beyond their capacities to love;
whether they are physicians criminally prosecuted for acting from
compassion for some of their patients; whether they are children
whose lives are ended though others similarly afflicted still live.
But for all its uncertainties, there is a larger social logic to
permitting the unfolding of this process over time. In this way,
we as a society can progressively, slowly, carefully come to terms
with the implications of our technology without giving our collective
identities over to the unexamined imperatives of that technology.

REFERENCES

1. See Freud, A., The doctor-patient relationship, in "Experimen-
    tation with Human Beings," J. Katz, (ed.), p. 643, Russell Sage
    Foundation, New York (1972); Callahan, D., "The Tyranny of
    Survival," p. 230, Macmillan, New York (1973).

2. Friedman, J., Legal implications of amniocentesis, Univ. Penn.
    Law Rev. 123:92, 93 (1974).

3. Roe v. Wade, 410 U.S. 113 (1973).

4. Duff, R.S. and Campbell, A.G.M., Moral and ethical dilemmas
    in the special-care nursery, New Eng. J. Med. 289:890 (1973.

5. Id. at p. 891.

6. Id. at p. 894.

7. Robertson, J., Involuntary euthanasia of defective newborns:
    A legal analysis, Stanford Law Rev. 27:213 (1975).

8. Id. at p. 217.

9. See id. at p. 243.

10. Regina v. Dudley and Stephens, 14 Queens Bench Division 273
    (1884).

11. Duff and Campbell report that, in their special-care nursery,
    an infant with Down syndrome was similarly permitted to die.
    See op. cit. supra note 4, at p. 891.

12. Kamisar, Y., Some non-religious views against proposed "mercy-
    killing" legislation, Minn. Law Rev. 42:969, 1014 (1958).

13. Op. cit. supra n. 7, at p. 267.

14. See the conditions described by the visibly shocked Federal
    judges in N.Y. State Asso. for Retarded Children v. Rockefeller,
    357 Federal Supplement 752 (Eastern District, NY 1973) and
    Wyatt v. Stickney, 344 Federal Supplement 387 (Middle District,
    Alabama, 1972).

15. See ibid.

16. See, e.g., Nicholas Hobbs (ed.), "The Futures of Children,"
    Jossey-Bass Publishers, San Francisco (1975).

17. Compare Burt, R., Reflections on the Detroit psychosurgery case:
    Why we should keep prisoners from the doctors, Hastings Cntr.
    Rep. 5:25, 34 (1975).

18. See Report of Committee for the Study of Inborn Errors of
    Metabolism, Division of Medical Sciences, National Research
    Council, Chapter 6, Section 2 (1975).

19. Gleitman v. Cosgrove, 49 N.J. 22, 227 A.2d 689, 693 (1967).

20. Op. cit. supra note 7, at pp. 230-35

21. See Bickel, A.M., "The Least Dangerous Branch," Bobbs-Merrill,
    Indianapolis (1962).

22. See Goldstein, J., Police Discretion Not to Invoke the Criminal
    Process, in "Crime, Law and Society," A, Goldstein and J.
    Goldstein (eds.), The Free Press, New York (1971); Morris, N.,
    "The Future of Imprisonment," p. 45, University of Chicago Press,
    Chicago (1974); Gaylin, W., "Partial Justice: A Study of Bias
    in Sentencing," Knopf, A.A., New York (1974).

23. Repouille v. United States, 165 F.2d 152 (2d Circuit, 1947).

24. Ibid.

25. Id. at p. 153.

26. Ibid.

27. Id. at p. 154.

DISCRETIONARY NON-TREATMENT OF DEFECTIVE NEWBORNS

John A. Robertson

University of Wisconsin Law School

Developments during the last decade in neonatal intensive care have drastically cut the infant mortality rate in the United States, and assured the survival of many infants who formerly would have died. Among the survivors are infants with spina bifida, Down's syndrome, hydrocephalus and a variety of other congenital and genetic defects which substantially impair the infant's capacity for full physical and social interaction. The reduction of neonatal death has thus starkly raised the question of whether the expected quality of life should influence treatment decisions, and whether intensive care resources may be withdrawn from newborns with minimal potential for a meaningful existence.

Among physicians, ethicists, lawyers, and others thinking about these questions, there appears to be a growing consensus that parents and physicians are socially and morally justified in selecting certain infants for non-treatment and an early death. Although proponents of this view recognize its conflict with principles of equality and respect for persons, and are uncomfortable in having to make this choice, they feel that parents and physicians should have the freedom to decide against the life of a child who has minimal capacity for human interactions. They cite the physical and social pain and suffering the child with grave physical and mental deficits will experience; the financial, psychic, and social costs to the family of having to care for an unwanted defective newborn; and finally, the high cost-benefit ratio, where the benefits appear so minimal and the costs so great. Given the unfortunate circumstances of the newborn, and the great drain on resources involved in maintaining the child's most marginal existence, many persons, with deep compassion and understanding, conclude that non-

treatment is justified in the interests of the child, the family,
and society.

    If the question were solely one of ethics, the debate might
very well end once all arguments were canvassed, and one reached a
considered judgment concerning standards to guide his own practices
and moral judgments. Those who differed would be free to decide
according to their own views of the morality of non-treatment.
Like the question of abortion during the first two trimesters, the
decision would be left to the privacy of parents and physicians,
to decide as they saw best in accordance with their own situations.
But we are not so secular a society that law and morals are irrevocably severed. Proponents of either position tend to seek legal
support for their views, thus raising the entirely separate set of
considerations that enter when the wisdom of enacting moral prescriptions into law is considered. The defective newborn situation,
however, does not need anyone to invite the law in. Although participants in the dilemma have largely ignored the law, the fact
is that the law is already there, looming large, with clear admoni-
tions and limitations on permissible action, backed with threats
for non-compliance. Indeed, the main problem for many who have
personally resolved the ethical issues may be to disinvite legal
intervention altogether. As Lorber recently put it, "Keep the law
out--we have done very well without it" (1).

    The need to disinvite the law arises because the law's pro-
tection of human life extends to defective newborns as well as
normal healthy adults. Under traditional principles of criminal
law, parents, physicians, nurses, supervisors, consultants, hospital administrators and the hospital itself, despite benevolent
motivations, are committing crimes that may include murder, manslaughter, child abuse, neglect, or conspiracy when they withhold
ordinary medical care which leads either to injury or death of the
newborn. The principles upon which liability are based may be
briefly summarized (2). The defective newborn, who is alive and
fully separate from the mother, is in the eyes of the law a person
with legal rights, the subject of legal duties, and fully protected
by the criminal and civil law. If another person has a legal duty
to care for or treat the child, and his failure to do so causes its
death,   he is   guilty of homicide by omission, the degree of homicide (first or second degree murder or manslaughter) dependent on
the amount of premeditation and intention. Parents by law in every
state have a legal duty to provide medical care to their children.
Physicians who undertake to care for them also have a legal duty
based on contract or their undertaking to care for them, a duty
which neither the parents nor physician may terminate if it will
jeopardize the life or health of the child. Nurses also have legal
duties of care to patients, again which cannot be abrogated by
parents or superiors, to the detriment of their patient. Hospital
supervisors, administrators, and the hospital itself also undertake
or contract to care for and protect patients, and if they knowingly

or grossly negligently acquiesce in parental or physician decision
of non-treatment, also may commit homicide by omission. While the
legal duty in many cases will require direct intervention to save
the child's life, in other cases it may be fulfilled by reporting
the case to public authorities specified in child abuse reporting
statutes. In any case, failure to take this minimal step could
lead to criminal liability for violation of those laws, neglect,
or even homicide. Advising or recommending various alternatives to
the parents may implicate one in a conspiracy to commit homicide
by omission, or lead to liability as an accessory.

While no parent or physician has yet been prosecuted for withholding care from a defective newborn (there have been prosecutions
for active killing of defectives), and the basis of liability may
appear overly technical or theoretical, one cannot safely counsel
parents, physicians and others to ignore the law. The recent
prosecution of Dr. Kenneth Edelin for omitting care for an allegedly
viable abortus was based on a similar theory in circumstances that
few thought could ever lead to prosecution. Constituent demands,
political motives, or moral zeal could lead prosecutors to file
charges, if only to clarify the law. Thus while physicians,
parents and others may decide that they are willing to risk prosecution, such a position may entail risks.

For physicians and hospitals unwilling to risk prosecution or
concerned with observance of the law, they are faced with several
alternatives none of which may seem an optimal solution to the
dilemma facing parents of defective newborns. First, physicians
caring for defective newborns could inform parents that criminal
liability may attach to a non-treatment decision, and that even
if the parents do not wish to keep the child, they are legally
obligated, at least until parental obligations are formally terminated, to provide it with medical care. If the parents insist on
risking prosecution, the physician might then inform them that he
is legally obligated to take steps toward saving the infant. In
some jurisdictions it would be sufficient to report the matter to
the child welfare or other authorities prescribed in the child abuse
reporting laws; in others the physician or the hospital might have
to initiate neglect proceedings. The parents cannot terminate the
physician's legal duties by withholding consent or even by discharg-
ing him. The law does not permit a physician to avoid criminal
liability by submitting to the wishes of the parents and doing nothing if this will lead to injury or death of his patient.

To avoid liability hospitals could adopt rules prohibiting
medical staff from not treating defective newborns, or at least,
for following certain procedures when faced with those decisions.
The procedure could include reporting such cases to hospital authorities who would then seek a judicial ruling authorizing treatment. Resort to judicial approval, however burdensome and painful

in this situation, would perform several useful functions. It shields parents, physicians, nurses, and hospitals from criminal liability; passes the burden of a difficult decision to an impartial decision-maker whose socially assigned role is to make such judgments; and provides an opportunity to test or challenge the law before rather than after criminal prosecution. If a court rules in favor of treatment, this decision could be appealed to state appellate courts, which could define more precisely the duties involved, and conceivably permit non-treatment in specific cases.

Although physicians and hospitals may be able to avoid criminal liability in this way, few would agree that a judicial ruling is an ideal solution. As has occurred in the several cases seeking judicial authority for treatment which have reached the courts, the chances are great that the courts will rule for treatment. Adherence to the law is thus likely to lead to non-selection decisions in most cases, with parents left with the care and custody of the unwanted defective newborn, or if parental custody or guardianship is terminated, with the child institutionalized at state expense.

EVALUATION OF LEGAL POLICY

Many persons who have struggled with the dilemma of caring for abnormal newborns, as well as those who coolly examine the expenditures involved, find the legal situation of parents and physicians in the neonatal intensive care intolerable. They would agree with Duff and Campbell who, in reporting cases of 43 infants allowed to die in the Yale-New Haven Pediatric I.C.U., argue that "if working out these dilemmas in ways we suggest is in violation of the law ... the law should be changed" (3). With Lorber and others, they presumably would grant parents and physicians the final discretion to decide whether a defective infant should be treated, and hence live or die:

> We believe the burdens of decision-making must be borne by families and their professional advisors because they are most familiar with the respective situations. Since families primarily must live with and are most affected by the decision, it therefore appears that society and the health professions should provide only general guidelines for decision-making. Moreover, since variations between situations are so great, and the situations themselves so complex, it follows that much latitude in decision-making should be expected and tolerated (4).

The proposal I want to examine is whether in fact it is wise social policy to allow those "most familiar with the respective situations (of families and professional advisors) ... much latitude

in decision-making." What are the implications of such a policy?
What consequences would flow from it? Should there be no limits
on parental decision-making? What limits would be desirable? More
specifically, I want to address the relative merits of alternative
ways in which the law may be disinvited from the neonatal intensive
care unit, that is to say, ways in which parents and their advisors
can be granted a sphere of autonomy in deciding the question of
treatment. This inquiry necessarily raises the question of the
impact which alternative legal devices authorizing the death of
one class of persons, whether for their benefit or the benefit of
others, would have on social policy toward non-infant defectives,
the institutionalized, the elderly, and physically disabled as well
as on our general attitudes toward life and the equality before the
law of all persons. Because law plays a major role in forming our
social and moral judgments, a legal change in the direction of permitting some persons to decide the death of others is a weighty
step, to be made only after careful consideration of its implications.

JUSTIFICATIONS FOR IDENTIFYING A NON-TREATMENT CLASS

The view that parents and their advisors should be given wide
latitude in the treatment decision necessarily rests on the assumption that there is a definable class of human offspring, such as
defective newborns, from whom ordinary medical care may be justifiably withheld, for it is not asserted that parents should have
this authority with regard to all infants. When the law authorizes
non-treatment decisions, it is taking the position that some lives
are less worthy of protection of the law than others. How can such
a radical departure from principles of respect for persons and
equal protection be justified?

One common justification is that non-treatment is in the best
interests of the child, who faces a painful life of psychosocial
handicap, and that parents and physicians are simply making the
choice which the child would make in this situation if able to
formulate and express a preference. The Sonoma Valley Conference
(5) for example, concluded that treatment may be withheld if

> in the context of certain irremediable life conditions, inten-
> sive care therapy appears harmful. These conditions are iden-
> tified ... as inability to survive infancy, inability to
> live without severe pain, and inability to participate,
> at least minimally, in human experience.

Treatment is viewed as harmful to the patient in those situations
because a reasonable person faced with those prospects would prefer
non-treatment and an early death.

An approach based solely on the best interests of the infant
is certainly preferable to one based on the needs of others, for it
adheres to the basic principle that no identified person should be
sacrificed to advance the interests of others. It is, however,
difficult to ascertain the child's best interests. The danger is
judging the infant's situation from the perspective of normal adults who were suddenly deprived of their capacities, rather than
from the perspective of one with no alternative but death. Even
if a reasonable person facing irremediable pain or minimal participation in the affairs of life might find treatment harmful, we
cannot be sure that one less well-endowed and experienced, would.
What appears to be a fate worse than death to a healthy, normal
adult, may be tolerable or a source of pleasure to one who has
never known those capacities. Curiously, proponents of non-treatment have not attempted to dispel the charge of egocentrism by asking defective children who have survived to adolescence or adulthood
whether they find their lives worse than death, and whether they
would have preferred non-treatment. The tendency to project our
own fears and needs on someone who is not similarly situated should
make one careful about advancing this justification for non-treatment.

A second justification for identifying a class not to be
treated is the burden which survival of defective newborns imposes
on families. This includes medical and special care expenses,
marital disruption, depression, neglect of siblings, and other
manifestations of familial pathology. In particular circumstances
each of these consequences may indeed occur, but their frequency
is unclear, and their occurrence perhaps preventable. Care may be
very expensive, and in the absence of adequate insurance coverage,
may drain a family's resources. But several federal programs provide
funds to families of defective newborns, and of course at many
income levels and consumption patterns, the cost of care is tolerable.

Nor is the extent to which the survival of a defective child
causes intra-family suffering clear. Parents and siblings will
face serious adjustments in self-esteem and social roles, but
these may be surmountable. Hunt (6) in interviews with 77 families
with children treated for myelomeningocele found only 6 cases of
broken marriage, with most families willing to make great efforts
and sacrifices for the child's sake. Similarly, a survey of
1,172 American spina bifida parents (46% response rate), albeit
equivocal, found that most parents are still in favor of treating
spina bifida babies (7). While further research is needed, these
studies do not suggest that survival of the defective child is always an unmitigated disaster for the family.

Even if the psychic and financial burdens of families were
substantial, it would not follow that the only feasible solution

is selection for non-treatment. More generous public support
for such families, including counseling assistance, could relieve
some of the burdens. Moreover, most jurisdictions have statutory
procedures through which parents may terminate their obligations
to care for and support a child, and transfer custody and guardianship to the state. While the termination alternative is no panacea
and poses problems in need of further research, it is surprising
how seldom it is mentioned in discussions of defective newborns.
For it does relieve the family of burdens which perhaps rightfully
the family ought not have to bear, while maintaining the state's
commitment to life.

If the burdens on parents can be limited or eliminated altogether, as through termination procedures, one may still justify
non-treatment on the ground that scarce resources, which could be
put to better use elsewhere, would be consumed in keeping defective
newborns alive at state expense. The same charge can, of course,
be made against all social programs providing services to the disabled, elderly, and institutionalized, and it is difficult to see
anomalous newborns as a distinct class. At the present time,
however, we are not in a position to assess this claim, for the
total resources consumed by defectives are not known, and by all
indications, are but a small portion of the health budget. Moreover, we cannot be certain that reallocation of these resources
would produce greater utility than now is achieved in treatment.
A clear trade-off between treating defective newborns and research
that would save normal lives would be a strong case for diverting
resources from defectives, but at the moment there is no certainty
as to either the size or existence of such a trade-off.

These justifications for non-treatment are suspect for a
further reason -- the difficulty of prediction in the first hours
after birth. In most instances parents must decide shortly after
birth whether to permit physicians to close the lesion of a myelomeningocele baby, to correct duodenal atresia in Down's syndrome,
or to shunt a hydrocephalic. A non-treatment decision at that
juncture assumes that enough information about an infant's deficits,
its chances in life, and the impact on the family are then known
to predict reliably the quality of its life several years hence,
as well as the potential impact on family and society. Physicians,
however, sharply disagree as to the predictive value of certain
physical indicators. Ames and Schut (8), for example, found that
infants who in Lorber's clinic would have been selected for non-
treatment do quite well when treated in theirs. Raimondi, a Chicago neurosurgeon who treats spina bifida, finds that it takes
about three weeks even to gather and assess complete data about
the infant's deficits (9). Predictions as to impact on family
also are generally made when the parents are most distraught about
the defective birth, and hence most unreliable about future effects.
While some of the difficulties of prediction could be eliminated

by making the non-treatment decision at a later point in time,
there will always be a potential for mistake.

While the justifications for non-treatment often appear
questionable, and may lead to mistakes, the policy itself of identifying a class of persons who are not entitled to the right to
life held by others may also be questioned. Such a policy estab-
lishes the principle that rights may be allocated according to
physical and mental characteristics, assessments of social utility,
or general usefulness to society. Such a principle clashes with
basic legal and cultural values of the equality of all persons,
whatever their natural endowments, before the law, and denigrates
the respect for persons generally accorded by society. Moreover,
it becomes a precedent for allocating rights by questionable standards of social utility, and may be the first step on to a slippery
slope the bottom of which threatens the security and personality
of all persons. Caring for defective newborns, on the other hand,
reinforces societal commitment to values of life, equality, and
the non-allocation of rights by meritocratic or other discriminatory
principles and thus produces respect for the life and moral equality
of all persons.

EVALUATION OF ALTERNATIVE DECISION PROCESSES FOR SELECTION FOR NON-TREATMENT

Despite the substantial costs flowing from identification of
a class of infants who are selected for non-treatment, many persons
might still reasonably conclude that the costs of treating all defective newborns is not worth the benefits of treatment and therefore should not be required. While they will differ as to which
situations justify non-treatment, and perhaps limit the practice
to a few extreme cases, they accept in principle a policy of
selection for non-treatment. The important question then for social and legal policy is the circumstances and process by which non-
treatment decisions are to be made. Since as Calabrese has said,
(10) "any process or system for choosing among lives has external
costs associated with the use of that process," it seems essential
that if non-treatment decisions are to be made, that they impose
the fewest external costs possible. Otherwise we risk creating
a non-treatment policy, the total costs of which are greater than
those of treatment, when the original justification for non-treatment was that it was the less costly method of resolving a tragic
dilemma.

Three types of costs associated with the decision for non-
treatment are relevant in evaluating alternative decision processes.
One cost is the frequency with which non-treatment decisions will
extend to infants from whom treatment cannot be justifiably withheld. The cost here is the loss or impairment of lives that most

people would want to be protected, even if non-treatment is permitted in other cases, because the disabilities involved will
neither prevent a meaningful life nor consume excessive resources.
Depending on the decision process, non-treatment decisions will
be more or less likely to include normal infants (because of mistake), or handicapped infants for whom non-treatment is hard to
justify (paraplegics with 150 I.Q.'s).

A second cost is the inequality and lessened respect for
persons which a social policy of involuntary euthanasia necessarily
implies. Depending again on the decision process invoked, non-
treatment will in varying degrees become a precedent that extends
involuntary euthanasia to other groups; encourages allocation of
rights by criteria of social worth; diminishes respect for life
generally; affects one's sense of personal worth and security; and
denigrates or causes suffering to present and future handicapped
or institutionalized persons.

A third set of costs, transactions costs, includes the time,
resources, and suffering involved in making non-treatment decisions.
Some decision processes will require more involvement of parents,
physicians, hospital officials, and societal institutions than
others. Some might require direct cash outlays, as in retaining
lawyers to present the case to a court; or considerable time, as in
a committee process; or considerable psychic strain, as when parents
may be required to wait a month before making a final decision.

However speculative and intangible these costs may be, the
directness and openness of the decision process will largely determine their importance. If official agencies of the state become
directly involved in the decision not to treat, then these costs
are likely to be very high, because the state will then be directly
involved in taking one life for the benefit of others. On the other
hand, complex control devices like the market or tort liability
system that would balance present versus future lives and still
put no one in the position of clearly deciding against individual
lives, may have many fewer costs, even if the same number of non-
treatment decisions is made. To minimize the costs then of deciding for one human life over another, it is essential, to quote
Calabrese again, to "create structures such that the lives are
taken before a judicial sentencing to death can occur" (11).

If, to avoid the costs of a formal decision process a less
open one is selected, a major difficulty now arises, for covert or
low visibility decisions increase the chance of discrimination and
arbitrariness, and enhance the risk that unacceptable treatment
decisions will result. The less open, the more indirect and private
the system, the more chance for abuse, partiality, and failure to
consider all relevant information. Policy seems caught between the
Syclla of governmental taking of life, and the Charybdis of roughly

exercised private discretion.

Let us examine this problem more closely in the context of four alternative ways of dealing with the present law, all of which illustrate the variability of and need to minimize the external costs of selection for non-treatment. The first alternative, recommended by Duff, Campbell, Lorber, and many others, would give parents and physicians broad discretion not to treat defective newborns. This approach would relieve parents and physicians of the risk of criminal prosecution, and enable them to make their decisions independent of the law. While the transaction costs are lower than any other alternative, costs of the first two types are high, since parents and physicians have total discretion through non-treatment to decide the fate of any infant. The risk would be great that infants whom we do not justifiably think should die would be selected for non-treatment, because nothing in the process assures that parental discretion will be carefully exercised. Parents and physicians are likely to continue to decide against treatment without full information, or an impartial evaluation of all relevant data, at a time when they are overcome with the emotional shock of the defective birth. Infants with minor defects, or with major defects which can be accommodated, will fall prey to parental prejudices and perceptions of familial suffering, which may have little support in fact.

The only safeguard or check on this decision would be the physician, who could seek legal authority for treatment if the parents refused. But whether he would depends on his attitudes, needs, relation to parents, views about disabilities and the like. The widespread tendency of many physicians, for example, to misunderstand Down's syndrome and recommend non-treatment, confirmed recently in Todres' survey of Massachusetts pediatricians which showed that 50% would not treat a Down's baby for duodenal atresia, does not inspire confidence in the physician as a check on arbitrary ill-informed parental decisions (12).

This approach would also be costly in terms of diminished respect for life. Since parents cannot now legally make non-treatment decisions, authorizing such decisions requires legislative or judicial action. Statutory authorization, however, might be unconstitutional as a violation of equal protection or deprivation of life without due process of law (13). Assuming that a statutory formulation can be developed that would pass constitutional muster, it would still represent adoption by the state of a policy that denigrated life generally, and the worth of the less productive in particular. Non-treatment authority would also lead easily to active euthanasia, as already appears to be the case in some neonatal units.

A second alternative would minimize the risks of mistakes and non-justified decisions by limiting non-treatment discretion to specified classes of defects, identified by clinical indicators associated with a prognosis deemed socially unacceptable. If non-treatment authority extended only to these specified classes, the risk of unacceptable decisions would be greatly reduced. By definition non-treatment could occur only where a societal consensus found that non-treatment was justified. However, some mistakes would still occur. The clinical indicators may be difficult to formulate and may not be reliable predictors, because social responses, so central to the quality of life of the disabled, may not be constant. The criteria may also be loosely applied, and may not be responsive to new developments in medicine.

Applying the criteria in particular cases need not entail substantial transaction costs, except in close cases where a more neutral judge of their applicability than the attending physician, would be desirable. The greatest cost under this model would be its diminution of governmental respect for persons. Unlike the first model, the state, either through direct legislative enactment of criteria or delegation of the task to the medical profession would be explicitly defining a class of citizens unworthy of the protection of the law, thus diluting the equality and respect for life to which the state is generally committed. Many persons would find this a serious cost, dangerously close to an explicit taking of life for the sake of others.

A third model of decision making would give the non-treatment decision to an impartial third-party, such as a court or a review committee. Non-treatment could occur only if the committee concurred with the decision of the parents and attending physicians. The advantage in this process is the likelihood of a detached, careful review of all relevant information by a group that more nearly approximates than do the parents alone societal consensus as to the propriety of non-treatment, and thus reduces the risk of unjustified non-treatment decisions. This risk would be further lessened if the decision-maker adopted and applied explicit criteria of non-treatment.

Transaction costs here unlike the first two models, might be considerable. Committees must be organized, procedures developed, and meetings held. Simply deciding who should sit on such a body, and assuring its availability to every hospital or neonatal unit will be a massive task. Individual decisions may also be onerous, depending on the review process established, the amount of evidence considered, and whether elements of due process are to be accorded the infant.

Formally designating an impartial decision-maker to approve non-treatment decisions also exacts a price in respect for life. Again, the state becomes implicated in relative assessments of life and explicitly or implicitly deviates from its commitment to the sanctity of all persons. State involvement is, of course, clearest where an organ of the state, such as a court, is making the non-treatment decision. But it occurs also when a review committee is established legislatively, or when legislatures or courts give validity to review processes which the medical profession itself develops.

A fourth model of decision-making is the present system of formal illegality, and through prosecutional decisions not to pro-secute, informal delegation to parents and physicians of discretion to make these decisions. Since the law formally condemns non-treat-ment, formal commitment to life and equality before the law is main-tained. Two substantial costs remain. One is the risk of arbitrary or abusive non-treatment decisions, and hence unjustifiable deaths. This risk is probably not as great as in the first alternative, because the unknown risk of prosecution might assure that treatment is not egregiously withheld. Physicians, for example, might be more cautious in acquiescing in parental decisions not to treat Down's syndrome, once it becomes known that they may be prosecuted. More unjustified deaths, however, are likely to occur than if expli-cit criteria guided the selection process.

A second set of costs involves the unequal treatment of some parents and physicians inevitable in a system of highly selective prosecution. While few prosecutors are likely to bring charges in cases where non-treatment appears clearly justified, there will be many unclear cases. It is likely at some point that parents and possibly physicians will be prosecuted in circumstances in which others have not been. While the risk of arbitrary or selec-tive prosecution may be minimal and not lead to conviction or sig-nificant penalties, it remains a cost of this approach, and should not be ignored by policy-makers.

CONCLUSION

What choice among these four alternatives should be made? The decision will depend on whether society finds the danger of the unstructured discretion of parents and physicians to be greater than the dangers of direct governmental involvement in the taking of life to benefit others (14), discounted by the greater accuracy of formal processes of selection for non-treatment. No one of course can answer that question -- it requires more research, analysis, experience, and the cleansing rays of public debate.

If Calabrese's point is valid that a complex structuring of the taking of life imposes the fewest costs, then we should consider whether the fourth model, the least formal and most indirect of all, might be preferable, despite the uncertain risk of prosecution.

If we were reasonably sure that parents and physicians would make roughly the same decisions that would occur in a system of decision criteria or formally designated decision-makers, we could retain the societal commitment to respect for persons by relying on the present system. Prosecutions would be very rare, and might not occur at all, since presumably physicians would not allow parental choice to dominate in questionable cases.

The chief risk -- that of erroneous decisions -- would be minimized if the physician reliably reviewed parental decisions. The physician should be more detached than the parents, and if equipped to think carefully about all relevant issues, could effectively screen out improper parental decisions either through further discussion with the parents, or by initiating judicial intervention. How reliable is the physician? Can he serve as a proxy for societal interests? Will not the rush of business, his own views and biases, and inadequate information lead him to concur in clearly wrong cases? Without a systematic evaluation of physician behavior in ethical dilemmas we do not know, though past experience raises considerable doubts as to whether physicians are well equipped to make ethical choices. We would feel more confident in the physician's capacity to assess non-medical factors if physicians did receive ethical training, or at least were accustomed to convene ethical conferences to work through difficult ethical issues in a systematic way. But no existing mechanism assures that this will occur, and the ethical training of physicians, though increasing, leaves much to be desired.

Medical expertise does not, of course, include the ability to weigh conflicting interests and values, nor to ascertain the relative value of life at various costs in resources. In practice, however, such decisions are often given to physicians, and if we were assured of their capacity to weigh them properly might feel secure doing so here. Absent renewed confidence in the physician's capacity to be society's proxy, however, it is likely that courts and legislatures will increasingly review the decisions of parents and physicians regarding treatment of defective newborns. A few authoritative rulings by the courts may clarify the rules sufficiently to minimize the external costs associated with formal sanctioning of non-treatment.

This analysis can only leave persons struggling with the dilemma of the defective newborn uncomfortable, particularly if they are sensitive to the consequences of formal state approval of non-treatment. Changes in existing law have costs, which appear to increase as the law attempts to confine discretion. Informally granting physicians and parents this authority, however, leaves them vulnerable to discriminatory prosecution, or risks leaving some infants unjustifiably to die.

The current situation can be tolerated only if, on the whole, treatment is desirable, and parents where they wish, can be relieved of the burden they find in the care and nuturing of the severely defective. Those who would deviate from the traditional notions of the equality and respect accorded all persons should properly have the burden of showing that compelling state interests require such a step -- that the costs of non-treatment are clearly worth its returns. At the present time we may reasonably conclude that they have not yet met their burden, and that existing legal arrangements enhance respect for the lives and rights of all persons at a price that society might very wisely pay.

REFERENCES

1. Statement at the New York University Medical Center Conference on Spina Bifida, Skytop, PA., May 6, 1975.

2. For a more complete analysis, see Robertson, J., Involuntary euthanasia of defective newborns: A legal analysis, Stanford Law Rev. 27:213 (1975).

3. Duff, R.S. and Campbell, A.G.M., Moral and ethical dilemmas in the special care nursery, New Eng. J. Med. 289:890 (1973).

4. Ibid.

5. Jonsen, A.R., Phibbs, R.H., Tooley, W.H. et al, Issues in newborn intensive care: A conference report and policy proposal, Pediatrics 55:756 (1975).

6. Hunt, G., Implications for the treatment of myelomeningocele for the child and his family, Lancet 2:1308 (1973).

7. Unpublished study by Chester Swinyard, et al.

8. Ames, M.D. and Schut, L., Results of treatment of 171 consecutive myelomeningoceles, 1963 to 1968, Pediatrics 50:466 (1972).

9. Statement at the New York University Medical Center Conference on Spina Bifida, Skytop, Pa., May 6, 1975.

10. Calabrese, G., Commentary, in "Ethics of Health Care, L. Tan-crecli (ed.), Vol. 55 (1975).

11. Id. at 53.

12. Statement at the New York University Medical Center Conference on Spina Bifida, Skytop, Pa., May 6, 1975.

It should be noted that the situation presented to pediatricians in the survey was whether they would operate when the
parents requested that surgery not be done. Mary C. Howell,
M.D., Ph.D. and Diane Krane collaborated with Dr. Todres in
this research.

13. I am grateful to Sylvia Law for a helpful discussion on this
     point.

14. The argument can be made that non-treatment is chosen to bene-
     fit the infant, rather than others. While this argument
     would be strongest if treatment would only assure the infant
     a life of irremediable pain, I am assuming that this is not
     the ordinary case confronting parents and physicians, and that
     treatment would necessarily, from the infant's perspective,
     be in its best interests.

FROM SOCIAL MOVEMENT TO CLINICAL MEDICINE - THE ROLE OF LAW AND

THE MEDICAL PROFESSION IN REGULATING APPLIED HUMAN GENETICS

James R. Sorenson

Boston University School of Medicine

INTRODUCTION

The role of law and medicine in controlling applied human genetics has been and continues to be complex in our society. It is not the intention of this discussion to analyze the multifaceted nature of the relationships among law, medicine, and genetics, but rather to select for purposes of discussion a limited facet of this large topic. Since the early 1900's the institutional base of applied human genetics has changed significantly. With these changes the role of law and medicine has varied in terms of controlling the uses of, or limiting access to human genetics in the solution of a large number of problems. It is the intent of this discussion to examine some of the major changes in the institutional base of applied human genetics, comparing the period from 1900 to 1930 with the period from the late 1950's up to the present. Our specific interest will be to analyze the manner in which law and medicine have acted as regulatory vehicles over applied human genetics during these two periods. It should be noted that in the following discussion attention is given primarily to control of the application of genetic knowledge and technologies. We are not concerned with the role of law and medicine as regulatory vehicles encouraging or imposing constraints on the discovery of genetic knowledge.

SOCIAL PROBLEMS, SOCIAL REFORMERS, AND GENETICS

To a large extent society, or more accurately various groups within society, have looked to human genetics as a total or partial solution to a variety of problems. In a practical sense this has

occurred primarily during two periods in our history. The first
was from about 1900 through 1930, a period referred to as the
Progressive Era by historians. This period witnessed the rise and
decline of the first concerted eugenics movement in this country.
The second period, beginning in the 1940's saw genetics take on
increased significance for medical and biological research and in
the process built the foundation for the increased import of genetics in medicine today. With respect to the earlier period, Haller
(1) suggests in his analysis of the history of the American eugenics
movement that one can see the movement as divided into three periods. The first, from the late 1800's to about 1905 was, to quote
Haller, "...a period of preparation during which hereditarian
attitudes took root" (1). The second period, from about 1905 to
approximately 1930 was the period of the greatest influence of eugenics in the early history of this country. Finally, after 1930
the eugenics movement faded, losing influence, prestige, and ultimately its effectiveness as a social movement.

It is our intention in the first part of this paper to concentrate singly on the period from about 1905 to 1930, the height
of the eugenics movement. In examining this period we will be interested in discussing three separate topics: (1) the types of
problems deemed controllable by systematic application of what was
then known about human genetics; (2) the institutional and professional affiliation of those applying genetics; and (3) the role of
law and the medical profession in regulating the application of
genetics during this period.

EARLY APPLICATIONS AND RATIONALES

A discussion of the early uses of human genetics must entail
at least three considerations. These are (1) the intellectual
climate of the period from the late 1900's up to the 1930's; (2)
the social setting of this period; and (3) developments in genetics
which provided support for viewing genetics as relevant to the
solution of pressing problems.

The latter part of the nineteenth century and the first part
of the twentieth century was a period during which there was
much concern with social problems in this country. A number of
intellectual developments shaped interest in such issues and directed attention to a consideration of the possible biological bases
of human behavior and social organization. These developments
included: (1) the intellectual ferment caused by the advance of
the theory of evolution; (2) a scientific orientation, reflected in
a philosophical naturalism, that promulgated the notion of an
analogy between human society and biological organisms; (3) a strong
commitment to scientific knowledge and technological advance as the
primary bases of social change and evolution; and (4) a legacy of

interest in the biology of social problems, based to a large extent on the Social Darwinism of the late 1800's (1-4).

During this period American society was undergoing signifi-cant social change. The industrial revolution had helped bring about considerable change, including rapid urbanization and with it the overcrowding in urban areas, slums, and the inflow of a large number of immigrants. Problems resulting from these and other developments combined to provide the basis for a sustained and potent interest in the control and alleviation of many social problems and various forms of social deviancy, including insanity, mental incapabilities, alcoholism, and criminality. Institutional programs to handle such problems developed rapidly, and almost as rapidly experienced failure and frustration (4, 5).

In addition to the intellectual and social climates of this period, there were advances more central to the developing science of genetics that made a eugenics posture seem both rationally sound as well as practically feasible. Ludmerer, in discussing the scientific input to the eugenic movement cites at least three im-portant developments (2). These were : (1) rediscovery of Mendels law in 1900. This theoretical underpinning of modern genetics pro-vided improved prediction of reproduction among plants and animals and was quickly extended to the prediction of the outcome of human reproduction; (2) a corollary development was the belief among some geneticists-eugenicists that most and perhaps all human traits were determined by single genes acting independently. This led to a belief in a one-to-one correspondence between gene and human trait and gave a specious view of the efficacy of breeding better humans; (3) finally there was the discrediting of the theory of acquired characteristics by the work of Weismann. Weismann's approach viewed germinal cells as distinct from somatic cells, and early, sometimes uncritical and overextended utilization of this view led eugenicists to posit genetic material as superior to environmental experiences in the shaping and determination of human traits. This led in turn to a rather pessimistic view of the extent to which man and society could be significantly altered through environmental manipulation, undercutting support for an institutional approach to social problems, and, at least for the eugenicists, pointing out the significance of a biological-genetic approach.

These three sets of factors, the intellectual climate, a grow-ing concern with social problems, and significant developments in the science of genetics, combined to provide a setting in which the eugenics movement could find a cause, a rationale, as well as a methodology. And it did, however limited and sometimes faulty was the then extant knowledge of human genetics, and however illo-gical were some of the deductions of eugenicists from the facts of genetics to the cure for social problems. It was in this intellec-tual, social, and scientific milieu that eugenicists found support for their two-part program in the United States. The first part, positive in orientation, sought racial improvement of the American population and general social betterment via encouragement of re-production among those believed to be biologically and socially fit. The second part, negative in view, sought restriction of re-production among those believed to be unfit, either biologically or socially. Who instituted such a sweeping agenda for the per-fection of man and society?

THE EUGENICISTS

Haller (1) in his discussion of the eugenics movement sites three major groups as constituting the basis for the eugenics movement. These were: (1) psychologists, psychiatrists, super-intendents of institutions and other institutional personnel, charged with the care and treatment of those considered to be biol-ogically or socially unfit; (2) a group of American citizens, alarmed at the influx of new immigrants into the United States and concerned with the heritage and heredity of old stock Americans; and (3) academics, primarily biological scientists, but social scientists and theorists as well, interested in genetic and social behavior research.

It is interesting to note that as one examines historical analyses of the eugenics movement and its personnel, it is im-pressive how many divergent professional people and non-professional groups were involved and the apparently small role of the medical profession as a systematic component of that movement. Certainly there were medical professionals who argued for a more active in-volvement of genetics in medicine at this early date. Ludmerer for example in an analysis of the professional backgrounds of 144 contributors to the pamphlet What I think About Eugenics indicates that ten were physicians (2). This publication reflected the views of many of the most influential eugenicists of this era. However, it was not until the late 1930's that the profession of medicine became more systematically involved in applying genetics, and by this time the eugenics movement was rapidly coming to an end (2).

To a large extent the eugenics movement was peopled by self-proclaimed experts in social and biological reform. Their prof-essional skills and interests were divergent, but their goals and aspirations as eugenicists were almost unitary. Never really a popular movement these experts led the battle against numerous enemies. What were their goals and how effective were they in implementing them?

LAW AND EUGENICS

As we have seen, to a large extent, the medical profession
played an insignificant role in the eugenics movement. While
there were limited writings exhorting physicians to employ eugenic
considerations in their practice, as a professional body they in
fact had little impact. This meant that by and large law as
promulgated through the activities of voluntary organizations was
the primary vehicle of control in administrating and regulating
the application of genetics during this era. The political-legal
side of the eugenics movement was complex in both intention and
scope and through various maneuvers achieved some successes among
many failures. From a legal perspective the eugenic movement
made its major impact through accomplishments involving three separate issues. These were: (1) the development of custodial care
for the feebleminded and provision of permanent institutional
facilities for those deemed socially and biologically unfit; (2)
passage of sterilization laws for people considered undesirable,
again either socially or biologically; and (3) the passage of laws
restricting immigration on the basis of assumed undesirable traits
among various ethnic-regional groups (1). These programs were
attempted at local, state, and federal levels, and their legal
thrust was based on court cases, administrative regulations, as
well as the passage of legislation. Each of these three issues
constituted a separate crusade, to some extent, under the umbrella
eugenics movement. And, as we will see, each employed somewhat
divergent strategies in attempting to achieve their particular
goals.

The legislative battles for increased custodial care of the
feebleminded were fought primarily at the state level with some
attention at the national level via educational programs. In some
states the drive for improved custodial care was coupled with the
screening of school children for early identification of mental
retardation and other possible problems.

The origin of interest in the creation of better state facilities resided in part in what was called the "menace of the
feebleminded." It was popularly believed that unless the feeble-
minded were institutionalized that they posed a threat by reprod-
ucing. This particular crusade existed to some extent prior to
the eugenic movement, as Haller notes, but at the same time, it
experienced considerable growth and success during the eugenics
movement. For example, according to Haller programs for improved
institutional facilities increased from 24 to 43 states during the
period from 1904 to 1923. In addition, the number of individuals
estimated to reside as inmates in these institutions increased
from about 14,000 to more than 42,000 during this same period (1).
During the post World War I era public concern about the feeble-
minded and their propagation lessened considerably and correspon-

dingly public support and drive for the provision of increased
facilities lost much of its strength.

Like most of the eugenics movement this particular crusade
was one limited largely to experts. On the other hand, as Haller
has noted, this particular crusade within the movement did achieve
considerable public support (1). This was so, perhaps because
there were fewer legal and moral objections to the purposes of
this crusade, especially the provision of better institutional
facilities, than for the other two major crusades we will discuss.

The crusade for sterilization was one which brought division
to the eugenics movement. In many respects the campaigns for
sterilization appeared to be less well-organized than had been the
crusades for improved custodial care. Nevertheless, through a
number of state organizations as well as some national groups,
sterilization laws were passed by several states. In fact by
1917 sixteen states had passed sterilization laws and by the close
of the eugenics movement more states had at one time or another
passed such legislation (6).

The crusade for sterilization drew support for both social
as well as eugenical reasons. Some people were concerned not only
with the germ plasm and society's interest in it, but they were
also interested in protecting those barely able to care for themselves from having additional children and thus burdening the
state even more.

Laws regulating sterilization and the grounds for the procedure
varied from state to state. In addition, as Haller has written,
there was variability in the enforcement of such laws (1). In
several states court decisions rendered the laws on the books
harmless. California was among the most active states in terms
of developing and implementing laws on sterilization. The sterilization laws also differed considerably from state to state in terms
of the extent to which they provided for due process. Some states
utilized panels of experts to declare individuals unfit for procreation, and others permitted sterilization on the basis of the
performance of various crimes, such as rape, highway robbery, and
even chicken stealing (1). Because many of the laws in the various
states were based in part or whole on punitive motives, they contained sufficient grounds for the charge of being cruel and unusual
punishment. In addition many of the laws did not provide for
due process, and accordingly there was considerably court-legisla-
tive battles over such laws. In the end the movement was only
partially successful in getting enforceable legislation passed
and acted upon (1).

Finally, it was in the area of restriction of immigration that
the eugenics movement obtained its most prominence on a national

basis and was able to affect legislation at a federal level. A
number of developments in the early part of the century, including
some of those already alluded to above, as well as the development
of I.Q. tests, the rapid growth of physical anthropology, and the
writings by a number of prominent sociologists, led to a widespread acceptance of the concept of race, in a typological rather
than a genetic-statistical sense, and a concommitant belief that
something must be done to protect the basic stock that founded
and settled America. Significant increases in immigration provided increased support for some consideration of immigration restriction. Congress appointed an Immigration Commission in 1907.
In 1921 Congress passed the first immigration restriction law, but
it was a temporary measure. This law, limiting immigration to 3
percent of the foreign born of each nationality in the United
States according to the 1910 census, was a temporary measure. It
was succeeded by more permanent legislation undertaken in 1924 limiting immigration to 2 percent of those nationalities represented
in the 1890 census. In fact, due to administrative problems the
law did not really go into effect until 1929 (1). There were
several prominent eugenicists involved in getting legislation on
immigration restriction, including Osborn and Laughlin, and the
instrumental role played by the eugenicists and their interests
in this issue was reflected not only in their input into the
House Committee on Immigration and Naturalization, but also in the
major theme of the Second International Congress of Eugenics held
in New York in 1921. It was devoted, to a significant degree, to
eugenic considerations of race (1).

This necessarily limited view of the eugenics movement and in
particular its political-legal thrusts provides for some important
observations. First, the application of genetics during this
period took the form of a social movement and to a great extent
private, voluntary organizations were a major mechanism for instituting and carrying on through legal procedures day-to-day activities of the various crusades within the movement. While a wide
array of professionals were involved with many different scientific
skills and interests, few professional organizations played a
significant role. Thus, the movement was supported and controlled
largely by self-proclaimed experts in social reform.

Second, the movement was a movement of experts, more so than
a popular movement. These experts took as problematic the restor-
ation and preservation of society, both biologically and socially.
It was a movement, at times divided within itself, but a movement
that did achieve some modicum of success. As a movement of experts
it faced, as does contemporary genetics, the problem of democratizing scientific knowledge, particularly when significant social
issues and public policies are at stake.

Thirdly, the eugenics movement was a social force in which law

played the major regulatory role. Built primarily on voluntary organizations, the movement relied on the mechanisms of law including
court decisions, administrative regulations, and legislative enactments to achieve its goals. The professions as entities in themselves played a secondary role to law in regulating, administrating and
limiting the application of genetics during this era. As we will see
below, this is significantly different than is the situation today.

     Finally, philosophically the eugenics movement was both
Arcadian as well as Utopian in temperament. It was Arcadian to
the extent that many within the movement looked to the past as an
ideal and were attempting to reconstruct the lost purity of the
American race or to recapture the simplicity of an earlier form
of social existence. The movement was also Utopian in that it
looked to the future as an opportunity to improve men and society,
through selective breeding and careful planning. In both its Arcadian dreams and its Utopian fantasies it looked to genetics as
the method. Contemporary genetics in the context of clinical medicine at least has lost this philosophical Janism, and while medicine no longer entertains dreams of Arcadia, genetics is increasingly an essential element in fantasies about society's future
health.

THE DECLINE OF EUGENICS AND THE RISE OF CLINICAL GENETICS

     The period from the 1930's through the 1950's was one during
which significant changes took place in applied genetics. The
application of genetics based on a eugenics rationale declined
rapidly, particularly scientific support for such programs. A
historical analysis by Ludmerer of social forces affecting geneticists'disenchantment with eugenic proposals cites two principal
factors (7). First, beginning as early as 1915, careful genetic
research as well as developing theories began to suggest that
inheritance was much more complex than previously assumed. The
postulation of the Hardy-Weinberg law in 1908 served to underscore
the difficulty of rapidly eliminating an undesirable trait from the
population. And, as Ludmerer documents, the research of Johannsen,
East, and Emerson served to undercut other basic assumptions of
the eugenics creed, in particular the concept of inheritance impervious to environmental effects and the notion of unit inheritance.

     While such developments internal to the science of genetics
resulted in the removal of scientific support for eugenic programs,
external factors were also undercutting support. For example, the
uncritical overextension of genetic principles to eugenics programs
offended many geneticists and provided a basis for withdrawing from
the movement. In addition, public concern about the unethical and
callous application of eugenics in Nazi Germany provided the basis
for scientific withdrawal from the movement, as well as public con-

demnation of such excesses (7).

The net result of such developments was the demise of the eugenics movement as a potent social force, and to some extent, a
lack of support for genetic research and work until the mid 1940's,
when interest in genetics once again began to develop. Ludmerer
argues that to a large extent the renewed interest was due to such
developments as the discovery of the genetic basis of a larger and
larger number of diseases as well as interest in mutation and its
genetic consequence, in light of the development of atomic weapons.
Also the discovery of blood groups as well as genetic linkage in
man highlighted the significance of genetics for medicine (7). To
quote Ludmerer:

> "These discoveries were important for more than
> purely intellectual reasons. They gave human
> genetics a start in medicine, which is an
> ideologically neutral field. Insofar as human
> genetics became part of medicine, it too became
> ideologically neutral, and this justified the
> faith of geneticists that human genetics could
> stand as an independent discipline apart from
> eugenics" (2).

Thus genetics made its second beginning as an applied science via
the profession of medicine. Applied genetics moved out of the
realm of social movement and of social reform, and into the world
of disease, the physician, and patient. To what extent, however,
is medicine and the entrepreneurs of the new genetics ideologically
neutral in their uses of the science of genetics, and if they
are not, what values are guiding present day application?

GENETICS IN MEDICINE

The movement of applied genetics into clinical medicine has
meant changes not only in institutional setting, but it has also
meant changes in the role of law as a regulatory vehicle in the
area of genetics. The designation of applied genetics as a medical
issue means that the values and the norms of the medical profession,
rather than legal proscriptions have become highly significant in
affecting access to the new genetics. In essence, law has taken a
passive reactive stance by and large in regulating applied genetics
and medicine has become the major control vehicle.

As several historians of genetics and medicine have commented,
it is only recently that medicine has become receptive, both ideologically as well as practically, to genetics (2, 8). It has been
noted that until medical science managed to conquer the immediate
threats posed by infectious disease, it had little time for genetics

and its concern with rare diseases. Practically genetics offered
little to the physician in the way of useful knowledge as long as
the physician was faced with the more immediate problems of infectious disease and death. In addition ideologically, as Ludmerer
has commented, medicine had to acquire a concern not just with
treatment, but it had to enlarge its view to include the prevention
of disease and disorder as well, before the full significance of
genetics could be appreciated (2). The dramatic success of medical
science in controlling infectious diseases has provided the practical impetus for the incorporation of genetics into medicine by
highlighting and increasing the significance of chronic, genetic
diseases as health problems. Secondarily, medicine's expansion of
its horizon to encompass prevention has provided the requisite
philosophical rationale to buttress the practical developments.
Together these changes have laid the foundation for the increasing
significance of applied human genetics in the practice of medicine
today.

        In our discussion above of the cultural, social, and scienti-
fic setting of the eugenics movement, it should have become
apparent that the rise of the eugenics movement was to a large extent a result of the coalescing of three sets of factors. The
eugenics movement rested on a special cultural milieu, a concern
with social problems, as well as developments in the science of
genetics. Contemporary applied genetics has a significantly different origin. While the eugenics movement was induced, so to
speak, by cultural, social, as well as scientific developments,
contemporary applied genetics has resulted perhaps almost totally
from the 'push' of developments in both the science of genetics and
corollary medical technological growth. There has been little
concerted public or private support for applying the new genetics.
And, while medicine has become more receptive ideologically to
taking a preventive stance, there has been generally little drive,
direction, or push from the medical establishment for more rapid
or extensive application of the new genetics, although some medical
geneticists have been voicing a concern for wider application for
some time.

        In brief, it appears that the current application of genetics
is due more to scientific and technological developments than was
the case during the eugenics era. Today, by and large this application has become much more centralized and localized within the
domain of a single institution. This is not to discredit the
role of such organizations as the National Foundation March of
Dimes, the National Genetics Foundation, or the numerous voluntary
organizations combating the many specific genetic disorders.
Rather, it is to suggest that, in terms of public contact with
genetic issues, it is most likely that this exposure will today
take place in a medical setting, be organized by health professionals, and most often run by a physician or a medical geneticist.

Genetics has become medical, and physicians have replaced social
reformers as the impresarios of the new applied genetics.

GENETIC COUNSELING, SCREENING AND AMNIOCENTESIS

Genetics has several roles in contemporary medicine. In considering its uses three applications, other than its part in the
diagnosis and treatment of genetic disease, seem most salient:
genetic counseling, genetic screening, and pre-natal diagnosis.
By genetic counseling we mean the provision of information about a
genetic disease to an individual or a couple, most frequently after
the birth of a genetically handicapped child (9). In this sense
most genetic counseling in this country today is retrospective.
Genetic screening refers to the provision of information to an
individual or a couple about the normalcy of their genotype. Most
such screening today takes place in large, public screening programs
and increasingly will add a prospective element to the prevention
of birth defects and genetic disease (10). Finally, pre-natal
diagnosis refers to the provision of information to a pregnant
couple about either or both the somatic and/or genetic status of
their fetus. It is most commonly applied after the birth of an
abnormal child, but is increasingly being used to monitor the pregnancies of mothers of advanced age (11).

For purposes of discussion I have decided to focus on genetic
counseling and pre-natal diagnosis. This is so in part because of
the three modes of utilization given, genetic screening is the
most marginally based in actual medical practice. Much genetic
screening is and has been the result of voluntary group activities
and some legislative enactments (12). To this extent genetic
screening programs in this country reflect a mode of application
similar to various facets of the eugenics movement. Genetic
counseling and prenatal diagnosis on the other hand reflect more
clearly the operation of medical rather than political norms and
values, and accordingly provide a better basis for examination of
applied genetics in the realm of medicine.

Genetic counseling dates back at least to the eugenics movement in this country. According to Ludmerer, it was provided as
part and parcel of the eugenics movement, and apparently, a considerable amount of counseling was done at the old Eugenic Record
Office in Cold Spring Harbor, New York (2). By the 1950's there
were at least 13 locations offering genetic counseling in this
country, ten of these were located in academic departments of
zoology and biology (13). By 1969 the number of settings in which
counseling was offered had increased to almost 200, and, according
to the National Foundation-March of Dimes International Directory
of Genetic Services, there were better than 350 counseling facilities in the United States in 1974 (14).

A reading of the clinical literature on genetic counseling as well as some results from a national survey of counselors we are presently completing at Boston University leads us to offer the following conclusions about genetic counseling in contemporary medicine. First, genetic counseling is an activity practiced by both medical and non-medical professionals, primarily M.D.'s and Ph.D.'s, and while there are professionals in genetic counseling, it is fair to say that with few exceptions today there are not yet any professional genetic counselors. For example in our study of some 500 professionals institutionally recognized as providing genetic counseling we found that for the vast majority counseling was a small component of their total activity. Most counseled about three couples a week, all seen in about three hours in one afternoon. When asked what was their primary area of professional interest the majority of our sample replied basic or clinical research. Only 13 precent said genetic counseling. In addition, there is still much discussion about appropriate qualifications for counseling (15) and no licensure is available, nor are there recognized courses or curriculum required for training to be a genetic counselor.

The movement of genetics into the medical domain has meant a significant change in the types of problems for which genetics is considered relevant, as well as the manner in which genetic abnormalities are viewed. Certainly our work suggests that most contemporary genetic counselors see little significance in their knowledge for social issues, nor in fact do many want to place genetic disease in a social framework. For example, when asked whether they thought it appropriate to discuss with parents the possible social burden that a diseased child may pose economically, only 23 percent indicated support for using this social framework to view the parents' problem. To some extent the traditional norms of the doctor-patient relationship may be operating here to induce counselors to take patient's view of the reproductive decisions involved, and to ignore or consider only secondary, such things as the cost to society of defective children (16).

Also, it was the case in our study that only 28 percent of the counselors held a reduction in the number of carriers of genetic defects as one of the goals of their counseling. While technically there would be problems in practically achieving this goal (17) the fact that 72 percent of the counselors did not endorse this as a goal suggests to us once again that the interests of the contemporary counselors are localized about the patient and his family, and generally extensions of this interest, either in time, so as to worry about the future generations, or even spacial extensions, so as to worry about social consequences, such as costs to society, are not viewed as legitimate interests of the counselors. These two concerns, of course, were fundamental to the earlier eugenics movement.

The goals that most counselors do endorse are (1) the alleviation of parental guilt and anxiety about being the carriers
of deleterious genes or having a defective child, and (2) the
prevention of disease. The latter goal, of course may pose problems for the counselor, in that while he may think parents at risk
for some specific disease should not reproduce, the parents may
desire to. In general, it appears that counselors do attempt to
permit parents to make their own decisions although they play a
significant role in this decision process. But the possible conflict in this situation highlights the issue of to what extent genetic counseling is preventive medicine, and if it is preventive
medicine, what is it attempting to prevent? Counselors express
a diversity of opinion on this issue.

While there may be limited agreement about the general goals
of counseling, there is much less agreement among counselors about
the manner in which counseling should be done or exactly how to
inform parents of such basic information as recurrence risk and
disease burden. For example, in our research, when asked to indicate how severe they believe galactosemia to be, in light of
present therapy, 21 percent of the counselors felt it to be very
severe, 30 percent thought it serious, 30 percent viewed it as
moderately serious, and 19 percent considered it not too severe
or only minor. This is a considerable amount of variation in opinion, particularly in light of the significance of the idea of
disease burden in parental reproductive decisionmaking, at least
as suggested by one study (18).

When asked to give their opinion as to the magnitude of various recurrence risk estimates, counselors once again exhibited
significant variation. For example, 48 percent felt a risk of 1
in twenty high or very high, 38 percent believe it to be only
moderate and 15 percent thought of it as low or very low. Once
again, several studies have suggested that parental sense of the
magnitude of a risk is a significant component in their reproductive
decisionmaking (18, 19). Undoubtedly, if counseled today, patients
would come away from different counselors with sometimes widely
varying views of the magnitude of their recurrence risk, and
supposedly, make significantly different decisions, often as a
function of their counselor's personal beliefs about the severity
of a specific disease and the magnitude of the recurrence risk.

While there is much variation in the delivery of genetic
counseling today, the goals it adheres to and its orientation are
much different than was the situation during the eugenics movement.
The significant variation that does exist in counseling reflects
in part the novelty of counseling as a medical practice. It is in
many respects experimental medicine. At the same time the variation
reflects to some extent the attitude of contemporary medicine
toward genetic counseling. Genetic counseling occupies a relatively

low position in medicine, as reflected for example in the amount
of time given to genetics in medical school curriculum, as well
as the relatively small number of departments of medical genetics
in medical schools. In addition, since much of genetic counseling
consists of simply talking to patients, and has been largely void
until recently of high technology, it has not had as much glamour
as the technologically dependent areas of medicine. Amniocentesis
is embedded in high technology, and we may now turn to a brief
examination of some aspects of prenatal diagnosis in contemporary
medicine.

     Amniocentesis is, of course, a much newer medical tool than
genetic counseling. Being a specific technological procedure,
control over access to amniocentesis has been much easier, from
the view of the medical profession, than concommitant control of
genetic counseling. The medical professionals who perform amniocentesis, or are instrumental in referring patients to the procedure, as are most genetic counselors, have held opinions about what
disorders, risks, or concerns warrant amniocentesis and which do
not. And these attitudes have probably been highly instrumental
in shaping public access. In our survey we asked counselors to
indicate if they thought amniocentesis was or was not appropriate
in a number of situations. Some of these situations and the percents
reporting approval or disapproval are reported in Table 1.

     As we can see, there is both considerable variability in op-
inion across possible situations, as well as significant variation in opinion as to use in a specific situation. The response to
the first question suggests to us that, as one would expect, a
'medical model' is guiding the thinking of counselors concerning
utilization of this new technology. Satisfying parental curiosity
to know the sex of their child is not considered appropriate at all,
while in utero screening among pregnant women of advanced age is
generally supported, probably because the latter can lead to some
reduction in the incidence of disorders associated with advanced
maternal age, while simply informing parents of the sex of their
fetus cannot lead to disease prevention. Interestingly counselors
do not consider it appropriate to use amniocentesis to inform
parents of the normality of their fetus if parents will not abort
an abnormal one. Apparently counselors see little value in providing parents at risk with such information, although it appears
that this attitude may be changing (20).

     The second part of the Table reflects variation in opinion
across specific genetic disease conditions. While there is considerable general agreement that couples at risk for Tay-Sachs
should be screened and affected fetuses aborted, this is not the
case for galactosemia. Only 56 percent consider amniocentesis
and abortion appropriate in the latter case, 27 percent consider
it inappropriate and 17 percent are uncertain. The case of galac-

TABLE I

COUNSELORS OPINIONS ABOUT APPROPRIATENESS OF AMNIOCENTESIS IN VARIOUS SITUATIONS

In your opinion, is it appropriate to use amniocentesis in order to:

	Appropriate	Not Appropriate	Uncertain	N
	%			
a. Evaluate the chromosomal status of fetuses of all women 35-40 and older	66	17	17	445
b. Determine the condition of a fetus at risk for a disorder, where parents will not abort but simply want to know if the child is normal	15	70	15	447
c. Determine the sex of a fetus to satisfy parental curiosity	1	95	4	448

In your opinion, if parents would abort an afflicted fetus, is it appropriate to use amniocentesis to:

	Appropriate	Not Appropriate	Uncertain	N
	%			
a. Determine the sex of a fetus with an older hemophiliac sib*	81	9	11	442
b. Determine the status of a fetus with an older sib who died of Tay-Sachs	95	2	3	443
c. Determine the status of a fetus with an older sib successfully treated for galactosemia	56	27	17	440
d. Determine the condition of a fetus with an older sib having Down's syndrome	84	4	12	439

*% is not equal to 100 due to rounding error

tosemia highlights a potential dilemma inherent in the new technology of amniocentesis that both counselors and parents must face.
When treatment is available, even if it does not restore the individual to complete 'normality', should amniocentesis be employed
and affected fetuses aborted? In striving for the prevention of
disease, should preference be given to avoiding the birth of a
child with a disease, or should the prevention come through therapy
when available? Both are preventive medicine in different senses,
but the consequences for the patient are obviously very different.

     Professional attitudes about limiting access to amniocentesis,
and concern about the validity and reliability of the procedure
appear to have been stronger than concern over similar issues with
respect to genetic counseling. For example when amniocentesis was
first becoming available as a diagnostic tool appeals were made to
limit access to the procedure on two general grounds. First, it
was argued that both the short and long term safety of the procedure for the mother and the fetus were unknown. In addition, it was
argued that the diagnostic reliability of the procedure was unknown
and hence access should be limited. In light of these uncertainties
professionals recommended access only when (1) the abnormality risk-
ed had a relatively high probability of occurring, and/or (2) the
severity of the abnormality was very great (21). To some extent
these general guidelines are reflected in the responses given in
Table 1. Access to amniocentesis appears to be changing. This is
due in part to more experience with the procedure, numerous small
studies reporting on the safety and diagnostic reliability of the
procedure, as well as collaborative efforts to assess the short term
biomedical aspects of the procedure for both the mother and the
fetus. To the extent that these studies report high levels of safety and reliability, one can assume that access to the procedure will
increasingly be permitted for other than medical reasons. At least
it would seem that there is a legal mandate for this direction to
be followed, based on such court decisions as Skinner v. Oklahoma,
Griswald v. Connecticut, Eisentadt v. Baird, and Roe v. Wade. As
Friedman has argued, inherent in these decisions is a legal mandate
providing for procreational privacy, one which extends to the termination of pregnancies for any reason whatsoever in the first few
months of pregnancy (22). As such, it is probable that while genetic counseling will remain fairly well embedded in the values and
norms of the medical profession, the utilization of amniocentesis
may increasingly reflect extramedical norms and values.

                              CONCLUSION

     This brief discussion of two major periods of applied human
genetics in this country provides for some comparisons between eugenics and clinical genetics. Applied human genetics has moved
from the realm of social problems and social reformers into the

world of medicine and physicians. Institutionally genetics was applied through numerous voluntary organizations during the eugenics era. It has become much more localized in the domain of medicine recently. Concommitantly, while law was a major vehicle in determining the application of genetics during the eugenics era, today the prerogative has fallen largely to the medical profession, with the exception of mass genetic screening programs. And, it appears that in the not too distant future pre-natal diagnosis also may begin to reflect values and norms other than those of the medical profession. Certainly the cultural, social, and scientific setting of our society have changed dramatically from the eugenics period. But in the application of genetics there are some communalities between the two eras. Primary among these is the problem, alluded to above, of democratizing scientific knowledge, particularly knowledge that has significant implications for both individuals and society. The early eugenics was a movement of experts, and the new genetics too is one administered largely by experts. How to make the public more informed, more accessible, and more willing to make decisions about how to best use this new knowledge remains a problem. Second, in guiding their uses of genetics, experts during both eras have appealed to various ideals. For the eugenicist the ideal was a dual-faced Janis-like god, looking both to the past and to the future. For clinical geneticists the past is of little use, but the future holds promise, a future with less disease, abnormality, expense, and human suffering.

In the practical application of these goals both sets of experts have had to concern themselves with defining acceptable limits of human variation. The eugenicists, having decided what were and were not acceptable human traits employed institutions and immigration restriction to achieve their desired ends. Clinical geneticists and parents today are engaged in some way in a similar task, using counseling and amniocentesis to make their decisions as to what is and is not acceptable human variation.

The movement of genetics into medicine has sharpened some of the issues about human variation, solved others, and raised new ones. Certainly some diseases are so terrible, and the quality of life they impose on both the affected as well as relatives such as to be avoided by almost all. But other disorders are not as serious, sometimes treatment is available, and an answer as to what should be done is far from clear. In such situations it is mandatory that we use our increasing capacity to measure man genetically with the tolerance demanded by such morally difficult situations.

ACKNOWLEDGEMENTS

Research on genetic counselors reported in this paper supported by a research grant from the Russell Sage Foundation, 230 Park Avenue New York.

REFERENCES

1. Haller, M.H., "Eugenics: Hereditarian Attitudes in American Thought," Rutgers University Press, New Brunswick (1963).

2. Ludmerer, K.M., "Genetics and American Society: A Historical Appraisal," The Johns Hopkins University Press, Baltimore (1972).

3. Allen, G.E., Science and society in the eugenic thought of H.J. Muller, in "Genetics and Society", J.B. Bressler (ed.), Addison-Wesley Publishing Company, Reading (1973).

4. Sarason, S. and Dorrs, J., "Psychological Problems in Mental Deficiency," Harper and Row, New York (1969).

5. Pickens, D.K., "Eugenics and the Progressives," Vanderbilt University Press, Nashville (1968).

6. Farrow, M., Juberg, R., Genetics and laws 'prohibiting' marriage in the United States, J.A.M.A. 209:534 (1969).

7. Ludmerer, K.M., The American geneticist and the eugenic movement; 1905-1935, J. Hist. Biol. 2:337 (1969).

8. Scheinfeld, A., The public and human genetics, Acta Genet. Stat. Med. 7:487 (1957).

9. Sorenson, J.R., "Social and Psychological Aspects of Applied Human Genetics: A Bibliography," Government Printing Office, Washington, D.C., 73-412 (1973).

10. Bergsma, D., Zappa, M., Roblin, R. et al (eds.), "Dimensions of Screening for Human Genetic Disease," Stratton Intercontinental Medical Book Corp., New York (1974).

11. Milunsky, A., "The Prenatal Diagnosis of Hereditary Disorders," Charles C. Thomas, Springfield (1973).

12. Powledge, T., Genetic screening as a political and social development, in "Dimensions of Screening for Human Genetic Disease," D. Bergsma, M. Zappa, R. Roblin et al (Eds.), Stratton Intercontinental Medical Book Corp., New York (1974).

13. Hammonds, H., "Hereditary Counseling," American Eugenics Society, New York (1957).

14. National Foundation-March of Dimes, "International Directory

of Genetic Services," New York (1974).

15. Epstein, C., Who should do genetic counseling and under what circumstances, in "Birth Defects Original Article Series," D. Bergsma (ed.), Vol. IX, p. 39.

16. Sorenson, J., Biomedical innovation, uncertainty, and doctor-patient interaction, J. Hlth Soc. Behav. 15(4):366 (1974).

17. Motulsky, A., Fraser, G., Felsenstein, J., Public health and long-term genetic implications of intrauterine diagnosis and selective abortion, in "Birth Defects: Original Article Series", Vol. VII, No. 5, p. 22.

18. Leonard, C., Chase, G. and Childs, B., Genetic counseling: a consumer's view, New Eng. J. Med. 287:433 (1972).

19. Carter, C., Evans, K., Fraser-Roberts, J.A. et al, Genetic clinic: a follow-up, Lancet 1:281 (1971).

20. Golbus, M., Conte, F., Schneider, E. et al, Intrauterine diagnosis of genetic defects, Amer. J. Obstet. Gynecol. 118: 897 (1974).

21. Hilton, B., Callahan, D., Harris, M. et al, "Ethical Issues in Human Genetics," Plenum Press, New York (1973).

22. Freidman, J., "Legal Implications of Amniocentesis," Univ. of Penn. Law Rev. 123:92 (1974).

DISCUSSION

Papers of Profs. R.A. Burt, J.A. Robertson, and J.R. Sorenson
<u>Moderator</u>: Prof. A.G. Steinberg

S. PRUZANSKY: Abraham Lincoln School of Medicine, Chicago:
Prof. Burt pointed out that photographs of the fetus were persuasive in convincing the jury in the Edelin case. He also suggested
that photographs might have a contrary effect in supporting the
position of Duff and Campbell for withholding care. For the benefit of the non-clinicians, I would want to point out that there is
a real hazard in using the aesthetic appearance of the newborn
for making such decisions in any way. There are a number of clinical entities, such as hemifacial microsomia, Down's, Crouzon's
and Apert's syndromes, which may be repulsive when they are seen by
the laity and are repugnant also to nurses and physicians. There
are many cases that we are aware of where out of ignorance the
physician advised the family to institutionalize these children
because they didn't look good.

We have rescued a number of such children and despite the deprivation of institutional life and despite the fact of a failure
to diagnose a middle ear deformity, we have been able to salvage
a good many. Recent advances in plastic surgery have resulted in
extraordinary cosmetic results. So what I would point out is
until we know what the natural history of many of these conditions
are, until we know what the potential for rehabilitation is, we
must exercise a great deal of caution.

Unquestionably, there are a number of patients for whom the
future is hopeless. There are a larger number of cases in the gray
area about which we know very little. What I fear is that some
well meaning physician with the consent of the parents may be
motivated by Duff and Campbell's article to withhold treatment when
this is not warranted.

M.W. STEELE: University of Pittsburgh School of Medicine,
Pennsylvania: Neither Prof. Burt nor Prof. Robertson address the
usual situation concerning withholding treatment - that is the
question of extraordinary versus ordinary care. The usual situation which you described as polar is not polar at all. The usual
situation is where life can be maintained only by the use of extraordinary measures.

Let me give you an example. Suppose a newborn is born with
cleft lip and palate, eye defects and other multiple congenital
anomalies, and it can't breathe without a respirator and its heart
keeps stopping so it needs a pacemaker. It can't feed and therefore needs intravenous therapy. It can't urinate so it has to have
a tube in the bladder. Then a chromosome study reveals the baby

has had trisomy 13. It is known that 100% of these babies will
not survive over one year, and all will be profoundly retarded.
In this situation don't you think that stopping extraordinary care
of all these mechanical devices is justified, and that those who
have to make this unpleasant decision ought to not be in fear of
personal jeopardy?

BURT: Let me respond in a couple of ways. I know that it is
usually fashionable in considering at least the ethics, if not
the legality, of withholding care across a broad range, to draw the
distinction that you have drawn between extraordinary and ordinary
means. Without rehashing the entire argument, the reason that I
avoided dealing with that proposition is that I am personally not
persuaded that that is a very helpful ethical straight line proposition. Certainly it is not helpful in the legal sphere.

What you are pointing to is the same kind of issue really that
the last commentator also addressed and which has to do with the
photographs of issue. Now, you are positing another case of a
terribly deformed child. All kinds of efforts are needed and you
are saying in 100% of those cases death comes by one year of age.
Under the existing regime, what the doctors and parents would say
to themselves, as anyone contemplating legal liability in the
future does, "When the moment of judgment would come what kind of
a case could I make? How persuasive would the case be to this jury
drawn from the general population. The judge whom I don't yet
know. The prosecutor whom I don't have in my hand." It seems to
me that in that case what they would all be led to do is first of
all take the photograph.

I am not advocating that ugly babies should be killed by any
means. What a physician who is worried, however, about the possibility of being criminally liable would have to say to himself
is, "Here is this photograph of a baby who looks just horrible -
very ugly - and yet will there be experts on the other side whom
the prosecutor can put forward to say, you know, you can correct
this in the following easy ways." If that kind of testimony is
brought forward, it seems to me that the impact of that photograph
is significantly diminished. On the other hand, if it is the kind
of proof that can be adduced of what you were describing as in
100% of the cases this baby has ultimately died, it seems to me
that there a parent and physician can say, "No matter what jury
we pull, that jury is going to understand." Even then it seems to
me the risk of liability and of an uncomprehending later reviewer
who would say to that parent and physician, "Are we willing to
take on this risk of suffering to ourselves?"

So what one ultimately comes to is the point Prof. Capron was
developing in his presentation earlier. How is it that you put
a proxy decision-maker - because that is what we are dealing with

here - who does not have an identity of interests in a position approximating identity of interest. It seems to me this technique for those kinds of decisions begins to approximate that, and that is its utility.

But it does not follow from what you are saying that there should be a kind of a standard raised that if at the end of one year in 100% of the cases the child will die, then ipso facto death will come, because of the psychological processes that I talked to about the consequences of drawing those kinds of visibly articulated in-advance standards.

D. TODRES: Massachusetts General Hospital: For the record and for the sake of accuracy, I need to direct my comments to Prof. Robertson, when he spoke of a study carried out in Boston, which was a questionnaire directed to the pediatricians of Massachusetts. This study included all the pediatricians in Massachusetts. There was a 57% response making a total of 230 replies. The question Prof. Robertson was alluding to and which I should clarify, was if the newborn baby has Down's syndrome and duodenal atresia, what would your choice of therapy be - skilled nursing, extended care or surgery? Some 50% opted for the operation and 50% for the remainder of choice of therapy.

DEYE: Prof. Burt posited the theoretical background for his intentional ambivalence on a case of Queen v. Dudley and Stevens back in 1884 and spoke of this example where there was cannibalism under this duress situation of potential starvation, and saying that in effect we have to keep up appearances legally. This strikes me as being a little bit presituation ethics and the recent similar situation resulted in a popular book and late night appearances on talk-shows. I would posit that possibly this sort of ambivalence will respond really with grossly unpredictive uneven enforcement of a law which is detached from reality, and that the purposeful societal assumption of the moral burden is indeed the route to at least aim toward in this situation. Because the problem is not going to go away as our position becomes a virtual certainty, the technology developing first of all at lengthening life artificially, the decision ultimately becomes an economic one.

I would propose that the internal inconsistency of your argument in first decrying the lack of social discussion leading to the Supreme Court's decision on abortion, and allowing the same judicial process to go on, will result in the opposite conclusion, that we will have a reason to open public debate and everyone will be happy.

I would propose that once national health insurance comes, it means a bureaucrat in Washington, deciding what will be covered and not covered, will indeed make the ultimate decision, and that this is not the most desirable solution.

BURT: I did not suggest that maintaining the regime will
make everybody happy. Quite the contrary, I think there is terrible
unhappiness on all sides of this question. It seems to me that I
was calling for definition in the Supreme Court decision on the
abortion matter. The Supreme Court ended the debate and said
here is the correctness of the matter. What I am arguing for in
this context at least is the inappropriateness of a conclusive
resolution of that question by any generalized social agency. The
virtue of this process to me is its very decentralization. I am
as opposed to a single bureaucrat in Washington making this decision as I am having the Supreme Court or a single-minded legislature do it. It's decentralization to preserve the dilemmatic
quality of this that seems to be truest to the enormous ambivalence
that those decisions inspire in all of us. I think we are untrue
to the dilemmatic quality of it if we say, "Let's just resolve the
issue."

W. JACOBS: Boston Area United Methodist Church: I now understand something that I didn't understand when I came. As a pastor
of the United Methodist Church, I have wondered about the ambivalence or even contradictory nature of statements on matters as
abortion, respect for life, and so forth. I understand that better
now, because I see that going on now here where these decisions have
to be made, and where the courts struggle with them, too, and I
take that away with me.

What I have heard is possibly more concern with defective
newborns, when that defect is rooted in the mental processes
rather than in physical defective categories. I partly ask this
question out of the reality that I am the father of a child with
cystic fibrosis, whether in the thinking of the dangers to society,
where the courts have their responsibility? Whether there is an
implicit concern more with mental defective than with physical
disorders or whether those are generally considered together?

ROBERTSON: I am not aware of courts making that distinction
as a matter of law. The rights of the retarded are undergoing
a very active phase because they have been so neglected in the past.
As you probably know, there is a similar movement on behalf of the
rights of the physically disabled for accessability, transportation,
and the like. As far as I know, courts are not making a distinction between the two, though many people in discussing these issues
tend to give lesser weight to the mentally retarded than just the
physically disabled.

N. SCRIBANU: Georgetown University Hospital, Washington, D.C.:
Profs. Robertson and Burt enlightened me that we are actually
functioning illegally in our universities. I had this hunch all

along, but nobody spelled it out that what we are doing is basically illegal. As a physician who has been in practice for
18 years, I can see things are not as simple. I have worked with
children with what we call birth defects all along and I would like
to stress the responsibility of the physician in the decision-
making process. He holds everything in his hands because the parents are overwhelmed when you tell them the bad news. They cannot
really grasp the reality. They are not in a position to make the
right decision. It depends upon us how we tell them, how we present the situation. I have had this experience before with conditions which have not been associated with severe mental retardation
or with diminished quality of life in which extraordinary means
were not offered only because the child was not whole. I should
say we should keep in mind that it is our responsibility. I feel
one person cannot make this decision. This is actually a multi-
disciplinary decision. I would like to see more involvement of
lawyers, people in the field of law and psychology, and social
work, in working with physicians and in educating us in those
problems.

MARX: Assuming that two mothers each have a D-trisomic
child that was described before. If one set of parents state that
they would not like lifesaving measures to be continued for the
child, is there a legal difference between this family saying this
and another family with a D-trisomic child who state that for religious reasons they do not want the child to be medically treated,
in both cases the child would die?

ROBERTSON: No, there is not. In fact, the cases in which
parents have been prosecuted for withholding care from newborns,
and I emphasize these are not cases of defective newborns, are
cases where they claimed that it clashed with their religious beliefs. In those cases parents have been successfully prosecuted.

M.D. LEVINE: Harbor General Hospital, Torrance, California:
I'd like to ask Profs. Robertson or Burt whether they advocate the
current laws - let society develop its consensus. If it wants to
change laws, doesn't this breed a disrespect for the law and the
social order which determines these laws?

BURT: One has to weigh a number of enormously complex criteria.
What breeds worse disrespect? The non-enforcement of law itself
is problematic and breeds disrespect. But on the other hand, for
a judge in his black robes to say, "You can kill that one, and
that one," breeds a different kind of disrespect. Or for the law
to say we are going to send policemen through the newborn nurseries
every week to check the records because we want to make sure that
nothing like this happens. I tried to suggest, the kind of hard-
heartedness toward the tragic qualities of these decisions that

that represents, also breeds a different kind of disrespect. If we use the disrespect principle, I think we end up pointing in a number of different directions.

LEVINE: I don't think too many physicians can approach continuing or not continuing life, the quality or quantity of life, with complete dispassion. I could understand this view if there were no law. But there is a law already, and I wondered, if this law is not working, shouldn't there be either no law or a new law?

BURT: There is an old law in a changed context, and the changed context is the Supreme Court's decision on abortion; and then the Edelin prosecution and the other prosecution that's about to be launched here in Boston. In essence, what I am saying, is that for me, balancing all of the different factors, that that is as good a situation I think as we can come up with, all things considered. Duff and Campbell say let's have a new law and the others say no, let's have a different law. But we can't go back. The question is, is this the best direction forward? I think it is.

R.L. INGRAHAM: Prof. Robertson suggested that it would be good to have input from defectives about how they feel regarding their status. We know that many people commit suicide for certainly less reasons. The county counsel in Santa Clara is now faced with a problem. He needs to make a decision with regard to a group interested in euthanasia. What would be the legal status of a document which one would sign, which would say, "I would not want any extraordinary measures taken to continue my life?" I am wondering if this kind of movement is going on elsewhere in the United States.

ROBERTSON: There is a very important distinction, which I am sure is obvious to everyone, between that case and the case of a defective newborn. The case you pose is one where one consents to non-treatment in his own case. The case of the defective newborn is where another is doing the consenting. I think there is a very good legal argument to be made that one perhaps does have this right to reject any kind of medical care for his or herself.

STEINBERG: I'd like to return to a point that Prof. Robertson made when he asked if we can identify a class of individuals who do not have all social rights that others do. I wonder if we have not already done so to some extent in redefining death as a flat EEG, to take care of transplantation.

ROBERTSON: In a sense we have, but by the very definition there, those people have died, they have ceased to be alive, so they could not constitute such a class. I realize that is not an adequate answer.

STEINBERG: Before abortion was legalized during the first two trimesters, it was common in various regions to permit abortion providing two psychiatrists and a physician agreed, or various combinations of that sort. The difficulty with that is that those who are wealthy enough to afford this treatment could have the abortion done properly, and those who could not had to go up the back alley. I wonder if a panel of that same sort couldn't handle the proposition of from whom should intensive care be retained.

ROBERTSON: It clearly is an alternative here. I am not persuaded that I would accept it. I would reiterate what some of the difficulties are. One of the difficulties is that we would as a society be explicitly sanctioning the position that some lives are not worth as much as others. Though just the transaction cost of organizing such committees and the time involved in running them, may indeed be worth it. That is one of the alternatives that is possible to work out. But I emphasize it does put us in a position as a society of taking the lives of a group of human beings for the benefit of the rest of us, and that may be unacceptable.

CONCLUDING COMMENT

SHAW: One of the problems which has come into sharp focus during yesterday's and today's discussions has been the difficulty of communication. Doctors, scientists, and lawyers speak different languages, and now we have the vocabulary of the ethicists to add to our new interdisciplinary lexicon.

We have heard new terms introduced: the "clonus," for example. We have been speaking glibly about "the fetus" without defining our meanings. Are we talking about a biological being, a legal being, or a religious being? Are we referring to a clone of cells which is differentiating, or a _potential_ legal "person" whose constitutional rights are ripening, or a sacred human being with a soul whose life is precious? We answer each other's questions with preconceived notions, based on different ethical positions.

One of Prof. Fletcher's chief contributions to the medical-ethical debate so alive today is his clarity of statement about his own ethical position. His code of ethics is _humanistic_ or _personalistic_. He has a value system that puts humanness and personal integrity above biological life and function.

Let me quote him directly instead of taking the chance of misquoting him:

"It makes no difference whether...an ethics system is grounded in a theistic or a naturalistic philosophy. We may believe that God wills human happiness or that man's happiness is, as Protagoras thought, a self-validating standard of the good and the right. But what counts ethically is whether human needs come first - not whether the ultimate sanction is transcendental or secular."*

Prof. Fletcher has commented on the responsibility of parent-hood.** He disagrees with those who hold that to reproduce is a legal, ethical, moral, or even a constitutional right. He believes that to decide to reproduce is the most important decision made in one's lifetime. He says:

"Genetics, molecular biology, fetology, and obstetrics have developed to a point where we now have effective control over the start of human life's continuum. And therefore from now on it would be irresponsible to leave baby-making to mere chance and impulse, as we once had to do. Modern men are trying to face up in a mature way to our emerging needs of quality control - medically, ecologically, legally, socially."*

When I studied Property in law school, wading through the complicated cases on "eminent domain" it occurred to me to question whether the gene pool of the next generation which resides in our gonads is the private property of the individual or the collective property of society. This question was not raised in the discussions of artificial insemination by donor or in vitro fertilization or sterilization.

Finally, Prof. Fletcher makes a statement about the nature of man which seems fitting in our deliberations where there is a lack of consensus on the problems we are addressing:

"The 'nature of man' question is of such depth and sensitivity that it is bound to raise controversy, and our task is to welcome the controversy but try to reduce it through analysis and synthesis. Said Heraclitus: Opposition brings concord. Out of discord comes the fairest harmony. It is by disease that health is pleasant; by evil that good is pleasant; by hunger, satiety; by weariness, rest."***

*Fletcher, J., Ethics and Euthanasia, Amer. J. Nursing 73:670 (1973).
**Fletcher, J., Humanness and Abortion, in "The Ethics of Genetic Control: Ending Reproductive Roulette," New York: Doubleday and Company, Inc. (1974).
***Fletcher, J., Medicine and the Nature of Man, in "Science, Medicine, and Man, Great Britain: Pergamon Press (1973).

SELECTED RECENT BIBLIOGRAPHY

THE FETUS AND THE NEWBORN

1. Hart, Fetal research and antiabortion politics: holding science hostage, Fam. Plan. Perspect. 7:72, 1975.
2. Powledge, Genetics research group conference. Fetal experimentation: Trying to sort out the issues, Hastings Cent. Rep. 5:8, 1975.
3. Kelsey, An interview with Dr. Raymond S. Duff. Which infants should live? Who should decide? Hastings Cent. Rep. 5:5, 1975.
4. Lappe, The moral claims of the wanted fetus, Hastings Cent. Rep. 5:11, 1975.
5. O'Rourke, The right to privacy: What next?, Hosp. Prog. 56: 58, 1975.
6. Fletcher, Abortion, euthanasia, and care of defective newborns, New Eng. J. Med. 292:75, 1975.
7. Horty, Guardianship: Death or life issue?, Mod. Health Care 3:72, 1975.
8. Curran, Law-medicine notes. Experimentation becomes a crime: Fetal research in Massachusetts, New Eng. J. Med. 292:300, 1975.
9. Report by a Working Party, Ethics of selective treatment of spina bifida, Lancet 1:85, 1975.
10. Stone, Guest Editorial: The rights of human beings participating as subjects in biochemical research, J. Lab. Clin. Med. 85: 183, 1975.
11. Shaw & Shapo, Legal, moral and ethical dilemmas in the newborn nursery, VA Med. Mon. 101:1059, 1974.
12. Culliton, National research act: Restores training, bans fetal research, Hastings Cent. Rep. 4:12, 1974.
13. Lennon, The God squad, RI Med. J. 57:334, 1974.
14. Guttman, On withholding treatment, Can. Med. Assoc. J. 111: 520, 1974.
15. Shepard & Fantel, Legislative threat to fetal research, Am. J. Dis. Child. 128:295, 1974.
16. Fantel & Shepard, Legislative threats to research on human congenital defects, Conn. Med. 38:535, 1974.
17. Editorial, Use of fetuses and fetal material for research, Conn. Med. 38:539, 1974.
18. Fost, Our curious attitude toward the fetus, Hastings Cent. Rep. 4:4, 1974.
19. Lieberman, Informed consent for parenthood, Am. J. Psychoanal. 34:155, 1974.
20. McCormich, Proxy consent in the experimentation situation. Perspect. Biol. Med. 18:2, 1974.
21. Ament, The right to be well born, J. Leg. Med. 2:24, 1974.
22. Fox, Ethical and existential developments in contemporaneous American medicine: Their implications for culture and society, Milbank Mem. Fund Q. 52:445, 1974.
23. Laurence, Clinical and ethical considerations of alpha-feto-

protein estimation for early prenatal diagnosis of neural tube malformations, Dev. Med. Child. Neurol. 16:117, 1974.

24. Pilpel, The fetus as a person: Possible legal consequences of the Hogan-Helms amendment, Fam. Plan. Perspect. 6:6, 1974.

25. Hayden et al, Custody of the myelodysplastic child - implications for selection for early treatment, Pediatrics 53: 253, 1974.

26. Rutkow & Lipton, Some negative aspects of state health departments' policies related to screening for sickle cell anemia, Am. J. Pub. Health 64:217, 1974.

27. Freeman, The shortsighted treatment of myelomeningocele - A long-term case report, Pediatrics 53:311, 1974.

28. Lorber, Selective treatment of myelomeningocele - To treat or not, Pediatrics 53:307, 1974.

29. Schulkind et al, Neonatal health insurance. Growing legislative involvement, Clin. Pediat. 13:209, 1974.

30. Blake, Sickle cell testing in the state laboratories, J. Med. Assoc. 63:52, 1974.

31. Schroeder, New life-person or property, Am. J. Psychiatry 131:541, 1974.

32. Gimbel, Editorial - Infanticide - Who makes the decision, Wis. Med. J. 73:10, 1974.

33. Curran, Legal abortion - The continuing battle, New Eng. J. Med. 290:1301, 1974.

34. McCormick, To save or let die. The dilemma of modern medicine, J.A.M.A. 229:172, 1974.

35. Dykes & Czapek, Regulations and legislation concerning abortus research, J.A.M.A. 229:1303, 1974.

36. College expresses concern on fetal research legislative proposals, J. Leg. Med. 2:45, 1974.

37. Lappe, Genetic knowledge and the concept of health, Hastings Cent. Rep. 3:1, 1973.

38. Reich & Smith, The anguish of decision-on the birth of a severely handicapped infant, Hastings Cent. Rep. 3:10, 1973.

39. Monreal, Abortion and legislation, Rev. Chil. Obstet. Ginecol. 38:76, 1973 (SPA.).

40. Gustafson, Mongolism, parental desires, and the right to life, Perspect. Biol. Med. 16:529, 1973.

41. Duff & Campbell, Moral and ethical dilemmas in the special-care nursery, New Eng. J. Med. 289:890, 1973.

42. Editorial, New horizons in medical ethics, Br Med. J. 2:680, 1973.

43. Christian, Malformations in newborn infants. New legal requirements for registration and statistical methods, Fortschr. Med. 28:1089, 1973 (GER.).

44. Freeman, To treat or not to treat - ethical dilemmas of the infant with a myelomeningocele, Clin. Neurosurg. 20:134, 1973.

45. Strang, Foetal medicine, Trans. Med. Soc. Lond. 89:164, 1973.

46. MacKeith, The Gavin Livingstone memorial lecture. The prevention of handicaps, Guys Hosp. Rep. 121:237, 1972.

47. Edwards, The problem of compensation for antenatal injuries, Nature 246:54, 1973.
48. Shepard et al, Editorial - Legislative threat to research on human congenital defects, Teratology 8:243, 1973.
49. Rozovsky, Rights before birth, Can. Hosp. 50:17, 1973.
50. Fischer, Mandatory legislation for the screening of newborns for PKU in the United States, Ment. Retard. 9:25, 1971.
51. Editorial, The use of human fetal material for research, Med. Leg. J. 40:75, 1972.
52. Editorial, Intensive care and low birth-weight, Lancet 2: 1183, 1972.
53. McWhirter, Legal rights of the unborn, Ariz. Med. 29:926, 1972.
54. Editorial, Right of fetal to sue, Br. Med. J. 1:244, 1973.
55. Editorial, Antenatal injury, Br. Med. J. 1:191, 1973.
56. Editorial, Early and periodic screening, diagnosis, and treatment, Pediatrics 51:741, 1973.
57. O'Beirn, Fetal rights and abortion laws, Br. Med. J., 1: 740, 1973.
58. Eckstein et al, New horizons in medical ethics. Severely malformed children, Br. Med. J. 2:284, 1973.
59. Hellegers, Amazing historical and biological errors in abortion decision, Hosp. Prog. 54:16, 1973.
60. Kelley, Role of the courts, Pediatrics 51:796, 1973.
61. Lanman, Population and politics, J. Pediat. 82:912, 1973.
62. Nadler, Fetal 'indications' for termination of pregnancy, Semin. Psychiat. 2:302, 1970.
63. Smithells & Beard, New horizons in medical ethics. Research investigations and the fetus, Br. Med. J. 2:464, 1973.
64. Cooke, Ethics and law on behalf of the mentally retarded. Pediat. Clin. North Am. 20:259, 1973.
65. Morison, Dying, Sci. Am. 229:54, 1973.
66. Ingelfinger, Bedside ethics for the hopeless case, New Eng. J. Med. 289:914, 1973.
67. Duff & Campbell, Moral and ethical dilemmas in the special-care nursery, New Eng. J. Med. 289:890, 1973.
68. Shaw, Dilemmas of 'informed consent' in children, New Eng. J. Med. 289:885, 1973.
69. Guttmacher & Pilpel, Abortion and the unwanted child, Fam. Plan. Perspect. 2:16, 1970.
70. Cutright, Illegitimacy - myths, causes and cures, Fam. Plan. Perspect. 3:25, 1971.
71. Luttger, Beginning of life and criminal law, Beitr.Gerichtl. Med. 27:23, 1970 (GER.).
72. Herzog, Proposed law for protection of life before birth, Beitr. Gerichtl. Med. 27:14, 1970.
73. Cooke, Is there a right to die -- quickly, J. Pediat. 80: 906, 1972.
74. Kahn et al, The impact of recent changes in therapeutic abortion laws, Clin. Obstet. Gynecol. 14:1130, 1971.

75. Burns, Rubella and abortion laws, Med. Leg. Bull. 208:1, 1970.
76. Saylor, Hemolytic disease of the newborn. A new law for prenatal blood test and disease reporting, Calif. Med. 112: 79, 1970.
77. Editorial, Interruption of pregnancy before the period of fetal viability. The opinion of the national medical council about the abortion, Presse Med. 78:2147, 1970 (FRE.).
78. Goodhart, The biologist's dilemma, Nature 229:213, 1971.
79. Veghelyi, Ethics of intensive treatment, Anaesthesist. 19: 468, 1970.
80. Editorial, Fetal rights, Can. Med. Assoc. J. 104:61, 1971.
81. Zuelzer, The pediatrician and the species - Some implications of our achievements, Pediatrics 47:339, 1971.
82. Curran, The thalidomide tragedy in Germany - The end of a historic medicolegal trial, New Eng. J. Med. 284:481, 1971.
83. Blei, Bodily injury by damage to the fetus, Munch Med. Wochenschr, 112:741, 1970 (GER.).
84. Ingelfinger, Medical obligations imposed by abortion, New Eng. J. Med. 284:727, 1971.
85. Dyck, Ethical issues in community and research medicine, New Eng. J. Med. 284:725, 1971.
86. Ramsey, The ethics of a cottage industry in an age of community and research medicine, New Eng. J. Med. 284:700, 1971.
87. Haynes, Preservation of the unfit, Med. J. Aust. 1:650, 1971.
88. Resnik & Wittlin, Abortion and suicidal behaviors - Observations on the concept of 'endangering the mental health of the mother, Ment. Hyg. 55:10, 1971.
89. Katzen, The decision to treat myelomeningocele on the first day of life, So. Afr. Med. J. 45:345, 1971.
90. The Committee of Physicians' Responsibility 1970, Lakartidningen 68:2393, 1971 (SWE.).
91. Heese, Thoughts on the ethics of treating or operating on newborns and infants with congenital abnormalities, So. Afr. Med. J. 45:631, 1971.
92. Klose et al, Cesarean section in the dying and the dead -- Medical and legal evaluation, Geburtshilfe Frauenheilkd 31: 778, 1971 (GER.).
93. Brocklehurst, Meningomyelocele - The price of treatment, Br. Med. J. 3:429, 1971.
94. Zachary, Moral and social problems in intensive treatment of myelomeningocele. Moral, philosophical, religious and social bases of intensive treatment of severe forms of myelomeningocele, Ann. Chir. Infant. 10:7, 1969 (FRE.).
95. Leone, Legislative regulations on the reporting of the birth of deformed infants, Minerva Med. 60:4485, 1969 (ITA.).
96. Diddle, Gravid women at work. Fetal and maternal morbidity, employment policy, and medicolegal aspects, J. Occup. Med. 12: 10, 1970.
97. Resnick, Murder of the newborn - A psychiatric review of neonaticide, Amer. J. Psychiat. 126:1414, 1970.

98. Editorial, New dimensions in legal and ethical concepts for
     human research. 2. Special problems of medical disciplines.
     Panel discussion, Ann. NY Acad. Sci. 169:382, 1970.
99. Ayd, Fetology - Medical and ethical implications of interven-
     tion in the prenatal period, Ann. NY Acad. Sci. 169:376, 1970.
100. Droegemueller & Taylor, Is therapeutic abortion preventable.
     Obstet. Gynec. 35:758, 1970.
101. Editorial, Experiments on the fetus, Brit. Med. J. 1:433, 1970.
102. Uhlenbruck, Refusal of consent for medical treatment on re-
     ligious grounds, Med. Klin. 63:1125, 1968 (GER.).
103. Resnick, Child murder by parents - A psychiatric review of
     filicide, Amer. J. Psychiat. 126:325, 1969.
104. Curran, Public health and the law. Illegal therapeutic
     abortions - The modern dilemma, Amer. J. Pub. Health 59:
     1434, 1969.

                        PRENATAL GENETIC DIAGNOSIS

105. Milunsky, The prenatal diagnosis of hereditary disorders,
     Charles C. Thomas, Springfield, 1973.
106. Nadler, Prenatal detection of genetic disorders, in Advances
     in human genetics, Vol. 3, H. Harris & K. Hirschhorn (eds.),
     Plenum Press, New York, 1972, p. 1.
107. Milunsky, The prevention of genetic disease and mental retard-
     ation. W.B. Saunders Company, Philadelphia, 1975.
108. Koch, Bibliographica genetica medica, Vol. 4, Verlag Palm und
     Enke, Erlangen, 1975.
109. Milunsky, et al, Prenatal genetic diagnosis, New Eng. J. Med.
     283:1370, 1441, 1498, 1970.
110. Milunsky & Reilly, The "new" genetics: Emerging medicolegal
     issues in the prenatal diagnosis of hereditary disorders,
     Am. J. L. Med. 1:71, 1975.
111. Hirschhorn, The role and the hazards of amniocentesis, Ann.
     NY Acad. Sci. 240:117, 1975.
112. Powledge & Sollitto, Prenatal diagnosis - The past and the
     future, Hastings Cent. Rep. 4:11, 1974.
113. Friedman, Legal implications of amniocentesis, U. Pa. L. Rev.
     123:92, 1974.
114. Ormrod, The medico-legal aspects of sex determination, Med.
     Leg. J. 40:78, 1972.
115. Adams, Amniocentesis - Medical and social implications,
     Rev. Med. Suisse Romande 91:389, 1971.
116. Epstein, Medical genetics: Recent advances with legal impli-
     cations, Hastings L. J. 21:35, 1969.
117. Lappe, How much do we want to know about the unborn?, Hastings
     Cent. Rep. 3:8, 1973

GENETIC COUNSELING

118. Sorenson, Social and psychological aspects of applied human genetics: A bibliography. Fogarty Internatl. Cntr., DHEW Publicat. No. 73-412 (NIH).
119. Koch, Bibliographica genetica medica, Vol. 4, Verlag Palm und Enke, Erlangen, 1975.
120. Milunsky, The prevention of genetic disease and mental retardation, W.B. Saunders Company, Philadelphia, 1975.
121. Shaw, Editorial - Genetic counseling, Science 184:751, 1974.
122. Singer, Impact of the law on genetic counseling, Birth Defects 9:34, 1973.
123. Lappe'et al, The genetic counselor: Responsible to whom?, Hastings Cent. Rep. #2, p. 6, 1971.
124. Parker, Some ethical and legal aspects of genetic counseling, Birth Defects 6:52, 1970.
125. Martin, Modern medical practice and malpractice litigation in relation to genetic counseling, Birth Defects 5:58, 1970.
126. Parker, Some legal aspects of genetic counseling, Prog. Med. Genet. 7:217, 1970.

GENETIC SCREENING

127. Bergsma, Ethical, social and legal dimensions of screening for human genetic disease, Birth Defects: Orig. Art. Ser., The National Foundation March of Dimes, Vol. X, Stratton Intercontinental Med. Book Corp., New York, 1974.
128. Genetic Screening. Programs, principles, and research. Committee for the Study of Inborn Errors of Metabolism. National Acad. Sciences, Washington, D.C., 1975.
129. Scriver & Rosenberg, Amino acid metabolism and its disorders, W.B. Saunders Company, Philadelphia, 1973.
130. Milunsky, The prevention of genetic disease and mental retardation, W.B. Saunders Company, Philadelphia, 1975.
131. Levy, Genetic screening in Advances in human genetics, Vol. 4, H. Harris & K. Hirschhorn (eds.), Plenum Press, New York, 1973, p. 1.
132. Annas & Coyne, Fitness for birth and reproduction: Legal implications of genetic screening, Fam. L.Q. 9: No. 3, 1975.
133. Reilly, Genetic screening legislation, Adv. Hum. Genet. 5: 319, 1975.
134. Dexter, Screening and prevention of high-grade mental retardation - To what purpose? Under what circumstances? On what premises?, Bull. NY Acad. Med. 51:169, 1975.
135. Curran, The questionable virtues of genetic screening laws, Am. J. Publ. Health 64:1003, 1974.
136. Schmidt, Hemoglobinopathy screening - Approaches to diagnosis, education and counseling, Am. J. Publ. Health 64:799, 1974.

137. Frankenburg, Pediatric screening, Adv. Pediat. 20:149, 1973.
138. Waltz & Thigpen, Genetic screening and counseling: The legal
      and ethical issues, NW U. L. Rev. 68:696, 1973.
139. Reilly, Sickle cell anemia legislation, J. Leg. Med. 1:36,
      1973.
140. Swazey, Phenylketonuria: A case study in biomedical legisla-
      tion, J. Urban L. 48:883, 1971.
141. Ashley, The Oregon program of screening for inborn errors of
      metabolism, Northwest Med. 70:268, 1971.
142. Mitchell, Legislation in the provision of mass screening and
      other medical services, Health Bull. 28:78, 1970.
143. Holm et al, Some factors influencing the development of a
      voluntary PKU screening program. Possible implication for
      other screening procedures for newborns, J.A.M.A. 212:1835,
      1970.
144. Rothenberg & Sills, Iatrogenesis - The PKU anxiety syndrome,
      J. Amer. Acad. Child Psychiat. 7:689, 1968.

GENETICS AND FAMILY LAW

a. Disputed paternity

145. Hawkins, The scope of blood genetic marker investigations in
      paternity testing in Chinese and Malays, Singapore Med. J.
      15:128, 1974.
146. Speiser et al, Exclusion of paternity in the HL-A system
      without testing the deceased accused man, Vox. Sang. 27:379,
      1974.
147. King et al, Pitfalls in paternity testing, Ohio State Med.
      J. 70:724, 1974.
148. Welch & Dodd, Red cell glutamate-pyruvate transaminase in
      studies of paternity cases in the United Kingdom, Forensic
      Sci. 3:39, 1974.
149. Mayr, The HL-A-system in paternity testing (Author's transl.),
      Z. Rechtsmed. 75:81, 1974(GER.).
150. Salmon, Estimation of probability of paternity from blood
      groups and genetic markers (Author's transl.), Nouv. Rev.
      Fr. Hematol. 14:477, 1974 (FRE.).
151. Salmon, Applications of blood groups to human genetics, Ann.
      Biol. Clin. 32:385, 1974 (FRE.).
152. King, Studies on exclusion of paternity, Cleve Clin. Q. 41:
      15, 1974.
153. Bias, Exclusion of paternity, Am. J. Hum. Genet. 27:245,
      1975.
154. Wiener, Chances of proving nonpaternity with tests for a
      sex-linked trait, Am. J. Hum. Genet. 27:243, 1975.
155. Welch, Red cell esterase D in studies of paternity cases in
      the United Kingdom, Vox. Sang. 28:366, 1975.

156. Salmon, Bayesian process for paternity diagnosis, Methods
      Inf. Med. 7:291, 1973.
157. Knubbmann, Differences between mother-child and father-child
      correlations of the dermatoglyphics in man (Author's transl.),
      Humangenetik 19:145, 1973 (GER.).
158. Farhud & Walter, Use of C3(Beta-1C-globulin) polymorphism in
      cases of disputed paternity (Author's transl.), Z. Rechtsmed.
      72:225, 1973 (GER.).
159. Paige & Paige, The politics of birth practices - A strategic
      analysis, Am. Sociol. Rev. 38:663, 1973.
160. Sussman, Medicolegal blood grouping tests (Parentage exclusion
      tests), Prog. Clin. Pathol. 5:143, 1973.
161. Ellis et al, Application of GM typing in cases of disputed
      paternity, J. Forensic Sci. 18:290, 1973.
162. Sussman, Blood grouping tests for non-paternity, J. Forensic
      Sci. 18:287, 1973.
163. Speiser, et al, An exclusion of paternity in the HL-A system
      without testing the deceased accused man (Author's transl.),
      Wien Klin. Wochenschr. 86:317, 1974 (GER.).
164. King, Studies on exclusion of paternity, Cleve. Clin. Q.
      41:15, 1974.
165. Heide et al, Forensic importance of spectrophotometric tests
      of the isoenzyme systems red cell acid phosphatase and glu-
      tamatic-pyruvic transaminase in settlement of paternity dis-
      putes (Author's transl.), Z. Rechtsmed. 74:177, 1974 (Ger.).
166. Spielmann & Seidl, The application of the HL-A-system in cases
      of disputed paternity. Studies on 110 families (Author's
      transl.), Z. Rechtsmed. 74:121, 1974 (GER.).
167. Chakraborty et al, exclusion of paternity - The current state
      of the art, Am. J. Hum. Genet. 26:477, 1974.
168. Kirk, The haptoglobin groups in man, Monogr. Hum. Genet. 4:
      1, 1968.
169. Jeannet et al, Use of the HL-A antigen system in disputed
      paternity cases, Vox. Sang. 23:197, 1972.
170. Mayr, The HL-A-system, Folia Haematol. 97:245, 1972 (GER.).
171. Soulier et al, Evaluation of paternity using the HL-A
      system, Rev. Fr. Transfus. 15:11, 1972 (FRE.).
172. Kellermann et al, Suitability of the PI-system in disputed
      paternity, Z. Rechtsmed. 71:24, 1972 (GER.).
173. Lefevre et al, Value of the adenosine deaminase (ADA) iso-
      enzyme system for forensic evidence - Statistical dependa-
      bility testing of paternity exclusion claims, Z. Rechtsmed.
      71:17, 1972 (GER.).
174. Sorgo, Problem of superfecundation in paternity testimonies,
      Beitr. Gerichtl. Med. 30:415, 1973 (GER.).
175. Sussman & Solomon, Another pitfall in blood group testing
      for nonpaternity, Transfusion 13:231, 1973.
176. Sussman & Bove, Disputed parentage, CRC Crit. Rev. Clin.
      Lab. Sci. 1:45, 1970
177. Wust, The red cell adenosine deaminase (ADA) polymorphism in

Vienna. Distribution and usefulness in disputed parentage.
Preliminary report, Vox. Sang. 20:267, 1971.

178. Rex-Kiss & Szabo, Experiences with M-N blood group examinations in cases of disputed paternity, Z. Rechtsmed. 69:
135, 1971 (GER.).

179. Mayr & Mickerts, Human gamma globulin polymorphism. Calculation of its distribution in Vienna and its suitability in
paternity cases, Acta Biol. Med. Ger. 25:473, 1970 (GER.).

180. Abe & Pausch, The kell-cellano blood group system in clinical
and medico-legal practice. A survey convering a period of
twenty years, Haematologia 5:217, 1971.

181. Endo, Laws concerning paternity, Jap. J. Midwife 25:52, 1971.

182. Jonasson et al, HL-A antigens and heteromorphic fluorescence
characters of chromosomes in prenatal paternity investigation,
Nature 236:312, 1972.

183. Rust, On the probability of detecting nonpaternity through the
Rh blood-group system, Am. J. Hum. Genet. 24:54, 1972.

184. Peritz & Rust, On the estimation of the nonpaternity rate
using more than one blood-group system, Am. J. Hum. Genet. 24:
46, 1972.

185. Trube-Becker, Expert testimony on gestational age, Z. Rechtsmed. 70:1, 1972 (GER.).

186. Bradbrook et al, AG(X) and AG(Y) antigens in studies of paternity cases in the United Kingdom, Hum. Hered. 21:493, 1971.

187. Teisberg, Application of the C3 system in paternity cases,
Vox. Sang. 22:213, 1972.

188. Dodd, Some recent advances in forensic serology, Med. Sci. Law.
12:195, 1972.

189. Keune & Rothe, Legal questions regarding human artificial
insemination. II, Z. Aerztl. Fortbild. 66:189, 1972 (GER.).

190. Zimmermann & Kaiser, Calculation of the probability of paternity by use of the binomial-formula, Z. Rechtsmed. 70:
93, 1972 (GER.).

191. Bauer et al, The frequency of adenylate kinase-(AK-) types
in Vienna - Application to forensic serology and value in
disputed paternity, Wien Klin Wochenschr. 84:369, 1972 (GER.).

b. Genetic Intervention

192. Murphy, Clinical genetics: Some neglected facets, New Eng.
J. Med. 292:458, 1975.

193. Lappe, The human uses of molecular genetics, Fed. Proc. 34:
1425, 1975.

194. Roblin, Ethical and social aspects of experimental gene
manipulation, Fed. Proc. 34:1421, 1975.

195. Eisinger, The ethics of human gene manipulation. Introductory
remarks, Fed. Proc. 34:1418, 1975.

196. Widdus & Ault, Progress in research related to genetic engineering and life, Int. Rev. Cytol. 38:7, 1974

197. Vaisrub, Editorial: Shaking hands with the future, J.A.M.A. 230:589, 1974.
198. Editorial, Hazards of genetic experiments, Br. Med. J. 3:483, 1974.
199. Davis, Editorial: Genetic engineering: How great is the danger?, Science 186:309, 1974.
200. Vaux, Generating man, Tex. Rep. Biol. Med. 32:351, 1974.
201. Moore, This is medical ethics?, Hastings Cent. Rep. 4:1, 1974.
202. Fox, Ethical and existential developments in contemporaneous American medicine: Their implications for culture and society, Milbank Mem. Fund Q. 52:445, 1974.
203. Stent, The dilemma of science and morals, Genetics 78: 41, 1974.
204. Dunlop, Genetic engineering -- A waste of valuable resources?, Publ. Health 89:13, 1974.
205. Callahan, Human rights - biogenetic frontier and beyond, Hosp. Prog. 54:80, 1973.
206. Snow, Human Care, J.A.M.A. 225:617, 1973.
207. Danks, Prospects for the prevention of genetic disease, Med. J. Aust. 1:573, 1973.
208. Editorial, Population and the new biology, Lancet 2:834, 1973.
209. Riga, Genetic experimentation - The new ethic, Hosp. Prog. 54:59, 1973.
210. Nichols, New directions in genetics utilizing tissue culture techniques, Hereditas 67:1, 1972.
211. Good, On the threshold of biologic engineering, Am. J. Med. Technol. 38:153, 1972.
212. Editorial, Gene therapy for human genetic disease, Science 178:648, 1972.
213. Klinger, Correction of genetic defects in vitro -- prospects and problems, Bull. Schweiz. Akad. Med. Wiss. 28:342, 1972.
214. Weber, Synthetic genes, Bull Schweiz. Akad. Med. Wiss. 28: 320, 1972 (GER.).
215. Luria, Ethical aspects of the new perspectives in biomedical research, Experientia 17:224, 1972.
216. Eppenberger, Genetic manipulation of the cell, Schweiz. Med. Wochenschr. 102:1777, 1972 (GER.).
217. Lappe', Genetic counseling and genetic engineering, Hastings Cent. Rep. #3, p. 13, 1971.
218. Vinokurova, Genetics: Today and tomorrow, Soc. Biol. 17: 54, 1970.

c. Artificial Insemination

219. Zvolsky et al, Psychiatric, genetic and gynecological charac- teristic features of a matrimony asking for artificial fertil ization (Author's transl.), Cesk. Gynekol. 39:199, 1974 (CZE.).
220. Beck, Artificial insemination and semen preservation, Clin.

Obstet. Gynecol. 17:115, 1974.
221. Sillo-Seidl, Opportunities and possibilities of artificial sperm transmission, Acta Ginecol. 25:701, 1974 (SPA.).
222. Barkey et al, A new, practical method of freezing and storing human sperm and a preliminary report on its use, Fertil. Steril. 25:399, 1974.
223. Schwalm, Legal comments on human artificial insemination, Med. Klin. 69:1554, 1974.
224. Warner, Artificial insemination. Review after thirty-two years' experience, NY State J. Med. 74:2358, 1974.
225. Frankel, Role of semen cryobanking in American medicine, Br. Med. J. 3:5931, 1974.
226. Lappe & Steinfels, Choosing the sex of our children: A dream come true or--?, Hastings Cent. Rep. 4:1, 1974.
227. Soupart, Experimental human fecundation. Status of the problem and future perspectives, Brux. Med. 54:473, 1974.
228. Frankel, Artificial insemination: The medical profession and public policy, Conn. Med. 38:476, 1974.
229. Carruthers, Artificial insemination with husband semen, Med. Gynaecol. Androl. Sociol. 8:4, 1974.
230. Fraser, The long-term genetical effects of recent advances in the treatment and prevention of inherited disease, Br. J. Psychiat. 125:521, 1974.
231. Barwin, Intrauterine insemination of husband's semen, J. Reprod. Fertil. 36:101, 1974.
232. Gigon, Medical and legal aspects of heterologous insemination, Schweiz. Med. Wochenschr. 104:48, 1974 (GER.).
233. Swaab, Results and experiences with donor insemination. Ned. Tijdschr. Geneeskd. 118:493, 1974 (DUT.).
234. Edwards, Fertilization of human eggs in vitro - Morals, ethics and the law, Q. Rev. Biol. 49:3, 1974.
235. Parkes, Sexuality and reproduction, Perspect. Biol. Med. 17: 399, 1974.
236. Lebech, Editorial - Problems with heterological insemination, Ugeskr. Laeger. 136:837, 1974 (DAN.).
237. Robertson, Donor insemination -- A substitute for the infertile male, NZ J. Obstet. Gynaecol. 13:224, 1973.
238. Goldman & Zuckerman, Artificial insemination and its problems, Harefuah. 85:377, 1973 (HEB.).
239. Editorial, Social implications of genetic engineering, Eng. Symp. Soc. Dev. Biol. 31:355, 1973.
240. Mohr, Social and ethical implications of recent developments in biology and medicine. A United Nations proposal for establishment of an international commission, Ugeskr, Laeger. 135:2536, 1973 (DAN.).
241. Sillo-Seidl, The number of pregnancies after artificial inseminations in relation to the number of donors, Acta Eur. Fertil. 4:105, 1973.
242. Fiumara, Transmission of gonorrhoea by artificial insemina-

tion, Br. J. Vener. Dis. 48:308, 1972.

243. Emperaire et al, Preservation of human sperm. Present status and prospects, Bord. Med. 5:1819, 1972 (FRE.).

244. Hershey, Legal and social policy issues pertaining to recent developments in genetics, Birth Defects 8:83, 1972.

245. Smith & Steinberger, Survival of spermatozoa in a human sperm bank. Effects of long-term storage in liquid nitrogen, J.A.M.A. 223:774, 1973.

246. Tyler & Berger, Cryobanking of semen, New Eng. J. Med. 288: 527, 1973.

247. Sherwood, Some legal aspects of semen storage and family planning programs, J. Reprod. Med. 10:208, 1973.

248. Hanack, Legal aspects of heterologous insemination, Geburtshilfe Frauenheilkd. 33:161, 1973 (GER.).

249. Editorial, A.I.D., Lancet 1:755, 1973.

250. Slome, Artificial insemination by donor, Br. Med. J. 2: 365, 1973.

251. McLaren & Parkes, Ciba foundation symposium. Legal and other aspects of artificial insemination by donor (AID) and embryo transfer, J. Biosoc.Sci. 5:205, 1973.

252. Scott, Artificial insemination by donor, Br. Med. J. 2: 781, 1973.

253. Schulz, Legal problems in artificial insemination, Med. Klin. 68:683, 1973 (GER.).

254. Schill, Sperm banks in the federal republic of Germany, Med. Klin. 68:683, 1973 (GER.).

255. Haderka, Current genetics and our contemporary family law, Cesk. Zdrav. 21:119, 1973.

256. Wadlington, Artificial insemination: The dangers of a poorly kept secret, NW U. L. Rev. 64:777, 1970.

257. McLaren, Biological regulation of reproduction. In the family and its future, Ciba Found. Symp. p. 101, 1970.

258. Sherwood, Some legal implications of frozen semen banks, J. Reprod. Med. 8:190, 1972.

259. Ramsey, Shall we 'reproduce' II. Rejoinders and future forecast, J.A.M.A. 220:1480, 1972.

260. Editorial, Genetic engineering-reprise, J.A.M.A. 220:1356, 1972.

261. Keune & Rothe, Legal questions regarding human artificial insemination. II. Z. Aerztl. Fortbild. 66:189, 1972 (GER.).

262. Keune & Rothe, Legal questions on artificial insemination in man. I, Z.Aerztl. Fortbild. 66:138, 1972.

d. In Vitro Fertilization

263. Thompson & Zamboni, Anomalous patterns of mammalian oocyte maturation and fertilization, Am. J. Anat. 142:233, 1975.

264. Petrovaamaslakov et al, Fertilization of human ova in vitro, Bull. Exp. Biol. Med. 76:12, 1974.

265. Cure et al, Growth characteristics of human embryonic cell lines with chromosomal anomalies, Biomedicine 21:233, 1974.
266. Lappé, Ethics of in-vitro fertilization: Risk-taking for the unborn, Wien Klin Wochenschr. 86:1, 1974.
267. Soupart, Experimental human fecundation. Status of the problem and future perspectives, Brux. Med. 54:473, 1974.
268. Rutkis, In vitro fertilization of rabbit oocytes, Arkh. Anat. Gistol. Embriol. 67:62, 1974.
269. Soupart & Strong, Ultrastructural observations on human oocytes fertilized in vitro, Fertil. Steril. 25:11, 1974.
270. Cassiman & Bernfield, Morphogenetic properties of human embryonic cells - Aggregation of dissociated cells and histogenesis in cultured aggregates, Pediat. Res. 8:184, 1974.
271. Tyler et al, Current status of in vitro fertilization and embryo transplantation, J. Reprod. Med. 11:200, 1973.
272. Editorial, In vitro fertilization of human ova and blastocyst transfer. An invitational symposium, J. Reprod. Med. 11: 192, 1973.
273. Petrov-Maslakov et al, In vitro fertilization of human ova, Biull Eksp. Biol. Med. 76:73, 1973 (RUS.).
274. Soupart & Morgenstern, Human sperm capacitation and in vitro fertilization, Fertil. Steril. 24:462, 1973.
275. Fowler & Edwards, The genetics of early human development, Prog. Med. Genet. 9:49, 1973.
276. De Kretzer et al, Transfer of a human zygote, Lancet 2: 728, 1973.
277. Editorial, Genetic engineering - reprise, J.A.M.A. 220: 1356, 1972.
278. Ramsey, Shall we 'reproduce' I. The medical ethics of in vitro fertilization, J.A.M.A. 220:1346, 1972.
279. Metz, Effects of antibodies on gametes and fertilization, Biol. Reprod. 6:358, 1972.
280. Edwards, Culture of human embryos in vitro, Acta Endocrinol. 166:131, 1972.
281. Kass, Babies by means of in vitro fertilization - Unethical experiments on the unborn, New Eng. J. Med. 285:1174, 1971.
282. Editorial, Rules and regulations for test-tube babies, Nature 231:69, 1971.
283. McLaren, Biological regulation of reproduction. In - the family and its future, Ciba Found. Symp. p. 101,1970.

EUGENICS, ETHICS, LAW, EXPERIMENTATION, AND GENETICS

284. Sj-Ovall, Voluntary versus compulsory sterilization in Sweden then and now, Lakartidningen 72:241, 1975 (SWE.).
285. Holt, Science as social and political reform. Monists and Nazis: A question of scientific responsibility, Hastings Cent. Rep. 5:37, 1975.
286. Martin, Ethical standards for fetal experimentation, Ford.

L. Rev. 43:547, 1975.
287. Robertson, Involuntary Euthanasia of the newborn, Stanford
      L. Rev. 27:213, 1975.
288. Note, Medical responsibility for fetal survival under Roe
      and Doe, Harv. Civ. Rights - Civ. Lib. L. Rev. 10:444, 1975.
289. Brodie, Marriage and the new biology, L. & Soc. Order 177,
      1970, Delgado & Keyes, Parental preferences and selective
      abortion: A commentary on Roe v. Wade, Doe v. Bolton and the
      shape of things to come, 1974 Wash. L.Q. 203.
290. Murdock, Sterilization of the retarded: A problem or a
      solution?, Calif. L. Rev. 62:917, 1974.
291. Shapiro, Who merits merit? Problems in distributive justice
      and utility posed by the new biology, Cal. L. Rev.48:318,
      1974.
292. Note, Governmental control of research in positive eugenics,
      J.L. Reform 7:615, 1974.
293. Note, XYY Syndrome and the judicial system, N.C. Central L.J.
      6:66, 1974.
294. Note, Fetal experimentation: Moral, legal, and medical
      implications, Stan. L. Rev. 26:1191, 1974.
295. Heymann & Barzelay, The forest and the trees: Roe v. Wade
      and its critics, B.U.L. Rev. 53:765, 1973.
296. Kindregan, State power over human fertility and individual
      liberty, Hastings L. J. 23:1401, 1972.
297. Spraic, Sexual selection and the law, Colo. Q. 20:516, 1972.
298. Greenwalt, Criminal law and population control, Vand. L. Rev.
      24:465, 1971.
299. Louisell, Biology, Law and Reason: Man as self-creator, Am.
      J. Juris 16:1, 1971.
300. Robinson, Genetics and society, Utah L. Rev. 487, 1971.
301. Rosenberg & Dunn, Genetics and criminal responsibility, Mass.
      L.W. 56:413, 1971.
302. Vukowich, Dawning of the brave new world - legal, ethical and
      social issues of eugenics, 1971 U. Ill. L. F. 189.
303. Friedman, Interference with human life: Some jurisprudential
      reflections, Columbia L. Rev. 70:1058, 1970.
304. Note, The XYY defense, Georgetown L. J. 57:892, 1969.
305. Note, Eugenic sterilization - A scientific analysis,
      Denver L.J. 46:631, 1969.
306. O'Hara & Sanks, Eugenic sterilization, Georgetown L. J. 45:
      20, 1956.
307. Paul, The return of punitive sterilization proposals, Law &
      Society 3:77, 1968.
308. Tedeschi, On tort liability for "wrongful life," Israel L.
      Rev. 1:513, 1966.
309. Means, The law of New York concerning abortions and the status
      of the foetus, 1664-1968: A case of cessation of constitution-
      ality, N.Y.L. Forum 14:411, 1968.
310. Forney, The new biology and the future of man, U.C.L.A.L. Rev.
      15:273, 1968.

311. Murphy, The normal, eugenics and racial survival, Johns
      Hopkins Med. J. 136:98, 1975.
312. Wendt, Genetics and society, Med. Klin. 69:1689, 1974.
313. Hartlmaier, Justified trust in the geneticist. Eugenics,
      conducted the right way, Zahnaerztl. Mitt. 64:172, 1974.
314. Twiss, Examining the pros and cons of parental responsibility
      for genetic health, Hastings Cent. Rep. 4:9, 1974.
315. Osborn, History of the American eugenics society, Soc. Biol.
      21:115, 1974.
316. Editorial, Ethics of selective abortion, Br. Med. J. 4:
      676, 1974.
317. Schultz & Henning, Comparative studies on the new legalization
      of legal abortion, Zentralbl. Gynaekol. 96:1217, 1974.
318. Pace, Eugenic consultation, Minerva Med. 65:4754, 1974.
319. Gibson, Involuntary sterilization of the mentally retarded-
      A western Canadian phenomenon, Can. Psychiat. Assoc. J.
      19:59, 1974.
320. Motulsky, Brave new world, Science 185:653, 1974.
321. Greenblatt, Class action and the right to treatment, Hosp.
      Commun. Psychiat. 25:449, 1974.
322. Schwartz, Litigating the right to treatment - Wyatt v.
      Stickney, Hosp. Commun. Psychiat. 25:460, 1974.
323. Kunitz, Some notes on physiologic conditions as social
      problems, Soc. Sci. Med. 8:207, 1974.
324. Mills, Abortions, sterilizations, and religion, J.A.M.A.
      229:338, 1974.
325. Editorial, Litigation tied to ligation, J. Leg. Med. 2:8, 1974.
326. Bernstein, Law in brief - Abortion - The unanswered questions,
      Hospitals 48:108, 1974.
327. Eaves & Eysenck, Genetics and the development of social
      attitudes, Nature 249:288, 1974.
328. Perlman, Human experimentation, J. Leg. Med. 2:40, 1974.
329. Israel, Current concepts in female sterilization, Clin.
      Obstet. Gynecol. 17:139, 1974.
330. Greenberg, Medicine and public affairs, New Eng. J. Med.
      290:977, 1974.
331. Begab, The major dilemma of mental retardation - Shall we
      prevent it (Some social implications of research in mental
      retardation), Am. J. Ment. Defic. 78:519, 1974.
332. Schulte, Challenges to individual and corporate rights,
      Hosp. Prog. 55:52, 1974.
333. O'Rourke, Rationale and implications of sanctity of life
      commitment, Hosp. Prog. 55:57, 1974.
334. Pickering, The Pickering report. V. A patient's bill or rights,
      Can. Med. Assoc. J. 110:344, 1974.
335. Holder, Recent decisions on pain and suffering, J.A.M.A.
      227:1204, 1974.
336. Editorial, Medicine and the law. Federal court holds Texas
      Catholic Hospital has right to deny hospital facilities for
      sterilization, Tex. Med. 70:99, 1974.

337. Smiley, Sterilization and therapeutic abortion counseling
      for the mentally retarded, Can. Psychiat. Assoc. J. 19:65,
      1974.
338. Romano, Reflections on informed consent, Arch. Gen. Psychiat.
      30:129, 1974.
339. Eisinger, The ethics of human gene manipulation. Introductory
      remarks, Fed. Proc. 34:1418, 1975.
340. McGarrah, Voluntary female sterilization: Abuses, risks and
      guidelines, Hastings Cent. Rep. 4:5, 1974.
341. Peck, Voluntary female sterilization: Attitudes and legisla-
      tion, Hastings Cent. Rep. 4:8, 1974.
342. Rosner, Modern medicine, religion, and law; Human experi-
      mentation, NY State J. Med. 75:758, 1975.
343. Fanconi, The problem of the medical indication for artifici-
      al abortion, Minerva Pediat. 27:455, 1975 (ITA).
344. Cruz-Coke, A genetic reform to the civil law (Author's
      transl.), Rev. Med. Chil. 102:711, 1974 (SPA.).
345. Zimmerly, Consent to sterilization: Are we creating new prob-
      lems?, J. Leg. Med. 3:4, 1975.
346. Shanklin, Editorial: It is time to take a stand, J. Reprod.
      Med. 14:41, 1975.
347. Blomquist & Giertz, Ethic aspects on treatment of children
      with spina bifida, Lakartidningen, 71:5283, 1974.
348. Stern, Presidential address. The domain of genetics,
      Genetics 78:21, 1974.
349. Stent, The dilemma of science and morals, Genetics 78:1, 1974.
350. Berman, Michigan pediatricians ponder care of congenitally
      defective and handicapped, Mich. Med. 73:675, 1974.
351. Leyhausen, The biological basis of ethics and morality,
      Sci. Med. Man. 1:215, 1974.
352. Cleland & Sluyter, The Alabama decision: Unequivocal blessing?,
      Comm. Ment. Health J. 10:409, 1974.
353. Moise, Will the real advocate for the retarded please stand
      up?, Child. Welfare 54:27, 1975.
354. Moore, This is medical ethics?, Hastings Cent. Rep. 4:1, 1974.
355. Simonaitis, Compulsory participation in voluntary steriliza-
      tion, J.A.M.A. 230:1453, 1974.
356. Davis, Editorial: Genetic engineering: How great is the
      danger?, Science 186:309, 1974.
357. Vaughan, Community, courts, and conditions of special edu-
      cation today - Why, Ment. Retard. 11:43, 1973.
358. Weingold, Rights of the retarded, Ment. Retard. 11:50, 1973.
359. Kaltreider, Contraception, sterilization, abd abortion legal
      interpretation of consent, MD State Med. J. 22:67, 1973.
360. Murphy, The normal, Am. J. Epidemiol. 98:403, 1973.
361. Ikonen, Sterilization, Duodecim. 89:1657, 1973 (FIN.).
362. Editorial, Medicine and the law, Tex. Med. 69:124, 1973.
363. Williams, Euthanasia, Med. Leg. J. 41:14, 1973.
364. Schneider, Counseling for sterilization, Obstet. Gynecol.
      42:778, 1973.

365. Hiersche, When does life begin, Gynaekol. Rundsch. 13:212,
      1973 (GER.).
366. Gullatte, Medico-legal insurance implications of sickle cell
      anemia, J. Natl. Med. Assoc. 65:415, 1973.
367. Keemer, Involuntary sterilization, J. Natl. Med. Assoc.
      65:458, 1973.
368. Riga, Genetic experimentation - The new ethic, Hosp. Prog.
      54:59, 1973.
369. Weisboro, Birth control and the Black American: A matter of
      genocide?, Demography 10:571, 1973.
370. Regan, Constitutional rights of Catholic hospitals, Hosp.
      Prog. 54:66, 1973.
371. Smiley, Sterilization and therapeutic abortion counselling
      for the mentally retarded, Curr. Ther. Res. 15:78, 1973.
372. Gelfman, 'Wrongful life' revisited - A question of fact,
      Forensic Sci. 2:169, 1973.
373. Diddle, Rights affecting human reproduction, Obstet. Gynecol.
      41:789, 1973.
374. Vogel, Risks and chances of progress for the genetic future
      of man (Author's transl.), Klin. Wochenschr. 51:575, 1973
      (GER.).
375. Hulka, Editorial - Eugenic sterilization in North Carolina,
      NC Med. J. 34:950, 1973.
376. Rollins & Wolfe, Eugenic sterilization in North Carolina,
      NC Med. J. 34:944, 1973.
377. Schroeder, New life - Person or property, Am. J. Psychiat.
      131:541, 1974.
378. Ackerman, Biological consequences of polulation control,
      Int. J. Fertil. 17:131, 1972.
379. Haderka, Modern genetics and our contemporary family law,
      Cesk. Epidemiol. Mikrobiol. Imunol. 21:119, 1973 (CHE.).
380. Lappe, Public policy toward environment 1973 - A review and
      appraisal. Human genetics, Ann. NY Acad. Sci. 216:152, 1973.
381. Enjolras, Traditional ethics and progress in genetics, Nouv.
      Presse. Med. 2:865, 1973.
382. Osborn, The emergence of a valid eugenics, Am. Sci. 61:
      425, 1973.
383. Sang, Nature, Nurture and eugenics, Postgrad. Med. J. 48:
      227, 1972.
384. Conterio, Limitations of eugenics, Ateneo Parmense Acta
      Biomed. 41:67, 1971.
385. Dubinin, Philosophical and sociological aspects of human
      genetics, Z. Aerztl. Fortbild. 66:437, 1972 (GER.).
386. Husquinet, Huntington's disease - social problem - eugenic
      problem, Arch Belg. Med. Soc. 30:65, 1972 (FRE.).
387. Li & Nei, Total number of individuals affected by a single
      deleterious mutation in a finite population, Am. J. Hum.
      Genet. 24:667, 1972.
388. D'Andrea, Eugenic legislation in the world, Minerva Med. 63:
      4644, 1972 (ITA.).

389. Borgaonkar, Recent developments in human genetics -- Their
      usefulness and impact on society, Birth Defects 8:8, 1972.
390. Crow, Advances in human genetics and their impact on society.
      Introductory remarks, Birth Defects 8:5, 1972.
391. Hirschhorn, Practical and ethical problems in human genetics,
      Birth Defects 8:17, 1972.
392. Lederberg, Biomedical frontiers - genetics, Experientia 17:
      231, 1972
393. Pfandler & Kalin, The selective effect of therapeutic abortion
      when children thus eliminated are carriers of a recessive
      autosomic or X-chromosome-linked defect, J. Genet. Hum.
      20:135, 1972 (FRE.).
394. Fraser, The implications of prevention and treatment of in-
      herited disease for the genetic future of mankind, J. Genet.
      Hum. 20:185, 1972.
395. Handler, In defense of science, Fed. Proc. 31:1569, 1972.
396. Largey, Sex control, sex preferences, and the future of the
      family, Soc. Biol. 19:379, 1972.
397. Osborn & Bajema, The eugenic hypothesis, Soc. Biol. 19:
      337, 1972.
398. Glass, Eugenic implications of the new reproductive technol-
      ogies, Soc. Biol. 19:326, 1972.
399. Editorial, the new eugenics, Lancet 2:751, 1971.
400. Stern, The place of genetics in medicine, Ann. Intern.
      Med. 75:623, 1971.
401. D'Andrea, Eugenic prophylaxis in the light of international
      legislation, Ann. Sanita Pubblica 32:25, 1971 (ITA.).
402. Hirschhorn, On re-doing man, Ann. NY Acad. Sci. 184:103,
      1971.
403. Guttentag et al, Genetic control, New Eng. J. Med. 286:
      48, 1972.
404. Krauss, Legal possibilities of pregnancy interruption for
      eugenic or fetal indications, Munch. Med. Wochenschr. 113:
      1505, 1971 (GER.).
405. Kass, The new biology - What price relieving man's estate,
      Science 174:779, 1971.
406. Languna, Scope and perspectives of genetics in medicine,
      Gac. Med. Mex. 100:975, 1970 (SPA.).
407. Townes, Preventive genetics and early therapeutic procedures
      in the control of birth defects, Birth Defects 6:42, 1970.
408. Friedmann & Roblin, Gene therapy for human genetic disease,
      Science 175:949, 1972.
409. Freese, Prospects of gene therapy, Science 175:1024, 1972.
410. Howie, The prevention of mental defect, NZ Med. J. 74:
      14, 1971.
411. Duval, Implications of advanced biomedical research and
      technology, J.A.M.A. 220:247, 1972.
412. Editorial, Ethical and social issues in screening for genetic
      disease, New Eng. J. Med. 286:1129, 1972.
413. Beckwith, Science for the people, Ann. NY Acad. Sci. 196:

236, 1972.
414. Emery & Smith, Ascertainment and prevention of genetic
     disease, Br. Med. J. 3:636, 1970.
415. Elkinton, The literature of ethical problems in medicine,
     Ann. Intern. Med. 73:662, 1970.
416. Davis, Prospects for genetic intervention in man, Science
     170:1279, 1970.
417. Huxley, Eugenics in evolutionary perspective, Perspect.
     Biol. Med. 6:155, 1963.
418. Edwards & Sharpe, Social values and research in human embry-
     ology, Nature 231:87, 1971.
419. Kass & Glass, What price the perfect baby, Science 173:
     103, 1971.
420. Cocks, Malthus on population quality, Soc. Biol. 18:84, 1971.
421. Dyke, Potential mates in a small human population, Soc. Biol.
     18:28, 1971.
422. Motulsky, The William Allan memorial award lecture, Human
     and medical genetics - A scientific discipline and an expand-
     ing horizon, Am. J. Hum. Genet. 23:107, 1971.
423. Davis, Ethical and technical aspects of genetic intervention,
     New Eng. J. Med. 285:799, 1971.
424. Fletcher, Ethical aspects of genetic controls. Designed
     genetic changes in man, New Eng. J. Med. 285:776, 1971.
425. Taylor & Merrill, Progress in the delivery of health care -
     genetic counseling, Amer. J. Dis. Child. 119:209, 1970.
426. LeJeune, The William Allan memorial award lecture. On the
     nature of men, Amer. J. Hum. Genet. 22:121, 1970.
427. Suter, Population crisis and extremism, Science 168:777, 1970.
428. Barrai, Human genetics and public health, Who Chron. 24:
     241, 1970.
429. Inge, Eugenics and religion, Eugen. Rev. 60:92, 1968.
430. Ellis, Birth-Control and Eugenics, Rugen. Rev. 60:76, 1968.
431. Webb, Eugenics and the poor law. The minority report, Eugen.
     Rev. 60:71, 1968.
432. Binney, Eugenic aspects of the English criminal law, Eugen.
     Rev. 60:118, 1968.
433. Matsunaga, Birth control policy in Japan - A review from
     eugenic standpoint, Jap. J. Hum. Genet. 13:189, 1968.
434. Lappe', Genetic counseling and genetic engineering, Hastings
     Cent. Rep. #3, p. 13, 1971.
435. Powledge, New trends in genetic legislation, Hastings
     Cent. Rep. 3:6, 1973.
436. Breslau & Bell, XYY, Health and Law, Southern Med. J. 63:
     831, 1970.
437. Money, XYY, the law, and forensic moral philosophy, J. Nerv.
     Ment. Dis. 149:309, 1969.
438. Rosenberg, The right to expert testimony, New Eng. J. Med.
     282:1308, 1970.
439. MacKay & Edey, The law concerning voluntary sterilization as
     it affects doctors, J. Urol. 103:482, 1970.

440. Hayt, Legal responsibility for unsuccessful sterilization, Hosp. Manage. 109:72, 1970.
441. Graham, The relation of genetics to control of human fertility, Perspect. Biol. Med. 14:615, 1971.
442. Aposhian, The use of DNA for gene therapy -- The need, experimental approach, and implications, Perspect. Biol. Med. 14: 98, 1970.
443. Polani, Science and man, Proc. R. Soc. Med. 63:969, 1970.
444. Becker, Sterilization in the new penal law bill, Med. Klin. 67:551, 1972 (GER.).
445. Krishef, State laws on marriage and sterilization of the mentally retarded, Ment. Retard. 10:36, 1972.
446. Clayton, Human rights, retardation, and research, Hosp. Comm. Psychiat. 23:81, 1972.
447. Ferster, Advances in human genetics and their impact on society, Birth Defects 8:102, 1972.
448. Engel, The making of an XYY, Am. J. Ment. Defic. 77:123, 1972.

---

449. Hilton et al, Ethical Issues in Human Genetics, Plenum Press, New York, 1973.
450. Katz, Experimentation With Human Beings, The Russell Sage Foundation, New York, 1972.
451. Rosenfeld, The Second Genesis, Arena Books, New York, 1972.
452. Hamilton et al, The New Genetics and the Future of Man, William B. Eerdmans Publishing Company, Grand Rapids, 1972.
453. Ramsay, Fabricated Man, Yale University Press, 1970.
454. Leach, The Biocrats, Jonathan Cape, London, 1970.
455. Fuller et al, The Social Impact of Modern Biology, Routledge and Kegan Paul, London, 1971.
456. Law and the Ethics of AID and Embryo Transfer. CIBA Foundation No. 17, New Series. Elsevier-Excerpta Medica, North Holland 1973.
457. The Challenge of Life, Roche Anniversary Symposium. Experienta Supplementum, 17. Birkhauser Verlag, Basel and Stuttgart, 1972.
458. Genetic Science and Man, Theological Studies, Volume 33, No. 3, September 1972.
459. Frankel, Genetic Technology: Promises and Problems. Washington, D.C.: The Goerge Washington University, Program of Policy Studies in Science and Technology, Monograph No. 15, March 1973.
460. Sollitto & Veatch, Bibliography of Society, Ethics and the Life Sciences, Hastings Center, Hastings-on-Hudson, New York 1974.
461. Fletcher, The Ethics of Genetic Control-Ending Reproductive Roulette, Anchor Press/Doubleday, Garden City, 1974.
462. Visscher, Birth Defects, Pemberton Publishing Company, London, 1972.
463. Jones & Bodmer, Our Future Inheritance: Choice or Chance?

Oxford University Press, London, 1974.
464.   Lipkin & Towley, Genetic Responsibility - On Choosing Our
       Children's Genes, Plenum Press, New York, 1974.
465.   McLaren, The future of the family, in The Future of Man
       (Inst. Biol. Symp. no. 20), Ebling & Health (eds.),
       p. 65, Academic Press, London, 1971.
466.   Edwards, The Social Impact of Modern Biology, Routledge &
       Kegan Paul, London, 1971.
467.   Haring, Medical Ethics, St. Paul Publications, Slough, p. 92,
       1972.
468.   Titmuss, The Gift Relationship: From Human Blood to Social
       Policy, Allen & Unwin, London, 1971.
469.   U.K. Law Commission, Injuries to Unborn Children, Published
       Working Paper no. 47, 1973.

CONTRIBUTORS

George J. Annas, J.D., M.P.H.
 Assistant Professor, Dept. of
 Socio-Medical Sciences, Director,
 Center for Law and Health Sci-
 ences, Boston University Schools
 of Law and Medicine
 Boston, Massachusetts

Charles H. Baron, LL.B., Ph.D.
 Professor of Law
 Boston College Law School
 Brighton, Massachusetts

Jonathan R. Beckwith, Ph.D.
 Professor of Microbiology
 and Molecular Genetics
 Harvard Medical School
 Boston, Massachusetts

Sissela Bok, Ph.D.
 Lecturer on Medical Ethics
 Harvard MIT Program in Health
 Sciences and Technology
 Harvard Medical School
 Boston, Massachusetts

Robert A. Burt, J.D.
 Professor of Law and of Law in
 Psychiatry, The University of
 Michigan Law School, Ann Arbor
 Michigan

Daniel Callahan, Ph.D.
 Director, Institute of Society,
 Ethics and the Life Sciences
 Hastings Center
 Hastings-on-Hudson, New York

Alexander M. Capron, J.D.
 Assistant Professor of Law, Univ.
 Pennsylvania School of Law
 Philadelphia, Pennsylvania

Neil L. Chayet, J.D.
 Attorney, Consultant in Health
 Law, Boston, Massachusetts and
 Washington, D.C.

Stephan L. Chorover, Ph.D.
 Professor of Psychology
 Department of Psychology, MIT
 Cambridge, Massachusetts

Catherine Damme, J.D.
 Research Associate
 Medical Genetics Center
 The University of Texas
 Health Sciences Center at
 Houston
 Houston, Texas

Bernard D. Davis, M.D.
 Adele Lehman Professor of Bac-
 terial Physiology, Bacterial
 Physiology Unit
 Harvard Medical School
 Boston, Massachusetts

Alan M. Dershowitz, J.D.
 Professor of Law
 Harvard Law School
 Cambridge, Massachusetts

Arthur J. Dyck, Ph.D.
 Mary B. Saltonstall Professor
 of Population Ethics
 Harvard School of Public Health
 Member, Harvard Divinity School
 Cambridge, Massachusetts

Leon Eisenberg, M.D.
 Professor of Psychiatry, Harvard
 Medical School; Chairman,
 Executive Committee, Department
 of Psychiatry, Harvard Medical
 School, Senior Associate in
 Psychiatry, Children's Hospital
 Medical Center
 Boston, Massachusetts

Richard W. Erbe, M.D.
 Assistant Professor of Pediatrics
 Harvard Medical School
 Chief, Genetics Unit
 Massachusetts General Hospital
 Boston, Massachusetts

Fredric D. Frigoletto, Jr., M.D.
 Assistant Professor of Obstet-
 rics and Gynecology, Harvard
 Medical School; Service Chief
 of Obstetrics and Director of
 Education, Boston Hospital for
 Women, Boston, Massachusetts

Sydney S. Gellis, M.D.
 Professor and Chairman, Department of Pediatrics, School
 of Medicine, Pediatrician-in-
 Chief, Boston Floating Hospital
 for Infants and Children
 Boston, Massachusetts

Leonard H. Glantz, J.D.
 Staff Attorney, Center for
 Law and Health Sciences
 Boston University School of Law
 Boston, Massachusetts

Donald P. Goldstein, M.D.
 Assistant Clinical Professor of
 Obstetrics and Gynecology
 Harvard Medical School
 Director, New England Tropho-
 blastic Disease Center
 Chief of Gynecology, Children's
 Hospital Medical Center
 Boston, Massachusetts

Harold P. Green, J.D.
 Professor of Law and Director
 of the Law, Science and
 Technology Program
 The George Washington University
 National Law Center
 Washington, D.C.

Wendy M. Greenfield, B.A.
 Manager of Information and
 Development, Blue Shield of
 Massachusetts
 Boston, Massachusetts

Joseph M. Healey, J.D.
 Kennedy Fellow in Medical Ethics
 Harvard Medical School
 Boston, Massachusetts

Kurt Hirschhorn, M.D.
 Professor of Pediatrics
 Mount Sinai School of Medicine
 of the City University of
 New York; Chief, Division of
 Medical Genetics
 Mount Sinai Hospital, New York

Lewis B. Holmes, M.D.
 Assistant Professor of Pediatrics
 Harvard Medical School
 Director, Genetics Clinic
 Massachusetts General Hospital
 Boston, Massachusetts

Ernest B. Hook, M.D.
 Associate Professor of Pediatrics
 Chief, Epidemiology and Human
 Ecology, Birth Defects Institute
 New York State Department of
 Health and Albany Medical College
 Albany, New York

Angelyn Konugres, Ph.D.
 Research Associate in Obstetrics
 and Gynecology, Harvard
 Medical School; Director of
 Blood Bank and Director of
 Research, Boston Hospital for
 Women
 Boston, Massachusetts

Marc Lappe, Ph.D.
 Associate for the Biological
 Sciences, Institute of Society,
 Ethics and the Life Sciences
 Hastings Center
 Hastings-on-Hudson, New York

Seymour Lederberg, Ph.D.
 Professor of Biology
 Division of Biological and Medi-
 cal Sciences, Brown University
 Providence, Rhode Island

Harvey L. Levy, M.D.
  Assistant Professor of Neurol-
  ogy, Harvard Medical School
  Assistant in Neurology
  Massachusetts General Hospital
  Assistant Director of the
  Division of Diagnostic State
  Laboratories
  State Laboratory Institute
  Boston, Massachusetts

Charles U. Lowe, M.D.
  Executive Director, National
  Commission on the Protection
  of Human Subjects
  National Institutes of Health
  Department of Health, Education
  and Welfare
  Bethesda, Maryland

Salvadore E. Luria, M.D.
  Institute Professor
  Director of the Center for
  Cancer Research, MIT
  Cambridge, Massachusetts

Maurice J. Mahoney, M.D.
  Associate Professor of Human
  Genetics and Pediatrics
  Yale University
  New Haven, Connecticut

George W. Melcher, Jr., M.D.
  Associate Professor of Clinical
  Medicine, College of Physicians
  and Surgeons, Columbia Univer-
  sity; Associate Attending
  Physician, Columbia Presbyter-
  ian Medical Center; President,
  National Genetics Foundation
  New York, New York

Aubrey Milunsky, MB.B.Ch.,
  M.R.C.P., D.C.H.
  Assistant Professor of Pediatrics
  Harvard Medical School
  Medical Geneticist
  Massachusetts General Hospital
  Director, Genetics Laboratory

Eunice Kennedy Shriver Center
  at the Walter E. Fernald
  State School, Boston and
  Waltham, Massachusetts

Philip Reilly, J.D.
  Adjunct Assistant Professor of
  Law, University of Houston Law
  School; Post-Doctoral Fellow in
  Medical Genetics, The University
  of Texas Health Science Center
  at Houston, Graduate School
  of Biomedical Sciences
  Houston, Texas

Stanley J. Reiser, M.D., Ph.D.,
  M.P.A.
  Assistant Professor of History
  of Medicine, Co-Director of
  Harvard Interfaculty Program
  in Medical Ethics
  Harvard Medical School
  Boston, Massachusetts

John A. Robertson, J.D.
  Assistant Professor of Law
  University of Wisconsin
  Law School
  Madison, Wisconsin

Leon E. Rosenberg, M.D.
  Professor of Human Genetics,
  Pediatrics and Medicine
  Chairman, Department of
  Human Genetics, Yale University
  School of Medicine
  New Haven, Connecticut

Margery W. Shaw, M.D., J.D.
  Director, Medical Genetics
  Center, The University of
  Texas Health Science Center at
  Houston
  Houston, Texas

James R. Sorenson, Ph.D.
  Associate Professor
  Boston University School of
  Medicine

Department of Socio-Medical
Science
Boston, Massachusetts

Arthur G. Steinberg, Ph.D.
  Herrick Professor of Biology
  Department of Biology
  Professor of Human Genetics
  Department of Reproductive
  Biology, Case Western Reserve
  University
  Cleveland, Ohio

John L. Thompson, J.D.
  President, Blue Shield of
  Massachusetts
  Boston, Massachusetts

Jon R. Waltz, J.D.
  Professor of Law, Northwestern
  University School of Law
  Chicago, Illinois

Marx W. Wartofsky, Ph.D.
  Professor of Philosophy
  Boston University
  Boston, Massachusetts

INDEX